SOCIOLOGY 86/87

Editor
Kurt Finsterbusch
University of Maryland, College Park

Kurt Finsterbusch received his bachelor's degree in history from Princeton University in 1957, and his bachelor of divinity degree from Grace Theological Seminary in 1960. His Ph.D. in Sociology, from Columbia University, was conferred in 1969. He is the author of several books, including *Understanding Social Impacts* (Sage Publications, 1980), and *Social Research for Policy Decisions* (Wadsworth Publishing, 1980, with Annabelle Bender Motz). He is currently teaching at the University of Maryland, College Park, and in addition to serving as editor for *Annual Editions: Sociology,* is also co-editor for The Dushkin Publishing Group's *Taking Sides: Clashing Views on Controversial Social Issues.*

Annual Editions

A Library of Information from the Public Press

Cover illustration by Mike Eagle

The Dushkin Publishing Group, Inc.
Sluice Dock, Guilford, Connecticut 06437

The Annual Editions Series

PUBLISHED

Africa
Aging
American Government
American History, Pre-Civil War
American History, Post-Civil War
Anthropology
Biology
Business
China
Comparative Politics
Computers in Education
Computers in Business
Computers in Society
Criminal Justice
Drugs and Society
Early Childhood Education
Economics
Educating Exceptional Children
Education
Educational Psychology
Environment
Geography

Global Issues
Health
Human Development
Human Sexuality
Latin America
Macroeconomics
Marketing
Marriage and Family
Middle East and the Islamic World
Personal Growth and Behavior
Psychology
Social Problems
Social Psychology
Sociology
Soviet Union and Eastern Europe
State and Local Government
Urban Society
Western Civilization,
    Pre-Reformation
Western Civilization,
    Post-Reformation
World Politics

FUTURE VOLUMES

Abnormal Psychology
Death and Dying
Congress
Energy
Ethnic Studies
Foreign Policy
Judiciary
Nutrition
Parenting
Philosophy

Political Science
Presidency
Religion
South Asia
Twentieth Century American
    History
Western Europe
Women's Studies
World History

Library of Congress Cataloging in Publication Data
Main entry under title: Annual editions: Sociology.
        1.   Sociology—Periodicals.   2.   United States—Social conditions—1960—Periodicals.
Title: Sociology.
HM1.A76   301'.05   72-76876
ISBN 0-87967 -635-3

Fifteenth Edition

Manufactured by The Banta Company, Menasha, Wisconsin 54952

Editors/Advisory Board

To The Reader

In publishing ANNUAL EDITIONS we recognize the enormous role played by the magazines, newspapers, and journals of the *public press* in providing current, first-rate educational information in a broad spectrum of interest areas. Within the articles, the best scientists, practitioners, researchers, and commentators draw issues into new perspective as accepted theories and viewpoints are called into account by new events, recent discoveries change old facts, and fresh debate breaks out over important controversies.

Many of the articles resulting from this enormous editorial effort are appropriate for students, researchers, and professionals seeking accurate, current material to help bridge the gap between principles and theories and the real world. These articles, however, become more useful for study when those of lasting value are carefully *collected, organized, indexed,* and *reproduced* in a *low-cost format,* which provides easy and permanent access when the material is needed. That is the role played by *Annual Editions.* Under the direction of each volume's *Editor,* who is an expert in the subject area, and with the guidance of an *Advisory Board,* we seek each year to provide in each *ANNUAL EDITION* a current, well-balanced, carefully selected collection of the best of the public press for your study and enjoyment. We think you'll find this volume useful, and we hope you'll take a moment to let us know what you think.

The 1980s have brought crises, changes, and challenges. Crime is running rampant. The public is demanding more police, more jails, and tougher sentences, but less government spending. The economy has experienced a major recession and the recovery has not eliminated high unemployment, trade deficits, budget deficits, and economic uncertainties. Government economic policies seem to create almost as many problems as they solve. Laborers, women, blacks, and many other groups complain of injustices and victimization. The use of toxic chemicals has been blamed for increases in cancer, sterility, and other diseases. Marriage and the family have been transformed, in part, by the women's movement, but new problems are surfacing. Schools, television, and corporations are commonly vilified. Add to this the problems of population and the threat of nuclear war and it is easy to despair.

The present generation may be the one to determine the course of history for the next two hundred years. Great changes are taking place and new solutions are being sought where old answers no longer work. The issues the current generation faces are complex and must be interpreted within a sophisticated framework. The sociological perspective provides such a framework. The articles that follow should help you develop the sociological perspective to determine how the issues of the day relate to the way society is structured. They will provide not only information, but also models of interpretation and analysis which will guide you as you form your own views.

Annual Editions depends upon reader response to develop and change. You are encouraged to select articles you think have sociological merit for subsequent issues, tell us what you think of existing articles, and advise us on how we can make the reader more useful as a teaching and learning tool by returning the article rating form located on the last page of this book.

Annual Editions: Sociology 86/87 emphasizes social change, institutional crises, and prospects for the future. It provides an intellectual preparation for acting for the betterment of humanity in times of critical changes. The sociological perspective is needed more than ever as humankind tries to find a way to peace and prosperity. The obstacles that lie in the path of these important goals seem to increase yearly. The goals of this edition are to communicate the excitement and importance of the study of the social world and provoke interest and enthusiasm among students for the study of sociology.

Kurt Finsterbusch

Editor

Contents

Unit 1

The Discipline

Two articles present several classic perspectives on the discipline of sociology and its impact on society.

Unit 2

Culture

Six selections consider the effect of American values, social conditions, and social mores on the individual and human culture.

The concepts in italics are developed in the article. For further expansion please refer to the Topic Guide, the Index, and the Glossary.

Unit 3

Socialization

Six articles examine the effects of social influences on childhood, personality, and human behavior with regard to the socialization of the individual.

Unit 4

Groups and Roles in Transition

Seven articles discuss some of the social roles and group relationships that are in transition in today's society.

The concepts in italics are developed in the article. For further expansion please refer to the Topic Guide, the Index, and the Glossary.

Unit 5

Social Institutions in Crisis and Change

Seven articles examine several social institutions that are currently in crisis. The political and economic spheres, as well as the family and traditional goals are considered.

Unit 6

Stratification and Social Inequalities

Six selections discuss the social stratification and inequalities that exist in today's society with regard to the rich, the poor, blacks, and other minorities.

The concepts in italics are developed in the article. For further expansion please refer to the Topic Guide, the Index, and the Glossary.

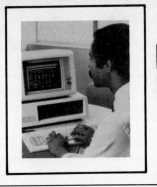

Unit 7

Social Change and the Future

Nine selections discuss the impact that technology, environmental degradation, nuclear war, and changing social values will have on society's future.

The concepts in italics are developed in the article. For further expansion please refer to the Topic Guide, the Index, and the Glossary.

Topic Guide

This topic guide suggests how the selections in this book relate to the topics of traditional concern to sociology students and professionals. It is very useful in locating articles which relate to each other for reading and research. The guide is arranged alphabetically according to topic. Articles may, of course, treat topics that do not appear in the topic guide. In turn, entries in the topic guide do not necessarily constitute a comprehensive listing of all the contents of each selection.

TOPIC AREA	TREATED AS AN ISSUE IN:	TOPIC AREA	TREATED AS AN ISSUE IN:
Abortion	28. Between Pro-Life and Pro-Choice	**Economy**	24. The Three Fiscal Crises
Adults/Adulthood	11. Erik Erikson's Eight Ages of Man		25. America's Management Crisis
	36. Snapshot of a Changing America		29. Who Owns America?
Blacks	5. Penny Capitalism		40. Technology and the Changing World of Work
	16. Restoring the Traditional Black Family		43. Window of Opportunity
	33. The Black Underclass	**Education**	13. Sexism in the Schoolroom of the '80s
	34. A Struggle for Freedom		27. Why Johnny Can't Think
Business	25. America's Management Crisis		36. Snapshot of a Changing America
	30. Corporate Welfare out of Control	**Elderly**	*See* Aging
	39. Technology out of Control	**Family/Marriage**	8. Radical Departures
Children/Childhood	6. The New Lost Generation		9. Childhood Through the Ages
	7. Brave New Wave of the '80s		10. The Loss of Childhood
	8. Radical Departures		15. The Secret of Strong Families
	9. Childhood Through the Ages		16. Restoring the Traditional Black Family
	10. The Loss of Childhood		17. Jonestown as a Perverse Utopia
	11. Erik Erikson's Eight Ages of Man		20. The Politics of Motherhood
	12. Growing Up as a Fore		21. Another Stereotype
	13. Sexism in the Schoolroom of the '80s		26. The American Family in the Year 2000
	14. What Is TV Doing to America?		36. Snapshot of a Changing America
	15. The Secret of Strong Families	**Future**	26. The American Family in the Year 2000
	16. Restoring the Traditional Black Family		38. We Can Prevent Nuclear Winter
Civil Rights	33. The Black Underclass		39. Technology out of Control
	34. A Struggle for Freedom		40. Technology and the Changing World of Work
Class	*See* Social Class		41. Copernican Politics
Communications	40. Technology and the Changing World of Work		42. 10 Forces Reshaping America
	48. Window of Opportunity		43. Window of Opportunity
Cults	8. Radical Departures	**Generations**	6. The New Lost Generation
	17. Jonestown as a Perverse Utopia		7. Brave New Wave of the '80s
Culture	3. Why I Love America		8. Radical Departures
	4. The Mountain People		15. The Secret of Strong Families
	5. Penny Capitalism		21. Another Stereotype
	6. The New Lost Generation	**Groups**	5. Penny Capitalism
	7. Brave New Wave of the '80s		8. Radical Departures
	8. Radical Departures		12. Growing Up as a Fore
	12. Growing Up as a Fore		17. Jonestown as a Perverse Utopia
	16. Restoring the Traditional Black Family		19. Work: The Right to Right Livelihood
Deinstitutionalization	31. Abandoned Americans		21. Another Stereotype
Demography	35. People, People, People		28. Between Pro-Life and Pro-Choice
	36. Snapshot of a Changing America		33. The Black Underclass
	37. The Changing Face of America	**Immigration**	36. Snapshot of a Changing America
	42. 10 Forces Reshaping America		37. The Changing Face of America
Discrimination	21. Another Stereotype	**Life-Styles**	5. Penny Capitalism
	33. The Black Underclass		6. The New Lost Generation
	34. A Struggle for Freedom		7. Brave New Wave of the '80s
Ecology/Environment	4. The Mountain People		16. Restoring the Traditional Black Family
	12. Growing Up as a Fore		40. Technology and the Changing World of Work
	18. Cities Won't Drive You Crazy		43. Window of Opportunity
	38. We Can Prevent Nuclear Winter	**Media**	6. The New Lost Generation
	39. Technology out of Control		14. What Is TV Doing to America?
			22. Where Have All the Heroes Gone?

The Discipline

To C. Wright Mills, the sociological imagination was the way by which ordinary people could understand what was happening to them. The need for such understanding is urgent at the present historical moment. Change has become so rapid that events of even a decade ago bewilder and amaze us: the energy crisis transformed global economics; new technologies are changing the workplace; and a complex, interdependent world threatens to explode into frightening wars.

Most people today are associated with large, complex, and impersonal organizations, which sometimes take actions that disturb one's sense of justice. Universities herd students through large classes and seldom create truly joyful intellectual work. The medical system extorts stupendous fees from patients, making them feel like victims. The tobacco industry enthusiastically markets their highly addictive and harmful drug which endangers the health of hundreds of thousands of Americans every year. Corporations close factories in New England and open factories in Taiwan. American banks invest in the Japanese industries which are invading the American market. Is it surprising, then, that individuals often feel powerless against such indignities?

There lie before us unprecedented opportunities to build a better world and improve the quality of life for many people. The study of sociology can help students figure out how society works and what they can do to change it by developing a sociological imagination and sociological perspective. The two articles in this section explain how the economic structures of society converge on our lives in the context of history. C. Wright Mills says the sociological imagination enables us to understand how we are shaped by society which in turn is shaped by historical forces. Nevertheless the individual also ". . . contributes, however minutely, to the shaping of this society and to the course of its history. . . ." Peter L. Berger focuses more on the common occurrences of everyday life. He challenges the student to use the sociological perspective to "see" in daily events the sociological truths which most people miss.

Looking Ahead: Challenge Questions

How can sociology contribute to our understanding of the contemporary world?

In what ways can the sociological imagination become a significant factor in political policies?

Can sociology contribute to personal growth?

THE SOCIOLOGICAL IMAGINATION

The Promise

C. WRIGHT MILLS

NOWADAYS men often feel that their private lives are a series of traps. They sense that within their everyday worlds, they cannot overcome their troubles, and in this feeling, they are often quite correct: What ordinary men are directly aware of and what they try to do are bounded by the private orbits in which they live; their visions and their powers are limited to the close-up scenes of job, family, neighborhood; in other milieux, they move vicariously and remain spectators. And the more aware they become, however vaguely, of ambitions and of threats which transcend their immediate locales, the more trapped they seem to feel.

Underlying this sense of being trapped are seemingly impersonal changes in the very structure of continent-wide societies. The facts of contemporary history are also facts about the success and the failure of individual men and women. When a society is industrialized, a peasant becomes a worker; a feudal lord is liquidated or becomes a businessman. When classes rise or fall, a man is employed or unemployed; when the rate of investment goes up or down, a man takes new heart or goes broke. When wars happen, an insurance salesman becomes a rocket launcher; a store clerk, a radar man; a wife lives alone; a child grows up without a father. Neither the life of an individual nor the history of a society can be understood without understanding both.

Yet men do not usually define the troubles they endure in terms of historical change and institutional contradiction. The well-being they enjoy, they do not usually impute to the big ups and downs of the societies in which they live. Seldom aware of the intricate connection between the patterns of their own lives and the course of world history, ordinary men do not usually know what this connection means for the kinds of men they are becoming and for the kinds of history-making in which they might take part. They do not possess the quality of mind essential to grasp the interplay of man and society, of biography and history, of self and world. They cannot cope with their personal troubles in such ways as to control the structural transformations that usually lie behind them.

Surely it is no wonder. In what period have so many men been so totally exposed at so fast a pace to such earthquakes of change? That Americans have not known such catastrophic changes as have the men and women of other societies is due to historical facts that are now quickly becoming 'merely history.' The history that now affects every man is world history. Within this scene and this period, in the course of a single generation, one sixth of mankind is transformed from all that is feudal and backward into all that is modern, advanced, and fearful. Political colonies are freed; new and less visible forms of imperialism installed. Revolutions occur; men feel the intimate grip of new kinds of authority. Totalitarian societies rise, and are smashed to bits—or succeed fabulously. After two centuries of ascendancy, capitalism is shown up as only one way to make society into an industrial apparatus. After two centuries of hope, even formal democracy is restricted to a quite small portion of mankind. Everywhere in the underdeveloped world, ancient ways of life are broken up and vague expectations become urgent demands. Everywhere in the overdeveloped world, the means of authority and of violence become total in scope and bureaucratic in form. Humanity itself now lies before us, the super-nation at either pole concentrating its most co-ordinated and massive efforts upon the preparation of World War Three.

The very shaping of history now outpaces the ability of men to orient themselves in accordance with cherished values. And which values? Even when they do not panic, men often sense that older ways of feeling and thinking have collapsed and that newer beginnings are ambiguous to the point of moral stasis. Is it any wonder that ordinary men feel they cannot cope with the larger worlds with which they are so suddenly confronted? That they cannot understand the meaning of their epoch for their own lives? That—in defense of selfhood—they become morally insensible, trying to remain altogether private men? Is it any wonder that they come to be possessed by a sense of the trap?

It is not only information that they need—in this Age of Fact, information often dominates their attention and overwhelms their capacities to assimilate it. It is not only the skills of reason that they need—although their struggles to acquire these often exhaust their limited moral energy.

What they need, and what they feel they need, is a quality of mind that will help them to use information and to develop reason in order to achieve lucid summations of what is going on in the world and of what may be happening within themselves. It is this quality, I am going to contend, that journalists and scholars, artists and publics, scientists and editors are coming to expect of what may be called the sociological imagination.

1

The sociological imagination enables its possessor to understand the larger historical scene in terms of its meaning for the inner life and the external career of a variety of individuals. It enables him to take into account how individuals, in the welter of their daily experience, often become falsely conscious of their social positions. Within that welter, the framework of modern society is sought, and within that framework the psychologies of a variety of men and women are formulated. By such means the personal uneasiness of individuals is focused upon explicit troubles and the indifference of publics is transformed into involvement with public issues.

The first fruit of this imagination—and the first lesson of the social science that embodies it—is the idea that the individual can understand his own experience and gauge his own fate only by locating himself within his period, that he can know his own chances in life only by becoming aware of those of all individuals in his circumstances. In many ways it is a terrible lesson; in many ways a magnificent one. We do not know the limits of man's capacities for supreme effort or willing degradation, for agony or glee, for pleasurable brutality or the sweetness of reason. But in our time we have come to know that the limits of 'human nature' are frighteningly broad. We have come to know that every individual lives, from one generation to the next, in some society; that he lives out a biography, and that he lives it out within some historical sequence. By the fact of his living he contributes, however minutely, to the shaping of this society and to the course of its history, even as he is made by society and by its historical push and shove.

The sociological imagination enables us to grasp history and biography and the relations between the two within society. That is its task and its promise. To recognize this task and this promise is the mark of the classic social analyst. It is characteristic of Herbert Spencer—turgid, polysyllabic, comprehensive; of E. A. Ross—graceful, muckraking, upright; of Auguste Comte and Emile Durkheim; of the intricate and subtle Karl Mannheim. It is the quality of all that is intellectually excellent in Karl Marx; it is the clue to Thorstein Veblen's brilliant and ironic insight, to Joseph Schumpeter's many-sided constructions of reality; it is the basis of the psychological sweep of W. E. H. Lecky no less than of the profundity and clarity of Max Weber. And it is the signal of what is best in contemporary studies of man and society.

No social study that does not come back to the problems of biography, of history and of their intersections within a society has completed its intellectual journey. Whatever the specific problems of the classic social analysts, however limited or however broad the features of social reality they have examined, those who have been imaginatively aware of the promise of their work have consistently asked three sorts of questions:

(1) What is the structure of this particular society as a whole? What are its essential components, and how are they related to one another? How does it differ from other varieties of social order? Within it, what is the meaning of any particular feature for its continuance and for its change?

(2) Where does this society stand in human history? What are the mechanics by which it is changing? What is its place within and its meaning for the development of humanity as a whole? How does any particular feature we are examining affect, and how is it affected by, the historical period in which it moves? And this period—what are its essential features? How does it differ from other periods? What are its characteristic ways of history-making?

(3) What varieties of men and women now prevail in this society and in this period? And what varieties are coming to prevail? In what ways are they selected and formed, liberated and repressed, made sensitive and blunted? What kinds of 'human nature' are revealed in the conduct and character we observe in this society in this period? And what is the meaning for 'human nature' of each and every feature of the society we are examining?

Whether the point of interest is a great power state or a minor literary mood, a family, a prison, a creed—these are the kinds of questions the best social analysts have asked. They are the intellectual pivots of classic studies of man in society—and they are the questions inevitably raised by any mind possessing the sociological imagination. For that imagination is the capacity to shift from one perspective to another—from the political to the psychological; from examination of a single family to comparative assessment of the national budgets of the world; from the theological school to the military establishment; from considerations of an oil industry to studies of contemporary poetry. It is the capacity to range from the most impersonal and remote transformations to the most intimate features of the human self—and to see the relations between the two. Back of its use there is always the urge to know the social and historical meaning of the individual in the society and in the period in which he has his quality and his being.

That, in brief, is why it is by means of the sociological imagination that men now hope to grasp what is going on in the world, and to understand what is happening in themselves as minute points of the intersections of biography and history within society. In large part, contemporary man's self-conscious view of himself as at least an outsider, if not a permanent stranger, rests upon an absorbed realization of social relativity and of the transformative power of history. The sociological imagination is the most fruitful form of this self-consciousness. By its use men whose mentalities have swept only a series of limited orbits often come to feel as if suddenly awakened in a house with which they had only supposed themselves to be familiar. Correctly or incorrectly, they often come to feel that they can now provide themselves with adequate summations, cohesive assessments, comprehensive orientations. Older decisions that once appeared sound now seem to them products of a mind unaccountably dense. Their capacity for astonishment is made lively again. They acquire a new way of thinking, they experience a transvaluation of values: in a word, by their reflection and by their sensibility, they realize the cultural meaning of the social sciences.

2

Perhaps the most fruitful distinction with which the sociological imagination works is between 'the personal troubles of milieu' and 'the public issues of social structure.' This distinction is an essential tool of the sociological imagination and a feature of all classic work in social science.

Troubles occur within the character of the individual and within the range of his immediate relations with others; they have to do with his self and with those limited areas of social life of which he is directly and personally aware. Accordingly, the statement and the resolution of troubles properly lie within the individual as a biographical entity and within the scope of his immediate milieu—the social setting that is directly open to his personal experience and to some extent his willful activity. A trouble is a private matter: values cherished by an individual are felt by him to be threatened.

1. THE DISCIPLINE

Issues have to do with matters that transcend these local environments of the individual and the range of his inner life. They have to do with the organization of many such milieux into the institutions of an historical society as a whole, with the ways in which various milieux overlap and interpenetrate to form the larger structure of social and historical life. An issue is a public matter: some value cherished by publics is felt to be threatened. Often there is a debate about what that value really is and about what it is that really threatens it. This debate is often without focus if only because it is the very nature of an issue, unlike even widespread trouble, that it cannot very well be defined in terms of the immediate and everyday environments of ordinary men. An issue, in fact, often involves a crisis in institutional arrangements, and often too it involves what Marxists call 'contradictions' or 'antagonisms.'

In these terms, consider unemployment. When, in a city of 100,000, only one man is unemployed, that is his personal trouble, and for its relief we properly look to the character of the man, his skills, and his immediate opportunities. But when in a nation of 50 million employees, 15 million men are unemployed, that is an issue, and we may not hope to find its solution within the range of opportunities open to any one individual. The very structure of opportunities has collapsed. Both the correct statement of the problem and the range of possible solutions require us to consider the economic and political institutions of the society, and not merely the personal situation and character of a scatter of individuals.

Consider war. The personal problem of war, when it occurs, may be how to survive it or how to die in it with honor; how to make money out of it; how to climb into the higher safety of the military apparatus; or how to contribute to the war's termination. In short, according to one's values, to find a set of milieux and within it to survive the war or make one's death in it meaningful. But the structural issues of war have to do with its causes; with what types of men it throws up into command; with its effects upon economic and political, family and religious institutions, with the unorganized irresponsibility of a world of nation-states.

Consider marriage. Inside a marriage a man and a woman may experience personal troubles, but when the divorce rate during the first four years of marriage is 250 out of every 1,000 attempts, this is an indication of a structural issue having to do with the institutions of marriage and the family and other institutions that bear upon them.

Or consider the metropolis—the horrible, beautiful, ugly, magnificent sprawl of the great city. For many upper-class people, the personal solution to 'the problem of the city' is to have an apartment with private garage under it in the heart of the city, and forty miles out, a house by Henry Hill, garden by Garrett Eckbo, on a hundred acres of private land. In these two controlled environments—with a small staff at each end and a private helicopter connection—most people could solve many of the problems of personal milieux caused by the facts of the city. But all this, however splendid, does not solve the public issues that the structural fact of the city poses. What should be done with this wonderful monstrosity? Break it all up into scattered units, combining residence and work? Refurbish it as it stands? Or, after evacuation, dynamite it and build new cities according to new plans in new places? What should those plans be? And who is to decide and to accomplish whatever choice is made? These are structural issues; to confront them and to solve them requires us to consider political and economic issues that affect innumerable milieux.

In so far as an economy is so arranged that slumps occur, the problem of unemployment becomes incapable of personal solution. In so far as war is inherent in the nation-state system and in the uneven industrialization of the world, the ordinary individual in his restricted milieu will be powerless—with or without psychiatric aid—to solve the troubles this system or lack of system imposes upon him. In so far as the family as an institution turns women into darling little slaves and men into their chief providers and unweaned dependents, the problem of a satisfactory marriage remains incapable of purely private solution. In so far as the overdeveloped megalopolis and the overdeveloped automobile are built-in features of the overdeveloped society, the issues of urban living will not be solved by personal ingenuity and private wealth.

What we experience in various and specific milieux, I have noted, is often caused by structural changes. Accordingly, to understand the changes of many personal milieux we are required to look beyond them. And the number and variety of such structural changes increase as the institutions within which we live become more embracing and more intricately connected with one another. To be aware of the idea of social structure and to use it with sensibility is to be capable of tracing such linkages among a great variety of milieux. To be able to do that is to possess the sociological imagination.

Invitation to Sociology
A Humanistic Perspective

Peter L. Berger

. . . The sociologist, then, is someone concerned with understanding society in a disciplined way. The nature of this discipline is scientific. This means that what the sociologist finds and says about the social phenomena he studies occurs within a certain rather strictly defined frame of reference. One of the main characteristics of this scientific frame of reference is that operations are bound by certain rules of evidence. As a scientist, the sociologist tries to be objective, to control his personal preferences and prejudices, to perceive clearly rather than to judge normatively. This restraint, of course, does not embrace the totality of the sociologist's existence as a human being, but is limited to his operations *qua* sociologist. Nor does the sociologist claim that his frame of reference is the only one within which society can be looked at. For that matter, very few scientists in any field would claim today that one should look at the world only scientifically. The botanist looking at a daffodil has no reason to dispute the right of the poet to look at the same object in a very different manner. There are many ways of playing. The point is not that one denies other people's games but that one is clear about the rules of one's own. The game of the sociologist, then, uses scientific rules. As a result, the sociologist must be clear in his own mind as to the meaning of these rules. That is, he must concern himself with methodological questions. Methodology does not constitute his goal. The latter, let us recall once more, is the attempt to understand society. Methodology helps in reaching this goal. In order to understand society, or that segment of it that he is studying at the moment, the sociologist will use a variety of means. Among these are statistical techniques. Statistics can be very useful in answering certain sociological questions. But statistics does not constitute sociology. As a scientist, the sociologist will have to be concerned with the exact significance of the terms he is using. That is, he will have to be careful about terminology. This does not have to mean that he must invent a new language of his own, but it does mean that he cannot naively use the language of everyday discourse. Finally, the interest of the sociologist is primarily theoretical. That is, he is interested in understanding for its own sake. He may be aware of or even concerned with the practical applicability and consequences of his findings, but at that point he leaves the sociological frame of reference as such and moves into realms of values, beliefs and ideas that he shares with other men who are not sociologists. . . .

We would say then that the sociologist (that is, the one we would really like to invite to our game) is a person intensively, endlessly, shamelessly interested in the doings of men. His natural habitat is all the human gathering places of the world, wherever men come together. The sociologist may be interested in many other things. But his consuming interest remains in the world of men, their institutions, their history, their passions. And since he is interested in men, nothing that men do can be altogether tedious for him. He will naturally be interested in the events that engage men's ultimate beliefs, their moments of tragedy and grandeur and ecstasy. But he will also be fascinated by the commonplace, the everyday. He will know reverence, but this reverence will not prevent him from wanting to see and to understand. He may sometimes feel revulsion or contempt. But this also will not deter him from wanting to have his questions answered. The sociologist, in his quest for understanding, moves through the world of men without respect for the usual lines of demarcation. Nobility and degradation, power and obscurity, intelligence and folly—these are equally *interesting* to him, however unequal they may be in his personal values or tastes. Thus his questions may lead him to all possible levels of society, the best and the least known places, the most respected and the most despised. And, if he is a good sociologist, he will find himself in all these places because his own questions have so taken possession of him that he has little choice but to seek for answers.

It would be possible to say the same things in a lower key. We could say that the sociologist, but for the grace of his academic title, is the man who must listen to gossip despite himself, who is tempted to look through keyholes, to read other people's mail, to open closed cabinets. Before some otherwise unoccupied psychologist sets out now to construct an aptitude test for sociologists on the basis of sublimated voyeurism, let us quickly say that we are speaking merely by way of analogy. Perhaps some little boys consumed with curiosity to watch their maiden aunts in the bathroom later become inveterate sociologists. This is quite uninteresting. What interests us is the curiosity that grips any sociologist in front of a closed door behind which there are human voices. If he is a good sociologist, he will want to open that door, to understand these voices. Behind each closed door he will anticipate some new facet of human life not yet perceived and understood.

The sociologist will occupy himself with matters that others regard as too sacred or as too distasteful for dispassionate investigation. He will find rewarding the company of priests or of prostitutes, depending not on his personal preferences but on the questions he happens to be asking at the moment. He will also concern himself with matters that others may find much too boring. He will be interested in the human interaction that goes with warfare or with great intellectual discoveries, but also in the relations between people employed in a restaurant or between a group of little girls playing with their dolls. His main focus of attention is not the ultimate significance of what men do, but the action in itself, as another example of the infinite richness of human conduct. . . .

Any intellectual activity derives excitement from the moment it becomes a trail of discovery. In some fields of learning this is the discovery of worlds previously unthought and unthinkable. This is the excitement of the astronomer or of the nuclear physicist on the antipodal boundaries of the realities that man is capable of conceiving. But it can also be the excitement of bacteriology or geology. In a different way it can be the excitement of the linguist discovering new realms of human expression or of the anthropologist exploring human customs in faraway countries. In such discovery, when undertaken with passion, a widening of awareness, sometimes a veritable transformation of consciousness, occurs. The universe turns out to be much more wonder-full than one had ever dreamed. The excitement of sociology is usually of a different sort. Sometimes, it is true, the sociologist penetrates into worlds that had previously been quite unknown to him—for instance, the world of crime, or the world of some bizarre religious sect, or the world fashioned by the exclusive concerns of some group such as medical specialists or military leaders or advertising executives. However, much of the time the sociologist moves in sectors of experience that are familiar to him and to most people in his society. He investigates communities, institutions and activities that one can read about every day in the newspapers. Yet there is another excitement of discovery beckoning in his investigations. It is not the excitement of coming upon the totally unfamiliar, but rather the excitement of finding the familiar becoming transformed in its meaning. The fascination of sociology lies in the fact that its perspective makes us see in a new light the very world in which we have lived all our lives. This also constitutes a transformation of consciousness. Moreover, this transformation is more relevant existentially than that of many other intellectual disciplines, because it is more difficult to segregate in some special compartment of the mind. The astronomer does not live in the remote galaxies, and the nuclear physicist can, outside his laboratory, eat and laugh and marry and vote without thinking about the insides of the atom. The geologist looks at rocks only at appropriate times, and the linguist speaks English with his wife. The sociologist lives in society, on the job and off it. His own life, inevitably, is part of his subject matter. Men being what they are, sociologists too manage to segregate their professional insights from their everyday affairs. But it is a rather difficult feat to perform in good faith.

The sociologist moves in the common world of men, close to what most of them would call real. The categories he employs in his analyses are only refinements of the categories by which other men live—power, class, status, race, ethnicity. As a result, there is a deceptive simplicity and obviousness about some sociological investigations.

One reads them, nods at the familiar scene, remarks that one has heard all this before and don't people have better things to do than to waste their time on truisms—until one is suddenly brought up against an insight that radically questions everything one had previously assumed about this familiar scene. This is the point at which one begins to sense the excitement of sociology.

Let us take a specific example. Imagine a sociology class in a Southern college where almost all the students are white Southerners. Imagine a lecture on the subject of the racial system of the South. The lecturer is talking here of matters that have been familiar to his students from the time of their infancy. Indeed, it may be that they are much more familiar with the minutiae of this system than he is. They are quite bored as a result. It seems to them that he is only using more pretentious words to describe what they already know. Thus he may use the term "caste," one commonly used now by American sociologists to describe the Southern racial system. But in explaining the term he shifts to traditional Hindu society, to make it clearer. He then goes on to analyze the magical beliefs inherent in caste tabus, the social dynamics of commensalism and connubium, the economic interests concealed within the system, the way in which religious beliefs relate to the tabus, the effects of the caste system upon the industrial development of the society and vice versa—all in India. But suddenly India is not very far away at all. The lecture then goes back to its Southern theme. The familiar now seems not quite so familiar any more. Questions are raised that are new, perhaps raised angrily, but raised all the same. And at least some of the students have begun to understand that there are functions involved in this business of race that they have not read about in the newspapers (at least not those in their hometowns) and that their parents have not told them—partly, at least, because neither the newspapers nor the parents knew about them.

It can be said that the first wisdom of sociology is this—things are not what they seem. This too is a deceptively simple statement. It ceases to be simple after a while. Social reality turns out to have many layers of meaning. The discovery of each new layer changes the perception of the whole.

Anthropologists use the term "culture shock" to describe the impact of a totally new culture upon a newcomer. In an extreme instance such shock will be experienced by the Western explorer who is told, halfway through dinner, that he is eating the nice old lady he had been chatting with the previous day—a shock with predictable physiological if not moral consequences. Most explorers no longer encounter cannibalism in their travels today. However, the first encounters with polygamy or with puberty rites or even with the way some nations drive their automobiles can be quite a shock to an American visitor. With the shock may go not only disapproval or disgust but a sense of excitement that things can *really* be that different from what they are at home. To some extent, at least, this is the excitement of any first travel abroad. The experience of sociological discovery could be described as "culture shock" minus geographical displacement. In other words, the sociologist travels at home—with shocking results. He is unlikely to find that he is eating a nice old lady for dinner. But the discovery, for instance, that his own church has considerable money invested in the missile industry or that a few blocks from his home there are people who engage in cultic orgies may not be drastically different in emotional impact. Yet we would not want to imply that sociological discoveries are always or even usually outrageous to moral sentiment. Not at all. What they have in common with exploration in distant lands, however, is the sudden illumination of new and unsuspected facets of human existence in society. This is the excitement and, as we shall try to show later, the humanistic justification of sociology.

People who like to avoid shocking discoveries, who prefer to believe that society is just what they were taught in Sunday School, who like the safety of the rules and the maxims of what Alfred Schuetz has called the "world-taken-for-granted," should stay away from sociology. People who feel no temptation before closed doors, who have no curiosity about human beings, who are content to admire scenery without wondering about the people who live in those houses on the other side of that river, should probably also stay away from sociology. They will find it unpleasant or, at any rate, unrewarding. People who are interested in human beings only if they can change, convert or reform them should also be warned, for they will find sociology much less useful than they hoped. And people whose interest is mainly in their own conceptual constructions will do just as well to turn to the study of little white mice. Sociology will be satisfying, in the long run, only to those who can think of nothing more entrancing than to watch men and to understand things human. . . .

Culture

- **American Values (Article 3)**
- **Culture and Conditions (Articles 4-5)**
- **Youth and Generational Cultures (Articles 6-8)**

The ordinary, everyday objects of living and the daily routines of life provide a structure to social existence that is regularly punctuated by festivals and celebrations. Both the routine and special times are the "stuff" of culture, for culture is the sum total of all pieces of one's social inheritance. Culture includes language, tools, values, habits, literature, and art.

Because culture is often overlooked and taken for granted, it helps to pause and reflect upon shared beliefs and the relationships that form the foundations of group life. In a similar way, an examination of exotic and different cultures is valuable for recognizing how cultural assumptions affect all facets of life. A great deal can be learned by observing how other people treat their elderly or raise their young. Moreover, through such observations, individuals can recognize how misunderstandings begin and can appreciate the problems of maintaining cultural continuities in a rapidly changing environment. Through an awareness of culture we can begin to "know" ourselves, for culture lies at the heart of our personal and collective identities. Culture is one of the most powerful and important concepts in the discipline.

This section includes articles which look at culture from different perspectives and which portray cultural differences between groups in America. Often it takes an outsider to see the peculiarities of a group. How do you think Americans look to outsiders? One vistor from England, Henry Fairlie, explains how unusual he thought Americans were because we say "Hi" to everyone. From this simple greeting Fairlie learned about American freedom and democracy. He also discusses other peculiarities of America and tells why he loves and adopted the country.

Specific cultures are shaped by the conditions of life. When those conditions change, the culture will also change over time. Colin Turnbull describes life with an Afri-

can tribe that was moved off of its original land and was forced to live in a harsh environment. Literally all aspects of life changed for them, in a disturbingly sinister direction. The following selection by Elliot Liebow describes another culture that developed as a response to difficult conditions. To some middle class Americans, this ghetto culture may seem more unusual than many foreign societies.

One facet of culture which is of perennial interest is the development of a new perspective and way of life by each new teenage generation. Obviously the continuity outweighs the diversity between generations, but the differences are fascinating to look at. The last three articles explore some of these differences. Leavitt describes the youth generation of the 1970s while Barnett examines the youth generation of the 1980s. The authors think their own generation is very unique, but that issue is debatable.

In the final article, Saul Levine describes the sudden flight of teenagers into cults as an escape from the culture of their parents. He concludes, however, that "more than ninety percent of these departures end in a return home within two years, and virtually all joiners eventually abandon their groups." The reason they leave in the first place, Levine suggests, is that "...they use their radical departures to grow up." Levine's argument for this thesis is an example of the use of the sociological imagination.

Looking Ahead: Challenge Questions

Why do individuals seldom question their cultural values?

What are the boundaries of a culture? How does one cross over boundaries?

What is the relationship between culture and identity?

What might a visitor from a primitive tribe describe as shocking and barbaric about American society?

Unit 2

Why I Love America

Henry Fairlie

I HAD REPORTED from some twenty-four countries before I set foot in America. I will never forget the first shock—even after having been in every country from the Sudan to South Africa—at realizing that I was in another place entirely, a New World. In the casbah of Algiers during the first referendum called by de Gaulle in 1959, when the women hurrying down the steep streets to vote for the first time pulled their yashmaks around their faces as they passed a man (which seemed to me only to make their dark eyes more fascinating), I was still in the Old World, however strange it was. But here in America it was all new.

I had been in the country about eight years, and was living in Houston, when a Texan friend asked me one evening: "Why do you like living in America? I don't mean why you find it interesting—why you want to write about it—but why you *like* living here so much." After only a moment's reflection, I replied, "It's the first time I've felt free." In the nine years that have passed since then, I have often reflected on that answer, and have found no reason to change it. What I mean by it is part of the story to be told here.

Other memories come to mind. One spring day, shortly after my arrival, I was walking down the long, broad street of a suburb, with its sweeping front lawns (all that space), its tall trees (all that sky), and its clumps of azaleas (all that color). The only other person on the street was a small boy on a tricycle. As I passed him, he said "Hi!"—just like that. No four-year-old boy had ever addressed me without an introduction before. Yet here was this one, with his cheerful "Hi!" Recovering from the culture shock, I tried to look down stonily at his flaxen head, but instead, involuntarily, I found myself saying in return: "Well—hi!" He pedaled off, apparently satisfied. He had begun my Americanization.

"Hi!" As I often say—for Americans do not realize it—the word is a democracy. (I come from a country where one can tell someone's class by how they say "Hallo!" or "Hello!" or "Hullo," or whether they say it at all.) But anyone can say "Hi!" Anyone does. Shortly after my encounter with the boy, I called on the then Suffragan Bishop of Washington. Did he greet me as the Archbishop of Canterbury would have done? No. He said, "Hi, Henry!" I put it down to an aberration, an excess of Episcopalian latitudinarianism. But what about my first meeting with Lyndon B. Johnson, the President of the United States, the Emperor of the Free World, before whom, like a Burgher of Calais, a halter round my neck, I would have sunk to my knees, pleading for a loan for my country? He held out the largest hand in Christendom, and said, "Hi, Henry!"

Small anecdotes? But I wish to suggest that it is there, in the small anecdotes, that the secret lies. America has—if one opens oneself to it—a bewitching power. From the very beginning the stranger feels its influence as a loosening. At first this can be disquieting. After all, one is not in an exotic land, where the differences are immediately striking, easy to see, so that one may be fascinated without really being touched by them. Yet from the beginning in America one feels this power, unsettling all that one had thought was familiar, fixed by the ages. To some—I have known them—it is alarming. For there do come moments when one realizes, more than in any other country not one's own, that here one may be being remade. If here history still invents itself, then here also, still, one may invent the future. But suppose that means that one may also invent oneself? Max Ascoli, the Italian Jew who fled from Fascism and founded and edited in America a remarkable magazine, *The Reporter*, once wrote: "It did not cause me any trouble to become an Italian, but my becoming an American is my own work." Every immigrant will know what he means; millions are still working on it in their own lives.

I remember also the time when I still resisted the very power of America to attract. After I had been here in

Washington, D.C., a little while, I noticed one day that all the Americans who had befriended me were preparing to participate in some ritual, and that I was not invited. It was the Fourth of July. I presumed that they were being tactful: How could they ask me to celebrate a British defeat? So I accepted an invitation from Patrick O'Donovan, then the Washington correspondent of *The Observer*. What could we do on the Fourth? We looked at the television listings, and were delighted to find that there was a midday rerun of the original *Scarlet Pimpernel*, with Leslie Howard as Sir Percy Blakeney. We may have been defeated by the Americans, but one Englishman, single-handedly, had outwitted Robespierre's police. So we sat with our elbows on the lunch table, watching Leslie Howard be English, brave, and debonair, and even when the table leaf gave way with a crash, it did not interrupt Sir Percy or our absorption.

Later in the afternoon, Patrick—who had been a strapping young Irish Guards officer during the Second World War, as handsome (as they say) as the devil—opened the screen door into his Georgetown garden, and peed. "It does one good," he proclaimed, "on the Fourth of July, to piss on American soil." But he let in an enormous bug— one of those gigantic bugs that make it all the more inexplicable why Americans like barbecuing on their patios in the fetid summer—which then banged from wall to wall, sometimes wheeling to dive-bomb us. "You shouldn't have pissed on America," I said to Patrick. "George III tried to piss on it, and look what happened to him." But Patrick was by now cowering behing the couch—all six-foot-four Irish Guards of him—shouting to his wife, " 'Mione, 'Mione, HELP!' " She came downstairs, took one pitying look at her brave Britishers, got a can of Raid, and destroyed the American intruder. Patrick got up from behind the couch, drew himself up again to his full height, and said as if he were addressing his troops in the desert, "Henry, I cannot *bear* the tropics." By the time the fireworks began on the mall— "More shots to be heard round the world, I suppose," grumbled Patrick—we had the Dutch courage to ignore them. We had drunk our way—what else for exiles to do?—through the Fourth of July.

But as I stayed and felt America drawing me to it, I inevitably began to think of the others who have come. The curiosity about the country which first brought and kept me here scarcely entitles me to claim that I have shared the experience of most immigrants. I have no right to make it seem as if I came here traveling steerage, like the political refugees or those who simply had neither food nor hope in their native lands. But I will say this about the Statue of Liberty. It was an act of imagination, when the French proposed raising the money for it to celebrate the American Revolution, to choose such a site, and not Washington or Mount Vernon or Philadelphia, and to put on it that inscription, recalling not the English colonists who made the Revolution, but the millions upon millions of others who have come here since. They were drawn by the promise of this land; the land has performed for many

more of them than it has failed; and they in turn have helped remake the nation. And still they come.

The story of the immigration cannot be told bloodlessly. It cannot be drained of what Osbert Sitwell caught so well, in this hauntingly lovely passage from his *The Four Continents*, published in 1954: "New York, with all its faults, is yet the greatest and the most moving of modern cities . . . built by refugees to shelter and protect their dreams on alien soil. . . . For that is what it is, a metropolis of dreams realized and unrealized . . . dreams of every age and intensity. . . . So when in the small hours you open the window, and the cool of the darkness flows into the heated room, it is on a beautiful and improbable city of dreams that you look, some tragic, some naive, but many of them practicable and to be achieved in the future, near or distant, by the labors of these same dreamers when awake during the working day. Thus in the main the dreams will be fulfilled, and the hopes that prevail over fears are justified." How can one lose the sense that something quite miraculous has happened in the making of one nation from so many different peoples?

No other immigration into any other country has had anything like the same meaning for the rest of the world, for those who did not migrate, lifting the imagination of the world to horizons beyond even the expanse of this continent. The name of America still lends to countless millions its own dreams for them to dream themselves.

An English economist once said that it was America that had taught the world that it need not starve. Consider that. It cannot be denied. The achievements of American agriculture are one of the wonders of the modern world. Americans consume each year only a third of the wheat which American farmers produce; there is no other valley in the world which has been made, by irrigation, as fertile as the Central Valley of California. But it is not only such facts and figures that tell the wonder. One must look down the vastness of the Middle West, as the English poet Louis MacNeice did in 1940, "astonished by its elegance from the air. Elegance is the word for it—enormous plains of beautifully inlaid rectangles, the grain running different ways, walnut, satinwood or oatcake, the whole of it tortoiseshelled with copses and shadows of clouds. . . ." It is common for the American when he is in Europe to gasp at the hedgerows of England or the terraced vineyards of Italy, kept for centuries. But the gasp of the Englishman is no less when he gazes on a continent, immense in scale, still fabulous in its diversity, which not only is cultivated but has by its cultivation been given its own coherence; which unlike Europe has been made one. Who but the Americans would, so early, have made the Great Plains yield so much—those semi-arid lands which even they, at first, called "the Great American Desert"?

But let us return to small things. If America was to produce, it had also to invent. The English critic T. R. Fyvel once told a story of a friend, also English, who had "found himself for a fantastic weekend in a society of Texas millionaires who whizzed around in their private aircraft, dropping in on parties hundreds of miles away."

2. CULTURE: American Values

The friend found this unexpectedly refreshing. He was even more impressed when he saw the children of his host "buzzing around in special little pedal motor cars which were air conditioned." But one night his Texan millionaire host turned to him and said something like: "You know, Bob, I ask myself if our machine civilization isn't shot all to hell." The Englishman, horrified, burst out to his host: "Don't have those decadent thoughts! Don't have any thoughts! Leave them to us—while you stay just as you are!" I understand his response. There seems to be nothing, however fanciful, that the American, with his unflagging inventive genius, will not attempt.

MATTHEW ARNOLD was amazed at the warmth of American houses. "We are full of plans," he wrote to his daughter from Philadelphia in 1883, "for putting an American stove into the Cottage," when he got back to England. In 1912 Arnold Bennett was amazed that, whereas "the European telephone is a toy," in America it was regarded as an indispensable convenience for everyone. In 1942 Sir Philip Biggs was amazed by the supermarket, "where you grab what you want and wheel it to the cashier in steel perambulators made for the purpose," and leave "laden with a variety of food, beyond the range of English households even in peacetimes, from the A & P stores." (Twenty-three years later, on my very first morning in America, the wife of the English friend with whom I was staying took me, not to the Washington Monument, but to a supermarket—just to stare.) In 1963 T. H. White, who made a lecture tour in his old age, accompanied by the eighteen-year-old sister-in-law of Julie Andrews as "my secretary, but really as a protectress," was amazed at the change machine in the automat restaurant on a train: "In went a dollar bill which was inspected and out come [sic] four silver quarters. Why couldn't we put in bits of newspaper cut to the right size?" But he found more to wonder at: "In Long Island fishermen can buy *worms* from slot machines"; and again: "I also learned of *tab-opening cans*. You can open a beer can and, it is to be hoped, you will soon be able to open any can, without a tin opener." They were all responding to something I could not imagine America without.

How I have come to take it all for granted was brought home to me not long ago, when I was sitting in my house with a friend visiting from England. It was a quiet afternoon in early summer, the windows were open, I could hear the birds chirping in the garden. My friend suddenly exclaimed: "How can you bear to live in all this noise?" What noise? "All this noise in the house," he said. "Something is always switching itself off or on, humming or purring." He had destroyed my own peace, for I noticed it from then on. It is no wonder that America consumes so much energy. The electric gadgetry in an American home makes it its own Disney World. But to most Englishmen it is the physical evidence of a society that does not tire of innovation; which by its inventiveness still seems to keep the future open; and in whose inventiveness ordinary people find convenience.

THE INVENTIVENESS and gadgetry of the American reflects the spirit of a society which echoes the song: "It ain't necessarily so." If houses are insufferably cold, you invent a stove, and then you invent central heating; and if anyone writes in to say that the Romans had central heating, the important point is that the common man in Rome did not have it. Ben Franklin invented a prefabricated stove which could be produced for the common man; such a stove in Europe at the time would have been produced by craftsmen for the few. But then it has always been the American way as well, when faced with any injustice or harshness in this society, to say that "it ain't necessarily so," and to do something about it. If ever this spirit is allowed to languish, whether in the invention of things or the improvement of its society, America will have ceased to be what it means to the rest of the world.

When the cafeteria was first invented, the English responded to it with delight, from Clare Sheridan first being taken to one by Upton Sinclair in 1921, when she followed him as "he first took a metal tray from a column of trays," to S.P.B. Mais's description in 1933:

> You put your tray on a slide, help yourself as you rush along to orange juice, puffed rice, eggs, rolls, coffee, marmalade, or whatever it is you eat for breakfast, and when you reach the end of the counter a girl checks your loaded tray with lightning calculation, says "Thirty cents"—or whatever it is—and you take your tray and eat your breakfast at a table. The whole time spent in getting your food is thirty seconds.

The cafeteria has, of course, spread all over the world. But what these first encounters tell, above all, is of their convenience, and the fact that this convenience is liberating, as electrical gadgets (or Clarence Birdseye's invention, frozen foods) are liberating in the home. What they tell secondly is that these conveniences are not for a privileged few. Like the Franklin stove or the Ford Model T, these amenities were meant for all.

What I am trying to show is that, to other Englishmen besides myself, there is a meaning to the material progress of America which has traveled, and is still traveling, to the rest of the world, beyond the physical benefits which it bestows. It was a critic of fastidious taste and judgment, Cyril Connolly, who said in 1952:

> All American influence on Europe, however vulgar, brings with it an improvement in the standard of living and the dissipation of certain age-old desires. Should Europe oppose this influence? Europe, which has destroyed so many exotic civilizations, without even providing them with the democratic optimism which America brings with its films, its gadgets, and its *lingua franca*, the demotic language which obliterates all class distinctions.

BUT CONNOLLY left out the most significant American influence of all: the spread of the manners of a society which has always been more informal, less stiff, less bound by convention, than any other in the world; in which a person is accepted, as Thackeray said during one of his visits, for what he is. The impetus to informality in

America is, at least in part, the source of one of the most striking changes in our century: the change in the relationship between one individual human being and another, and so in their relationship to their society.

The informality is one characteristic which at first both jarred and drew me. By far the most infectious account of this characteristic of America was given by Dom Hubert van Zeller, an English monk who often preached retreats in both countries, and enjoyed America, but was still astonished at this scene:

In a hall at Denver I had the privilege of being listened to by upwards of six hundred nuns, assembled from different communities, all of whom were eating ices off the ends of sticks. The distribution of the ices, effectively conducted by a member of the home team, took place during the earlier phase of my address, so from the elevated position which I occupied on the platform, I was able to lay bets with myself as to which religious order would finish first.

This is the public informality—often noticed in Congress, in the courts—but the training begins early, with the freedom given the American child.

The children, like the informality, can at first jar. But the true mark of American society is that its informality forms its own patterns and codes. Although the outsider cannot at first detect it, there is a rhythm of American life. This rhythm is a constant improvisation, a flexibility that will accommodate the wishes and whims of every member of the group. No one voice in the typical American family takes precedence over the rest. Someone is always leaving or coming back; someone is always asking if he or she can have the car; someone is always going to the refrigerator for a snack instead of a meal; someone is always arriving late at a meal or leaving it early. The rhythm of the American family is to be found in a system of communications by which the improvised activities of each of its members is made known to all so that they can be taken into account. What holds the home together is a pattern of wires and castings, as hidden from view as the inside of a transistor radio, along which a ceaseless flow of messages is carried, and accommodations made to them. Messages left on the refrigerator door can for days be the only visible form of communication between members of a family who otherwise succeed in never running into each other as they come and go.

This is one reason why Mom and Dad, Lois and Junior, are so noticeable as tourists, and look so uncomfortable. They are not used to doing things as a unit. One can notice this even in an ordinary restaurant in America, when a whole family has for once come out to have dinner together: one by one, each grows restless to get away, and the meal degenerates into a pitiless nagging of the one person (usually, the mother) who is actually having a good time, and so is holding up the rest. What has happened is that they are not using their transistors; since they are all together, the flow of messages has been interrupted; having to do the same thing, at the same time, their common life has lost its rhythm.

I NOTICED AT ONCE the general American aversion to sitting down to a meal, and the time spent, if you are a guest, sitting in an armchair, or a canvas chair on the porch, always with a low table within handy reach. What then happens was perfectly caught in 1952 by the English journalist Mervyn Jones:

Darting in and out of the kitchen, your hostess keeps the table constantly loaded with sandwiches, plates of cheese, nice little things on crackers, bowls of fruit, nuts, olives, pretzels, rolls, cakes, cookies, and other refreshments. Gin, whisky, beer, and coffee are on tap without a moment's break. You are urged, in case there should be anything you lack, to help yourself from the two or three vast refrigerators. . . . People arrive in cars, sit down, stretch out their hands with the same air of unthinking habit as a horse reaching for a clump of grass, nibble for a while, get into their cars, and go—to be replaced, no matter what the hour, by other nibblers. All sense of time is lost. . . . You have, however, eaten twice as much as though you had sat round the table for three square meals.

The fact is that a wholly different manner of life was invented in America, contrasted with that of Europe (before it began to spread there from America): with more flexibility, more activity, more fragmentation, but still with its own patterns. American society is a kaleidoscope, in which the original pattern is always being rearranged. This is itself freeing, simply in day-to-day behavior, in the opportunities to meet other people, but also in deeper ways.

Though there are classes in America, there is no *class system*. When I answered, "The first time I've felt free," one thing I meant was that I was free of class. How could a class system be fastened onto a shifting kaleidoscope? If you imagine that you have discovered some symmetrical pattern in American society, you have only to change the angle at which you stand to it and the pattern changes. As Martin Green wrote in 1961, "America is not dominated by any single type, much less [a] class-limited one"; and he added, referring to Britain, "In these two ways, America stands for health, and we for sickness." This is strong, but it is just. Class—accent, vocabulary, dress, manners—not only confines the lower class in England, it also confines the upper class. It is much easier to mix here with people who are unlike oneself. To whom can this be more important than the immigrant making his way into the mainstream? Why the barriers remain so difficult for blacks to cross is too large a question to go into here; and the disappointing results so far of the Puerto Rican immigration (of which Nathan Glazer and Daniel Patrick Moynihan expected so much in *Beyond the Melting Pot*) also raise disconcerting questions which are beyond the scope of personal response. I will merely say that the sheer rise of the present colored—Asian, Latin American, Caribbean—immigration seems bound to present challenges which will make Americans again consider the virtues of assimilation.

OTHER LINES than those of class are also more easily crossed: those of sex, for example, and of age. When the English have come to America they have always written at length about American women. "And what luncheons," exclaimed Clare Sheridan, ". . . and apparently all for themselves. There is never a man. They even pay one another compliments. I wonder if they can be contented." (There has often been this ambivalence in the consistent praise of American women.) I too would comment when I first came here on the numbers of women lunching together in restaurants. But I soon came to believe that it is partly from her associations with other women that the American woman draws, not only a strength and subtlety of feeling for her own existence (a part of her superiority which almost every English visitor has acknowledged), but also her capacity for friendship with men. It is the American man's capacity for friendship with women which is in doubt, and I attribute it to the shallowness of his associations and lack of intimacy with his own sex. In a moment I will show why that last observation is not thrown in just to provoke a riot.

But first I must emphasize what it is in American women which, especially when they began to arrive in England in large numbers a century ago, took the English by storm. In 1907, Lady Dorothy Nevill calling her "bright and vivacious," said, "it is by the American girl we have been conquered." As early as 1864 Lord Bryce, who later married one, thought that American women had "so much more freedom in their manners; . . . the absence of primness was a very agreeable relief." To Rudyard Kipling in 1891, "the girls of America are above and beyond them all. . . . They have societies, and clubs . . . where all the guests are girls. . . ; they understand; they can take care of themselves; they are superbly independent." But the essential point was made by Jerome K. Jerome in 1904: "The American girl has succeeded in freeing European social intercourse from many of its hide-bound conventions. There is still work for her to do. But I have a faith in her."

The barrier of age is also crossed. My first editor in 1945 had lectured to a party of American students on the liner bringing them to observe postwar Europe. He exclaimed to me: "They are so different. They ask questions. They say what they think. They are not afraid to talk." Since I was twenty-one myself, and had never been afraid to talk, I thought he was a little gone in the head. There are few things more delightful than the way in which young Americans all over the country are willing to engage openly and freely in conversation and even friendship with someone perhaps more than twice their age. There is a democracy of manners in America which I would miss terribly if I ever left here.

I have been describing a society that is freeing. But there is no doubt it is also demanding. For if the immigrant feels here that he may invent himself, then is he not in that only being an American already? So much in the Old World is fixed for one: not only one's position but so much of one's life and even one's self. This is what weighs in the first part of Ascoli's remark: "It did not cause me any trouble to become an Italian." But even for an American born here, is it not his "own work" to become an American? This accounts for the one unease I still feel.

WITH THE CONTRAST I am about to draw, it is worth saying, I know many Americans who agree. It is much easier at first—and it is here that I am thinking of the men—to get to know an American. The welcoming "Hi!," the first names, the ready handshake, the quick generosity. You do not get through these first layers with an Englishman nearly as easily or as quickly. But once through them with an American, you come soon to a dead end, you are not admitted to the core or to any real intimacy. With the Englishman, whereas it is hard to get through the initial reserve, once through those outer layers, all resistance crumbles, and you find that you are sharing a level of extraordinary intimacy.

Julián Marías, the disciple of Ortega y Gasset, who spent much time here in the 1950s and 1960s, observed that although Americans get more mail than any other people in the world, they receive far fewer personal letters. An American friend of mine, Howard Higman, a professor of sociology, makes the point well. A letter from an American is like an itinerary, he says, a letter from an Englishman is like a diary. There is no questioning this, and I have often wondered what it is that Americans fear to expose, even whether they fear that there is nothing at the core to expose at all. But the answer, I believe, is simpler. If there has been so much freedom and informality in which to make oneself, if it really is one's "own work" to be an American, then one is bound to guard jealously a self which must often feel isolated and fragile, far more than in a society where so much of who one is has been determined for one. (For if one has been made by that society, it has made others like oneself, so what is there to fear?) This is the significance of the women's associations on which the English observers at once fixed their attention. The men's associations are far more likely to be centered on some activity—sports, watching football, hunting—anything to avoid having to talk about themselves and bare their souls. This is where one comes to a dead stop. These are the personal letters one misses. Almost all letters from American men are typed, even those from my friends, even those meant to be warmly personal. They might be dictated to a secretary, for the little they dare to say.

There is in all of this one reason why so many American attempts to describe the experience of being an American fall back on myth and metaphor, whereas almost all the English descriptions of what it seems to them to mean to be an American stick to the details and small encounters of everyday life. Americans take too much for granted the details of American life in which may often be found the meaning of the freedom and equality and opportunity which still draw people to it. We all know the wretched side of the life of the immigrants: the rough, menial, even dangerous work; the abysmally low wages; the abject conditions in which they lived, in the notorious dumbbell tenements of New York, for example, honeycombed with tiny rooms. And we know that those wretched conditions, whether in the large cities or in the acres of the Southwest baking under the sun, still exist. Yet there was and is another side. It was not all that long after the Italians began to arrive that, in their communities on the Upper East Side, there were shoulders of meat in the butcher's windows at twelve cents a pound; outside the macaroni shops, under improvised shelters, the macaroni was hung out to dry; along the curbs were the pushcarts with artichokes and asparagus, early melons and tomatoes; and a round of cheese cost twenty-four cents. And although only a third of the Italian immigrants had ever cast a vote in their native country, before the first generation had reached middle age they had politicians courting them; and Fiorello La Guardia was elected to Congress from East Harlem on his second attempt in 1916. As they shopped on their streets, where did their allegiance lie? To Genoa? We can still catch from that picture of their streets the smell of freedom.

As a young officer, George C. Marshall was surprised, when he inspected his troops on landing in France in 1917, at how many of them spoke broken English. But of their stake in America, in its industry, in its freedom, there could be little doubt; this was borne out by the astonishing lack of sedition in America throughout the war. I have tried from my own experience to explain some of the small but revealing reasons why America worked its influence so quickly and so deeply on them. It now seems to be working on some of the new immigrants. In my observa-tion, the East Asians especially (and who would have predicted it?) are responding wholeheartedly to American life—their children are into the Little League almost as soon as they are out of the cradle—as they work their way, often by traditional routes such as running neighborhood stores, into the mainstream. This third wave of immigra-tion is repeating, quite remarkably, many of the charac-teristics of the first two waves. America is still open, and it will be a tragedy if those who wish it to "think small," who will to keep America as a playground for those already here, have their way, and close America down.

I will give the last words to an American. Daniel Patrick Moynihan wrote in 1978: ". . . while the matter has not received much attention, the United States is quietly but rapidly resuming its role as a nation of first- and second-generation immigrants, almost the only one of its kind in the world, incomparably the largest, and for the first time in our history or any other, a nation drawn from the entire world. The Immigration Act of 1965 altered the shape of American immigration and increased its size. . . . Our immigrants in wholly unprecedented proportions come from Asia, South America, and the Caribbean. In fiscal year 1973 the ten top visa-issuing ports were Manila, Monterrey, Seoul, Tijuana, Santo Domingo, Mexico City, Naples, Guadalajara, Toronto, Kingston. I would expect Bombay to make this top ten list before long. . . . In short, by the end of the century, the United States will be a multi-ethnic nation the like of which even we have never imagined."

In this vision, America is still open. And America is about to be remade by its immigrants—again—as they become enthusiastic Americans. And what will the immi-grants write home about? The gadgets, I beg, the gadgets.

The Mountain People

Colin M. Turnbull

Anthropologist Colin M. Turnbull, author of The Forest People *and* The Lonely Africans, *went to study the Ik of Uganda, who he believed were still primarily hunters, in order to compare them with other hunting-and-gathering societies he had studied in totally different environments. He was surprised to discover that they were no longer hunters but primarily farmers, well on their way to starvation and something worse in a drought-stricken land.*

In what follows, there will be much to shock, and the reader will be tempted to say, "how primitive, how savage, how disgusting," and, above all, "how inhuman." The first judgments are typical of the kind of ethno- and egocentricism from which we can never quite escape. But "how inhuman" is of a different order and supposes that there are certain values inherent in humanity itself, from which the people described here seem to depart in a most drastic manner. In living the experience, however, and perhaps in reading it, one finds that it is oneself one is looking at and questioning; it is a voyage in quest of the basic human and a discovery of his potential for inhumanity, a potential that lies within us all.

Just before World War II the Ik tribe had been encouraged to settle in northern Uganda, in the mountainous northeast corner bordering on Kenya to the east and Sudan to the north.

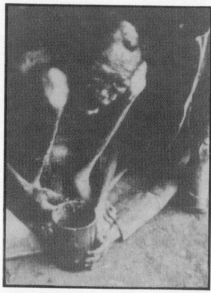

Until then they had roamed in nomadic bands, as hunters and gatherers, through a vast region in all three countries. The Kidepo Valley below Mount Morungole was their major hunting territory. After they were confined to a part of their former area, Kidepo was made a national park and they were forbidden to hunt or gather there.

The concept of family in a nomadic society is a broad one; what really counts most in everyday life is community of residence, and those who live close to each other are likely to see each other as effectively related, whether there is any kinship bond or not. Full brothers, on the other hand, who live in different parts of the camp may have little concern for each other.

It is not possible, then, to think of the family as a simple, basic unit. A child is brought up to regard any adult living in the same camp as a parent, and age-mate as a brother or sister. The Ik had this essentially social attitude toward kinship, and it readily

lent itself to the rapid and disastrous changes that took place following the restriction of their movement and hunting activities. The family simply ceased to exist.

It is a mistake to think of small-scale societies as "primitive" or "simple." Hunters and gatherers, most of all, appear simple and straightforward in terms of their social organization, yet that is far from true. If we can learn about the nature of society from a study of small-scale societies, we can also learn about human relationships. The smaller the society, the less emphasis there is on the formal system and the more there is on interpersonal and intergroup relations. Security is seen in terms of these relationships, and so is survival. The result, which appears so deceptively simple, is that hunters frequently display those characteristics that we find so admirable in man: kindness, generosity, consideration, affection, honesty, hospitality, compassion, charity. For them, in their tiny, close-knit society, these are necessities for survival. In our society anyone possessing even half these qualities would find it hard to survive, yet we think these virtues are inherent in man. I took it for granted that the Ik would possess these same qualities. But they were as unfriendly, uncharitable, inhospitable and generally mean as any people can be. For those positive qualities we value so highly are no longer functional for them; even more than in our own society they spell ruin and disaster. It seems that, far from being basic human qualities, they are luxuries we can afford in times of plenty or are mere mechanisms for survival and security. Given the situation in which the Ik found

themselves, man has no time for such luxuries, and a much more basic man appears, using more basic survival tactics.

Turnbull had to wait in Kaabong, a remote administration outpost, for permission from the Uganda government to continue to Pirre, the Ik water hole and police post. While there he began to learn the Ik language and became used to their constant demands for food and tobacco. An official in Kaabong gave him, as a "gift," 20 Ik workers to build a house and a road up to it. When they arrived at Pirre, however, wages for the workers were negotiated by wily Atum, "the senior of all the Ik on Morungole."

The police seemed as glad to see me as I was to see them. They hungrily asked for news of Kaabong, as though it were the hub of the universe. They had a borehole and pump for water, to which they said I was welcome, since the water holes used by the Ik were not fit for drinking or even for washing. The police were not able to tell me much about the Ik, because every time they went to visit an Ik village, there was nobody there. Only in times of real hunger did they see much of the Ik, and then only enough to know that they were hungry.

The next morning I rose early, but even though it was barely daylight, by the time I had washed and dressed, the Ik were already outside. They were sitting silently, staring at the Land Rover. As impassive as they seemed, there was an air of expectancy, and I was reminded that these

were, after all, hunters, and the likelihood was that I was their morning's prey. So I left the Land Rover curtains closed and as silently as possible prepared a frugal breakfast.

Atum was waiting for me. He said that he had told all the Ik that Iciebam [friend of the Ik] had arrived to live with them and that I had given the workers a "holiday" so they could greet me. They were waiting in the villages. They were very hungry, he added, and many were dying. That was probably one of the few true statements he ever made, and I never even considered believing it.

There were seven villages in all. Village Number One was built on a steep slope, and even the houses tilted at a crazy angle. Atum rapped on the outer stockade with his cane and shouted a greeting, but there was no response. This was Giriko's village, he said, and he was one of my workers.

"But I thought you told them to go back to their villages," I said.

"Yes, but you gave them a holiday, so they are probably in their fields," answered Atum, looking me straight in the eye.

At Village Number Two there was indisputably someone inside, for I could hear loud singing. The singing stopped, a pair of hands gripped the stockade and a craggy head rose into view, giving me an undeniably welcoming smile. This was Lokelea. When I asked him what he had been singing about, he answered, "Because I'm hungry."

Village Number Three, the smallest of all, was empty. Village Number Four had only 8 huts, as

against the 12 or so in Lokelea's village and the 18 in Giriko's. The outer stockade was broken in one section, and we walked right in. We ducked through a low opening and entered a compound in which a woman was making pottery. She kept on at her work but gave us a cheery welcome and laughed her head off when I tried to speak in Icietot. She willingly showed me details of her work and did not seem unduly surprised at my interest. She said that everyone else had left for the fields except old Nangoli, who, on hearing her name mentioned, appeared at a hole in the stockade shutting off the next compound. Nangoli mumbled toothlessly at Losike, who told Atum to pour her some water.

As we climbed up to his own village, Number Five, Atum said that Losike never gave anything away. Later I remembered that gift of water to Nangoli. At the time I did not stop to think that in this country a gift of water could be a gift of life.

Atum's village had nearly 50 houses, each within its compound within the stout outer stockade. Atum did not invite me in.

A hundred yards away stood Village Number Six. Kauar, one of the workers, was sitting on a rocky slab just outside the village. He had a smile like Losike's, open and warm, and he said he had been waiting for me all morning. He offered us water and showed me his own small compound and that of his mother.

Coming up from Village Number Seven, at quite a respectable speed, was a blind man. This was Logwara, emaciated but alive and remarkably active. He had heard us and had come to greet me, he said, but he added the inevitable demand for tobacco in the same breath. We sat down in the open sunlight. For a brief moment I felt at peace.

After a short time Atum said we should start back and called over his shoulder to his village. A muffled sound came from within, and he said, "That's my wife, she is very sick—and hungry." I offered to go and see her, but he shook his head. Back at the Land Rover I gave Atum some food and some aspirin, not knowing what else to give him to help his wife.

I was awakened well before dawn by the lowing of cattle. I made an extra pot of tea and let Atum distribute it, and then we divided the workers into two teams. Kauar was to head the team building the house, and Lokelatom, Losike's husband, was to take charge of the road workers.

While the Ik were working, their heads kept turning as though they were expecting something to happen. Every now and again one would stand up and peer into the distance and then take off into the bush for an hour or so. On one such occasion, after the person had been gone two hours, the others started drifting off. By then I knew them better; I looked for a wisp of smoke and followed it to where the road team was cooking a goat. Smoke was a giveaway, though, so they economized on cooking and ate most food nearly raw. It is a curious hangover from what must once have been a moral code that Ik will offer food if surprised in the act of eating, though they now go to enormous pains not to be so surprised.

I was always up before dawn, but by the time I got up to the villages they were always deserted. One morning I followed the little *oror* [gulley] up from *oror a pirreï* [Ravine of Pirre] while it was still quite dark, and I met Lomeja on his way down. He took me on my first illicit hunt in Kidepo. He told me that if he got anything he would share it with me and with anyone else who managed to join us but that he certainly would not take

anything back to his family. "Each one of them is out seeing what he can get for himself, and do you think they will bring any back for me?"

Lomeja was one of the very few Ik who seemed glad to volunteer information. Unlike many of the others, he did not get up and leave as I approached. Apart from him, I spent most of my time, those days, with Losike, the potter. She told me that Nangoli, the old lady in the adjoining compound, and her husband, Amuarkuar, were rather peculiar.

They helped each other get food and water, and they brought it back to their compound to eat together.

I still do not know how much real hunger there was at that time, for most of the younger people seemed fairly well fed, and the few skinny old people seemed healthy and active. But my laboriously extracted genealogies showed that there were quite a number of old people still alive and allegedly in these villages, though they were never to be seen. Then Atum's wife died.

Atum told me nothing about it but kept up his demands for food and medicine. After a while the beady-eyed Lomongin told me that Atum was selling the medicine I was giving him for his wife. I was not unduly surprised and merely remarked that

that was too bad for his wife. "Oh no," said Lomongin, "she has been dead for weeks."

It must have been then that I began to notice other things that I suppose I had chosen to ignore before. Only a very few of the Ik helped me with the language. Others would understand when it suited them and would pretend they did not understand when they did not want to listen. I began to be forced into a similar isolationist attitude myself, and although I cannot say I enjoyed it, it did make life much easier. I even began to enjoy, in a peculiar way, the company of the silent Ik. And the more I accepted it, the less often people got up and left as I approached. On one occasion I sat on the *di* [sitting place] by Atum's rain tree for three days with a group of Ik, and for three days not one word was exchanged.

The work teams were more lively, but only while working. Kauar always played and joked with the children when they came back from foraging. He used to volunteer to make the two-day walk into Kaabong and the even more tiring two-day climb back to get mail for me or to buy a few things for others. He always asked if he had made the trip more quickly than the last time.

Then one day Kauar went to Kaabong and did not come back. He was found on the last peak of the trail, cold and dead. Those who found him took the things he had been carrying and pushed his body into the bush. I still see his open, laughing face, see him giving precious tidbits to the children, comforting some child who was crying, and watching me read the letters he carried so lovingly for me. And I still think of him probably running up that viciously steep mountainside so he could break his time record and falling dead in his pathetic prime because he was starving.

Once I settled down into my new home, I was able to work more effectively. Having recovered at least some of my anthropological detachment, when I heard the telltale rustling of someone at my stockade, I merely threw a stone. If when out walking I stumbled during a difficult descent and the Ik shrieked with laughter, I no longer even noticed it.

Anyone falling down was good for a laugh, but I never saw anyone actually trip anyone else. The adults were content to let things happen and then enjoy them; it was probably conservation of energy. The children, however, sought their pleasures with vigor. The best game of all, at this time, was teasing poor little Adupa. She was not so little—in fact she should have been an adult, for she was nearly 13 years old—but Adupa was a little mad. Or you might say she was the only sane one, depending on your point of view. Adupa did not jump on other people's play houses, and she lavished enormous care on hers and would curl up inside it. That made it all the more jump-on-able. The other children beat her viciously.

Children are not allowed to sleep in the house after they are "put out," which is at about three years old, four at the latest. From then on they sleep in the open courtyard, taking what shelter they can against the stockade. They may ask for permission to sit in the doorway of their parents' house but may not lie down or sleep there. "The same thing applies to old people," said Atum, "if they can't build a house of their own and, of course, if their children let them stay in their compounds."

I saw a few old people, most of whom had taken over abandoned huts. For the first time I realized that there really was starvation and saw why I had never known it before: it was confined to the aged. Down in Giriko's village the old ritual priest, Lolim, confidentially told me that he was sheltering an old man who had been refused shelter by his son. But Lolim did not have enough food for himself, let alone his guest; could I . . . I liked old Lolim, so, not believing that Lolim had a visitor at all, I brought him a double ration that evening. There was a rustling in the back of the hut, and Lolim helped ancient Lomeraniang to the entrance. They shook with delight at the sight of the food.

When the two old men had finished eating, I left; I found a hungry-looking and disapproving little crowd clustered outside. They muttered to each other about wasting food. From then on I brought food daily, but in a very short time Lomeraniang was dead, and his son refused to come down from the village above to bury him. Lolim scratched a hole and covered the body with a pile of stones he carried himself, one by one.

Hunger was indeed more severe than I knew, and, after the old people, the children were the next to go. It was all quite impersonal—even to me, in most cases, since I had been immunized by the Ik themselves against sorrow on their behalf. But Adupa was an exception. Her madness was such that she did not know just how vicious humans could be. Even worse, she thought that parents were for loving, for giving as well as receiving. Her parents were not given to fantasies. When she came for shelter, they drove her out; and when she came because she was hungry, they laughed that Icien laugh, as if she had made them happy.

Adupa's reactions became slower and slower. When she managed to find food—fruit peels, skins, bits of bone, half-eaten berries—she held it in her hand and looked at it with wonder and delight. Her playmates caught on quickly; they put tidbits in her way and watched her simple drawn little face wrinkle in a smile. Then as she raised her hand to her mouth, they set on her with cries of excitement, fun and laughter, beating her savagely over the head. But that is

not how she died. I took to feeding her, which is probably the cruelest thing I could have done, a gross selfishness of my part to try to salve my own rapidly disappearing conscience. I had to protect her, physically, as I fed her. But the others would beat her anyway, and Adupa cried, not because of the pain in her body but because of the pain she felt at the great, vast, empty wasteland where love should have been.

It was *that* that killed her. She demanded that her parents love her. Finally they took her in, and Adupa was happy and stopped crying. She stopped crying forever because her parents went away and closed the door tight behind them, so tight that weak little Adupa could never have moved it.

The Ik seem to tell us that the family is not such a fundamental unit as we usually suppose, that it is not essential to social life. In the crisis of survival facing the Ik, the family was one of the first institutions to go, and the Ik as a society have survived.

The other quality of life that we hold to be necessary for survival—love—the Ik dismiss as idiotic and highly dangerous. But we need to see more of the Ik before their absolute lovelessness becomes truly apparent.

In this curious society there is one common value to which all Ik hold tenaciously. It is *ngag*, "food." That is the one standard by which they measure right and wrong, goodness and badness. The very word for "good" is defined in terms of food. "Goodness" is "the possession of food," or the "*individual* possession of food." If you try to discover their concept of a "good man," you get the truly Icien answer: one who has a full stomach.

We should not be surprised, then, when the mother throws her child out at three years old. At that age a series of *rites de passage* begins. In this environment a child has no chance of survival on his own until he is about 13, so children form age bands. The junior band consists of children between three and seven, the senior of eight- to twelve-year-olds. Within the band each child seeks another

21

close to him in age for defense against the older children. These friendships are temporary, however, and inevitably there comes a time when each turns on the one that up to then had been the closest to him; that is the *rite de passage,* the destruction of that fragile bond called friendship. When this has happened three or four times, the child is ready for the world.

The weakest are soon thinned out, and the strongest survive to achieve leadership of the band. Such a leader is eventually driven out, turned against by his fellow band members. Then the process starts all over again; he joins the senior age band as its most junior member.

The final *rite de passage* is into adulthood, at the age of 12 or 13. By then the candidate has learned the wisdom of acting on his own, for his own good, while acknowledging that on occasion it is profitable to associate temporarily with others.

One year in four the Ik can count on a complete drought. About this time it began to be apparent that there were going to be two consecutive years of drought and famine. Men as well as women took to gathering what wild fruits and berries they could find, digging up roots, cutting grass that was going to seed, threshing and eating the seed.

Old Nangoli went to the other side of Kidepo, where food and water were more plentiful. But she had to leave her husband, Amuarkuar, behind. One day he appeared at my *odok* and asked for water. I gave him some and was going to get him food when Atum came storming over and argued with me about wasting water. In the midst of the dispute Amuarkuar quietly left. He wandered over to a rocky outcrop and lay down there to rest. Nearby was a small bundle of grass that evidently he had cut and had been dragging painfully to the ruins of his village to make a rough shelter. The grass was his supreme effort to keep a home going until Nangoli returned. When I went over to him, he looked up and smiled and said that my water tasted good. He lay back and went to sleep with a smile on his face. That is how Amuarkuar died, happily.

There are measures that can be taken for survival involving the classical institutions of gift and sacrifice. These are weapons, sharp and aggressive. The object is to build up a series of obligations so that in times of crisis you have a number of debts you can recall; with luck one of them may be repaid. To this end, in the circumstances of Ik life, considerable sacrifice would be justified, so you have the odd phenomenon of these otherwise singularly self-interested people going out of their way to "help" each other. Their help may very well be resented in the extreme, but is done in such a way that it cannot be refused, for it has already been given. Someone may hoe another's field in his absence or rebuild his stockade or join in the building of a house.

The danger in this system was that the debtor might not be around when collection was called for and, by the same token, neither might the creditor. The future was too uncertain for this to be anything but one additional survival measure, though some developed it to a fine technique.

There seemed to be increasingly little among the Ik that could by any stretch of the imagination be called social life, let alone social organization. The family does not hold itself together; economic interest is centered on as many stomachs as there are people; and cooperation is merely a device for furthering an interest that is consciously selfish. We often do the same thing in our so-called "altruistic" practices, but we tell ourselves it is for the good of others. The Ik have dispensed with the myth of altruism. Though they have no centralized leadership or means of physical coercion, they do hold together with remarkable tenacity.

In our world, where the family has also lost much of its value as a social unit and where religious belief no longer binds us into communities, we maintain order only through coercive power that is ready to uphold a rigid law and through an equally rigid penal system. The Ik, however, have learned to do without coercion, either

spiritual or physical. It seems that they have come to a recognition of what they accept as man's basic selfishness, of his natural determination to survive as an individual before all else. This they consider to be man's basic right, and they allow others to pursue that right without recrimination.

In large-scale societies such as our own, where members are individual beings rather than social beings, we rely on law for order. The absence of both a common law and a common belief would surely result in lack of any community of behavior; yet Ik society is not anarchical. One might well expect religion, then, to play a powerful role in Icien life, providing a source of unity.

The Ik, as may be expected, do not run true to form. When I arrived, there were still three ritual priests alive. From them and from the few other old people, I learned something of the Ik's belief and practice as they had been before their world was so terribly changed. There had been a powerful unity of belief in Didigwari—a sky god—and a body of ritual practice reinforcing secular behavior that was truly social.

Didigwari himself is too remote to be of much practical significance to the Ik. He created them and abandoned them and retreated into his domain somewhere in the sky. He never came down to earth, but the *abang* [ancestors] have all known life on earth; it is only against them that one can sin and only to them that one can turn for help, through the ritual priest.

While Morungole has no legends attached to it by the Ik, it nonetheless figures in their ideology and is in some ways regarded by them as sacred. I had noticed this by the almost reverential way in which they looked at it—none of the shrewd cunning and cold appraisal with which they regarded the rest of the world. When they talked about it, there was a different quality to their voices. They seemed incapable of talking about Morungole in any other way, which is probably why they talked about it so very seldom. Even that weasel Lomongin became gentle the only time he talked about it to me. He said, "If Atum and I were there, we would not argue. It is a good place." I asked if he meant that it was full of food. He said yes. "Then why do Ik never go there?" "They do go there." "But if hunting is good there, why not live there?" "We don't hunt there, we just go there." "Why?" "I told you, it is a good place." If I did not understand him, that was my fault; for once he was doing his best to communicate something to me. With others it was the same. All agreed that it was "a good place." One added, "That is the Place of God."

Lolim, the oldest and greatest of the ritual priests, was also the last. He was not much in demand any longer, but he was still held in awe, which means kept at a distance. Whenever he approached a *di*, people cleared a space for him, as far away from themselves as possible. The Ik rarely called on his services, for they had little to pay him with, and he had equally little to offer them. The main things they did try to get out of him were certain forms of medicine, both herbal and magical.

Lolim said that he had inherited his power from his father. His father had taught him well but could not give him the power to hear the *abang*—that had to come from the *abang* themselves. He had wanted his oldest son to inherit and had taught him everything he could. But his son, Longoli, was bad, and the *abang* refused to talk to him. They talked instead to his oldest daughter, bald Nangoli. But there soon came the time when all the Ik needed was food in their stomachs, and Lolim could not supply that. The time came when Lolim was too weak to go out and collect the medicines he needed. His children all refused to go except Nangoli, and then she was jailed for gathering in Kidepo Park.

Lolim became ill and had to be protected while eating the food I gave him. Then the children began openly ridiculing him and teasing him, dancing in front of him and kneeling down so that he would trip over them. His grandson used to creep up behind him and with a pair of hard sticks

drum a lively tattoo on the old man's bald head.

I fed him whenever I could, but often he did not want more than a bite. Once I found him rolled up in his protective ball, crying. He had had nothing to eat for four days and no water for two. He had asked his children, who all told him not to come near them.

The next day I saw him leaving Atum's village, where his son Longoli lived. Longoli swore that he had been giving his father food and was looking after him. Lolim was not shuffling away; it was almost a run, the run of a drunken man, staggering from side to side. I called to him, but he made no reply, just a kind of long, continuous and horrible moan. He had been to Longoli to beg him to let him into his compound because he knew he was going to die in a few hours, Longoli calmly told me afterward. Obviously Longoli could not do a thing like that: a man of Lolim's importance would have called for an enormous funeral feast. So he refused. Lolim begged Longoli then to open up Nangoli's *asak* for him so that he could die in *her* compound. But Longoli drove him out, and he died alone.

Atum pulled some stones over the body where it had fallen into a kind of hollow. I saw that the body must have lain parallel with the *oror*. Atum answered without waiting for the question: "He was lying looking up at Mount Meraniang."

Insofar as ritual survived at all, it could hardly be said to be religious, for it did little or nothing to bind Icien society together. But the question still remained: Did this lack of social behavior and communal ritual or religious expression mean that there was no community of belief?

Belief may manifest itself, at either the individual or the communal level, in what we call morality, when we behave according to certain principles supported by our belief even when it seems against our personal interest. When we call ourselves moral, however, we tend to ignore that ultimately our morality benefits us even as individuals, insofar as we are social individuals and live in a

society. In the absence of belief, law takes over and morality has little role. If there was such a thing as an Icien morality, I had not yet perceived it, though traces of a moral past remained. But it still remained a possibility, as did the existence of an unspoken, unmanifest belief that might yet reveal itself and provide a basis for the reintegration of society. I was somewhat encouraged in this hope by the unexpected flight of old Nangoli, widow of Amuarkuar.

When Nangoli returned and found her husband dead, she did an odd thing: she grieved. She tore down what was left of their home, uprooted the stockade, tore up whatever was growing in her little field. Then she fled with a few belongings.

Some weeks later I heard that she and her children had gone over to the Sudan and built a village there. This migration was so unusual that I decided to see whether this runaway village was different.

Lojieri led the way, and Atum came along. One long day's trek got us there. Lojieri pulled part of the brush fence aside, and we went in and wandered around. He and Atum looked inside all the huts, and Lojieri helped himself to tobacco from one and water from another. Surprises were coming thick and fast. That households should be left open and untended with such wealth inside . . . That there should have been such wealth, for as well as tobacco and jars of water there were baskets of food, and meat was drying on racks. There were half a dozen or so compounds, but they were separated from each other only by a short line of sticks and brush. It was a village, and these were homes, the first and last I was to see.

The dusk had already fallen, and Nangoli came in with her children and grandchildren. They had heard us and came in with warm welcomes. There was no hunger here, and in a very short time each kitchen hearth had a pot of food cooking. Then we sat around the central fire and talked until late, and it was another universe.

There was no talk of "how much better it is here than there"; talk revolved around what had happened on the hunt that day. Loron was lying on the ground in front of the fire as his mother made gentle fun of him. His wife, Kinimei, whom I had never seen even speak to him at Pirre, put a bowl of fresh-cooked berries and fruit in front of him. It was all like a nightmare rather than a fantasy, for it made the reality of Pirre seem all the more frightening.

The unpleasantness of returning was somewhat alleviated by Atum's suffering on the way up the stony trail. Several times he slipped, which made Lojieri and me laugh. It was a pleasure to move rapidly ahead and leave Atum gasping behind so that we could be sitting up on the *di* when he finally appeared and could laugh at his discomfort.

The days of drought wore on into weeks and months and, like everyone else, I became rather bored with sickness and death. I survived rather as did the young adults, by diligent attention to my own needs while ignoring those of others.

More and more it was only the young who could go far from the village as hunger became starvation. Famine relief had been initiated down at Kasile, and those fit enough to make the trip set off. When they came back, the contrast between them and the others was that between life and death. Villages were villages of the dead and dying, and there was little difference between the two. People crawled rather than walked. After a few feet some would lie down to rest, but they could not be sure of ever being able to sit up again, so they mostly stayed upright until they reached their destination. They were going nowhere, these semianimate bags of skin and bone; they just wanted to be with others, and they stopped whenever they met. Perhaps it was the most important demonstration of sociality I ever saw among the Ik. Once they met, they neither spoke nor did anything together.

Early one morning, before dawn, the village moved. In the midst of a hive of activity were the aged and crippled, soon to be abandoned, in danger of being trampled but seemingly unaware of it. Lolim's widow, Lo'ono, whom I had never seen before, also had been abandoned and had tried to make her way down the mountainside. But she was totally blind and had tripped and rolled to the bottom of the *oror a pirre'i;* there she lay on her back, her legs and arms thrashing feebly, while a little crowd laughed.

At this time a colleague was with me. He kept the others away while I ran to get medicine and food and water, for Lo'ono was obviously near dead from hunger and thirst as well as from the fall. We treated her and fed her and asked her to come back with us. But she asked us to point her in the direction of her son's new village. I said I did not think she would get much of a welcome there, and she replied that she knew it but wanted to be near him when she died. So we gave her more food, put her stick in her hand and pointed her the right way. She suddenly cried. She was crying, she said, because we had reminded her that there had been a time when people had helped each other, when people had been kind and good. Still crying, she set off.

The Ik up to this point had been tolerant of my activities, but all this was too much. They said that what we were doing was wrong. Food and medicine were for the living, not the dead. I thought of Lo'ono. And I thought of other old people who had joined in the merriment when they had been teased or had a precious morsel of food taken from their mouths. They knew that it was silly of them to expect to go on living, and, having watched others, they knew that the spectacle really was quite funny. So they joined in the laughter. Perhaps if we had left Lo'ono, she would have died laughing. But we prolonged her misery for no more than a few brief days. Even worse, we reminded her of when things had been different, of days when children had cared for parents and parents for children. She was already dead, and we made her unhappy as well. At the time I was sure we were right, doing the only "human" thing. In a way we *were*—we were making life more comfortable for ourselves. But now I wonder if the Ik way was not right, if I too should not have laughed as Lo'ono flapped about, then left her to die.

Ngorok was a man at 12. Lomer, his older brother, at 15 was showing signs of strain; when he was carrying a load, his face took on a curious expression of pain that was no physical pain. Giriko, at 25 was 40, Atum at 40 was 65, and the very oldest, perhaps a bare 50, were centenarians. And I, at 40, was younger than any of them, for I still enjoyed life, which they had learned was not "adult" when they were 3. But they retained their will to survive and so offered grudging respect to those who had survived for long.

Even in the teasing of the old there was a glimmer of hope. It denoted a certain intimacy that did not exist between adjacent generations. This is quite common in small-scale societies. The very old and the very young look at each other as representing the future and the past. To the child, the aged represent a world that existed before their own birth and the unknown world to come.

And now that all the old are dead, what is left? Every Ik who is old today was thrown out at three and has survived, and in consequence has thrown his own children out and knows that they will not help him in his old age any more than he helped his parents. The system has turned one full cycle and is now self-perpetuating; it has eradicated what we know as "humanity" and has turned the world into a chilly void where man does not seem to care even for himself, but survives. Yet into this hideous world Nangoli and her family quietly returned because they could not bear to be alone.

For the moment abandoning the very old and the very young, the Ik as a whole must be searched for one last lingering trace of humanity. They appear to have disposed of virtually all the qualities that we normally think of as differentiating us from other primates, yet they survive without seeming to be greatly different from ourselves in terms of behavior.

Their behavior is more extreme, for we do not start throwing our children out until kindergarten. We have shifted responsibility from family to state, the Ik have shifted it to the individual.

It has been claimed that human beings are capable of love and, indeed, are dependent upon it for survival and sanity. The Ik offer us an opportunity for testing this cherished notion that love is essential to survival. If it is, the Ik should have it.

Love in human relationships implies mutuality, a willingness to sacrifice the self that springs from a consciousness of identity. This seems to bring us back to the Ik, for it implies that love is self-oriented, that even the supreme sacrifice of one's life is no more than selfishness, for the victim feels amply rewarded by the pleasure he feels in making the sacrifice. The Ik, however, do not value emotion above survival, and they are without love.

But I kept looking, for it was the one thing that could fill the void their survival tactics had created; and if love was not there in some form, it meant that for humanity love is not a necessity at all, but a luxury or an illusion. And if it was not among the Ik, it meant that mankind can lose it.

The only possibility for any discovery of love lay in the realm of interpersonal relationships. But they were, each one, simply alone, and seemingly content to be alone. It was this acceptance of individual isolation that made love almost impossible. Contact, when made, was usually for a specific practical purpose having to do with food and the filling of a stomach, a single stomach. Such contacts did not have anything like the permanence or duration required to develop a situation in which love was possible.

The isolation that made love impossible, however, was not completely proof against loneliness. I no longer noticed normal behavior, such as the way people ate, running as they gobbled, so as to have it all for themselves. But I did notice that when someone was making twine or straightening a spear shaft, the focus of attention for the spectators was not the person but the action. If they were caught watching by the one being watched and their eyes met, the reaction was a sharp retreat on both sides.

When the rains failed for the second year running, I knew that the Ik as a society were almost certainly finished and that the monster they had created in its place, that passionless, feelingless association of individuals, would spread like a fungus, contaminating all it touched. When I left, I too had been contaminated. I was not upset when I said good-bye to old Loiangorok. I told him I had left a sack of *posho* [ground corn meal] with the police for him, and I said I would send money for more when that ran out. He dragged himself slowly toward the *di* every day, and he always clutched a knife. When he got there, or as far as he could, he squatted down and whittled at some wood, thus proving that he was still alive and able to do things. The *posho* was enough to last him for months, but I felt no emotion when I estimated that he would last one month, even with the *posho* in the hands of the police. I underestimated his son, who within two days had persuaded the police that it would save a lot of bother if he looked after the *posho*. I heard later that Loiangorok died of starvation within two weeks.

So, I departed with a kind of forced gaiety, feeling that I should be glad to be gone but having forgotten how to be glad. I certainly was not thinking of returning within a year, but I did. The following spring I heard that rain had come at last and that the fields of the Ik had never looked so prosperous, nor the country so green and fertile. A few months away had refreshed me, and I wondered if my conclusions had not been excessively pessimistic. So, early that summer, I set off to be present for the first harvests in three years.

I was not surprised too much when two days after my arrival and installation at the police post I found Logwara, the blind man, lying on the roadside bleeding, while a hundred yards up other Ik were squabbling over the body of a hyena. Logwara had tried to get there ahead of the others to grab the meat and had been trampled on.

First I looked at the villages. The lush outer covering concealed an inner decay. All the villages were like this to some extent, except for Lokelea's. There the tomatoes and pumpkins were carefully pruned and cleaned, so that the fruits were larger and healthier. In what had been my own compound the shade trees had been cut down for firewood, and the lovely hanging nests of the weaver birds were gone.

The fields were even more desolate. Every field without exception had yielded in abundance, and it was a new sensation to have vision cut off by thick crops. But every crop was rotting from sheer neglect.

The Ik said that they had no need to bother guarding the fields. There was so much food they could never eat it all, so why not let the birds and baboons take some? The Ik had full bellies; they were good. The *di* at Atum's village was much the same as usual, people sitting or lying about. People were still stealing from each other's fields, and nobody thought of saving for the future.

It was obvious that nothing had really changed due to the sudden glut of food except that interpersonal relationships had deteriorated still further and that Icien individualism had heightened beyond what I thought even Ik to be capable of.

The Ik had faced a conscious choice between being humans and being parasites and had chosen the latter. When they saw their fields come alive, they were confronted with a problem. If they reaped the harvest, they would have to store grain for eating and planting, and every Ik knew that trying to store anything was a waste of time. Further, if they made their fields look too promising, the government would stop famine relief. So the Ik let their fields rot and continued to draw famine relief.

The Ik were not starving any longer; the old and infirm had all died the previous year, and the younger survivors were doing quite well. But the famine relief was administered in a way that was little short of criminal. As before, only the young and well were able to get down from Pirre to collect the relief; they were given relief for those who could not come and told to take it back. But they never did—they ate it themselves.

The facts are there, though those that can be read here form but a fraction of what one person was able to gather in under two years. There can be no mistaking the direction in which those facts point, and that is the most important thing of all, for it may affect the rest of mankind as it has affected the Ik. The Ik have "progressed," one might say, since the change that has come to them came with the advent of civilization to Africa. They have made of a world that was alive a world that is dead—a cold, dispassionate world that is without ugliness because it is without beauty, without hate because it is without love, and without any realization of truth even, because it simply is. And the symptoms of change in our own society indicate that we are heading in the same direction.

Those values we cherish so highly may indeed be basic to human society but not to humanity, and that means that the Ik show that society itself is not indispensable for man's survival and that man is capable of associating for purposes of survival without being social. The Ik have replaced human society with a mere survival system that does not take human emotion into account. As yet the system if imperfect, for although survival is assured, it is at a minimal level and there is still competition between individuals. With our intellectual sophistication and advanced technology we should be able to perfect the system and eliminate competition, guaranteeing survival for a given number of years for all, reducing the demands made upon us by a social system, abolishing desire and consequently that ever-present and vital gap between desire and achievement, treating us, in a word, as individuals with one basic individual right—the right to survive.

Such interaction as there is within this system is one of mutual exploitation. That is how it already is with the Ik. In our own world the mainstays of a society based on a truly social sense of mutuality are breaking down, indicating that perhaps society as we know it has outworn its usefulness and that by clinging to an outworn system we are bringing about our own destruction. Family, economy, government and religion, the basic categories of social activity and behavior, no longer create any sense of social unity involving a shared and mutual responsibility among all members of our society. At best they enable the individual to survive as an individual. It is the world of the individual, as is the world of the Ik.

The sorry state of society in the civilized world today is in large measure due to the fact that social change has not kept up with technological change. This mad, senseless, unthinking commitment to technological change that we call progress may be sufficient to exterminate the human race in a very short time even without the assistance of nuclear warfare. But since we have already become individualized and desocialized, we say that extermination will not come in our time, which shows about as much sense of family devotion as one might expect from the Ik.

Even supposing that we can avert nuclear holocaust or the almost universal famine that may be expected if population keeps expanding and pollution remains unchecked, what will be the cost if not the same already paid by the Ik? They too were driven by the need to survive, and they succeeded at the cost of their humanity. We are already beginning to pay the same price, but we not only still have the choice (though we may not have the will or courage to make it), we also have the intellectual and technological ability to avert an Icien end. Any change as radical as will be necessary is not likely to bring material benefits to the present generation, but only then will there be a future.

The Ik teach us that our much vaunted human values are not inherent in humanity at all but are associated only with a particular form of survival called society and that all, even society itself, are luxuries that can be dispensed with. That does not make them any less wonderful, and if man has any greatness, it is surely in his ability to maintain these values, even shortening an already pitifully short life rather than sacrifice his humanity. But that too involves choice, and the Ik teach us that man can lose the will to make it. That is the point at which there is an end to truth, to goodness and to beauty, an end to the struggle for their achievement, which gives life to the individual and strength and meaning to society. The Ik have relinquished all luxury in the name of individual survival, and they live on as a people without life, without passion, beyond humanity. We pursue those trivial, idiotic technological encumbrances, and all the time we are losing our potential for social rather than individual survival, for hating as well as loving, losing perhaps our last chance to enjoy life with all the passion that is our nature.

Penny capitalism on an urban streetcorner

Elliot Liebow

A pickup truck drives slowly down the street. The truck stops as it comes abreast of a man sitting on a cast-iron porch and the white driver calls out, asking if the man wants a day's work. The man shakes his head and the truck moves on up the block, stopping again whenever idling men come within calling distance of the driver. At the Carry-out corner, five men debate the question briefly and shake their heads no to the truck. The truck turns the corner and repeats the same performance up the next street. In the distance, one can see one man, then another, climb into the back of the truck and sit down. It starts and stops, the truck finally disappears.

What is it we have witnessed here? A labor scavenger rebuffed by his would-be prey? Lazy, irresponsible men turning down an honest day's pay for an honest day's work? Or a more complex phenomenon marking the intersection of economic forces, social values, and individual states of mind and body?

Let us look again at the driver of the truck. He has been able to recruit only two or three men from each twenty or fifty he contacts. To him, it is clear that the others simply do not choose to work. Singly or in groups, belly-empty or belly-full, sullen or gregarious, drunk or sober, they confirm what he has read, heard and knows

Editor's note: Mr. Liebow's study was conducted in Washington, D.C., and its environs.

from his own experience: these men wouldn't take a job if it were handed to them on a platter.[1]

Quite apart from the question of whether or not this is true of some of the men he sees on the street, it is clearly not true of all of them. If it were, he would not have come here in the first place; or having come, he would have left with an empty truck. It is not even true of most of them, for most of the men he sees on the street this weekday morning do, in fact, have jobs. But since, at the moment, they are neither working nor sleeping, and since they hate the depressing room or apartment they live in, or because there is nothing to do there,[2] or because they want to get away from their wives or anyone else living there, they are out on the street, indistinguishable from those who do not have jobs or do not want them. Some, like Boley, a member of a trash-collection crew in a suburban housing development, work Saturdays and are off on this weekday. Some, like Sweets, work nights cleaning up middle-class trash, dirt, dishes, and garbage, and mopping the floors of the office buildings, hotels, restaurants, toilets, and other public places dirtied during the day. Some men work for retail businesses such as liquor stores which do not begin the day until ten o'clock. Some laborers, like Tally, have already come back from the job because the ground was too wet for pick and shovel or because the weather was too cold for pouring concrete. Other employed men stayed off the job

today for personal reasons: Clarence to go to a funeral at eleven this morning and Sea Cat to answer a subpoena as a witness in a criminal proceeding.

Also on the street, unwitting contributors to the impression taken away by the truck driver, are the halt and the lame. The man on the cast-iron steps strokes one gnarled arthritic hand with the other and says he doesn't know whether or not he'll live long enough to be eligible for Social Security. He pauses, then adds matter-of-factly, "Most times, I don't care whether I do or don't." Stoopy's left leg was polio-withered in childhood. Raymond, who looks as if he could tear out a fire hydrant, coughs up blood if he bends or moves suddenly. The quiet man who hangs out in front of the Saratoga apartments has a steel hook strapped onto his left elbow. And had the man in the truck been able to look into the wine-clouded eyes of the man in the green cap, he would have realized that the man did not even understand he was being offered a day's work.

Others, having had jobs and been laid off, are drawing unemployment compensation (up to $44 per week) and have nothing to gain by accepting work which pays little more than this and frequently less.

Still others, like Bumdoodle the numbers man, are working hard at illegal ways of making money, hustlers who are on the street to turn a dollar any way they can: buying and selling sex, liquor, narcotics, stolen goods, or anything else that turns up.

Only a handful remains unaccounted for. There is Tonk, who cannot bring himself to take a job away from the corner, because, according to the other men, he suspects his wife will be unfaithful if given the opportunity. There is Stanton, who has not reported to work for four days now, not since Bernice disappeared. He bought a brand new knife against her return. She had done this twice before, he said, but not for so long and not without warning, and he had forgiven her. But this time, "I ain't got it in me to forgive her again." His rage and shame are there for all to see as he paces the Carry-out and the corner, day and night, hoping to catch a glimpse of her.

And finally, there are those like Arthur, able-bodied men who have no visible means of support, legal or illegal, who neither have jobs nor want them. The truck driver, among others, believes the Arthurs to be representative of all the men he sees idling on the street during his own working hours. They are not, but they cannot be dismissed simply because they are a small minority. It is not enough to explain them away as being lazy or irresponsible or both because an able-bodied man with responsibilities who refuses work is, by the truck driver's definition, lazy and irresponsible. Such an answer begs the question. It is descriptive of the facts; it does not explain them.

Moreover, despite their small numbers, the don't-work-and-don't-want-to-work minority is especially significant because they represent the strongest and clearest expression of those values and attitudes associated with making a living which, to varying degrees, are found throughout the streetcorner world. These men differ from the others in degree rather than in kind, the principal difference being that they are carrying out the implications of their values and experiences to their logical, inevitable conclusions. In this sense, the others have yet to come to terms with themselves and the world they live in.

Putting aside, for the moment, what the men say and feel, and looking at what they actually do and the choices they make, getting a job, keeping a job, and doing well at it is clearly of low priority. Arthur will not take a job at all. Leroy is supposed to be on his job at 4:00 P.M. but it is already 4:10 and he still cannot bring himself to leave the free games he has accumulated on the pinball machine in the Carry-out. Tonk started a construction job on Wednesday, worked Thursday and Friday, then didn't go back again. On the same kind of job, Sea Cat quit in the second week. Sweets had been working three months as a busboy in a restaurant, then quit without notice, not sure himself why he did so. A real estate agent, saying he was more interested in getting the job done than in the cost, asked Richard to give him an estimate on repairing and painting the inside of a house, but Richard, after looking over the job, somehow never got around to submitting an estimate. During one period, Tonk would not leave the corner to take a job because his wife might prove unfaithful; Stanton would not take a job because his woman had been unfaithful.

Thus, the man-job relationship is a tenuous one. At any given moment, a job may occupy a relatively low position on the streetcorner scale of real values. Getting a job may be subordinated to relations with women or to other non-job considerations; the commitment to a job one already has is frequently shallow and tentative.

The reasons are many. Some are objective and reside principally in the job; some are subjective and reside principally in the man. The line between them, however, is not a clear one. Behind the man's refusal to take a job or his decision to quit one is not a simple impulse or value choice but a complex combination of assessments of objective reality on the one hand, and values, attitudes and beliefs drawn from different levels of his experience on the other.

Objective economic considerations are frequently a controlling factor in a man's refusal to take a job. How much the job pays is a crucial question but seldom asked. He knows how much it pays. Working as a stock clerk, a delivery boy, or even behind the counter of liquor stores, drug stores, and other retail businesses pays one dollar an hour. So, too, do most busboy, car-wash, janitorial, and other jobs available to him. Some jobs, such as dishwasher, may dip as low as eighty cents an hour and others, such as elevator operator or work in a junk yard, may offer $1.15 or $1.25. Take-home pay for jobs such as these ranges from $35 to $50 a week, but a take-home pay of over $45 for a five-day week is the exception rather than the rule.

One of the principal advantages of these kinds of jobs is that they offer fairly regular work. Most of them involve essential services and are therefore somewhat less responsive to business conditions than are some higher paying, less menial jobs. Most of them are also inside jobs not dependent on the weather, as are construction jobs and other higher-paying outside work.

Another seemingly important advantage of working in hotels, restaurants, office and apartment buildings, and retail establishments is that they frequently offer an opportunity for stealing on the job. But stealing can be a two-edged sword. Apart from increasing the cost of the goods or services to the general public, a less obvious result is that the practice usually acts as a depressant on the employee's own wage level. Owners of small retail establishments and other employers frequently anticipate employee stealing and adjust the wage rate accordingly. Tonk's employer explained why he was paying Tonk $35 for a 55–60 hour workweek. These men will all steal, he said. Although he keeps close watch on Tonk, he estimates that

Tonk steals from $35 to $40 a week.[3] What he steals, when added to his regular earnings, brings his take-home pay to $70 or $75 per week. The employer said he did not mind this because Tonk is worth that much to the business. But if he were to pay Tonk outright the full value of his labor, Tonk would still be stealing $35–$40 per week and this, he said, the business simply would not support.

This wage arrangement, with stealing built-in, was satisfactory to both parties, with each one independently expressing his satisfaction. Such a wage-theft system, however, is not as balanced and equitable as it appears. Since the wage level rests on the premise that the employee will steal the unpaid value of his labor, the man who does not steal on the job is penalized. And furthermore, even if he does not steal, no one would believe him; the employer and others believe he steals because the system presumes it.

Nor is the man who steals, as he is expected to, as well off as he believes himself to be. The employer may occasionally close his eyes to the worker's stealing but not often and not for long. He is, after all, a businessman and cannot always find it within himself to let a man steal from him, even if the man is stealing his own wages. Moreover, it is only by keeping close watch on the worker that the employer can control how much is stolen and thereby protect himself against the employee's stealing more than he is worth. From this viewpoint, then, the employer is not in wage-theft collusion with the employee. In the case of Tonk, for instance, the employer was not actively abetting the theft. His estimate of how much Tonk was stealing was based on what he thought Tonk was able to steal despite his own best efforts to prevent him from stealing anything at all. Were he to have caught Tonk in the act of stealing, he would, of course, have fired him from the job and perhaps called the police as well. Thus, in an actual if not in a legal

sense, all the elements of entrapment are present. The employer knowingly provides the conditions which entice (force) the employee to steal the unpaid value of his labor, but at the same time he punishes him for theft if he catches him doing so.

Other consequences of the wage-theft system are even more damaging to the employee. Let us, for argument's sake, say that Tonk is in no danger of entrapment; that his employer is willing to wink at the stealing and that Tonk, for his part, is perfectly willing to earn a little, steal a little. Let us say, too, that he is paid $35 a week and allowed to steal $35. His money income—as measured by the goods and services he can purchase with it—is, of course, $70. But not all of his income is available to him for all purposes. He cannot draw on what he steals to build his self-respect or to measure his self-worth. For this, he can draw only on his earnings—the amount given him publicly and voluntarily in exchange for his labor. His "respect" and "self-worth" income remains at $35—only half that of the man who also receives $70 but all of it in the form of wages. His earnings publicly measure the worth of his labor to his employer, and they are important to others and to himself in taking the measure of his worth as a man.[4]

With or without stealing, and quite apart from any interior processes going on in the man who refuses such a job or quits it casually and without apparent reason, the objective fact is that menial jobs in retailing or in the service trades simply do not pay enough to support a man and his family. This is not to say that the worker is underpaid; this may or may not be true. Whether he is or not, the plain fact is that, in such a job, he cannot make a living. Nor can he take much comfort in the fact that these jobs tend to offer more regular, steadier work. If he cannot live on the $45 or $50 he makes in one week, the longer he works, the longer he cannot live on what he makes.[5]

Construction work, even for

unskilled laborers, usually pays better, with the hourly rate ranging from $1.50 to $2.60 an hour.[6] Importantly, too, good references, a good driving record, a tenth grade (or any high school) education, previous experience, the ability to "bring police clearance with you" are not normally required of laborers as they frequently are for some of the jobs in retailing or in the service trades.

Construction work, however, has its own objective disadvantages. It is, first of all, seasonal work for the great bulk of the laborers, beginning early in the spring and tapering off as winter weather sets in.[7] And even during the season the work is frequently irregular. Early or late in the season, snow or temperatures too low for concrete frequently sends the laborers back home, and during late spring or summer, a heavy rain on Tuesday or Wednesday, leaving a lot of water and mud behind it, can mean a two or three day workweek for the pick-and-shovel men and other unskilled laborers.[8]

The elements are not the only hazard. As the project moves from one construction stage to another, laborers—usually without warning—are laid off, sometimes permanently or sometimes for weeks at a time. The more fortunate or the better workers are told periodically to "take a walk for two, three days."

Both getting the construction job and getting to it are also relatively more difficult than is the case for the menial jobs in retailing and the service trades. Job competition is always fierce. In the city, the large construction projects are unionized. One has to have ready cash to get into the union to become eligible to work on these projects and, being eligible, one has to find an opening. Unless one "knows somebody," say a foreman or a laborer who knows the day before that they are going to take on new men in the morning, this can be a difficult and disheartening search.

Many of the nonunion jobs are in suburban Maryland or Virginia. The newspaper ads say, "Report ready to work to the trailer at the intersection of Rte. 11 and Old Bridge Rd., Bunston, Virginia (or Maryland),'' but this location may be ten, fifteen, or even twenty-five miles from the Carry-out. Public transportation would require two or more hours to get there, if it services the area at all. Without access to a car or to a car-pool arrangement, it is not worthwhile reading the ad. So the men do not. Jobs such as these are usually filled by word of mouth information, beginning with someone who knows someone or who is himself working there and looking for a paying rider. Furthermore, nonunion jobs in outlying areas tend to be smaller projects of relatively short duration and to pay somewhat less than scale.

Still another objective factor is the work itself. For some men, whether the job be digging, mixing mortar, pushing a wheelbarrow, unloading materials, carrying and placing steel rods for reinforcing concrete, or building or laying concrete forms, the work is simply too hard. Men such as Tally and Wee Tom can make such work look like child's play; some of the older work-hardened men, such as Budder and Stanton, can do it too, although not without showing unmistakable signs of strain and weariness at the end of the workday. But those who lack the robustness of a Tally or the time-inured immunity of a Budder must either forgo jobs such as these or pay a heavy toll to keep them. For Leroy, in his early twenties, almost six feet tall but weighing under 140 pounds, it would be as difficult to push a loaded wheelbarrow, or to unload and stack 96-pound bags of cement all day long, as it would be for Stoopy with his withered leg.

Heavy, backbreaking labor of the kind that used to be regularly associated with bull gangs or concrete gangs is no longer characteristic of laboring jobs, especially those with the larger, well-equipped construction companies. Brute strength is still required from time to time, as on smaller jobs where it is not economical to bring in heavy equipment or

where the small, undercapitalized contractor has none to bring in. In many cases, however, the conveyor belt has replaced the wheelbarrow or the Georgia buggy, mechanized forklifts have eliminated heavy, manual lifting, and a variety of digging machines have replaced the pick and shovel. The result is fewer jobs for unskilled laborers and, in many cases, a work speed-up for those who do have jobs. Machines now set the pace formerly set by men. Formerly, a laborer pushed a wheelbarrow of wet cement to a particular spot, dumped it, and returned for another load. Another laborer, in hip boots, pushed the wet concrete around with a shovel or a hoe, getting it roughly level in preparation for the skilled finishers. He had relatively small loads to contend with and had only to keep up with the men pushing the wheelbarrows. Now, the job for the man pushing the wheelbarrow is gone and the wet concrete comes rushing down a chute at the man in the hip boots who must "spread it quick or drown."

Men who have been running an elevator, washing dishes, or "pulling trash" cannot easily move into laboring jobs. They lack the basic skills for "unskilled" construction labor; familiarity with tools and materials, and tricks of the trade without which hard jobs are made harder. Previously unused or untrained muscles rebel in pain against the new and insistent demands made upon them, seriously compromising the man's performance and testing his willingness to see the job through.

A healthy, sturdy, active man of good intelligence requires from two to four weeks to break in on a construction job.[9] Even if he is willing somehow to bull his way through the first few weeks, it frequently happens that his foreman or the craftsman he services with materials and general assistance is not willing to wait that long for him to get into condition or to learn at a glance the difference in size between a rough 2" x 8" and a finished 2" x 10". The foreman and the craftsman are themselves "under

the gun" and cannot "carry" the man when other men, who are already used to the work and who know the tools and materials, are lined up to take the job.

Sea Cat was "healthy, sturdy, active and of good intelligence." When a judge gave him six weeks in which to pay his wife $200 in back child-support payments, he left his grocery-store job in order to take a higher-paying job as a laborer, arranged for him by a foreman friend. During the first week the weather was bad and he worked only Wednesday and Friday, cursing the elements all the while for cheating him out of the money he could have made. The second week, the weather was fair but he quit at the end of the fourth day, saying frankly that the work was too hard for him. He went back to his job at the grocery store and took a second job working nights as a dishwasher in a restaurant,[10] earning little if any more at the two jobs than he would have earned as a laborer, and keeping at both of them until he had paid off his debts.

Tonk did not last as long as Sea Cat. No one made any predictions when he got a job in a parking lot, but when the men on the corner learned he was to start on a road construction job, estimates of how long he would last ranged from one to three weeks. Wednesday was his first day. He spent that evening and night at home. He did the same on Thursday. He worked Friday and spent Friday evening and part of Saturday draped over the mailbox on the corner. Sunday afternoon, Tonk decided he was not going to report on the job the next morning. He explained that after working three days, he knew enough about the job to know that it was too hard for him. He knew he wouldn't be able to keep up and he'd just as soon quit now as get fired later.

Logan was a tall, two-hundred-pound man in his late twenties. His back used to hurt him only on the job, he said, but now he can't straighten up for increasingly longer periods of time. He said he had traced this to the awkward walk he was forced to adopt by the loaded wheelbarrows which pull him down into a half-stoop. He's going to quit, he said, as soon as he can find another job. If he can't find one real soon, he guesses he'll quit anyway. It's not worth it, having to walk bent over and leaning to one side.

Sometimes, the strain and effort is greater than the man is willing to admit, even to himself. In the early summer of 1963, Richard was rooming at Nancy's place. His wife and children were "in the country" (his grandmother's home in Carolina), waiting for him to save up enough money so that he could bring them back to Washington and start over again after a disastrous attempt to "make it" in Philadelphia. Richard had gotten a job with a fence company in Virginia. It paid $1.60 an hour. The first few evenings, when he came home from work, he looked ill from exhaustion and heat. Stanton said Richard would have to quit, "he's too small [thin] for that kind of work." Richard said he was doing O.K. and would stick with the job.

At Nancy's one night, when Richard had been working about two weeks, Nancy and three or four others were sitting around talking, drinking, and listening to music. Someone asked Nancy when was Richard going to bring his wife and children up from the country. Nancy said she didn't know, but it probably depended on how long it would take him to save up enough money. She said she didn't think he could stay with the fence job much longer. This morning, she said, the man Richard rode to work with knocked on the door and Richard didn't answer. She looked in his room. Richard was still asleep. Nancy tried to shake him awake. "No more digging!" Richard cried out. "No more digging! I can't do no more God-damn digging!" When Nancy finally managed to wake him, he dressed quickly and went to work.

Richard stayed on the job two more weeks, then suddenly quit, ostensibly because his pay check was three dollars less than what he thought it should have been.

In summary of objective job considerations, then, the most important fact is that a man who is able and willing to work cannot earn enough money to support himself, his wife, and one or more children. A man's chances for working regularly are good only if he is willing to work for less than he can live on, and sometimes not even then. On some jobs, the wage rate is deceptively higher than on others, but the higher the wage rate, the more difficult it is to get the job, and the less the job security. Higher-paying construction work tends to be seasonal and, during the season, the amount of work available is highly sensitive to business and weather conditions and to the changing requirements of individual projects.[11] Moreover, high-paying construction jobs are frequently beyond the physical capacity of some of the men, and some of the low-paying jobs are scaled down even lower in accordance with the self-fulfilling assumption that the man will steal part of his wages on the job.[12]

Bernard assesses the objective job situation dispassionately over a cup of coffee, sometimes poking at the coffee with his spoon, sometimes staring at it as if, like a crystal ball, it holds tomorrow's secrets. He is twenty-seven years old. He and the woman with whom he lives have a baby son, and she has another child by another man. Bernard does odd jobs—mostly painting—but here it is the end of January, and his last job was with the Post Office during the Christmas mail rush. He would like postal work as a steady job, he says. It pays well (about $2.00 an hour) but he has twice failed the Post Office examination (he graduated from a Washington high school) and has given up the idea as an impractical one. He is supposed to see a man tonight about a job as a parking attendant for a large apartment house. The man told him to bring his birth certificate and driver's license, but his license was suspended because of a backlog of unpaid traffic fines. A friend promised to lend him some money this evening. If he gets it, he will pay the fines tomorrow morning and have his license reinstated. He hopes the man with the job will wait till tomorrow night.

A "security job" is what he really wants, he said. He would like to save up money for a taxicab. (But having twice failed the postal examination and having a bad driving record as well, it is highly doubtful that he could meet the qualifications or pass the written test.) That would be "a good life." He can always get a job in a restaurant or as a clerk in a drugstore but they don't pay enough, he said. He needs to take home at least $50 to $55 a week. He thinks he can get that much driving a truck somewhere . . . Sometimes he wishes he had stayed in the army . . . A security job, that's what he wants most of all, a real security job . . .

When we look at what the men bring to the job rather than at what the job offers the men, it is essential to keep in mind that we are not looking at men who come to the job fresh, just out of school perhaps, and newly prepared to undertake the task of making a living, or from another job where they earned a living and are prepared to do the same on this job. Each man comes to the job with a long job history characterized by his not being able to support himself and his family. Each man carries this knowledge, born of his experience, with him. He comes to the job flat and stale, wearied by the sameness of it all, convinced of his own incompetence, terrified of responsibility—of being tested still again and found wanting. Possible exceptions are the younger men not yet, or just, married. They suspect all this but have yet to have it confirmed by repeated personal experience over time. But those who are or have been married know it well. It is the experience of the individual and the group; of their fathers and probably their sons. Convinced of their inadequacies, not only do they not seek out those few better-paying jobs which test their resources, but they actively avoid them, gravitating in a mass to the menial routine jobs which offer no challenge—and therefore pose no threat—to the already diminished images they have of themselves.

Thus Richard does not follow through on the real estate agent's offer. He is afraid to do on his own—minor plastering, replacing broken windows, other minor repairs, and painting—exactly what he had been doing for months on a piecework basis under someone else (and which provided him with a solid base from which to derive a cost estimate).

Richard once offered an important clue to what may have gone on in his mind when the job offer was made. We were in the Carry-out, at a time when he was looking for work. He was talking about the kind of jobs available to him.

I graduated from high school [Baltimore] but I don't know anything. I'm dumb. Most of the time I don't even say I graduated, 'cause then somebody asks me a question and I can't answer it, and they think I was lying about graduating. . . . They graduated me but I didn't know anything. I had lousy grades but I guess they wanted to get rid of me.

I was at Margaret's house the other night and her little sister asked me to help her with her homework. She showed me some fractions and I knew right away I couldn't do them. I was ashamed so I told her I had to go to the bathroom.

And so it must have been, surely, with the real estate agent's offer. Convinced that "I'm dumb . . . I don't know anything," he "knew right away" he couldn't do it, despite the fact that he had been doing just this sort of work all along.

Thus, the man's low self-esteem generates a fear of being tested and prevents him from accepting a job with responsibilities or, once on a job, from staying with it if responsibilities are thrust on him, even if the wages are commensurately higher. Richard refuses such a job, Leroy leaves one, and another man, given more responsibility and more pay, knows he will fail and proceeds to do so, proving he was right about himself all

along. The self-fulfilling prophecy is everywhere at work. In a hallway, Stanton, Tonk and Boley are passing a bottle around. Stanton recalls the time he was in the service. Everything was fine until he attained the rank of corporal. He worried about everything he did then. Was he doing the right thing? Was he doing it well? When would they discover their mistake and take his stripes (and extra pay) away? When he finally lost his stripes, everything was all right again.

Lethargy, disinterest, and general apathy on the job, so often reported by employers, has its streetcorner counterpart. The men do not ordinarily talk about their jobs or ask one another about them.[13] Although most of the men know who is or is not working at any given time, they may or may not know what particular job an individual man has. There is no overt interest in job specifics as they relate to this or that person, in large part perhaps because the specifics are not especially relevant. To know that a man is working is to know approximately how much he makes and to know as much as one needs or wants to know about how he makes it. After all, how much difference does it make to know whether a man is pushing a mop or pulling trash in an apartment house, a restaurant, or an office building, or delivering groceries, drugs, or liquor, or, if he's a laborer, whether he's pushing a wheelbarrow, mixing mortar, or digging a hole. So much does one job look like every other that there is little to choose between them. In large part, the job market consists of a narrow range of nondescript chores calling for nondistinctive, undifferentiated, unskilled labor. "A job is a job."

A crucial factor in the streetcorner man's lack of job commitment is the overall value he places on the job. *For his part, the streetcorner man puts no lower value on the job than does the larger society around him.* He knows the social value of the job by the amount of money the employer is

willing to pay him for doing it. In a real sense, every pay day, he counts in dollars and cents the value placed on the job by society at large. He is no more (and frequently less) ready to quit and look for another job than his employer is ready to fire him and look for another man. Neither the streetcorner man who performs these jobs nor the society which requires him to perform them assess the job as one "worth doing and worth doing well." Both employee and employer are contemptuous of the job. The employee shows his contempt by his reluctance to accept it or keep it, the employer by paying less than is required to support a family.[14] Nor does the low-wage job offer prestige, respect, interesting work, opportunity for learning or advancement, or any other compensation. With few exceptions, jobs filled by the streetcorner men are at the bottom of the employment ladder in every respect, from wage level to prestige. Typically, they are hard, dirty, uninteresting, and underpaid. The rest of society (whatever its ideal values regarding the dignity of labor) holds the job of the dishwasher or janitor or unskilled laborer in low esteem if not outright contempt.[15] So does the streetcorner man. He cannot do otherwise. He cannot draw from a job those social values which other people do not put into it.[16]

Only occasionally does spontaneous conversation touch on these matters directly. Talk about jobs is usually limited to isolated statements of intention, such as "I think I'll get me another gig [job]," "I'm going to look for a construction job when the weather breaks," or "I'm going to quit. I can't take no more of his shit." Job assessments typically consist of nothing more than a noncommittal shrug and "It's O.K." or "It's a job."

One reason for the relative absence of talk about one's job is, as suggested earlier, that the sameness of job experience does not bear reiteration. Another and more important reason is the emptiness of the job experience itself. The man sees middle-class occupations as a primary source of prestige, pride, and self-respect; his own job affords him none of these. To think about his job is to see himself as others see him, to remind him of just where he stands in this society.[17] And because society's criteria for placement are generally the same as his own, to talk about his job can trigger a flush of shame and a deep, almost physical ache to change places with someone, almost anyone, else.[18] The desire to be a person in his own right, to be noticed by the world he lives in, is shared by each of the men on the streetcorner. Whether they articulate this desire (as Tally does below) or not, one can see them position themselves to catch the attention of their fellows in much the same way as plants bend or stretch to catch the sunlight.[19]

Tally and I were in the Carry-out. It was summer, Tally's peak earning season as a cement finisher, a semi-skilled job a cut or so above that of the unskilled laborer. His take-home pay during these weeks was well over a hundred dollars—"a lot of bread." But for Tally, who no longer had a family to support, bread was not enough.

"You know that boy came in last night? That Black Moozlem? That's what I ought to be doing. I ought to be in his place."

"What do you mean?"

"Dressed nice, going to [night] school, got a good job."

"He's no better off than you, Tally. You make more than he does."

"It's not the money. [Pause] It's position, I guess. He's got position. When he finish school he gonna be a supervisor. People respect him. . . . Thinking about people with position and education gives me a feeling right here [pressing his fingers into the pit of his stomach]."

"You're educated, too. You have a skill, a trade. You're a cement finisher. You can make a building, pour a sidewalk."

"That's different. Look, can anybody do what you're doing? Can anybody just come up and do your job? Well, in one week I can teach you cement finishing. You won't be as good as me 'cause you won't have the experience but you'll be a cement finisher. That's what I mean. Anybody can do what I'm doing and that's

what gives me this feeling. [Long pause] Suppose I like this girl. I go over to her house and I meet her father. He starts talking about what he done today. He talks about operating on somebody and sewing them up and about surgery. I know he's a doctor 'cause of the way he talks. Then she starts talking about what she did. Maybe she's a boss or a supervisor. Maybe she's a lawyer and her father says to me, 'And what do you do, Mr. Jackson?' [Pause] You remember at the courthouse, Lonny's trial? You and the lawyer was talking in the hall? You remember? I just stood there listening. I didn't say a word. You know why? 'Cause I didn't even know what you was talking about. That's happened to me a lot."

"Hell, you're nothing special. That happens to everybody. Nobody knows everything. One man is a doctor, so he talks about surgery. Another man is a teacher, so he talks about books. But doctors and teachers don't know anything about concrete. You're a cement finisher and that's your specialty."

"Maybe so, but when was the last time you saw anybody standing around talking about concrete?"

The streetcorner man wants to be a person in his own right, to be noticed, to be taken account of, but in this respect, as well as in meeting his money needs, his job fails him. The job and the man are even. The job fails the man and the man fails the job.

Furthermore, the man does not have any reasonable expectation that, however bad it is, his job will lead to better things. Menial jobs are not, by and large, the starting point of a track system which leads to even better jobs for those who are able and willing to do them. The busboy or dishwasher in a restaurant is not on a job track which, if negotiated skillfully, leads to chef or manager of the restaurant. The busboy or dishwasher who works hard becomes, simply, a hard-working busboy or dishwasher. Neither hard work nor perseverance can conceivably carry the janitor to a sitdown job in the office building he cleans up. And it is the apprentice who becomes the journeyman electrician, plumber, steam fitter or bricklayer, not the common unskilled Negro laborer.

Thus, the job is not a stepping-stone to something better. It is a dead end. It promises to deliver no more tomorrow, next month or next year than it does today.

Delivering little, and promising no more, the job is "no big thing." The man appears to treat the job in a cavalier fashion, working and not working as the spirit moves him, as if all that matters is the immediate satisfaction of his present appetites, the surrender to present moods, and the indulgence of whims with no thought for the cost, the consequences, the future. To the middle-class observer, this behavior reflects a "present-time orientation"—an "inability to defer gratification." It is this "present-time" orientation—as against the "future orientation" of the middle-class person—that "explains" to the outsider why Leroy chooses to spend the day at the Carry-out rather than report to work; why Richard, who was paid Friday, was drunk Saturday and Sunday and penniless Monday; why Sweets quit his job today because the boss looked at him "funny" yesterday.

But from the inside looking out, what appears as a "present-time" orientation to the outside observer is, to the man experiencing it, as much a future orientation as that of his middle-class counterpart.[20] The difference between the two men lies not so much in their different orientations to time as in their different orientations to future time or, more specifically, to their different futures.[21]

The future orientation of the middle-class person presumes, among other things, a surplus of resources to be invested in the future and a belief that the future will be sufficiently stable both to justify his investment (money in a bank, time and effort in a job, investment of himself in marriage and family, etc.) and to permit the consumption of his investment at a time, place and manner of his own choosing and to his greater satisfaction. But the streetcorner man lives in a sea of want. He does not, as a rule, have a surplus of resources, either economic or psychological. Gratification of hunger and the desire for simple creature comforts cannot be long deferred. Neither can support for one's flagging self-esteem. Living on the edge of both economic and psychological subsistence, the streetcorner man is obliged to expend all his resources on maintaining himself from moment to moment.[22]

As for the future, the young streetcorner man has a fairly good picture of it. In Richard or Sea Cat or Arthur he can see himself in his middle twenties; he can look at Tally to see himself at thirty, at Wee Tom to see himself in his middle thirties, and at Budder and Stanton to see himself in his forties. It is a future in which everything is uncertain except the ultimate destruction of his hopes and the eventual realization of his fears. The most he can reasonably look forward to is that these things do not come too soon. Thus, when Richard squanders a week's pay in two days it is not because, like an animal or a child, he is "present-time oriented," unaware of or unconcerned with his future. He does so precisely because he is aware of the future and the hopelessness of it all.

Sometimes this kind of response appears as a conscious, explicit choice. Richard had had a violent argument with his wife. He said he was going to leave her and the children, that he had had enough of everything and could not take any more, and he chased her out of the house. His chest still heaving, he leaned back against the wall in the hallway of his basement apartment.

"I've been scuffling for five years," he said. "I've been scuffling for five years from morning till night. And my kids still don't have anything, my wife don't have anything, and I don't have anything.

"There," he said, gesturing down the hall to a bed, a sofa, a couple of chairs and a television set, all shabby, some broken. "There's everything I have and I'm having trouble holding onto that."

Leroy came in, presumably to petition

Richard on behalf of Richard's wife, who was sitting outside on the steps, afraid to come in. Leroy started to say something but Richard cut him short.

"Look, Leroy, don't give me any of that action. You and me are entirely different people. Maybe I look like a boy and maybe I act like a boy sometimes but I got a man's mind. You and me don't want the same things out of life. Maybe some of the same, but you don't care how long you have to wait for yours and *I—want—mine—right—now*."[23]

Thus, apparent present-time concerns with consumption and indulgences—material and emotional—reflect a future-time orientation. "I want mine right now" is ultimately a cry of despair, a direct response to the future as he sees it.[24]

In many instances, it is precisely the streetcorner man's orientation to the future—but to a future loaded with "trouble"—which not only leads to a greater emphasis on present concerns ("I want mine right now") but also contributes importantly to the instability of employment, family and friend relationships, and to the general transient quality of daily life.

Let me give some concrete examples. One day, after Tally had gotten paid, he gave me four twenty-dollar bills and asked me to keep them for him. Three days later he asked me for the money. I returned it and asked why he did not put his money in a bank. He said that the banks close at two o'clock. I argued that there were four or more banks within a two-block radius of where he was working at the time and that he could easily get to any one of them on his lunch hour. "No, man," he said, "you don't understand. They close at two o'clock and they closed Saturday and Sunday. Suppose I get into trouble and I got to make it [leave]. Me get out of town, and everything I got in the world layin' up in that bank? No good! No good!"

In another instance, Leroy and his girl friend were discussing "trouble." Leroy was trying to decide how best to go about getting his hands on some "long green" (a lot of money), and his

girl friend cautioned him about "trouble." Leroy sneered at this, saying he had had "trouble" all his life and wasn't afraid of a little more. "Anyway," he said, "I'm famous for leaving town."[25]

Thus, the constant awareness of a future loaded with "trouble" results in a constant readiness to leave, to "make it," to "get out of town," and discourages the man from sinking roots into the world he lives in.[26] Just as it discourages him from putting money in the bank, so it discourages him from committing himself to a job, especially one whose payoff lies in the promise of future rewards rather than in the present. In the same way, it discourages him from deep and lasting commitments to family and friends or to any other persons, places or things, since such commitments could hold him hostage, limiting his freedom of movement and thereby compromising his security which lies in that freedom.

What lies behind the response to the driver of the pickup truck, then, is a complex combination of attitudes and assessments. The streetcorner man is under continuous assault by his job experiences and job fears. His experiences and fears feed on one another. The kind of job he can get—and frequently only after fighting for it, if then—steadily confirms his fears, depresses his self-confidence and self-esteem until finally, terrified of an opportunity even if one presents itself, he stands defeated by his experiences, his belief in his own self-worth destroyed and his fears a confirmed reality.

NOTES

[1] By different methods, perhaps, some social scientists have also located the problem in the men themselves, in their unwillingness or lack of desire to work: "To improve the underprivileged worker's performance one must help him to learn to *want* . . . higher social goals for himself and his children. . . . The problem of changing the work habits and motivation of [lower class] people . . . is a problem of changing the goals, the ambitions, and the level of cultural and occupational aspiration of the underprivileged worker." (Emphasis in

original.) Allison Davis, "The Motivation of the Underprivileged Worker," p. 90.

[2]The comparison of sitting at home alone with being in jail is commonplace.

[3]Exactly the same estimate as the one made by Tonk himself. On the basis of personal knowledge of the stealing routine employed by Tonk, however, I suspect the actual amount is considerably smaller.

[4]Some public credit may accrue to the clever thief but not respect.

[5]It might be profitable to compare, as Howard S. Becker suggests, gross aspects of income and housing costs in this particular area with those reported by Herbert Gans for the low-income working class in Boston's West End. In 1958, Gans reports, median income for the West Enders was just under $70 a week, a level considerably higher than that enjoyed by the people in the Carry-out neighborhood five years later. Gans himself rented a six-room apartment in the West End for $46 a month, about $10 more than the going rate for long-time residents. In the Carry-out neighborhood, rooms that could accommodate more than a cot and a miniature dresser—that is, rooms that qualified for family living—rented for $12 to $22 a week. Ignoring differences that really can't be ignored—the privacy and self-contained efficiency of the multi-room apartment as against the fragmented, public living of the rooming-house "apartment," with a public toilet on a floor always different from the one your room is on (no matter, it probably doesn't work, anyway)—and assuming comparable states of disrepair, the West Enders were paying $6 or $7 a month for a room that cost the Carry-outers at least $50 a month, and frequently more. Looking at housing costs as a percentage of income—and again ignoring what cannot be ignored: that what goes by the name of "housing" in the two areas is not at all the same thing—the median income West Ender could get a six-room apartment for about 12 percent of his income, while his 1963 Carry-out counterpart, with a weekly income of $60 (to choose a figure from the upper end of the income range), often paid 20-33 percent of his income for one room. See Herbert J. Gans, *The Urban Villagers*, pp. 10-13.

[6]The higher amount is 1962 union scale for building laborers. According to the Wage Agreement Contract for Heavy Construction Laborers (Washington, D.C., and vicinity) covering the period from May 1, 1963 to April 30, 1966, minimum hourly wage for heavy construction laborers was to go from $2.75 (May 1963) by annual increments to $2.92, effective November 1, 1965.

[7]"Open-sky" work, such as building overpasses, highways, etc., in which the workers and materials are directly exposed to the elements, traditionally begins in March and ends around Thanksgiving. The same is true for much of the street repair work and the laying of sewer, electric, gas, and telephone lines by the city and public utilities, all important employers of laborers. Between Thanksgiving and March, they retain only skeleton crews selected from their best, most reliable men.

[8]In a recent year, the crime rate in Washington for the month of August jumped 18 percent over the preceding month. A veteran police officer explained the increase to David L. Bazelon, Chief Judge, U.S. Court of Appeals for the District of Columbia. "It's

quite simple. . . . You see, August was a very wet month. . . . These people wait on the street corner each morning around 6:00 or 6:30 for a truck to pick them up and take them to a construction site. If it's raining, that truck doesn't come, and the men are going to be idle that day. If the bad weather keeps up for three days . . . we know we are going to have trouble on our hands—and sure enough, there invariably follows a rash of purse-snatchings, house-breakings and the like. . . . These people have to eat like the rest of us, you know." David L. Bazelon, Address to the Federal Bar Association, p. 3.

[9]Estimate of Mr. Francis Greenfield, President of the International Hod Carriers, Building and Common Laborers' District Council of Washington, D.C., and Vicinity. I am indebted to Mr. Greenfield for several points in these paragraphs dealing with construction laborers.

[10]Not a sinecure, even by streetcorner standards.

[11]The overall result is that, in the long run, a Negro laborer's earnings are not substantially greater—and may be less—than those of the busboy, janitor, or stock clerk. Herman P. Miller, for example, reports that in 1960, 40 percent of all jobs held by Negro men were as laborers or in the service trades. The average annual wage for nonwhite nonfarm laborers was $2,400. The average earning of nonwhite service workers was $2,500 (*Rich Man, Poor Man*, p. 90). Francis Greenfield estimates that in the Washington vicinity, the 1965 earnings of the union laborer who works whenever work is available will be about $3,200. Even this figure is high for the man on the streetcorner. Union men in heavy construction are the aristocrats of the laborers. Casual day labor and jobs with small firms in the building and construction trades, or with firms in other industries, pay considerably less.

[12]For an excellent discussion of the self-fulfilling assumption (or prophecy) as a social force, see "The Self-Fulfilling Prophecy," Ch. XI, in Robert K. Merton's *Social Theory and Social Structure*.

[13]This stands in dramatic contrast to the leisure-time conversation of stable, working-class men. For the coal miners (of Ashton, England), for example, "the topic [of conversation] which surpasses all others in frequency is work—the difficulties which have been encountered in the day's shift, the way in which a particular task was accomplished, and so on." Josephine Klein, *Samples from English Cultures*, Vol. I, p. 88.

[14]It is important to remember that the employer is not entirely a free agent. Subject to the constraints of the larger society, he acts for the larger society as well as for himself. Child labor laws, safety and sanitation regulations, minimum wage scales in some employment areas, and other constraints, are already on the books; other control mechanisms, such as a guaranteed annual wage, are to be had for the voting.

[15]See, for example, the U.S. Bureau of the Census, *Methodology and Scores of Socioeconomic Status*. The assignment of the lowest SES ratings to men who hold such jobs is not peculiar to our own society. A low SES rating for "the shoeshine boy or garbage man . . . seems to be true for all [industrial] countries." Alex Inkeles, "Industrial Man," p. 8.

[16]That the streetcorner man downgrades

manual labor should occasion no surprise. Merton points out that "the American stigmatization of manual labor . . . *has been found to hold rather uniformly in all social classes*" (emphasis in original; *Social Theory and Social Structure*, p. 145). That he finds no satisfaction in such work should also occasion no surprise: "[(There is] a clear positive correlation between the over-all status of occupations and the experience of satisfaction in them." Inkeles, "Industrial Man," p. 12.

[17]"[In our society] a man's work is one of the things by which he is judged, and certainly one of the more significant things by which he judges himself. . . . A man's work is one of the more important parts of his social identity, of his self; indeed, of his fate in the one life he has to live." Everett C. Hughes, *Men and Their Work*, pp. 42-43.

[18]Noting that lower-class persons "are constantly exposed to evidence of their own irrelevance," Lee Rainwater spells out still another way in which the poor are poor: "The identity problems of lower class persons make the soul-searching of middle class adolescents and adults seem rather like a kind of conspicuous consumption of psychic riches" ("Work and Identity in the Lower Class," p. 3).

[19]Sea Cat cuts his pants legs off at the calf and puts a fringe on the raggedy edges. Tonk breaks his "shades" and continues to wear the horn-rimmed frames minus the lenses. Richard cultivates a distinctive manner of speech. Lonny gives himself a birthday party. And so on.

[20]Taking a somewhat different point of view, S.M. Miller and Frank Riessman suggest that "the entire concept of deferred gratification may be inappropriate to understanding the essence of workers' lives" ("The Working Class Subculture: A New View," p. 87).

[21]This sentence is a paraphrase of a statement made by Marvin Cline at a 1965 colloquium at the Mental Health Study Center, National Institute of Mental Health.

[22]And if, for the moment, he does sometimes have more money than he wants to spend or more food than he wants to eat, he is pressed to spend the money and eat the food anyway since his friends, neighbors, kinsmen, or acquaintances will beg or borrow whatever surplus he has or, failing this, they may steal it. In one extreme case, one of the men admitted taking the last of a woman's surplus food allotment after she had explained that, with four children, she could not spare any food. The prospect that consumer soft goods not consumed by oneself will be consumed by someone else may be related to the way in which portable consumer durable goods, such as watches, radios, television sets, or phonographs, are sometimes looked at as a form of savings. When Shirley was on welfare, she regularly took her television set out of pawn when she got her monthly check. Not so much to watch it, she explained, as to have something to fall back on when her money runs out toward the end of the month. For her and others, the television set or the phonograph is her savings, the pawnshop is where she banks her savings, and the pawn ticket is her bankbook.

[23]This was no simple rationalization for irresponsibility. Richard had indeed "been scuffling for five years" trying to keep his family going. Until shortly after this episode,

Richard was known and respected as one of the hardest-working men on the street. Richard had said, only a couple of months earlier, "I figure you got to get out there and try. You got to try before you can get anything." His wife Shirley confirmed that he had always tried. "If things get tough, with me I'll get all worried. But Richard get worried, he don't want me to see him worried. . . . He *will* get out there. He's shoveled snow, picked beans, and he's done some of everything . . . . He's not ashamed to get out there and get us something to eat." At the time of the episode reported above, Leroy was just starting marriage and raising a family. He and Richard were not, as Richard thought, "entirely different people." Leroy had just not learned, by personal experience over time, what Richard had learned. But within two years Leroy's marriage had broken up and he

was talking and acting like Richard. "He just let go completely," said one of the men on the street.

[24]There is no mystically intrinsic connection between "present-time" orientation and lower-class persons. Whenever people of whatever class have been uncertain, skeptical or downright pessimistic about the future, "I want mine right now" has been one of the characteristic responses, although it is usually couched in more delicate terms: e.g., Omar Khayyam's "Take the cash and let the credit go," or Horace's "*Carpe diem.*" In wartime, especially, all classes tend to slough off conventional restraints on sexual and other behavior (i.e., become less able or less willing to defer gratification). And when inflation threatens, darkening the fiscal future, persons who formerly husbanded their resources with

commendable restraint almost stampede one another rushing to spend their money. Similarly, it seems that future-time orientation tends to collapse toward the present when persons are in pain or under stress. The point here is that, the label notwithstanding (what passes for) present-time orientation appears to be a situation-specific phenomenon rather than a part of the standard psychic equipment of Cognitive Lower Class Man.

[25]And proceeded to do just that the following year when "trouble"—in this case a grand jury indictment, a pile of debts, and a violent separation from his wife and children—appeared again.

[26]For a discussion of "trouble" as a focal concern of lower-class culture, see Walter Miller, "Lower Class Culture as a Generating Milieu of Gang Delinquency," pp. 7, 8.

The New Lost Generation

It's post-Sixties, pre-Eighties, and forever in between

DAVID LEAVITT

David Leavitt's *first book*, Family Dancing, *is published by Knopf.*

On Saturday nights in 1971, when I was ten years old, I used to go folk dancing with my brother and sister in Tresidder Plaza at Stanford University. They were both undergraduates at Stanford, and my father taught there; I was what was known as a facbrat. I remember vividly those warm nights, the stone surface of the plaza illuminated like a skating rink and the little tinny record player blaring "Hava Nagila." As we approached I would start running. The air smelled of pot. Then we were there, and in the magic center a circle whirled madly in perfect step—the men long-haired, dirty, barefoot; the women wrapped in bolts of brightly patterned gypsy fabric, swathed in scarves, their hair held back by turquoise pins. Everyone reeked; deodorant, I suppose, was politically incorrect, like leg-shaving. Inevitably, in the course of the evening, someone would offer me a joint. I always refused. I only wanted to watch the dancers and learn the intricate patterned steps—the particular twining of ankles and arms, the systems for switching partners. The few times I actually joined in, I remember being shocked at the sudden intimacy I was thrown into with hand after hand, some bony and fragile, others heavy and lumbering and sweaty. Sometimes, in the more reckless dances, I would feel my feet quite literally lifted off the ground by their momentum.

Usually I did not dance, because usually I did not know the steps. Instead I would stand on the periphery, with a few other hesitant loners, behind one of the accomplished dancers, and I would falteringly, clumsily try to follow. Just as I was beginning to get it, the dance would end. The next week I would wait for the same dance to be played again, but it never was—at least not before 11:00, when I would hear a horn honking in the parking lot and see the glaring lights of my mother's car, come to fetch me home. "Did you have fun?" my mother would ask me as she opened the door. "Yes," I'd say, sliding in next to her. All that night the music drummed in my head. I knew the dancing went on and on after I had to go to bed, possibly all night, possibly until dawn, and as I fell asleep I tried to imagine what kinds of dances, what weirdly erotic configurations, those people would try in those late hours, the hours I had yet to witness, for I was just too young.

THE FIRST AND only time I ever saw a President, I was fourteen. The President was Gerald R. Ford, one year into his term, and he came to Stanford University to participate in a ceremony inaugurating the new law school. *Saturday Night Live* was in its first season that year, but I wouldn't get to see Chevy Chase's famous dunderhead imitations of the President until the series went into reruns. I had hardly heard of the show, which was on too late for me to watch. I remember thinking of President Ford as an only mildly evil character, at

least in comparison with Nixon, whose hateful image on the kitchen television had more than once sent my mother into screaming fits so loud I had been convinced she was being murdered. "Conservative, but honest" was my father's estimation of Ford the man. My sister disagreed. She was a senior at Stanford and lived at Columbae House, a communal student residence devoted to radical thinking. I remember standing next to my sister that afternoon in a crowd of serious-looking young people holding signs and banners. In unison and with great dedication, they chanted: "The people—united—will never be defeated! The people—united—will never be defeated!" I listened. I loved the rhythm of the chant. At some point I joined in. A long time later than we'd been told, a helicopter came into view, hovered, and landed on the law school roof. It was like the arrival of a rock star at an outdoor concert. For a moment, even the demonstrators quieted and stood on tiptoe, straining to catch a glimpse of a real President. When he started to speak, the demonstrators increased the volume of their chant in an effort to drown him out. They were hundreds strong, but he was amplified.

It's hard to say, in retrospect, which meant less—the speech, or the protesters' endless declaration that the people, united, would never be defeated. But I was caught up in the spirit of the thing. When some of the demonstrators turned their eyes toward the SWAT men who stood armed on the roofs of the surrounding buildings and began to chant "Jump! Jump! Jump!," "I was thrilled. From the TV show I knew they were SWAT men. I didn't like their uniforms, or the fact that their guns were pointed at us. I joined in and shouted "Jump!" at the top of my lungs, until I felt a sharp tugging at my elbow. It was my sister. "Shut up," she said to me. "You don't have any idea what you're saying."

Ten years later my sister lives in San Francisco. After many different kinds of therapy, she has settled into marriage and a career as a social worker that almost fulfills her old ideals. She says she wants to have children but wonders if it would be selfish to bring new life into a world that is sure to end in the next twenty years. Gerald Ford, himself the most in-between of Presidents, has faded from public view, taking a backseat to his famous wife. Each week the *New York Post* carries news of another celebrity checking into the Betty Ford Center for treatment of "drug and alcohol dependency." My mother screams at Reagan on the television, but at a somewhat reduced volume in comparison with the Nixon days.

One evening during my freshman year at college, I was walking to the dining hall with my roommate, when I noticed a small group of students holding a sit-in on a square of carefully trimmed grass outside the president's office. There were only five of them. A sign explained that they were protesting President Carter's newly announced program for draft registration. They had a guitar and they were singing "We Shall Overcome." Although little frightened me at the age of eighteen more than the thought of getting drafted, I still felt an aversion toward the protestors. How ridiculous, I thought as I passed—a sit-in, in 1980, at Yale. "Throwbacks," I said to my roommate, unable to think of a word that carried more disdain. "Don't they realize their style is going to alienate people from their cause?" He nodded in agreement, and we continued on our way. My roommate wore small tortoiseshell glasses. My hair was short, and I was wearing a Brooks Brothers tweed jacket I had bought myself, but somehow it didn't occur to me that we were throwing back even further than they were. Then, as we approached the Freshman Commons, I heard the protestors begin to chant quietly: "The people—united—will never be defeated." For a moment I stopped, remembering that afternoon when Gerald Ford had visited Stanford. I knew that those demonstrators I had stood among, who had seemed so glorious to me, were themselves a mere shadow of Berkeley, or Kent State, or Harvard five years earlier. I had witnessed only the tail end of something that had once been great. It seemed easy to me, these days, for five Yale stu-

dents to chant, "The people, united, will never be defeated." What astonished me was that there had actually been a time when someone believed it.

MY GENERATION HAS always resisted definition. The younger siblings of the Sixties, we watched riots from a distance, sneaked peeks at the *Zap Comix* lying around our older siblings' bedrooms, grew our hair long, and in prepubescent droves campaigned door to door for McGovern. When I was ten I played the guitar and wanted to be like Joni Mitchell. A friend of my sister's, a fellow who must have fancied himself a Bill Graham in the making, arranged for me to sing my own compositions in a series of little concerts given in the communal dining hall of Columbae House. By the time I was old enough to take part in any real way, disillusion had set in, people had given up, cocaine was the drug of choice. Tail end. We have always been the tail end—of the Sixties, of the baby boom. We hit our stride in an age of burned-out, restless, ironic disillusion. With all our much-touted youthful energy

first generation whose members usually cannot remember their first plane trip. And the first in recent history that has never seen its friends missing in action or lost in combat or living and working in Canada.

It should have been perfect, the perfect time and place. As our parents always reminded us, we had so much they had not even been able to imagine as children. So little harm came to us. And yet, on those bright afternoons of my childhood, when I sat indoors, watching sunlight reflect off the face of *Speed Racer* on the television, I was already aware that rips were being made in the fabric of perfection. When my parents shouted at each other, their voices sounded like fabric ripping. My friends sat in the cafeteria of our middle school reading brightly colored books with titles like *The Kids' Book of Divorce*. On television the Brady Bunch and the Partridge Family continued on their merry ways. Sometimes I closed my eyes and tried to will myself through the television's scrim of glass and into their world. It was, in its own way, as appealing and as inaccessible as the world of the folk dancers, of my brother and sis-

---

WE hit our stride in an age of burned-out, restless, ironic disillusion. With all our much-touted youthful energy boiling inside us, where were we supposed to go? What were we supposed to do?

---

boiling inside us, where were we supposed to go? What were we supposed to do?

Now the Rainbows and the Moon Units of the world (conceived at love-ins, "birthed" in birthing rooms) are hitting their teens. They are computer-literate. They own their own Apple Macintoshes. They watch MTV on VCRs. Those with an artistic inclination rent video cameras, make their own films, and proclaim that written language will soon degenerate until it serves only as a vehicle for nostalgia, eclipsed by the shot—videotape and its new alphabet of images.

My generation is somewhere in between. Born too late and too early, we are partially what came before us and partially what followed. But we can make certain claims. We are the first generation, for instance, that is younger than television. We knew the Vietnam War as something about as real as the *Mannix* episodes it seemed to interrupt so often. We learned stealth by figuring out how to get around our parents' efforts to ration the number of hours we watched each day. And we are the

ter, who went to college and were free of the big house with its burden of memories. But I knew that if I broke through the television, I wouldn't instantly emerge in that magical community of Sherman Oaks, with its homecoming dances, ice-cream floats, and wise maids. Instead I'd find circuits and wires, the complicated brainworks of the famous "tube."

In the real world, real parents were splitting up, moving out, questioning and in some cases rejecting the commandments to marry and have a family, commandments that had been the foundation of their parents' lives. In my family it was happening against our wishes. In a community where the divorce rate had reached a record high, and every family seemed to have at least one child in prison, or in a hospital, or dead of an overdose, my parents had never even separated. Still, there were sharp words, often, and a sense of desperate effort and hard, unrewarded labor through it all. We felt it in the politics of playing records, of who did the dishes, and who really cared around here, and who had slaved for whom for how long. Sometimes it seemed to me that we walked around the house opened up and bleeding, yet talking, laughing, smiling, like actors in a horror movie who, during a break in the shooting, simply forget to remove the prop knives from their backs or mop up the imitation blood. In this case the blood was real, though we pretended it wasn't.

I watched. During *Star Trek* my mother brought me dinner on a tray. Sometimes, after watching for hours and hours, I would have to get very close to the screen in order to focus, even though I knew it was bad for my eyes. Sometimes I'd see how close I could get, let the lenses of my eyes touch the hot lens of the television, soak in the pure light.

WHEN MY BROTHER and sister were my age, they had already seen much more of the world than I will probably ever see. They'd gone to India, Guatemala, Cuba, Hong Kong. They'd worked in prisons, and organized striking farm workers, and driven across the country half a dozen times each. They'd read Kerouac, Castaneda, *Zen and the Art of Motorcycle Maintenance*. And when, as a child, I'd ask them about their lives, they'd tell me about the movement. Movement. It seemed an appropriate word, since they moved all the time, driven by exploratory wanderlust into the vast American wilderness. I possess no similar desire whatsoever, and neither, I think, do most members of my generation. Rather than move, we burrow. We are interested in stability, neatness, entrenchment. We want to stay in one place and stay in one piece, establish careers, establish credit. We want good apartments, fulfilling jobs, nice boy/girl friends. We want American Express Gold Cards. Whereas my brother and sister, at the same age, if asked, would probably have said that their goals were to expand their minds, see the world, and encourage revolutionary change.

I've never thought of myself as naive; I've never imagined that I might lead a sheltered life. I am, after all, "sophisticated," have been to Europe, understand dirty jokes and the intricacies of sexually transmitted diseases. This is my milieu, the world I live in, and I have almost never stepped beyond its comfortable borders. A safety net surrounds my sophisticated life, and the question is, of course, how did it get there? Did I build it myself? Was it left for me? Sometimes I feel as if I live in a room with mirrored walls, imagining that the tiny space I occupy is in fact endless, and constitutes a real world. I remember when I first moved to New York, and I was looking for work, I dropped my résumé off with the manager of the Oscar Wilde Memorial Bookshop—a political gay bookstore—and he asked me to tell him about

my "movement experience." For a few seconds I just blanked out. I thought he was talking about dance.

LAST YEAR I went with three friends to see the film *Liquid Sky*, which was enjoying a cult following in lower Manhattan. The film portrays a culture of young people who live in lower Manhattan, dress in outlandish costumes, and spend most of their nights in wildly decorated clubs—a culture of young people very much like the young people in the theater that night watching the film. Margaret, the heroine, explains that she has moved beyond the suburban dream of having a husband, and also moved beyond the middle-urban dream of having an agent (and hence a career), and has now recognized the pointlessness of striving for anything. Her new dream lover is an alien creature that thrives on the chemicals released in the brain during orgasm and that will ultimately devour Margaret in the course of a final, quite literally cosmic climax. Perhaps the moment in the film that stuck most to my ribs is the one in which Margaret's ex-lover and ex-acting teacher, a man in his late forties, accuses her of dressing like a whore. She retaliates with a childish sneer that his jeans (throwbacks to his own heyday) are just as much a costume as her push-up bras and red leather skirts. Of her peers, she says something like, "At least we don't pretend we aren't wearing costumes."

own green youthfulness; it is a generation. In performance spaces, bars that double as art galleries, clubs with names like 8 B.C. or Save the Robots, on the darkest and most dangerous streets of New York, a culture is being born out of the claim that there is no culture—that it's all mere dress-up, mere fakery, mere whooping-it-up-before-the-plague. This culture is downtown. It basks in the limelight of the present moment. It avoids tall buildings. Poverty is its kin, its company, and sometimes its reality, but it draws the curious rich like flies. Then real estate possibilities emerge out of nowhere: tenements turn into town houses, yet another chic and colorful neighborhood for the new rich emerges. Sometimes I wonder whether my generation's lunatic fringe of trendsetters keeps moving into more and more dangerous parts because the gentrified keep pushing them out of the neighborhoods they've pioneered, or because they're attracted to the hopeless edge of the city, where the future means finding food and drugs to get you through tomorrow. That is about as far as you can get from long-term investments. And the irony is, of course, that where they have gone, the rich young future-mongers of the generation ahead have followed, attracted by the scent of potential development. Farther east, and farther down, their world keeps moving. It is sometimes decadent, destructive, dangerous. It is some-

---

WE have inserted into our minds the image of the mushroom cloud and the world in flames in order to justify a blind spot in us—an inability to conceive of any future at all.

At least we don't pretend we aren't wearing costumes? Well, yes, I guess they don't, I thought. For Margaret, to pretend one isn't wearing a costume is contemptible. She rejects the idea that the way one dresses might represent a claim made about the world today, or project an idea for the world tomorrow. Hell, there probably won't be a world tomorrow. Clothes have to do with what we aren't, not what we are. Screw art, let's dance.

And yet Margaret lets something slip when she makes this claim. She implicates herself by referring to her friends, her cronies, as "we." The "we" in *Liquid Sky* is disloyal, backstabbing, bitchy, and violent. But it is still a "we"; it is a group, defined by its belief in its own newness, its

times gloriously, extraordinarily fun.

I've seen that world. Good yuppie that I am, I've even dipped my toe in its freezing waters on select Saturday nights and Sunday mornings when an urge to dance came over me like an itch. When I was an undergraduate I was friends with a couple of women who became lovers and took to walking around the campus with dog collars around their necks connected by a link chain. And I remember going with them once to have tea at the home of one of their mothers—a big brownstone in the East Sixties, on the same block where Nixon used to live. They marched defiantly through the foyer, their very entrance a calculated affront, me following meekly, while the mother strove not to notice the white-blond tint of her daughter's hair, or the double nose ring (she had pierced the nostril herself, in the bathroom), and offered to take my jacket. "So how is school going, honey?" the mother said. In the course of tea she made a valiant effort to call her daughter "Max," as Max currently insisted. (Her real name was Elizabeth.) And a year later, in New York, I walked home from a party one night with an NYU student and her friend, a boy dressed like Boy George—eyeliner, dreadlocks, lipstick. And they were going to steal the boy's sister's food stamps so they could get something to eat. They said this matter-of-factly. And when I expressed amazement that the girl's affluent parents didn't send her enough money to buy food, she said equally matter-of-factly, "Oh, they send me plenty of money, but I use it all up on booze and drugs." Without a trace of self-consciousness she said it; but with more than a trace of self-pity.

It was Saturday night and we were going to a party. It was always Saturday night and we were always going to a party. Someone was stoned. Someone was drunk, lying snoring on the big sofa in the library. Someone was wearing Salada tea-bag fortunes as earrings. In their rooms, the boys were experimenting with eye makeup. In their rooms, the girls were experimenting with mushrooms. It was Saturday night and we were going to a dress party (everyone had to wear a dress), to a gender-transcendence party, to a party supporting the women's center, supporting the Marxist Literary Group, supporting the Coalition Against Apartheid. My friends were not active in these organizations; we expressed our support by giving the parties. For days beforehand we'd trade twelve-inch singles, mix them on our stereos, compete to produce the greatest dance tape ever, the one that would bring the dancers to the floor in an orgiastic heap.

The favorite songs that year, I think, were "Dancing with Myself," by Billy Idol, and "I Wanna Be Sedated," by the Ramones. But "Rock Lobster" seemed to turn up on every tape, as did "We Got the Beat" and "I Love a Man in a Uniform."

A photographer friend of mine used to come to all the parties that year, throw her camera out into the pulsating dark as arbitrarily as Richard Misrach, who was known for blindly aiming his camera out into the dark Hawaiian jungle. It became a kind of joke, Jennie's presence at every party. You could count on seeing yourself a few days later, stoned or drunk or vomiting, or making out with someone you didn't recognize on a sofa you couldn't remember. In the photographs bodies were frozen in the midst of flight, heads shook in beady haloes of light and sweat, clothes flew and were suspended, forever revealing small patches of white skin. There was

a quality of ecstasy. But when I see those pictures these days, I think *I was mad*.

I don't remember ever feeling as much joy as I did that year, when, on any Saturday night, on a crowded dance floor I'd hear my favorite song begin. It was as if my body itself had become an instrument, pulled and plucked and wrenched by the music, thrown beyond itself. This was no love-in of the Sixties, no drug-hazed ritual of communion. We were dancing with ourselves. Someone joked that each of us could have had on his own individual Walkman.

The mornings after such evenings always began around two in the afternoon. Exhausted and hung over, we would go back to the big rooms where the parties had taken place to confront the hundreds of empty beer cans and cigarette stubs, the little clots of lost sweaters stuffed into corners, forgotten, never to be retrieved. Sunlight streamed in. While the guests slept in late, and Jennie toiled in her darkroom, frenzied with creation, the partygivers took out their mops.

LIKE OUR OLDER brothers and sisters, my generation belongs to gyms. We find Nautilus equipment consoling. Nothing gets in your way when you're bench pressing, or swimming, or running, not even the interfering subconscious that tended to muck up all those Seventies efforts at psychological self-improvement. Muscles appear as a manifestation of pure will.

In contrast to our older brothers and sisters, however, the fact that we believe in health does not necessarily mean that we believe in the future. The same bright young person who strives for physical immortality also takes for granted the imminence of his destruction. At Brown University, students voted last October on a referendum to stock poison tablets in the school infirmary, so that in the event of a nuclear catastrophe, they could commit suicide rather than die of fallout. As if nuclear disaster, rather than being a distant threat, were a harsh reality, an immediacy, something to prepare for. I am reminded of Grace Paley's description of an eighteen-year-old in her story "Friends": "His friends have a book that says a person should, if properly nutritioned, live forever.... He also believes that the human race, its brains and good looks, will end in his time."

Brains and good looks. Last year I went dancing at Area for the first time, arguably the chicest dance club in New York. (A friend of mine who is more of an expert than I in these matters insists that the club called Save the Robots is chicer, since it is frequented by the people who work at Area and does not open until after Area has closed.) At this point Area was dressed in its nuclear holocaust garb. On our way in,

we passed tableaux vivants of people in Karen Silkwood suits, peeling lurid green candy off sheets on a conveyor belt. Women danced inside fantastic, menacing pseudo-reactors. Signs reading DANGER— RADIOACTIVE MATERIAL glowed above the dance floor. Later, at a bar, I was introduced to an artist who had been asked to create a work of art in support of the nuclear freeze, and was thinking of carving a mushroom cloud out of a block of ice. It was hard for me to keep from wondering about the famed holocaust anxiety of my postnuclear generation. The world after the bomb, it seemed to me, had become a cliché, incorporated into our dialogue and our culture with an alarming thoughtlessness. Do most of us dream, like Eddie Albert as the President in the movie *Dreamscape*, of a parched postholocaust landscape, peopled by weird halfhuman monsters and scarred children wailing, "It hurts! It hurts!" I doubt it. I think we purport to worry about the world ending much more than we actually do.

Because the terror of knowing the world could end at any moment haunts them so vividly, older people seem to believe that it must be ten times worse for the young. The realization that nuclear disaster is not only possible, but possibly imminent, writes the noted essayist Lewis Thomas, "is bad enough for the people in my generation. We can put up with it, I suppose, since we must. We are moving along anyway.... What I cannot imagine, what I cannot put up with... is what it would be like to be young. How do the young stand it? How can they keep their sanity?"

Well, I want to say, we do. Indeed, I think we are more sane and less hysterical about the issue of nuclear holocaust than are the generations ahead of us. We do not go crazy, because for us the thought of a world with no future—so terrifying to Dr. Thomas—is completely familiar; is taken for granted; is nothing new.

I have tried time and again to explain this to people who are older than I. I tell them that no matter how hard I try—and I have closed my eyes tightly, concentrated, tried to will my mind to do it—I simply cannot muster an image of myself fifty, or twenty, or even ten years in the future. I go blank. I have no idea where or what or even *if* I'll be. Whereas my parents, when they were young, assumed vast and lengthy futures for themselves, a series of houses, each larger than the one before, and finally the "golden years" of retirement, knitting by fires, bungalows in Florida. I think we have inserted into our minds the commercialized image of the mushroom cloud and the world in flames in order to justify a blind spot in us—an inability to think beyond the moment, or conceive of any future at all, which makes us immune to the true horror felt by older people. This blind spot has more to do with our attitude toward the nuclear family than with nuclear disaster—with the fact that our parents, as they now reach the golden years they once looked forward to, are finding themselves trapped in unhappy marriages or divorced, are too bitter to ever consider loving again, or are desperate to find a new mate with whom they can share those last happy years that they were promised, that they worked so hard for, that they were so unfairly cheated out of.

And we—well, we aren't going to make the same mistakes they did. Alone at least we're safe—from pain, from dependency, from sexually transmitted diseases. Those who belong to no one but themselves can never be abandoned.

IT IS 1983. I have just graduated from college and, like most of my friends, lead the sort of life that makes a good biographical note in the back of a literary magazine—"living and working in Manhattan." Most mornings, I have to get up at 7:30 A.M.—unnaturally early for someone like me, who finds it hard to fall asleep before 3:00. I don't eat breakfast, I shower in three minutes, timed. From inside my apartment, where it is warm, I head out into the cold, begin the long trek to the subway. My station is famous for its poor design. If I have a token, I must run down one staircase and up another to get to the train. Sometimes the train doors close on my nose. Other times I'm lucky. I squeeze in, find a space to stand. The train begins to move, and there are newspapers in my eyes, painted fingernails, noses, the smell of toothpaste and coffee everywhere around me. People are nodding, falling asleep on their feet. For six months now, this subway ride in the morning and afternoon has been the closest I have come physically to another human being.

I arrive at my office. For the length of the morning, I work, taking frequent breaks. I visit the cookie lady in publicity. I visit the water cooler. I gossip with friends on the phone, thinking about lunch.

I used to think there was something gloriously romantic about the nine-to-five life. I used to imagine there could be no greater thrill than being part of the crush riding the escalator down from the Pan Am Building into Grand Central at 5:00. The big station ceiling, with its map of stars, would unfold above you, the escalator would slip down under your feet—you, so small, so anonymous in all that hugeness and strangeness. Yet you'd know you were different. Light on your feet at rush hour, you'd dodge and cut through the throng, find your way fast to the shuttle. Like the north-or-south-going Zax in Doctor Seuss, you'd have one direction, and no choice but to move in it.

Ha, as the old woman who has worked

forty years in accounting says to everyone. *Ha-ha.*

It's 5:30. Outside the sun has set. Inside other people are still typing, still frenzied. Everyone works harder than you, no matter how hard you work. Everyone makes more than you do, no matter how much you make. You slip out silently, guilty to be leaving only a half hour late, wondering why you're not as ambitious as they are, why you don't have it in you to make it.

But when you get outside, the wind is cold on your face, the streets are full of people herding toward the subway. You put on your Walkman. You think that tonight you might like to go dancing. Then the Pointer Sisters come on, and you realize that, like John Travolta tripping down the streets of Brooklyn in *Saturday Night Fever,* you already are.

A FEW YEARS after I stopped going, the Saturday night folk-dancing ritual at Stanford ceased. Lack of interest, I suppose. The women wrapped in gypsy fabric and the boys with dirty feet were getting cleaned up and prepping for their GMATs. Today they are baby-boomers. They are responsible, says a *People* magazine ad, for "the surge in microchips, chocolate chips, and a host of special services to help Boomers run their two-career households." They work, live, love in offices. They have "drive."

My generation, in the meantime, still trots outside their circle, eager to learn the steps. In every outward way we are perfect emulators. We go to work in corporations right out of college. We look good in suits. But we also have haircuts that are as acceptable at East Village early-hours clubs as they are at Morgan Stanley. And (of course) at least we don't pretend we're not wearing costumes.

There are advantages to growing up, as we did, on the cusp of two violently dislocated ages; advantages to becoming conscious just as one decade is burning out, and another is rising, phoenixlike, from the ashes of its dissolution—or disillusion. If the Sixties was an age of naive hope, then the Eighties is an age of ironic hopelessness—its perfect counterpart, its skeptical progeny. We are the children of that skepticism. We go through all the motions. But if we tried then to learn the steps from our brothers and sisters because we believed in what they were doing, we follow in their footsteps now for almost the opposite reason—to prove that we can sell out just as well as they can, and know it too.

I remember, as a child, listening to my mother talk about fashion. "Once you've seen stiletto heels come and go three times, you'll realize how little any of it means," she said. I don't think I knew yet what a stiletto heel was, but I understood already and perfectly how little any of it meant. It came to me very early, that ironic and distanced view on things, and it's stayed.

The voice of my generation is the voice of David Letterman, whose late-night humor—upbeat, deadpan, more than a little contemptuous—we imitate because, above all else, we are determined to make sure everyone knows that what we say might not be what we mean. Consider these words, from Brett Duval Fromson, in an op-ed piece for *The New York Times:* "Yuppies, if we do anything at all, respect those who deliver the goods. How else are we going to afford our Ferragamo pumps, Brooks Brothers suits, country houses, European cars, and California chardonnays?" The balance of the irony is perfect—between self-mockery and straight-faced seriousness, between criticism and comfy self-approval. "If we do anything at all," Fromson writes, leaving open the possibility that we don't. Certainly, he acknowledges, during the recession we "didn't give much thought to those who wouldn't make it." And now I am thinking about a headline I read recently in *The Village Voice,* above one of a series of articles analyzing Reagan's victory last November. It read DON'T TRUST ANYONE UNDER THIRTY.

Mine is a generation perfectly willing to admit its contemptible qualities. But our self-contempt is self-congratulatory. The buzz in the background, every minute of our lives, is that detached, ironic voice telling us: At least you're not faking it, as they did, at least you're not pretending as they did. It's okay to be selfish as long as you're up-front about it. Go ahead. "Exercise your right to exercise." Other people are dying to defend other people's rights to speak, to vote, and to live, but at least you don't pretend you're not wearing a costume.

What is behind this bitterness, this skepticism? A need, I think, for settledness, for security, for home. Our parents imagined they could satisfy this urge by marrying and raising children; our older brothers and sisters through community and revolution. We have seen how far those alternatives go. We trust ourselves, and money. Period.

Fifteen years ago you weren't supposed to trust anyone over thirty. For people in my generation, the goal seems to be to get to thirty as fast as possible, and stay there. Starting out, we are eager, above all else, to be finished. If we are truly a generation without character, as is often claimed, it is because we have seen what has happened to generations with character. If we are without passion or affect, it is because we have decided that passion and affect are simply not worth the trouble. If we stand crouched in the shadows of a history in which we refuse to take part, it is because that's exactly where we've chosen to stand.

Characterlessness takes work. It is defiance and defense all at once.

DURING MY FRESHMAN year in college I remember going to see Mary Tyler Moore as a woman paralyzed from the neck down in *Whose Life Is It Anyway?* At intermission I ran into a friend from school who was practically in tears. "You don't know what it's like for me to see her like that," he said. "Mary's a metaphor for my youth. And looking at her on that stage, well, I can't help but feel that it's my youth lying paralyzed up there." Later, a woman I know told me in all earnestness, "When I'm in a difficult situation, a real bind, I honestly think to myself, 'What would Mary have done?' I really do." I know people who significantly altered the shape of their lives so that they could stay up every weeknight for a 2:30 to 4:00 A.M. Mary tripleheader on Channel 4 in New York. Even John Sex, the East Village's reigning club maven, is famous for his early-morning rendition, at the Pyramid club, of the Mary theme.

Remember those words? "Who can take the world on with her smile? Who can take a nothing day and suddenly make it all seem worthwhile?" And of course, at the end of the opening credits, there is the famous epiphany, the throw of the hat. "You're gonna make it after all," sings Sonny Curtis, who faded quickly into obscurity, but whose dulcet voice will live forever in reruns, and in our hearts. She throws the red cap into the air; the frame freezes, leaving Mary's hat perpetually aloft, and Mary perpetually in the bloom of youthful anticipation. The great irony of that shot, underscoring the show's tender, melancholy tone, is that as the seasons wore on, and new images of a shorter-haired Mary were spliced into the opening credit sequence, it always remained the same. So that even in the last, saddest seasons, with Mary pushing forty and wanting a raise and still not married, we are still given a glimpse of Mary as she used to be, young Mary, full of youthful exuberance, and that image of Mary and her hat and her hope gently plays against the truth of what her life has given her. The fact is that Mary's life stinks. She is underpaid in a second-rate job at a third-rate television station.

Her best friends, Rhoda and Phyllis, have both left her to fail in spin-offs in other cities, and she doesn't even have a boyfriend. That's Mary's life, and even the clever tactic of changing the last line of the theme song from "You're gonna make it after all" to "Look's like you've made it after all" fails to convince us that it's anything but rotten.

But Mary presses on, and the great epic film, which all the episodes of the Mary show comprise, ends as it began—with Mary not getting married. The camaraderie of the newsroom has provided her less with a bond of strength than with a buffer against sorrow. Mary and her friends share one another's loneliness, but they don't cure it. The station closes down, the lights go out, and still young Mary throws her hat.

I see Marys often these days; the other day I saw one going into a deli on Third Avenue in the Eighties, just after work. She's younger, a bit fatter, better paid, so she wears silk blouses with ruffles and bows. And because she lives in New York, she's a bit more desperate, the pain is a little closer to the surface. It's 9:00, and she's just gotten off from work. She buys herself dinner—chicken hot dogs, Diet Coke, Häagen-Dazs—and heads home to the tiny apartment, with a bathtub in the kitchen, for which she pays far too much. And I can't help but think that, even as a child, when the goings-on in that Minneapolis newsroom were the high point of her week, she knew she was going to end up here. Remember the episodes where Mary and Lou quit in order to protest how little money they make? Mary is forced to borrow from Ted. Nothing upsets her more than the realization that, for the first time in her life, she's in debt. She never asked for more than a room to live in, after all, and someplace to go each day, and perhaps a little extra money for a new dress now and then.

Here in New York, all the prime-time shows of my childhood have found their way, like memories or dreams, to the darkest part of the night. First there's *Star Trek* and the familiar faces of the *Enterprise* crew. Tonight they are confronted with an android that has become human because it has felt the first pangs of love. Once again, no woman can win Kirk, be-

cause he's already married to the most beautiful woman of them all—his ship. At 1:00 *The Twilight Zone* comes on, another lost astronaut wanders a blank landscape, the world before or after man. At 1:30, only an hour before Mary begins, I watch the *Independent News*. I am, by this time, on the floor, and close to sleep. The newscaster's voice clucks amicably, telling us that Mary Tyler Moore has checked herself into the Betty Ford Center. She has bravely admitted to having a problem, and she is battling it.

I leap up. I stare at the screen. The image has already passed, the newscaster moved on to another story. And I think, how sad that Mary's life has come to this. And yet, how good that she is bravely admitting to having a problem, and battling it. And I wonder if Mary Tyler Moore sat and looked at herself in the mirror before she made the decision; sat and looked at herself in the mirror and asked herself, "What would Mary do?"

Mary would do the right thing. And that is a comfort to me, this dark night, as I drag myself from the living room floor and click the television into silence. We have learned a few things from Mary. We have learned, on a day-to-day basis, how to do the right thing. We have learned to be kind and patient with one another, to give comfort. We have learned how to be good and generous friends.

It is late. The apartment is close and quiet. Tonight I am alone, but this weekend I will be with my friends. Like the folks in Mary's newsroom or the crew of the *Enterprise* bridge, we are a gang. We go dancing, and afterward, to an all-night deli for babkas and French toast, our clothes permeated with the smell of cigarettes. We walk five abreast, arm-in-arm, so that other people must veer into the street to avoid hitting us. When we decide the time has come to head back uptown, we pile into a cab, sometimes five or six of us, and sit on each other's laps and legs, and feel happy that we have friends, because it means we can take cabs for less than the price of the subway. It is nearly dawn, and a few sour-looking prostitutes are still marching the sidewalks of the West Side Highway in the cold. In a moment when we're not looking a sun will appear, small and new and fiery, as if someone had thrown it into the air.

*The children of the flower children
may be rebelling against—guess what?
—the values of the 1960s.*

Brave New Wave of the '80s

Steve Barnett

Steve Barnett is vice president of the Cultural Analysis Group at Planmetrics Inc., which has offices in Chicago, New York and San Francisco. Barnett, a Ph.D. in cultural anthropology, has taught at Princeton and Brown Universities and the Massachusetts Institute of Technology.

In the background a rock band is playing "White Wedding," sung by Billy Idol. What viewers are watching on the TV screen is a wedding unlike any they've ever seen. A coffin is slowly nailed closed. The bride cuts her finger and screams hysterically. Explosions of unknown origin shake the church. The scene shifts to the happy couple's kitchen—appliances start blowing up.

Such bizarre, montage sequences are not unusual for MTV—Music Television—the two-year-old cable network created by Warner Amex, which claims a growing audience of 15½ million viewers around the country. MTV features rock bands playing nonstop music 24 hours a day and illustrated by "concept tapes"—film footage of people and scenes, often speeded up; fragments of action, flickering lights and displays of primary colors; imaginary worlds of space creatures (usually band members or actors). "The results are silly, pretentious, weird, and fun, like eavesdropping on playacting children in unselfconscious parody of adult behavior," wrote critic Helen Dudar in *The Wall Street Journal.*

Whether it's art or "the most exalted junk on the box" (as Dudar called it), MTV is saying something important to a new generation of American consumers. With its high-tech visual tricks (much like those used in TV commercials) and surreal fantasy worlds, the MTV format corresponds closely to what I call the "New-Wave mindset" of American youth. Although New-Wave teenagers now constitute less than half the teenage population, recent studies by Planmetrics, a consulting firm that specializes in strategic planning, suggest that this segment is growing and may be in the vanguard of their generation's changing tastes.

The emergence of a significant teenage group with very different values and behavior from the young people of the late 1960s and 1970s has received relatively little attention so far. Just as the "flower children" were initially thought to be marginal to American society, but went on to reshape many consumption patterns in the U.S., these New-Wave youth of the 1980s will change the product and service market for young people in the coming decade.

Believing that many companies were not yet reacting to changing styles among young Americans, the Cultural Analysis Group at Planmetrics has been studying attitudes of young Americans since 1980. Our research methods are anthropological and linguistic, relying on careful observation (with their permission) of 120 teenagers interacting in small groups across the country. Our team of researchers, led by two anthropologists (myself and one other) and a psychologist, has observed them in their homes, at school, in video-game parlors and other hangouts for a week or two at a time. We have recorded and analyzed many of their conversations and interviewed them at length about their behavior and habits.

This qualitative data provided us with hypotheses to be tested in a telephone survey of 350 teenagers conducted by a nationwide polling organization using standard sampling methods. The questions we asked employed language that they use in their everyday lives. First, we took an inventory of their tastes: What clothes did they wear, what music did they like, who did they look up to. Then we probed their attitudes on a range of issues, with questions like: "Do you think conserving energy is important to ensure a prosperous future for the U.S.?" "Do you favor or oppose nuclear

From *Across the Board*, December 1983, pp. 5-12. Reprinted by permission of the author and The Conference Board.

Their styles—A recent "Rockabilly-'50s" event in Los Angeles. "Many young people who share New-Wave attitudes dress in ways their parents find vaguely reminiscent of the 1950s."

Their rules—Below, a scene from Dungeons & Dragons. "In their retreat into fantasy worlds, the new generation is rejecting many of their parents' values from the 1960s."

energy?" "Do your parents understand your views on dating, school, jobs, and what matters to you in general?" "Do you try to explain your views to your parents when they disagree with you?" When we analyzed the results, we found that certain responses tended to go together in a statistically significant "cluster." We labeled this set of tastes, attitudes and other characteristics "New Wave." From both the qualitative analysis and the national survey, we found that in 1980 about 25 percent of American teenagers from ages 12 to 16 shared New-Wave characteristics. By this year, the figure had risen to 39 percent.

So-called New-Wave styles originated with punk-rock groups and teenage culture in England, and have spread to the U.S. In their extreme form they are associated with bizarre dress—multicolored hair, men with earrings and safety pins stuck in their skin—and drug taking.

But it would be a mistake to dismiss such styles simply as aberrations. Indeed, appearances are deceptive. Many young people who share New-Wave attitudes dress in less ostentatious ways which their parents would find vaguely reminiscent of the 1950s, including wearing pegged pants, charcoal gray and pink combinations, pedal pushers, bobby socks, and so on. There is even a "drugged preppy" look—combining preppy clothes and sustained drug taking.

New-Wave youth are deeply involved in creating an alternative identity through stylistic extremes. Moreover, when compared with previous generations, they are, even for their age, less political, much less con-

cerned with conservation and environmental issues, and very much protechnology. To a limited extent, their outlook corresponds to a general conservative swing in the United States. But it is important to remember that New-Wave youth are concerned with their own hermetically sealed world and do not easily adapt to current social rules and values.

As one articulate New-Wave representative put it: "We are searching for an identity outside of your society. Some things that we do may look outrageous, but it is the only way left to us to say we are not part of your crazy world. You won't let us in [he was referring to a lack of jobs], and so we can make another world outside yours that we can control." This overwhelming feeling of exclusion is at the heart of the New-Wave culture.

The easiest way to get an overall sense of how New-Wave teenagers think is to contrast their attitudes on several key issues with those of the previous generation of teenagers:

Protechnology/Antitechnology. Planmetrics developed a technology value scale for the national teenage survey and found that the respondents who identified themselves as New Wave consistently evaluated new technology positively, while "straight" respondents were more cautious about endorsing new technology (like robots, computerized homes, artificial environments).

Younger people have generally been ill-disposed to technology since the middle 1960s, when they asso-

New-Wave Lyrics
KNOW YOUR RIGHTS*

This is a public service announcement—with guitar
Know your rights—all three of them, I say
You have the right not to be killed
Murder is a crime
Unless it was done by a policeman or aristocrat
You have the right to food and money
Providing of course you don't mind a little humiliation,
Investigation and if you cross your fingers
Rehabilitation
Young offenders! Know your rights
You have the right to freeee speech
As long as your not dumb enough
To actually try it

ciated it with an unpopular war and with unfeeling, hierarchical bureaucratic control. During the late 1960s, for example, students at the University of Rochester attacked and set fire to computers. In other schools students intentionally crumpled computer registration forms in defiance of the forms' instructions: "Do not bend, fold, spindle, or mutilate."

New-Wave youth, however, are genuinely fascinated by the technology behind computers and computer games, space exploration, robotics, electronic forms of music and communication, the creation of artificial environments through lighting and sound systems at concerts and dances. Increasingly, they see technology as a value-neutral conduit that can provide them with the sensory and emotional stimulation they seek.

Oddly enough, teenagers understand little of how technology actually works. For example, we found that very few can explain the basics of computers, even though most are adept at computer games. Most of the youngsters we studied did not even know how a simple light bulb works — or even that it has a filament (nowadays, most bulbs are frosted and the filament is not visible).

For many New-Wave youth, technology has become a magical part of their surroundings. They have no particular need to master its technical secrets, but neither do they understand the radical antitechnology stance of their parents. In California we observed this conversation between two teenagers after they were given printouts of their class schedules at the beginning of the semester:

"My mother told me that when she was in college,

they used to burn forms that came out of computers," one said.

"Why the hell would anyone do that? It [the printouts] makes things easier," the other student replied.

"Beats me. She gave me that old '60s line, but I don't know what she's talking about."

Environmental Unconcerns. Young people of the late 1960s and the 1970s were environmentally concerned, basically supporting all nature-preservation issues and strongly endorsing energy conservation. Now, many teenagers are becoming apathetic toward environmental issues. For example, they are turning away from traditional camping activities. (One small sign of the trend: To continue to attract families with teenagers, some campground owners have been forced to install electronic-game rooms at campsites.)

In a study of how Americans actually set their thermostats (versus what they *say* their thermostat setting is), Planmetrics found, in a study of homes with heating and air conditioning on the same system, that teenagers consistently and surreptitiously move the thermostat up in winter and down in summer, showing little concern for energy conservation. In addition, we surveyed teenagers on whether they would participate in political action around a specific environmental issue (for respondents near a coast, offshore exploratory drilling for oil; for inland respondents, exploratory drilling for oil on publicly owned parkland). The sample as a whole was significantly apathetic toward such issues. But of those identified as New Wave, only 5 percent said they would participate in environmental political action, versus 27 percent for the entire sample.

Natural vs. Artificial. Young people in the 1960s and '70s endorsed the notion of "small is beautiful," as a way of expressing a basic value of living in harmony with nature. The concept of harmony was a reaction against the dominance of a basic Western cultural value which tends to view nature as something to be subdued and controlled.

Throughout the '70s, teenagers preferred casual clothing made with natural fibers and downplayed makeup and hair dye. Now, many teenagers wear clothing made of heavily dyed artificial fabrics rather than natural yarns in low-key colors, and teenage girls typically become interested in makeup at age 12 or 13. New-wave youth ridicule "natural" or "health" food as tasting terrible, and identify it as the food that their parents prefer. Indeed, health food is to this generation of teenagers what spinach was to previous generations. As one teenager we observed said, "My parents want me to eat health food . . . ugh! I want food with artificial additives; that kind of food tastes good."

Actually measuring the concept of living in harmony with nature is elusive, since survey questions on such subjects contain too many implicit assumptions. Therefore, we relied on qualitative observations of teenagers in small groups. To stimulate discussions of living in harmony with nature, we introduced the idea of small is beautiful and asked the young people what they felt about it. Typical was this exchange among a group of New-Wave young people in Boston:

First person: "You mean I got to grow things and look like a nature freak?"

Second person: "No, no, they're saying, 'Don't get too big so that you ruin the air and water.'"

Third person: "That's gone already—maybe it will produce mutations. Excellent! Sounds like our neighbor who tells me to lower my radio because it's not natural to play it loud. You can't get too big for me—imagine stereo speakers on every street corner."

First person: "Farmers are dumb; their kids can't wait to get off the farm and ditch that hick look."

Third person: "That small-is-beautiful stuff sounds like what my teachers say—maybe farmers believe it, but it can't work here."

Political Apathy. To measure political involvement, the Planmetrics teenage survey used a "political-efficacy scale," a modified version of similar scales used in the classic study by political scientist Donald Stokes and his colleagues in *American Voter* (University of Chicago Press). The survey asked such questions as "Would you vote if you could?" and "Would you express your opinion to your Congressperson on a political issue of importance to you?"

When we compared our results with similar data collected by various political scientists over the past 25 years, we found that today's teenagers felt significantly more alienated than previous generations. While feelings of political efficacy for just about all segments of the population have declined during that period, the New-Wave group's feelings were even more striking. Sixty-two percent of them felt that they have no political efficacy at all now—and will not have when they reach voting age either; another 26 percent perceived only a minimal effect on the political process. Clearly, New-Wave youth see themselves as outside the mainstream of the political process.

In their political attitudes, today's teenagers are more apathetic and cynical than were people their age in recent decades. They seem to be well aware of events during the Vietnam and Watergate eras, though they were mere children in those years. They see politicians as dishonest, but are not disposed to seek remedies through political action. In contrast, the previous generation often began active participation in causes and demonstrations from the age of 13 or 14.

This is not to say they are law-abiding, middle-of-the-road citizens who simply want to mind their own business. On the contrary, they appear to be indifferent to laws, and will often violate a rule if it suits them. Unlike young people in the 1960s who sought to

Their parents—Antiwar march in San Francisco (1967). The New Wave "is not disposed to seek remedies through political action."

Eugene Anthony/Black Star

change the rules, the new generation sees rules as obstacles to be gotten around, especially school rules regarding behavior in general and smoking and drug use in particular. Again, this attitude suggests that the new generation is withdrawing from the larger social arena into a smaller universe where they can create new values and where only these values have moral significance.

In our survey, we did not ask our young respondents how they felt about the prospects of a nuclear war; it's difficult to frame questions that don't sound trite or tendentious. However, in our field studies, we observed that many New-Wave youth seemed to view nuclear war with passivity, as almost inevitable. Indeed, a few talked about nuclear war and the atomic bomb as metaphors for creating an exciting undefined future; a few mentioned that the biological mutations that might ensue from such a war could bring changes for the better.

One sign of what is perhaps a chilling shift in attitudes was a recent advertisement for the movie, *A Boy and His Dog*, a tale about the survivors of a nuclear disaster, among them a talking dog. The ad, which ran in newspapers across the country, showed a mushroom cloud beaming like a happy face—an unthinkable image a generation ago.

Substitute Worlds. From our observations, we concluded that New-Wave youth have shorter attention spans than their peers, are bored more quickly, and find sustained involvement in anything difficult. In their daily lives, they often move from one imaginary world to another in rapid succession.

For example, teenagers play one computer game after another, and each time they drop another quarter into the machine they are lured into an imaginary world. A typical remark of our young subjects, while discussing the games, was: "Wow, look at that score. I am one ace space pilot; move over Buck Rogers, I'm taking over the galaxy." (This from a stoned 15-year-old in Santa Monica.) Identification with an imaginary alter ego is strong, even though the world created in most computer games is rudimentary and not especially compelling.

Therefore, it is not surprising that Dungeons & Dragons (and all its spin-offs) is an extremely important game for New-Wave youth. Unlike most other games, Dungeons & Dragons has few rules; the players not only dream up characters but create in their own heads virtually an entire medieval universe, complete with monsters, heroic knights, damsels in distress, sinister dukes and barons (though the plot basically involves a hunt for treasure and battles against creatures who are protecting it).

But New-Wave youth substitute activities in real life as quickly as they do in games. "Substitution" here means that each activity can be replaced by almost any other activity — even its opposite — with ease. Thus, doing schoolwork tends to be the same as not

doing schoolwork, getting stoned on drugs is the same as being high on alcohol, and so on. Rather than sustain a connection with an environment they don't like, New-Wave youth are ceaselessly experimenting with alternate environments.

Why have teenage values shifted so drastically in the past few years? What accounts for the New Wave's feelings of exclusion? Identifying causes in social research is extremely difficult, but the Planmetrics research team believes that much of what we are seeing is a demographic reversal: In the 1960s, young people were a disproportionately large percentage of the population as a whole. Now, they are a relatively small portion of the total population. Unlike the 1960s rebels who felt the strength of their numbers and flexed their muscles in social action, the New Wave recognizes demographic realities and has withdrawn, at least at this stage of their lives, into a private, nonpolitical world.

That withdrawal, however, is itself a form of rebellion. For in their retreat into fantasy worlds, the new generation is, in effect, rejecting many of their parents values from the 1960s. In the Planmetrics national survey, we found that young people who identified themselves as New Wave consistently had younger parents

Their future?—The movie ad below may reflect a chilling shift in young people's attitudes toward nuclear war. The beaming mushroom cloud would have been "an unthinkable image a generation ago."

than other teenagers. The parents of New-Wave youth tend to come from the baby-boom generation. Thus, the idea of a generation gap broadly defines the New-Wave rebellion; the values of the 1960s, instead of becoming the guideposts for future generations of Americans (as some futurists have mistakenly predicted) have, instead, become the old-fashioned, to-be-rejected values of one's parents.

As a much smaller percentage of the population, the new cohort of Americans feels correspondingly isolated and powerless. After a decade of affirmative action, other groups—minorities, older people, the handicapped—have apparently won a greater degree of power and social acceptance. But more than pre-vious generations, New-Wave youth tend to see action as futile in a world where so many other groups are demanding and getting attention. "No one listens to us," we often heard from them, "so let's just do what we have to do for ourselves." For New-Wave youth, the idea of powerlessness does not only lead to the negative emotion of frustration, but to the positive sense of being free to create alternate identities.

The specific feeling of powerlessness is magnified by a perception that good jobs may not be waiting for them. In the 1970s, members of the baby-boom generation were optimistic about job opportunities; it was only when they began to reach maturity in the economy that they realized they might have to settle for less

The New-Wave Market

Just as the values of the '60s rebels did not persist and come to dominate America in the '80s, so the values of New-Wave youth will probably be significant for the remainder of this decade and then fade away or become fundamentally transformed in ways that cannot be anticipated now. New-Wave values, however, will be with us for some time, and companies would be well-advised to understand the implications of that for their products and marketing strategies.

A good example of the difficulties in communicating with New-Wave youth is the jeans and jean-jacket market. Traditional American companies assumed teenagers would reject highly styled jean jackets and jeans, as teenagers had done in the past. But New-Wave youth, who want to look different from their parents, favor highly styled clothes, and one company, Guess Inc., has taken advantage of this attitude. By creating assorted jean colors and using denim in a wider range of styles, Guess is beginning to penetrate the market. Highly styled clothes in general (especially from Japan, England, and Italy) are making significant gains in the New-Wave market.

Manufacturers of computer games misjudged the scope of teenage demand for expensive video-arcade and repetitious home-computer games. As a marketing executive of a major computer company said, "Arcades are growing cobwebs; we goofed by developing only six basic game types and using those to produce endless variations of games they already had." The movement away from arcades to home games enabled teenagers to put their money to other uses since parents typically paid for personal computers and games. Then, the home-game market slumped as teenagers didn't buy the next clone of a game they were already playing.

But the potential attraction of computer games for creating substitute worlds is still very real. New microchip capabilities will result in more realistic and flexible video presentations. We can expect a sales boom of second- and third-generation games that are visually compelling and that require players to move through open-ended, symbolically rich environments rather than simply scoring a "kill" over a rudimentarily sketched enemy.

Anticipating and meeting the needs of New-Wave consumers is not easy. The following are a few basic guidelines:
• Do not assume that young people today think and act like previous generations.
• New-Wave teenagers respond to products and services clearly directed at them (and not immediately suitable for other markets) as an indicator that they are taken seriously. Thus, the market is sharply segmented.
• Style is critical; a clear, identifiable style for a product (especially for movies, clothes, records, computer games, and food) is necessary.
• Advertise the concrete, immediate rewards of a product, not abstract values of health or environmental quality.
• Given an emphasis on substitute worlds, products can be expected to have a relatively short life cycle, and new-product planning should begin even though an existing product is doing well.
• Monitor carefully trends in Europe and Japan, which have been the source of several New-Wave styles.

New-Wave values have recently begun to spread to adult America. We are starting to see advertisements for automobiles and perfume in stark, overdone primary colors, with surrealist scenes and music, and with a close interweaving of fantasy and reality. A better understanding of the New Wave is important for all companies, not just those marketing directly to younger people.

—S.B.

in their careers than their parents—because of their numbers and a stagnating economy.

Now teenagers are acutely aware that good jobs are scarce and usually require intensive preparation. Many New-Wave youth seem to feel that they must become career-oriented very early—as young even as age 11—or they will have to abandon hope for getting a reasonably steady, well-paying, interesting job. Given the glamorous, inflated media images of some kinds of work (everyone wants to be *Star Wars* director George Lukas or members of a rock group like "The Police"), the group tends to look down on routine, blue-collar work. Or they perceive their job prospects as so bleak that they discount the future and concentrate obsessively on their friends and entertainment.

In the national survey, New-Wave youth were somewhat less likely than other teenagers to believe that they would be able to find a job acceptable to them. Just as significant was our finding that 72 percent of the entire teenage sample felt that the future would be bleaker than the present. In Los Angeles, a young person we observed at a music club said, "My dad keeps telling me how he's gonna get laid off, and how horrible things are, and how I should study all the time so I won't be in that fix. But I can't study that good. I'm gonna wind up just like him or worse probably."

Radical Departures

Leaving home to join an ideological commune is a desperate move, but in the end it is usually a benign, even therapeutic, experience.

Saul V. Levine

Saul V. Levine is head of the department of psychiatry at Sunnybrook Medical Center in Toronto, where he is a professor in the department of psychiatry and also has a clinical practice. This article is adapted from his book Radical Departures: Desperate Detours to Growing Up *(Harcourt, Brace, Jovanovich), 1984.*

June 27, 1983, was a cloudy, breezy day in the San Francisco Bay area. Around a breakfast table in the Thomas home in an affluent suburb, good-humored conversation was interrupted by the honk of a horn. Mark got up from the table and made for the door to join his friends waiting in the car.

His father stopped him. Pressing a $20 bill into Mark's hand, he rested his arm on his son's shoulder for a moment and made an embarrassed joke about the money. "Just in case you get in trouble in the big city," he winked. He could afford to make such jokes. Mark, as clean-cut a blond as any middle-class family could hope for, had never been in trouble in his life. He was willing and reliable, the kind of boy who had been given responsibilities since elementary school.

After kissing his mother good-bye, Mark strode out the door to the waiting car. It was the Monday after high school graduation, and Mark and his friends were on their way to celebrate for a day in San Francisco. When the group returned that evening, Mark wasn't with them. His friends had last seen him late that afternoon in Golden Gate Park, where they had gone to share a six-pack of beer and watch the sun go down. The Thomases weren't worried. He had probably missed his train; he would call them from the station shortly.

But Mark didn't call his parents that night, nor the next night. After 72 hours, the Thomases finally heard from Mark. They weren't to worry, he told them during the collect call from Oregon. He said he was fine. Mark had joined the followers of Bhagwan Shree Rajneesh. He had made a "radical departure."

Every year thousands of young people abruptly turn their backs on family, friends and future to join one or another of an estimated 2,500 communal groups in North America whose values, dress and behavior seem totally alien to everything the joiner has stood for. Practitioners of Rajneeshism wear clothes in the "sunrise colors." Around their necks hang pendants bearing a portrait of their enlightened Master. When the Thomases next saw their son, he was on a street corner in Portland chanting in a circle dance, robed in red. He refused to acknowledge his father's greeting; indeed, he showed no sign of recognizing his parents.

Mark Thomas is a composite of several young men among the hundreds I have studied since the late 1960s (see the "Questions and Answers" box). In my book, *Radical Departures*, I follow nine such young men and women through their journeys into and out of communal groups.

Radical departures are a fact of life, a cultural phenomenon that has inspired more fear, agony, anger, disgust—and misinterpretation—than almost any other. When I started my studies, most people agreed that the groups were hostile to the fundamental standards of middle-class conduct, but beyond that judgment there was a lot of confusion. Were the joiners troubled, academic failures; loners from embattled homes; drug addicts? Certainly there was a subpopulation of

such dropouts, and mental-health professionals were quick to indict all radical departures as a manifestation of pathology. The most charitable judgment was that kids who joined charismatic fringe groups were gullible innocents who had been brainwashed.

Given this widespread sentiment, I was surprised to find, as my research got under way, that these young people, massed in urban communes or converted to a variety of intensely ideological groups, came right off the cover of *The Saturday Evening Post*. There were no more signs of pathology among them than among any group of youngsters. They came from warm, concerned families that had given them every material, social and intellectual benefit. They were, in short, Mark Thomases—good kids with everything to look forward to.

Those who followed press reports on these "cults," as they were invariably called, were treated to a first impression much like what I at first perceived. Such groups were controlled by a charismatic leader who used his power to enrich himself unconscionably. The beliefs he perpetrated were counterfeit, and those who followed him had been duped into serving against their will. They might be held captive by force, deprived of financial means to escape and prevented from communicating with their families.

The details varied from group to group, but the press reports were uniformly negative. One cult censored incoming and outgoing mail and prevented privacy through an intrusive "buddy system." It used the words of the Bible, "For I am come to set a man at variance against his father, and the daughter against her mother," to turn children against their parents. Young girls were encouraged to be "happy hookers in Christ"—that is, to seduce new members sexually.

Another group practiced "heavenly deception," begging donations in public places by selling flowers to benefit a fictional home for the retarded or some other nonexistent cause. Their tactic was to bar the way of hurried travelers with smiling entreaty, making it clear that it would be easier to reach for some change than to brush them off.

Other cults practiced extreme asceticism, foisting inadequate nutrition, clothing and housing on their converts. A zealous leader of one group considered five hours of sleep a night sufficient for members, some of them still growing children.

As I gradually became involved in the study of communal groups, first in the United States, and later in Europe, Israel and my native Canada, I found that the reality of the ones I dealt with simply did not accord with press sensationalism. I have seen bad things, but in the hundreds of groups I know of firsthand, I have never seen excesses worthy of the pejorative label of "cult." Furthermore, not all of these intense groups are religious; some are political, therapeutic or social in nature.

Because these groups don't easily lend themselves to existing terminology, I have chosen the rather inexact term "radical" to describe both the groups and the joining that makes them possible. It is a relative term: To the families of joiners, their children's beliefs and behavior seem radically opposed to the families' own intellectual, spiritual and social standards.

Although there is an underlying structure that makes these groups similar—the fantasized omniscience of leaders, rigid belief systems opposed to the outside world and a studied strangeness—the earmark of a radical departure is less the specific characteristics of the group than the rapid, total transformation of the joiner. Mark Thomas could not say when, if ever, he would return. His previous plans for college no longer meant a thing to him. Similarly, voracious readers stop reading; musicians abandon their instruments; athletes stop exercising. There is an ominous narrowing of horizons, and their absolute commitment is, they believe, for the rest of their lives.

*M*ORE THAN 90 PERCENT OF THESE DEPARTURES END IN A RETURN HOME WITHIN TWO YEARS, AND VIRTUALLY ALL JOINERS EVENTUALLY ABANDON THEIR GROUPS.

I have worked among radical departers and their families since 1969, thoroughly studying more than 400 subjects in 15 groups. In no case was the sudden leave-taking expected by those who knew them best. These departures are called "out of character" by people who can make no sense of them; the radical departers appear to have taken leave of their senses.

I have come to realize how much sense radical departures make, despite their appearance of irrationality, as desperate attempts to grow up in a society that places obstacles in the way of normal youthful yearnings. The strangeness that unnerves, the hostility that enrages and even the euphoria that puzzles are expressions of belief and belonging that adolescents use as catalysts in growing up.

To understand what this means, we must consider the entire history of a radical departure, beginning with the months just prior to it, then the moment of first approach, the screening process the groups employ and on through life in the group during the peak period of commitment. This history helps us understand the remarkable endings to radical departures: More than 90 percent end in a return home within two years, and virtually all joiners eventually abandon their groups. Most important, they resume their previous lives and find gratification in the middle-class world they had totally abjured. In short, they use their radical departures to grow up.

Radical departers share certain characteristics. While there are exceptions, the majority are between 18 and 26 years of age, unmarried, affluent, well-educated, white and from intact families. But only a few such adolescents make radical departures; to understand what makes them different,

one must examine what normally happens during these years.

The school years up to about age 12 are ordinarily a time of smooth progress. By each birthday, a child has grown taller, reads at a grade level higher and acts with measurably greater sophistication. But in the following six years, adolescents' bodies change so radically and rapidly that they must constantly look in the mirror to see who they are and how they like it. Nature dumps on adolescents the makings of adulthood but doesn't tell them what to make of it.

In our middle-class culture, we strongly believe that during these years, children must separate from their families and establish their individuality both practically and psychologically. No radical departer I have known has been able to separate gradually to everyone's satisfaction. All of them are still so closely tied to their parents that I tend to refer to joiners as children despite their true age.

Normally, as children become teenagers, parents begin to diminish control. They no longer try to supervise homework or to act as constant chaperones. Even if they wish to, they can no longer control their children's aggressiveness and sexual impulses, so adolescents are forced to a degree of independence. At the same time, parents also make it clear to high school students that adult responsibilities loom ahead. They are asked to think about college and to make tentative career choices; most are expected to leave home. These challenges, unlike most challenges of childhood, smack of permanence.

At the same time that parents withdraw control, their children withdraw the unconditional love and faith that typify childhood. But because they

UNITED NATIONS/NORMAN PRINCE

Eastern religions have, in recent years, engendered a great deal of interest for the youth of many western countries. The spartan life of these Buddhist monks in Bangkok, Thailand, is a model for the Hari Krishna in the United States.

cannot proceed into adulthood without love and without faith, they seek intimacy with friends and lovers.

That is the normal course. But of the radical departers I have studied, few have been involved in relationships that were more than exploitive or tentative. None felt committed to a value system at the time of joining.

Joiners look to belief as a way to avoid their personal dilemma. Feeling so little self-esteem, they can't shoulder the responsibility of perhaps making a wrong moral choice and thereby feeling even more worthless. They are looking for ideology that will bolster whatever is admirable in them and purge whatever is bad.

Everyone must experience self-doubt, disillusion and loneliness on the way to adulthood. Radical departers are notable not only for the degree of their pain, but for the fact that everything seems to hit them at once. Too much has been put off, and the confluence of unfaced dilemmas causes a developmental logjam. They open the

dam of their own development by the abrupt and violent breaking away that is a radical departure.

The final ingredient is often an accident. At just this critical period in their lives, they are offered what seems a magical solution: separation without accompanying pain. It is very common to make a radical departure while away from home, sometimes for the first time. These children wish to be back at home, safe from the frightening freedom of travel, but then how can they be separate? Separate, they feel empty—a word frequently used by radical departers—as if there is not enough to fill them. The departure is a compromise solution to this conflict.

Despite the public perception that teenagers are somehow tricked into joining radical groups, the initial encounter is actually only the beginning of a screening process that will sort out those who do belong from those who might be alien to the group. The process varies from group to group, but it often involves three basic steps.

The first step is for a member of the group to approach a youth of about the same age and background as the members themselves. Anyone may be the target of propaganda or solicitation, but approaches are made only to those who appear interested, who ask questions or linger longer than most passersby. Friendly conversation leads quite naturally to an invitation to spend an evening with the group.

Only about 5 of every 100 approached in this way feel so attracted to these new friends that they consent to the first visit. Direct proselytizing is rare, but members and candidate are indirectly checking one another's values for a match. Those who are not screened out by the group or themselves are invited for a two- or three-day retreat.

The retreat is usually held in a secluded, rural and often strikingly beautiful spot away from the busy city that surrounds most groups' central meeting place. There is ordinarily no television, radio or telephone. It is as though there were no outside—no appointments, no hassles to endure, no criticism to answer, no worldly chores, schedules, deadlines or expectations.

Joiners have told me that during the retreat, the group's ideology, which seemed mere background noise before, suddenly makes immense sense. They feel a new clarity to their thoughts; the words they hear seem rich with significance and truth. Meaning dawns: This is the way that they and the world are to be seen. Interestingly, as gripping as the euphoria is, fewer than 10 percent of those who attend the first retreat decide to stay within the group. Indeed, the screening process is so accurate that, while only 1 in 500 of those originally approached chooses to join, those who do usually stay at least six months.

I have spent hundreds of hours reading the voluminous works of all the many ideological groups I've studied in an effort to understand what their beliefs are and why radical departers should be so moved by them. The vocabulary is theological, political or therapeutic, depending on the avowed nature of the group, but they all sound the same. They are replete with tautologies ("Being here as a group brings us together") and truisms ("Life can be difficult"). Mostly the beliefs are incomprehensible to outsiders and, I suspect, to most members as well. But in a curious way, it doesn't matter. There is even relief in not understanding, comfort in knowing that there are those at the top who do understand.

One common characteristic of these various belief systems is that they closely match the ideals of the joiner's family. One young woman who joined the Children of God could just as well have joined two other sects whose teachings echoed perfectly the Sunday School lessons of her childhood. Beneath the verbiage there inevitably lie the goals all mankind has always wished for, but the rationale for achieving this peace and unity is lost in anti-intellectualism. To me, this smacks of the innocence of early childhood when, in union with one's parents who need not be understood to be trusted utterly, prayers are answered and endings are always happy.

Belonging is the heart of radical departure. They are a unity, all doing the same things, believing the same be-

QUESTIONS AND ANSWERS

In the 15 years I have been studying radical departures, I have developed a methodology that balances the need for objective data with an equal need for subjective impressions. I first meet with the local leader of a group to ask permission to study the membership, making clear that my purpose is to understand, not to pass judgment on the group's beliefs or activities. No leader has ever turned down my request.

Individual participation is voluntary. To screen out members who aren't fully committed to a group, I study only individuals who have belonged for at least six months. I usually meet most members first during the height of their commitment, then as their intensity and single-mindedness begin to give way to doubt and, finally, within the first six months of their return home. For many, I have brief follow-ups some years later.

I first take a demographic profile: age, education, residence, parents' occupations and marital status, siblings, prior religious training and previous interests. The interview proper starts with rather formal questions that usually elicit pat answers as to why they joined this group, what they feel to be significant about their activities and so on. As members gradually begin to feel more comfortable with me, I can usually investigate further for their feelings in the months before their departure, how they are getting along now with their parents

and their relationships within the group. Subsequent meetings explore similar territory in relation to later phases of membership or the return to their families. Altogether, I usually spend about five hours talking to each person during the course of the study.

When I first started, I also gave several standard psychological inventories to check my personal impressions of members' mental health. I no longer do so for two reasons: There was never a discrepancy between test results and my own assessment, and the young people considered the testing so nefarious that it interfered with a trusting relationship.

If a participant agreed, I also interviewed their families. When possible, I spent some time with other relatives and with peers who had been close friends of the joiner.

Using this technique, I have thoroughly studied a total of 15 radical groups ranging from the drug cults of the 1960s to the religious, political and therapeutic groups most active today.

In addition, because of my interest and expertise in this area (I served on a government commission that examined the issue), I have received letters and referrals from hundreds of people in Western Europe, the British Isles, North America and Israel. Through these contacts, I have been involved with members of at least 100 other groups—a total of more than 1,000 individuals in all.

liefs, speaking the same stock phrases, eating the same food, wearing the same clothes and working for the same cause. For the period of their commitment, they give up the usual adolescent struggle to form an independent self and instead participate with relief in a flawless group self.

But this is by no means a complete retreat from growing up. The departers have taken a giant step. Be-

cause the group self is vehemently not bound up with that of the parents, psychological separation from them has begun. For these children, however, separation can be accomplished only within the safety of joining. Or perhaps rejoining is more accurate, because these groups are built along the lines of an exaggerated and idealized family. Careful attention is given to serving good, nutritious food, for example, an emphasis that closely echoes a mother's care in assuring that her children have a wholesome diet. Health in general is high on the list of most groups' concerns, and in fact my studies revealed a bunch of unusually healthy youngsters, who are free from stress, anxiety and depression.

I don't believe, however, that these radical departers are happy in the way that happiness is generally understood. As much as I have looked at beatific faces and witnessed gushes of joy, something has always prevented me from being swept up. Again and again, with hundreds of committed group members, I have felt that theirs is a performance, a case of bad acting in which the actor is himself carried away by the ringing truth of his role yet fails to convince the audience.

It is this spurious air, I think, that leads parents to the mistaken conclusion that their children have been brainwashed and to the public perception that joiners were weird to begin with. They are not brainwashed or weird, but neither are they quite whole. The happy face that joiners wear is uncontagious precisely because it does not accurately represent their inner dynamics. Conflict, fear and resentment may have the weight of bad baggage, but these feelings cannot be dumped so easily outside the mind. They can, however, be put temporarily in the unconscious while the radical departer goes through the psychological adjustment necessary for dealing with those feelings.

One of the most fascinating findings about radical departures, given the impenetrable commitment of group members, is that nine out of ten members leave their group within two years. After a period of some months, subtle but unmistakable changes begin. Dogmatic attitudes relax; there are fewer unequivocal opinions and less inflexible faith. This is quickly followed by a siege of doubt about the perfection of the group and its leader, an upwelling of longing for the family and, finally, a return to the world.

Some joiners are able to identify the specific event that triggered or crystallized their doubts. Others describe instead a gradual creeping of ambiguity into a faith that had been absolute. During this period of doubt, criticism of the group by the family and society that previously had been ignored is

DEPROGRAMMING, DESIGNED TO WHIP AWAY THE GROUP MEMBER'S DEFENSES WITH DUPLICITY AND DURESS, CAN CAUSE PERMANENT PSYCHOLOGICAL DAMAGE.

suddenly reheard. In many ways this echoes the joiners' period of self-doubt just prior to their radical departures. The leader of the group, once perceived to be as perfect as a child supposes his parents to be, is revealed as flawed. Beliefs, once accepted with childlike faith and lack of understanding, begin to seem less significant, then hypocritical, finally nonsensical. Formerly committed members now entertain rebellious thoughts and contemplate another departure, with an important difference: This time they know what they are doing and feel the conflict of impending separation.

What has happened to create this difference? I'm convinced that a radical departure is a rehearsal for separation, practice for the real task of growing up. While the departers appear to be passively frozen into their narrow mold of commitment, they are actively rehearsing for their coming out. The new perceptions that intrude upon them during this second period of doubt mark the reentry into their conscious minds of the unwanted feelings that were cast out during the time of commitment. They are now psychologically fortified to deal with conflict.

The fact that the original departure is never accompanied by conflict gives away its play-like nature. Now the young people are ready to come out of rehearsal and try the painful thrust to adulthood for real. All the fears and failures that had prevented them from taking a more direct path earlier now come back to trouble them.

The most overwhelming feeling the returnees have to deal with is guilt, not about making the departure but about how they treated family and friends. They sometimes say that if they had it to do over again they would handle departures differently—less suddenly and with more careful

explanations—but they rarely feel that joining was a mistake. Former members seldom vilify the group to which they once belonged or look back on the experience with shock and distaste. I have found quite the opposite: Former members almost always extract from their experience permanent values which they integrate into their present lives.

To understand this, it is important to appreciate the voluntary nature of both the radical departure and the return. Going back to the very beginning, we have seen that the percentage of potential joiners who drop out at each escalation of group pressure also escalates; of every 500 youngsters who are approached, only one actually joins. If recruitment techniques are so sinister, why do they so rarely work? The answer is that very few children are looking for what radical groups have to offer. They don't buy it because they don't want it. Those who do usually get what they want.

This doesn't mean that radical groups don't use group-pressure techniques to assure conformity. They do. But so do corporations intent on whipping up the enthusiasm of the sales force, preachers who seek generous donations from their congregation and football coaches eager for a winning season. The short-term outcome of a young person's recruitment into a group is not likable, and some mental-health professionals even consider the characteristic "symptoms," from tunnel vision to uncontagious bliss, to be pathological. But such judgments are inaccurate. Mourning takes extreme forms in many societies, but it would be inaccurate to label such a crucial period of psychological reorganization pathological. Radical departure, like mourning, is in the end therapeutic, although excesses can occur in both.

Just as the original departure is voluntary, so must the return be. In my experience, if there is no voluntary homecoming, physical or emotional, the joiner who has left a group is merely "between jobs" and has not set for himself the task of resolution. Some radical departers stay with a group not because they are able to use it in a true resolution of their problems, but because any resolution at all has been cut off by the brutality of the parents' response.

One dramatic, and rare, kind of brainwashing I have come upon during 15 years of research is that practiced by deprogrammers. Frustrated by their children's departure, thousands of parents have resorted to kidnapping and deprogramming, practices that are expensive, illegal and developmentally harmful. Designed to whip away the group member's defenses with duplicity and duress, the method does just that; and whether it "works" or fails, it can cause permanent psychological damage.

More often, deprogramming does not work. Or, more accurately, it works against the possibility that the joiners will resolve their conflicts, leave the group and rejoin their families in the kind of mature relationship that cements generations. Deprogramming interferes with the natural rhythm of a radical departure, and it can drive young people back into their group, or into a pattern of cult-hopping, for years. The grotesque experience of young adults suing their parents for unlawful acts of deprogramming has been played out too often.

When deprogramming works—brings the joiner back to the family—the loss is even greater. Halted before they have been able to utilize the group self in their own behalf, former members are thrown back upon their psychological dependency on parents. The more clearly they perceive their "mistake," the less trust former members have in their own ability to make wise choices and the more dangerous freedom seems to them.

Like other reformed "sinners," successfully deprogrammed group members feel great hostility toward the group they once found congenial and now preach against it with the same fervor with which they once proselytized for it. They exhibit exactly the alarming traits of intolerance, rigidity and closed-minded hostility that society finds unsettling in the groups themselves.

This can be avoided only by letting radical departures run their course. Although many returning group members experience severe emotional upheaval in the first few months, my experience indicates that a reassuring majority have not been damaged. To be certain, there is a cost: Families suffer extreme pain, some relationships suffer irrevocably and time lost from school and other goals may be irretrievable. To say that nine out of ten children who make radical departures return within a few years to pick up the threads of their lives successfully is not to wish a radical departure on anyone. It is a desperate move.

But by understanding what it is that joiners seek, why they find commitment gratifying and—most important—how the experience is of genuine psychological use to them, we are in a better position to judge what we as a society should do. While most radical groups disappear within a few years, new groups spring up to supplant them. This cultural phenomenon may be telling us what we can and should be doing as a society to enable our youth to emancipate themselves and find meaning in their lives.

Socialization

- Stages of Development (Articles 9-11)
- Influences on Personality and Behavior (Articles 12-14)

Belonging is as essential to human survival as breathing. Recent studies confirm the threat to health and well-being caused by social isolation. Learning how to belong is one of the most fundamental lessons of socialization: the lifetime process of adapting to others and learning what is the expected behavior in particular situations. Through contact with others, one learns who he or she is and gains self-knowledge. Socialization may take place in many contexts. The most basic socialization begins in the family, but churches, schools, communities, the media, and workplaces also play major roles in the process.

This section contains articles which deal with the conditions of childhood and both the negative and positive socialization of children. In the first article, Elin McCoy explains that parents were calloused and indifferent toward children hundreds of years ago. Before the eighteenth century, many children were punished severely for triffling offenses, many died in their first year, and many spent little time with their parents.

Marie Winn describes another major shift in the conditions of childhood since the 1950s when children were shielded from the experiences of adulthood. The sexual revolution, the drug epidemic, the women's movement, high divorce rates, television, and the spread of psychoanalytic thinking have changed the relations between adults and children. Children are treated as little adults, shown as little adults on TV, and act like little adults to a surprising degree. Winn explores the influence of new ideas in psychology on child-rearing practices. She concludes that the ideas guiding parents as they socialize their children have changed, and some negative consequences are evident.

David Elkind's article, ''Erik Erikson's Eight Ages of Man,'' about the stages of psychosocial development, has become a classic. A child learns to be an adult in stages. Erikson identifies five stages of childhood and explains what is learned in each stage. If these stages are navigated successfully the child develops a sense of trust, autonomy, initiative, industry, and identity by age eighteen. If problems are encountered in these stages, the child may develop feelings of mistrust, self-doubt, guilt, inferiority, and role confusion. The final three stages of development are young adulthood, middle age, and advanced middle age or old age. Growth in these stages produces intimacy, generativity, and integrity.

The last three articles in this section diagnose some of the major influences on personality development and behavior patterns. Richard Sorenson, an anthropologist, takes us to New Guinea to observe a tribe with very permissive and successful child-rearing patterns that are very dissimilar to our own. The article compares the influences of peers, parents, and styles of interaction on personality formation in this foreign tribe with the child-rearing practices of our own society.

The next article examines aspects of sex role socialization in grade schools. Myra and David Sadker focus on the differential treatment of boys and girls by their teachers. Boys participate more than girls because they are encouraged more by teachers who, according to the report, are unaware of their biases.

The final article discusses the effects of television as a major socializing agent in America. There is evidence that it increases violence and decreases traditional learning. On the other hand, there are claims that television brings families together, increases social awareness, teaches tolerance, provides company for lonely people, and entertains. The article reviews many other positive and negative effects of television and explores ways in which television will expand its role in American life in the future.

Socialization suggests learning and adaptation. It is a dynamic and ever changing process. In many ways, it is synonymous with living.

Looking Ahead: Challenge Questions

How can we improve the ways in which children are socialized in America?

In what ways are people alone some of the time, as well as members of a group some of the time?

Why is socialization a lifetime process?

What are the principal factors that make us what we are?

Childhood Through the Ages

Elin McCoy

Elin McCoy is the author of "The Incredible Year-Round Playbook" (Random House).

A gentleman-in-waiting and the nurse of little Comte de Marle often amused themselves tossing the swaddled infant back and forth across the sill of an open window. One day one of them failed to catch him, and the infant landed on a stone step and died.

The surgeon of the newborn Louis XIII cut the "fiber" under his tongue a few days after he was born, believing that if it remained uncut, Louis would be unable to suck properly and would eventually stutter.

These aren't atypical examples of child rearing in the past. Recent historical research indicates that for most of the past 2,500 years, childhood was a brief, grim period in most people's lives, especially when judged against contemporary views of child rearing.

A new field—family history.

Through a new field of historical research, known as family history, we now know that family life and childhood in the previous centuries were startlingly different from what most people, including historians, had imagined them to be. Scores of historians are currently probing such questions as: How were children treated in the past? What concept of childhood did people have in different centuries? How important were children to their parents? Is there such a thing as "instinctual" parental behavior? What do the prevailing child-rearing beliefs and practices of the past tell us about the political, social, and psychological ideals of society? And

what kind of adults resulted from such child-rearing practices?

"Family history is the most explosive field of history today," says Professor Lawrence Stone—director of Princeton University's Shelby Cullom Davis Center for Historical Studies—whose 1977 book, *The Family, Sex and Marriage in England 1500–1800,* came out in an abridged paperback last year. "In the 1930s only about 10 scholarly books and articles on the family and childhood in history were published each year, but, incredibly, between 1971 and 1976 over 900 important books and articles were published on that subject, just covering America, England, and France." Two scholarly journals devoted to the subject were also started in the 1970s.

Why, suddenly, have so many historians focused on the family? "A whole series of contemporary anxieties has contributed to this new interest," explains Professor Stone. "General anxiety about the state of the family and whether it's breaking down, concern about the rising divorce rate, anxieties about current permissiveness in raising children, and concern about what effects women's liberation will have on children, the family, and society. And underlying all of these anxieties are two questions: Are we really doing so badly? Was it better in the past?"

In addition, two other trends in historical research have focused attention on childhood and the family. The first is social historians' growing interest in the daily lives of ordinary people in history, which has meant a greater concern with children, parenting, marriage, disease, death, and aging. The second is historians' recent efforts to employ psychological concepts as

a research tool in order to understand human motivations and experiences in the past.

Although all family historians agree that child-rearing patterns influence what happens in history, they disagree about how much and in what precise ways the treatment of children shapes history. Some researchers in the field, like Lloyd deMause, founder of *The Journal of Psychohistory: A Quarterly Journal of Childhood and Psychohistory,* go so far as to say that, in deMause's words, "child-rearing practices have been *the* central force for change in history." Along with some other psychohistorians, deMause believes that "if you want to understand the causes of historical events like the growth of Nazism, you have to look at how the children who became Nazis as adults were treated as children." But many scholars have reservations about attributing the character of a society solely to the relations between parents and children, pointing out that these relations must be understood in the context of the society as a whole and that such factors as economics must also be taken into account.

Surprising discoveries.

Family historians have recently exploded many long-standing myths about childhood and the nature of the family throughout history. It's now clear that the functions and structure of the family have changed continuously over the years and that a variety of family types coexisted in each historical period in different regions and classes. Scholars have found, surprisingly, that the prevailing family mode in America today (the small nuclear family of parents and children living apart from other relatives)—a struc-

From *Parents,* January 1981, pp. 60-65. Reprinted by permission of Elin McCoy and her agents, Raines & Raines, 71 Park Avenue, New York, N.Y. 10016. Copyright ©1981 Elin McCoy.

ture that is under much attack—is not as new to our culture as they had previously thought. Even as long ago as thirteenth-century England, as many as half of all families consisted of only a mother and/or father and two to three children. In fact, the large, loving extended families we tend to picture, with eight to ten children and several generations of relatives living under the same roof, were more the exception than the rule, even in Colonial America.

According to Professor Tamara Hareven—founder and head of the first History of the Family program in the country, at Clark University in Worcester, Massachusetts, and founding editor of the *Journal of Family History*—one of the great surprises for today's historians was "finding out that in the past, the concept of childhood and children was not the same in all centuries, classes, and countries. While the middle classes were 'discovering' childhood and becoming interested in children," she explains, "the working classes still regarded children as small adults with the same responsibilities. And in the past, childhood as we know it lasted for a much shorter time." In medieval England, for example, children as young as seven were sent to live in other households as apprentices, and for peasant children, childhood was even briefer—they joined their parents to work in the fields as soon as they could.

Infants were regarded in medieval times as unimportant, unformed animals, in the sixteenth century as "exasperating parasites," and even as late as the seventeenth century they were not seen as individuals with their own identities. Children were considered interchangeable, and frequently were given the same name as an older sibling who had died. Small children were not even viewed as interesting; Montaigne, the French essayist, summed up the prevailing attitudes of a few hundred years ago when he dismissed infants as having "neither movement in the soul, nor recognizable form in the body by which they could render themselves lovable."

Scholars tell us that infants and small children were important only insofar as they could benefit their parents. Considered possessions with no individual rights, they were used to further adult aims, and they ended up as security for debts, as ways of increasing property holdings through arranged marriages, as political hostages, and even as slaves sold for profit.

Infancy in the past.

Throughout history, parents' treatment of infants and very small children has been characterized by psychological coldness and physical brutality that horrify most of us today. But this behavior becomes at least comprehensible when we realize some of the conditions of people's lives. The physical realities of life were oppressive. And there were severe parental limitations as well: in addition to being influenced by unscientific medical knowledge and religious views about the nature of man, most adults had to concentrate so much of their energy on mere survival that they had little time to care for or worry about infants and small children. Abusive and violent behavior was common among adults and, therefore, not looked on with disapproval when it appeared in the treatment of children.

In view of the following facts, consider what your experience as a parent and your child's experience as an infant would have been if you had lived prior to the eighteenth century.

Your child probably wouldn't have been wanted. Lack of birth control meant that having children was not a choice. For poverty-stricken peasants, an infant meant another mouth to feed—and food was precious—as well as interference with the mother's role as a worker whose contribution was necessary to the family's ability to survive. In all classes, the high risk of maternal mortality made the birth of a child a traumatic event. Even in the relatively healthy conditions enjoyed by the inhabitants of Plymouth Colony, 20 percent of women died from causes related to childbirth (compared with under 1 percent today), and in seventeenth-century England and France, the rates were much higher. It's no wonder that most children were probably unwanted. In fact, Professor Stone suggests that the availability of birth control was probably one of the necessary conditions for the increase in affection for children that began in England and America in the eighteenth century.

Your infant would have had a good chance of dying before his or her first birthday. In medieval England and seventeenth-century France, for example, between 20 and 50 percent of all infants died

within the first year after birth. Complications of childbirth, prematurity, diseases such as smallpox and the plague, and generally unsanitary living conditions, as well as such customs as baptism in icy water in freezing churches, took a heavy toll among vulnerable newborns. America was healthier for infants—in Plymouth Colony, infant mortality was only 10 to 15 percent (which is still ten times higher than it is in America today). The likelihood that one's infants would die discouraged parents from investing much affection or interest in them and from regarding them as special, unique individuals until it appeared more certain that they might live to adulthood.

Illegitimate infants and infants of poverty-stricken parents (and parents who felt they already had enough children) were often the victims of infanticide through deliberate murder, abandonment, or neglect. In ancient Greece, for example, infants who seemed sickly or didn't have a perfect shape or cried too much or too little were "exposed," or abandoned to die, a decision that was made by the father shortly after birth. In mid-eighteenth-century England, so many babies—both legitimate and illegitimate—were abandoned to die in the streets of cities and towns that the first foundling home established in London received several thousand babies a year. In early America, infanticide seems to have affected only illegitimate children.

If you were well-off, your baby probably would have been breast-fed by someone else. In spite of the fact that all medical advice since Roman times had stressed that babies breast-fed by their own mothers had a better chance of survival, for eighteen centuries any woman who could afford it sent her infant to a wet nurse.

Recuperation from a difficult childbirth prevented some women from breast-feeding, but many others thought it too demanding, especially since it was customary for infants to breast-feed for as long as two years. Also, many husbands would not allow their wives to breast-feed, partly because medical opinion held that women who were breast-feeding should not engage in sexual intercourse.

Underlying these reasons may have been parents' desire to distance themselves emotionally from their infants.

3. SOCIALIZATION: Stages of Development

In Renaissance Italy, middle-class infants were delivered to the *bália*, or wet nurse, immediately after baptism—two or three days after birth—and, if they survived, remained there for two years. Rarely did mothers visit their infants, and thus a baby was returned home at the end of that time to a stranger.

Although some wet nurses moved in with the family, most women left their babies at the wet nurse's home, where the child was often neglected and starved because wet nurses commonly took on too many babies in order to make more money. Frequently wet nurses ran out of milk, and infants had to be sent to a series of different nurses and thus were deprived even of a single surrogate mother.

The first groups of middle-class women to change this 1,800-year-old pattern on a large scale were the Puritans in the seventeenth century. Eventually, in the eighteenth century, there was a widespread cult of maternal breast-feeding in both America and England. Scholars have suggested that this shift may have contributed substantially to the shift in parental feelings for infants that began in the eighteenth century; certainly it reduced infant mortality.

Your infant would have spent little time with you. In the past, parents spent much less time with their children than even working parents do today and clearly did not feel the need to arrange supervision for them. Peasant women commonly left their infants and toddlers alone all day at home while they worked elsewhere. In one area of England during the thirteenth century, for example, half the infant deaths involved infants in cradles being burned while no one was home. Unsupervised toddlers frequently wandered off and drowned. In the middle and upper classes, parental neglect took the form of turning toddlers over to the servants to raise.

Your infant would have been swaddled in tightly bound cloths from birth to as old as eight months. Emotional distancing, economic necessity, and faulty medical knowledge are also evident in another common practice—swaddling. In England this practice continued up to the eighteenth century; in France, the nineteenth century; and in Russia, into the twentieth century. Kept in tightly bound bandages, swaddled infants were totally isolated from their surroundings for the first four months or so. After that, only their legs were bound. They couldn't turn their heads, suck their own thumbs for comfort, or crawl. Swaddling that was too tight occasionally caused suffocation. Although doctors advocated changing the infant two or three times a day, this apparently was uncommon, and even Louis XIII developed severe rashes because of his swaddling bands.

Medical reasons for the practice included the beliefs that if free, the infant might tear off his ears or scratch out his eyes, that swaddling was necessary to keep infants warm in cold, draughty cottages, houses, and castles, and that it ensured that the infant's pliable limbs would grow straight so he would be able to stand erect. Even when the swaddling bands were removed from their legs, children were not allowed to crawl "like an animal," but were forced to stand with the help

THE BETTMANN ARCHIVE

Mother's helper: The "roundabout" was a 19th-century gadget designed to keep baby out of mother's way. But it sacrificed a freedom of movement that today we know is crucial to a child's development.

of bizarre contraptions. Convenienc was another reason for swaddling: caused infants to sleep more and cr less, so they could be left for lon periods of time while mother worked. Also, swaddled infant were easier to carry and could eve be hung on a peg on the wall out o the way.

Your infant or child would pr bably have received harsh beating regularly—from you or a servant— even for such "normal" behavior a crying or wanting to play. For man centuries, discipline and teaching o the infant and young child con centrated on "breaking the child' will," which meant crushing all as sertiveness and instilling complet obedience. This was accomplished through physical and psychologica maltreatment that today we woul consider "child abuse." Susanna Wesley, mother of John Wesley, th founder of the Methodist Church records her treatment of her chil dren: "When turned a year old, and some before, they were taught to fear the rod and cry softly." Louis XIII was whipped every morning starting at the age of two, simply fo being "obstinate," and was even whipped on the day of his corona tion at the age of nine. The Puritans believed that "the newborn babe is full of the stains and pollutions of sin" and saw the first strivings of a one- and two-year-old to indepen dence—which we now recognize as essential to a child's growing mas tery of himself and understanding of the world—as a clear manifesta tion of that original sin. It was considered the duty of parents to use physical harshness and psy chological terrorization—locking children in dark closets for an entire day or frightening them with tales of death and hellfire, for example—to wipe this sin out.

These child-rearing practices, a well as the difficult realities of life in the past, had important psychologica effects on children's development. Ac cording to Professor Stone, the isola tion, sensory deprivation, and lack o physical closeness that resulted from swaddling; the absence of a mother because of death in childbirth or the practice of wet-nursing; the common experience for small children of losing parents and siblings; and the suppression of self-assertion through whipping and other fear-producing techniques all resulted in an "adult world of emotional cripples."

A change for the better.

In the late seventeenth and eighteenth centuries, many of these child-rearing practices began to change among wealthy merchants and other groups in the upper middle classes of England and America. Some changes can be traced to the Puritans, who, even though they advocated harsh disciplinary measures, focused a new attention on children and the importance of their upbringing. By the late eighteenth century, among some groups, methods of contraception were available, swaddling had been abandoned, maternal breast-feeding had become the fashion, and "breaking the will" had given way to affection and a degree of permissiveness that seems extraordinary even by today's standards. In England the indulgent Lord Holland, for example, intent on gratifying his little son Charles's every whim, allowed him to jump and splash in the large bowl of cream intended for dessert at a grand dinner while the guests, a group of foreign ministers, looked on. Many adults feared the effect on society when these spoiled children reached maturity. And in fact, many of them did spend their lives in lifelong dissipation and often became followers of evangelical religions. While the Victorian era varied from harsh to permissive in the treatment of children, by the end of the nineteenth century the child-oriented family became a reality for all classes in Western society.

What it all means for us.

Were childhood and family life better in the past? The answer—obviously—is a resounding no. One is tempted to agree with Lloyd deMause that "the history of childhood is a nightmare from which we have only recently begun to awaken."

Nevertheless, Professor Hareven feels that there *were* some good aspects to childhood in the past, which we can learn from today. "Children were not so segregated from adults and responsibility," she points out. "The historical record shows children grew up in households that included servants, other workers employed by the family, lodgers, visiting relatives, and siblings of widely differing ages, as well as parents. They were exposed to a greater variety of adult roles than children usually are today and they interacted with a greater variety of people of all ages. They also knew more about their parents' work. And unlike today, children were working, contributing members of families and the society from an early age—as they are in contemporary China. Today's child-oriented family and the postponement of responsibility and work limit children's experience. The models are there in history for us to borrow and shape to today's ideals."

Historical research on childhood helps us view our own ideas about parenthood from a perspective in which it is clear that there are no absolutes. The new facts that are available to us show that assumptions behind child rearing change and that what we think of as parents' "instincts" actually depend on the beliefs and experiences of their society. The possessiveness and affection toward infants, which we take for granted, is a recent development. Even the "maternal instinct" to breast-feed one's own child was not instinctive for many women for over 1,800 years.

Family history also gives us an informative view of family structure. Those who are worried about the high divorce rate and the effect of parental separation on children, for example, should realize that in the past, approximately the same percentage of families were separated—only it was by the death of one of the parents instead of by divorce.

Although problems with child rearing will probably always be with us,

"The Human Comedy": That's the name of this 19th-century sketch—but the partially-swaddled child, left alone hanging on a wall, isn't finding anything in his situation to laugh about.

the very existence of family history means that we have come to the point where we are much more self-conscious about how we raise children, and, in turn, this may help us to be more thoughtful about the way we treat them. By examining childhood in the past, we become aware that our own attempts to do things differently—"nonsexist" child rearing, co-parenting, and different mixes of permissiveness and discipline—may have profound effects on society. If we can avoid the mistakes of the past, borrow what was good, and continue to examine our own aims and practices, the society our children make may be a better one than ours.

The Loss Of Childhood

Marie Winn

Once upon a time and not so long ago, the second Sunday in May celebrated a very different image of women and motherhood from the one that prevails today. When today's parents were children, Mother's Day still honored a domesticated little woman waiting with milk and cookies after school, a mother as unlikely to become a single parent during the course of her children's childhood as to become a coal miner.

That bygone era set store by a very different image of children and childhood as well. Children, at least until they reached the "terrible teens," were seen as innocent, playful, *childlike* creatures in need of special protection, and parents were fiercely determined to keep childhood a carefree Golden Age.

Today, in a time when nearly two-thirds of all mothers with children over 6 have left home for the workplace—some even for the mines—in a time when one out of two marriages ends in divorce, something is decidedly different about children as well.

In their everyday demeanor, the language they use, the things they know and above all in their relations with the adult world, children have changed. This was confirmed in almost every one of hundreds of interviews with fourth, fifth, sixth and seventh graders. The ease and aplomb these children demonstrated in their talks with an interviewer were quite as indicative of change as

This article is adapted from Marie Winn's "Children Without Childhood," (Pantheon Books).

anything they actually said, although some of their testimony about marijuana, sex and pornographic movies on cable television would have deeply shocked parents a decade or two ago. The reticence and shyness once associated with childhood have clearly gone the way of curtsies and pinafores. As a Denver fourth-grade teacher reports, "Kids are a lot freer now. Even in the 10 years I've been at this school, there's been a change. The other day, a very innocent-looking little boy came up to me and casually asked me whether a certain sexual act was 'for real.' He used a crude word for it. I asked him to whisper in my ear what he thought the word meant. Well, he knew more details than I myself knew until about five years ago."

The greatest change of all, however, is not that children have lost their innocence. (An article on that subject, "What Became of Childhood Innocence?" by Marie Winn, appeared in this magazine Jan. 25, 1981.) It is a change in our conception of childhood itself. We have seen, in an amazingly short span of time, a transformation of society's most fundamental attitudes toward children. Where parents once felt obliged to shelter their children from life's vicissitudes, today, great numbers of them have come to operate according to a new belief: that children must be exposed early to adult experience in order to survive in an increasingly uncontrollable world. The Age of Protection has ended. An Age of Preparation has set in. And children have suffered a loss. As they are integrated at a young age into the adult world, in every way their lives have become more difficult, more confusing—in short, more like adult lives.

We are beginning to hear a bitter reaction from that first generation of children to grow up in the new era—today's young adults. In a recent issue of a newsmagazine, a college student writes: "We are the kids who were 'so adult.' . . . Our parents expected us to understand their problems and frustrations. . . . What we missed was the chance to be childish, immature and unafraid to admit we didn't have it all together."

The Age of Protection did not end because of a deliberate decision to treat kids in a new way; it ended out of necessity. For children's lives are always a mirror of adult life. The great social upheavals of the late 1960's and early 1970's—the so-called sexual revolution, the drug epidemic, the women's movement, the breakdown of the conventional two-parent family, the spread of psychoanalytic thinking and the proliferation of television—each of these created changes in adult life that necessitated new ways of dealing with children.

No one of these changes alone could have brought about the emergence of a brave new relationship between adults and children. It was the confluence of these factors in the beginning of the 1970's that swiftly altered children's lives. Only with the rise in two-career families and with the mounting divorce rate did parents have cause to withdraw their close attention from children and reduce the careful supervision that had once made the very possibility of sixth graders drinking or smoking marijuana unthinkable. Only with the help of television was the actual decrease in supervision made possible: With the kids sedated into reliable passivity, parents could more easily pursue their own imperatives. Only as the fatalistic principles of Freudian psychology became part of every adult's general knowledge did parents' confidence in their basic ability to supervise their school-age children begin to fail them.

And yet a decline in supervision is not the entire story. Even in the 1950's, there were undersupervised schoolchildren, who nevertheless did not "go all the way" or smoke anything more than an experimental Lucky Strike. The difference is that, in those days before "The Joy of Sex" and X-rated movies, sex was still in the closet and drugs were unavailable outside the lower reaches of society. It took a combination of unsupervised children *and* a permissive, highly charged sexual atmosphere *and* an influx of easily acquired drugs *and* the wherewithal to buy them to bring about, by the mid-1970's, precocious experimentation by younger and younger children.

Women and children first!" was the cry on the decks of a sinking ship. Just so, for at least two centuries, women's and children's lives were inextricably bound together as a symbiotic entity. In many ways, the Golden Age of Childhood owed its existence to this bond.

Before the 18th century, before industrialization and urbanization altered ancient work patterns by taking men away from the household to distant workplaces, women were as vital to the proper functioning of the economy as men. Then, as the various articles they had once produced came to be manufactured outside the household and as their agricultural chores were taken over by men and machines, women lost their direct economic function and became more and more isolated within the home. Not surprisingly, as they grew increasingly dependent on men both economically and emotionally, women came to be seen as vulnerable creatures in need of protection.

As Grace Greenwood, an advice writer of the 1850's, wrote: "True feminine genius is ever timid, doubtful and clingingly dependent; a perpetual childhood." From hardy helpmates to clinging vines, women certainly had gone a long way—though not necessarily forward. Children underwent a similar metamorphosis, from expendable, relatively independent cogs in the feudal economic system to tender dependents in need of care and protection.

It must be understood that this situation did not hold true for all mothers and children. At first, only the relatively privileged classes could afford to protect and isolate women and children; older ways prevailed among the lower classes. At the height of the sentimentalization of childhood in the 19th century, great numbers of needy women and children labored in factories and mills. But, as the 20th century progressed and protective labor laws removed children from the workforce, the new family model became increasingly common among all classes of society.

By the 1950's, the transformation of the family into a domestic haven was complete. Postwar prosperity and the growth of suburbia isolated childlike women and innocent children in what seemed a paradise of material comforts and almost pastoral safety. Men reserved strong language for the company of their peers; cultural media adhered to standards of purity such that the delicate sensibilities of women, to say nothing of children, would not be offended.

It was television that first penetrated the protective cocoon and thrust the long-hidden outside world into women's and children's lives. The new freedom and openness of the 1960's and 1970's allowed programs to grow more violent and sexually explicit—more adult, as they say. But soon parents made a troubling discovery: It was not easy to keep these programs out of the reach of their children; television was too hard to control. Parents consequently began to abandon some of their former protection of children—if only to prepare them to some degree for what they were bound to see on television anyway. "Yesterday, on 'Guiding Light,' this married guy got in an argument with his wife and went to an island and had sex with another lady," relates a fifth-grader in upper New York State about a soap opera she watches regularly. It is easy to understand that her parents are casual about protecting her from adult knowledge.

3. SOCIALIZATION: Stages of Development

But television was not the whole story. The liberation movement as well, gaining momentum in the mid-1960's played a role in bringing children out of their former seclusion from the adult world. Inevitably, as mothers rejected their roles as child-women and objected to being protected and treated like little pets, they began to resist dealing with their own children in a similar manner. Recognizing that the protective circle of secrecy surrounding them was also preventing them from fully developing their strengths and abilities, they began to wonder whether such treatment might similarly hamper their children's development.

As women became less emotionally dependent upon their husbands, they began, perhaps unconsciously at first, to encourage their children to be independent and assertive. It was as if mothers could not challenge an unequal relationship with their husbands and still demand subservience or deference from their kids. It didn't seem fair. But while mothers urged the kids to express their feelings openly, just as they themselves were learning to do in their consciousness-raising groups, they nevertheless could not suppress their distress about some of the behavior that their new attitudes also seemed to be encouraging: rudeness, whiny irritability, defiance. When the 6-year-old who has been asked to go to bed looks his mother in the eye and says, "No, I won't, and you can't make me!" parents understand that they're involved in a different sort of relationship from the one they once had with their own parents.

□

There was a time when parents confidently believed that as long as they fed their children properly, kept them out of harm's way and gave them the proper advantages they would grow up well. In those days, a parent's major task was to teach children to conform to the requirements of the society they were born into.

By the late 1950's, as Freudian theorists—Erik Erikson and Bruno Bettelheim, for example—as well as a host of popular child experts including Selma H. Fraiberg and Haim G. Ginott began applying psychoanalytic principles to practical aspects of child rearing, a new element of uncertainty was introduced into parents' minds. And it came at a time when uncertainty was assailing them from other directions—uncertainty about their sexuality, their marriage, their government, their economic future. Suddenly, parents were struck with the fearful knowledge that they alone stood between their child's growing up "normal" and his growing up to be a neurotic adult. A single false step, a traumatic experience, an inadvertent peek at the "primal scene" might cause a child to develop insomnia, impotence or an irrational fear of horses many years later.

The very fact that between the trauma and the neurosis could lie a seemingly normal childhood made the situation all the more unnerving. Like those long-incubating viruses that produce minor symptoms when they first enter the body and may, 20 years later, result in multiple sclerosis, so parental miscalculations, missteps, misunderstandings might lead, after a long hiatus, to the most untoward consequences.

This new knowledge, when it finally penetrated by the end of the 1960's, helped to facilitate the widespread adoption of a new child-rearing style, one no longer focused on the child's socialization but on its mental health. From the benevolent despotism it had been for centuries, child rearing changed, for many parents, into a more perilous, more collaborative, more *democratic* process, one that they felt instinctively was beyond their powers to pull off successfully.

A mother of two preteenagers epitomizes the new parental insecurity when she confides ruefully, "We always tell our kids to remember what happens today so that they can tell their therapist in the future. It's inevitable that they'll spend hours on the couch someday, obsessing about how awful we were and so forth."

One has only to listen to the particular tone of so many parents today who negotiate with their children, even preschoolers, in an almost conspiratorial manner, to recognize that this is not exactly the way parents spoke to their children a generation ago.

To be sure, the good parent of the 1950's or 1960's also spent considerable time patiently explaining things to his child. But it was the ways of the world the parent clarified—the world of nature, of politics, of social relations. A great many of today's laborious parental explanations, however, refer not to the causality of natural or social phenomena but to the parent's own feelings, anxieties and insecurities.

No longer does the parent operate from a vantage point of superior knowledge, of adult convictions. Such confidence, it seems, no longer sits well with the *Zeitgeist* of the 1970's and 1980's. Now, the child is enlisted as an accomplice in his own upbringing. And everywhere parents are explicating the texts of themselves, pleading for their children to agree, to forgive, to *understand,* instead of simply telling them what to do. The child has come to seem a psychological equal.

This parity between adults and children forms a hidden base of today's less authoritative style of child rearing. It is illuminating to compare Selma Fraiberg's influential 1959 book for parents, "The Magic Years," with Benjamin M. Spock's earlier child-care manual. Though published only 13 years apart, each represents a very different view of childhood.

Dr. Spock's renowned book was informed by a simple but crucial presumption: Sharp boundaries exist between children and adults. Parents are adult, children are children, and different rules apply to each group. Dr. Spock's very title, "The Common Sense Book of Baby and Child Care," emphasizes the adultness of the audience being addressed, adults having among their natural gifts enough common sense to deal successfully with those less sensible creatures, children. The first words of the book, "You know more than you think you do," stressed parental capability and established Dr. Spock's basic premise: Parents, in their ability to nurture, to protect, to use strategies of one sort or another, are a breed apart from children. (It is interesting to note that in the revised edition of the book published in 1968, the words "common sense" were excised from the title, making it simply "Baby and Child Care." It is as if the very notion of common sense had now become alien to a new consciousness abroad in the land.)

The title of Dr. Fraiberg's book, "The Magic Years," carried less reassuring overtones, implying that there is something beyond a parent's control, something irrational, weird, indeed "magic" about a child's development.

Consider Dr. Fraiberg's and Dr. Spock's very different opinions on that controversial child-rearing issue, to spank or not to spank. Dr. Spock is quite complaisant about spanking. "If an angry parent keeps himself from spanking, he may show his irritation in other ways; for instance, by nagging the child for half the day, or trying to make him feel deeply guilty. I'm not particularly advocating spanking," he writes, "but I think it is less poisonous than lengthy disapproval, because it clears the air, for parent and child."

Dr. Spock's unquestioning assumption that the child is essentially different from the adult becomes clear if we try to extend the pro-spanking argument to *adult* human relations. We know perfectly well that Dr. Spock would not advocate that a husband smack his wife in order to "clear the air." For adults, the "lengthy disapproval" strategy is clearly preferable. But different rules apply, according to Dr. Spock, in parent-child relations.

Dr. Fraiberg condemns spanking unequivocally. "The 'lessons' which a spanking is supposed to teach somehow fail to be integrated in the form of conscience," she writes. "The motive for controlling the naughty impulse is a motive that comes from the outside, a fear of external authority and a fear of punishment, and we will find that a conscience which functions on this basis is not a very reliable conscience. . . . But the child who is capable of developing guilt feelings when he considers doing something which is 'bad' has a signal system within himself which will warn him and inhibit the act. Unlike the child whose control system is 'outside,' this child with a conscience does not need a policeman around in order to control his behavior. The child with a conscience has his policeman inside."

But wait a moment. This "child" Dr. Fraiberg describes doesn't sound much like a child. In fact, he sounds suspiciously like an adult.

Once, people *expected* children to be naughty, to get into trouble. Part of the definition of a child that distinguished him from a grown-up was an impulsiveness and willingness to chance punishment in order to explore or experiment or gratify a desire. For today's adult, however, it is preferable to live with a 5-year-old who doesn't need a "policeman" around to control his behavior, a child with an internalized conscience. And for a divorced or working parent who cannot be around in any case to monitor the child's behavior, it is less a matter of preference than of dire necessity.

□

While the impact of Freud's ideas upon the practical realities of child rearing may have served to diminish some of the traditional boundaries between childhood and adulthood, Freud's own view of childhood, as it happens, was a highly differentiated one. Indeed, in his theoretical construct of a "latency period," Freud revealed an attitude that bears a distinct kinship to the standard thinking of the era he was born into. Freud's writings introduced the startling new concept of infant sexuality and investigated the sexual realities of *early* childhood. But his views of the later years between toddlerhood and adolescence present a picture of childhood innocence that is as idealized as any Victorian's.

According to Freud's theoretical structure of personality development, there is a period of heightened sexuality during the first four or five years of life—the so-called Oedipal stage, when the child develops a sexual passion for the parent of the opposite sex. This, however, is followed by a period in which that sexual energy diminishes, or at least goes into deep hiding, not to reappear until adolescence. This calm between two sexual storms covers the years between 5, approximately, and the onset of puberty—the very years that make up the heart of childhood.

There is something odd about this particular part of Freud's theory. Among all other creatures in the animal kingdom, development generally proceeds in a steady line from immaturity to maturity. Why, then, in the human species alone should there be this sudden interruption between two spurts of sexual growth?

Freud developed a remarkable answer to this self-created enigma. The latency period, he believed, has an evolutionary purpose. It serves the growth of civilization by allowing the child to devote his childhood to learning instead of to the development of his sexual capacities. The two, apparently, cannot go on simultaneously. In other words, if the sex drive were allowed free expression during childhood, the child wouldn't be able to apply himself to less exciting tasks such as memorizing the multiplication tables or learning the five principal products of Brazil.

In "Three Essays on the Theory of Sexuality," Freud spelled out his belief that the two processes—intellectual development and sexual development—would interfere with each other: "Historians of civilization appear to be at one in assuming that powerful components are acquired for every kind of cultural achievement by this diversion of sexual, instinctual forces from sexual aims and their direction to new ones—a process which deserves the name of 'sublimation.' "

3. SOCIALIZATION: Stages of Development

Freud's latency theory reminds us that he was in many ways a product of the thinking of his times, an era when a fearful society believed manifestations of sexuality in childhood would lead to hideous physical deformities and inevitable mental breakdown. Freud, too, showed a deep fear of child sexuality when he wrote, in "The Question of Lay Analysis": "Among races at a low level of civilization, and among the lower strata of civilized races, the sexuality of children seems to be given free rein. This probably provides a powerful protection against the subsequent development of neuroses in the individual. But does it not at the same time involve an extraordinary loss of the aptitude for cultural achievements? There is a good deal to suggest that here we are faced by a new Scylla and Charybdis."

There is little question but that Freud chose the Scylla of repression over the Charybdis of cultural loss. For while the fearful anti-masturbationists of the 19th century predicted a population of hairy-palmed lunatics if childhood sexuality were not suppressed, Freud feared an end to civilization itself and a return to a savage state of nature if this force were unleashed during the course of childhood.

Freud's concept of a latency period and especially its connection to the child's educational future has been challenged in recent years. "I reject Freud's notion that there is a relation between sexual latency and an ability to learn," says Anke Erhardt, a psychologist and expert on children's sexual development at Columbia University's New York Psychiatric Institute. "Latency has never existed. Children were always, to a certain degree, sexually active. There is certainly no basic shift of energy from intellectual aspects to sexual ones, when children are not repressed sexually."

While the physiological reality of a childhood latency period as well as the one-drive-at-a-time explanation of why sexual latency might make the child more educable are subject to debate, there is still reason to suppose that a culturally imposed period of sexual latency might have great bearing on the child's educational future.

Consider the outcome of certain progressive schools founded on misguided understandings of Freudian theories that sprang up during the early days of the psychoanalytic movement in the 1920's and 1930's. In spite of the fact that Freud accepted the need of repression in childhood, these schools hoped to prevent the development of adult neuroses by allowing the child to behave according to the dictates of his own instinctual drives. Teachers were encouraged to give sexual information freely, to place no restrictions on masturbation or sex play and to replace all authoritarian rules with permissive methods emphasizing reasoning and explanation. But the results were disastrous. According to Willi Hoffer, a founder of one such experimental institution in Vienna, the Kinderheim Baumgarten, children in these schools often showed themselves to be "less curious about the more complicated world of objects" and generally disinclined to learn. As he

With the loss of a traditional family structure through divorce or separation, today's children are often forced to become independent. This premature responsibility to cope with life's problems impacts on the children's experience in school as well as their role in society.

described them further in a 1945 paper, "Psychoanalytic Education": "They had no perseverance . . . They seemed egocentric; group demands affected them little. They were extremely intolerant of the demands of adults; timetables, mealtimes, table manners, routine hygienic measures, even if leniently handled, became sources of conflict." None of the changes Freud ascribed to the onset of latency seemed to materialize—no greater docility, no eagerness to learn. Indeed, Hoffer observed that the children showed "an unexpected degree of irritability, a tendency to obsession, depression and anxiety."

Anxiety, irritability, suspiciousness—these, as it happens, are all traits we associate more with adults than with children. Children are usually angry, not irritable; persistent rather than obsessive; unhappy rather than depressed. Yet it appears that these are just as natural to children when they are unrepressed. In a state of nature, children cannot afford to be childlike, to relax, to romp and play, to explore, to be "curious about the more complicated world of objects," above all to *learn.* Alertness, caution, as in a jungle, must be the watchwords in the unprotected world where children are given instinctual and emotional freedom.

Although few children today are exposed to the dangerous freedom of schools such as the Kinderheim Baumgartner, for certain children, an equivalent world without rules and repressions looms large: the children of divorce. Inevitably, in the course of a marital breakup, as parents' attention turns away from matters of child rearing and toward their own suddenly imperative needs, the familiar structure of family life is suspended. At such times, children are often casually included in adult situations once considered unsuitable for the young—taking on advisory roles, for example, in their newly single parents' sex lives.

Studies such as the National Association of Elementary School Principals' longitudinal survey of children growing up in one-parent families clearly attest to the negative impact of divorce on children's school careers. Children of divorce show lower achievement in school than do their two-parent classmates. The same study uncovered a statistical increase in tardiness among single-parent children, as well as a higher rate of absenteeism, expulsion and truancy.

The connection between family breakdown and the child's educational outcome is becoming ominously clear. Writing last month in the New England Journal of Medicine, the psychiatrist Armand M. Nicholi Jr., in an article on the drug epidemic in America, says, "The accelerating divorce rate in the United States has closely paralleled the rise in drug use . . . Moreover, poor academic performance, susceptibility to peer influence and delinquent behavior (all characteristic of drug users), as well as suicide and homicide, have been found to be more pronounced among children from homes with one or both parents missing or frequently absent."

☐

There may be another, less obvious advantage to preserving sexual latency: It may profoundly influence adult behavior toward children. That is, if cultural influences encourage repression of children's sexuality, the child's consequent appearance and behavior may inspire the adults around him to act in a more protective manner. Some biological evidence lends strength to the idea that the way adults perceive children *does* profoundly affect the way they behave toward them.

As Konrad Lorenz has observed, the young of all species possess certain physical characteristics unique to them that disappear as they grow older—"neotenic

traits," Lorenz has called them. Among humans, neotenic traits are the child's outsize head relative to the rest of the body, his outsize eyes relative to the size of the head, the short, rounded proportions of his arms and legs. Lorenz proposed that these juvenile differences serve an evolutionary purpose: They act as "innate releasing mechanisms," causing adults instinctively to nurture and protect the child.

In addition to these special *physical* neotenic characteristics, Lorenz describes certain neotenic *behavior* traits displayed by the young that have a powerful, genetically programmed effect on the adults of that species. The wide-beaked clamor of baby birds in the nest, for instance, so different from the normal singing of mature birds, has been shown to trigger especially attentive feeding behavior from the parent birds. Experiments have demonstrated that when baby birds are prevented from opening their beaks extra wide, their parents do not feed them with reliability, and the fledglings perish.

There are obvious neotenic behavior patterns among humans just as there are among birds or beasts, things children do that differ significantly from things adults normally do. Among them might be classified young children's "cute" mispronunciations that adults have long smiled at, as well as the romping and playing children spontaneously engage in. And just as young animals have programmed into their behavior patterns certain signs of dependence and submissiveness that they display to older and stronger animals in order to avoid being treated aggressively—laying the ears back, dropping the head, placing the tail between the legs—so children not so long ago were obliged to show submissive and dependent behavior to adults: certain formulas of "respect," such as the use of "sir" and "please" and "thank you"—learned behaviors that also fall into the neotenic category.

All these "childish" ways—not only deferent manners, but distinctively childlike styles of walking, talking and playing—have an importance in children's lives that goes beyond simple tradition: They promote among adults a particular kind of protectiveness toward the child. This, in turn, allows the child to pursue his various activities, his exploration, and play—indeed, his entire education—in safety.

☐

There are those who see childhood as a form of deprivation. The literary critic Helen Vendler, for instance, refers in passing to "the poverty of every child's restricted early life" when she describes "the passage from a sequestered childhood to a forcibly socialized adulthood." The implication of the word "poverty" in conjunction with the idea of a "sequestered" childhood is this: Were the child to be offered the full wealth of experience that is available to the adult, he would be enriched by it. Because he is protected from it, however, the child must be seen as poor and incomplete. Yet there is reason to think that this is a misguided sentiment.

Part of that wealth from which children were once sequestered was a questionable enrichment: the knowledge of evil, violence, human helplessness, futility, injustice, misery, death. Today, as parents struggle for economic survival and search for sexual fulfillment, as they divorce, remarry, work out their primitive conflicts with their "shrinks," rail against political corruption, agonize over depleting natural resources and ecological destruction, tremble at the nuclear threat, many do not try to shield their children from these complex affairs. It is not always because they are no longer capable of hiding these difficult subjects, but also because they believe it is harmful to do so.

Yet those who believe that to protect children is to impoverish them, are making a questionable assumption: that children have the same capacity as adults to assimilate and utilize knowledge and experience. Annie Hermann, former educational director of New York's Child Development Center, disagrees. Indeed, she connects some of the problems that seem almost to define today's youth with just this failure to differentiate children's needs from those of adults:

"Trying to do away with the discrepancies between children and adults is more prevalent in America than in Europe. We rather feel it is helping to promote equality and democracy to treat children as equal, and for this reason we feel obliged to share all our adult knowledge with them. But it's like feeding a 2-day-old child a delicious steak, justifying our action by saying that we love to eat steak and therefore it's only fair to give it to our child. The trouble is that the child has no teeth and cannot eat the steak. He chokes on it."

Moreover, Annie Hermann continues, "innocence, once considered the right of children, may be seen as simply the absence of weight and burden. Maturity, meanwhile, may be defined as the capacity to carry a burden successfully. But if you are given the heavy burden of knowledge before you have the capacity to deal with it—and knowledge *is* burdensome, because it requires mental and psychological work to deal with it— the results may be those distressing signs parents and teachers are observing among children today: confusion, fear, feelings of incompetence. Children grow up not really able to deal with difficulties, and they learn that the best way to deal with problems is to escape, through drugs or drink or whatever."

Because of the precocious knowledge, independence, assertiveness and "adultness" that characterize so many children today—especially, it appears, those who have had to "grow up faster" because their parents have divorced or are both absorbed in their careers, it is easy to get the impression that children are also more mature these days. Indeed, the child growing up under more protective, old-fashioned circumstances may seem more "bratty," more "spoiled," more demanding than the hardy, self-sufficient child of absent parents. But while a certain level of sophistication is inevitably achieved when a child is forced to take care of himself much of the time, it is not the same thing as maturity. As the child grows older, true maturity, defined by an ability to share, to sacrifice, to be generous, to love unselfishly, and to nurture and care for children of his own, may prove elusive, and in its place, attention-seeking and narcissism become the characteristics that define his adult life. While those children whose childhoods are enriched by a bounty of adult experiences end up the poorer for it, those "poor" protected children have received a treasure in disguise—one, however, that will reveal itself only when they have grown up.

A 13-year-old girl whose parents divorced when she was 9 points out the connection between an unprotected childhood and subsequent difficulties achieving maturity: "When my parents split, things were a mess. They were too upset to pay much attention to me, and I guess in a lot of ways I had to bring myself up. I really did grow up very fast. But actually this didn't make me end up more mature. If anything, it worked the other way. I need a lot of attention—really a lot more than most of my friends who grew up more slowly."

□

It would be foolish to suggest that childhood in the bygone Age of Protection was a continuously happy state. Rare indeed was the child whose childhood was completely free of jealousy or shame or anger or any of the other forms of human misery. In his prize-winning memoir "Growing Up," Russell Baker describes his childhood during the Depression years, darkened by poverty, marital discord, illness and death. And yet he is able to write: "The occasional outbursts of passion that flickered across my childhood were like summer storms. The sky clouded suddenly, thunder rumbled, lightning flashed and I trembled a few moments, then just as swiftly the sky turned blue again and I was basking contentedly in the peace of innocence."

It is not by chance that when Baker paints a scene of his childhood days he fills it with adults sitting on a porch, pronouncing beliefs such as, "Children should be seen and not heard," adults who interrupt their gossip with reminders that "little pitchers have big ears." For it was not the complete absence of unhappiness that allowed him to look back on his childhood as an island of peace and innocence. It was the secure certainty that he was a child and that adults were adults, and that in spite of the wretchedness he might glimpse in their world he could still remain, in his different state, untouched by it. This is the essence of adult protectiveness: transmitting to children the sense that they are separate and special and under the adults' careful supervision. This understanding allowed children of the past, even those growing up a mere 10 or 15 years ago, to enjoy the simple pleasures of childhood—of play, imagination, curiosity, and pursuit of adventure—in the most adverse circumstances.

Can the boundaries between adulthood and childhood be once again restored? Can parents today, sensing uneasily that something is missing, try to recreate the different sort of childhood that they themselves once were granted? In an Age of Preparation, can individual parents hope to buck the tide and try to bring their children up protectively?

The social processes that helped bring about children's new integration into adult life—changes in family stability and employment patterns, most notably, along with the increasing dominance of television in children's lives—cannot be reversed. We will never return to the old-style family with the bread-earning father and the childlike, stay-at-home mother minding the house and kids. Nor would we desire such a step backward. The liberation movement has brought a new maturity and independence to women, impelling them to seek fulfillment of a greater potential than they had understood in the past. The hope of a simple turning of the tide is an unrealistic and indeed a retrogressive one.

Nevertheless, while social change cannot be reversed, it may indeed be modified and made to work better for families.

Perhaps an understanding of the irreversible consequences of family breakdown on children's lives will cause parents to readjust some of their original goals for marriage, and to focus greater attention on their children's well-being than on those ambitions, desires and dreams of personal fulfillment they had when they were single. The future holds the possibility of a variety of partnerships for men and women, only some of which will be seen as conducive to the raising of children.

Perhaps an understanding that children and adults are *not* equal, and that children do not prosper when treated as equal, will encourage parents to take a more authoritative—authoritative, not authoritarian—position in the family.

Perhaps the recognition that a highly complicated civilization cannot afford to shorten the period of nurture and protection of its immature members will restore a real childhood to the children of coming generations.

Erik Erikson's Eight Ages Of Man
One man in his time plays many psychosocial parts

David Elkind

DAVID ELKIND *is professor of psychology and psychiatry at the University of Rochester.*

At a recent faculty reception I happened to join a small group in which a young mother was talking about her "identity crisis." She and her husband, she said, had decided not to have any more children and she was depressed at the thought of being past the child-bearing stage. It was as if, she continued, she had been robbed of some part of herself and now needed to find a new function to replace the old one.

When I remarked that her story sounded like a case history from a book by Erik Erikson, she replied, "Who's Erikson?" It is a reflection on the intellectual modesty and literary decorum of Erik H. Erikson, psychoanalyst and professor of developmental psychology at Harvard, that so few of the many people who today talk about the "identity crisis" know anthing of the man who pointed out its pervasiveness as a problem in contemporary society two decades ago.

Erikson has, however, contributed more to social science than his delineation of identity problems in modern man. His descriptions of the stages of the life cycle, for example, have advanced psychoanalytic theory to the point where it can now describe the development of the healthy personality on its own terms and not merely as the opposite of a sick one. Likewise, Erikson's emphasis upon the problems unique to adolescents and adults living in today's society has helped to rectify the one-sided emphasis on childhood as the beginning and end of personality development.

Finally, in his biographical studies, such as "Young Man Luther" and "Gandhi's Truth" (which has just won a National Book Award in philosophy and religion), Erikson emphasizes the inherent strengths of the human personality by showing how individuals can use their neurotic symptoms and conflicts for creative and constructive social purposes while healing themselves in the process.

It is important to emphasize that Erikson's contributions are genuine advances in psychoanalysis in the sense that Erikson accepts and builds upon many of the basic tenets of Freudian theory. In this regard, Erikson differs from Freud's early co-workers such as Jung and Adler who, when they broke with Freud, rejected his theories and substituted their own.

Likewise, Erikson also differs from the so-called neo-Freudians such as Horney, Kardiner and Sullivan who (mistakenly, as it turned out) assumed that Freudian theory had nothing to say about man's relation to reality and to his culture. While it is true that Freud emphasized, even mythologized, sexuality, he did so to counteract the rigid sexual taboos of his time, which, at that point in history, were frequently the cause of neuroses. In his later writings, however, Freud began to concern himself with the executive agency of the personality, namely the ego, which is also the repository of the individual's attitudes and concepts about himself and his world.

It is with the psychosocial development of the ego that Erikson's observations and theoretical constructions are primarily concerned. Erikson has thus been able to introduce innovations into psychoanalytic theory without either rejecting or ignoring Freud's monumental contribution.

The man who has accomplished this notable feat is a handsome Dane, whose white hair, mustache, resonant accent and gentle manner are reminiscent of actors like Jean Hersholt and Paul Muni. Although he is warm and outgoing with friends, Erikson is a rather shy man who is uncomfortable in the spotlight of public recognition. This trait, together with his ethical reservations about making public even disguised case material, may help to account for Erikson's reluctance to publish his observations and conceptions (his first book appeared in 1950, when he was 48).

In recent years this reluctance to publish has diminished and he has been appearing in print at an increasing pace. Since 1960 he has published three books, "Insight and Responsibility," "Identity: Youth and Crisis" and "Gandhi's Truth," as well as editing a fourth, "Youth: Change ·and Challenge." Despite the accolades and recognition these books have won for him, both in America and abroad, Erikson is still surprised at the popular interest they have generated and is a little troubled about the possibility of being misunderstood and misinterpreted. While he would prefer that his books spoke for themselves and that he was left out of the picture, he has had to accede to popular demand for more information about himself and his work.

The course of Erikson's professional career has been as diverse as it has been unconventional. He was born in Frankfurt, Germany, in 1902 of Danish parents. Not long after his birth his father died, and his mother later married the pediatrician who had cured her son of a childhood illness. Erikson's stepfather urged him to become a physician, but the boy declined and became an artist instead—an artist who did portraits of children. Erikson says of his post-adolescent years, "I was an artist then, which in Europe is a euphemism for a young man with some talent and nowhere to go." During this period he settled in Vienna and worked as a tutor in a family friendly with Freud's. He met Freud on informal occasions when the families went on outings together.

These encounters may have been the impetus to accept a teaching appointment at an American school in Vienna founded by Dorothy Burlingham and directed by Peter Blos (both now well known on the American psychiatric scene). During these years (the late nineteen-twenties) he also undertook and completed psychoanalytic training with Anna Freud and August Aichhorn. Even at the outset of his career, Erikson gave evidence of the breadth of his interests and activities by being trained and certified as a Montessori teacher. Not surprisingly, in view of that training, Erikson's first articles dealt with psychoanalysis and education.

It was while in Vienna that Erikson met and married Joan Mowat Serson, an American artist of Canadian descent. They came to America in 1933, when Erikson was invited to practice and teach in Boston. Erikson was, in fact, one of the first if not the first child-analyst in the Boston area. During the next two decades he held clinical and academic appointments at Harvard, Yale and Berkeley. In 1951 he joined a group of psychiatrists and psychologists who moved to Stockbridge, Mass., to start a new program at the Austen Riggs Center, a private residential treatment center for disturbed young people. Erikson remained at Riggs until 1961, when he was appointed professor of human development and lecturer on psychiatry at Harvard. Throughout his career he has always held two or three appointments simultaneously and has traveled extensively.

Perhaps because he had been an artist first, Erikson has never been a conventional psychoanalyst. When he was treating children, for example, he always insisted on visiting his young patients' homes and on having dinner with the families. Likewise in the nineteen-thirties, when anthropological investigation was described to him by his friends Scudder McKeel, Alfred Kroeber and Margaret Mead, he decided to do field work on an Indian reservation. "When I realized that Sioux is the name which we |in Europe| pronounced "See us" and which for us was *the* American Indian, I could not resist." Erikson thus antedated the anthropologists who swept over the Indian reservations in the post-Depression years. (So numerous were the field workers at that time that the stock joke was that an Indian family could be defined as a mother, a father, children and an anthropologist.)

Erikson did field work not only with the Oglala Sioux of Pine Ridge, S. D. (the tribe that slew Custer and was in turn slaughtered at the Battle of Wounded Knee), but also with the salmon-fishing Yurok of Northern California. His reports on these experiences revealed his special gift for sensing and entering into the world views and modes of thinking of cultures other than his own.

It was while he was working with the Indians that Erikson began to note syndromes which he could not explain within the confines of traditional psychoanalytic theory. Central to many an adult Indian's emotional problems seemed to be his sense of uprootedness and lack of continuity between his present life-style and that portrayed in tribal history. Not only did the Indian sense a break with the past, but he could not identify with a future requiring assimilation of the white culture's values. The problems faced by such men, Erikson recognized, had to do with the ego and with culture and only incidentally with sexual drives.

The impressions Erikson gained on the reservations were reinforced during World War II when he worked at a veterans' rehabilitation center at Mount Zion Hospital in San Francisco. Many of the soldiers he and his colleagues saw seemed not to fit the traditional "shell shock" or "malingerer" cases of World War I. Rather, it seemed to Erikson that many of these men had lost the sense of who and what they were. They were having trouble reconciling their activities, attitudes and feelings as soldiers with the activities, attitudes and feelings they had known before the war. Accordingly, while these men may well have had difficulties with repressed or conflicted drives, their main problem seemed to be, as Erikson came to speak of it at the time, "identity confusion."

It was almost a decade before Erikson set forth the implications of his clinical observations in "Childhood and Society." In that book, the summation and integration of 15 years of research, he made three major contributions to the study of the human ego. He posited (1) that, side by side with the stages of psychosexual development described by Freud (the oral, anal, phallic, genital, Oedipal and pubertal), were psychosocial stages of ego development, in which the individual had to establish new basic orientations to himself and his social world; (2) that personality development continued throughout the whole life cycle; and (3) that each stage had a positive *as well as* a negative component.

Much about these contributions—and about Erikson's way of thinking—can be understood by looking at his scheme of life stages. Erikson identifies eight stages in the human life cycle, in each of which a new dimension of "social interaction" becomes possible—that is, a new dimension in a person's interaction with himself, and with his social environment.

TRUST vs. MISTRUST

The first stage corresponds to the oral stage in classical psychoanalytic theory and usually extends through the first year of life. In Erikson's view, the new dimension of social interaction that emerges during this period involves basic *trust* at the one extreme, and *mistrust* at the other. The degree to which the child comes to trust the world, other people and himself depends to a considerable extent upon the quality of the care that he receives. The infant whose needs are met when they arise, whose discomforts are quickly removed, who is cuddled, fondled, played with and talked to, develops a sense of the world as a safe place to be and of people as helpful and dependable. When, however, the care is inconsistent, inadequate and rejecting, it fosters a basic mistrust, an attitude of fear and suspicion on the part of the infant toward the world in general and people in particular that will carry through to later stages of development.

It should be said at this point that the problem of basic trust-versus-mistrust (as is true for all the later dimensions) is not resolved once and for all during the first year of life; it arises again at each successive stage of development. There is both hope and danger in this. The child who enters school with a sense of mistrust may come to trust a particular teacher who has taken the trouble to make herself trustworthy; with this second chance, he overcomes his early mistrust. On the other hand, the child who comes through infancy with a vital sense of trust can still have his sense of mistrust activated at a later stage if, say, his parents are divorced and separated under acrimonious circumstances.

This point was brought home to me in a very direct way by a 4-year-old patient I saw in a court clinic. He was being seen at the court clinic because his adoptive parents, who had had him for six months, now wanted to give him back to the agency. They claimed that he was cold and unloving, took things and could not be trusted. He was indeed a cold and apathetic boy, but with good reason. About a year after his illegitimate birth, he was taken away from his mother, who had a drinking problem, and was shunted back and forth among several foster homes. Initially he had tried to relate to the persons in the foster homes, but the relationships never had a chance to develop becuase he was moved at just the wrong times. In the end he gave up trying to reach out to others, because the inevitable separations hurt too much.

Like the burned child who dreads the flame, this emotionally burned child shunned the pain of emotional involvement. He had trusted his mother, but now he trusted no one. Only years of devoted care and patience could now undo the damage that had been done to this child's sense of trust.

AUTONOMY vs. DOUBT

Stage Two spans the second and third years of life, the period which Freudian theory calls the anal stage. Erikson sees here the emergence of *autonomy*. This autonomy dimension builds upon the child's new motor and mental abilities. At this stage the child can not only walk but also climb, open and close, drop, push and pull, hold and let go. The child takes pride in these new accomplishments and wants to do everything himself, whether it be pulling the wrapper off a piece of candy, selecting the vitamin out of the bottle or flushing the toilet. If parents recognize the young child's need to do what he is capable of doing at his own pace and in his own time, then he develops a sense that he is able to control his muscles, his impulses, himself and, not insignificantly, his environment—the sense of autonomy.

When, however, his caretakers are impatient and do for him what he is capable of doing himself, they reinforce a sense of shame and doubt. To be sure, every parent has rushed a child at times and children are hardy enough to endure such lapses. It is only when caretaking is consistently overprotective and criticism of "accidents" (whether these be wetting, soiling, spilling or breaking things) is harsh and unthinking that the child develops an excessive sense of shame with respect to other people and an excessive sense of doubt about own abilities to control his world and himself.

If the child leaves this stage with less autonomy than shame or doubt, he will be handicapped in his attempts to achieve autonomy in adolescence and adulthood. Contrariwise, the child who moves through this stage with his sense of autonomy buoyantly outbalancing his feelings of shame and doubt is well prepared to be autonomous at later phases in the life cycle. Again, however, the balance of autonomy to shame and doubt

set up during this period can be changed in either positive or negative directions by later events.

It might be well to note, in addition, that too much autonomy can be as harmful as too little. I have in mind a patient of 7 who had a heart condition. He had learned very quickly how terrified his parents were of any signs in him of cardiac difficulty. With the psychological acuity given to children, he soon ruled the household. The family could not go shopping, or for a drive, or on a holiday if he did not approve. On those rare occasions when the parents had had enough and defied him, he would get angry and his purple hue and gagging would frighten them into submission.

Actually, this boy was frightened of this power (as all children would be) and was really eager to give it up. When the parents and the boy came to realize this, and to recognize that a little shame and doubt were a healthy counterpoise to an inflated sense of autonomy, the three of them could once again assume their normal roles.

INITIATIVE vs. GUILT

In this stage (the genital stage of classical psychoanalysis) the child, age 4 to 5, is pretty much master of his body and can ride a tricycle, run, cut and hit. He can thus initiate motor activities of various sorts on his own and no longer merely responds to or imitates the actions of other children. The same holds true for his language and fantasy activities. Accordingly, Erikson argues that the social dimension that appears at this stage has *initiative* at one of its poles and *guilt* at the other.

Whether the child will leave this stage with his sense of initiative far outbalancing his sense of guilt depends to a considerable extent upon how parents respond to his self-initiated activities. Children who are given much freedom and opportunity to initiate motor play such as running, bike riding, sliding, skating, tussling and wrestling have their sense of initiative reinforced. Initiative is also reinforced when parents answer their children's questions (intellectual initiative) and do not deride or inhibit fantasy or play activity. On the other hand, if the child is made to feel that his motor activity is bad, that his questions are a nuisance and that his play is silly and stupid, then he may develop a sense of guilt over self-initiated activities in general that will persist through later life stages.

INDUSTRY vs. INFERIORITY

Stage Four is the age period from 6 to 11, the elementary school years (described by classical psychoanalysis as the *latency phase*). It is a time during which the child's love for the parent of the opposite sex and rivalry with the same sexed parent (elements in the so-called family romance) are quiescent. It is also a period during which the child becomes capable of deductive reasoning, and of playing and learning by rules. It is not until this period, for example, that children can really play marbles, checkers and other "take turn" games that require obedience to rules. Erikson argues that the psychosocial dimension that emerges during this period has a sense of *industry* at one extreme and a sense of *inferiority* at the other.

The term industry nicely captures a dominant theme of this period during which the concern with how things are made, how they work and what they do predominates. It is the Robinson Crusoe age in the sense that the enthusiasm and minute detail with which Crusoe describes his activities appeals to the child's own budding sense of industry. When children are encouraged in their efforts to make, do, or build practical things (whether it be to construct creepy crawlers, tree houses, or airplane models—or to cook, bake or sew), are allowed to finish their products, and are praised and rewarded for the results, then the sense of industry is enhanced. But parents who see their children's efforts at making and doing as "mischief," and as simply "making a mess," help to encourage in children a sense of inferiority.

During these elementary-school years, however, the child's world includes more than the home. Now social institutions other than the family come to play a central role in the developmental crisis of the individual. (Here Erikson introduced still another advance in psychoanalytic theory, which heretofore concerned itself only with the effects of the parents' behavior upon the child's development.)

A child's school experiences affect his industry-inferiority balance. The child, for example, with an I.Q. of 80 to 90 has a particularly traumatic school experience, even when his sense of industry is rewarded and encouraged at home. He is "too bright" to be in special classes, but "too slow" to compete with children of average ability. Consequently he experiences constant failures in his academic efforts that reinforces a sense of inferiority.

On the other hand, the child who had his sense of industry derogated at home can have it revitalized at school through the offices of a sensitive and committed teacher. Whether the child develops a sense of industry or inferiority, therefore, no longer depends solely on the caretaking efforts of the parents but on the actions and offices of other adults as well.

IDENTITY vs. ROLE CONFUSION

When the child moves into adolescence (Stage Five—roughly the ages 12-18), he encounters, according to traditional psychoanalytic theory, a reawakening of the family-romance problem of early childhood. His means of resolving the problem is to seek and find a romantic partner of his own generation. While Erikson does not deny this aspect of adolescence, he points out that there are other problems as well. The adolescent matures mentally as well as physiologically and, in addition to the new feelings, sensations and desires he experiences as a result of changes in his body, he develops a multitude of new ways of looking at and thinking about the world. Among other things, those in adolescence can now think about other people's thinking and wonder about what other people think of them. They can also conceive of ideal families, religions and societies which they then compare with the imperfect families, religions and societies of their own experience. Finally, adolescents become capable of constructing theories and philosophies designed to bring all the varied and conflicting aspects of society into a working, harmonious and peaceful whole. The adolescent, in a word, is an impatient idealist who believes that it is as easy to realize an ideal as it is to imagine it.

Erikson believes that the new interpersonal dimension which emerges during this period has to do with a sense of *ego identity* at the positive end and a sense of *role confusion* at the negative end. That is to say, given the adolescent's newfound integrative abilities, his task is to bring together all of the things he has learned about himself as a son, student, athlete, friend, Scout, newspaper boy, and so on, and integrate these different images of himself into a whole that makes sense and that shows continuity with the past while preparing for the future. To the extent that the young person succeeds in this endeavor, he arrives at a sense of psychosocial identity, a sense of who he is, where he has been and where he is going.

In contrast to the earlier stages, where parents play a more or less direct role in the determination of the result of the developmental crises, the influence of parents during this stage is much more indirect. If the young person reaches adolescence with, thanks to his parents, a vital sense of trust, autonomy, initiative and industry, then his chances of arriving at a meaningful sense of ego identity are much enhanced. The reverse, of course, holds true for the young person who enters adolescence with considerable mistrust, shame, doubt, guilt and inferiority. Preparation for a successful adolescence, and the attainment of an integrated psychosocial identity must, therefore, begin in the cradle.

Over and above what the individual brings with him from his childhood, the attainment of a sense of personal identity depends upon the social milieu in which he or she grows up. For example, in a society where women are to some extent second-class citizens, it may be harder for females to arrive at a sense of psychosocial identity. Likewise at times, such as the present, when rapid social and technological change breaks down many traditional values, it may be more difficult for young people to find continuity between what they learned and experienced as children and what they learn and experience as adolescents. At such times young people often seek causes that give their lives meaning and direction. The activism of the current generation of young people may well stem, in part at least, from this search.

When the young person cannot attain a sense of personal identity, either because of an unfortunate childhood or difficult social circumstances, he shows a certain amount of *role confusion*—a sense of not knowing what he is, where he belongs or whom he belongs to. Such confusion is a frequent symptom in delinquent young people. Promiscuous adolescent girls, for example, often seem to have a fragmented sense of ego identity. Some young people seek a "negative identity," an identity opposite to the one prescribed for them by their family and friends. Having an identity as a "delinquent," or as a "hippie," or even as an "acid head," may sometimes be preferable to having no identity at all.

In some cases young people do not seek a negative identity so much as they have it thrust upon them. I remember another court case in which the defendant was an attractive 16-year-old girl who had been found "tricking it" in a trailer located just outside the grounds of an Air Force base. From about the age of 12, her mother had encouraged her to dress seductively and to go out with boys. When she returned from dates, her sexually frustrated mother demanded a kiss-by-kiss, caress-by-caress description of the evening's activities. After the mother had vicariously satisfied her sexual needs, she proceeded to call her daughter a "whore" and a "dirty tramp."

As the girl told me, "Hell, I have the name, so I might as well play the role."

Failure to establish a clear sense of personal identity at adolescence does not guarantee perpetual failure. And the person who attains a working sense of ego identity in adolescence will of necessity encounter challenges and threats to that identity as he moves through life. Erikson, perhaps more than any other personality theorist, has emphasized that life is constant change and that confronting problems at one stage in life is not a guarantee against the reappearance of these problems at later stages, or against the finding of new solutions to them.

INTIMACY vs. ISOLATION

Stage Six in the life cycle is young adulthood; roughly the period of courtship and early family life that extends from late adolescence till early middle age. For this stage, and the stages described hereafter, classical psychoanalysis has nothing new or major to say. For Erikson, however, the previous attainment of a sense of personal identity and the engagement in productive work that marks this period gives rise to a new interpersonal dimension of *intimacy* at the one extreme and *isolation* at the other.

When Erikson speaks of intimacy he means much more than love-making alone; he means the ability to share with and care about another person without fear of losing oneself in the process. In the case of intimacy, as in the case of identity, success or failure no longer depends directly upon the parents but only indirectly as they have contributed to the individual's success or failure at the earlier stages. Here, too, as in the case of identity, social conditions may help or hinder the establishment of a sense of intimacy. Likewise, intimacy need not involve sexuality; it includes the relationship between friends. Soldiers who have served together under the most dangerous circumstances often develop a sense of commitment to one another that exemplifies intimacy in its broadest sense. If a sense of intimacy is not established with friends or a marriage partner, the result, in Erikson's view, is a sense of isolation—of being alone without anyone to share with or care for.

GENERATIVITY vs. SELF-ABSORPTION

This stage—middle age—brings with it what Erikson speaks of as either *generativity or self-absorption,* and stagnation. What Erikson means by generativity is that the person begins to be concerned with others beyond his immediate family, with future generations and the nature of the society and world in which those generations will live. Generativity does not reside only in parents; it can be found in any individual who actively concerns himself with the welfare of young people and with making the world a better place for them to live and to work.

Those who fail to establish a sense of generativity fall into a state of self-absorption in which their personal needs and comforts are of predominant concern. A fictional case of self-absorption is Dickens's Scrooge in "A Christmas Carol." In his one-sided concern with money and in his disregard for the interests and welfare of his young employee, Bob Cratchit, Scrooge exemplifies the self-absorbed, embittered (the two often go together) old man. Dickens also illustrated, however, what Erikson points out: namely, that unhappy solutions to life's crises are not irreversible. Scrooge, at the end of the tale, manifested both a sense of generativity and of intimacy which he had not experienced before.

INTEGRITY vs. DESPAIR

Stage Eight in the Eriksonian scheme corresponds roughly to the period when the individual's major efforts are nearing completion and when there is time for reflection—and for the enjoyment of grandchildren, if any. The psychosocial dimension that comes into prominence now has *integrity* on one hand and *despair* on the other.

The sense of integrity arises from the individual's ability to look back on his life with satisfaction. At the other extreme is the individual who looks back upon his life as a series of missed opportunities and missed directions; now in the twilight years he realizes that it is too late to start again. For such a person the inevitable result is a sense of despair at what might have been.

These, then, are the major stages in the life cycle as described by Erikson. Their presentation, for one thing, frees the clinician to treat adult emotional problems as failures (in part at least) to solve genuinely adult personality crises and not, as heretofore, as mere residuals of infantile frustrations and conflicts. This view of personality growth, moreover, takes some of the onus off parents and takes account of the role which society and the person himself play in the formation of an individual personality. Finally, Erikson has offered hope for us all by demonstrating that each phase of growth has its strengths as well as its weaknesses and that failures at one stage of development can be rectified by successes at later stages.

The reason that these ideas, which sound so agreeable to "common sense," are in fact so revolutionary has a lot to do with the state of psychoanalysis in America. As formulated by Freud, psychoanalysis encompassed a theory of personality development, a method of studying the human mind and, finally, procedures for treating troubled and unhappy people. Freud viewed this system as a scientific one, open to revision as new facts and observations accumulated.

The system was, however, so vehemently attacked that Freud's followers were constantly in the position of having to defend Freud's views. Perhaps because of this situation, Freud's system became, in the hands of some of his followers and defenders, a dogma upon which all theoretical innovation, clinical observation and therapeutic practice had to be grounded. That this attitude persists is evidenced in the recent remark by a psychoanalyst that he believed psychotic patients could not be treated by psychoanalysis because "Freud said so." Such attitudes, in which Freud's authority rather than observation and data is the basis of deciding what is true and what is false, has contributed to the disrepute in which psychoanalysis is widely held today.

Erik Erikson has broken out of this scholasticism and has had the courage to say that Freud's discoveries and practices were the start and not the end of the study and treatment of the human personality. In addition to advocating the modifications of psychoanalytic theory outlined above, Erikson has also suggested modifications in therapeutic practice, particularly in the treatment of young patients. "Young people in severe trouble are not fit for the couch," he writes. "They want to face you, and they want you to face them, not a facsimile of a parent, or wearing the mask of a professional helper, but as a kind of over-all individual a young person can live with or despair of."

Erikson has had the boldness to remark on some of the negative effects that distorted notions of psychoanalysis have had on society at large. Psychoanalysis, he says, has contributed to a widespread fatalism—"even as we were trying to devise, with scientific determinism, a therapy for the few, we were led to promote an ethical disease among the many."

Perhaps Erikson's innovations in psychoanalytic theory are best exemplified in his psycho-historical writings, in which he combines psychoanalytic insight with a true historical imagination. After the publication of "Childhood and Society," Erikson undertook the application of his scheme of the human life cycle to the study of historical persons. He wrote a series of brilliant essays on men as varied as Maxim Gorky, George Bernard Shaw and Freud himself. These studies were not narrow case histories but rather reflected Erikson's remarkable grasp of Europe's social and political history, as well as of its literature. (His mastery of American folklore, history and literature is equally remarkable.)

While Erikson's major biographical studies were yet to come, these early essays already revealed his unique psycho-history method. For one thing, Erikson always chose men whose lives fascinated him in one way or another, perhaps because of some conscious or unconscious affinity with them. Erikson thus had a sense of community with his subjects which he adroitly used (he calls it *disciplined subjectivity)* to take his subject's point of view and to experience the world as that person might.

Secondly, Erikson chose to elaborate a particular crisis or episode in the individual's life which seemed to crystallize a life-theme that united the activities of his past and gave direction to his activities for the future. Then, much as an artist might, Erikson proceeded to fill in the background of the episode and add social and historical perspective. In a very real sense Erikson's biographical sketches are like paintings which direct the viewer's gaze from a focal point of attention to background and back again, so that one's appreciation of the focal area is enriched by having pursued the picture in its entirety.

This method was given its first major test in Erikson's study of "Young Man Luther." Originally, Erikson planned only a brief study of Luther, but "Luther proved too bulky a man to be merely a chapter in a book." Erikson's involvement with Luther dated from his youth, when, as a wandering artist, he happened to hear the Lord's Prayer in Luther's German. "Never knowingly having heard it, I had the experience, as seldom before or after, of a wholeness captured in a few simple words, of poetry fusing the esthetic and the moral; those who have suddenly 'heard' the Gettysburg Address will know what I mean."

Erikson's interest in Luther may have had other roots as well. In some ways, Luther's unhappiness with the papal intermediaries of Christianity resembled on a grand scale Erikson's own dissatisfaction with the intermediaries of Freud's system. In both cases some of the intermediaries had so distorted the original teachings that what was being preached in the name of the master came close to being the opposite of what he had himself proclaimed. While it is not possible to describe Erikson's treatment of Luther here, one can get some feeling for Erikson's brand of historical analysis from his sketch of Luther:

"Luther was a very troubled and a very gifted young man who had to create his own cause on which to focus his fidelity in the Roman Catholic world as it was then.... He first became a monk and tried to solve his scruples by being an exceptionally good monk. But even his superiors thought that he tried much too hard. He felt himself to be such a sinner that he began to lose faith in the charity of God and his superiors told him, 'Look, God doesn't hate you, you hate God or else you would trust Him to accept your prayers.' But I would like to make it clear that someone like Luther becomes a historical person only because he also has an acute understanding of historical actuality and knows how to 'speak to the condition' of his times. Only then do inner struggles become representative of those of a large number of vigorous and sincere young people—and begin to interest some troublemakers and hangers-on."

After Erikson's study of "Young Man Luther" (1958), he turned his attention to "middle-aged" Gandhi. As did Luther, Gandhi evoked for Erikson childhood memories. Gandhi led his first nonviolent protest in India in 1918 on behalf of some mill workers, and Erikson, then a young man of 16, had read glowing accounts of the event. Almost a half a century later Erikson was invited to Ahmedabad, an industrial city in western India, to give a seminar on the human life cycle. Erikson discovered that Ahmedabad was the city in which Gandhi had led the demonstration about which Erikson had read as a youth. Indeed, Erikson's host was none other than Ambalal Sarabahai, the benevolent industrialist who had been Gandhi's host—as well as antagonist—in the 1918 wage dispute. Throughout his stay in Ahmedabad, Erikson continued to encounter people and places that were related to Gandhi's initial experiments with nonviolent techniques.

The more Erikson learned about the event at Ahmedabad, the more intrigued he became with its pivotal importance in Gandhi's career. It seemed to be the historical moment upon which all the earlier events of Gandhi's life converged and from which diverged all of his later endeavors. So captured was Erikson by the event at Ahmedabad, that he returned the following year to research a book on Gandhi in which the event would serve as a fulcrum.

At least part of Erikson's interest in Gandhi may have stemmed from certain parallels in their lives. The 1918 event marked Gandhi's emergence as a national political leader. He was 48 at the time, and had become involved reluctantly, not so much out of a need for power or fame as out of a genuine conviction that something had to be done about the disintegration of Indian culture. Coincidentally, Erikson's book "Childhood and Society," appeared in 1950 when Erikson was 48, and it is that book which brought him national prominence in the mental health field. Like Gandhi, too, Erikson reluctantly did what he felt he had to do (namely, publish his observations and conclusions) for the benefit of his

Erikson in a seminar at his Stockbridge, Mass., home.

"Young analysts are today proclaiming a 'new freedom' to see Freud in historical perspective, which reflects the Eriksonian view that one can recognize Freud's greatness without bowing to conceptual precedent."

ailing profession and for the patients treated by its practitioners. So while Erikson's affinity with Luther seemed to derive from comparable professional identity crises, his affinity for Gandhi appears to derive from a parallel crisis of generativity. A passage from "Gandhi's Truth" (from a chapter wherein Erikson addresses himself directly to his subject) helps to convey Erikson's feeling for his subject.

"So far, I have followed you through the loneliness of your childhood and through the experiments and the scruples of your youth. I have affirmed my belief in your ceaseless endeavor to perfect yourself as a man who came to feel that he was the only one available to reverse India's fate. You experimented with what to you were debilitating temptations and you did gain vigor and agility from your victories over yourself. Your identity could be no less than that of universal man, although you had to become an Indian—and one close to the masses—first."

The following passage speaks to Erikson's belief in the general significance of Gandhi's efforts:

"We have seen in Gandhi's development the strong attraction of one of those more inclusive identities: that of an enlightened citizen of the British Empire. In proving himself willing neither to abandon vital ties to his native tradition nor to sacrifice lightly a Western education which eventually contributed to his ability to help defeat British hegemony—in

all of these seeming contradictions Gandhi showed himself on intimate terms with the actualities of his era. For in all parts of the world, the struggle now is for *the anticipatory development of more inclusive identities* . . . I submit then, that Gandhi, in his immense intuition for historical actuality and his capacity to assume leadership in 'truth in action,' may have created a ritualization through which men, equipped with both realism and strength, can face each other with mutual confidence."

There is now more and more teaching of Erikson's concepts in psychiatry, psychology, education and social work in America and in other parts of the world. His description of the stages of the life cycle are summarized in major textbooks in all of these fields and clinicians are increasingly looking at their cases in Eriksonian terms.

Research investigators have, however, found Erikson's formulations somewhat difficult to test. This is not surprising, inasmuch as Erikson's conceptions, like Freud's, take into account the infinite complexity of the human personality. Current research methodologies are, by and large, still not able to deal with these complexities at their own level, and distortions are inevitable when such concepts as "identity" come to be defined in terms of responses to a questionnaire.

Likewise, although Erikson's life-stages have an intuitive "rightness" about them, not everyone agrees with his formulations. Douvan and Adelson in their book, "The Adolescent Experience," argue that while his identity theory may hold true for boys, it doesn't for girls. This argument is based on findings which suggest that girls postpone identity consolidation until after marriage (and intimacy) have been established. Such postponement occurs, says Douvan and Adelson, because a woman's identity is partially defined by the identity of the man whom she marries. This view does not really contradict Erikson's, since he recognizes that later events, such as marriage, can help to resolve both current and past developmental crises. For the woman, but not for the man, the problems of identity and intimacy may be solved concurrently.

Objections to Erikson's formulations have come from other directions as well. Robert W. White, Erikson's good friend and colleague at Harvard, has a long standing (and warmhearted) debate with Erikson over his life-stages. White believes that his own theory of "competence motivation," a theory which has received wide recognition, can account for the phenomena of ego development much more economically than can Erikson's stages. Erikson has, however, little interest in debating the validity of the stages he has described. As an artist he recognizes that there are many different ways to view one and the same phenomenon and that a perspective that is congenial to one person will be repugnant to another. He offers his stage-wise description of the life cycle for those who find such perspectives congenial and not as a world view that everyone should adopt.

It is this lack of dogmatism and sensitivity to the diversity and complexity of the human personality which help to account for the growing recognition of Erikson's contribution within as well as without the helping professions. Indeed, his psycho-historical investigations have originated a whole new field of study which has caught the interest of historians and political scientists alike. (It has also intrigued his wife, Joan, who has published pieces on Eleanor Roosevelt and who has a book on Saint Francis in press.) A recent issue of Daedalus, the journal for the American Academy of Arts and Sciences,

was entirely devoted to psycho-historical and psycho-political investigations of creative leaders by authors from diverse disciplines who have been stimulated by Erikson's work.

Now in his 68th year, Erikson maintains the pattern of multiple activities and appointments which has characterized his entire career. He spends the fall in Cambridge, Mass., where he teaches a large course on "the human life cycle" for Harvard seniors. The spring semester is spent at his home in Stockbridge, Mass., where he participates in case conferences and staff seminars at the Austen Riggs Center. His summers are spent on Cape Cod. Although Erikson's major commitment these days is to his psycho-historical investigation, he is embarking on a study of preschool children's play constructions in different settings and countries, a follow-up of some research he conducted with preadolescents more than a quarter-century ago. He is also planning to review other early observations in the light of contemporary change. In his approach to his work, Erikson appears neither drawn nor driven, but rather to be following an inner schedule as natural as the life cycle itself.

Although Erikson, during his decade of college teaching, has not seen any patients or taught at psychoanalytic institutes, he maintains his dedication to psychoanalysis and views his psycho-historical investigations as an applied branch of that discipline. While some older analysts continue to ignore Erikson's work, there is increasing evidence (including a recent poll of psychiatrists and psychoanalysts) that he is having a rejuvenating influence upon a discipline which many regard as dead or dying. Young analysts are today proclaiming a "new freedom" to see Freud in historical perspective—which reflects the Eriksonian view that one can recognize Freud's greatness without bowing to conceptual precedent.

Accordingly, the reports of the demise of psychoanalysis may have been somewhat premature. In the work of Erik Erikson, at any rate, psychoanalysis lives and continues to beget life.

Freud's "Ages of Man"

Erik Erikson's definition of the "eight ages of man" is a work of synthesis and insight by a psychoanalytically trained and worldly mind. Sigmund Freud's description of human phases stems from his epic psychological discoveries and centers almost exclusively on the early years of life. A brief summary of the phases posited by Freud:

Oral stage—roughly the first year of life, the period during which the mouth region provides the greatest sensual satisfaction. Some derivative behavioral traits which may be seen at this time are *incorporativeness* (first six months of life) and *aggressiveness* (second six months of life).

Anal stage—roughly the second and third years of life. During this period the site of greatest sensual pleasure shifts to the anal and urethral areas. Derivative behavioral traits are *retentiveness* and *expulsiveness*.

Phallic stage—roughly the third and fourth years of life. The site of

greatest sensual pleasure during this stage is the genital region. Behavior traits derived from this period include *intrusiveness* (male) and *receptiveness* (female).

Oedipal stage—roughly the fourth and fifth years of life. At this stage the young person takes the parent of the opposite sex as the object or provider of sensual satisfaction and regards the same-sexed parent as a rival. (The "family romance.") Behavior traits originating in this period are *seductiveness* and *competitiveness*.

Latency stage—roughly the years from age 6 to 11. The child resolves the Oedipus conflict by identifying with the parent of the opposite sex and by so doing satisfies sensual needs vicariously. Behavior traits developed during this period include *conscience* (or the internalization of parental moral and ethical demands).

Puberty stage—roughly 11 to 14. During this period there is an integration and subordination of oral, anal and phallic sensuality to an overriding and unitary genital *sexuality*. The genital sexuality of puberty has another young person of the opposite sex as its object, and discharge (at least for boys) as its aim. Derivative behavior traits (associated with the control and regulation of genital sexuality) are *intellectualization* and *estheticism*.

—D.E.

Growing up as a Fore

E. Richard Sorenson

Dr. Sorenson, director of the Smithsonian's National Anthropological Film Center, wrote The Edge of the Forest *on his Fore studies.*

Exploring, two youngsters walk confidently past men's house in hamlet. Smaller women's house is at right.

Untouched by the outside world, they had lived for thousands of years in isolated mountains and valleys deep in the interior of Papua New Guinea. They had no cloth, no metal, no money, no idea that their homeland was an island—or that what surrounded it was salt water. Yet the Fore (for'ay) people had developed remarkable and sophisticated approaches to human relations, and their child-rearing practices gave their young unusual freedom to explore. Successful as hunter-gatherers and as subsistence gardeners, they also had great adaptability, which brought rapid accommodation with the outside world after their lands were opened up.

It was alone that I first visited the Fore in 1963—a day's walk from a recently built airstrip. I stayed six months. Perplexed and fascinated, I returned six times in the next ten years, eventually spending a year and a half living with them in their hamlets.

Theirs was a way of life different from anything I had seen or heard about before. There were no chiefs, patriarchs, priests, medicine men or the like. A striking personal freedom was enjoyed even by the very young, who could move about at will and be where or with whom they liked. Infants rarely cried, and they played confidently with knives, axes, and fire. Conflict between old and young did not arise; there was no "generation gap."

Older children enjoyed deferring to the interests and desires of the younger, and sibling rivalry was virtually undetectable. A responsive sixth sense seemed to attune the Fore hamlet mates to each other's interests and needs. They did not have to directly ask, inveigle, bargain or speak out for what they needed or wanted. Subtle, even fleeting expressions of interest, desire, and discomfort were quickly read and helpfully acted on by one's associates. This spontaneous urge to share food, affection, work, trust, tools and pleasure was the social cement that held the Fore hamlets together. It was a pleasant way of life, for one could always be with those with whom one got along well.

Ranging and planting, sharing and living, the Fore diverged and expanded through high virgin lands in a pioneer region. They hunted out their gardens, tilled them while they lasted, then hunted again. Moving ever away from lands peopled and used they had a self-contained life with its own special ways.

The underlying ecological conditions were like those that must have encompassed the world before agriculture set its imprint so broadly. Abutting the Fore was virtually unlimited virgin land, and they had food plants they could introduce into it. Like hunter-gatherers they sought their sources of sustenance first in one locale and then another, across an extended range, following opportunities provided by a providential nature. But like agriculturalists they concentrated their effort and attention more narrowly on selected sites of production, on their gardens. They were both seekers and producers. A pioneer people in a pioneer land, they ranged freely into a vast territory, but they planted to live.

Cooperative groups formed hamlets and gardened together. When the fertility of a garden declined, they abandoned it. Grass sprung up to cover these abandoned sites of earlier cultivation, and, as the Fore moved on to other parts of the forest, they left uninhabited grasslands to mark their passage.

The traditional hamlets were small, with a rather fluid system of social relations. A single large men's house provided shelter for 10 to 20 men and boys and their visiting friends. The several smaller women's houses each normally sheltered two married women, their unmarried daughters and their sons up to about six years of age. Formal kinship bonds were less important than friendship was. Fraternal "gangs" of youths formed the hamlets; their "clubhouses" were the men's houses.

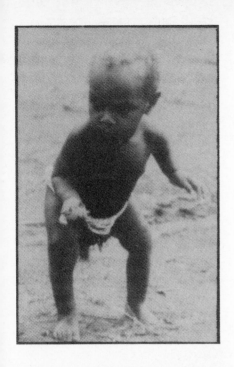

Learning to be a toddler, a Fore baby takes its first experimental steps. No one urges him on.

During the day the gardens became the center of life. Hamlets were virtually deserted as friends, relatives and children went to one or more garden plots to mingle their social, economic and erotic pursuits in a pleasant and emotionally filled Gestalt of garden life. The boys and unmarried youths preferred to explore and hunt in the outlying lands, but they also passed through and tarried in the gardens.

Daily activities were not scheduled. No one made demands, and the land was bountiful. Not surprisingly the line between work and play was never clear. The transmission of the Fore behavioral pattern to the young began in early infancy during a period of unceasing human physical contact. The effect of being constantly "in touch" with hamlet mates and their daily life seemed to start a process which proceeded by degrees: close rapport, involvement in regular activity, ability to handle seemingly dangerous implements safely, and responsible freedom to pursue individual interests at will without danger.

While very young, infants remained in almost continuous bodily contact with their mother, her house

mates or her gardening associates. At first, mothers' laps were the center of activity, and infants occupied themselves there by nursing, sleeping and playing with their own bodies or those of their caretakers. They were not put aside for the sake of other activities, as when food was being prepared or heavy loads were being carried. Remaining in close, uninterrupted physical contact with those around them, their basic needs such as rest, nourishment, stimulation and security were continuously satisfied without obstacle.

By being physically in touch from their earliest days, Fore youngsters learned to communicate needs, desires and feelings through a body language of touch and response that developed before speech. This opened the door to a much closer rapport with those around them than otherwise would have been possible, and led ultimately to the Fore brand of social cement and the sixth sense that bound groups together through spontaneous, responsive sharing.

As the infant's awareness increased, his interests broadened to the things his mother and other caretakers did and to the objects and materials they used. Then these youngsters began crawling out to explore things that attracted their attention. By the time they were toddling, their interests continually took them on short sorties to nearby objects and persons. As soon as they could walk well, the excursions extended to the entire hamlet and its gardens, and then beyond with other children. Developing without interference or supervision, this personal exploratory learning quest freely touched on whatever was around, even axes, knives, machetes, fire, and the like. When I first went to the Fore, I was aghast.

Eventually I discovered that this capability emerged naturally from Fore infant-handling practices in their milieu of close human physical

In infancy, Fore children begin experimental play with knives and other lethal objects. Sorenson never saw a child warned away or injured by them.

proximity and tactile interaction. Because touch and bodily contact lend themselves naturally to satisfying the basic needs of young children, an early kind of communicative experience fostered cooperative interaction between infants and their caretakers, also kinesthetic contact with the activities at hand. This made it easy for them to learn the appropriate handling of the tools of life.

The early pattern of exploratory activity included frequent return to one of the "mothers." Serving as home base, the bastion of security, a woman might occasionally give the youngster a nod of encouragement, if he glanced in her direction with un-certainty. Yet rarely did the women attempt to control or direct, nor did they participate in the child's quests or jaunts.

As a result Fore children did not have to adjust to rule and schedule in order to find their place in life. They could pursue their interests and whims wherever they might lead and still be part of a richly responsive world of human touch which constantly provided sustenance, comfort, diversion and security.

Learning proceeded during the course of pursuing interests and exploring. Constantly "in touch" with people who were busy with daily activities, the Fore young quickly learned the skills of life from example. Muscle tone, movement and mood were components of this learning process; formal lessons and commands were not. Kinesthetic skills developed so quickly that infants were able to casually handle knives and similar objects before they could walk.

Even after several visits I continued to be surprised that the unsupervised Fore toddlers did not recklessly thrust themselves into unappreciated dangers, the way our own children tend to do. But then, why should they? From their earliest days, they enjoyed a benevolent sanctuary from which the world could be confidently

Babies have free access to the breast and later, like this toddler being helped to kernels of corn by an older girl, can help themselves to whatever food is around—indulged by children and grown-ups.

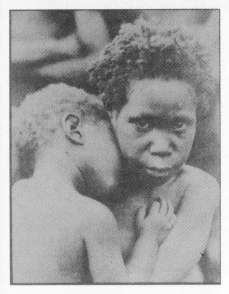

Close, constant body contact, as between this baby and older girl, creates security in Fore children.

On the way to hunt birds, cuscus (a marsupial) or rats, Fore boys stride through a sweet-potato garden.

viewed, tested and appreciated. This sanctuary remained ever available, but did not demand, restrain or impose. One could go and come at will.

In close harmony with their source of life, the Fore young were able confidently, not furtively, to extend their inquiry. They could widen their understanding as they chose. There was no need to play tricks or deceive in order to pursue life.

Emerging from this early childhood was a freely ranging young child rather in tune with his older and younger hamlet mates, disinclined to act out impulsively, and with a capable appreciation of the properties of potentially dangerous objects. Such children could be permitted to move out on their own, unsupervised and unrestricted. They were safe.

Such a pattern could persist indefinitely, re-creating itself in each new generation. However, hidden within the receptive character it produced was an Achilles heel; it also permitted adoption of new practices, including child-handling practices, which did *not* act to perpetuate the pattern. In only one generation after Western contact, the cycle of Fore life was broken.

Attuned as they were to individual pursuit of economic and social good, it did not take the Fore long to recognize the value of the new materials,

practices and ideas that began to flow in. Indeed, change began almost immediately with efforts to obtain steel axes, salt, medicine and cloth. The Fore were quick to shed indigenous practices in favor of Western example. They rapidly altered their ways to adapt to Western law, government, religion, materials and trade.

Sometimes change was so rapid that many people seemed to be afflicted by a kind of cultural shock. An anomie, even cultural amnesia, seemed to pervade some hamlets for a time. There were individuals who appeared temporarily to have lost memory of recent past events. Some Fore even forgot what type and style of traditional garments they had worn only a few years earlier, or that they had used stone axes and had eaten their dead close relatives.

Remarkably open-minded, the Fore so readily accepted reformulation of identity and practice that suggestion or example by the new government officers, missionaries and scientists could alter tribal affiliation, place names, conduct and hamlet style. When the first Australian patrol officer began to map the region in 1957, an error in communication led him to refer to these people as the "Fore." Actually they had had no name for themselves and the word, Fore, was their name for a quite different group, the Awa, who spoke another language and lived in another valley. They did not correct the patrol officer but adopted his usage. They all now refer to themselves as the Fore. Regional and even personal names changed just as readily.

More than anything else, it was the completion of a steep, rough, always muddy Jeep road into the Fore lands that undermined the traditional life. Almost overnight their isolated region was opened. Hamlets began to move down from their ridgetop sites in order to be nearer the road, consolidating with others.

The power of the road is hard to overestimate. It was a great artery where only restricted capillaries had existed before. And down this artery came a flood of new goods, new ideas

and new people. This new road, often impassable even with four-wheel-drive vehicles, was perhaps the single most dramatic stroke wrought by the government. It was to the Fore an opening to a new world. As they began to use the road, they started to shed traditions evolved in the protective insularity of their mountain fastness, to adopt in their stead an emerging market culture.

THE COMING OF THE COFFEE ECONOMY

"Walkabout," nonexistent as an institution before contact, quickly became an accepted way of life. Fore boys began to roam hundreds of miles from their homeland in the quest for new experience, trade goods, jobs and money. Like the classic practice of the Australian aborigine, this "walkabout" took one away from his home for periods of varying length. But unlike the Australian practice, it usually took the boys to jobs and schools rather than to a solitary life in traditional lands. Obviously it sprang from the earlier pattern of individual freedom to pursue personal interests and opportunity wherever it might lead. It was a new expression of the old Fore exploratory pattern.

Some boys did not roam far, whereas others found ways to go to distant cities. The roaming boys often sought places where they might be welcomed as visitors, workers or students for a while. Mission stations and schools, plantation work camps, and the servants' quarters of the European population became way-stations in the lives of the modernizing Fore boys.

Some took jobs on coffee plantations. Impressed by the care and attention lavished on coffee by European planters and by the money they saw paid to coffee growers, these young Fore workers returned home with coffee beans to plant.

Coffee grew well on the Fore hillsides, and in the mid-1960s, when the first sizable crop matured, Fore who previously had felt lucky to earn a few dollars found themselves able to earn a few hundred dollars. A rush to coffee ensued, and when the new gardens became productive a few years later, the Fore income from coffee jumped to a quarter of a million dollars a year. The coffee revolution was established.

At first the coffee was carried on the backs of its growers (sometimes for several days) over steep, rough mountain trails to a place where it could be sold to a buyer with a jeep. However, as more and more coffee was produced, the villagers began to turn with efforts to planning and constructing roads in association with neighboring villages. The newly built roads, in turn, stimulated further economic development and the opening of new trade stores throughout the region.

Following European example, the segregated collective men's and women's houses were abandoned. Family houses were adopted. This changed the social and territorial arena for all the young children, who hitherto had been accustomed to living equally with many members of their hamlet. It gave them a narrower place to belong, and it made them more distinctly someone's children. Uncomfortable in the family houses, boys who had grown up in a freer territory began to gather in "boys' houses," away from the adult men who were now beginning to live in family houses with their wives. Mothers began to wear blouses, altering the early freer access to the breast. Episodes of infant and child frustration, not seen in traditional Fore hamlets, began to take place along with repeated incidents of anger, withdrawal, aggressiveness and stinginess.

So Western technology worked its magic on the Fore, its powerful materials and practices quickly shattering their isolated autonomy and lifestyle. It took only a few years from the time Western intruders built their first grass-thatched patrol station before the Fore way of life they found was gone.

Fortunately, enough of the Fore traditional ways were systematically documented on film to reveal how unique a flower of human creation they were. Like nothing else, film made it possible to see the behavioral patterns of this way of life. The visual record, once made, captured data which was unnoticed and unanticipated at the time of filming and which was simply impossible to study without such records. Difficult-to-spot subtle patterns and fleeting nuances of manner, mood and human relations emerged by use of repeated reexamination of related incidents, sometimes by slow motion and stopped frame. Eventually the characteristic behavioral patterns of Fore life became clear, and an important aspect of human adaptive creation was revealed.

The Fore way of life was only one of the many natural experiments in living that have come into being through thousands of years of independent development in the world. The Fore way is now gone; those which remain are threatened. Under the impact of modern technology and commerce, the entire world is now rapidly becoming one system. By the year 2000 all the independent natural experiments that have come into being during the world's history will be merging into a single world system.

One of the great tragedies of our modern time may be that most of these independent experiments in living are disappearing before we can discover the implication of their special expressions of human possibility. Ironically, the same technology responsible for the worldwide cultural convergence has also provided the means by which we may capture detailed visual records of the yet remaining independent cultures. The question is whether we will be able to seize this never-to-be repeated opportunity. Soon it will be too late. Yet, obviously, increasing our understanding of the behavioral repertoire of humankind would strengthen our ability to improve life in the world.

Sexism in the Schoolroom of the '80s

THINGS HAVEN'T CHANGED.
BOYS STILL GET MORE ATTENTION, ENCOURAGEMENT
AND AIRTIME THAN GIRLS DO.

MYRA AND DAVID SADKER

Myra and David Sadker are professors of education at American University, Washington, D.C.

If a boy calls out in class, he gets teacher attention, especially intellectual attention. If a girl calls out in class, she is told to raise her hand before speaking. Teachers praise boys more than girls, give boys more academic help and are more likely to accept boys' comments during classroom discussions. These are only a few examples of how teachers favor boys. Through this advantage boys increase their chances for better education and possibly higher pay and quicker promotions. Although many believe that classroom sexism disappeared in the early '70s, it hasn't.

Education is not a spectator sport. Numerous researchers, most recently John Goodlad, former dean of education at the University of California at Los Angeles and author of *A Place Called School*, have shown that when students participate in classroom discussion they hold more positive attitudes toward school, and that positive attitudes enhance learning. It is no co-incidence that girls are more passive in the classroom and score lower than boys on SAT's.

Most teachers claim that girls participate and are called on in class as often as boys. But a three-year study we recently completed found that this is not true; vocally, boys clearly dominate the classroom. When we showed teachers and administrators a film of a classroom discussion and asked who was talking more, the teachers overwhelmingly said the girls were. But in reality, the boys in the film were out-talking the girls at a ratio of three to one. Even educators who are active in feminist issues were unable to spot the sex bias until they counted and coded who was talking and who was just watching. Stereotypes of garrulous and gossipy women are so strong that teachers fail to see this communications gender gap even when it is right before their eyes.

Field researchers in our study observed students in more than a hundred fourth-, sixth- and eighth-grade classes in four states and the District of Columbia. The teachers and students were male and female, black and white, from urban, suburban and rural communities. Half of the classrooms covered language arts and English—subjects in which girls traditionally have excelled; the other half covered math and science—traditionally male domains.

We found that at all grade levels, in all communities and in all subject areas, boys dominated classroom communication. They participated in more interactions than girls did and their participation became greater as the year went on.

Our research contradicted the traditional assumption that girls dominate classroom discussion in reading while boys are dominant in math. We found that whether the subject was language arts and English or math and science, boys got more than their fair share of teacher attention.

Some critics claim that if teachers talk more to male students, it is simply because boys are more assertive in grabbing their attention—a classic case of the squeaky wheel getting the educational oil. In fact, our research shows that boys are more assertive in the classroom. While girls sit patiently with their hands raised, boys literally grab teacher attention. They are eight times more likely than girls to call out answers. However, male assertiveness is not the whole answer.

Teachers behave differently, depending on whether boys or girls call out answers during discussions. When boys call out comments without raising their hands, teachers accept their answers. However, when girls call out, teachers reprimand this "inappropriate" behavior with messages such as, "In this class we don't shout out answers, we raise our hands." The message is subtle but powerful: Boys should be academically assertive and grab teacher attention; girls should act like ladies and keep quiet.

Teachers in our study revealed an interaction pattern that we called a "mind sex." After calling on a student, they tended to keep calling on students of the same sex. While this pattern applied to both sexes, it was far more pronounced among boys and allowed them more than their fair share of airtime.

It may be that when teachers call on someone, they continue thinking of that sex. Another explanation may be found in the seating patterns of elementary, secondary and even postsecondary classrooms. In approximately half of the classrooms in our study, male and female students sat in separate parts of the room. Sometimes the teacher created this segregation, but more often, the students segregated themselves. A teacher's tendency to interact with same-sex students may be a simple matter of where each sex sits. For example, a teacher calls on a female student, looks around the same area and then continues questioning the students around this girl, all of whom are female. When the teacher refocuses to a section of the classroom where boys are seated, boys receive the series of questions. And because boys are more assertive, the teacher may interact with their section longer.

Girls are often shortchanged in quality as well as in quantity of teacher attention. In 1975 psychologists Lisa Serbin and K. Daniel O'Leary, then at

WHILE GIRLS SIT PATIENTLY WITH THEIR HANDS RAISED, BOYS LITERALLY GRAB TEACHER ATTENTION.

the State University of New York at Stony Brook, studied classroom interaction at the preschool level and found that teachers gave boys more attention, praised them more often and were at least twice as likely to have extended conversations with them. Serbin and O'Leary also found that teachers were twice as likely to give male students detailed instructions on how to do things for themselves. With female students, teachers were more likely to do it for them instead. The result was that boys learned to become independent, girls learned to become dependent.

Instructors at the other end of the educational spectrum also exhibit this same "let me do it for you" behavior toward female students. Constantina Safilios-Rothschild, a sociologist with the Population Council in New York, studied sex desegregation at the Coast Guard Academy and found that the instructors were giving detailed instructions on how to accomplish tasks to male students, but were doing the jobs and operating the equipment for the female students.

Years of experience have shown that the best way to learn something is to do it yourself; classroom chivalry is not only misplaced, it is detrimental. It is also important to give students specific and direct feedback about the quality of their work and answers. During classroom discussion, teachers in our study reacted to boys' answers with dynamic, precise and effective responses, while they often gave girls bland and diffuse reactions.

Teachers' reactions were classified in four categories: praise ("Good answer"); criticism ("That answer is wrong"); help and remediation ("Try again—but check your long division"); or acceptance without any evaluation or assistance ("OK" "Uh-huh").

Despite caricatures of school as a harsh and punitive place, fewer than 5 percent of the teachers' reactions were criticisms, even of the mildest sort. But praise didn't happen often either; it made up slightly more than 10 percent of teachers' reactions. More than 50 percent of teachers' responses fell into the "OK" category.

Teachers distributed these four reactions differently among boys than among girls. Here are some of the typical patterns.

Teacher: "What's the capital of Maryland? Joel?"
Joel: "Baltimore."
Teacher: "What's the largest city in Maryland, Joel?"
Joel: "Baltimore."
Teacher: "That's good. But Baltimore isn't the capital. The capital is also the location of the U.S. Naval Academy. Joel, do you want to try again?"
Joel: "Annapolis."
Teacher: "Excellent. Anne, what's the capital of Maine?"
Anne: "Portland."
Teacher: "Judy, do you want to try?"
Judy: "Augusta."
Teacher: "OK."

In this snapshot of a classroom discussion, Joel was told when his answer was wrong (criticism); was helped to discover the correct answer (remediation); and was praised when he offered the correct response. When Anne was wrong, the teacher, rather than staying with her, moved to Judy, who received only simple acceptance for her correct answer. Joel received the more specific teacher reaction and benefited from a longer, more precise and intense educational interaction.

Too often, girls remain in the dark about the quality of their answers. Teachers rarely tell them if their answers are excellent, need to be improved or are just plain wrong. Unfortunately, acceptance, the imprecise response packing the least educational punch, gets the most equitable sex distribution in classrooms. Active students receiving precise feedback are more likely to achieve academically. And they are more likely to be boys. Consider the following:

☐ Although girls start school ahead

of boys in reading and basic computation, by the time they graduate from high school, boys have higher SAT scores in both areas.

☐ By high school, some girls become less committed to careers, although their grades and achievement-test scores may be as good as boys'. Many girls' interests turn to marriage or stereotypically female jobs. Part of the reason may be that some women feel that men disapprove of their using their intelligence.

☐ Girls are less likely to take math and science courses and to participate in special or gifted programs in these subjects, even if they have a talent for them. They are also more likely to believe that they are incapable of pursuing math and science in college and to avoid the subjects.

☐ Girls are more likely to attribute failure to internal factors, such as ability, rather than to external factors, such as luck.

The sexist communication game is played at work, as well as at school. As reported in numerous studies it goes like this:

☐ Men speak more often and frequently interrupt women.

☐ Listeners recall more from male speakers than from female speakers, even when both use a similar speaking style and cover identical content.

☐ Women participate less actively in conversation. They do more smiling and gazing; they are more often the passive bystanders in professional and social conversations among peers.

☐ Women often transform declarative statements into tentative comments. This is accomplished by using qualifiers ("kind of " or "I guess") and by adding tag questions ("This is a good movie, isn't it?"). These tentative patterns weaken impact and signal a lack of power and influence.

Sexist treatment in the classroom encourages formation of patterns such as these, which give men more dominance and power than women in the working world. But there is a light at the end of the educational tunnel. Classroom biases are not etched in stone, and training can eliminate these patterns. Sixty teachers in our study received four days of training to establish equity in classroom interactions. These trained teachers succeeded in eliminating classroom bias. Although our training focused on equality, it improved overall teaching effectiveness as well. Classes taught by these trained teachers had a higher level of intellectual discussion and contained more effective and precise teacher responses for all students.

There is an urgent need to remove sexism from the classroom and give women the same educational encouragement and support that men receive. When women are treated equally in the classroom, they will be more likely to achieve equality in the workplace.

What Is TV Doing To America?

In its 43 years, television has been praised as a miracle and damned as a distorter of reality. Now, new evidence is emerging about the medium and how it affects the people who watch it.

Soon after 28-year-old David Radnis watched the movie "The Deer Hunter" on TV in his Chicago-area home, he was dead—one of at least 29 viewers in the U.S. who shot themselves imitating the show's Russian-roulette scene.

When Hoang Bao Trinh fled from Vietnam to Silver Spring, Md., he spent months baby-sitting his grandchildren in front of the TV set. Soon the whole family was speaking English, much of it learned by imitating speech heard on the televised programs.

Such cases reflect TV's increasingly pervasive influence on America, both for good and bad. In a country where television has become a major—and in some cases primary—force determining how people work, relax and behave, the consequences are staggering. Recent studies show that the lives of Americans, from their selection of food to their choice of political leaders, are deeply affected by TV, and that influence is growing.

In an age when millions of inexperienced young people are growing up in front of the tube without close guidance of elders, many Americans worry that the nation could be ruined by a generation that gets its moral values from "Flamingo Road," its cultural standards from "Laverne & Shirley" and its sense of family relationships from "Dallas."

Most broadcasters, with support from some researchers, maintain that TV is unfairly blamed for merely conveying what the public demands and argue that the medium's power is exaggerated. They contend that most people treat television simply as one of many sources of information, and that most homes have basically been unaltered since the first modern home-TV set was marketed in 1939.

Others in the industry are worried that what author and actor Steve Allen calls the "amoral force" of TV and other popular media is helping to weaken old values. "It's horrendous," says Allen. "That our nation, our society, our culture is in some state of moral and ethical collapse is absolutely undeniable. In about 50 years, you could create what we already have a good percentage of—people who think it's perfectly OK to grab what they want, to do what they want, and the only bad thing is getting caught."

Linking the Tube and Violence

A report released in May by the National Institute of Mental Health says that "violence on television does lead to aggressive behavior by children and teenagers who watch the programs." In one five-year study of 732 children, "several kinds of aggression—conflicts with parents, fighting and delinquency—were all positively correlated with the total amount of television viewing." Defenders of TV have long held that there is no clear link between viewing and violence.

The findings covered a wide range of topics. In one survey, more than half the parents thought their children learned more about sex from TV than from any other source except the parents themselves. TV also was cited for fostering bad habits by glamorizing highly advertised junk foods and frequent use of alcohol.

The federally sponsored study noted that almost all Americans watch TV, many for hours each day. Some of the most avid watchers are the very young and very old, women and minorities. Heavy viewers are usually less educated.

"Television can no longer be considered as a casual part of daily life, as an electronic toy," the report stated. "Research findings have long since destroyed the illusion that television is merely innocuous entertainment."

TV is also partly blamed for a sharp slide in traditional learning. Since television became nearly universal in the early 1960s, average scores for high-school students taking the Scholastic Aptitude Test, the broadest measure of academic ability, have plunged from 478 to 424 on the verbal exam and from 502 to 466 in mathematics.

A panel of educators appointed to study the decline noted that by age 16 most children have spent 10,000 to 15,000 hours watching television—more time than they have spent in school. The panel's conclusion: "Is television a cause of the SAT-score decline? Yes, we think it is. . . . Television has become surrogate parent, substitute teacher."

As TV's children graduated in the 1960s and '70s, an Adult Performance Level test found that "20 percent of the American population was functionally incompetent, that is, could not perform the basic kinds of reading, writing or computing tasks—such as calculating the change on a small purchase, addressing an envelope, reading a want ad or filling out a job application." The result, says Paul Copperman, president of the Institute of Reading Development in San Francisco, is that "society may be compelled to support an increasing percentage of dysfunctional or only marginally functional citizens."

TV Has Brought Americans Together

Even the severest critics admit that television has achieved unprecedented results in making the public aware of a huge variety of developments—from war in Lebanon and the Falkland Islands to the plight of migrant workers.

Veteran broadcaster Eric Sevareid argues that television has had an enormously positive influence on America in

Reprinted from *U.S. News & World Report,* August 2, 1982. Copyright 1982, U.S. News & World Report, Inc.

three main areas: It has brought families together more, it has counteracted the country's tendency toward fragmentation, and it has stayed independent of government.

Says Severeid: "On balance, TV is better for us than bad for us. When Gutenberg printed the Bible, people thought that invention would put bad ideas in people's heads. They thought the typewriter would destroy the muse, that movies would destroy legitimate theater, that radio would destroy newspapers and that TV would destroy everything. But it doesn't happen that way."

A main virtue of TV, according to scholars, is that the medium is a powerful force for freedom—a far better source of information and motivation than the party apparatus that used to dominate politics in many sections of the country.

Television's broadening of perspectives also is credited with boosting worthwhile causes and diminishing the ethnic, religious and geographic prejudices that have plagued American history. Cited as a key example are the "freedom marches" that caught the attention of TV viewers in the early 1960s. Laws were then passed guaranteeing civil rights that blacks had sought for more than a century.

Many educators add that television has given Americans a wealth of experience and knowledge that isn't being measured by today's school tests. The National Education Association, the nation's biggest teachers' organization, has called for cultivation of "electronic literacy" and has distributed guides to help teachers solidify what students learn from programs like "Holocaust" and "Shogun."

Millions of young Americans have been led through the alphabet and rudiments of algebra by the educational series "Sesame Street" and "Electric Company" of the Children's Television Workshop. One study suggested that children who watch a lot of TV in their early years tend to read more widely later on than children who were lighter viewers when they were young.

The medium also provides an invaluable window on the world for invalids and the elderly. Steve Allen recalls a series of visits he made to hospitals where Vietnam veterans were being treated: "What was helping to pull them through the day was television. The television set does provide company for lonely people, a voice in the house."

Broadcasters point out that, no matter what sociologists think, the public likes what it is getting on television. The A.C. Nielsen Company, an audience-measuring firm, announced that, despite a decline in network viewing, America's 80 million television households averaged a record level of 6 hours and 44 minutes a day in front of the tube in 1981—up 9 minutes from 1980. That's three times the average rate of increase during the 1970s.

Observes one network executive: "It's all there, good and bad. All you have to do is change the dial."

How the Brain Reacts to TV

Until recently, there was little research on how the human brain absorbs information from TV. Many scholars long have been convinced that viewers retain less from television than from reading, but evidence was scarce.

Now, a research project by Jacob Jacoby, a Purdue University psychologist, has found that more than 90 percent of 2,700 people tested misunderstood even such simple fare as commercials or the detective series "Barnaby Jones." Only minutes after watching, the typical viewer missed 23 to 36 percent of the questions about what he or she had seen.

One explanation is that TV's compelling pictures stimulate primarily the right half of the brain, which specializes in

emotional responses, rather than the left hemisphere, where thinking and analysis are performed. By connecting viewers to instruments that measure brain waves, researcher Herbert Krugman found periods of right-brain activity outnumbering left-brain activity by a ratio of 2 to 1.

Another difficulty is the rapid linear movement of TV images, which gives viewers little chance to pause and reflect on what they have seen. Scientists say this torrent of images also has a numbing effect, as measured electronically by the high proportion of alpha brain waves, normally associated with daydreaming or falling asleep.

The result is shortened attention spans—a phenomenon increasingly lamented by teachers trying to hold the interest of students accustomed to TV. To measure attention spans, psychophysiologist Thomas Mulholland of the Edith Nourse Rogers Memorial Veterans Hospital in Bedford, Mass., attached 40 young viewers to an instrument that shut off the TV set whenever the children's brains produced mainly alpha waves. Although the children were told to concentrate, only a few could keep the set on for more than 30 seconds.

Other researchers have found unrealistic career expectations among young people who watch a lot of TV. According to "Television and Behavior," the new federal report: "Heavy viewers want high-status jobs but do not intend to spend many years in school. For girls, there is even more potential for conflict between aspirations and plans; the girls who are heavy viewers usually want to get married, have children and stay at home to take care of them, but at the same time they plan to remain in school and have exciting careers."

Frustration of these expectations, according to social scientists, can spill over into communities, helping to fuel destructive outbursts, ranging from disruption of schools to ghetto riots. Once civil disturbances are telecast, they may spread through imitation, as they did from Washington, D.C., to dozens of other cities in 1968.

Fictional shows can have a similar effect. An airplane bomb threat on "Doomsday Flight" was followed by a rash of similar occurrences across the nation.

"Facts" Are Not Always as They Seem

Another concern is the growing number of Americans who rank television as their main source of news and information—more than two thirds, according to the Roper Poll.

Some complain that "facts" on TV are not always what they seem. A new form of program, the "docudrama," is cited as a potential source of confusion. Mixing established facts and conjecture, a docudrama often is accepted as totally accurate. One such program, "King," was criticized by associates of the Rev. Martin Luther King, Jr., for allegedly misrepresenting

Who Watches TV the Most?
Weekly TV Usage

Older women (ages 55 and over)	36 hr., 33 min.
Older men	33 hr., 15 min.
Younger women (ages 18-55)	31 hr., 49 min.
Younger men	28 hr., 3 min.
Teenagers	22 hr., 59 min.
Children (ages 2-11)	25 hr., 10 min.

USN&WR—Basic data: A. C. Nielsen Company

the personality of the late civil-rights leader.

In his objections to video coverage of budget cutting and poverty, President Reagan joined a long list of politicians who charge that their efforts have been distorted by TV's need for dramatic pictures, rather than factual analysis. The late Chicago Mayor Richard Daley complained that "protesters" against various causes often would show up outside his office door, unknown to him inside, wanting not to present their grievances to him but to get coverage by TV crews whom they had notified in advance.

Television also is blamed for making viewers impatient by distorting their notions of what to expect from life. "TV teaches that all problems can be resolved quickly—within 30 minutes on a sitcom, 30 seconds in a commercial," says Neil Postman, a communications professor at New York University. When that doesn't happen in real life, he adds, "many people become frustrated or depressed."

Author Ben Stein, a speech writer during the Nixon administration, says the fictional creations of TV have tended to make Americans contemptuous and suspicious of their leaders. In his book, *The View From Sunset Boulevard: America as Brought to You by the People Who Make Television,* Stein notes that most "heavies" in TV shows are conservative authority figures such as high-ranking officials and business executives. And a recent study by the Media Institute in Washington, D.C., concludes that two thirds of business leaders in entertainment series are portrayed as foolish, greedy or immoral, and half their actions as illegal.

Helping to Reshape Democracy

Scholars have grown increasingly troubled by some of the effects of TV on democratic government.

More than two decades ago, Richard Nixon's sweat during a televised debate with John F. Kennedy weighed heavily against the Republican candidate for President, and apparently became a factor in his defeat. Since then, other TV debates during political campaigns also have been judged as much for cosmetics as for content, and are regarded as having contributed to winning or losing.

Even in the midst of ballot counting, TV's effects are far-reaching. In 1980, networks declared Ronald Reagan the projected winner soon after polls in Eastern states closed but before balloting ended in the West. Experts say some prospective voters never went to the polls in the West, believing their choices would make no difference.

A lesser-known issue that worries many political scientists is the frequent satirizing of public officials by entertainers such as Johnny Carson and Mark Russell.

According to some scholars, widely viewed TV skits poking fun at former President Jerry Ford's occasional clumsiness may have contributed to his defeat in 1976 by popularizing the notion that Ford was too awkward to lead the nation. Subsequent Presidents—Jimmy Carter and Ronald Reagan—also have been the objects of ridicule on TV—not a laughing matter if, as some believe, the satire prejudices a candidate's chance for election. Humorous commentary on politics in this country dates back to colonial times, but the immediacy and pervasiveness of television have given such satire added potency. "Now, one or two comics can start nationwide waves of derision that are almost impossible to overcome," says Robert Orben, a humor consultant to many politicians.

Worries About Morality

Concern also is growing about the sexual content of programs flooding cable systems and videocassette machines now installed in more than one third of American homes.

Until recently, X-rated shows made up a heavy majority of the sales of prerecorded videotapes for exhibition on home sets. Among the three-dozen pay-cable networks, at least three—the *Playboy* channel, Eros and Private Screenings—include explicit sexual material. Depending on which channel they select, viewers can find everything from partial nudity to simulated intercourse.

Mainstream-movie channels, such as Home Box Office and Showtime Entertainment, also owe some of their success to occasional airings of unedited theatrical films intended for adults only. Such films often contain obscene language, gore and degrees of undress that would never make it past the in-house censors of conventional TV.

All this has prompted a backlash by communities trying to limit what can be brought into homes via cable. In Manhattan, officials have tried to deny use of the "public access" channel to amateur producers who air programs with footage of people who were persuaded to undress or even engage in sex acts in front of the camera.

Peggy Charren, president of Action for Children's Television, urged Congress to head off a wave of local censorship by requiring cable systems to offer free lock boxes—devices that keep children from watching certain channels.

Others have suggested antiobscenity statutes similar to the rules governing over-the-air television. Many constitutional experts believe, however, that cable will continue to be protected by the First Amendment in the same manner as theatrical movies, books and magazines—especially in light of a recent U.S. district-court ruling that Utah's ban on "indecent" cable programs was unconstitutionally vague.

Some scholars also are concerned about another aspect of moral values that may have been distorted by TV. Lois DeBakey, communications professor and head of a nationwide literacy movement, lists the television industry among "profit-hungry pleasure peddlers" who have created a national tendency to exalt entertainment above crucial needs such as health and education. Noting that highly televised sports stars are paid an average of $250,000 a year and teachers only $20,000, DeBakey asks: "Do we honestly

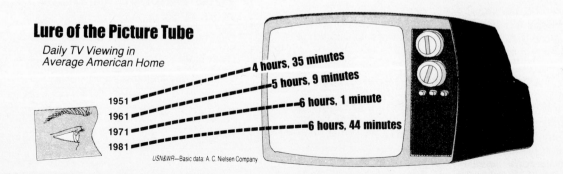

Lure of the Picture Tube

Daily TV Viewing in Average American Home

1951 — 4 hours, 35 minutes
1961 — 5 hours, 9 minutes
1971 — 6 hours, 1 minute
1981 — 6 hours, 44 minutes

USN&WR—Basic data: A. C. Nielsen Company

expect to motivate young people to take school seriously when the highest monetary and social rewards are reserved for occupations in which education is often unnecessary?"

Bigger Role for Special Interests?

Many business and political leaders are troubled by recent developments in video communications, including a movement toward deregulation of TV.

In conventional broadcasting, stations have always been licensed by the Federal Communications Commission to use a scarce public commodity, the airwaves. As a result, they are bound by laws and policies that strictly limit obscenity and prohibit any company from owning more than seven stations, as well as by the fairness and equal-time doctrines requiring free time for opposing views and candidates when controversial opinions are aired.

None of those rules applies, however, to the new outlets of cable, videocassettes and pay TV. Moreover, a drive is under way, backed by the Reagan administration, to repeal those rules for all broadcasters and leave ownership and program content up to what FCC Chairman Mark S. Fowler calls the new "competitive pressures of the marketplace." Fowler's proposals have drawn fire from critics, who call the deregulation movement an invitation for companies and organizations with the most money to control what people see on TV.

Already, various ideological groups are rushing to buy their way onto the tube. By raising as much as 70 million dollars a year from viewers and using the money to purchase air time, conservative evangelists such as Jerry Falwell and Pat Robertson have virtually drowned out the broadcasting voices of the major denominations. Falwell's TV operation launched the Moral Majority, cornerstone of a religious right wing that was active in the conservative shift of the last elections. A Falwell ally, Texas-based TV preacher James Robison, has aired two hour-long specials—"Wake Up, America" and "Attack on the Family"—in more than 50 cities. This spring, producer Norman Lear's liberal group, "People for the American Way," countered with "I Love Liberty," a 3-million-dollar extravaganza.

Local stations have taken the lead in what they call "issue-oriented advertising," commercials espousing political views. Participation so far has mostly been by big firms, such as Mobil Oil, attacking what they regard as excessive government regulation.

Backers of "message programing" maintain that rules of fairness and equal time are no longer needed because the many cable channels, independent stations and networks using relay satellites offer affordable soapboxes to almost anybody.

Opponents, however, say that is wishful thinking, because reaching a large portion of the national audience is too expensive except for a few rich organizations and individuals.

Do Viewers Respond Too Quickly?

Fresh criticism is being leveled at the potential for abuse in two-way cable systems spreading across the country.

These systems allow viewers with home computers or push-button consoles to communicate with central computers in requesting data, ordering merchandise, conducting banking transactions and responding to opinion polls.

Because computers can build dossiers from viewers' responses, civil libertarians fear violations of privacy by businesses or government agencies.

"Two-way systems are hitched to computers that scan each household every 6 seconds, recording all manner of information," explains Les Brown, editor of *Channels of Communication* magazine. "They know what we watch, what we buy through television, how we vote in public-opinion polls."

More than 90,000 homes now have two-way systems, and rapid expansion into a fully "wired society" is expected eventually. Already, there are TV alarm systems tied to police stations and customers' homes that can turn on TV sets and record when people enter or leave a home. Although these processes are now aimed solely at detecting intruders, the possibility of other uses is alarming to some observers.

Brown says he discovered one unsettling ramification of the cable age when he was discussing the issue of privacy in two-way-cable systems during an interview on the Cable News Network. Suddenly, the interviewer called for an instant plebiscite on Brown's concern, and an undetermined number of noontime viewers on the Columbus, Ohio, QUBE system pushed response buttons on their sets.

Eighty-five percent rejected Brown's suggestion that there was anything to worry about.

Knowing that daytime audiences are frequently dominated by preschoolers who may not understand what they are doing but who are capable of pushing the response button, Brown comments: "What's frightening to contemplate is that such polls are routinely conducted on every kind of important national issue, and their results cited as public opinion.

"You will never hear a cable newscaster say, 'QUBE took a poll today, and here's what some 4-year-olds think about the sale of AWACS to Saudi Arabia.' But some poor congressman may think he hears the voice of his constituents" in those results.

Despite the uncertainties, there is widespread hope that the new video age will benefit from the industry's past mistakes and triumphs and do the country far more good than harm.

As Benjamin Barber, a Rutgers University professor of political science, observes: "It is difficult to imagine the Kennedy generation, the '60s, Watergate, the Woodstock generation or even the Moral Majority in the absence of national television."

Now, he adds, those concepts "belong to history, for we stand—prepared or not—on the threshold of a new television age that promises to revolutionize our habits as viewers, as consumers and ultimately as citizens."

JAMES MANN

Groups and Roles in Transition

- **Primary Groups (Articles 15-17)**
- **Secondary Groups (Articles 18-19)**
- **Questioning Roles (Articles 20-21)**

Primary groups are small, intimate, spontaneous, and personal. In contrast, secondary groups are large, formal, and impersonal. Often primary groups are formed within a factory, school, or business. Primary groups are the main source for developing an individual's values and self-identity. The family, couples, gangs, cliques, teams, and small tribes or rural villages are examples of primary groups. Secondary groups include most of the organizations and bureaucracies in a modern society, and carry out most of its instrumental functions.

Urbanization, geographic mobility, centralization, bureaucratization, and other aspects of modernization have had an impact on the nature of groups, the quality of the relationships between people, and individuals' feelings of belonging. Some of the issues explored in this section include the place of tradition in family life, the failure of neighbors and neighborhoods in metropolitan areas to provide primary group support, the alienation that blue collar and white collar workers are experiencing in the workplace, and the unfair assignment of traditional sex roles on females and males.

The issues discussed in this section are sometimes identified as the loss of community. Individuals often try to solve their own loss of community through an intense commitment to a group which provides structure and meaning to their lives. These primary group attachments often serve deep psychological needs. Their results, however, can be either beneficial or harmful.

The first selection concerns the family—the basic primary group—and its contribution to our socialization. Alex Haley presents an autobiographical sketch of an extremely strong family. He explains that families can be strengthened but it requires work and commitment.

The second selection also focuses on the family—the black family. However, the author is not concerned with strong black families like Haley's, but the many black families under severe stress in the ghetto. Eleanor Holmes Norton describes an alarming family situation which she blames on the ghetto conditions.

The Cosers describe a cult which tried to totally absorb its members into the group. Though more than nine hundred people lived in the Jonestown community, the leader, Jim Jones, tried to make them live as one primary group. He wanted all members to be more committed to him than to their "real" family members. All individuals were subordinated to the group and to the group leader, and their capacity for independent judgment was systematically destroyed. The perversity and fanaticism of this primary group forces upon our consciousness some of the negative features of intense primary groups. At the same time, however, the article delineates many positive functions the group performed for its members.

The next two articles emphasize the shift from primary to secondary groups in modern society. A century ago most neighborhoods or communities and most work settings shared more characteristics of primary groups than secondary groups.

The city, typical of a secondary group, is berated for producing pathologies and social problems. It is viewed as impersonal at best and dangerous at worst. Creekmore calls this view a myth. His argument is based on literature that density is good for us. According to his report, cities are more beneficial than rural areas for improving our physical and mental health. They are not bad environments generally, but rather complex ones which require complex adaptations. Nevertheless they stimulate activity, increase social ties, and generally produce higher quality lives.

Theodore Roszak explores the workplace as a secondary group. He blasts the modern American workplace for its emptiness and meaninglessness. His father, a skilled carpenter, longed to make quality houses or fine furniture. Instead he was forced to slapdash houses together for builders who were after a "fast buck." Roszak believes this portrait of his father symbolizes the reality of modern work. Even when workers are paid well, they are often exploited and dehumanized.

Social roles generally make social life much easier, but many roles are being questioned today. This is reflected in two articles in this section. Deborah Fallows tries to present a balanced view of the debate over the roles of housewives and mothers. The feminists are questioning traditional definitions of these roles and the anti-feminists are questioning the feminists' definitions.

Another segment of society that is burdened with a stereotypical role is the elderly. They are being placed in a childish role by the media and others in society. Arluke

and Levin contend that when they are defined as child-like and treated as childlike, they are more likely to exhibit childlike behavior. They explore what the group is doing to change its image.

The lesson here is certainly not to view all changes in primary and secondary groups with alarm, but to look for both the positive and negative aspects of changes.

Looking Ahead: Challenge Questions

What has been lost and what has been gained in the process of modernization?

What kind of community do most people want?

How can work and life in general be made meaningful?

In what ways are social relationships between men and women changing?

Alex Haley: The Secret of Strong Families

Alex Haley

I was only four years old, and so nobody told me the mysterious look I sometimes saw my Mama and Dad exchange in our little church on Sunday mornings had anything to do with that word "love." During those long-ago Sunday mornings, I'd be seated in the front pew beside my Grandma, and my Mama would be up alongside the choir at the piano. She'd be playing some opening bars, but without looking down at her fingers on the keys because she'd be gazing straight across the piano's top at my Dad who would be standing waiting to sing. His head would be turned just enough to look straight back at Mama, and as I watched, their looks would seem to fuse.

Every time they shared that particular look, it seemed to me so strong that somebody could just reach out and touch it. It also seemed clear they didn't care that the whole congregation was seated right before them, watching. I wasn't entirely sure if I should feel embarrassed about how they were acting up there. They *were* so close to our preacher seated in his pulpit in his big wing-backed, brown leather-covered chair.

And then Mama would strike a certain chord, and Dad would quickly turn his head and, smiling out at our congregation, start singing his baritone solo. I know one thing today, over fifty years later: That image of my Mama and Dad gazing across the top of the piano at each other remains for me synonymous with a man and a woman truly *loving* one another.

I have another image I carry from that time when I was growing up in my little hometown of Henning, Tennessee. I remember watching a strange thing that went on at our dining room table when Grandpa would say the prayer before

we'd eat our meals. In our 1930s Bible Belt South, neither our family nor, I guess, any others—black or white, that considered themselves decent—would ever think of eating any meal which hadn't first been prayed over by the head of the house. In our family that was Grandpa, although he would sometimes delegate to Dad with a quick glance or a nod.

But the thing that the little boy who was me found so bemusing was that always when nearing the end of the prayer, Grandpa would say, "And, please, O Lord, bless the hands that prepared this meal." I just couldn't help squinching open one eye and peeping across the tablecloth at Grandma's hands, so as not to miss if the Lord might decide to bless them *right then!* But always Grandma just sat as if she were carved, her graying head bowed over her wrinkled hands. On one of those loosely-clasped fingers was her worn gold wedding band about which she liked to say, "Ain't never been off since Will stuck it there."

I'd wonder how Grandma must feel when she'd be out in the kitchen using those hands to cook with, knowing that the Lord was soon going to be asked to bless them. And I hoped that if He would, that He'd also bless mine, so I'd know how something as powerful as that would feel. Anyhow, when any food blessing prayer ended, we'd eat and I'd feel once again there within our home a second variety of that word "love," which somehow this time seemed to me even more solemn and sacred.

During some portion of each summer, my Dad would catch a train and ride off up North to a Cornell University that was in an Ithaca, N.Y., to study some more toward obtaining what he'd often proudly tell people would eventually be his "master's

degree." I didn't understand what such a degree was. Neither did most of the people in the town. Finally our church's good sister, Miss Scrap Green, figured it out for herself and made it her business to tell everybody that the real meaning was "'Fesser Haley's just takin' all the educatin' that any one man's head can stand." Her explanation kind of settled that matter for most of our Henning people.

Anyhow, during those periods when Dad was gone off up North to do his studying, another memorable thing would happen. With Dad not there to help him, Grandpa generally got home much later than usual from his Will E. Palmer Lumber Company. Sometimes when he got home he'd say to Grandma that there was someone he needed to see before it got dark. I'd be hanging around practically under their feet, and always they'd frustrate me by acting as if I were nowhere in sight. But then Grandpa would give Grandma, or Mama, an exaggerated questioning look. If they nodded back, it meant that I'd acted pretty fair that day. Then Grandpa, with still not a glance at me, would just thrust down his right hand extending stiffly its big index finger. I'd jump like a watch spring to clutch it tightly within my fist. And we'd leave the house with Grandpa striding and me struttin'. I would be so happy and proud.

Grandpa was real black and he walked tall and erect. As we progressed, I'd sometimes look down at our feet and count silently to myself how it was taking three of my short, quick steps to keep up with his long, slow one. I remember that each step he took sent one of his pants cuffs jerking backward over one of his dully-shined, black hightop shoes, then just as that foot would set down, the other foot would have swung forward over the usually dusty footpath.

And somehow after we'd gone a pretty good distance with me steadily holding onto Grandpa's forefinger, I'd begin having a feeling that kind of resembled my Mama's and Dad's fusion of gazes. It would feel like something was flowing from deeply within my Grandpa and through his finger into my fist and on down within me. And an image would start up in my head, that Grandpa was our family's tall, strong tree. My Dad, Grandma and Mama each were stout limbs on it, while obviously I was still just a twig. But at least I knew that every day I was eating all that I could hold, trying my best to grow as strong and as big as I could.

Finally, let me share one further incident from my boyhood there in Henning. It remains for me *so* indelible, principally because at intervals ever since I've continued to realize with new insights and new gratitude how hard my family, a loving, protective Southern black family, tried to rear me in a positive manner. It wasn't easy in that time, amid the intense racial prejudices of the 1930s, which were at their most overt, of course, in the South. Anyway, I was still four and my forthcoming fifth birthday had me very excited. I was very anxious to get older, although that situation had been helped because I had a baby brother named George. Since his arrival I had seized every opportunity to observe to whomever I could that I had become a "*big* brother," which somewhat elevated my status.

But during the days immediately preceding my birthday, my frustration had steadily mounted because I somehow simply *knew* I'd soon be receiving some sort of *big* birthday present. I especially sensed this from my elders who had begun acting as if they were unaware that I even existed. I did my very best discreet searching within the house, both upstairs and down, and found absolutely nothing, whereupon I launched into my very best wheedling efforts for even any little hint, but that didn't get me anything more than my poor elders' blank, deadpan expression.

Awakening and bursting from the bed and snatching on my clothes, I fairly flew downstairs before breakfast on that August 11th morning. I met four impassive adults who then began walking solemnly out onto the back porch, clearly meaning that I should, as I did, follow, falling in behind Grandma, who was carrying baby George. Our little procession had crossed the backyard when I noticed

Grandpa's Model-A Ford truck was parked by the cowbarn instead of its usual spot inside the garage, whose door now bore a shiny big new iron lock.

My Dad unlocked and swung wide open the garage door. Astonished, I saw a maybe foot-thick tree slice leaning up against a wall. It stood wider than I was tall, and had maybe twelve to fifteen round, white markers stuck on here and there, each bearing some small handprinting. I stood staring at it, wondering what on earth some tree slice could have to do with my birthday, when my Dad began pointing and explaining how each year a tree acquired one more of the clearly visible "annual growth rings," and this tree's many rings meant it had been cut down after growing for nearly 200 years. Then Dad told me how each one of those round, white markers represented how big and how old that tree was when whatever was printed on each marker happened.

Pointing out a marker that was positioned deep within the tree slice, Dad said that one represented—and it was the first time I ever heard the words—"the Emancipation Proclamation that freed the slaves." It was still confusing, even though I'd heard Grandma speak a whole lot about "slaves." She had often told me that her parents, then their parents, and plenty more before them, too, living away back in time, had been slaves working on plantations for white people who had owned them. What confused me was that I just couldn't understand how any person could go around *owning* other people.

Another marker represented the founding year of Lane College, in Jackson, Tennessee, where I'd heard countless times that Mama and Dad first met when he'd asked to walk her back to her dormitory after a choir practice. Another familiar Lane College story was that when Dad and Mama got married, Grandpa, sparing no expenses, had phoned the Lane College president and paid for the college choir to ride in a bus to Henning where they sang at the wedding.

Yet another marker showed how big and how old that tree was in the birth-year of my famous rooster-fighter great-grandpa. Although he was a slave, he was known and respected wherever he went as "Chicken George," and Grandma loved to tell stories about him. Some markers were for people of whom I'd never heard, like a Harriet Tubman, a Frederick Douglass and a Sojourner Truth, for instance. Dad told me they were important persons I'd be needing to learn a lot more about. And

there were other birth-year markers representing Grandpa, Grandma, Dad and Mama—and even *me*. And I remember how strange I felt, looking at the marker of when I'd entered the world, because it was placed at just five years of those growth rings, practically right beneath the tree's bark!

Looking back on that August morning, I can see my parents' and grandparents' reasons for giving me that singularly imaginative gift for a fifth birthday. For one, they wanted me to have a useful perspective on history, and they also wanted to start broadening my vistas. Concurrent with those aims, their intention was to start—that early—shielding me the best they could against the racial harshnesses I'd inevitably meet. Young black persons suffered most when they were not girded in advance with some knowledge of their ethnic past coupled with pride in being black—or "colored," as was the ethnic term used at that time. My Dad later told me that often when I slept, the four of them would sit and discuss such concerns for hours, and that after Mama presented the tree slice idea, the actual thick cross-section of a California redwood was obtained by Grandpa through his lumberyard connection, but just barely in time for my birthday.

For me, I know that a tree slice, a symbol of a family's concern and love, certainly did implant my boyhood concept of history as a drama of people, some gone, others living, and of events as real as any in the present but which had actually happened during the past. And I know that my tree slice gift had the further effect of getting me to read all the books that I could as my desire grew to find somebody else worthy of yet another marker's placement, preferably away down within the tree slice. Most of my suggestions (such as Cinderella!) didn't qualify, but now and then something would, and my pride swelled. Before I reached age six, no one visiting us escaped my using my cut-down teacher's pointer in explaining all about trees' annual growth rings, then what each of my eventually fifty or more markers represented. As I sit here remembering this, I've no question that my fifth birthday's tree slice set into motion a whole long interrelated chain of events which turned me into a writer who prefers historical subjects.

Certainly it is this habit of looking at things with a historical perspective that makes me realize that in today's advanced society too many of us are losing our once-strong family ties, such as those I had as a boy in Henning. The symptomatic sounds of our loss are already familiar. Two pervasive examples are the common expressions, "I'm trying to find myself," or, "I need my own space." Whether these popular statements are made in a tone conveying matter-of-factness or sophisticated élan, to me the bottom-line translation is rootlessness. And also, a word that bothers me is "relationship," popularly applied across the whole range of human unions. To me it seems to avoid stating solid commitment, a fact reflected in today's unprecedented divorce rate. (Pray forgive my flashback to the most moving words I think I ever heard my Grandma utter. One evening during her last years, with Grandpa long dead, she sat quietly listening to several of us family members discuss new sexual mores, then abruptly she offered, "Ain't never knowed no man but Will." Thinking about it, I later wept at its simple majesty.)

Today I believe that we must pursue ways to rebuild our families, which may have eroded during the swiftly changing past years. We must recapture the values that interacting, interdependent, loving families once had. And I also believe that there *are* specific ways families can indeed strengthen themselves. For instance, while I'm a fourth-generation Methodist, I believe that any family will benefit by adopting the weekly tradition known as "Family Night" which is widely practiced by Mormons. Family members set aside an hour one night every week to get reacquainted with each other and to work and pray together and exchange candid views. Mormon bookstores usually carry a booklet, called *Family Time,* which is filled with concrete suggestions on how to spend that hour together. A characteristic gathering might see the family talking about traditions and how they were started or parents telling youngsters about their own childhood experiences. Group discussion of a recent movie or television show can richly fill an evening hour together as well. Finally, Family Nights end with a prayer of thanks for the gathering.

Another good way to strengthen a family is to research its history. This is best accomplished when youthful family members query elders and pursue the nigh-mystical interrelations of the past and the present. For some reason, grandparents and other aged folk will tell their own children far less than they will reveal to their grandchildren.

Attics of old family homes should be searched. Precious treasures are probably lying in wait. (Imagine me the morning I blew dust off what turned out to be my ex-slave great-grandfather Tom Murray's ledger of his charge account as a free blacksmith.) Don't overlook any packets of letters. My most cherished old letter was Grandpa's written proposal to Grandma, herewith literally: "Dear Cynthia: We have been keeping company for two years. I feel it is now time we should discuss the contract of marriage. Yours sincerely, Will E. Palmer." Later, Grandma confessed to me that upon receipt of that letter, she, in her words, "went tearing out all through the house, hollerin' to my Mama and sisters, 'I got him! I got him!'"

Finally, nothing strengthens a family more than a planned reunion. Something almost mystical happens when numerous and widely-dispersed family groups converge somewhere en masse—and are suddenly a *clan*.

For all the thrills that happen during a reunion, I believe the most emotional moment of all is when the professional photographer starts arranging for the formal full-family portrait. Classically, all front-row steps are reserved for those of the eldest generation. Would you like to test your capacity for tearfulness? Then you just stand quietly watching as some two young members each gently takes an arm and starts carefully guiding an elder whose vision wavers now, whose footsteps falter, to a front seat.

Next, your clan's newest members are set into those elders' laps. Likely your tears will freshen, looking at sagging, aged ones clutching the lively, plump babies—and you realize that probably you will never again witness that particular pair occupying that seat of honor in that graphic generational contrast.

When at last the camera clicks, the resulting photograph will capture, at least for a moment, your clan, which is unique on this earth. With that experience and that photograph as evidence of the generational ties, every family involved can scarcely miss feeling a wellspring of new strength.

RESTORING THE TRADITIONAL BLACK FAMILY

Alone and on welfare in New York. Today, well over half of black infants are born to single women, and the vast majority are brought up in poverty.

Eleanor Holmes Norton

Eleanor Holmes Norton, chairman of the Equal Employment Opportunity Commission during the Carter Administration, is a professor at the Georgetown University Law Center.

What would society be like if the family found it difficult to perform its most basic functions? We are beginning to find out. Half of all marriages in this country end in divorce, and half of all children will spend a significant period with only one parent.

Startling and unsettling changes have already occurred in black family life, especially among the poor. Since the 1960's, birth rates among blacks have fallen dramatically, but two out of every three black women having a first child are single, compared to one out of every six white women. Today, well over half of black children in this country are born to single women. Why are female-headed households multiplying now, when there is less discrimination and poverty than a couple of generations ago, when black family life was stronger?

The disruption of the black family today is, in exaggerated microcosm, a reflection of what has happened to American family life in general. Public anxiety has mounted with the near-doubling of the proportion of white children living with one parent (from 9 percent to 17 percent) since 1970. Single parents of all backgrounds are feeling the pressures—the sheer economics of raising children primarily on the depressed income of the mother (a large component of the so-called "feminization of poverty"); the psychological and physical toll when one person, however advantaged, must be both mother and father, and the effects on children.

The stress on American family life was recently addressed by Senator Daniel P. Moynihan, Democrat of New York, on the 20th anniversary of his controversial "Moynihan Report." The original report confined its analysis to the black family. Moynihan, who in April delivered a series of lectures at Harvard on the family, said, "I want to make clear this is not a black issue." Indeed, just last month, the problem of increasing poverty among all the nation's children was underscored in a major report from two Federal agencies.

Yet until recently, many blacks have had an almost visceral reaction to mention of black family problems. Wounds to the family were seen as the most painful effect of American racism. Many blacks and their supporters have regarded talk of black family weaknesses as tantamount to insult and smear. Some conservatives have taken signs of trouble in the black family as proof that the remaining problems of race are internal and have announced the equivalent of "Physician, heal thyself."

At the heart of the crisis lies the self-perpetuating culture of the ghetto. This destructive

ethos began to surface 40 years ago with the appearance of permanent joblessness and the devaluation of working-class black men. As this nation's post-World War II economy has helped produce a black middle class, it has also, ironically, been destroying the black working class and its family structure. Today, the process has advanced so far that renewal of the black family goes beyond the indispensable economic ingredients. The family's return to its historic strength will require the overthrow of the complicated, predatory ghetto subculture, a feat demanding not only new Government approaches but active black leadership and community participation and commitment.

WHILE THIS crisis was building, it received almost no public attention, in part because of the notorious sensitivity of the subject. Yet 20 years ago, Martin Luther King Jr. spoke candidly about the black family, spelling out the "alarming" statistics on "the rate of illegitimacy," the increase in female-headed households and the rise in families on welfare. The black family, King asserted, had become "fragile, deprived and often psychopathic."

King relied in part on the Moynihan report, written when the Senator was an Assistant Secretary of Labor. Many were stunned by what one critic called the report's "salacious 'discovery' " — its discussion of illegitimacy, matriarchy and welfare and its view that black family structure had become, in its own words, a "tangle of pathology" capable of perpetuating itself without assistance from the white world. As a result, the report's concern with remedies, including jobs, and its call for a national family policy were eclipsed.

The delay has been costly to blacks and to the country. When King spoke out, the statistics he characterized as alarming showed that two-and-a-half times as many black families as white ones were headed by women. Today, it is almost three-and-a-half times as many — 43 percent of black families compared with 13 percent of white families. Since 1970, out-of-wedlock births have become more prevalent throughout society, almost doubling among whites to 11 percent. But among blacks, births to single women have risen from 38 percent in 1970 to 57 percent in 1982.

While families headed by women have often proved just as effective as two-parent families in raising children, the most critical danger facing female-headed households is poverty. Seventy percent of black children under the age of 18 who live in female-headed families are being brought up in poverty. In 1983, the median income for such households was $7,999, compared to almost $32,107 for two-parent families of all races, in which both spouses worked. Without the large increase in female-headed households, black family income would have *increased* by 11 percent in the 1970's. Instead, it fell by 5 percent.

As last month's report from the Congressional Research Service and the Congressional Budget Office pointed out, "The average black child can expect to spend more than five years of his childhood in poverty; the average white child, 10 months."

Buried beneath the statistics is a world of complexity originating in the historic atrocity of slavery and linked to modern discrimination and its continuing effects. What has obscured the problem is its delicacy and its uniqueness. The black family has been an issue in search of leadership. Discussion of problems in the black family has been qualitatively different from debates on voting rights or job discrimination. Fear of generating a new racism has foreclosed whatever opportunity there may have been to search for relief, driving the issue from the public agenda and delaying for a generation the search for workable solutions. Today, when nearly half of all black children are being raised in poverty, further delay is unthinkable.

Blacks themselves have been stunned by recent disclosures of the extent of the growth of poor, alienated female-headed households. The phenomenon is outside the personal experience of many black adults. Many have overcome deep poverty and discrimination only because of the protection and care of stable traditional and extended families. As recently as the early 1960's, 75 percent of black households were husband-and-wife families. The figure represents remarkable continuity — it is about the same as those reported in census records from the late 19th century. Indeed, the evidence suggests that most slaves grew up in two-parent families reinforced by ties to large extended families.

The sharp rise in female-headed households involves mostly those with young children and began in the mid-1960's. The phenomenon — while by no means a trend that permeates the entire black community — affects a significant portion of young people today, many of whom are separated economically, culturally and socially from the black mainstream. They have been raised in the worst of the rapidly deteriorating ghettos of the 1960's, 1970's and 1980's, in cities or neighborhoods that lost first the white and then the black middle and working classes. Drugs, crime and pimps took over many of the old communities. Blacks remaining were often trapped and isolated, cut off from the values of the black working poor and middle class — where husbands often work two jobs, wives return to work almost immediately after childbirth and extended families of interdependent kin are still more prevalent than among whites.

A complete explanation of black family disruption does not emerge from a roundup of the usual suspects, including the many factors that make American family life generally less stable these days: the ease and relative acceptance of separation, divorce and childbirth outside of marriage; the decline of religion and other traditional family-reinforcing

96

institutions, and welfare rules that discourage family unity and penalize economic initiative. Anecdotal explanations — the girl-mothers are said to want to love and receive affection from a baby; the boy-fathers reportedly brag about making babies — are also inadequate. Such anecdotes do not explain how the strong presumption in favor of marriage before childbearing has been overcome so often.

The emergence of single women as the primary guardians of the majority of black children is a pronounced departure that began to take shape following World War II. Ironically, the women and children — the most visible manifestations of the change — do not provide the key to the transformation. The breakdown begins with working-class black men, whose loss of function in the post-World War II economy has led directly to their loss of function in the family.

In the booming post-World War I economy, black men with few skills could find work. Even the white South, which denied the black man a place in its wage economy, could not deprive him of an economic role in the farm family. The poorest, most meanly treated sharecropper was at the center of the work it took to produce the annual crop.

As refugees from the South, the generation of World War I migrants differed in crucial respects from the World War II generation. The World War I arrivals were enthusiastic, voluntary migrants, poor in resources but frequently middle class in aspiration. They were at the bottom of a society that denied them the right to move up very far, but they got a foothold in a burgeoning economy.

Family stability was the rule. According to a 1925 study in New York City, five out of six children under the age of six lived with both parents. Nationally, a small middle class emerged, later augmented by the jobs generated by World War II, service in the armed forces and the postwar prosperity that sometimes filtered down to urban blacks.

Today's inner-city blacks were not a part of these historical processes. Some are the victims of the flight of manufacturing jobs. Others were part of the last wave of Southern migrants or their offspring, arriving in the 1950's and 1960's. They often migrated not because of new opportunities but because of the evaporation of old ones. Mechanized farming made their labor superfluous in agriculture, but unlike the blacks of earlier generations and European immigrants, later black migrants were also superfluous in the postwar cities as manufacturing work for the less-skilled and poorly educated declined. Today's postindustrial society, demanding sophisticated preparation and training, has only exacerbated these problems.

This permanent, generational joblessness is at the core of the meaning of the American ghetto. The resulting, powerful aberration transforms life in poor black communities and forces everything else to adapt to it. The female-headed household is only one consequence. The underground economy, the drug culture, epidemic crime and even a highly unusual disparity between the actual number of men and women — all owe their existence to the cumulative effect of chronic joblessness among men. Over time, deep structural changes have taken hold and created a different ethos.

An entire stratum of black men, many of them young, no longer performs its historic role in supporting a family. Many are unemployed because of the absence of jobs, or unemployable because their ghetto origins leave them unprepared for the job market. Others have adapted to the demands of the ghetto — the hustle, the crime, the drugs. But the skills necessary to survive in the streets are those least acceptable in the outside world.

The macho role cultivated in the ghetto makes it difficult for many black men, unable to earn a respectable living, to form households and assume the roles of husband and father. Generationally entrenched joblessness joined with the predatory underground economy form the bases of a marginal life style. Relationships without the commitments of husband and father result.

This qualitative change in fundamental family relationships could have occurred only under extreme and unrelentingly destructive conditions. Neither poverty nor cyclical unemployment alone could have had this impact. After all, poverty afflicts most of the world's people. If economic and social hardships could in themselves destroy family life, the family could not have survived as the basic human unit throughout the world.

The transformation in poor black communities goes beyond poverty. These deep changes are anchored in a pervasively middle-class society that associates manhood with money. Shocking figures show a long, steep and apparently permanent decline in black men's participation in the labor force, even at peak earning ages. In 1948, before the erosion of unskilled and semiskilled city and rural jobs had become pronounced, black male participation in the labor force was 87 percent, almost a full point higher than that of white males.

In the generation since 1960, however, black men have experienced a dramatic loss of jobs — dropping from an employment rate of 74 percent to 55 percent in 1982, according to the Center for the Study of Social Policy in Washington. While white male employment slipped in that period, much of the white decline, unlike that of the blacks, is attributed to early retirement. Since 1960, the black male population over the age of 18 has doubled, but the number employed has lagged badly.

These figures tell a story not only of structural unemployment, but of structural changes in low-income black families. The unemployment rates of young blacks have been the most devastating and militate against the establishment of stable marriages. This year, for instance, black teen-agers overall had an unemployment rate of 39 percent, two-and-a-half times that of white teen-agers. The loss of roles as workers has led to the acceptance of other roles for financial gain, many of them antisocial. Aside from the fact that large numbers of young men are imprisoned, disabled by drugs or otherwise marginal or unavailable as marriage partners, there is an unusual disparity between the sheer numbers of black men and black women. Among whites, the ratio of men to women does not change significantly until age 50, when men's shorter life expectancy creates a gap. But among blacks, beginning at age 20, women outnumber men significantly enough to have a major impact upon the possibility of marriage.

Some argue persuasively that the female-headed family is an adaptation that facilitates coping with hardship and demographics. This seems undeniable as an explanation, but unsatisfactory as a response. Are we willing to accept an adaptation that leaves the majority of black children under the age of 6 — the crucial foundation years of life — living in poverty? Given a real choice, poor blacks, like everybody else, would hardly choose coping mechanisms over jobs, educational opportunity and family stability.

YET, THE REMEDY for ghetto conditions is not as simple as providing necessities and opportunities. The ghetto is not simply a place. It has become a way of life. Just as it took a complex of social forces to produce ghetto conditions, it will take a range of remedies to dissolve them. The primary actors unavoidably are the Government and the black community itself.

The Government is deeply implicated in black family problems. Its laws enforced slavery before the Civil War and afterward created and sanctioned pervasive public and private discrimination. The effects on the black family continue to this day. Given the same opportunities as others, blacks would almost certainly have sustained the powerful family traditions they brought with them from Africa, where society itself is organized around family.

Quite apart from its historical role, the Government cannot avoid present responsibility. It can choose, as it now does, to ignore and delay the search for ways to break the hold of the ghetto, such as early intervention with young children and training and education for the hard-core poor. Although programs capable of penetrating ghetto conditions have proved elusive, the current Government posture of disengagement is folly. With the poor growing at a faster rate than the middle class, the prospect is that succeeding generations will yield more, not fewer, disadvantaged blacks. An American version of a *lumpenproletariat* (the so-called underclass), without work and without hope, existing at the margins of society, could bring down the great cities, sap resources and strength from the entire society and, lacking the usual means to survive, prey upon those who possess them.

Perhaps the greatest gap in corrective strategies has been the failure to focus on prevention. Remedies for deep-rooted problems — from teen-age pregnancy to functional illiteracy — are bound to fail when we leave the water running while we struggle to check the overflow. A primary incubator for ghetto problems is the poor, female-headed household. Stopping its proliferation would prevent a spectrum of often-intractable social and economic problems.

Remedies often focus at opposite ends — either on the provision of income or of services. Neither seems wholly applicable to entrenched ghetto conditions. Public assistance alone, leaving people in the same defeatist environment, may reinforce the status quo. The service orientation has been criticized for using a disproportionate amount of the available resources relative to the results obtained.

More appropriate solutions may lie between income and service strategies. Programs are likely to be more successful if they provide a rigorous progression through a series of steps leading to "graduation." This process, including a period of weaning from public assistance, might prove more succesful in achieving personal independence. Such programs would be far more disciplined than services to the poor generally have been. They would concentrate on changing life styles as well as imparting skills and education. The test of their effectiveness would be the recipients' progress in achieving economic self-sufficiency.

To reach boys and men, especially the hard-core unemployed, more work needs to be done to cull the successful aspects of training and job programs. Effective training models need to be systematically replicated. It is untenable to abandon the hard-core unemployed, as the Reagan Administration has done, by moving to a jobs program that focuses on the most, rather than the least, trainable. Ghetto males will not simply go away. As we now see, they will multiply themselves.

The welfare program — a brilliant New Deal invention now stretched to respond to a range of problems never envisioned for it — often deepens dependence and lowers self-esteem. Although welfare enjoys little support anywhere along the political spectrum, it continues for lack of an alternative.

Reconceived, a public-assistance program could reach single mothers and offer them vehicles to self-sufficiency. The counterparts of young women on welfare are working downtown or attending high school or junior college on grants to low-income students. Far from foreclosing such opportunities because a woman has a child, public assistance should be converted from the present model of passive maintenance to a program built around education or work and prospective graduation.

Studies of the hard-core unemployed have shown women on welfare to be the most desirous of, open to and successful with training and work. Some, especially with young children, will remain at home, but most want work or training because it is the only way out of the welfare life. Some promising experiments in work and welfare are underway in such cities as San Diego and Baltimore. But the old "workfare" approach, when administered as another form of welfare with no attempt to break the cycle of dependency, is self-defeating. Gainful employment, even if in public jobs for those unaccommodated by the private sector, would have beneficial effects beyond earning a living. Jobs and training would augment self-esteem by exposing women to the values and discipline associated with work, allowing them to pass on to their children more than their own disadvantages.

The ghetto, more than most circumscribed cultures, seeks to perpetuate itself and is ruthless in its demand for conformity. However, it contains institutions of the larger society—schools, churches, community groups. With minor additional resources, schools, for example, could incorporate more vigorous and focused ways to prevent teen-age pregnancy. If pregnancy occurs, girls could be motivated to remain in school, even after childbirth, thus allowing an existing institution to accomplish what training programs in later life do more expensively and with greater difficulty.

Schools and other community institutions also need to become much more aggressive with boys on the true meaning and responsibilities of manhood, and the link between manhood and family. Otherwise, many boys meet little resistance to the ghetto message that associates manhood with sex but not responsibility.

Most important, nothing can substitute for or have a greater impact than the full-scale involvement of the black community. Respect for the black family tradition compels black initiative. Today, blacks are responding. Many black organizations are already involved, including the National Urban League, the National Association for the Advancement of Colored People, the National Council of Negro Women and the National Urban Coalition. In 1983, the country's major black leaders endorsed a frank statement of the problems of the black family and a call for solutions. The statement, published by the Joint Center for Political Studies, a black research center in Washington, represented the first consensus view by black leadership on the problems of the black family. Significantly, it went beyond a call for Government help, stressing the need for black leadership and community efforts.

With the increase in the number of black public officials, many black mayors, legislators and appointed officials control some of the resources that could help shape change. Although they cannot redesign the welfare system by themselves, for example, some are in a position to experiment with model projects that could lead to more workable programs—such as supplementing welfare grants with training or work opportunities for single mothers; promoting family responsibility and pregnancy prevention for boys and girls through local institutions, and encouraging the completion of school for single teen-aged parents.

The new black middle class, a product of the same period that saw the weakening of the black family, still has roots in the ghetto through relatives and friends. From churches, Girl Scout troops and settlement houses to civil-rights organizations, Boys' Clubs and athletic teams, the work of family reinforcement can be shared widely. The possibilities for creative community intervention are many—from family planning and counseling and various roles as surrogate parents and grandparents, to sex education, community day care and simple, but crucial, consciousness-raising. Most important is passing on the enduring values that form the central content of the black American heritage: hard work, education, respect for family, and, notwithstanding the denial of personal opportunity, achieving a better life for one's children.

Jonestown as a Perverse Utopia

Rose Laub Coser and Lewis Coser

For 20 days, until December 8, the Jonestown horror story made first-page news in the *New York Times*. In the course of five hours, 911 adults and children were killed or killed themselves. There had been no threat on their lives from the outside, nor was there any strong transcendental cause that leader or followers meant to serve. The leader had claimed he wanted "socialism" and "Marxism," and had mixed his missionary zeal with religion because he allegedly believed the followers "needed it." So for years he gave them "opium for the people," and in the end cyanide.

The questions that are usually being asked are: What kind of people were those commune members? Were they without roots? Were they the rejects of society—the drug addicts, the convicts, the prostitutes, those not embedded in the social fabric of their society? And who was the leader? What manner of man commanded such obedience? How did he grow up in the small town where he was born? Had he given signs of such wickedness earlier in his life?

It turned out that the followers were of all kinds. There were the poor, the rich, and those of the middle. There were convicts and there were lawyers; there were the elderly and young prostitutes; there were physicians and nurses, blacks and whites. There were those with weak moral beliefs, and those with a strong social conscience. The answers about the characteristics of the members are not satisfactory. At best they tell us who was attracted to Jim Jones, but they cannot tell us why they obeyed him unto death.

Nor do the characteristics of the leader tell us much. It is interesting to hear that as a child he killed animals, and said mass after their death; and that his mother had predicted her son would be a messiah. But surely, the Jekyll-Hyde personality is a frequent figure, and many people have fantasies of omnipotence. Some even become murderers, and occasionally there is one who manages to kill as many as a dozen people. But they do not kill, or are not capable of killing, almost a thousand people in one sweep. This is hard work. While psychological predispositions in the leader and his followers explain some of their mutual attraction, they cannot fully explain this horrible success story.

Let us turn from personal to structural characteristics. Perverse as it was, Jonestown was a species of the genus, *utopian commune*. Ever since the industrial revolution and earlier—already in antiquity—usually at times of widespread discontent with the quality of life, blueprints for a more satisfying social organization were drawn up, from *The Republic* to *Utopia* (which coined the generic name) to *Looking Backward*. These utopias transcended the here-and-now, served as guidelines for social criticism and as foci for human strivings. Yet, as Lewis Coser and Henry Jacoby wrote years ago, "We are appalled to discover that many of the rationalistic fantasies of the world improvers contain a large admixture of what we now recognize as totalitarianism" (*Common Cause*, February 1951).

Not only blueprints but actual experiments in utopian living attracted over the years the socially committed and the morally courageous, the physically and psychologically deprived, and those yearning for a new morality. Yet, in most communes morals and social relations tended to become regulated from above; personal and public allegiances were monopolized by a central authority; and what had started out as an experiment in liberation usually ended in an experiment in the total absorption of personality. Communes have an innate tendency to become, as one of the authors wrote, *greedy institutions*.

Communes did not usually end in the destruction of their members, and some of those inspired by vigorous religious beliefs even managed to survive for several

 "Jonestown as a Perverse Utopia," Rose Laub Coser and Lewis Coser, *Dissent,* Spring 1979, pp. 158-163. Reprinted by permission.

generations. But most ended in splits, fights between factions, acrid disputes, mutual recriminations, and sordid intrigues between rival leaders. Their isolation from other social institutions, their inward orientation, the absorption of the members' total personality often led to a disintegration of the commune, even as it deprived members of the ability to sustain personal relations both within and without.

Jonestown was a community isolated by design. In a sense, if not literally, it was an incestuous community. To survive for even the short period it did, it operated in secrecy, erected strong barriers around itself. Rank-and-file members had to break all ties with the outside. This prevented interference from nonbelievers, but mainly it prevented reality testing. Any personal or social values members brought with them from their previous lives were destroyed. Finally, any personal relations, whether sexual or otherwise affective, were broken up. This assured the absence of interpersonal allegiances. It also assured complete dependency, similar to the dependency of a newborn child, on one person, and one person only.

The Isolated Society: "We Had Nowhere to Go."

Anthropologists and sociologists are generally agreed on the proposition that society is possible because libidinal energies and affective orientations, within or between generations, are directed outward, so that self-sufficiency is prevented. This is the basis for the incest taboo. A certain amount of what Philip Slater has called "libidinal diffusion" (*American Sociological Review*, 1963) is necessary for social survival, since it facilitates exchange among various units of a society. Groups that monopolize affective energies within themselves tend to be subject to inner decay and to have low survival value. Jonestown is a case in point. Isolated from any but the minimum contact with the outside world, Jonestown's members had no place to go: no place to go to test reality, no place to go with libidinal cathexis except to one man, no place to go to obtain or receive support except from him.

Jonestown seems to have been incestuous in more than the figurative sense. The leader, who was called "Dad," had sexual relations with the commune's members, that is, his "children," men or women, sometimes as many as 16 a day, as he bragged to Charles Gary. He explained that he did this "to assure their loyalty to him." By working to monopolize the affect of the community's members, and making them withdraw their libidinal energy not only from outside relationships but inside as well, Jones completed his efforts at reducing his followers to a narcissistic stage of infantile dependency that Bruno Bettelheim had shown to develop among inmates of concentration camps.

There was hardly any contact with the outside on the part of rank-and-file members. Nobody could leave the premises except some trusted aides who could go as far as the Georgetown headquarters, where control of movement was as tight as it could possibly be. Ron Javers describes the physical isolation from the plane that took him to Port Kaituma—a six-mile jeep ride from Jonestown:

> At some points the trees were so thick we couldn't see the ground. . . . Elsewhere there were large stretches of flat, deep, red mud. There were no roads. It was startling to realize how isolated people could be only 150 miles from the capital. There was no way to get to Jonestown except by air or by a long boat trip along the Atlantic coast and up the Kaituma River.*

The isolation of the site was a criterion for selection when Jones first conceived of the settlement. From its early days, the People's Temple tried to erect boundaries or break relations with the rest of society (even as Jones tried to influence, cajole, or threaten politicians and the press). Several times he had picked up and moved when outside intrusions became threatening. Around 1965 in Redwood City, it became known that there were guards around the Temple church and dogs along the fences.

There was isolation from the media as well. Jones controlled the news and the members' access to it. When *New West* magazine was to appear with disclosures about the doings at the Temple, and he departed for Guayana, he instructed his aides to buy out the magazine from newsstands in Oakland, San Francisco, and Los Angeles, where a copy might fall into the hands of Temple members or their relatives. He also instructed his aides to forbid followers to read newspapers or watch television. Later, in Jonestown, members were asked to listen to news broadcasts selectively, and had to write out their reactions and send them to "Dad."

Without newspapers and with only occasional news that had to be "understood" in a prescribed manner, surrounded by the jungle—how would it ever be possible for any rank-and-file member to test reality? How could anyone have looked for evidence of the alleged fact that mercenaries were waiting in the woods to invade the settlement and torture its members? There was no place to go with one's cognitive assessments if not into the jungle—even if, as is doubtful, the need for such assessment were perceived by the members who anyhow "knew" that they must depend on "Dad."

Isolation could not be maintained without secrecy. In the mid-'60s in Redwood Valley, the Temple members' children were said to lie, and to be evasive at school about what they did at the Temple. Isolation and secrecy, if they are to be organizational requirements,

---

*Marshall Kilduff and Ron Javers, *Suicide Cult* New York: Bantam Books, 1978). All subsequent quotes and factual material not otherwise identified are from this book.

must be enjoined upon and upheld by all individual members. Temple members often had to forgo bidding their relatives good-bye when they left for Guayana. Often departing members were called in the morning and told they would leave for Guayana the same night. People would call their children to tell them they would be leaving on a trip immediately, and refuse to say where they were going or how long they would be gone. Relatives of those who had gone to Jonestown without leaving word were met with silence when they made inquiries at the San Francisco Temple.

While isolation and secrecy were organizational requirements for Jones's designs, they served social and psychological purposes as well. Group members who break up all relationships on the outside will be dependent on staying with that group. Not only will it be difficult for them to return home if they so desire, but their whole cognitive and affective orientation will be inward-directed so that the outside world fades from view—much as in cases of confinement to concentration camps, long-term imprisonment or hospitalization, even though in these cases the inmates do not join voluntarily.

Temple members who made the trip signed away to the church, as many before them had done, their cars, homes, and other possessions. When they arrived at Jonestown, whatever money they had left was confiscated together with their passports. Already in San Francisco church members had been talked into cashing their life-insurance policies and turning the money over to the Temple, or into signing over power-of-attorney. Way back in Indiana couples had been persuaded to sell their houses and turn the money over to the church. The well-to-do had to give up their means of survival on the outside. The poor had to contribute an ever larger percentage of meager earnings.

All this money made the People's Temple a viable operation. But it served other purposes as well: it deprived members of all means of independence. Jones wanted the money not only for selfish or organizational purposes: it became a problem merely to dispose of the wealth that piled up. "Jim was giving the stuff away just to get rid of it," one former member said. People who were deprived of their money would have no options but to stay with the Temple. "The Temple ended up with everything I had," said Jeannie Mills. "That's what made it so hard to leave. *We had nowhere to go* and nothing to fall back on."

Having no place to go, and having invested all their emotional life in the Temple, the stage was set for binding people to the Total Institution that was to be Jonestown. To assure its survival, however, two more things had to be accomplished: the remaking of personal values, and the prevention of solidarity within the settlement. These, paradoxically, led to its destruction.

The Invertebrate: "I Know I'm Like a Banana."

Having no place to go was not enough. Not *wanting* to

go would be better. And so we read in one of those required letters of confession: "I'm an elitist and anarchist. . . . I've come a little way. . . . Here I don't have any intention of becoming a traitor or going back to the United States" (Avis G., quoted in the *New York Times,* November 29).

People's behavior as well as their personal attitudes and moral values had to come under the scrutiny of all. Individuals had to submit to physical and mental humiliations and more: they had to humiliate themselves. Former Temple members report that men and women would be forced to strip off their clothes at the public meetings and say they were homosexuals or lesbians.

Already in San Francisco Jones spent much of his time presiding over such "catharsis" sessions, which were grueling, drawn-out spells of emotional dissection by the followers:

Why did she wear such new clothes when there were millions of people starving? Wasn't it true that he wanted to make love to another man's wife? Admit it! How could anyone complain about working until dawn after getting off work when Father is in such pain for us all.

Beatings, torture, mutual accusations and confessions—techniques that had started way back in San Francisco—remind us of the social-psychological processes in the concentration camps as described by Bruno Bettelheim. At Jonestown, those who, like Bettelheim's camp inmates,

did not develop a childlike dependency were accused of threatening the security of the group. . . . The regression into childlike behavior was inescapable. . . . [They] lived, like children, only in the immediate present; they lost their feeling for the sequence of time; they became unable to plan for the future. . . . They were unable to establish durable object relations. Friendships developed as quickly as they broke off. [*Journal of Abnormal and Social Psychology,* 1943.]

For the acceptance of the new life, everything that had to do with the personal life of the past or of the present—relatives, friends, social, personal, and intimate values—had to be defiled. "When your name was called, people would scream, 'Get down there,' and swear. It was hostile," said a former member. "Everyone related to you was required to run up and accuse you." Any loyalties, any solidarity, any relatedness between the members of the Temple had to be broken up, and mutual accusations, hostilities, and mandatory denunciations were used to bring this about. Nobody could trust anybody. Not being permitted to establish relationships with one another, they soon became incapable of doing so, like Don F., who wrote in one of his mandatory letters of confession: "Now I know I'm like a banana, just one of the bunch. I have come a long way" (*New York Times,* November 29).

"Sex Was One of Jim's Specialties for Pulling People Apart."

Children were removed from their parents, spouses separated, matches made and broken up. Family ties within the church were always kept under Jones's direct control. Jones knew that the most effective way to control personal relationships is to control libidinal attractions. When he bragged to his lawyer, Charles Gary, about having sex with 14 women and 2 men in that one day, he explained that this was to assure their loyalty to him.

Jones ordered marriages ended and rearranged. Many of his marathon six-hour sermons dwelled on sex, including directions to members to swear off relations. Already in the church he had established a kind of spy group that regulated everything including hand holding, forced divorces and shotgun marriages. A high school boy seen talking to a girl who did not belong to the Temple would be called before the assembly to talk at length about his sex life.

"Sex was one of Jim's specialties for pulling people apart," said a former member. For married couples, Jones would often have another form of advice: abstention. Couples were forced apart and told not to engage in sexual intercourse because it was evil.

Lewis Coser has argued elsewhere that such manifestly opposite sexual patterns as abstinence and sexual promiscuity serve the same purposes (*Greedy Institutions,* Free Press, 1974). Both promiscuity and celibacy help prevent stable dyadic bonds, for such bonds detract from emotional attachment to the community and its leaders. Whether members refrain from all sexual relations, as did the Shakers, or whether there is a controlled form of promiscuity, as in Oneida, is sociologically unimportant. What these communities share is a deliberate attempt to prevent dyadic personal relationships so that emotional energies will be purposely channeled. A similar pattern prevails in other totalistic communes today, for example, at Synanon. A recent *New York Times* report (December 10, 1978) describes the policies introduced by its leader, Mr. Dederich. They include forced vasectomies for male members, mandatory abortions for women, and orders from Mr. Dederich for more than 230 married couples to divorce and switch to other partners within the group.

"I'm Dead Inside"

The problem, it seems to us, is that emotional energies cannot simply be "channeled" for the common or not so common good. Arbitrary and unpredictable interference with them leads to their being damaged at best and destroyed at worst. The latter happened in Jonestown. When people are cut off from emotional bonds with their fellows they have no psychic energies left that can be mobilized even in situations of extreme peril. How many were there among the hundreds of adults in line for cyanide who asked themselves like Odell Rhodes, "How can I get out of here?" as he later reported? Could he not at least have made eye contact with someone who had similar feelings? It seems that at the high point of the ceremony of self-immolation everyone was but an atom unto itself, unable to relate even in imagination to others who might share some doubts. They must all have felt, as Odell Rhodes later stated about himself, "dead inside" (*New York Times,* November 29).

Jonestown was more "greedy" an institution than has probably ever existed. It successfully "devoured" its members by making total claims on them and by encompassing their whole personality. By claiming, and receiving, undivided loyalty, and by reducing the claims of competing roles and allegiances, it succeeded not merely in totally absorbing members within its boundaries but in reducing them to human pulp as well. Not only did it erect insurmountable boundaries between the inside and the outside, between the "reborn" collective present of the members and their "disreputable" private past; it also succeeded in maiming them by breaking up any mutual attachments, sexual or otherwise. The stable relationship, *voilà l'ennemi.*

Even as we recoil in horror at the unfolding of the Jonestown story it behooves us not to look at it in isolation. It did, after all, unfold at this time and in this place. While it would be fatuous to blame what happened on "American society," we must keep in mind that the damned and the lost and the hopeful who flocked to Jones and the People's Temple did so because the society in which they lived had failed to provide satisfactory bonds, meaningful community, and fraternal solidarities. To Jones's followers, the society felt like a desert devoid of love; so they turned to the People's Temple, which they saw as an oasis. Although their quest turned out to be a delusion, we cannot deny that their need was acute.

Cities Won't Drive You Crazy

NOT IF YOU LEARN THE TRICK: MAKE STRESS A STIMULUS RATHER THAN A THREAT.

C. R. CREEKMORE

C. R. Creekmore is a freelance writer who lives in Amherst, Massachusetts.

Trapped in one of those Olympian traffic jams on the Garden State Parkway in New Jersey, I waited to pay my toll for the Newark exit. Horns, insults and exhaust fumes had settled in a noisy, dark-tempered cloud. As I finally reached the end of the exact-change line, I faced a sudden dilemma. There was the automatic toll collector, side-by-side with a human toll taker standing in his little booth. I stared into the impersonal mouth of the collection machine, then at the person, and chose him. The man looked shocked. He regarded the quarter I thrust at him as if it were a bug. "Grow up!" he screamed at me with a sense of indignation that I assumed was generated by a life dedicated to the parkway system. "Grow up and use the machine!"

To me, the incident has always summed up the essence of what cities are: hotbeds of small embarrassments, dehumanizing confrontations, monetary setbacks, angry people and festering acts of God.

Many Americans agree with this stereotype and believe firmly that the dirty, crowded, dangerous city must gradually destroy an urbanite's psyche. This belief has a corollary: Rural life, haven of natural purity, wholesome values and the spirit of self-reliance, is the wellspring of physical and mental health.

A large body of research, conducted in the past 15 years by a diverse group of social scientists, challenges these heartfelt prejudices. These studies conclude that metropolitan living is more than OK. In many ways, researchers have found, city pavements outshine the sticks as healthy places to live and work.

Jonathan Freedman, chairperson of the psychology department at the University of Toronto, is an authority on how cities affect those who live in them. On the physical side, he believes that life expectancy is higher for people in urban areas and infant mortality rates are lower. The potentially unhealthy aspects of city life, such as pollution, stress and crime, are more than offset by better medical care, better water supplies and sewage systems and better systems for handling emergencies of all kinds.

What about mental illness? Surely the fabled rat race must eventually sap mental endurance and lead to breakdowns. Not according to mental-

IN MANY WAYS, CITY PAVEMENTS OUTSHINE THE STICKS AS HEALTHY PLACES FOR PEOPLE TO LIVE AND WORK.

health statistics. In a now classic study of the subject, *Mental Health in the Metropolis: The Midtown Manhattan Study*, sociologist Leo Srole and five colleagues compared mental-health statistics in Manhattan with those in small towns. They concluded that small towns have a slightly higher rate of mental illness.

This doesn't mean that cities are easy to live in. Manhattan psychiatrist Herbert E. Walker and C. Ray Smith, a writer on urban planning, point out in an article that certain environmental stress comes with the urban territory: automobile traffic, air pollution, high noise levels, lack of privacy and such architectural faults as poor lighting, tight spaces and inadequate seating.

With all this to contend with, why don't cities drive more people around the bend? One answer is that we learn to cope with the multiple problems. "It's not a bad environment, just a very complex one," says Gerda McCahan, chairperson of the department of psychology at Furman University in Atlanta, who once worked as a clinical psychologist in New York City. "An effect of living in the big city is that with time people learn to insulate themselves in a psychological sense. They learn not to allow a lot of stimuli to impinge on their consciousness. They sift out things that do not concern them."

Another answer is that mental illness goes deeper than environmental stress. "Severe mental illness is not caused by the kinds of environmental stimuli char-

 From *Psychology Today*, January 1985, pp. 46-50, 52-53.

UNPLEASANT CITY STIMULI MIGHT AFFECT YOUR MOOD TEMPORARILY, BUT THEY ARE UNLIKELY TO CAUSE REAL MENTAL ILLNESS.

acteristic of a city—loud noises, noxious odors, density of population and high levels of activity, for instance," Freedman explains. "Rather, it is caused by complex human and social problems such as genetic defects, interpersonal relationships and the stresses of dealing with one's needs. And these problems are carried wherever you go. City stimuli might affect your mood temporarily, but they are unlikely to cause real mental illness."

Crowding is perhaps the most studied problem of city living. As urbanites do battle with blitzing cabdrivers, crammed subway cars, the frustrations of traffic and deadly competition for parking spaces, they have one big thing going for them. As McCahan suggests, their saving grace is superior adaptability.

Take some of the ways city folk deal with common crowding situations. They live on many levels, so the entire population is not constantly milling together on the ground. They have complex social rules (walk on the right; stop at red lights; wait in line for services) for pedestrian traffic. Cities now install bicycle, horse and foot paths that connect parks and open space and make movement safer and more pleasant. Freeways are built to travel to and from downtown faster. And planners use a variety of methods (rotaries, coordinated traffic lights, one-way roads) to improve traffic flow in the most crowded areas.

Other improvements are on the way. "One feature now becoming standard on urban expressways is noise barriers," says Dorn McGrath Jr., a professor of urban and regional planning at George Washington University. "That's because research carried on over the last 15 years has determined that highway noise is not only annoying to nearby residents, but can be psychologically and physiologically harmful."

This type of human adaptability is one reason Freedman is skeptical about the relevance of experiments that test the effect of crowding on rats and other animals—research that typically shows heightened levels of aggression, competitiveness, infant neglect and early death. Freedman feels that these findings can't be usefully applied to human crowding conditions. "Humans are much more adaptable creatures than other animals," he explains. Additionally, "the level of density you are talking about with laboratory animals is extraordinary, a level that would never appear in the real world."

Other researchers are less certain about the harmlessness of crowding to humans. For example, psychologists Janice Zeedyk-Ryan and Gene F. Smith report that crowding took its toll when 16 undergraduates volunteered to stay in a 12-foot-by-18-foot civil-defense shelter for 18 hours. Compared to a group of six students who occupied the same shelter in a second test, the densely packed students became markedly more hostile and anxious as the hours passed.

In another experiment, psychologists Yakov M. Epstein, Robert L. Woolfolk and Paul M. Lehrer created an environment that approximated the close conditions found in rush-hour mass-transit systems. They then compared the students' reactions under these conditions to what happened when they were put with the same number of strangers in a normal-sized room. The researchers found that the crowded students had higher blood pressure, reported that they felt unfriendlier and less in control and were rated by the strangers (who were actually working with the experimenters as observers) as tenser and more uncomfortable and annoyed than the uncrowded students.

Studies such as these suggest that crowding cramps the style of city dwellers and produces stress. Freedman has another interpretation. "Density intensifies people's reactions to events around them," he explains. "If you get people who are feeling aggressive for other reasons—who have been angered at home or work, for instance—and you put them under high-density conditions, they are likely to be more aggressive. On the other hand, if the same people are feeling good and cooperative, density will also intensify that."

Freedman uses loud music as an analogy. If people like the music being played, turning it up usually enhances the experience. If they don't, increased volume makes the experience even more unpleasant.

Thus, when crowding occurs in situations normally considered negative, such as commuting to work or waiting in line for service in a bank or store, it intensifies those negative feelings. But place the same crowds in an amusement park, at a cocktail party or in a basketball arena, and crowding enhances the fun.

One recent study indicates that under the right conditions, population density can actually improve relations in a neighborhood. Sociologists Lois M. Verbrugge and Ralph B. Taylor explained how this worked in a study they did in Baltimore. As population density increases, some environmental resources diminish and people start to compete for limited space, ease of movement, services and other resources.

The ultimate result of this competition, however, is that people adapt. They add services, make adjustments in how they live and increase social interaction to make up for scarce resources. Think of the Guardian Angels, patrolling neighborhoods to augment police services. Or consider those neighborhood characters who direct people to vacant parking spaces and act as traffic cops for alternate-side-of-the-street parking changes. In

UNDER THE RIGHT CONDITIONS, POPULATION DENSITY CAN ACTUALLY IMPROVE RELATIONS IN A NEIGHBORHOOD.

adaptive ways of this kind, neighbors get together.

"Local social resources actually increase," Verbrugge and Taylor point out. "High density provides opportunities for informal contact and assistance because people are more accessible. . . . It is very possible that increasing density enhances social ties."

Crowding aside, it seems obvious that other stimuli peculiar to cities can

CROWDING INTENSIFIES PEOPLE'S REACTIONS— BOTH GOOD AND BAD— TO EVENTS HAPPENING AROUND THEM.

be harmful to many people. In their article on urban stress, Walker and Smith list anxiety, depression, back pain, ulcers and heart attacks as diseases that can be traced to the high level of environmental stress in the city. "But for those people equipped to handle it," McCahan argues, "the city is the absolute optimum habitat." And, she adds, people can find their share of stress in the country as well. The boredom, lack of variety and low level of stimulation can be just as stressful as city living for those not accustomed to it.

Cities can also provide ties that help inhabitants handle stress better than their country cousins do. Home economist David Imig of the University of Missouri investigated the impact of life stress on 37 rural and 64 urban families with similar economic and educational backgrounds. He discovered that when the families suffered unemployment, money problems, relocation, illness and divorce, the city people suffered considerably less disruption in family relationships than did the rural families.

The difference seems to lie in the support systems that influence people's perception of stress. Urban families, Imig says, usually have closer

Telegraph Hill in San Francisco: a strong sense of neighborhood identity.

CARL MYDANS/BLACK STAR

connections to their social environment. They operate within a wide-ranging network of secondary relationships that may not involve close kinship or friendship, but which do offer informal support and exchange of services. You take my kid to dance class; I take yours to the ball game.

By contrast, rural families usually limit their support networks to a few close primary ties. This means that urban families have more outlets to diffuse stress. "Rural families don't have the large support system that urban families do," Imig believes. "They don't have anyone to turn to, to fall back on, when stress concentrates on their few close ties."

Another popular urban myth was depicted humorously in the movie *Terms of Endearment.* In one scene,

an Iowa banker chastises a rude and insensitive cashier by noting, "You must be from New York."

Many studies contradict this stereotype of the cold, impersonal city. We have already seen that dense population can improve social ties, and that the city support network often works better than that in the country. In a study reported in *Psychology Today* (April 1981), environmental psychologist Karen Franck and two colleagues at the City University of New York found that although good friends come slowly in the city, friendships there eventually seem to become more intimate and more highly valued than those in nonurban settings. City friendships also tend to be more varied, broadening people's perspectives and opportunities.

*I*N THE CITY, A NETWORK OF SECONDARY RELATIONSHIPS OFFERS INFORMAL SUPPORT AND EXCHANGE OF SERVICES. YOU TAKE MY KID TO DANCE CLASS; I TAKE YOURS TO THE BALL GAME.

"You have access to people at your own level in intellectual pursuits, sports, artistic interests—any area that you select," McCahan explains. "And you can seek out people at or above your own level who stimulate your growth."

Another measure of an area's elusive sense of warmth and personality is whether its inhabitants help one another in times of need. Do people help less in cities than in the country? The jury is still out on that one.

"A majority of studies find more help in rural areas," says Erwin Staub, a professor of psychology at the University of Massachusetts who has studied helping behavior extensively. "But some find no difference. And a minority even find more help in urban areas.

"The more confusing a situation, the more complex the stimuli, the more people's attention tends to be distracted," Staub says. "So the complexity of a city situation might distract people from helping." But, he points out, some areas also feature helping networks that can spur onlookers to come to the aid of victims.

People living in an urban neighborhood with a strong sense of identity— a Little Italy, a Chinatown or a rehabilitated neighborhood, for example— see emergency situations as their responsibility. After all, it's their turf. Cities also have concentrations of people with special helping skills such as CPR expertise, civil-defense training or medical backgrounds, and these people help in emergencies because they are conditioned to do so.

One of the most important mechanisms for triggering a person's helping response, Staub proposes, is a "prosocial orientation," previous experience being helpful. Since cities are the regional centers for charitable causes, social campaigns and reform efforts, many people learn to be helpers.

Thus, the whole process of solving city problems is part of a healthy cycle of activity. "If you want to look for problems that need addressing," says urban planner McGrath, "cities are the places where they tend to accumulate." Among the problems that he lists are "the awesome fabric of despair and difficulty" that covers our ghettos; bad traffic flow with its accompanying pollution and psychological frustration; noise; pollution of the environment; and frightening rises in already frightening urban crime rates.

"As one consequence, there are people drawn to deal with these problems. The whole process acts to revitalize a city," McGrath continues. "And the very problems that accumulate also serve to get meaning and satisfaction into the lives of the people who live there by giving them causes."

McGrath's viewpoint is another indication that the key to living in a city is adaptability. Stress is in the eye and mind of the beholder. An urbanite must be able to take apparently unpleasant stimuli and use them to his or her advantage.

Can people learn this psychological backflip? Yes, according to Walker and Smith, who tell in their article how to manipulate city stress. "Urban stress should be seen as a stimulus," they say. And to relieve pressure, they advise exercising regularly in enjoyable, varied places, attending a wide range of entertainments, living in a pleasant, well-lighted space, being assertive when a situation demands it and adopting a positive attitude about the city and its complexity.

"To flourish in the city, you must have a good sense of self-esteem and be able to tolerate competition," McCahan adds. "You must be able to pit yourself against the best and, win or lose, learn something positive about yourself. And you must be relatively assertive. If you are a shy person, the city can eat you up."

The city can also do you in if you are saddled with competitive handicaps; if you are financially, socially, physically or mentally restricted from competing. But for those geared to compete, city life can be a horn of plenty. "I always think of living in the city as a potential growth center for human beings," McCahan says. "One reason is that cities attract the best of everything."

There are good jobs. The city offers the opportunity, according to McCahan, of "seeking your own milieu" and level of competence, whatever your calling. You can see good plays and artsy movies. Professional and collegiate sports abound. You can go to street fairs and ethnic festivals in the park. Take your pick of music, art galleries and cultural exhibits. Or you can spend your days wandering among various periods of architecture, testing Lewis Mumford's observation that "In the city, time becomes visible."

And, of course, you can always take advantage of a city's most notable amenity—going out for Chinese food at 3 a.m.

All of this activity is what makes a city go: a great, roiling, collective energy. "It is as if, far down in the rocky bowels ... some vast, secret turbine were generating an extra source of power, capable of being shared by all the inhabitants of the city," wrote author Brendan Gill about New York's psychic energy. "It is a power that gives them the means of meeting the city on its own fierce terms of constant stress. And it is profoundly the case that your true (urbanite) rejoices in stress; the crowds, the dirt, the stench, the noise. Instead of depressing him, they urge him onto an unexpected 'high,' a state of euphoria in which the loftiest of ambitions seems readily attainable."

Work: The Right to Right Livelihood

Theodore Roszak

. . . In my family, with its almost proverbial American immigrant background, nobody ever entertained the notion that there might be cultural styles of work, that our livelihood, like the food we eat, should be a material we shape and flavor to our taste. Nobody could have afforded to see things that way. My grandparents arrived from Eastern Europe with one fixed star in their universe: their willingness to work, without raising questions, without making trouble. Work was their one chance to prove themselves and to make good as Americans. They stepped off the boat straight into the mines and shops and factories of Wilkes Barre, West Wheeling, Akron, Chicago, grateful and glad for any employment they could find.

Eventually, by dint of steady toil and fanatical thrift, they raised themselves into the lower margins of that sprawling social conurbation called the American middle class. From first to last, work was the center and substance of their lives; it was their validation as useful citizens. Even more, the work ethic, as they honored it in their every waking moment, was the bedrock of their security and their self-respect. When all else failed or collapsed—as it did for them in the Great Depression—or whenever injustice or discrimination touched them, they could always fall back upon their willingness to work unstintingly and at anything until they dropped.

Yet it was a strange, contradictory pride they took in their work. I remember vividly how my father would rehearse the family litany whenever he had been bruised by insult or injustice. "I had to sweat for every nickel I ever earned . . . I never got something for nothing . . . nobody in this family ever asked for any handouts. . . ." It was pride mixed darkly with bitterness, because, for all he might say for himself as a hard worker, my father, like his father before him, never took satisfaction in the work he was hired to do. He loathed and cursed all his jobs. He was a gifted cabinetmaker, but—with the exception of a few failed business efforts of his own—he spent his entire working life as an underpaid carpenter, with never a good word for any job he held. He despised his bosses and the work they assigned him, which always had to be done on the quick and cheap, making no use of his best skills. Worst of all, he came to despise himself as one of the hundred million American nobodies who were stuck on the bottom rungs of the social ladder with no way up.

"Working poor" is the quaint social category we now have for families like mine, the sort of people who only get a little ahead of their debts by putting in ten or twenty hours a week of overtime. "OT" was like manna from heaven in our household; my father would announce its arrival like a portent of better days. But then he wound up working harder than ever, and it always showed. He would drag home dog-tired and short-tempered at night, leave bleary-eyed and unshaven the next morning, grumble as he ate warmed-over meals at how much less he was bringing home in his pay check than he deserved. And there was always the lament: The work wasn't worthy of him. It was slapdash and stupid and shoddy, none of it done with care or craftsmanship.

Hard work killed my father young—at forty-six. He died of heart failure and (I believe) of demoralization, with not enough money in the bank for a good funeral. My mother had to use up his life insurance to bury him.

My father was pugnaciously proud of being "hard-working." But his constant advice to me was, "Never work with your hands. Go to college. Become a professional man. If you work with your hands, you're not worth shit in this world." His pride, like that of all the working poor I have ever met, was the best face he could put upon his sense of helpless victimization. He had every right to the self-respect he claimed; he was the possessor of a noble and useful skill. He was a builder, a man who could make houses and fine furniture. He knew the true use of his tools. I have worked with executive paper shufflers and "decision makers" who will not contribute anything to the world as valuable as a single good table or chair my father made. In another age he would have been highly honored for his craft. But his pride could no longer be based on that, because he knew he was somebody's misused employee, the hireling of people who valued him only as a means to a fast dollar. So his self-esteem was infected with anger and envy; when he boasted of being "hard-working," he was making a slender virtue of a hated necessity. At last, his pride was an expression of belligerent and powerless resentment.

Whenever I hear politicians and labor leaders talk about "putting people to work," I wonder if they realize, as I suspect a great many working people do, what a pathetically minimal ideal that has become. What does "full employment" mean to men like my father whose daily work is an insult and a torment? Is it enough any longer for the economic index to measure how many people have jobs, without asking whether they take pride in the jobs they have? I wonder, when do we begin talking about the quality of employment, as well as its quantity? Another way of asking, when do we stop treating people like statistics and start treating them like persons?

There is one more thing I remember about my father's work life—something that always puzzled me in my youth. Every year my father got two meager weeks of paid vacation. When it came around, he swore he was going to lie out in the back yard and rot. And he would do just that . . . for perhaps the first two or three days he was off work. He would sit under a tree with some beer and a radio and do very nearly nothing. But soon enough, he would be banging away in some part of the house, remodeling a room; or he would be out in the garage, building a piece of furniture; or he would be clambering about under the floor boards, repairing the foundation. He would finish those long hours of work as tired and grimy as he ever came home from his job. But now he wasn't morose, he didn't complain. He would be talking about how well the job was going, or making sketches and puzzling out better ways to design the project.

One summer he used up his entire vacation working ten and twelve hours a day to help an incompetent neighbor put up a new porch. He finally took over the job, redesigned the porch, and pretty well did it all himself. All he got in payment was a bottle of whiskey. When my mother asked him why he was going to the trouble, he answered, "Because I can't sit out there and watch him do a half-assed job. It drives me nuts."

The True Dimensions of Alienation

If there was ever an example of alienation in the classic Marxist sense of the word, my father was it. He was the quintessential proletarian: totally vulnerable both economically and psychologically. He never even found his way into an effective labor union to defend his interests. He was a man with nothing to sell for his livelihood but his labor; and at last even that was not enough. He had to surrender his self-respect as well. In that act of resignation, there is more than personal pathos. A noble tradition of craftsmanship is poisoned to death by such self-contempt, and the meaning of honest work is hideously distorted for all of us.

Yet, over the years, I have come to see, in large part through my own work experience at a variety of jobs, unskilled, white collar, and professional, that the problem of dehumanized labor barely begins with my father's example. His experience is really only the base line from which the further reaches of alienation may be measured. From the personalist viewpoint we adopt here, the hard core of the problem is not to be found among those who are, like my father, miserable and embittered, but among those who are exploited and acquiescent, alienated and yet complacent. It is only when we begin to appreciate how effectively people can be persuaded to will their own alienation from the work they do that we grasp the true dimensions of the problem.

One need not reach beyond a conventional left-wing analysis to recognize that a worker whose discontent is softened by a pay raise and shorter hours is still an exploited worker. Similarly, if working conditions are redesigned to make life on the job more relaxed and diverting (for example, the office is air-conditioned and carpeted, music is piped in, the day is strategically punctuated with coffee breaks in the handsome company lounge), we may still see this as alienated employment, even if those who work in this mellowed environment are unexceptionally cheerful. How so? Because their work still does not belong to them; it is still not an act of their own choosing done to their own standard. Instead, they remain dependent on the favor of employers and bosses; they are still powerless to determine the use to which their work is put; they own neither the means nor the fruits of their labor. They are still working as productive instruments at the disposal of forces they do not control and may not even understand.

In the years before I became a teacher and writer, I worked in factories that were unutterably dismal and hazardous. I worked in a chrome-plating plant where I was forever over shoes in muck and constantly breathing the fumes of boiling acid. I worked in a boiler factory where I was expected to sacrifice my eardrums to a hot and heavy riveting job that paid the dead minimum wage. The boss had to yell at the nearly deaf worker I was replacing (Dummy George, everyone called him) to tell him he was off the job. When I asked for a raise to do the work, I was fired. The plain wretchedness of work like this is obvious to all concerned; nobody needs to be persuaded that it is exploitive and humiliating.

But I have also worked at white-collar jobs—for both private and public organizations—where every effort was made to provide amenities. At one insurance company, the personnel department never let a week pass without announcing a busy agenda of activities and amusements: picnics and theater parties, baseball outings and amateur talent shows, tours and charter flights. There were company programs for everything: savings, mutual fund investments, discount purchasing, medical and dental care, retirement. Every pregnant typist was treated to a lunchtime baby shower by the firm; births, deaths, engagements, retirements were noted in the weekly bulletin, along with the company's generous contribution to the occasion. The corridors were carpeted; lunches in the well-upholstered cafeteria were kept cheap and nutritious; on one's birthday, everybody in one's department got a cupcake with a lighted candle on top.

There were people I worked with in that office who loved the company. They joined in on all the fun, subscribed to all the programs. It was the joy and mainstay of their lives. They *cared* whether "our" company caught up with Prudential or Mutual of Omaha in gross sales. From my work in the claims department, I could tell that the company sold some of the most dishonest health and accident insurance on the market. It also refused employment to Jews and blacks. But that, of course, was supposed to be none of *my* business. Nor were the totally reactionary politics which determined the company's influence in the city. There was no union; it was universally understood that there was no need for a union. And while the personnel office was always available to hear complaints or suggestions, there was no grievance procedure, no right of appeal upon dismissal. Without surrendering a fraction of its capitalist prerogatives, the company had found the secret of winning the hearts and minds of its employees.

Perhaps white-collar labor has always been the most coddled sector of the work force, but my guess is that, in the next generation, we will see ever more intensive efforts at morale-boosting of this sort in all areas of the economy. The literature documenting boredom, resentment, recalcitrance on the job grows by the year. Absenteeism, high turnover, industrial sabotage are prominently recognized as major obstacles to discipline and productivity. In response, "job enrichment" and "job restructuring" have become high priorities on the industrial agenda; academic study centers have been set up by government and the corporations to research the subjects, and imaginative experiments have been launched. No doubt there are tedious and dirty jobs which are very nearly intractable to any form of "enrichment": mining, waste collection, assembly-line and construction work, clerk-typing. But even here there are possibilities for blunting the edge of discontent: flex-time scheduling, profit sharing, job sharing, work-gang assignments, more breaks, greater variety of job assignments. Recent contracts in the auto industry have stressed sabbatical leaves, paid time off, and more union participation in decision making, especially with respect to working conditions, quite as much as higher wages and overtime rates.[1]

If we can take Japan as an example, there is room for a good deal of enrichment and amelioration within industrial capitalism. There, a suave paternalism has managed to co-opt most of the services of the Western welfare state and has thereby done much to capture the loyalty and enthusiasm of workers. It may well be that the next phase of advanced capitalist expansion will, ironically enough, hark back to Robert Owen's enlightened experiments at New Lanark in Scotland, which proved at the very beginning of the Industrial Revolution that a major investment in employee morale more than paid for itself in productivity. Owen was

prophetically right, but, in the early nineteenth century, the compulsions of primitive accumulation blinded his fellow capitalists to his insight—with the result that capitalism came to be indelibly marked in the eyes of radical critics by physical degradation and brutality.

But that was never the essence of capitalist employment, as Marx, in his best analytical passages, recognized. The fundamental act of alienation during the Industrial Revolution was the subordination of work to money, so that work—any work and all work—came to be an abstract commodity valued only as a means of earning the wages that purchased subsistence and (perhaps) some leisured enjoyment. "Alienation," as Marx put it, "shows itself not merely in the result, but also in the process of production, within productive activity itself. . . . The work is *external* to the worker, . . . it is not part of his nature, . . . consequently, he does not fulfill himself in his work but denies himself. . . ."[2]

At their most perceptive, both Marx and Engels noted that alienation in this deeper sense may be characteristic, not simply of capitalism, but of any high industrial system—especially one that serves the needs of a major economic power. But, convinced as they were (and, of course, Lenin and Stalin after them) that the medicine of revolution would somehow cure all the ills of society, they did not press the point or give it full theoretical scope. It was left to their despised radical opposition, the anarchists, to warn that such big systems, sunk as they are in a competitive nationalist ethos and the eternal arms race, are bound to overwhelm the human scale of life and so to subordinate work-as-personal-fulfillment to work-as-productivity. The sheer physical burden of work may then be ameliorated; but in its place, both in privatized and in collectivized economies, we discover that our work life has been infiltrated by clever strategies invented by planners and managers to seduce our allegiance and manipulate our energy for the greater glory of the system.

We may even progress then toward forms of workers' control and industrial democracy, but always with the understanding that our participation is constrained by certain abstract imperatives: efficiency, the rate of growth, the balance of world power, etc. "Participation" (by workers, consumers, investors, planners) has become a vogue word and prominent policy objective in many Western European governments; there, it is understood to be a major means of oiling away the discontent that inhibits planning on the scale of the Common Market. It may even be a sincere intention; but we should remember that every Nazi concentration camp was based on "participation," using inmates to police inmates in return for special favors.

Responsibility and Vocation

I want to argue that none of the enrichments and inducements mentioned here, not even the ingenious methods the Chinese have developed for collectivizing the altruism of the work force, goes to the root of alienation. I do not mean to say these reforms make no difference; they obviously render life on the job more pleasant and secure than it was in the worst days of wage slavery. But they do not make the *right kind* of difference. They may be necessary changes in many respects, but they are not sufficient. They alter the atmosphere and incentives of work, but they do not in themselves redeem work by any acceptable personalist standard, because they do not place the whole and unique person at the center of economic life. . . .

Responsibility—there we have the missing factor in both capitalist job enrichment and collectivist work morale, the crucial distinction that separates mere employment from true vocation. To have a vocation is to work with responsibility—not in any merely legal sense, nor in the sense of fearing that one will be pointed out as a slacker by one's workmates and reported to the party—but in the sense that our work is ourselves; we are at one with it because it grows from all that we have chosen to become in this life. It is our personal emblem and pledge of honor before the world. We *care* about our vocation, because if it is misused or proves inadequate, all that gives our life distinction and meaning is called into question.

It is a stubborn fact of human experience: Except in the most technical legal sense, I cannot hold myself responsible for work that is personally meaningless, let alone for work I despise. Meaningless work, despicable work, is work I blame on others; I treat it as a mere necessity, an imposed duty, I may even feel ashamed that I waste my life at such work. So I say to myself (and secretly to the world), "I am only doing this because I need the money, or I need the grade, or I need the credit, or reputation, or publicity. I am doing something my boss wants to have done, or the system needs to have done. I did not invent this job; I do not believe in it; I do not endorse it. If I had *my* way, I would be doing something else. So don't hold me responsible for its waste, its shoddiness, its criminality."

In this way, I seek to distance myself from the job. And that, essentially, is what alienation is: the withdrawal of self from action, the retreat of the person from the performance. Work then becomes a foreign object in one's life which is, at most, a means to an end, but no proper part of one's real identity. Alienation is not—as left-wing radicalism customarily contends—an estrangement merely from the means and fruits of production. It is also estrangement from the activity itself which allows us to deny our responsibility for what we do. And this is what surely follows when work has no *craft* to it: no challenge, no taste, no personal style. Work of that kind is a zero, a hole in the middle of one's life. . . .

Responsibility, as I intend the word here, is double-edged. It means being responsible *to* and being responsible *for*. If we have a vocation, we are responsible *to* our work that it should be well done; we are responsible *for*

our work that it should be well used. We want it to be intrinsically excellent by the highest standards of our craft or profession; we also want it to be of good and honorable service in the world. In our vocation, we wish to see *the good* achieved in both its senses: the well crafted and the ethically right. Only one force will provide this double-edged sense of responsibility—and that is love: the love we bear toward the work we do. . . .

The Buddha, in his wisdom, made "right livelihood" (another word, I think, for vocation) one of the steps to enlightenment. If we do not pitch our discussion that high, we have failed to give work its true dimension, and we will settle for far too little—perhaps for no more than a living wage. Responsible work is an embodiment of love, and love is the only discipline that will serve in shaping the personality, the only discipline that makes the mind whole and constant for a lifetime of effort. There hovers about a true vocation that paradox of all significant self-knowledge—our capacity to find ourselves by losing ourselves. We lose ourselves in our love of the task before us, and, in that moment, we learn an identity that lives both within and beyond us.

What else should the highest yoga be, after all, but the work we turn to each day?

"Take This Job and Shove It"

Each day I move through a world at work, an ocean of human activity as pervasively and as unobtrusively there as the ocean of air that surrounds me. I breathe in the labor of people around me; I live by it, yet I take it for granted like some free resource. People work, I work. That is what we are here to do; it is how we pass the time.

But our work is more than a pastime. It is our life. It takes up years of the portion we have been allotted on this Earth to work out our salvation. And not many of us work at a true vocation . . . sometimes I think very nearly none. Some, like my father, grind their substance away at hard and dirty work for too little pay and appreciation. Most are toiling at jobs whose worst burden is deadly and impersonal routine: typing, filing, checking groceries, selling across a counter, filling out forms, processing papers.

I have done such jobs myself. I still do them. A deal of what I do as a teacher in a colossal state college system is stale paper work and routine committee assignments that have nothing to do with education or scholarship, little enough to do with simple intelligence. Did any of us really have to read Studs Terkel's report *Working* to know what the daily deadly toll of alienated labor is? "I feel like a machine," "I feel like a robot," Terkel's interviewees complain. As I sit down to the task of revising this chapter, the record at the top of the American charts is Johnny Paycheck singing "Take This Job and Shove It." When we do not hear that lamentation from the people around us, it is only because we are not listening to what they say behind the heroic good humor that is the shield of their self-respect. Only look, and you can see their stifled personhood written in their faces; you can see it in the distraction that carries their thoughts to imaginary pleasures and leads to slip-ups and mistakes each day on the job; it is there in their surliness and bad temper. I have seen it in myself whenever I have felt the vital hours of my life being turned to dust by work that did not use the best I have to offer, whenever I have had to carry out the orders of employers who had no interest in the bright and extraordinary powers I could feel within me yearning to be hard-worked for all they were worth.

All of us have a gift, a calling of our own whose exercise is high delight, even if we must sweat and suffer to meet its demands. That calling reaches out to find a real and useful place in the world, a task that is not waste or pretense. If only that life-giving impulse might be liberated and made the whole energy of our daily work, if only we were given the chance to be *in* our work with the full force of our personality, mind and body, heart and soul . . . what a power would be released into the world! A force more richly transformative than all the might of industrial technology.

But *they*—the company, the system—rarely have any use for that calling. Our bosses do not even look for it in themselves. It makes no difference to the profit and loss; it does not show up (so the experts believe) in the economic indicators. So they sweep it out of sight and continue to work us as personnel, not persons. That is very nearly the prerequisite for being a successful boss in this warped economy: to blind oneself to the personhood of one's workers, to insist that business is business. That is treatment fewer workers will now accept; and the trend is by no means limited to middle-class, college-educated workers. In a recent statistical study, Daniel Yankelovich concludes that, in growing numbers through the seventies, "noncollege youth . . . take up the quest of their college peers for a new definition of success in which the emphasis is on self-fulfillment and quality of life, as well as on money and security."[3] Thus, the Department of Labor reports that, even in a tight job market, twice as many people quit their jobs in disgust as did a decade ago; the number has gone from 200,000 per year to 400,000 and continues to rise.

Yet somehow we carry on. I am always astonished at how resourcefully most people find ways to stick at their jobs without becoming bitter or corrupt. . . .

But there are so many others I meet who miraculously manage to stay human on the job. They invent little strategies of self-encouragement and compensation to get them through the day. They decorate their work space with trinkets and placards of their own choosing. They smuggle a transistor radio into the shop to play "their" kind of music, though most of what they hear is idiotic commercials and payola disk jockeys. They divide the day's work into so many little contests and competitions that will pace them along. They secretly challenge themselves to absurdly high standards of neatness and precision to put some sport in the work. They organize games with workmates, they gossip, they flirt, they kid around, they kibbitz with the customers, they exchange jokes and novelties. Perhaps most of all, they gripe. Mutual griping always helps. It relieves the conscience to let someone know that *you* know this is a bitch of a job. That is a way to remind yourself and the world that you are bigger and smarter and better than this dumb job. And if you had *your* way . . .

When I worked as a teller for the Bank of America, I kept my head busy all day long repeating Greek declensions and memorizing poems. It kept my brain alive—and also made me a miserably bad teller. But even my mistakes were a secret gratification—a tiny way of obstructing B of A's smooth flow of high financial banditry. I imagine strategies like these have sustained people through all the most suffocating kinds of toil since the factory bells pealed in the first dawn of industrialism. They are symptoms of our vocational instinct fighting to survive: little sparks and flashes of our thwarted personhood. The pathos of the matter is that no private strategy of this kind will ever turn an empty or fraudulent job into a vocation—nor, for that matter, will any social reform. And far too many of us are entrammeled by just such work, struggling to avoid the embarrassment of acknowledging our entrapment. A phony job is a phony job; a wicked job is a wicked job. These are not matters of morale or social organization; not even revolutionary workers' control can change them. They are objective moral facts attached to certain forms of employment that have become the only jobs many industrial societies seem able to offer millions of workers.

Work that produces unnecessary consumer junk or weapons of war is wrong and wasteful. Work that is built upon false needs or unbecoming appetites is wrong and wasteful. Work that deceives or manipulates, that exploits or degrades is wrong and wasteful. Work that wounds the environment or makes the world ugly is wrong and wasteful. There is no way to redeem such work by enriching it or restructuring it, by socializing it or nationalizing it, by making it "small" or decentralized or democratic. It is a sow's ear that will yield no silk purses.

Here we have an absolute criterion that must enter any discussion of work. *Is the job honest and useful? Is it a real contribution to human need?* These are questions that can only be answered by a worker's own strong sense of responsibility. That is why the struggle for right livelihood is as important as the struggle for industrial democracy. For it does not matter how democratically controlled our work life is: If a job is inherently worthless, it cannot be a vocation. So, if we encourage people to search for responsible work—for work they can love as an image of their personal destiny—then we must not expect them to continue doing what is stupid or ugly. We must not expect them to go on working for the military-industrial complex or for Madison Avenue, to continue producing "people's bombs" or printing party propaganda. One cannot build a vocation on a lie.

The hard truth is that the world we live in, the high industrial world we presume to hold up as the standard of "development," is immensely committed to proliferating work that is wrong and wasteful. It does this in the name of growth, or the national security, or the standard of living; but at the bottom it all comes down to creating jobs that are unworthy of our best energies:

Huckstering jobs—inventing, advertising, selling expensive trash to gullible customers

Busywork jobs—sorting, recording, filing, computerizing, endless amounts of data, office memos, statistical figments

Mandarin-administrative jobs—co-ordinating, overseeing, supervising clerical battalions and bureaucratic hierarchies, many of which—especially in government operations—exist merely to spin their own wheels

Financial sleight-of-hand jobs—juggling cash and credit, sniffing out tax loopholes and quick speculative windfalls in real estate, arbitrage, stocks and bonds

Compensatory amusements jobs—marketing the vicarious glamour and escapist pleasures whose one use is to relieve the tedium and frustration of workaday life: spectator sports, mass media distractions, superstar entertainments, package tours, the pricey toys and accoutrements of "creative leisure"

Cop jobs—providing security against the theft and violence of society's have-nots, policing the streets, hassling the riffraff through the courts, guarding the prisons, snooping into credit ratings, school records, personnel evaluations

Welfare processing jobs—picking up the economy's casualties, keeping them on the public assistance treadmill, holding the social discontent below the boiling point

And at the dizzy top of the heap, we have the billion-dollar boondoggling—the cartel building, multinational maneuvering, military-industrial back scratching—which is the corrupted soul of our corporate economy. The list could go on indefinitely, a spreading network of waste and corruption that touches very nearly everybody's work life. How many of us could not finally be tied into it in at least some peripheral way—like it or not, know it or not? My own profession of university teaching has fattened enormously over the past generation by educating (or training) the personnel who have become the executive functionaries and white-collar rank and file in this flourishing surplus economy.

Many who are utterly dependent upon this dense congestion of socially useless getting and spending may never see the full context of the work they do. That is the peculiar moral dodge made available by our social complexity. It allows us to work in the blind at little, seemingly innocent fractions of big, dishonorable projects. The full extent of culpability may be nearly impossible to delineate; there are so many degrees and shadings. But the ethical issue is nevertheless there at the heart of our economy, and it must be addressed by any honest discussion of work. There is work that is good and useful; and there is work that is not. Work that is not good and useful is work that wastes the lives of people and the resources of the Earth—and industrial society generates a scandalous amount of that kind of work. Perhaps it is what our society does most. In our search for a true vocation, here is indeed a Himalayan obstacle. For it may mean there is a prodigious amount of work we are involved in which no healthy sense of responsibility should permit us to do at all. . . .

Notes

The books I have drawn upon in preparing this chapter include the following: Folkert Wilken, *The Liberation of Work* (London: Routledge & Kegan Paul, 1969), and David Jenkins, *Job Power* (Garden City, N.Y.: Doubleday, 1973), which survey experiments in workers' control in America and Europe. Laile Bartlett, *New Work/New Life* (New York: Harper & Row, 1976), reports on new forms of self-management in the United States and offers a helpful resource kit of "networks" dealing in work reform. Fred Blum, *Work and Community* (London: Routledge & Kegan Paul, 1968), is a study of the Scott-Bader Commonwealth, one of the long-standing British experiments in industrial democracy. Clare Huchet Bishop, *All Things Common* (New York: Harper & Row, 1950), deals with the postwar French communities of work, especially Boimondau. David and Elena French, *Working Communally* (New York: Russell Sage Foundation, 1975), is a perceptive critique of contemporary collectives and communes, especially with respect to their need to create viable, communal workplaces. I have also found the following helpful: Ivan Illich, *Tools for Conviviality* (New York: Harper & Row, 1973); Studs Terkel, *Working* (New York: Pantheon, 1974); Stanley Aronowitz, *False Promises: The Shaping of the American Working-class Consciousness* (New York: McGraw-Hill, 1973), the last for its shrewd criticism of organized labor's failure to take industrial democracy as a serious social goal. Louis Davis et al., eds., *The Quality of Working Life* (New York: Free Press, 1974), is a good introductory collection of papers dealing with contemporary reforms of work.

1. Among the major centers of job-enrichment research are the Center for the Quality of Working Life at the Institute for Industrial Relations, University of California at Los Angeles, the Quality of Work Program at the University of Michigan, and the Work in America Institute in New York City. The Tavistock Institute of Human Relations in London has also issued a large body of literature dealing with the reform of working life. The Ford Foundation has financed a deal of job-enrichment programs. See its *Newsletter* for September 1, 1975.

2. Marx, from the *Economic and Philosophical Manuscripts,* in Karl Marx, *Early Writings,* trans. and ed. T. B. Bottomore (New York: McGraw-Hill, 1964), pp. 124–25.

3. Daniel Yankelovich, *The New Morality: A Profile of American Youth in the Seventies* (New York: McGraw-Hill, 1974), p. 29.

the *Politics* of *Motherhood*

Deborah Fallows

Deborah Fallows is the mother of two sons. This article is adapted from her book, A Mother's Work, *published by Houghton Mifflin.*

Betty Friedan launched the contemporary women's movement in 1963 by depicting the home as a domestic penal institution for women. In *The Feminine Mystique* she wrote that housewives "baked their own bread, sewed their own and their children's clothes, kept their new washing machines and dryers running all day. They changed the sheets on the beds twice a week instead of once, took the rug-hooking class in adult education. Their only dream was to be perfect wives and mothers; their highest ambition to have five children and a beautiful house; their only fight to get and keep their husbands."

Over the past 20 years, the women's movement has carefully proclaimed its intention to give women the "opportunity to choose" their own lives—as professionals, as wage earners, or as housewives. But in feminists' eyes, the real challenges lay outside the home—in the workplace. A career offered all the answers: Dependent on your spouse? Get an income, become self-sufficient. No power to back up your opinion? Money talks. Bored and lonely? Get out of the house and in with interesting people. Everyone taking you for granted? Find recognition with an official-sounding job.

One thing was missing from this strategy, however, and that was a concern for how it would affect the children. Leaders of the women's movement have never quite said that jobs should come before family. Those from the mainstream of the movement have taken care to point out that many of their guiding lights are young mothers. Still, their battles for political and economic equality have inevitably led them to prize achievement on the job above all else. Understanding as they might be of women who choose not to work, feminists tend to see such a choice as a step backwards for the cause. By questioning women's place in society, the women's movement threw motherhood into the political arena.

In the late 1970s, conservative forces coalesced to challenge feminism. The right offered women a clear, complete explanation of the wife's place at home. It is "good" to be there (it is traditional, Christian); the wife has a responsibility to be there (to husband and to children); she enjoys security in her position (her right to support by her husband); she should find all of her satisfaction there (from raising her children); it is important that she be there (to her family, she is irreplaceable).

While some leaders of the so-called "pro-family" forces concede that women may have to work for economic reasons, this doesn't shake the right's faith in an "ideal" division of labor and authority in the family. In the "ideal family"—a concept referred to routinely in pro-family literature—the husband is the breadwinner and decisionmaker. Next to him is his wife, a helpmate but not an equal.

Neither the women's movement nor the pro-family movement offers an adequate, or even honest prescription for mothers. The right preaches complaince and subservience. It discourages women from seeking challenges in the world beyond the home, thereby reducing the spiritual resources that could enrich mothers' years with their children. Many conservatives have also succumbed to the familiar temptation of the comfortable to forget about or condemn those on whom fortune has not smiled.

The women's movement, with which I sympathize much more than I do with the right, defines success in terms of professional achievement, thereby implicitly downgrading the idea that parents should care for their children themselves. In coming to grips with the realities of motherhood, women will have to see through the symbolism and rhetoric of both sides of this debate.

Right-wing sweetheart

Phyllis Schlafly, leader of the anti-ERA movement and founder of the conservative Eagle Forum, reigns as first lady of the pro-family movement. What Schlafly would have for all other women is her version of a perfect life—that is, a life much like her own.

From what I'd read about Schlafly in *Ms.* magazine and elsewhere, I expected her to be a harpy, or at least an excessively brisk woman. Instead, she is attractive and professional-looking—calm as an executive, warm as my best friend's mother. She ushered me into her Capitol Hill office, like a hostess having me in for coffee. "Hello, Debbie. Sorry to keep you waiting. Tell me about your book. Have you got a copy of *Sweetheart*?"

I have read her biography, *Sweetheart of the Silent Majority*, and many issues of her monthly newsletter, the *Phyllis Schlafly Report*, although neither publication is easy to locate. The proprietor of one women's bookstore I called told me she didn't know whether Schlafly had written anything, adding, "and we certainly wouldn't carry it if she did."

From talking with her, I soon knew many things about Schlafly's personal life: for example, she worked her way through college toiling in a munitions factory and taught her six children to read. She wrote and published her own numerous books, lives in financial security with her wealthy husband, and has waged several unsuccessful campaigns to hold political office. Her husband is much older than she is, and she employed a governess for her children for at least one summer.

In between the lines of her conversation lurk the prerequisites to the "perfect" life she has led: education, money, a healthy family, and a supportive husband.

But life doesn't work for most women the way Schlafly thinks it should. Half the women getting married today can expect to be divorced; by 1990, one child out of four under ten years old—almost nine million children—will have lived with a single parent at some point in his life. Over one-fourth of the women who are legally entitled to child support payments do not receive them. In hard economic times, husbands will lose jobs, and women can still expect to earn about 60 percent of what men earn. We know these things to be facts. And we can pretty well guess that during the days when divorce was rare and when women kept their own counsel, similar discontent and trouble existed—only secretly.

But Schlafly ignores statistics like these, and turns a judgmental ear to the stories of troubled women. She complacently advises wives to stay home, resting assured that "since God ordained that women have babies, our laws properly and realistically establish that men must provide financial support for their wives and children."

Connaught Marshner, director of the Family Policy Division of the Free Congress and Education Foundation, is a generation younger than Schlafly but, like her, a mother and a major power in the conservative movement. Marshner, like many conservative young women raising families, speaks with more realism than Schlafly does.

Marshner is an attractive, kind-looking woman in her mid-thirties, with dark, shoulder-length hair pinned back from her face. She has a company phone in her car so she can conduct business on her long commutes from Washington to Virginia, where she lives with her husband, who is a college professor, and her two elementary school-age sons. On her desk sits a photo of one of her sons bathing her infant daughter, who, she tells me at a difficult moment in our talk, has died from heart disease. Unlike Schlafly, Marshner has seen life's rougher side.

Like Schlafly, however, Marshner lives something of a contradiction. She agrees with the right's version of the "ideal" family, in which the mother stays home with the children. But, she says, "ideal" comes with two large qualifications: *if* a family can afford for the mother to stay home, and *if* she can be fulfilled at home. For Marshner and many younger conservative women, the fact of working mothers is just that—a fact. It is not a goal or an opportunity or a promising development. According to Marshner, women work because they are called upon to work, either for economic reasons or for community needs. Women, being "other-oriented" by nature, as Marshner describes them, are responding to a call from others to work, rather than to inner drives.

A mother who works or who is divorced or single, according to Marshner, can still raise a "traditional" family. The idea of "tradition" rests much less on the structure of the family or the detailed division of family labor than on a sense of mission about moral standards. The family must live by "a system of moral norms which, once well-defined, are taken to be without exception."

Conservatives may love their kids, but their view of children is remote, studied, and at odds with the reality of daily life.

In some general sense, it's hard to quibble with Marshner's morality. It sounds like an effort to raise honest, generous children—something all of us, conservative or liberal, strive to do. But Marshner's definitions of "traditional" morality are more specific than this and include prominently her staunch belief that, when push may come to shove, the father is the figure of authority in the family. "The husband is the head of the household," she says. "He *should* have responsibility for making final decisions. That *should* be the case."

Somewhere between Schlafly and Marshner the conservative pendulum rests. Much of the right still ignores the basic truth about women at home: that they are in a state of financial dependency. This is not necessarily evil—it is the situation in my household, by my husband's and my own choice—but it requires something more than Schlafly's pacifying assertions that little ladies should not trouble their pretty heads with thoughts about money.

Every woman needs to make sure she can take care of herself, and the children, if circumstances should change—and to this need the conservatives seem blind. Women owe it to themselves and their children to make financial provisions for such unforeseen but common occurrences as divorce or illness or death. Women should also at least be thinking of contingency plans for intolerable situations at home, such as infidelity or physical abuse.

For their self-protection, women need some form of insurance. It may be education, which would equip them to earn a living, even if they prefer not to while the children are young; it may be extra money, from an insurance policy or pension; it may also be a network of extended family or friends, who can help absorb the shock.

This need not imply what Schlafly suggests—that women who make such preparations are spurning their families. She characterizes the provoking call of the feminists as: "Come, leave your home, husband, and children and join all those unhappy females in a new sisterhood of togetherness." But wise precautions do not imply any less love, trust, or confidence in a marriage or family situation. Behind every statistic of divorce, widowhood, or poverty, is the story of a woman whose life did not turn out the way she planned.

The right ignores not only these provisions for the unexpected but also plans for the inevitable. The responsibility of caring for children, consuming as it may be, has limits even while it is going on—and someday it will be over. What are women to do then?

Schlafly implies that such concerns stem from women with attitude problems— "whether you wake up in the morning with a chip on your shoulder or whether you have a positive mental attitude." Once you stop moping around the house and letting yourself get big ideas about meeting challenges in the outside world, then your troubles will disappear. "If you think diapers and dishes are a never-ending repetitive routine," says Schlafly, "just remember that most of the jobs outside the home are just as repetitious, tiresome, and boring." She writes that "if you complain about servitude to a husband, servitude to a boss will be more intolerable. Everyone in the world has a boss of some kind. It is easier for most women to achieve a harmonious working relationship with a husband than with a foreman, supervisor, or office manager."

Rita Kramer, author of *In Defense of the Family*, suggests that some feminists "attempt to substitute one form of tyranny [childrearing] with another [working at a job]." She argues that a mother's "natural desire to be with her baby may give way to the social pressure to 'be somebody' in a society that is increasingly telling women that what counts is achievement, however trivial, outside the home, just so it is outside the home and apart from childrearing."

Social pressures certainly do play a large part in many women's decisions to work, but Kramer underestimates the depth of feeling and the scope of the ambivalence that many women have about their desire to broaden themselves beyond motherhood.

With no grasp of how tearing an issue this is for many women, the right blithely offers an array of milquetoast alternatives for ways of keeping yourself busy outside the home. Schlafly proposes that women try volunteer work: "welfare, hospital, educational, cultural, civic, and political. All these avenues provide opportunities for women to perform useful services to the community—and in so doing to become happier, more interesting, and more fulfilled."

Volunteerism certainly meets a basic human need. It can be deeply satisfying to help others when they cannot help themselves. Attending community service club meetings, participating in museum benefits, doing library work—all have their place. The shortcoming of the conservatives is not their recognition of the merits of volunteerism; it is their simplistic notion that it can and should be enough for all women. Not everyone can find a life of fulfillment in volunteer work, just as not everyone can find fulfillment in a boardroom, a courtroom, a university, or at home.

To hear the right's hymns of praise to the family, one might guess that the welfare of children is the first and last item on their list of concerns. The reason that mothers and fathers must take their assigned places in the family hierarchy is that the children will thereby benefit.

But the details of the right's position—for example, pro-family opposition to day care (see sidebar, p.45)—reveal a seeming lack of interest in children and their needs. The right presents an abstract, peculiar sense of what children are like. I can't claim that conservatives don't love their children as much as anyone else does. But their view of children is remote, studied, and at odds with the realities of daily life.

Once again, Phyllis Schlafly is a remarkable example. As she tells it, she was able to write books while her children played contentedly at her feet. "I was able to compose and write with children right around me," she explains, adding, "My husband can't do that."

Having spent the last three years in such an effort myself, with my children ranging from as young as one year old to as old as seven during that time, I know the difficulties of writing with children around. I can do it only when my children are away—taking naps, at school, at friends' houses. Surely Schlafly has forgotten: could her children really have colored or built with blocks around her feet for sustained periods without interrupting with questions, requests for glasses of water, trips to the bathroom, or fights? Perhaps she closed her study door and the children knew not to enter. Some mothers boast that this is their secret to working at home and "caring" for their children at the same time. The technique might work for a ten-year-old, but it certainly won't—and shouldn't—for a child of three.

Schlafly's reminiscences of children greatly resemble those of Marabel Morgan's. In her book, *The Total Woman,* Morgan recommends, among other things, that women lift the spirits of their tired breadwinners by greeting hubby at the front door clad only in saran wrap. She counsels mothers to "draw out the venom inside a person" as a tactic for dealing with a recalcitrant child. "When a close friend spanked his three-year-old for hitting the baby, he did it in a loving way," Morgan writes. "Afterward the child hugged him and said, 'Thank you for saying no, Daddy!' "

As any parent knows, this scene is make-believe. Bearing and raising a child is far more complex and far less programmable than Morgan or Schlafly would have us think. Moreover, there isn't much room for bad luck in the pro-family world. What if a child is born ill or impaired in some way? Does it mean you have failed if you have nothing to show off to your friends and neighbors? What if you raise a plumber or a short-order cook instead of a lawyer or a business executive? What if you raise a liberal instead of a conservative? Just as you can't control the sex of your child, the skills she is born with, or the beauty he inherits, you can affect but not determine your child's future, his personality, her "success." You can do your best while raising your child, but you can't claim or bear complete responsibility for the life your child leads.

Yet this is the burden Schlafly seems to put on mothers who spend all their energy raising children. She implies that a perfect life with a perfect mother will automatically produce a perfect child. "A mother can see the results of her own handiwork in the good citizen she has produced and trained," Schlafly writes. She congratulates mothers on successes they aren't responsible for—and implicitly charges them with failures they can't control.

Ms.-*ing the point*

While conservatives have in recent years reasserted a vision of the ideal homemaker, the women's movement has continued to look with a suspicious eye at women who stay at home. Feminist leaders are quick to deny this accusation, arguing that the press is to blame for unfairly depicting their position as being hostile to homemakers.

"Infuriating," says Letty Cottin Pogrebin, a founder and editor of *Ms.* magazine. "It's not a club with membership cards on behalf of women's interests," Pogrebin tells me one afternoon in the New York offices of *Ms.* Liberal women's groups include strong contingents of women at home; many of their leaders are mothers themselves. Feminists have pushed for legislative reform that directly assists homemakers. "Her issues are our issues," says Pogrebin, citing child care, healthcare, drug addiction, divorce reform, domestic violence, displaced homemakers, and comparable worth.

To its credit, the women's movement has made great progress for women in general, including mothers at home. To understand Pogrebin's pride

Who'll Mind the Children?

In the political battle over motherhood, day care is a central point of contention, but one largely obscured by the passion of ideology. In feminists' eyes, day care is indispensable to the formula for women's equality. Conservatives see it as a threat to the foundation of the family.

The debate focuses on day care—meaning the organized care for large groups of children—more often than other forms of child care, in part because large centers are where government is involved and where innovations and regulations can most easily be applied. Large facilities are also the most economical and efficient way for caring for children.

Often the area of disagreement extends even to what "day care" is. Some people who "don't believe in day care" really mean that they wouldn't consign their children to large, impersonal facilities, yet they happily send them to family homes or nursery schools. Meanwhile, some people who say that "day care is fine for children" are thinking about several hours a day in a family home.

The most familiar conservative criticism of day care is that it amounts to a near-totalitarian separation of child from parent and should in no way be encouraged. For example, when the House of Representatives Select Committee on Children, Youth, and Families recently recommended more federal support of day care, four Republican committee members dissented, arguing that government-sponsored day care is unacceptable as a matter of first principles. "Let's look for a moment at the real subject of our discussion—children," the congressmen said. "When we talk about the comparative costs of care for infants, toddlers, and pre-school children, we ought never to forget that we are talking about children who will be taken from their mothers and cared for primarily by strangers from the first months of their lives." Of primary concern, they added, is the question, "how does day care affect our children?" This is certainly a good question, but it will not be answered with confidence

anytime soon. In the meantime, 2 million children are in day care centers, and 6.5 million under the age of 13 go without any supervision at home.

Often, conservative opponents of day care say they recognize that some mothers have to work and even sound broad-minded about it. The Rev. Jerry Falwell has said, "My pastoral advice is, if the wife must work, the husband should make the extra effort to compensate in any way possible for her absence . . . .The husband is as much responsible for rearing the children as the wife."

Yet the logical progression seems to come to a halt at this point. If Falwell really believed that mothers must sometimes work, would it not follow that someone else must look after their children? If day care is therefore necessary, shouldn't the right join in supporting improvements in the institutions where these children will spend so many hours? Apparently not, if that means further expansion of federal power. Rochelle Beck of the Children's Defense Fund points out that Falwell's Moral Majority is part of the network of "'pro-family' interest groups [whose]. . .effective lobbying and fundraising efforts go to oppose federal funds for child-care services."

The conservative spokesmen do not explicitly block improvements in day care, but they oppose all the steps—especially further regulation and subsidy—that would make improvement possible. They support the kind of laissez-faire child care system we have today, whereby some combination of luck or money is the only answer to finding good care.

For example, Paul Weyrich, president of the far right Coalition for America, has said: "If a mother has to work, she should see to it her children are cared for by another family or by other family members. It is detrimental when so many kids are left in day care operations with strangers. . . .A child learns to hide the things he's worried about from some day care attendant."

Does Weyrich know what it is like to "try to see to it" that a friend or relative can handle

in these accomplishments, it helps to examine some specific examples.

In insurance and pensions, women's groups have worked to reform rates, terms, and conditions that discriminate on the basis of gender. For instance, women often pay more than men for

the same health insurance coverage. Pregnancy and childbirth are often excluded from coverage or qualify only for very inadequate coverage. Women who take time off to raise children don't fit the rules and provisions of retirement systems.

In the area of Social Security, feminist groups

all the day care? He is right about the drawbacks of large day-care centers but is content to push the problem away, since this fits conveniently with his overall political views.

Phyllis Schlafly, leader of the anti-ERA movement, touched on day care in her 1977 book, *The Power of the Positive Woman*. Her arguments still stand as a fair reflection of the "pro-family" attitude: "The energies and dedication of the Positive Woman are needed as never before to fend off the attacks on the moral, the social and economic integrity of the family. Take, for example, the tremendous drive to set up child-care centers—taxpayer-financed, government-managed, 'universally' available for 'all socioeconomic groups' regardless of means. This adds up to an attempt to make it public policy to remove babies from the family unit and place them in an institutional environment."

Obviously the government should not "substitute" for parents; but there are certain families in which parents cannot or will not care adequately for their children. To what extent will those parents' sins be visited upon their children? By defining those parents as morally unworthy—which in some cases they may be—the conservatives have successfully excluded the innocent *children* of those families from the universe of those deserving public help. This leads easily to a dismissal of subsidized day care as a national need.

As is so often the case in political life, the inflexibilities and excesses of one extreme are fully matched by the other. Leaders of the women's movement, who have done so much to remove barriers to women's occupational success, naturally view day care in a special light. Unless children can be left safely and happily in someone else's care, how will women continue to advance in the workplace?

The feminists don't delude themselves with dreams about fathers quitting work to tend the children while their wives move up. Day care has to be the answer.

According to the women's movement, the only people who object to day care are those who feel threatened by the idea of women succeeding in the workplace. Feminists may be willing to entertain private comments about the defects of certain facilities or certain approaches, as long as everyone understands that they all believe in day care as an institution. But when criticism is conducted in public,

where the gains made by the women's movement still seem so fragile, it's inevitably seen as a hostile act. For feminists it is but a short step from criticizing day care to suggesting that there are fundamental conflicts between parenthood and career.

Bettye Caldwell, president of the National Association for the Education of Young Children, reflects this doctrinaire attitude, denouncing even the most troubling reports about day care. No doubt Caldwell, who represents those who work in centers, is sincerely concerned about the conditions that make large group day care difficult for many children. But she reserves her public fury for something else—the *reports* about bad conditions, which she says give day care a bad name.

Caldwell was particularly outraged by a 1983 article by Dominique Browning published in *Texas Monthly* magazine. Browning described day-care centers in and around Houston:

"Workers are paid the minimum wage, and many of them take a job in a center only long enough to make money for a special purpose; then they quit....All day long, 11 to 15 babies from about eight weeks to 12 months old lie in their cribs or sit in their pens and scream for attention, stare at the ceiling, gurgle quietly, or sleep....The sitters cannot play with any child for very long because, as one of them explained, the child would get used to the attention and scream whenever he didn't get it."

In her remarks to the 1983 Junior League Parenting Conference in Washington, D.C., Caldwell said that in all her travels, she had never seen any day-care center like that. Caldwell has written that "the media need to highlight more of the positive aspects of quality child care if the public interest is to be served."

Bettye Caldwell may never have seen day-care centers like those Browning described, but I have, and I did not have to look very hard. Liberals in general have found it hard to confess the limitations of their social programs, even though such warts and imperfections are inevitable in even the best-run organizations. For this reluctance they have paid a steep political price. There is a lot of very bad day care out there, and the institution of outside-the-home child care must be strong enough to withstand scrutiny or it will not improve and flourish. —*D.F.*

such as the Women's Equity Action League (WEAL) advocate improving the fairness and adequacy of provisions for *all* women. In 1982, WEAL points out, the average man received $430 per month in benefits; the average woman, $308. Retired female workers averaged $335 per month

compared to $438 for retired male workers. These inequities arise, the feminists say, from historically low wages for working women and an undervalued estimation of homemakers' contributions to a family's income. To correct the situation, WEAL has supported a system of "earnings shar-

*T*he tensions between the women's movement and nonworking mothers stems from politics, but the hostility is deeply personal.

ing." Under earnings sharing, a husband and wife would, for Social Security purposes, each be credited with half the family's total earnings during the marriage, whether both of them were working or not, plus individual earnings gained before or after the marriage. Later, each would receive pensions based on his or her own personal account. For the homemaker, earnings sharing could also provide disability benefits and survivor protection through the Social Security system, even though she may never have worked for pay.

But none of this addresses the question of spirit and tone. The deepest tensions between the women's movement and nonworking mothers are based on the attitudes the mothers perceive in the movement. Although its origin is in politics, the hostility is also personal.

Working mothers often feel that nonworking mothers are trying to drown them in guilt. They perceive homemakers sneering at them for being irresponsible toward home and family. On the other hand, nonworking mothers assume that working mothers look down on them, making them feel like weak sisters who just can't keep up. The withering comments are familiar to every at-home mother: "What's an educated young woman like you doing at home?" Or: "I'd go out of my mind if I stayed at home all day."

There is, of course, no inherent incompatibility between women reaching out for equality and women staying at home. But, as any woman under the age of 40 knows, there is an imposed incompatibility. The women's movement has not yet had the time or made the effort to understand and explore what life at home can be like for women today. Feminists may officially say that "choice" is at the top of their agenda for women, but there are too many hints suggesting that this talk comes fairly cheap. Throughout my years at home and well before that, I have gotten the message from the feminists that there is only one "right" choice that a progressive woman and young mother can make. Why did I feel that? Because of signals like these:

• Gloria Steinem is promoting her latest book, *Outrageous Acts and Everyday Rebellions* on a radio talk show in mid-1984. During a phone-in session, a caller asks, "What do you *really* think

of women who stay home?" The host of the show, a droll, forthright character named Joel E. Spivak, points out that on every show with a prominent feminist, at least one caller asks some version of this question. Steinem's answer, of course, is that the feminist movement created the choice for women to lead their lives as they want to. She even says that staying home is just as valid and reputable a choice as working. And yet, only minutes earlier, perhaps forgetting that housewives are listening, she has referred to the "narrow and stifled" lives of women at home.

• I am speaking with a spokeswoman for the National Women's Political Caucus about Social Security and insurance as well as about my children and my book. On the way out, she asks me, in a sister-to-sister tone, "Well, when *are* you going to go back to work?"

• A full-time mother writes to *Ms.*, complaining, "I get the feeling you look down on me, condescend to me because I'm not working." *Ms.* replies with a straight face, "We were surprised to hear this. We have tried to present topics of interest to women at home—childbirth, pregnancy, housework, daily lives, etc. We all have children ourselves and know what it's been like to face the decisions."

To prove its bona fides, *Ms.* sends writer Jane Lazarre to spend a morning with Jane Broderick, author of the challenging letter. Lazarre describes a meeting at the crossroads of feminism that takes place in a Long Island kitchen. A full-time mother of eight, Broderick lays out her positions on feminist issues: birth control, child-rearing, housework. Lazarre professes a closeness to Broderick, but the closest the writer comes to finding a key to Broderick's spirit is to focus on two things: her strong Catholicism, which has a lot to do with becoming a mother of eight children but very little to do with feminism, and Broderick's explanation that she sometimes finds it necessary "to hide. And I do just that. I really have to sit very still. Just be alone with myself. And become whole again."

All mothers can recognize that sitting very still is Broderick's gimmick for maintaining sanity. But they also understand that it reveals little about her method of sustaining herself as a

*O*ne of the reasons to push ahead
with the feminist campaign for fairer pay
is that it would permit fathers to take a
few years off to care for the children.

mother to eight children. Lazarre, and *Ms.*, are content with the superficial view and do not search for any real insights into full-time motherhood.

To be fair, an occasional insight slips into the feminist literature. For example, in a diary of a day with her small children, published in *Ms.*, Phyllis Rosser describes motherhood minute-by-minute:

"9:50. Stopped to feed the cat because she was making so much noise."

"10:28. Sat down again. Sam asked me to watch her turn somersaults."

"5:10. Took Sam to the toy store to buy birthday present for Tim while the boys stayed home with Bill."

Her days are not that interesting to read about, but the insights she gleans from examining her own diary are. They offer an important message to full-time mothers of small children:

"I was beginning to understand why raising children was so much harder than working in an office. I was allowing my children to dominate my life with trivia, and that left no time to do the things I wanted to do with them, like painting and hiking. It also kept me from having any blocks of time for projects of my own."

Betty Friedan has come closest to taking the scorn out of the word "housewife," much of which she introduced in the first place with *The Feminine Mystique.* In her sequel, *The Second Stage,* Friedan writes:

"We must at least admit and begin openly to discuss feminist denial of the importance of family, of women's own need to give and get love.... It would seem to me that in the second stage we should move for some very simple aids that make it possible for mothers (or fathers) who want to stay home and take care of their own children to do so, with some economic compensation that might make the difference."

The women's movement has addressed many issues of concern to women at home. But the heart of the matter—how women can lead rich and independent lives at home—is left hanging. Feminists offer women in the workplace a great

sense of having asked the difficult questions about life: whether to work, what to expect on the job, what professional goals to set. The women's movement has not done the same for women at home. Feminists have not asked the questions that matter: Why stay at home? How can I find satisfaction there? How does life at home fit with important things in my family's life or the fabric of a larger community?

Diapering is man's work

What, then, am I recommending? For people who are troubled by the blind spots and omissions in the standard political formulas, is there a better alternative? I think there is. It is possible at least to outline a political approach to children and parenthood that would emphasize the things that make a difference in children's lives.

The first principle is that parents should strive to care for their children themselves. It will not always be possible, and many children will get along fine in any case. Still, other conditions being equal, children are more likely to thrive when they spend most of their day with a parent rather than a hired caretaker. One of our political goals, therefore, should be to create the circumstances that allow more parents to care for their young children themselves.

Simply stating that as a goal would be important in itself. "Parenthood" is supposed to be one of our bedrock societal values, but it really isn't. I have heard many more speeches about inflation, taxes, the deficit, nuclear war, and the Sandinistas than about parenthood. Recognizing the potential political power of a rational approach to parenthood could lead to many practical steps: for example, encouraging businesses to change their policies on maternity leave, paternity leave, part-time work, and job-sharing.

The second principle is an insistence that the balance between parenthood and career be worked out by both parents. In part this is a practical economic problem. Because most women earn less money than most men, when it comes time to decide which spouse stays home, the choice is obvious. How can the family afford to lose its main breadwinner? One of the reasons to push ahead with the feminist campaign for fairer pay is that it would make it more feasible for fathers to take a few years off to care for the children.

Unfortunately, this issue transcends economics. Too many men view the parenthood/career balance as their wives' problem, of no concern to them. For the sake of the children, and the mothers, *and* the fathers, we need to remind men, day after day until it takes, that it is their concern, too. They are as responsible as their wives for finding a way to reconcile their professional ambitions with the welfare of their children.

Third, we must recognize that if spouses—for the time being, mainly mothers—are to stay out of the work force for a while, they need certain practical protections. Here, many of the steps toward reform already have been proposed by the feminists. Pension reform and enforcement of child-support orders will allow parents to care for their children without becoming too vulnerable to fate.

Fourth, we must have day care—more of it, and more of high quality. Day care has become a permanent feature of American life. Millions of children will spend billions of hours in these institutions. Those hours can be relatively productive, or they can be actively damaging, depending on how the day care centers are run. If we are serious about improving day care, we must raise the regulatory standards imposed on the centers and put more money into their operation. Increased federal spending is unlikely at a time when government programs of all kinds are being cut back. But if the care of our children is important, we should find ways to improve day care that do not add to the federal deficit—perhaps by enlisting businesses to subsidize day care, or by using our talents more creatively in volunteer efforts.

Finally, we should insist on a principle missing from all the political manifestos about women and families I have seen. Women who stay home with their children should feel just as great an obligation to use their intellect and energy wisely as any young doctor or teacher of either sex. The women's movement and the pro-family forces seem to agree that a woman who ends up at home with the children ("by choice" according to the feminists, "by natural order" according to the right) has stepped off of life's main road. She's spending these years "at home," and there's not much more to say about her. But the exhortations feminists direct at careerists—to bring out the best in themselves, to be responsible, independent, and strong—should also be issued as challenges to women at home.

Another Stereotype: Old Age As A Second Childhood

Arnold Arluke Ph.D.
and Jack Levin Ph.D.

Dr. Jack Levin is a professor of sociology at Northeastern University in Boston and is the co-author of Ageism: Prejudice and Discrimination Against the Elderly. *Dr. Arnold Arluke is Associate Professor of Sociology, also at Northeastern University, and is co-author of the forthcoming book,* Division of Labor As Marketplace: Rehabilitation Medicine, 1890-1980.

Stereotypes are more than privately held "pictures in our heads." They are more often culturally shared and institutionalized negative images which are used to justify unequal treatment, or discrimination, directed against minority groups, ranging from perpetrating, petty indignities in everyday life to slavery and genocide.

One common and particularly damaging stereotype, "infantilization," reduces minority group members to the status of children, ranging from infants to adolescents, who lack moral, intellectual, or physical maturity. According to this image, they are typically depicted as "irresponsible," "impulsive," "fun-loving," and "immature." In sum, they are seen as dependent on the "more mature" dominant group for guidance to accomplish the tasks to which they are assigned or even to survive.

The antebellum South provides an appropriate example. The "Little Black Sambo" image was extensively

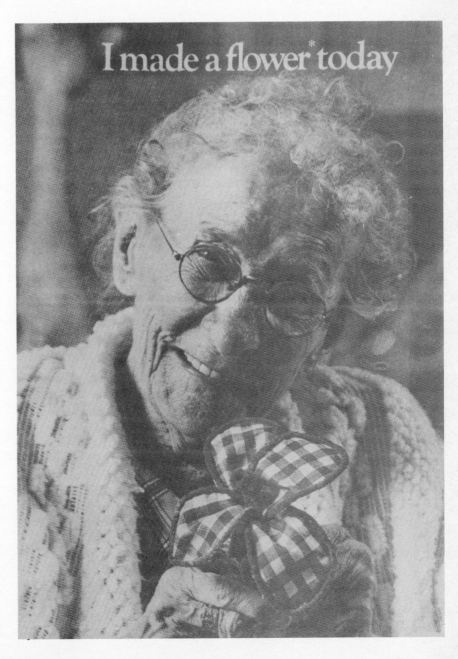

I made a flower* today

From *Aging*, August 1984, pp. 7-11. U.S. Department of Health, Education & Welfare.

123

applied to sell the ideology of a "white man's burden," whereby slaves would actually perish if denied the paternalistic "protection" of their masters who administered corporal punishment and withheld rewards to assure that tasks were accomplished. To this day, the epithet "boy" remains as a vestige of the infantilization of the slave (Blassingame, 1972). In the same manner, women before the liberation movement of the 1960's were often called "baby," "girl," "honey," and "sweety." Their fashions were made to reflect the fashions of children, frequently imitating the clothing worn by infants or teenagers of a previous generation (Lurie, 1982).

Similarly, many stereotypes currently portray old age as a time of second childhood. This dim view of the elderly suggests that they are losing, or have lost, the very things a growing child gains. It implies a backward movement to earlier developmental stages, with no recognition of the lifetime of experience that unquestionably separates the elderly from children (Gresham, 1973).

The image of old people as childlike has been with us for a long time. Tuckman and Lorge (1953) asked graduate students in psychology to indicate their agreement or disagreement with a number of statements about old people. Despite the fact that the students were well acquainted with psychology and enrolled in a course involving the aging process, there was a high level of agreement that old people are unproductive, have to go to bed early, need a nap every day, are in the "happiest" period of their lives, cannot manage their own affairs, and are in their second childhood.

More recent research indicates that stereotyping continues to be an integral part of public images of the aged, and that one of the major stereotypes still perpetuates the second childhood image. McTavish (1971) found considerable acceptance for an image of old people that is distinctly reminiscent of the view of toddlers during the stage known as "the terrible two's." Many of his subjects

felt that old people are likely to be annoying, obstinate, and unreasonable. In 1975, the National Council on the Aging reported the results of a survey of 4,254 adult Americans (Harris, 1975). Old people were generally thought of as useless and inactive by participants in the survey. They viewed the elderly as spending most of their time watching television or "doing nothing," in the true spirit of directionless adolescence.

Viewing the Old as Childlike

The ubiquitousness of the "second childhood" stereotype becomes apparent when we examine its common forms.

First, old people are given the personality and moods of children. It is common, for example, in prescription drug ads to describe senility in terms normally associated with children. An ad for a tranquilizer "for the agitated geriatric" shows an elderly man angrily waving his fist. "TANTRUMS" is printed large across the page. Other tranquilizer ads use terms such as "nuisance," "disruptive," and "obstreperous" to describe the actions of elders. Even in a recent children's book, which was written to acquaint children with old age, the elderly woman who is explaining to a young girl what it is like to be old describes herself as sometimes "cranky," a word usually reserved for children. Television shows and movies characterize the personality of older people as childlike whether it is "Mother Jef-

He's out of diapers for the second time in his life.

ferson's" cantankerousness, the silliness of Johnny Carson's "Aunt Blabby," or the impulsiveness and recklessness of Ruth Gordon in the film, *Harold and Maude*.

Second, old people are given the dress and appearance of children. On the cover of one birthday card is a blackboard with "You're only young once!" chalked on it along with various doodles. Inside, an overweight, unshaven elderly man smoking a cigar is wearing a summer camp tee shirt, shorts, sneakers and cap and is playing with a yo-yo and a baseball bat. Above his grinning face the card says "Happy Birthday Playboy." In addition to its other connotations, the card suggests that when you get old, you are at liberty to play like a child again. One of the worst examples of attributing childlike qualities to the elderly is the appearance of an older man—dressed in pajamas and a birthday hat and blowing a noisemaker—in an advertisement for a "geriatric highchair." On the chair's tray is a birthday cake.

Third, old people are given the physical problems of children. One ad for catheters, which appears in a geriatric nursing journal, shows the forearms and hands of a baby as its model instead of an elder. A prescription drug ad for a stool-softener features a smiling bifocaled older woman. The text reads: "Minnie moved her bowels today. The day started right for Minnie. That young doctor feller gave her a stool softener to take last night. And it worked!. . .Minnie figures she's got the smartest doctor in town." It is not too farfetched to imagine that Minnie's smile not only expresses her physical relief but also her pride at being told she moved her bowels.

Fourth, old people are given parties in the spirit of children's parties. In a suburban smalltown newspaper, a recent article reported that the patients at a local nursing home "held their very own Christmas party." The article went on to indicate that patients "planned the party, made the invitations, decorated the cookies

made by the chef, and took part in the entertainment, which included a group singing of Christmas Carols." The article thanked a local drugstore for supplying "Santa's gifts." The intentions were admirable, but the message rang loud and clear: Old people are like big children.

Posters in a popular chain of fast-food restaurants urge customers to "Have a Senior Birthday Party." For the "birthday kid" who is "young at heart," the fast food chain offers to provide the cake, hats, and party favors. Also consider a telephone company ad for custom phones which can be given as gifts to "celebrate any occasion." One such occasion is "Gertrude's" retirement party, complete with colorful ribbons and balloons. In honor of her retirement, Gertrude is shown receiving her own Snoopy phone from her co-workers. A similar ad shows an elder receiving a Mickey Mouse phone at a party.

Fifth, old people are encouraged to pursue the activities of children. In an article called "The Fun Life for Young and Old," a major city newspaper provided "a guide to August activities for senior citizens and children." Pictures were shown of a puppet show and a magic act. Even the "Kiddies' Menu" of a popular Massachusetts ice cream parlor portrays an older man walking hand-in-hand with a young boy. As clearly stated on the face of the menu, "for all kids under 10 and over 65," the bill of fare consists of a "hot doggie," "kiddie burger," and "peanut butter and jelly samwhich."

Advice books for the elderly often treat them as children by advising them to reduce the work-related activities associated with adulthood (Arluke, et al., 1984). Programs in nursing homes and hospitals intended to make life more interesting for elderly patients also become infantilizing at times (Levin at al., 1983). One handbook of activities and recreational programs for nursing homes recommends discussing such topics as "growing things," "boys," "sunshine," "stones," and "favorite story."

Kiddies' Menu

For all kids under 10 and over 65 offers the following Bill of Fare

HOT DOGGY .99
KIDDIE BURGER .99
PEANUT BUTTER &
JELLY SAMWHICH .75

all of the above served with Steak Fries

Sixth, old people are given the playthings of children. A department store ad in *TV Guide* shows an elderly man riding a child's three wheeler. The caption reads: "Wish they had Hot Cycles when I was a kid. . .Yep, kids sure are lucky today. Hey, maybe when no one's around. . ."

A prescription drug used to treat symptoms associated with organic brain syndrome, claims in an ad that it "Usually leaves the disturbed elderly patient in the nursing home more alert, more responsive." In the ad, the photograph of an elderly woman shows her smiling limply and holding a large red and white checked cloth flower. Above her is the caption: "I made a flower today." A similar arts-and-crafts portrayal of the aged appears in an ad for a drug used to improve circulation. Three elders who are "deficient in peripheral circulation" but "proficient in the 'home' " are shown hard at work making ceramics—which is evidently considered to be a higher level activity in the nursing home. A major newspaper recently ran an article entitled "Latest Trends from Toyland," in which the reporter suggests that dolls can be a "companion to the elderly as they are to children."

Implications

"Infantilization" justifies the paternalistic treatment of minority group members with the consequence that they may be "kept in their place" as dependent inferiors. Forms of discrimination supported by infantilization include slavery, forcing women to stay at home and various forms of institutionalization.

Casting old people as children has detrimental effects on old and young alike. The "second childhood" stereotype tends to make young people feel distant from their elders. Having just graduated from childhood, what adolescent wants to endure it again by associating with the old? The stereotype may well also encourage gerontophobia, the neurotic fear of old age. How many adults want to be thought of one day as a six-year-old who isn't toilet trained?

For old people, the second-childhood stereotype creates a self-fulfilling prophecy. Many elderly people come to accept the second-childhood stereotype and play the role with enthusiasm. But is that because they fail to see any alternative? Our society has traditionally offered certain rewards to those elderly citizens who are willing to "stay in their place." Riding on a special bus for senior citizens, or dancing with other seniors to the tune of Yankee Doodle, may isolate elderly people. But it may be preferable to watching re-runs of "Marcus Welby."

Acting like children has three negative consequences for old people.

First, such behavior lowers their social status because their individual responsibility has been diminished, while their dependency has increased. Secondly, the perception of infantile behavior in the elderly may allow certain things to be done to them that would otherwise not be considered: the prescription of psychoactive medications, institutionalization, and declaration of legal incompetency. Thirdly, infantilization robs the "gray power" movement of adults who might otherwise work for political change and social betterment.

Not all old people buy the second-childhood stereotype. A large number of elderly Americans are thoroughly offended by infantilization and seek to avoid the consequences of the stereotype. For many, this means making efforts to "pass" for middle-age by dying hair, lying about their age, and using youth-oriented cosmetics. A positive form of avoidance is reengagement, whereby old people seek to become either re-employed or remarried after the loss of a job or spouse.

On the damaging side, an unknown number of cases of apparent senility may actually represent a refusal to accept the second-childhood syndrome. Rather than comply, some elders may retreat into a more comfortable, more secure psychological state which ironically has the appearance of infantile behavior. So, for example, we might see lack of sexual interest, giddiness, forgetfulness, inability to maintain a stable relationship, and lack of control over bodily functions.

A Warning

In contemporary America, stereotyped images of the elderly may one day include less emphasis on infantilization and more emphasis on dehumanization. There is a tendency to view some aged people as mere "vegetables" —totally beyond the age of productivity and usefulness. They are viewed as no longer alive in the sense that we understand what it means to be human and therefore not worthy of the medical and social services available to those who are younger—such as expensive dialysis or lengthy rehabilitation for fractures, stroke, and other problems.

Another aspect of this dehumanization of the elderly may be "to color them all gray" and see them as a group that presents a threat. In periods of economic retrenchment, a large and growing elderly population may to an increasing extent be regarded as a major threat to the economic well-being of younger Americans. Those Americans who feel especially frustrated may look for a justification to reduce the power of their older competitors. Substantial reductions in social security and health benefit payments might be a first step.

Stereotypical or dehumanizing views of the elderly (or any age group) damage the social fabric of our nation even though they may not be held by all Americans. Much is being done currently to counter these views through education and advocacy in the public and private sectors. As the examples in this article illustrate, however, much remains to be done.

REFERENCES

Arluke, A., Levin, J., and Suchwalko, J. "Sexuality and Romance in Advice Books for the Elderly." *Gerontologist.* In press, 1984.

Blassingame, J. *The Slave Community.* New York: Oxford University Press, 1972.

Gresham, M. "The Infantilization of the Elderly." *Nursing Forum* 15, 1976, pp. 196-209.

Harris, L., and Associates. *The Myth and Reality of Aging in America.* New York: National Council on Aging, 1975.

Helmreich, W. *The Things They Say Behind Your Back.* New York: Doubleday, 1982.

Levin, J., and Arluke, A. "Our Elderly's Fate?" *New York Times,* September 29, 1983, p. A31.

Levin, J. Arluke, A., and Cheren, C. "The Challenge of Ageism." *American Health Care Association Journal* 9, March 1983, pp. 47-50.

Lurie, A. *The Language of Clothing.* New York: Random House, 1982.

McTavish, D. "Perceptions of Old People: A Review of Research Methodologies and Findings." *Gerontologist* 11 (4, Part 2), 1971, pp. 90-101.

Tuckman, J. and Lorge, I. "Attitudes Toward Old People." *Journal of Social Psychology* 37, 1953, pp. 249-260.

Social Institutions in Crisis and Change

- The Political Sphere (Articles 22-23)
- The Economic Sphere (Articles 24-25)
- The Social Sphere (Articles 26-28)

Social institutions are the building blocks of social structure. They represent the ways in which the important tasks of society are accomplished. The regulation of reproduction, socialization of children, production and distribution of economic goods, enforcement of social control, and organization of religion and other value systems are examples of social tasks performed by social institutions.

Social institutions are not rigid arrangements; they reflect changing social conditions. Institutions generally change slowly. At the present time, however, many of the social institutions in the United States are in a state of crisis and are undergoing rapid change. The political system is ineffective; it does not generate great leaders. Public consensus seems to be the less government intervention the better. American foreign policy sometimes appears to be guided more by fear than by reason. The United States economy is on shaky ground. The management of American businesses has been blamed for the decline in productivity. Medical care in some cases is uncaring. Institutional crisis is found everywhere. Even the family as an institution is under attack. Critics of the system complain that our institutions are not meeting the needs of society. Whether this is because institutions are changing too rapidly or too slowly will continue to be debated. However, in order to appreciate how social institutions endure, it is necessary to understand the development and process of such changes.

The selections in this section examine some changing institutions. Joshua Meyrowitz presents a provoking thesis that America has not had great political leaders because the political process prevents great leadership. He maintains that the main culprit is television because it keeps leaders and potential leaders constantly in the spotlight and it is difficult to remain a hero when watched too closely and too constantly. Meyrowitz concludes that the styles of leaders who are appealing on television are not the styles of great leaders.

Henry Steel Commager debates the conventional wisdom that the least government intervention possible is the best government. He points out that the federal government is not the great threat to individual freedoms feared by many Americans but rather the great defender of freedoms. Furthermore, only the federal government can address many of the issues which plague the United States today.

Though America has recovered from the recession of the early 1980s, the economy is still facing some major problems. James Fallows explains how large budget and trade deficits and heavy borrowing from abroad may cause hardships in the future in the form of higher taxes and inflation. He says the United States lacks the political will to correct its current economic course. David Vogel, on the other hand, looks at the businesses which affect our economy and points out how badly they are managed. The major cause for this failure, he believes, is the short run perspective which is reflected in the way managers are rewarded.

The litany of failure spills over into the social sphere as well. Cherlin and Furstenberg do not proclaim the death of the family as did David Cooper in 1970, but they do review the statistics on divorce, unmarried couples, working wives, single parent families, and other changing family patterns and conclude that "the traditional family will no longer predominate." They expect family patterns of the future to accommodate frequent divorce and remarriages.

Karp's article on education criticizes the system for training students to be passive and for stiffling creative thinking. While schools are shown to be failing in several other areas such as SAT testing, he emphasizes the school's lack of responsibility in teaching Johnny to think.

Finally Victoria Sackett examines the public's opinion on one of the most divisive issues of our day—abortion. Rather than finding two opposing camps, she discovers an ambivalent public which is troubled by abortion but at the same time is concerned with freedom to choose.

Looking Ahead: Challenge Questions

Why is it important to preserve some continuity in institutions?

Can institutions outlive their usefulness?

Why are institutions so difficult to change? Cite examples where changes are instituted from the top, down, and others where they are instituted from the bottom, up. Do you see a similar pattern of development for these changes?

Unit 5

<u>Politics in the Video Eye:</u>

Where Have All the Heroes Gone?

THERE'S NO SHORTAGE OF POTENTIALLY GREAT LEADERS, JUST AN OVERABUNDANCE OF INFORMATION ABOUT THEM.

Joshua Meyrowitz

Joshua Meyrowitz is an associate professor of communication at the University of New Hampshire. This article is adapted from his book, No Sense of Place: The Impact of Electronic Media on Social Behavior *(Oxford University Press).*

To hide in plain sight: Walter Mondale in Chicago, March 1984.

The towns and cities of this country once served as "back stages" or rehearsal halls for national political figures. By the time William Jennings Bryan, for example, delivered his powerful "cross-of-gold" speech to win the Democratic nomination for President in 1896, he had practiced the speech before many different audiences. Bryan's legendary oratory and the treasured images of many of our other political heroes were made possible by the opportunity to rehearse and modify the way they performed in public. Early mistakes could be limited to small forums, minor changes could be tested and speeches and presentations could be honed to perfection. Politicians could thrill many different crowds on different days with the same well-turned phrase.

That was before television became such a pervasive force in the political arena. Today a national politician often faces a single audience. Wherever Walter Mondale, Gary Hart or Ronald Reagan speak, they are "overheard" by people everywhere. Major speeches, therefore, cannot be pretested, and because they are presented only once, they tend to be relatively coarse and undramatic. Further, politicians can no longer easily enhance their positions with different promises to different audiences. Because politicians now confront so many types of people simultaneously, they cannot speak in specifics. And any mistake or slip of the tongue is amplified in significance because of the millions of people who have seen and heard it.

Many people still hope for the emergence of an old-style, dynamic, "great

THE SPEAKER'S PLATFORM ONCE RAISED POLITICIANS UP AND AWAY FROM THE PEOPLE—LITERALLY AND SYMBOLICALLY.

Hi-yo silver: William Jennings Bryan and his "cross of gold."

leader," but television is making it virtually impossible to find one. There is no lack of potential leaders but rather an overabundance of information about them. The great-leader image depends upon distance, mystery and careful management of public impressions. Through television, we see too much of our politicians, and they are losing control over their images.

Our national leaders once had much greater control over their public images. Reporters were not even allowed into the White House until the 20th century, for example, and could not quote a President without permission until the mid 1950s. Few people ever heard Thomas Jefferson's slight speech impediment; few were aware of Lincoln's frequent bouts of depression. Grover Cleveland had his entire upper jaw removed in a secret operation in 1893. Although he was out of sight for many days (including July 4) and spoke with bandages in his mouth for almost a month, the facts surrounding his ordeal remained secret for nearly 25 years. The public barely realized that Franklin Roosevelt was badly disabled. On radio, FDR was a powerful, disembodied voice. Even Eisenhower, the first President to be watched frequently on television, could linger near death in a hospital while the public witnessed an apparent flurry of presidential activity through the news releases of his press secretary. But by the time Lyndon Johnson had his gall bladder removed, he felt obliged to smile broadly and reveal his scars to the nation. And in recent years, we have had the dubious honor of watching President Carter nearly collapse while jogging and of seeing President Reagan nod off during an audience with the Pope.

We can better appreciate television's impact on politicians' control of their images by examining what it takes to successfully "stage" our own public images. Regardless of competence or desire, there is a limit to how long we can play out an idealized version of a social role, whether it be dedicated worker, dutiful child, concerned parent or trustworthy friend. We all need to sleep, to make love and to go to the bathroom. We must take time to think about our behavior in social situations, prepare for social encounters and rest from them. Most of us play many different roles each day and must highlight different aspects of our personalities in different situations. We behave differently with co-workers, with friends, with children and with spouses. The performance of social roles, then, is in many ways like a drama: The success of the performance "onstage" depends not only upon keeping the audience from "backstage," where we rehearse and relax, but also upon keeping people away from performances aimed at another audience. Opening up the backstage area does not give us a truer picture of the actor, just a different, more confusing performance.

Television has steadily eroded the traditional barriers between politicians' onstage and backstage areas. We see politicians address crowds of well-wishers, then greet their families "in private." We join candidates as they speak with their advisers, and we sit with them as they watch the political conventions on television. We see candidates address many different types of audiences in many different settings. We watch politicians move from backstage to onstage to backstage. Revealing both traditional onstage and traditional backstage activities, television could be said to provide a "sidestage" view of public figures.

By definition, the "private" behavior now exposed is no longer truly backstage activity, simply because it is exposed. Politicians are certainly losing some aspects of their privacy—a

THE GRANGER COLLECTION

A voice of iron: Despite his polio, FDR conveyed an image of strength.

complaint we often hear—but, more important, they are simultaneously losing the backstage time necessary to play traditional onstage roles.

Our leaders once had many hours, sometimes even weeks or months, to consult with advisers, formulate policy statements and respond to crises. In live, televised press conferences today, even a five-second pause for thought can destroy a leader's credibility. Speaking before millions of people, politicians often must begin a sentence before the end of the sentence is fully formed in their minds. The apparent inarticulateness of all of our recent Presidents may be related more to changes in the press than to a decline in their basic abilities.

The sidestage perspective offered by television makes normal differences in behavior appear to be evidence of inconsistency and dishonesty. We all behave differently in different situations, depending on who is there and who is not. Yet when television news programs edit together videotape sequences that show Reagan or Mondale saying and doing different

things in different places and before different audiences, they appear, at best, indecisive and, at worst, dishonest. This element of television coverage may be at the core of the "crisis of credibility" that has plagued all our recent Presidents.

Part of the problem is that politicians have lost a great deal of control over their messages and performances. When they ask that the television camera or tape recorder be turned off, politicians appear to have something to hide. When a camera or microphone is on, they cannot separate their exchanges with the press from their exchanges with the public. And unlike the reports of journalists or other witnesses, quotes taken from tapes of public or private conversations are impossible to deny.

President Nixon was the archetypal victim of the new sidestage politics. Nixon tried to play the role of an old-style great leader in blissful ignorance of the communication environment in which he performed. A good speaker and an excellent debater, he was extremely effective in person and on ra-

dio. On television, however, Nixon's finely tuned verbal arguments were often undermined by a clenched fist, shifty eyes and a contemptuous scowl. He seemed tense and untrustworthy. What ultimately undid Nixon were blatant inconsistencies between his onstage claims and his exposed backstage behavior. Tapes of his private conversations confirmed what many had inferred from his televised slips of the tongue and disturbing nonverbal style. Nixon had made public proclamations of his greatness and his dedication to law and order; his backstage behavior revealed his pettiness and his use of the language of gangsters.

To be carried off smoothly, the new sidestage political arena requires a synthesis: behavior that lacks both the extreme formality of traditional onstage political behavior and the extreme informality of traditional backstage behavior. The political performance remains a performance, but the demand for consistency among all exposed behavior has led to a bland and uninspiring political drama.

Our first sidestage President was Jimmy Carter, who abandoned the traditional dramatic style of most of his predecessors. Carter usually spoke quietly and slowly in simple phrases and in a tone and manner well-suited to the sensitive microphone and close-up lens. In his first Presidential campaign, Carter avoided making specific promises to different audiences. His message all over the country was nearly the same, basically "Just trust me." While the imperial Richard Milhous Nixon spoke about clean language in public and cursed in private, low-key Jimmy (not James Earl) Carter attempted to project an image that could not be easily undermined by anything the press could reveal. He spoke of screwing and shacking up in an interview in *Playboy,* and he claimed few uncommon virtues beyond a strong faith in God and a willingness to work hard. Even in his inaugural address he spoke about his weaknesses and the likelihood of his making mistakes. Yet while Carter adapted to the sidestage political arena, many people came to resent his "lowering" of the Presidency and his lackluster style.

Before television, relatively few people closely observed the personal characteristics of national politicians.

*T*ELEVISION NOT
ONLY REDUCES OUR
AWE OF POLITICAL
LEADERS, IT INCREASES
THEIR SELF-DOUBT
AND LOWERS THEIR
SELF-ESTEEM.

When you least expect it: Johnson bares scar; Carter barely stands.

Even when in public, politicians were usually seen at a distance; they were able to maintain a "personal space" that was reserved only for those close to them. Television, however, allows each of us to be a spy in the personal spaces of politicians. The television camera allowed us to watch Richard Nixon sweating under pressure, it showed us Gerald Ford grimacing at his own ill-phrased remarks and it coolly recorded Jimmy Carter as he aged and tired during the Iranian hostage crisis. The speaker's platform once raised a politician up and away from the people, both literally and symbolically. The camera now brings the politician close for the people's inspection. And in this sense, it lowers politicians to the level of their audience. Is it any wonder that politicians who try to orate and gesticulate like traditional great leaders, as Ted Kennedy frequently did in his 1980 Presidential campaign, now appear high-strung, overzealous or even fanatical on television?

The "messages" we receive from politicians on television are not the same as the political messages the public once received through printed statements in newspapers. A typical response to a printed message is to ask whether it is true or false, whether the arguments it presents are logical. Print messages are related to "issues" and "concepts." But the messages we receive through television often lead to a different response. The camera exposes a rich range of personal features and idiosyncracies; it highlights politicians' humanity and mutes abstract and conceptual rhetoric. Television's images are tied more

to the speaker than to the ideas discussed. A common response to a speech on television, therefore, is to think or say: "He seems nervous"; "She looks like she's going to cry"; "I don't trust him"; or "She's tough!"

When presidential candidate Edmund Muskie stood on the steps of the Manchester *Union Leader* in 1972 to denounce a newspaper story attacking his wife, the response to the televised message was based primarily on his emotional behavior rather than on his verbal message. Most people remember that Muskie cried; few can remember what he said. Similarly, few people remember what Jimmy Carter said during his televised "energy speech" but many people remember that he sported a sweater at the time.

Politicians' demeanor on television is often more important than their political programs, and this fact is not lost on political advisers. The night of the Carter-Reagan debate, for example, Reagan aide James Baker passed Reagan an index card with one word of advice: "Chuckle!" When most people think back on such televised debates, they tend to remember the general style and emotional state of the participants rather than their specific arguments. Hence, John F. Kennedy's ability to use his televised debates with Richard Nixon to win a firm place

in the hearts of Americans, while many of those who listened to the same debates on radio—where the focus was on words and issues—thought Nixon had won.

While the public and politicians are often blamed for being more concerned with images than with issues, the image bias may be inherent in the way we now get political information. Through television, we come to feel we "know" politicians personally, and our response to them has become similar to our response to friends and lovers. Just as we would not marry someone on the basis of a résumé or a writing sample, so are we now unwilling to choose Presidents merely on the basis of their stands on the issues. We want, instead, to know what they are "really like." However, the current drive toward intimacy with our leaders involves a fundamental paradox. In pursuing our desire to be close to great people or to confirm their greatness through increased exposure, we destroy the distance that enabled them to appear great in the first place.

Television has also changed how politicians perceive their own performances. In face-to-face behavior, people get a sense of themselves from how others respond, but they can never see themselves quite the way others see them. With television, in contrast, politicians can see exactly what the public sees. A speaker's nervousness and mistakes usually are politely ignored by "live" audiences and therefore soon forgotten by the speaker too. With videotape, politicians have permanent records of themselves sweating, stammering or anxiously licking their lips. Television not only reduces our awe of politicians, it increases politicians' self-doubt and lowers their self-esteem. Television may be a prime cause of the complaints of indecisive leadership and hesitant "followership" that we have heard since the mid 1960s.

Television has led us to vote for candidates who avoid trying to act like traditional great leaders and who have a low-key, sidestage style that can stand constant media exposure. It is no surprise that our most durable recent President is a veteran actor. Ronald Reagan almost always maintains an even-tempered, "nice-guy" demeanor. Even when dodging a question, the "Great Communicator" often humbly cocks his head, smiles and waves. Still, polls suggest that a surprisingly large number of the people who say that they "personally like" Reagan also disagree strongly with his policies, doubt his intelligence and question his control of his administration's activities. Reagan usually is not embarrassing to watch, but he is not an awe-inspiring leader reminiscent of Washington, Jefferson or Lincoln. We still hunger for something more.

By and large, Americans continue to wait for the hero who will gallantly rush from the wings onto the political stage and rescue America. Yet the proscenium arch has been expanded by television and the wings have been opened to public view. Now visible backstage, the hero has less time to rehearse the rescue and build up confidence. Now visible, the hero has to begin running too soon. As a result, the hero comes to the rescue out of breath, barely trotting, with sword undrawn and armor unpolished. In the new communication environment, the national political leader faces a disquieting paradox: to audition for the role of traditional hero is to end up playing the fool, and yet to eschew the trappings of a hero is also to fail for seeming lack of ability.

TOCQUEVILLE'S MISTAKE

A defense of strong central government

Henry Steele Commager

Henry Steele Commager, Simpson Lecturer at Amherst College, has edited an edition of Democracy in America *and is finishing a study of Alexis de Tocqueville.*

Alexis de Tocqueville was a statesman, a historian, a political philosopher, and the first modern sociologist. Like his mentor Montesquieu—indeed, like all judicious political philosophers, from Plato to Croce—he was first and last a moral philosopher. *Democracy in America*, the first volume of which was published 150 years ago, was far more than an interpretation of the American mind and character, or even of the institutions of democracy. It was a nineteenth-century *Spirit of the Laws*, designed to make clear to the people of all Western nations the kind of government, society, economy, and morality they must cultivate if they wished to be saved. Ostensibly, Tocqueville visited America in 1831 to study its prisons, then the model for the Western world; but his true goal was to study the form of government and of society that he took for granted represented the wave of the future.

"In America," he would later write, "I saw more than America; I sought the image of democracy itself, with its inclinations, its character, its prejudices, and its passions." America was the laboratory—the only one on the globe at that time—that might provide some insight into the fate that awaited those nations of the Old World that would move irresistibly toward democracy. What was happening in America, Tocqueville believed, was "interesting not only to the United States, but to the whole world. It concerns not a nation, but mankind."

Democracy in America, eight years in the writing, is a comprehensive analysis of American life and character, and of American institutions. It is the most profound book that has ever been written about America or democracy, and its unique quality is its interplay of shrewdness, sagacity, and moral earnestness. It was thought through by what is now acknowledged to be the most affluent mind ever to reflect on either the American character or the character of democracy. What still excites our interest is its clairvoyance. For in his study of American democracy Tocqueville submitted questions, sounded warnings, and made prophecies that have to do with the threats to any democracy: the tyranny of the majority, the vulgarization of culture, the centralization of power, the rise of a "manufacturing aristocracy, potentially the harshest that ever existed," racial injustice, an unwieldy military, and the corruption of individualism by ambition and greed.

The so-called neoconservatives of our own time have seized upon certain of the entries in this catalogue of dangers with uncritical enthusiasm; no wonder Tocqueville is the cow from which they draw their milk. To consider all the threats that Tocqueville submitted would require a volume; I confine myself here to what is the King Charles's head of neoconservatism: the threat of centralization.

Tocqueville had an almost congenital distrust of central authority, the roots of which extended deep into the soil of Normandy. His family had suffered impoverishment and violence during the French Revolution and under Napoleon. Centralization was the theme of his masterly *The Old Regime and the French Revolu-*

5. SOCIAL INSTITUTIONS: The Political Sphere

What Tocqueville failed to see was that in a federal system like the American, the problem of the role of local and central governments had taken on a new character

tion; here, he traced its disastrous history from the days of Louis XIV through the Revolution and the Restoration.

America, and especially New England, did not so much confirm Tocqueville in his fears as in his hopes. For, with the help of the most distinguished body of teachers any young man has ever enjoyed—three past or future presidents of Harvard (Josiah Quincy, Jared Sparks, and Edward Everett); the most learned justice of the Supreme Court, Joseph Story; and Story's disciple, the philosopher-scholar Francis Lieber—he was able to appreciate to the full the virtues of town government, the local militia, jury trials, and that remarkable institution he was the first to celebrate, the voluntary association. He was able to see local government in action, and nowhere did he see centralization as either dangerous or effective. His view here was so determined by his *point* of view that he regarded Andrew Jackson as a weak executive and predicted that the American president would never pose a threat!

But what about the future of centralization: "Who shall bridle Behemoth, who shall curb Leviathan?" That, Tocqueville knew, was the oldest question in the history of government. Could democracy come up with an answer, or would democracy itself be transformed into a Behemoth and thus justify Alexander Hamilton's alleged taunt: "Your people, sir, is a great beast"?

It is against this background that we read Tocqueville's seemingly paradoxical maxim: "While liberty is the product of *Art* and can be achieved therefore only by the most scrupulous calculations, centralization is the product of *Nature*, and as such enlists the passions of all men." In the Old World, he argued, Nature had triumphed over Art. But in America, Art—by which Tocqueville meant intelligence, inventiveness, ingenuity, skill—might still contain or reverse the dictates of Nature. For America, which had come late onto the stage of history, was not the slave of history and might even be its master. That is what Jefferson meant when he asserted that in America, history might be prospective rather than merely retrospective. "I like dreams of the future," he said, "better than the history of the past."

America was then the only place in which the elusive secret of the reconciliation of liberty and order might be discovered. A risky experiment, this. As Tocqueville wrote, "Political liberty is a difficult food to digest. It is only extremely robust constitutions that can take it."

True enough. Even in Tocqueville's day Americans had enjoyed a longer experience in the *art* of government than any other people. Could they be counted on to employ that art to enlarge liberty? They had indeed done this for almost all of America's white males; but how

did it happen that a people committed to liberty had so eagerly imposed slavery on others? After all, even countries with centralized governments like France and Britain had abolished slavery by the time *Democracy* was published.

Yet, historically, Tocqueville's assumption that liberty had a closer connection with local than with centralized governments had much to be said for it. France, Prussia, Russia, Spain, and most of the Italian states confessed governments that were tyrannical. Where the central government was comparatively weak—in the Low Countries, the Swiss cantons, and, above all, England, which was Tocqueville's spiritual home—the people enjoyed a large measure of liberty. So, too, there had been a larger measure of freedom in the American colonies (in the realm of religion, for example) than in the Mother Country.

Here, however, Tocqueville's propensity for deductive rather than inductive reasoning misled him, as it has misled so many of his present-day mockingbirds. In 1789, Americans had created a "more perfect union" by giving essential authority to a central government. That historic shift toward centralization had not made for a diminution but for an enhancement of liberty. The framers of the Constitution had been mindful of John Dickinson's admonition:

> For who are a free people? Not those over whom government is reasonably and equitably exercised, but those who live under a government so constitutionally checked and controlled that provision is made against it being otherwise exercised.

There was no perceptible threat to liberty from centralization in the America that Tocqueville observed. There was an ardent nationalist in the White House, but he had distributed a federal tax surplus to the states to spend as they pleased, vetoed a bill for an extension of the National Road, and declared war on the "Monster" Bank of the United States, thus putting an end to a promising national bank system.

What Tocqueville failed to take in as he looked over the jumble of American governmental bodies was that in a federal system like the American, where many states were larger than some nations of the Old World, the problem of the role of local and central governments had taken on a new character.

Once again it was John Dickinson who warned his colleagues at the Constitutional Convention of 1787 that "Reason may mislead us; experience must be our guide." Experience must be *our* guide, too, as we reflect on the drawbacks and advantages of centralization and on the extent to which centralization threatens or enhances liberty. It is easy enough to sound the tocsin of alarm—that is one of the noisiest of our bells—but we cannot avoid the conclu-

From the beginning, it has not been the states that have been the chief instruments of democracy but the central government in Washington

sion that those who today declaim against Big Government as the enemy of liberty are ignorant of America's history. The most elementary and overshadowing fact of that history is that there has been a causal connection between the enlargement and the deepening of liberty in America and the growth of a strong national government.

What is meant by "strong national government"? Perhaps the most astonishing feature of the current attack on centralization—an attack that President Reagan has turned into a crusade—is the argument that the United States today has not a strong national government but a Big Government. This notion has been so bolstered by repetition that it is unthinkingly accepted by most Americans. Yet what is most interesting to the foreign observers who have followed in Tocqueville's tracks is how meager, outside of what is involved in "national security," are the responsibilities and activities of the American national government compared with those assumed by most other national governments. In almost every country of Europe and Asia, the national government owns and controls all forms of transportation. It owns or controls the banks, the utilities, most radio and television stations, and most natural resources. All institutions of higher learning are government administered, as are opera companies and orchestras. The national government provides or finances medical services, a far broader range of social services than in our country, and much of the housing. This is not a phenomenon of communist nations; it is a matter of course in Britain, France, Holland, Denmark, Sweden, Australia, Italy, Japan, and scores of other nations. In short, Americans do not have a Big Government.

It is an interesting paradox that the passionate adversaries of centralization today are generally not ardent champions, as was Tocqueville, of the town meeting, the county court, the local militia. Most of those who are in public life appear to prefer life in Washington to life in their state capitals. Their devotion to states' rights has taken the form of devotion to white supremacy (Alabama) or to revenues from coal (Montana), oil (Texas), or tobacco (North Carolina). Many of them seem to be successors to those distinguished senators of the 1890s who were known as the senator from Standard Oil, the senator from the Sugar Trust, and the senator from the Pennsylvania Railroad. But today's "conservatives" have made some progress: popular hostility toward economic centralization has been deflected in the direction of political centralization.

Not that these "conservatives" are critical of all forms of centralization. They lend their support almost automatically to what has been the

most centralizing force in American history: the military. It was the veterans of the American Revolution who were the most ardent champions of a strong national government. It was the Civil War that dramatized the need for centralization and that led to the passage of legislation nationalizing transportation, finance, and industry.

This experience, of course, was duplicated in World War I and World War II. President Eisenhower, who viewed the problem from both a military and a civilian vantage point, warned in his farewell address against the "military-industrial complex." It is almost superfluous to add that this "complex" is celebrated with unrestrained enthusiasm by precisely those whose energies are otherwise devoted to deploring centralization and celebrating states' rights and localism.

But let us turn again to the growth of liberty that has resulted from the growth of the national government. From the beginning, it has not been the states that have been the chief instruments of democracy but the central government in Washington. It was the states that maintained slavery, the national government that abolished it. It was the states that fought for slavery and tried to reinstate it, through "black codes," even after Appomatox. It was the national government that intervened with the Thirteenth, Fourteenth, and Fifteenth amendments and a succession of civil rights acts designed to emancipate and free. It would be asking a great deal to expect blacks to look to the states or to their communities for the protection of their rights.

It would also be asking a great deal to expect women, so long denied not only their political and property rights but even access to the professions and control over their children, to look to the states for their equality. From *Muller v. Oregon* in 1908 to *Roe v. Wade* in 1973, it was the federal not the state courts that vindicated the rights of women. Suffrage, too, though first granted by the federal territory of Wyoming in 1869, required in the end a federal amendment, which was bitterly fought by those states that, half a century later, defeated the Equal Rights Amendment.

Further, it would be asking a great deal to expect labor to take its chances with state rather than national legislation. It is Congress that, over more than half a century, has enacted various charters of freedom for labor. It should be sufficient to note here the Clayton Antitrust Act of 1914, the La Follette Seamen's Act of 1915, the Civilian Conservation Corps Act of 1933, the National Labor Relations Act of 1935, the revolutionary Social Security Act of 1935, and the Fair Labor Standards Act of 1938. These laws did more to

*As every
natural resource
is continental, if
not global, local
governments
cannot control
any one of
them*

establish social justice than the whole corpus of state labor legislation since the Civil War. Nor should we forget that it was Congress and the Supreme Court that, over the vociferous opposition of state economic interests, put an end to the disgrace of child labor.

This record of the role of the national government in promoting justice and the general welfare is mirrored in federal efforts to encourage the conservation of natural resources. It was President Jefferson who launched the Lewis and Clark expedition and several others, whose mission it was to explore and chart the whole of America. And it was Jefferson who celebrated the providential blessing of "land enough for our descendants to the thousandth and thousandth generation." Alas, the people nullified that prediction, often with the connivance of the states. Theodore Roosevelt launched a conservation movement early in this century, and Franklin Roosevelt reinvigorated it. FDR did more to save and restore America's natural resources—through the Civilian Conservation Corps, the hundred-mile tree belt on the border of the Great Plains, and the Tennessee Valley Authority—than had been achieved in a hundred years. As every natural resource is continental, if not global, local governments cannot control any one of them. By neglect or exploitation, however, they can damage all of them.

In the arena of education the story is much the same. Ever since Massachusetts Bay enacted the first education laws in modern history, education has been the responsibility of local communities. But not all communities have fulfilled that responsibility. Our greatest educator, Thomas Jefferson, drafted ordinances making land grants to help support public schools and universities. That policy was expanded by the Morrill Act of 1862, which provided federal contributions to state universities throughout the nation, and by the Hatch Act of 1887, which set up scores of agricultural experiment stations. Those who now assert that education is a purely local matter are as wanting in logic as in a familiarity with history. The nation has an interest in the education of all children, each of whom, when an adult, can vote for congressmen and for president, and each of whom, therefore, can legislate for the whole of the nation, and for posterity.

Montesquieu had formulated what came to be widely accepted as a law of History. He held that the supreme principle of a monarchy was power, of an aristocracy, honor, and of a republic, virtue. Tocqueville was sagacious enough to give an American rather than a classical application to this law. "What Montesquieu meant by virtue," he wrote, "is the moral power which each individual exercises upon himself and which prevents him from violating another's right . . . those turbulent virtues which sometimes bring glory but more often trouble to society rank low in [American] public opinion."

Americans readily embraced this tribute while reserving judgment on its qualification. It appeared to most of them to be the common sense of the matter. The Founding Fathers themselves were all but obsessed with the idea of virtue; no public address, scarcely a private letter, failed to invoke it. A single sample must suffice, and that from the most exalted source. "There is no truth more thoroughly established," Washington said in his first inaugural address, "than that there exists in the economy and course of nature an indissoluble union between virtue and happiness, between duty and advantage, between the genuine maxims of an honest and magnanimous policy and the solid rewards of public prosperity and felicity. . . . The propitious smiles of Heaven can never be expected on a nation that disregards the eternal rules of order and right which Heaven itself has ordained."

Why was the ideal of virtue so essential to the American experiment? The answer to that was elementary. America was, after all, the only democratic nation in the world. It was, therefore, as Jefferson put it in his first inaugural address, "the world's best hope." Its success, its very survival, depended on the ascendance of virtue in its people. If they were not prepared to cherish and practice virtue, the audacious enterprise of democracy was foredoomed to failure.

The Founding Fathers were realists—even, with John Adams and Alexander Hamilton, somewhat cynical realists. They knew human nature and did not think highly of it. Most of them were closer to Edmund Burke than to Tom Paine. History had taught them that all men were creatures of ambition, passion, pride, envy, intemperance, greed, and inconsistency. How then could they be expected to conduct themselves collectively with prudence, dignity, honor, virtue, and magnanimity?

Tocqueville confronted that problem at its most troublesome. Only a virtuous people could make democracy work, and the American people were no more virtuous than any other people. How could America succeed where so many had failed?

Tocqueville put the question another way: What was the distinguishing characteristic of American democracy? It was, he concluded, individualism. Quite right, too, for never before had circumstances been so propitious for the exercise of (or the indulgence of) individualism by the common people, and never before had a people been so eager to indulge themselves in that exercise. To the average white American,

A host of new dangers confronts America. We can no longer count on those immunities that we enjoyed when Tocqueville contemplated our destiny

individualism was a simple matter. It meant that he could live where he would, marry whom he would, worship as he would, have children as he wished—confident that they would not want—and associate with whom he would. He could work on a farm, follow the sea, keep a shop, or embrace a profession, and if one of these ceased to suit him, he could shift easily to another. He could sit on juries, elect his own magistrates, and himself aspire to any office in the town, the county, the state, or the nation. Where else on the face of the earth did individualism have such scope?

But was an individualism so extreme compatible with an orderly society? Tocqueville thought not. Yet he acknowledged that the system had worked for half a century: in the early years of the Republic, Americans had resisted the temptations of ambition, self-indulgence, and corruption.

Was there any reason to suppose that the good fortune that had attended America would continue? Yes, Tocqueville believed, but only if Americans could overcome the seductions of majority tyranny, the menace of militarism, the threat of an industrial oligarchy, and the dangers of centralization. Only if Americans were ready to embrace what he called "enlightened self-interest."

What might enable American democracy to escape the fate of other democracies?

First of all, a religious toleration more profound than was to be found in any other country. Then education that would promote enlightenment—an education more widespread than elsewhere on the globe. Add to these a

boundless territory; resources bountiful enough to meet the needs of all and thus discourage selfish competition; a prosperity that might be expected to satisfy all ambitions, or at least to moderate them; immunity from wars; a government in which all could participate and which was encumbered with so many and intricate checks and balances that it was all but incapable of exercising tyranny. And then there is Tocqueville's homely observation that "in America it is not virtue that is great, but temptation that is small.... It is not disinterestedness that is great, it is interest that is taken for granted."

It is not only the same formidable threats that Tocqueville saw in the 1830s that now confront America, but a host of new dangers. Alas, we can no longer count on those dispensations and immunities that we enjoyed when Tocqueville contemplated our destiny. We no longer have limitless resources or immunity from attack; we are no longer confident that our democratic system works or that our system is indeed democratic. Nor, no matter how audaciously our leaders declaim it, is there any reason to believe that we are "God's chosen people."

Do we have the ingenuity to adapt to the realities of a global economy? Do we have the common sense to adjust our nationalism to a world of technology and science that is totally indifferent to national frontiers? Do we have the wisdom to realize that our fate is inextricably bound up with the fate of all the peoples of the globe? Can we practice a self-interest that is enlightened?

WASHINGTON

THE THREE FISCAL CRISES

Unprecedented budget and trade deficits, combined with unprecedented borrowing from other nations, darken the nation's future

—*James Fallows*

ECONOMICS DOES NOT easily accept the idea of irreversibility. In principle, almost no change is so permanent that it cannot be undone. If people are no longer eager to buy your goods and services, if your nation's comparative advantage has waned, you need only lower your price. It is all a matter of adjustment; at some point—which is to say, at some price—the curves of supply and demand will intersect.

Real life is not always so flexible as economic theory would suppose. For instance, wages sometimes stop rising but they rarely decline, because people cannot stand to live under circumstances in which the price of labor fluctuates like the spot price for oil. But there is an even more important exception to the economists' contention that what goes up must eventually come down.

Because of the relentless workings of compound interest—the mathematical formula under which the interest earned in each period is added to the principal sum, so that the interest is larger in the next period than it was in the last— when things start moving in a certain direction, they can gain rather than lose speed. A debtor who has a little trouble meeting this year's interest payments will have a lot of trouble next year. Because compound interest introduces a momentum of its own, trends subject to its influence behave very differently from normal equations of supply and demand. By the time a trend of this kind is detected, it will rapidly be getting worse.

The magic of compound interest is becoming the central explanatory fact about the American economy. In three fundamental and related areas the United States is quite suddenly shifting to the wrong side of the interest curve. Taken one by one, the changes are familiar; taken all together, they tell us something about the economy which we'd rather not know.

The first change is the sudden disappearance of America's surplus in the international balance of trade. During the 1970s the United States managed to sell almost exactly as much to other countries as it bought from them—even though it was unexpectedly obliged to spend astronomical sums for imported oil, and even though foreign competitors had already made deep inroads into traditional American bastions, from radios to steel. The trade deficit for the entire decade of the seventies was $20 billion.

Now things have changed so drastically that the deficit for 1985 alone will be more than $120 billion.

To make quickly the point that Walter Mondale made ad nauseam but to no effect in last year's campaign: the sudden collapse of the United States in international trade may have something to do with poor management or shoddy workmanship or unfair trade restrictions, but it mainly has to do with ballooning federal deficits. Because of the deficits, the government needs to borrow more money; because it has borrowed more, real interest rates have gone up; because U.S. interest rates are higher, foreigners are depositing more money in American banks; and because so much foreign money has been coming into the country, the exchange rate for the dollar became and has stayed unreasonably high. By most estimates, the dollar is worth about 40 percent more than its "natural" value against European and Japanese currencies. This is the equivalent of a 40 percent export tax on U.S. products, and it has had predictable results.

As recently as 1980 the merchandise category of U.S. trade accounts—which includes automobiles, shoes, and all the other manufactured goods in which the

United States has psychologically conceded defeat—showed a $20 billion *surplus*. By last year that had changed to an $80 billion deficit, a swing of $100 billion in four years. According to Peter Peterson, a former secretary of commerce and a present-day Jeremiah about deficit spending, the decline in exports has cost the United States 2.5 million jobs. Roy E. Moor, of the First National Bank of Chicago, has pointed out that of all the dozens of categories of American industry, only five managed to sell more goods abroad in 1984 than they sold in 1981—and even in those "successful" industries imports grew much faster than exports. The greatest American success stories were in the "business and office machine" category, notably computers. But even there imports grew almost four times faster than exports. Apart from the five successful groups (the others were cars, non-medicinal chemicals, non-food consumer goods, and electrical and electronic products), *all* other categories of American industry exported less in 1984 than they had in 1981. By the middle of 1984 the United States was importing 60 percent more than it was exporting—the most unfavorable ratio in our modern history, and one found more often among developing countries than among major industrial powers.

THE COMPETITIVE position of the United States might theoretically be brighter than the balance-of-payments figures would imply. American companies might conceivably be building efficient new plants overseas, with which they would defend their market share, even though they would not be restoring American jobs. But since American exports have collapsed so suddenly, such long-term investments would be slow to take up the slack—and in fact the flow of investments has been running the opposite way. Rather than sending capital abroad to build new plants and equipment, the United States has started borrowing from other nations, to subsidize its own consumption. This in turn helps explain the second radical change in America's economic position: the virtually instantaneous disappearance of the financial credits the United States had slowly accumulated around the world.

During the nineteenth century, when the United States was expanding its railway network and establishing its industrial base, foreign investors made loans and bought stock to provide much of the necessary capital. Late in the century, when the United States emerged as a pre-eminent industrial and agricultural power, it began to reverse the flow, using its new earnings to make loans and start businesses overseas. By the beginning of the First World War the United States had become a net international creditor for the first time in its history, meaning that the value of its loans and investments in other countries exceeded the value of foreign investments here. For the next sixty-five years its standing as a creditor improved, until in 1982 it enjoyed an international-investment surplus of $150 billion.

Then, in less than three years, everything changed. In the world as economists usually imagine it, the United States could not have gone into debt as rapidly as it in fact has. If the country developed a grievous balance-of-trade problem, the obvious next step would be for the value of the dollar to fall. The Japanese and Germans, having sold their wares to Americans and bought little in return, would find themselves with unwanted surpluses of dollars. When they exchanged them for the yen or Deutschmarks they preferred to have, the pressures of supply and demand would drive down the value of the dollar relative to other currencies. This, in turn, would make imports more expensive in the United States and American exports more attractive. The trade imbalance would be self-correcting.

But that is not what the Japanese and others have done with their dollars. For a variety of reasons—lack of investment opportunities in their own countries, persistently high interest rates in the United States, other factors whose influence economists are now debating—they have deposited their dollars in U.S. banks and bought U.S. bonds, rather than trading the dollars for yen. Several consequences have followed. Japanese VCRs and Italian shoes seem artificially cheap in the United States, since the value of the dollar has been held artificially high. Credit is artificially easy for Americans to obtain, since the Bank of America can use the deposits it has received from Japanese investors to make loans to families that want to buy Japanese cars. When all the complications are boiled away, what's left is a cycle in which the United States started borrowing money from foreigners to buy cut-rate foreign goods—and has kept borrowing and buying at faster and faster rates.

By the end of last year the international debts of the United States had grown so quickly that they had come to equal its investments. And they kept on growing; indeed, because of the workings of compound interest they gathered speed as the United States moved deeper into the debtor category. By the end of this year the United States will stand roughly $100 billion in debt to the rest of the world, which will make it the largest debtor nation, eclipsing the Mexicos and Argentinas—and this less than three years after being the largest creditor. By the end of next year it will owe at least $100 billion more.

One crucial technical measure of the velocity at which a country is moving into debt is the ratio between two financial indicators, the current-account deficit and the exports of goods and services. Roughly speaking, the equivalent measure for a household is the ratio between how much new money it is borrowing each year and how much it earns. In 1982, when the Third World's "debt crisis" was widely publicized and feared, this ratio reached a peak of 24 percent for the major debtors. Peter Peterson points out that in 1984 the United States' ratio rose above 25 percent.

THE THIRD AND most familiar of the economic changes is the phenomenal growth of federal deficits during the past four years. "Deficit spending" has been such a traditional bogey in U.S. politics that it is surprising to realize how modest most previous deficits have been. Before 1980, only twice in America's peacetime history had the annual federal deficit equaled more than three percent of the gross national product. The deficit for 1983, the largest in American history in both relative and absolute terms, equaled 6.4 percent of the GNP. According to most projections, the deficit will remain indefinitely in the five-percent range, unless federal taxing or spending policies change far more dramatically than any politician has yet proposed.

The previous "large" deficits all occurred either during wars or during economic recessions, when tax receipts are unusually low and social-welfare spending is high. These new deficits are much less cyclical. Indeed, the Administration's projections show sustained high deficits despite an assumption that the economy will grow smoothly and uninterruptedly in the future, as it never has grown in the past. Politicians such as Congressmen Jack Kemp and Newt Gingrich, and journalists such as Robert Novak and Robert Bartley, the influential editorial writer for *The Wall Street Journal*, have said that warnings about the deficits are more of the old leftist defeatism. Why concentrate on the bad news, when with the correct, optimistic policies we can grow our way out of the deficit? True, the deficit may shrink if the tonic effects of Reaganomics are so powerful and long-lasting that the American economy moves onto an entirely different plane, like an underdeveloped country reaching "take-off," in W.W. Rostow's famous model. If unemployment goes below four percent and stays there, and if real growth reaches five or six percent a year and stays there, then the nation's greatest concern will be managing its affluence and leisure time. But short of that, the deficit won't "grow" away. The basic mathematics of today's tax and spending policies will leave a chronic gap between what the government takes in and what it pays out.

As RONALD REAGAN understands, Walter Mondale learned, and the U.S. Congress demonstrates each day, debt and deficits are practically meaningless as political issues. "Nobody has successfully translated the evils of debt and deficits from the abstract to the real," Representative Jim Jones, of Oklahoma, a former chairman of the House Budget Committee, told me this summer. "Once it's shown to be a pocketbook issue, it will be dealt with. But for now it's all downside."

In the White House and Congress early this spring there was a flurry of concern over the deficits. The Administration's pollsters determined that with Mondale safely interred, the public was starting to express worry about the deficits. But once Congress had passed mild anti-deficit measures, which would stop the defense buildup and cut about $50 billion from the 1986 deficit (leaving it at about $170 billion), the issue resumed its accustomed seat in the rear.

The unsexiness of dealing with deficits is hardly surprising. When the workings of compound interest are considered, it becomes obvious why the sudden recent shifts in our economic standing have not yet registered as a national crisis—indeed, have done so

much for our recent prosperity—and why they will cause so much harm for so many years to come.

Of the three recent changes, one can be depended on to correct itself, sooner or later. At some point we'll have sent more dollars to Japan than the Japanese care to deposit in American banks or sink into U.S. Treasury bills. Then the value of the dollar will fall, imports will become more expensive, and the trade deficit will be reduced. The main uncertainty is how this will occur. Will the United States carry out its threats to retaliate against the Japanese with protectionist laws? (It may seem quaint now, but in 1971 Richard Nixon's revolutionary package of protectionist measures was provoked by fears of a *two*-billion-dollar annual trade deficit, or roughly six days' worth at today's pace.) Will foreign investors decide to do us a favor, by shifting their capital to other nations gradually, thereby decreasing demand for the dollar slowly and letting its value drift gently down, in turn making U.S. exports more attractive? Will there instead be a panicked run on the dollar, suddenly disrupting certain industries and reintroducing us to our old nemesis, inflation?

Whenever and however the inevitable adjustment occurs, the years of grotesque trade deficits will have done some damage, perhaps even of the "irreversible" variety. How much goodwill and market position will the Caterpillars and IBMs have sacrificed? And will other countries be so thoroughly accustomed to our insatiable demand for imports as to have difficulty in adjusting to its disappearance? Bankers and economists point out that for the past four years the U.S. trade deficit has been a powerful, if imprecisely directed, anti-poverty weapon. Our imports are everyone else's exports, so the booming demand here has given developing countries (along with Japan and Europe) a chance to sell their wares. All we have asked in return is that they lend us the money with which to make the purchases. By creating a debt crisis of its own the United States has helped other countries solve theirs.

While the adjustment may be rocky and the damage to U.S. exporters profound, the trend of the trade imbalance has to be toward correction. It is hard to be so confident, if that is the word, about what will become of the country's newly accumulated foreign debts and federal deficits.

From the beginning of the First World War to 1982 the position of the United States as an international creditor generated a steady stream of dividends and profits for U.S. investors. Money deposited in English banks caused interest payments to be sent back to the United States. Investments that helped build oil wells in Indonesia or computer factories in France or clothing works in Taiwan came back to America as profits. Some of the money was taxed away and used by our government; some was reinvested at home or abroad; some was spent on goods from cars to caviar; some may have been stashed in Swiss bank accounts, which pay little or no interest but offer the comfort of anonymity, or simply squandered. Whatever its precise disposition, all of it was money that the nation did not have to generate by other means. Taxes were lower, government benefits more generous, the standard of living higher than would otherwise have been the case. Whenever the United States had trouble exporting merchandise, the profits and dividends streaming back from overseas helped the nation pay for the imports it desired.

Now the situation is exactly the reverse. The $300 billion in foreign loans that have come into the country in the past three years have given us Hondas and Beaujolais we could not otherwise have afforded and (to the extent that foreigners have lent money to cover the federal deficit) government benefits for which we would otherwise have had to tax ourselves. In exchange for these three years of subsidized consumption we have obligated ourselves to send profits and dividends the other way from now on. Whatever benefit our six decades of foreign investment represented, our rapidly growing foreign debt now constitutes an equivalent handicap.

The increase in federal indebtedness arises from the same exchange—subsidized consumption now, in return for a lower standard of living in the future—but is on an even grander scale. During the Second World War the United States took on an enormous debt, in the attempt to defeat Hitler and Tojo. But for the next thirty-five years federal debt gradually declined relative to the rest of the American economy. That trend reversed itself with the coming of the Reagan Administration, and because of what has happened from 1981 to 1985, the United States for the indefinite future will see its freedom of action reduced. Because of just these four years of debt,

Ronald Reagan's successors will find it hard to do anything other than meet the government's interest obligations, and the nation as a whole will have more difficulty investing in education, technology, or other sources of happiness and wealth.

In 1980 one dollar of each ten the federal government spent was to pay interest on the national debt. Now interest consumes one dollar of each seven. To put it another way, nearly four dollars of each ten the government collects in individual income taxes goes not for Trident submarines or National Park rangers or even for Social Security benefits but for the premiums on Treasury bills. As interest payments continue to rise, the government must collect more in taxes, reduce its other functions, or borrow more money—and borrowing more of course means that interest payments will rise even faster the following year.

As the House Budget Committee summarized the situation, in a report last May:

> The rising interest burden makes the distribution of income more unequal; it will eventually lead to higher taxes which may affect economic efficiency; and it means less room in the budget for Federal programs which meet genuine national security, investment, or social needs, rather than just servicing debt.

Already the federal budget is showing signs of being squeezed by interest payments—and, of course, by defense and Social Security. Ronald Reagan continues to talk as if he were holding the line on spending for everything except defense, but in fact his legacy will be to have presided over large increases in interest payments, Social Security, and Medicare, in addition to defense. (Defense spending has risen from 5.8 percent of the GNP in 1975 to 6.5 percent now, on its way to the Administration's goal of 7.8 percent in 1990. Social Security and Medicare have risen from 5.2 percent in 1975 to 6.6 percent now.) The radical reductions have come only in the small part of the budget left over after these big-ticket accounts have been funded. Even though federal spending, as a proportion of the GNP, is higher under Ronald Reagan than it has been under any other President except Franklin Delano Roosevelt in wartime, spending for everything except interest, Social Security plus Medicare, and defense has shrunk. In 1975 this "other" category of federal spending accounted for 11.1 percent of the GNP; it is now 9.3 percent and according to the Administration's projections should fall to 6.0 percent by 1990.

Some conservatives claim that a hidden virtue of deficits is precisely that they starve the government and thereby keep the liberals from dreaming up any crazy new ways to waste money. Twenty years ago politicians were arguing about which programs to expand; now everyone argues about where to cut. If the deficits ever shrank, the conservatives say, those irrepressible liberals would be trying to start programs again.

Useful as it may be for the conservatives at this moment, this endorsement of deficits does seem shortsighted, both for their own political interests (what greater enemy do the defense budget and lower taxes have than the deficit?) and for the nation's ability to compete economically. Far beyond the effect that the government deficit has on the federal budget, it is beginning to encroach on the entire society's ability to invest in its future. One measure of how much capital is available for productive investment is the U.S. "net savings rate"—private savings, minus depreciation, plus surpluses generated by state and local governments. Since 1960 this measure has held remarkably constant, at about eight percent of the GNP. But after the demands of the federal deficit have been satisfied, there has been less and less capital left for other purposes. For the period 1961 to 1970, 7.4 percent of the GNP, or better than 90 percent of net savings, was available for investment and capital formation, after covering the deficit. From 1981 to 1984, 2.7 percent, or about a third of net savings, was. Federal deficits now consume two thirds of the nation's net savings. Only one third is available for investment in future growth.

Many types of federal spending, of course, result in what should be considered productive investments—highways, schools, hospitals, agricultural-research stations, and even space missions are obvious examples. The public debt might be less worrisome if its growth could be explained by projects like these, which can in various ways eventually help cover their own costs. But today the government is spending and borrowing much more but investing less. The only increases in government spending have been for interest, retirement, and the military. (Caspar Weinberger often claims that defense spending is "productive," since it creates jobs, technical spin-offs, and so forth, but few economists take this idea seriously. Almost any other type of spending creates more jobs. And money devoted to commercial research and development is more likely to produce usable technical innovations—otherwise, how would the Japanese, with virtually no military establishment, have stayed in the technical race?)

F EW EXPERTS PRETEND to understand fully the forces that have kept the dollar rising in value even as U.S. exports have fallen, thereby aggravating the accumulation of debt and confounding the underlying logic of economics. Still, it's hard not to conclude that something fundamental has changed in the U.S. economy in the past four years—namely, the assumption about how, and whether, we will pay our way.

As the President and his representatives have often emphasized, the United States has enjoyed a kind of economic renaissance in the past two years. After the severe recession of 1982 the United States began creating new jobs and generating new opportunities at a tremendous clip. Income is up; inflation is down; the Europeans are mad with envy. The bath of resultant good feelings helps explain the President's overwhelming re-election a year ago.

Part of the credit for the economic recovery must go to changes that the Reagan Administration deliberately made. Everyone likes lower taxes. Those intangible but undeniable feelings of confidence and optimism have increased. Still, a look at the balance sheets suggests a more obvious explanation for America's feeling good about itself. Why shouldn't we feel good, when we're paying only eighty cents for every dollar of government benefits we receive? What's not to like, when we can buy a dollar's worth of imports with exports worth sixty cents? Everyone feels optimistic on an expense account—and everyone is ready to believe that he deserves every comfort he's been offered, and then some. The genius of Ronald Reagan has been to play to these natural vanities, helping us believe that what looks very much like a subsidy is in fact proof that we are standing tall. Such is the emerging idea of "service" under President Reagan (they also serve who only stand and spend). We will bear any burden, except those that are inconvenient. We will do whatever it takes to re-arm the United States—except draft the soldiers or raise taxes to pay for the weapons. We will do all that's necessary to rebuild the American economy, by getting used to being subsidized.

If we could count on the boom to last forever—if other nations would subsidize us indefinitely in order to create a market for their goods—we'd have no source of discomfort except dreary puritanical reminders that we had turned into freeloaders. Or if we were sure we could readjust to the old ways whenever the boom came to an end, then even as we paid the bills we could think back fondly to a free ride that lasted a few years. But given the ratchet effect of democratic politics—it's much harder to give something up than to keep doing

without something you never had in the first place—how can we ever go back to the old days? Given the humiliation of Walter Mondale, how many politicians will run on a platform calling for higher taxes?

The House of Representatives—like the Senate, and like President Reagan—has not made any significant dent in the deficits. But the House Budget Committee at least made clear in its report on deficit spending that the ultimate cost of chronic deficits was "the way citizens view their government":

> In the short term, [Americans] may find it an attractive "bargain" to receive $100 in national defense and government services for only $80 in

taxes, as at present. In the longer term they will react in anger and disappointment when they find the deficit must be paid for, after all, with higher taxes and inflation. As this process proceeds, confidence in government and the competence of fiscal management will erode, further weakening the political institutions of our society. That may be the final and most costly burden placed on future generations.

Ronald Reagan's supporters contend that his Administration has restored confidence and patriotism to a nation that lacked them. Maybe so; but it may be remembered longer for conditioning us to the free lunch.

America's Management Crisis

David Vogel

David Vogel teaches in the school of business administration at Berkeley. He is the author of *Lobbying the Corporation* (Basic Books).

The creativity of American management has been one of the historic strengths of the American business system. Most of the technological innovations underlying the industrial revolution were developed in England, but it was the United States that pioneered new organizational techniques for improving productivity. Innovations such as standardized parts, introduced by Eli Whitney, the moving assembly line, conceived by Henry Ford, and the principles of scientific management developed by Frederick Taylor were responsible for much of the dramatic gains in America's industrial output during the 19th and early 20th centuries. The modern form of corporate organization now in use throughout the world was developed by railroad executives in the United States before the Civil War. The United States still has the world's most extensive and prestigious system of professional management education.

But American business managers, traditionally an important source of competitive strength, now have become a cause of national decline, even though business executives continue to blame government policies for the poor performance of the American economy. A widely quoted recent article in the *Harvard Business Review* asserted that much of the "competitive listlessness" of the US economy is due to the "attitudes, preoccupations, and practices of American managers." The article charged that preoccupation with "short-term results" and quantitative measurements of performance has led American managers to neglect the kinds of investments and innovations necessary to increase the nation's capacity to generate wealth. The authors, two Harvard Business School professors, conclude that many American managers "have effectively forsworn long-term technological superiority as a competitive weapon." *Business Week*'s special issue on reindustrialization a few months ago featured a similar indictment, specifically criticizing American managers

for their lack of technical skills and for their non-entrepreneurial mentality.

Even many corporate executives have become self-critical on this score. In a recent poll, three out of four US executives criticized corporate incentive plans for rewarding short-term performance and thus discouraging risky long-term projects. One out of three believed that senior managers didn't know enough about technology and underemphasized innovation.

There is some hard evidence to support these perceptions. Industry spending for basic research declined 12 percent in real terms between 1966 and 1976. A 1969 survey of manufacturing companies revealed that 20 percent had a policy requiring all capital expenditures for modernization and replacement to pay for themselves within three years. A decade later this policy had been adopted by 25 percent of the companies polled. The change is small, but the trend is significant.

Senior managers have been spending more energy trying to increase their companies' short-term profits through financial manipulation. In 1979 companies spent more than $40 billion in cash on acquiring other companies. This is far more than they spent on research and development. Some of these mergers may have led to improved efficiency, but most of them were little more than private sector transfer payments —money passing from one set of balance sheets to another without producing any net increase in actual wealth. The most striking (though admittedly least interesting) aspect of the recent Agee-Cunningham flap at Bendix Corporation was what it revealed about the way many senior executives are spending their time. Evidently William Agee, the head of one of America's largest industrial corporations, spent most of his life running around the country buying and selling various parts of Bendix, rather than improving the productivity of operators the company already owned. These escapades may ultimately benefit Bendix's shareholders, or may not, but they add nothing to America's ability to compete with the Japanese.

MORE AND MORE chief executive officers have only the most casual familiarity with what their companies actually make and how. They are more likely than ever before to have been hired away from another company, often in a completely unrelated line of business. And they are less likely than before to have had any operating or line experience. Since the mid-1950s, the proportion of American chief executives trained in either law or finance has increased by nearly half while the proportion with technical backgrounds has declined by nearly 15 percent. *Business Week* writes: "Just as the general practitioner who made house calls is a dim memory, so is the hands-on corporate leader who rose through the ranks, learning every aspect of the business before managing it." In a survey of 1,700 American corporate vice presidents, 47 percent began their careers in either marketing or finance. American executives are far more likely to possess an MBA than their foreign counterparts, but German, French, Swiss, and Swedish top executives are far more likely to have had technical training. The only nation where executives have less technical education than the United States is the United Kingdom.

Critical business decisions too often are made not on the basis of a true understanding of the technology but on elegant formulas learned in business school. Increasingly, executives manage their companies in the detached way that investors manage their portfolios.

The typical chief executive officer now holds office for an average of five years, compared to 10 years a generation ago. Since CEOs tend to be judged and judge themselves by the profits reported while they are in charge, they are understandably reluctant to pursue long-term projects that depress current earnings and won't pay off until after they retire. Executives frequently criticize politicians for making decisions on the basis of short-term considerations in order to ensure their reelection. But the same indictment applies even more to managers in the private sector. Elected officials have a time horizon of at least two years, but executive promotions within companies often are based on earnings calculated on an annual basis. Akio Morita, the chairman of Sony, recently observed: "The annual bonus some American executives receive depends on annual profit, and the executive who knows his firm's production facilities should be modernized isn't likely to make a decision to invest in new equipment if his own income and managerial ability are judged based only on annual profit. . . . I have heard many American managers say, 'Why should I sacrifice my profit for my successor?'"

For many years, a powerful piece of evidence against British management has been that American owned and managed companies in Great Britain have higher productivity than other firms in the British economy. A similar unflattering comparison now may be made between the productivity of native-run and foreign-run companies in the United States. The best known example is a television plant in Illinois. When it was run

by Motorola, inspectors found 140 defects for every 100 television sets. Since the plant was bought by Matsushita Electric Industrial Company in 1974, the number of defects declined to less than six per 100 sets. The number of warranty claims dropped by seven-eighths. American managers frequently attribute Japanese efficiency to values peculiar to Japanese culture; but one assembly line at Sony's San Diego plant holds the company's worldwide record for production: 200 days without a serious defect.

The contrast in quality between American and Japanese products has become increasingly obvious over the last decade. American consumers continue to prefer Japanese products (often as not made in Taiwan and South Korea) even as the Japanese price advantage has all but disappeared. According to a recent article in *Fortune*, a new American car is almost twice as likely to have a problem as a Japanese model, and American-made computer chips are three times more likely to fail than Japanese ones.

Both our slow productivity growth and the relatively poor quality of many American goods are connected to the training and incentives of American managers. It is difficult for MBAs—trained to measure discounted cash flow and capital asset pricing models —to work closely with employees in search of ways to improve procedures and equipment. The incentives for managers to make productivity improvements actually declined during the 1970s, as many companies switched from a strategy of expanding sales to one emphasizing immediate return of assets. According to the *Wall Street Journal*, the consequence of rewarding executives by this second measure encouraged them to make small investments that paid off quickly, rather than larger outlays that might greatly improve productivity eventually, but that were riskier and would take longer to show results.

MANY LARGE corporations have made the transition from founder-entrepreneur to professional management without suffering any decline of entrepreneurial vigor. Firms such as IBM, Dupont, Boeing, Texas Instruments, and Minnesota Mining and Manufacturing have demonstrated both a willingness to make investments in risky new technologies and patience in waiting for the pay-off. A company run by a scientist is not guaranteed continued success, as Polaroid's recent experiences indicate. Nor, as the history of the steel industry reveals, does a policy of promoting from within the ranks ensure informed management decisions. Various companies and plants throughout the United States have demonstrated impressive increases in productivity by involving workers in the decision-making process at the plant level. But the overall picture remains discouraging.

Managers are not completely at fault, of course. Just one special problem they face is that American industry is far more dependent on the stock market as a source of capital than our foreign competitors are. Japanese and German firms are financed mostly by borrowing, not selling shares. This frees them to make long-term investments without Wall Street money-managers scrutinizing each quarterly earnings report. It is impossible to determine the precise role played by any one factor in America's economic difficulties. But it is important that public discussion of the economy's poor performance not focus exclusively on the need for changes in government policy.

UNDER PRESIDENT Reagan the business community may get many of the changes in tax and regulatory policies that it claims it needs. But unless the private sector's own pattern of incentives and training is reformed, US-managed companies are likely to continue to lose market shares to foreign competitors. Instead of hiring more lobbyists, American companies should promote more engineers. We need to reexamine the kind of education that those to whom we entrust our economic future are getting. Has the notion of a professional manager—an individual who learns a set of general analytical, abstract, decision-making skills that can be applied equally well to the problems faced by any institution—become as irrelevant as the British classical Oxbridge education

became several generations ago? Why are the nations with the most developed systems of professional management education, the United States and Great Britain, performing so poorly, when two nations that provide almost no professional management training, Germany and Japan, have been the outstanding successes of the postwar period? Virtually none of the nation's major business schools require courses in production or offer adequate training in the management of human resources. Business schools ignore foreign language training and place little emphasis on teaching students to understand foreign cultures. The popularity of finance courses at business schools probably has contributed to the preoccupation of recently graduated MBAs with short-term time horizons.

Corporate critics also need to redirect their thinking. Except in cases of particularly gross blunders, like the recent bloopers of the automobile and steel industries, critics of business tend to take the competence of US management for granted. They most often criticize companies for being *too* successful in their pursuit of profits, and thereby neglecting other legitimate social needs. But Milton Friedman is right in saying that the most important social responsibility of business is in fact to produce wealth. We need to be as critical about the inability of companies to grow and innovate as we are about their failures of social responsibility.

The American Family in the Year 2000

Andrew Cherlin
and Frank F. Furstenberg, Jr.

Andrew Cherlin is associate professor of sociology at The Johns Hopkins University, Baltimore, Maryland 21218. The author of *Marriage, Divorce, Remarriage* (Harvard University Press, 1981), he has published many articles on trends in American family life.

Frank F. Furstenberg, Jr., is a sociology professor at the University of Pennsylvania, 3718 Locust Walk-CR, Philadelphia, Pennsylvania 91104.

"Diversity" is the word for the future of the American family. There will be more divorces, single-parent families, and mixed families from remarriages, but the ideal of marrying and having children is still very much a part of the American experience.

• At current rates, half of all American marriages begun in the early 1980s will end in divorce.

• The number of unmarried couples living together has more than tripled since 1970.

• One out of four children is not living with both parents.

The list could go on and on. Teenage pregnancies: up. Adolescent suicides: up. The birthrate: down. Over the past decade, popular and scholarly commentators have cited a seemingly endless wave of grim statistics about the shape of the American family. The trends have caused a number of concerned Americans to wonder if the family, as we know it, will survive the twentieth century.

And yet, other observers ask us to consider more positive developments:

• Seventy-eight percent of all adults in a recent national survey said they get "a great deal" of satisfaction from their family lives; only 3% said "a little" or "none."

• Two-thirds of the married adults in the same survey said they were "very happy" with their marriages; only 3% said "not too happy."

• In another recent survey of parents of children in their middle years, 88% said that if they had to do it over, they would choose to have children again.

• The vast majority of the children (71%) characterized their family life as "close and intimate."

Family ties are still important and strong, the optimists argue, and the predictions of the demise of the family are greatly exaggerated.

Neither the dire pessimists who believe that the family is falling apart nor the unbridled optimists who claim that the family has never been in better shape provide an accurate picture of family life in the near future. But these trends indicate that what we have come to view as the "traditional" family will no longer predominate.

Diverse Family Forms

In the future, we should expect to see a growing amount of diversity in family forms, with fewer Americans spending most of their life in a simple "nuclear" family consisting of husband, wife, and children. By the year 2000, three kinds of families will dominate the personal lives of most Americans: families of first marriages, single-parent families, and families of remarriages.

In first-marriage families, both spouses will be in a first marriage, frequently begun after living alone for a time or following a period of cohabitation. Most of these couples

From *The Futurist*, June 1983. THE FUTURIST, published by the World Future Society, 4916 St. Elmo Avenue, Washington, D.C. 20014.

will have one, two, or, less frequently, three children.

A sizable minority, however, will remain childless. Demographer Charles F. Westoff predicts that about one-fourth of all women currently in their childbearing years will never bear children, a greater number of childless women than at any time in U.S. history.

One other important shift: in a large majority of these families, both the husband and the wife will be employed outside the home. In 1940, only about one out of seven married women worked outside the home; today the proportion is one out of two. We expect this proportion to continue to rise, although not as fast as it did in the past decade or two.

Single-Parent Families

The second major type of family can be formed in two ways. Most are formed by a marital separation, and the rest by births to unmarried women. About half of all marriages will end in divorce at current rates, and we doubt that the rates will fall substantially in the near future.

When the couple is childless, the formerly married partners are likely to set up independent households and resume life as singles. The high rate of divorce is one of the reasons why more men and women are living in single-person households than ever before.

But three-fifths of all divorces involve couples with children living at home. In at least nine out of ten cases, the wife retains custody of the children after a separation.

Although joint custody has received a lot of attention in the press and in legal circles, national data show that it is still uncommon. Moreover, it is likely to remain the exception rather than the rule because most ex-spouses can't get along well enough to manage raising their children together. In fact, a national survey of children aged 11 to 16 conducted by one of the authors demonstrated that fathers have little contact with their children after a divorce. About half of the children whose parents had divorced hadn't seen their father in the last year; only one out of six had managed to see their father an average of once a week. If the current rate of divorce persists, about half of all

children will spend some time in a single-parent family before they reach 18.

Much has been written about the psychological effects on children of living with one parent, but the literature has not yet proven that any lasting negative effects occur. One effect, however, does occur with regularity: women who head single-parent families typically experience a sharp decline in their income relative to before their divorce. Husbands usually do not experience a decline. Many divorced women have difficulty reentering the job market after a long absence; others find that their low-paying clerical or service-worker jobs aren't adequate to support a family.

Of course, absent fathers are supposed to make child-support payments, but only a minority do. In a 1979 U.S. Bureau of the Census survey, 43% of all divorced and separated women with children present reported receiving child-support payments during the previous year, and the average annual payment was about $1,900. Thus, the most detrimental effect for children living in a single-parent family is not the lack of a male presence but the lack of a male income.

Families of Remarriages

The experience of living as a single parent is temporary for many divorced women, especially in the middle class. Three out of four divorced people remarry, and about half of these marriages occur within three years of the divorce.

Remarriage does much to solve the economic problems that many single-parent families face because it typically adds a male income. Remarriage also relieves a single parent of the multiple burdens of running and supporting a household by herself.

But remarriage also frequently involves blending together two families into one, a difficult process that is complicated by the absence of clear-cut ground rules for how to accomplish the merger. Families formed by remarriages can become quite complex, with children from either spouse's previous marriage or from the new marriage and with numerous sets of grandparents,

stepgrandparents, and other kin and quasi-kin.

The divorce rate for remarriages is modestly higher than for first marriages, but many couples and their children adjust successfully to their remarriage and, when asked, consider their new marriage to be a big improvement over their previous one.

The Life Course: A Scenario for the Next Two Decades

Because of the recent sharp changes in marriage and family life, the life course of children and young adults today is likely to be far different from what a person growing up earlier in this century experienced. It will not be uncommon, for instance, for children born in the 1980s to follow this sequence of living arrangements: live with both parents for several years, live with their mothers after their parents divorce, live with their mothers and stepfathers, live alone for a time when in their early twenties, live with someone of the opposite sex without marrying, get married, get divorced, live alone again, get remarried, and end up living alone once more following the death of their spouses.

Not everyone will have a family history this complex, but it is likely that a substantial minority of the population will. And many more will have family histories only slightly less complex.

Overall, we estimate that about half of the young children alive today will spend some time in a single-parent family before they reach 18; about nine out of ten will eventually marry; about one out of two will marry and then divorce; and about one out of three will marry, divorce, and then remarry. In contrast, only about one out of six women born in the period 1910 to 1914 married and divorced and only about one in eight married, divorced, and remarried.

Without doubt, Americans today are living in a much larger number of family settings during their lives than was the case a few generations ago.

The life-course changes have been even greater for women than for men because of the far greater likelihood of employment during the childbearing years for middle-class women today compared with their mothers and grandmothers. Moreover, the increase in life expectancy has increased the difference between men's and women's family lives. Women now tend to outlive men by a wide margin, a development that is new in this century. Consequently, many more women face a long period of living without a spouse at the end of their lives, either as a widow or as a divorced person who never remarried.

Long-lived men, in contrast, often find that their position in the marriage market is excellent, and they are much more likely to remain married (or remarried) until they die.

Convergence and Divergence

The family lives of Americans vary according to such factors as class, ethnicity, religion, and region. But recent evidence suggests a convergence among these groups in many features of family life. The clearest example is in childbearing, where the differences between Catholics and non-Catholics or between Southerners and Northerners are much smaller than they were 20 years ago. We expect this process of convergence to continue, although it will fall far short of eliminating all social class and subcultural differences.

The experiences of blacks and whites also have converged in many respects, such as in fertility and in patterns of premarital sexual behavior, over the past few decades. But with respect to marriage, blacks and whites have diverged markedly since about 1960.

Black families in the United States always have had strong ties to a large network of extended kin. But in addition, blacks, like whites, relied on a relatively stable bond between husbands and wives. But over the past several decades—and especially since 1960—the proportion of black families maintained by a woman has increased sharply; currently, the proportion exceeds four in ten. In addition, more young black women are having children out of wedlock; in the late 1970s, about two out of three black women who gave birth to a first child were unmarried.

These trends mean that we must qualify our previously stated conclusion that marriage will remain central to family life. This conclusion holds for Americans in general. For many low-income blacks, however, marriage is likely to be less important than the continuing ties to a larger network of kin.

Marriage is simply less attractive to a young black woman from a low-income family because of the poor prospects many young black men have for steady employment and because of the availability of alternative sources of support from public-assistance payments and kin. Even though most black women eventually marry, their marriages have a very high probability of ending in separation or divorce. Moreover, they have a lower likelihood of remarrying.

Black single-parent families sometimes have been criticized as being "disorganized" or even "pathological." What the critics fail to note is that black single mothers usually are embedded in stable, functioning kin networks. These networks tend to center around female kin—mothers, grandmothers, aunts—but brothers, fathers, and other male kin also may be active. The members of these networks share and exchange goods and services, thus helping to share the burdens of poverty. The lower-class black extended family, then, is characterized by strong ties among a network of kin but fragile ties between husband and wife. The negative aspects of this family system have been exaggerated greatly; yet it need not be romanticized, either. It can be difficult and risky for individuals to leave the network in order to try to make it on their own; thus, it may be hard for individuals to raise themselves out of poverty until the whole network is raised.

The Disintegrating Family?

By now, predictions of the demise of the family are familiar to everyone. Yet the family is a resilient institution that still retains more strength than its harshest critics maintain. There is, for example, no evidence of a large-scale rejection of marriage among Americans. To be sure, many young adults are living together outside of marriage, but the evidence we have about cohabitation suggests that it is not a lifelong alternative to marriage; rather, it appears to be either another stage in the process of courtship and marriage or a transition between first and second marriages.

The so-called "alternative lifestyles" that received so much attention in the late 1960s, such as communes and lifelong singlehood, are still very uncommon when we look at the nation as a whole.

Young adults today do marry at a somewhat older age, on average, than their parents did. But the average age at marriage today is very similar to what it was throughout the period from 1890 to 1940.

To be sure, many of these marriages will end in divorce, but three out of four people who divorce eventually remarry. Americans still seem to desire the intimacy and security that a marital relationship provides.

Much of the alarm about the family comes from reactions to the sheer speed at which the institution changed in the last two decades. Between the early 1960s and the mid-1970s, the divorce rate doubled, the marriage rate plunged, the birthrate dropped from a twentieth-century high to an all-time low, premarital sex became accepted, and married women poured into the labor force. But since the mid-1970s, the pace of change has slowed. The divorce rate has risen modestly and the birthrate even has increased a bit. We may have entered a period in which American families can adjust to the sharp changes that occurred in the 1960s and early 1970s. We think that, by and large, accommodations will be made as expectations change and institutions are redesigned to take account of changing family practices.

Despite the recent difficulties, family ties remain a central part of American life. Many of the changes in family life in the 1960s and 1970s were simply a continuation of long-term trends that have been with us for generations.

The birthrate has been declining since the 1820s, the divorce rate has been climbing since at least the Civil War, and over the last half century a growing number of married women have taken paying jobs. Employment outside the home has been gradually eroding the patriarchal system of values that was a part of our early history, replacing it with a more egalitarian set of values.

The only exception occurred during the late 1940s and the 1950s. After World War II, Americans raised during the austerity of depression and war entered adulthood at a time of sustained prosperity. The sudden turnabout in their fortunes led them to marry earlier and have more children than any generation before or since in this century. Because many of us were either parents or children in the baby-boom years following the war, we tend to think that the 1950s typify the way twentieth-century families used to be. But the patterns of marriage and childbearing in the 1950s were an aberration resulting from special historical circumstances; the patterns of the 1960s and 1970s better fit the long-term trends. Barring unforeseen major disruptions, small families, working wives, and impermanent marital ties are likely to remain with us indefinitely.

A range of possible developments could throw our forecasts off the mark. We do not know, for example, how the economy will behave over the next 20 years, or how the family will be affected by technological innovations still at the conception stage. But, we do not envision any dramatic changes in family life resulting solely from technological innovations in the next two decades.

Having sketched our view of the most probable future, we will consider three of the most important implications of the kind of future we see.

Growing Up in Changing Families

Children growing up in the past two decades have faced a maelstrom of social change. As we have pointed out, family life is likely to become even more complex, diverse, unpredictable, and uncertain in the next two decades.

Even children who grow up in stable family environments will probably have to get along with a lot less care from parents (mothers in particular) than children received early in this century. Ever since the 1950s, there has been a marked and continuous increase in the propor-

tion of working mothers whose pre-school children are cared for outside the home, rising from 31% in 1958 to 62% in 1977. The upward trend is likely to continue until it becomes standard practice for very young children to receive care either in someone else's home or in a group setting. There has been a distinct drop in the care of children by relatives, as fewer aunts, grandmothers, or adult children are available to supplement the care provided by parents. Increasingly, the government at all levels will be pressured to provide more support for out-of-home daycare.

How are children responding to the shifting circumstances of family life today? Are we raising a generation of young people who, by virtue of their own family experiences, lack the desire and skill to raise the next generation? As we indicated earlier, existing evidence has not demonstrated that marital disruption creates lasting personality damage or instills a distinctly different set of values about family life.

Similarly, a recent review on children of working mothers conducted by the National Research Council of the National Academy of Sciences concludes:

> If there is only one message that emerges from this study, it is that parental employment in and of itself—mothers' employment or fathers' or both parents'—is not necessarily good or bad for children.

The fact that both parents work *per se* does not adversely affect the well-being of children.

Currently, most fathers whose wives are employed do little child-care. Today, most working mothers have two jobs: they work for pay and then come home to do most of the childcare and housework. Pressure from a growing number of harried working wives could prod fathers to watch less television and change more diapers. But this change in fathers' roles is proceeding much more slowly than the recent spate of articles about the "new father" would lead one to expect. The strain that working while raising a family places on working couples, and especially on working mothers, will likely make childcare and a more equitable shar-

ing of housework prominent issues in the 1980s and 1990s.

Family Obligations

Many of the one out of three Americans who, we estimate, will enter a second marriage will do so after having children in a first marriage. Others may enter into a first marriage with a partner who has a family from a previous marriage. It is not clear in these families what obligations remain after divorce or are created after remarriage. For one thing, no clear set of norms exists specifying how people in remarriages are supposed to act toward each other. Stepfathers don't know how much to discipline their stepchildren; second wives don't know what they're supposed to say when they meet their husbands' first wives; stepchildren don't know what to call their absent father's new wife.

The ambiguity about family relations after divorce and remarriage also extends to economic support. There are no clear-cut guidelines to tell adults how to balance the claims of children from previous marriages versus children from their current marriages. Suppose a divorced man who has been making regular payments to support his two small children from a previous marriage marries a woman with children from her previous marriage. Suppose her husband isn't paying any child support. Suppose further that the remarried couple have a child of their own. Which children should have first claim on the husband's income? Legally, he is obligated to pay child support to his ex-wife, but in practice he is likely to feel that his primary obligation is to his stepchildren, whose father isn't helping, and to his own children from his remarriage.

Our guess, supported by some preliminary evidence from national studies, is that remarriage will tend to further reduce the amount of child support that a man pays, particularly if the man's new family includes children from his new wife's previous marriage or from the current marriage. What appears to be occurring in many cases is a form of "childswapping," with men exchanging an old set of children from a prior marriage for a new set from their new wife's prior marriage and from the remarriage.

Sociologist Lenore J. Weitzman provides a related example in her book *The Marriage Contract*. Suppose, she writes, a 58-year-old corporate vice president with two grown children divorces his wife to marry his young secretary. He agrees to adopt the secretary's two young children. If he dies of a heart attack the following year:

> In most states, a third to half of his estate would go to his new wife, with the remainder divided among the four children (two from his last marriage, and his new wife's two children). His first wife will receive nothing—neither survivors' insurance nor a survivors' pension nor a share of the estate—and both she and his natural children are likely to feel that they have been treated unjustly.

Since the rate of mid-life divorce has been increasing nearly as rapidly as that of divorce at younger ages, this type of financial problem will become increasingly common. It would seem likely that there will be substantial pressure for changes in family law and in income security systems to provide more to the ex-wife and natural children in such circumstances.

Intergenerational Relations

A similar lack of clarity about who should support whom may affect an increasing number of elderly persons. Let us consider the case of an elderly man who long ago divorced his first wife and, as is fairly typical, retained only sporadic contact with his children. If his health deteriorates in old age and he needs help, will his children provide it? In many cases, the relationship would seem so distant that the children would not be willing to provide major assistance. To be sure, in most instances the elderly man would have remarried, possibly acquiring stepchildren, and it may be these stepchildren who feel the responsibility to provide assistance. Possibly the two sets of children may be called upon to cooperate in lending support, even when they have had little or no contact while growing up. Currently, there are no clear guidelines for assigning kinship responsibilities in this new type of extended family.

Even without considering divorce, the issue of support to the elderly is likely to bring problems that are new and widespread. As is well known, the low fertility in the United States, which we think will continue to be low, means that the population is becoming older. The difficulties that this change in age structure poses for the Social Security system are so well known that we need not discuss them here. Let us merely note that any substantial weakening of the Social Security system would put the elderly at a great disadvantage with regard to their families, for older Americans increasingly rely on Social Security and other pensions and insurance plans to provide support. A collapse of Social Security would result in a large decrease in the standard of living among older Americans and a return to the situation prevailing a few decades ago in which the elderly were disproportionately poor.

The relations between older people and their children and grandchildren are typically close, intimate, and warm. Most people live apart from their children, but they generally live close by one or more of them. Both generations prefer the autonomy that the increased affluence of the older generation has recently made possible. Older people see family members quite often, and they report that family members are their major source of support. A survey by Louis Harris of older Americans revealed that more than half of those with children had seen them in the past day, and close to half had seen a grandchild. We expect close family ties between the elderly and their kin to continue to be widespread. If, however, the economic autonomy of the elderly is weakened, say, by a drop in Social Security, the kind of friendly equality that now characterizes intergenerational relations could be threatened.

One additional comment about the elderly: Almost everyone is aware that the declining birthrate means that the elderly will have fewer children in the future on whom they can rely for support. But although this is true in the long run, it will not be true in the next few decades. In fact, beginning soon, the elderly will have more children, on average, than they do today. The reason is the postwar baby boom of the late 1940s and 1950s. As the parents of these large families begin to reach retirement age near the end of this century, more children will be available to help their elderly parents. Once the next generation—the baby-boom children—begins to reach retirement age after about 2010, the long-term trend toward fewer available children will sharply reassert itself.

Were we to be transported suddenly to the year 2000, the families we would see would look very recognizable. There would be few unfamiliar forms—not many communes or group marriages, and probably not a large proportion of lifelong singles. Instead, families by and large would continue to center around the bonds between husbands and wives and between parents and children. One could say the same about today's families relative to the 1960s: the forms are not new. What is quite different, comparing the 1960s with the 1980s, or the 1980s with a hypothetical 2000, is the distribution of these forms.

In the early 1960s, there were far fewer single-parent families and families formed by remarriages after divorce than is the case today; and in the year 2000 there are likely to be far more single-parent families and families of remarriage than we see now. Moreover, in the early 1960s both spouses were employed in a much smaller percentage of two-parent families; in the year 2000, the percentage with two earners will be greater still. Cohabitation before marriage existed in the 1960s, but it was a frowned-upon, bohemian style of life. Today, it has become widely accepted; it will likely become more common in the future. Yet we have argued that cohabitation is less an alternative to marriage than a precursor to marriage, though we expect to see a modest rise in the number of people who never marry.

WHY JOHNNY CAN'T THINK

The politics of bad schooling

The following books are discussed in this essay:

A Place Called School, by John I. Goodlad. 396 pages. McGraw-Hill. $9.95

The Good High School, by Sara Lawrence Lightfoot. 399 pages. Basic Books. $19.95.

Horace's Compromise: The Dilemma of the American High School, by Theodore R. Sizer. 241 pages. Houghton Mifflin. $16.95.

High School: A Report on Secondary Education in America, by Ernest L. Boyer and the Carnegie Foundation for the Advancement of Teaching. 363 pages. Harper & Row. $16.95.

A Nation at Risk: The Imperative for Educational Reform, by the National Commission on Excellence in Education. 65 pages. U.S. Government Printing Office. $4.50.

The Great School Debate: Which Way for American Education?, edited by Beatrice and Ronald Gross. 481 pages. Simon & Schuster. $17.45.

The Challenge to American Schools, edited by John Bunzel. 256 pages. Oxford University Press. $19.95.

The Troubled Crusade: American Education 1945–1980, by Diane Ravitch. 384 pages. Basic Books. $19.95.

Walter Karp

Walter Karp is a contributing editor of Harper's *and the author of* The Politics of War. *He is at work on a book about the Korean War,* The Empire and the Mob.

Until very recently, remarkably little was known about what actually goes on in America's public schools. There were no reliable answers to even the most obvious questions. How many children are taught to read in overcrowded classrooms? How prevalent is rote learning and how common are classroom discussions? Do most schools set off gongs to mark the change of "periods"? Is it a common practice to bark commands over public address systems in the manner of army camps, prisons, and banana republics? Public schooling provides the only intense experience of a public realm that most Americans will ever know. Are school buildings designed with the dignity appropriate to a great republican institution, or are most of them as crummy looking as one's own?

The darkness enveloping America's public schools is truly extraordinary considering that 38.9 million students attend them, that we spend nearly $134 billion a year on them, and that foundations ladle out generous sums for the study of everything about schooling—except what really occurs in the schools. John I. Goodlad's eight-year investigation of a mere thirty-eight of America's 80,000 public schools—the result of which, *A Place Called School*, was published last year—is the most comprehensive such study ever undertaken. Hailed as a "landmark in American educational research," it was financed with great difficulty. The darkness, it seems, has its guardians.

Happily, the example of Goodlad, a former dean of UCLA's Graduate School of Education, has proven contagious. A flurry of new books sheds considerable light on the practice of public education in America. In *The Good High School*, Sara Lawrence Lightfoot offers vivid "portraits" of six distinctive American secondary schools. In *Horace's Compromise*, Theodore R. Sizer, a former dean of Harvard's Grad-

Overcrowded classrooms inevitably debase instruction, yet they are the rule in America's public schools

uate School of Education, reports on his two-year odyssey through public high schools around the country. Even *High School*, a white paper issued by Ernest L. Boyer and the Carnegie Foundation for the Advancement of Teaching, is supported by a close investigation of the institutional life of a number of schools. Of the books under review, only *A Nation at Risk*, the report of the Reagan Administration's National Commission on Excellence in Education, adheres to the established practice of crass special pleading in the dark.

Thanks to Goodlad et al., it is now clear what the great educational darkness has so long concealed: the depth and pervasiveness of political hypocrisy in the common schools of the country. The great ambition professed by public school managers is, of course, education for citizenship and self-government, which harks back to Jefferson's historic call for "general education to enable every man to judge for himself what will secure or endanger his freedom." What the public schools practice with remorseless proficiency, however, is the prevention of citizenship and the stifling of self-government. When 58 percent of the thirteen-year-olds tested by the National Assessment for Educational Progress think it is against the law to start a third party in America, we are dealing not with a sad educational failure but with a remarkably subtle success.

Consider how effectively America's future citizens are trained *not* to judge for themselves about anything. From the first grade to the twelfth, from one coast to the other, instruction in America's classrooms is almost entirely dogmatic. Answers are "right" and answers are "wrong," but mostly answers are short. "At all levels, [teacher-made] tests called almost exclusively for short answers and recall of information," reports Goodlad. In more than 1,000 classrooms visited by his researchers, "only *rarely*" was there "evidence to suggest instruction likely to go much beyond mere possession of information to a level of understanding its implications." Goodlad goes on to note that "the intellectual terrain is laid out by the teacher. The paths for walking through it are largely predetermined by the teacher." The give-and-take of genuine discussion is conspicuously absent. "Not even 1%" of instructional time, he found, was devoted to discussions that "required some kind of open response involving reasoning or perhaps an opinion from students. . . . The extraordinary degree of student passivity stands out."

Sizer's research substantiates Goodlad's. "No more important finding has emerged from the inquiries of our study than that the American high school student, *as student*, is all too often docile, compliant, and without initiative."

There is good reason for this. On the one hand, notes Sizer, "there are too few rewards for being inquisitive." On the other, the heavy emphasis on "the right answer . . . smothers the student's efforts to become an effective intuitive thinker."

Yet smothered minds are looked on with the utmost complacency by the educational establishment—by the Reagan Department of Education, state boards of regents, university education departments, local administrators, and even many so-called educational reformers. Teachers are neither urged to combat the tyranny of the short right answer nor trained to do so. "Most teachers simply do not know how to teach for higher levels of thinking," says Goodlad. Indeed, they are actively discouraged from trying to do so.

The discouragement can be quite subtle. In their orientation talks to new, inexperienced teachers, for example, school administrators often indicate that they do not much care what happens in class so long as no noise can be heard in the hallway. This thinly veiled threat virtually ensures the prevalence of short-answer drills, workbook exercises, and the copying of long extracts from the blackboard. These may smother young minds, but they keep the classroom quiet.

Discouragement even calls itself reform. Consider the current cry for greater use of standardized student tests to judge the "merit" of teachers and raise "academic standards." If this fake reform is foisted on the schools, dogma and docility will become even more prevalent. This point is well made by Linda Darling-Hammond of the Rand Corporation in an essay in *The Great School Debate*. Where "important decisions are based on test scores," she notes, "teachers are more likely to teach to the tests" and less likely to bother with "nontested activities, such as writing, speaking, problem-solving or real reading of real books." The most influential promoter of standardized tests is the "excellence" brigade in the Department of Education; so clearly one important meaning of "educational excellence" is greater proficiency in smothering students' efforts to think for themselves.

Probably the greatest single discouragement to better instruction is the overcrowded classroom. The Carnegie report points out that English teachers cannot teach their students how to write when they must read and criticize the papers of as many as 175 students. As Sizer observes, genuine discussion is possible only in small seminars. In crowded classrooms, teachers have difficulty imparting even the most basic intellectual skills, since they have no time to give students personal attention. The overcrowded classroom inevitably debases instruction, yet it is the rule in America's public schools. In the first three grades of elementary school, Goodlad notes, the average class has

Public-address systems teach the huge student mass to respect the rule of remote and invisible agencies

twenty-seven students. High school classes range from twenty-five to forty students, according to the Carnegie report.

What makes these conditions appalling is that they are quite unnecessary. The public schools are top-heavy with administrators and rife with sinecures. Large numbers of teachers scarcely ever set foot in a classroom, being occupied instead as grade advisers, career counselors, "coordinators," and supervisors. "Schools, if simply organized," Sizer writes, "can have well-paid faculty and fewer than eighty students per teacher [16 students per class] without increasing current per-pupil expenditure." Yet no serious effort is being made to reduce class size. As Sizer notes, "Reducing teacher load is, when all the negotiating is over, a low agenda item for the unions and school boards." Overcrowded classrooms virtually guarantee smothered minds, yet the subject is not even mentioned in *A Nation at Risk*, for all its well-publicized braying about a "rising tide of mediocrity."

Do the nation's educators really want to teach almost 40 million students how to "think critically," in the Carnegie report's phrase, and "how to judge for themselves," in Jefferson's? The answer is, if you can believe that you will believe anything. The educational establishment is not even content to produce passive minds. It seeks passive spirits as well. One effective agency for producing these is the overly populous school. The larger schools are, the more prison-like they tend to be. In such schools, guards man the stairwells and exits. ID cards and "passes" are examined at checkpoints. Bells set off spasms of anarchy and bells quell the student mob. PA systems interrupt regularly with trivial fiats and frivolous announcements. This "malevolent intruder," in Sizer's apt phrase, is truly ill willed, for the PA system is actually an educational tool. It teaches the huge student mass to respect the authority of disembodied voices and the rule of remote and invisible agencies. Sixty-three percent of all high school students in America attend schools with enrollments of 5,000 or more. The common excuse for these mobbed schools is economy, but in fact they cannot be shown to save taxpayers a penny. Large schools "tend to create passive and compliant students," notes Robert B. Hawkins Jr. in an essay in *The Challenge to American Schools*. That is their chief reason for being.

"How can the relatively passive and docile roles of students prepare them to participate as informed, active and questioning citizens?" asks the Carnegie report, in discussing the "hidden curriculum" of passivity in the schools. The answer is, they were not meant to. Public schools introduce future citizens to the public world, but no introduction could be more disheartening. Architecturally, public school buildings range

from drab to repellent. They are often disfigured by demoralizing neglect—"cracked sidewalks, a shabby lawn, and peeling paint on every window sash," to quote the Carnegie report. Many big-city elementary schools have numbers instead of names, making them as coldly dispiriting as possible.

Public schools stamp out republican sentiment by habituating their students to unfairness, inequality, and special privilege. These arise inevitably from the educational establishment's longstanding policy (well described by Diane Ravitch in *The Troubled Crusade*) of maintaining "the correlation between social class and educational achievement." In order to preserve that factitious "correlation," public schooling is rigged to favor middle-class students and to ensure that working-class students do poorly enough to convince them that they fully merit the lowly station that will one day be theirs. "Our goal is to get these kids to be like their parents," one teacher, more candid than most, remarked to a Carnegie researcher.

For more than three decades, elementary schools across the country practiced a "progressive," non-phonetic method of teaching reading that had nothing much to recommend it save its inherent social bias. According to Ravitch, this method favored "children who were already motivated and prepared to begin reading" before entering school, while making learning to read more difficult for precisely those children whose parents were ill read or ignorant. The advantages enjoyed by the well-bred were thus artificially multiplied tenfold, and 23 million adult Americans are today "functional illiterates." America's educators, notes Ravitch, have "never actually accepted full responsibility for making all children literate."

That describes a malicious intent a trifle too mildly. Reading is the key to everything else in school. Children who struggle with it in the first grade will be "grouped" with the slow readers in the second grade and will fall hopelessly behind in all subjects by the sixth. The schools hasten this process of falling behind, report Goodlad and others, by giving the best students the best teachers and struggling students the worst ones. "It is ironic," observes the Carnegie report, "that those who need the most help get the least." Such students are commonly diagnosed as "culturally deprived" and so are blamed for the failures inflicted on them. Thus, they are taught to despise themselves even as they are inured to their inferior station.

The whole system of unfairness, inequality, and privilege comes to fruition in high school. There, some 15.7 million youngsters are formally divided into the favored few and the ill-favored many by the practice of "tracking."

About 35 percent of America's public secondary-school students are enrolled in academic programs (often subdivided into "gifted" and "non-gifted" tracks); the rest are relegated to some variety of non-academic schooling. Thus the tracking system, as intended, reproduces the divisions of the class system. "The honors programs," notes Sizer, "serve the wealthier youngsters, and the general tracks (whatever their titles) serve the working class. Vocational programs are often a cruel social dumping ground." The bottom-dogs are trained for jobs as auto mechanics, cosmeticians, and institutional cooks, but they rarely get the jobs they are trained for. Pumping gasoline, according to the Carnegie report, is as close as an auto-mechanics major is likely to get to repairing a car. "Vocational education in the schools is virtually irrelevant to job fate," asserts Goodlad. It is merely the final hoax that the school bureaucracy plays on the neediest, one that the federal government has been promoting for seventy years.

The tracking system makes privilege and inequality blatantly visible to everyone. It creates under one roof "two worlds of schooling," to quote Goodlad. Students in academic programs read Shakespeare's plays. The commonality, notes the Carnegie report, are allowed virtually no contact with serious literature. In their English classes they practice filling out job applications. "Gifted" students alone are encouraged to think for themselves. The rest are subjected to sanctimonious wind, chiefly about "work habits" and "career opportunities."

"If you are the child of low-income parents," reports Sizer, "the chances are good that you will receive limited and often careless attention from adults in your high school. If you are the child of upper-middle-income parents, the chances are good that you will receive substantial and careful attention." In Brookline High School in Massachusetts, one of Lightfoot's "good" schools, a few fortunate students enjoy special treatment in their Advanced Placement classes. Meanwhile, students tracked into "career education" learn about "institutional cooking and clean-up" in a four-term Food Service course that requires them to mop up after their betters in the school cafeteria.

This wretched arrangement expresses the true spirit of public education in America and discloses the real aim of its hidden curriculum. A favored few, pampered and smiled upon, are taught to cherish privilege and despise the disfavored. The favorless many, who have majored in failure for years, are taught to think ill of themselves. Youthful spirits are broken to the world and every impulse of citizenship is effectively stifled. John Goodlad's judgment is severe but just: "There is in the gap between our highly idealistic goals for schooling in our society and the differentiated opportunities condoned and supported in schools a monstrous hypocrisy."

The public schools of America have not been corrupted for trivial reasons. Much would be different in a republic composed of citizens who could judge for themselves what secured or endangered their freedom. Every wielder of illicit or undemocratic power, every possessor of undue influence, every beneficiary of corrupt special privilege would find his position and tenure at hazard. Republican education is a menace to powerful, privileged, and influential people, and they in turn are a menace to republican education. That is why the generation that founded the public schools took care to place them under the suffrage of local communities, and that is why the corrupters of public education have virtually destroyed that suffrage. In 1932 there were 127,531 school districts in America. Today there are approximately 15,840 and they are virtually impotent, their proper role having been usurped by state and federal authorities. Curriculum and textbooks, methods of instruction, the procedures of the classroom, the organization of the school day, the cant, the pettifogging, and the corruption are almost uniform from coast to coast. To put down the menace of republican education its shield of local self-government had to be smashed, and smashed it was.

The public schools we have today are what the powerful and the considerable have made of them. They will not be redeemed by trifling reforms. Merit pay, a longer school year, more homework, special schools for "the gifted," and more standardized tests will not even begin to turn our public schools into nurseries of "informed, active and questioning citizens." They are not meant to. When the authors of *A Nation at Risk* call upon the schools to create an "educated work force," they are merely sanctioning the prevailing corruption, which consists precisely in the reduction of citizens to credulous workers. The education of a free people will not come from federal bureaucrats crying up "excellence" for "economic growth," any more than it came from their predecessors who cried up schooling as a means to "get a better job."

Only ordinary citizens can rescue the schools from their stifling corruption, for nobody else wants ordinary children to become questioning citizens at all. If we wait for the mighty to teach America's youth what secures or endangers their freedom, we will wait until the crack of doom.

The education of a free people will not come from federal bureaucrats crying up 'excellence' for 'economic growth'

Between Pro-Life and Pro-Choice

Victoria A. Sackett

No subject is so certain as abortion to silence a room or incite verbal warfare. Because disagreements about it revolve around the most fundamental, hence the most volatile, issues—sex, religion, the meaning of life—the disputes rarely lend themselves to compromise. And adding to the furor is that the opposing sides, whose disagreements with one another are irreconcilable, can *both* insist that public opinion agrees with them. Until recently, abortion rights advocates have been more successful than their anti-abortion opponents at convincing us that they have public sentiment on their side. We have heard few challenges to the notion that most people are in favor of legalized abortion and have taken the 1973 *Roe* v. *Wade* decision in stride.

Lately, though, the pro-choice faction has noticed that—public opinion aside—certain things aren't going their way. They've watched the overwhelming election and even more overwhelming reelection of an anti-abortion president. They've seen that same president break precedent and address the annual pro-life march on Washington. They've seen anti-abortion legislation narrowly defeated. How can this be happening, they ask, when, as one of them put it, "public support and acceptance of abortion seem to be increasing?"

One answer to the question is that the pro-choice side has mistaken public acquiescence for public enthusiasm. They can claim some aspects of public opinion and be correct, but that ignores a large body of equally convincing evidence on the other side. It may not be that the anti-abortion forces have been successful in dimming abortion's appeal, but that it was never terribly appealing in the first place. If this is true, what led abortion's defenders to believe they had not only the legal but the popular position? A look at the twelve years that have passed since the Supreme Court tried to settle the matter may help explain what has confused things.

Before the Court Decided

Roe v. *Wade* came as a great shock to those who disapproved of abortion. They were less than an organized group in 1973 when the Supreme Court handed down the twin rulings that sanctioned abortion on demand. It was these decisions, in fact, that moved many to band together to protest what seemed to them the court's outrageous and immoral act. ". . . [W]e felt as though the bottom had been pulled out from under us," recalled a woman in an interview with author Kristin Luker (*Abortion and the Politics of Motherhood*). "It was an incredible thing. I couldn't believe it. In fact, I didn't." Many shared this woman's sense of shock, unable to believe that a climate of opinion or a court could differ so radically with the views that were to them so obviously and indisputably correct.

But the climate of opinion *had* grown more receptive to abortion over the years, whether or not its opponents had noticed. The people who had noticed were those who had been pushing for the changes *Roe* v. *Wade* signalled. It was possible in 1973 for those who cheered the Supreme Court decision to believe that organized opposition to abortion was only "small and sectarian." It looked like everything was going the way the reformers wanted.

The most comprehensive collection of questions on abortion, posed by the National Opinion Research Center (NORC), showed that from 1965 to 1972, support for abortion had increased. NORC asked people whether they thought it should be possible for a pregnant woman to obtain a legal abortion for each of six reasons: "if the woman's health is seriously endangered by the pregnancy," "if she became pregnant as a result of rape," "if there is a strong chance of a serious defect in the baby," "if the family has a very low income and cannot afford any more children," "if she is not married and does not want to marry the man," and "if she is married and does not want any more children." The first three circumstances have been called the "hard" reasons and the last three the "soft" reasons for abortions. Between 1965 and 1972, support for abortion increased for all reasons. There was a greater willingness to approve it for the hard than for the soft reasons, though the gap in approval for the two sets of reasons had narrowed.

Other surveys offered the same kind of encouragement to the reformers. Whereas a Gallup inquiry in 1969 had found a minority of 44 percent of its sample in favor of a law that "would permit a woman to go to a doctor to end pregnancy at any time during the first three months," by 1972 that had climbed to 51 percent. And the belief that the decision to abort should be reached by a woman and her physician had climbed from 57 to 64 percent within five months in 1972. Louis Harris found 48 percent that same year in favor of "allowing legalized abortions to take place up to four months of pregnancy" (43 percent opposed it). Though this support slipped 6 percentage points two months later, most of it went to the undecided category and not to the opposition.

It is small wonder, then, that the pro-choice side congratulated the Supreme Court in 1973 for issuing a decision that paralleled public preferences as well as their own. Many thought the battle had been won.

What Meets Public Approval

Certain aspects of favorable opinion about a liberalized abortion law continued to grow following the Supreme Court decision, so that by 1982, an overwhelming 80 percent agreed mildly or strongly that "the decision to have an abortion should be left to the woman and her physician." By 1983, 54 percent supported the Court when a Gallup question explained *Roe* v. *Wade* as allowing "a woman [to] go to a doctor to end pregnancy at any time during the first three months of pregnancy." (A similarly worded description in a 1969 Gallup question had elicited 56 percent *dis*approval of a hypothetical law.) And by 1984, 62 percent agreed (either strongly or somewhat) that "a woman should be able to get an abortion if she decides she wants one," (ABC/*Post*) up from 61 percent in a comparable NBC question two years earlier.

More than a decade of NORC questions, following the Court's action, 1973-1982, further reassured the pro-choice side. These polls were among those cited most frequently as demonstrations of public support for abortion. With few dramatic fluctuations, approval of abortion under six circumstances ranged from around 50 percent at the low end (the lowest was the 49 percent who believed in 1982 that it should be possible for a woman to obtain a legal abortion if "she is married and does not want any more children") to a high of 93 percent in a case where the woman's health is seriously endangered. (See p. 27 of Opinion Roundup.) Support for abortion in cases of rape or a strong chance of a serious defect in the baby hovered in the realm of 83 percent.

Not only did the support for abortion look strong, but the opposition also looked weak. Gallup had been asking a question since 1975 that probed some of the subtleties of approval or disapproval—"Do you think abortions should be legal under any circumstances, legal under only certain circumstances, or illegal in all circumstances?"—and since 1975, no more than 23 percent had ever insisted upon absolute illegality. In 1983, that number was down to an all-time low of 16 percent.

The Muddle

So, in the eyes of those who wish to maintain the current abortion laws, their beliefs were and are right in line with the public mood. Neither the public nor pro-choice advocates wishes abortion to be made illegal; neither favors a constitutional amendment to ban it; neither wishes to make a woman bear a child who might be deformed, might threaten her health, or who was conceived in a rape. If this is true, and if these things the public wants are on the anti-abortion hit list, then it would be easy for the pro-choice side to believe that their opposition couldn't succeed. But, of course, the pro-choice forces have begun to fear that their opposites *are* succeeding, and they seem to have no clue why.

Selective readings of statistics can make it appear that the Supreme Court made its abortion decision in harmony with the sentiments of the general public, and they can make it look as if the abortion opposition was bucking the majority. It's no wonder, then, that abortion rights advocates have been able to see their opinions reflected by the populace. What the pro-choice side failed to notice was the *magnitude* of sentiment on the other side—it is indeed a minority on many questions, but a sizable one.

What the pro-choice side seems to underestimate, as does the anti-abortion side, is the degree to which Americans have mixed feelings about abortion. Most think of abortion as a necessary, though not very attractive, evil. They endorse it only reluctantly. The tale of this reluctance can be told with the public opinion numbers that are less often cited.

Abortion's Troubling Aspects

One culprit in the misunderstanding of public opinion about abortion is polling itself. It's possible to believe people support the Supreme Court decision simply because questions about it fail to tell the whole story. Queries about the Supreme Court decision, for example, most often specify that abortion is legal in the first three months of pregnancy. The decision, though, actually allows abortion far beyond that time, and this makes a difference to the public. The Gallup poll used to ask a series of questions (1979) in order to determine how opinion on abortion under varied circumstances might be affected by specifying first, second, or third trimesters. Once past the first trimester, it was impossible to muster a majority for any situation other than danger to the mother's life. (The question was posed to those who believed that abortion should be legal under only certain circumstances, not those who felt it should be legal or illegal at all times.) Because such a question allows us to see how people qualify their support, it is a truer test of their approval for *Roe* v. *Wade*.

Most, in fact, did not fall in with the opinions of either extreme on the abortion question—they thought it should be neither legal nor illegal all the time. And most people did not believe that most circumstances justify abortion. The possibility of a deformed baby (44 percent approved of abortion), or impairment of the mother's mental health (42 percent) or family financial trouble (15 percent) were all considered insufficient grounds for abortion even in the first trimester in this Gallup poll. In the second and third trimester, these disapproved situations expanded to include the possibility of severe physical health damage to the mother and a pregnancy that resulted from rape or incest. Though we have no more recent data to track the effect of adding advancing trimesters to questions, there is ample evidence from other surveys to buttress what Gallup found for the first trimester.

The NORC questions mentioned earlier are asked of the general population. They help demonstrate that people are troubled by certain occasions for abortion. In the cases of most severe hardship (threat to mother's health or life, chance of defect in the baby, cases of rape) most people approve abortion in these polls. In past years, there usually has also been a bare majority who supported abortion for a woman whose family has a very low income and cannot afford any more children. This turned around in 1983, when a 56 percent majority opposed abortion for financial reasons, as did 54 percent in 1984. Opposition in all three cases is at or close to a twelve-year high.

Abortion on demand has never been popular in anything but theory. At the same time that people supported the idea of relegating decisions about abortion to a woman and her physician, they have balked at circumstances that suggest this might be undertaken too lightly—for what people consider insufficient reason. Most people do not want to outlaw abortion (80 percent opt for legality in at least some circumstances), but it is also true in approximately equal proportions that they do not support abortion under *all* circumstances (also about 80 percent). Twenty percent would like abortion to be legal always, and 20 percent would like it to be illegal always. The bulk of the public (usually more than 50 percent) falls in the middle, which is a decidedly different spot from where the Supreme Court landed.

Where the Public Draws the Line

Seventy-nine percent of the abortions these days are performed on unmarried women, most of whom are in their early twenties. Most abortions take place in the first trimester (91 percent, according to the Guttmacher Institute, the statistical arm of Planned Parenthood). It's impossible to be certain why these women decided on abortion, but one can tell from other data that most were not the victims of rape, nor were they faced with threats to their lives or physical health, or to their babies' health. If all this is correct, then most abortions that take place do so for precisely the reasons most Americans disapprove: financial or psychological reasons or convenience.

Polling analyst William Schneider has explained that people draw the line between approving and disapproving abortion where "the pregnancy was, at least to some degree, a deliberate decision." The public believes that once the decision is made, abortion is an unacceptable "way of getting out of it." In other words, says Schneider, "the American public does not endorse abortion as a form of birth control."

To the extent that the right-to-life movement can emphasize these circumstances as the ground upon which they disagree with present law, they will have the public on their side. The most current information reinforces this. Two polls taken in January 1985 showed majorities in favor of abortion only in cases of rape, incest, or a threat to the mother's life. In Gallup's poll for *Newsweek*, 62 percent approved a ban on abortion in all but those cases, up from 53 percent a year earlier. A January CBS News/*New York Times* poll asked whether people thought abortion should be "legal as it is now; legal only in such cases as saving the life of the mother, rape, or incest; or should it not be permitted at all?" Forty-five percent believed abortion should be allowed only in the situations named; 38 percent wanted things as they are; and 13 percent wanted abortion outlawed.

People are extremely uncomfortable with the idea of abortion. They think it is wrong, but they seem reluctant to make moral decisions about it for others. Fifty-three percent in 1982 (the last NBC query) personally believed that abortion is wrong, though only a little more than half of *them* thought it should be illegal. At the same time, in the same poll, 80 percent agreed that the decision to have an abortion should be left to the woman and her physician, and 61 percent agreed that "every woman who wants to have an abortion should be able to have one."

There are reasons for this lack of willingness to endorse laws that reflect one's own opinions about abortion. Part of the explanation must be our national tradition of individualism, but more specific to the abortion issue is probably the fear of the consequences. People do not believe that outlawing abortion would eliminate abortions. Ninety-three percent said this year that women would get abortions anyway. But perhaps most telling is that 92 percent believe now (as did 83 percent in 1973) that outlawing abortion would be dangerous; women would be forced to seek unsafe procedures performed by incompetent people, and they would be harmed.

People are reluctant to impose their standards on others, especially if it may cause damage, and they hesitate to curtail others' freedom to choose. When asked for their views, they don't care much for abortion, but when asked what ought to be done about it, they often opt for the status quo. Public debates about the subject tend to take place at the extremes, where people are most certain of themselves and where things are simplest. It's important to remember that the public itself, unlike some of its spokesmen, is far less single-minded.

Stratification and Social Inequalities

- The Rich (Articles 29-30)
- The Poor (Articles 31-32)
- Blacks (Articles 33-34)

People are ranked in many different ways: by physical strength, education, wealth, or other characteristics. Those who are rated highly usually enjoy special privileges and opportunities. They often have power over others, special status, and prestige. The differences among people constitute their life chances, or the probability that an individual or group will be able to obtain the valued and desired goods in a society. These differences are referred to as stratification, or the system of structured inequalities that pattern social relationships.

In most industrialized societies income is one of the most important divisions among people, whereas in agricultural societies kinship has a major influence on life chances. Karl Marx described stratification in different terms. He used the term social class to refer to two distinct groups: those who control the means of production and those who do not. These groups overlap extensively with the rich and poor. This section examines the life chances of the rich and the poor and of various disadvantaged groups because they best demonstrate the crucial features of the stratification system in the United States.

The article by Maurice Zeitlin on the excessive power of the rich is already a classic. It analyzes the income and power distribution in the United States before and during the Reagan administration. It attacks the image of America as the land of democracy, equality, and opportunity, and finds that America is unfair to the majority of its citizens.

While Zeitlin focuses on the ownership of the rich, Gregory Fossedal considers welfare for the rich, or at least for corporations. Government handouts to rich corporations dwarf aid to poor people. Unfortunately efforts to trim corporate welfare will meet with powerful opposition and probably will not succeed.

In the 1980s the homeless, or street people, are very much in the public eye. Street people were primarily alcoholics and inveterate drifters until the economy became

so troubled and before mental institutions began releasing large numbers of people to reduce their patient load. As a result, many who are mentally unstable and others who have been squeezed by hard times and deserted by the government make up a majority of the homeless today. Wickenden explains their plight and discusses how governments and other groups have responded.

A major issue today is whether welfare for the poor does more harm than good. The National Council of State Human Service Administrators defends the benefits of welfare and calls for greater government investment in poor children. It argues that the budget cuts have badly hurt the "truly needy."

The inequality of blacks is the subject of the last two articles. William Julius Wilson calls on black leaders to recognize that civil rights activism can do little for the black underclass. Instead he recommends that they should push policies which benefit all poor peoples in the nation. Race is no longer the key issue but class is. Vincent Harding promotes the same theme by reviewing the black struggle for freedom from the 1950s to the Jesse Jackson campaign. He describes it as an heroic struggle with many heroes.

The six articles in this section vividly portray tremendous differences in wealth and life chances among Americans. Systems of inequality affect what a person does and when and how he or she does it. An important contribution of this section is to help you become more aware of how stratification operates in social life.

Looking Ahead: Challenge Questions

Will technology reduce or increase social inequalities?

Why is stratification such an important theme in sociology?

What social groups are likely to rise in the stratification system in the next decade? Which groups will fall? Why?

Who Owns America?
The Same Old Gang

MAURICE ZEITLIN

Maurice Zeitlin is a professor of sociology at the University of California, Los Angeles. Detailed references for the facts cited in this article are available from the author.

Do you remember those full-page newspaper ads that showed a little old lady stroking *her* locomotive, supposedly owned by millions of ordinary Americans just like her? Or Standard Oil's gushing claim, "Yes, the people own the tools of production.... How odd to find that it is here, in the capitalism [Karl Marx] reviled, that the promise of the tool has been fulfilled." Well, it's happening again.

A current Texaco television commercial has Bob Hope asking us to "take a look at the owners of America's oil companies," and then leads us on a tour of a typical community made up of just plain folks like you and me. A recent book, received with much fanfare in the press, repeats the refrain. Its author, long-time management consultant and publicist Peter Drucker, tells us that an "unseen revolution" has wrought "a more radical shift in ownership than Soviet communism." Even more amazing, "the socialism of Marxist theory has been realized for the first time on American soil."

Not only are the means of production now in everyone's hands, but the U.S. Chamber of Commerce confides that the United States has become a "post-industrial society." College textbooks inform us that a "dramatic shift from blue collar to white collar, from brawn to brain [has] occurred," and the best-seller *Future Shock* rhapsodizes that "for the first time in human history," a society — *our* society — has "managed within a few short decades to throw off the yoke of manual labor." A book on "power in America" celebrates the passing of classes and suggests that we organize popular visits to "Newport, and bus tours through Grosse Pointe, for purely educational purposes — like seeing Carlsbad Caverns once." It is time, the author advises us, to shout, "The Working Class is dead. Long live the memory of the Working Class." And, summing it all up, a popular book on how to be a politician announces that "the economic class system is disappearing.... Redistribution of wealth and income...has ended economic inequality's political significance."

So, what has happened to classes? Who does own America, and how has it all been changing? Has the capitalist class really been "lopped off" at the top, as Harvard's Talcott Parsons once pithily put it? Has the ownership of American corporations become so dispersed that control has shifted to "professional managers" who are merely the "trustees" for all of us — "stockholders, employes, suppliers, consumers, and the public" — as Donald S. McNaughton, the chairman of Prudential Life, announced in a recent speech? Has the yoke of manual labor really been lifted? Is the working class now a mere memory? Or are the claims that prompt these questions really pseudofacts that are as plausible and persuasive as they are deceptive? The answer, I think, is clear: Economic inequality weighs as heavily and cuts as deeply as ever, and neither capitalists nor workers have vanished from American life.

Let's look first at who owns what. It's certainly hard enough to find out, even if, like Government economists, you have access to Internal Revenue Service (IRS) data. No law requires Americans to report their net worth, and besides, wealth is deliberately hidden, whether out of modesty or to avoid taxes. Still, an ingenious method of estimating wealth has been devised, to make the dead disclose what the living conceal. It is called the "estate multiplier technique," and it uses IRS data on estate tax returns. It treats those who die in any year as a "stratified sample" of the living on whose estates tax returns would have to be filed if they died during the year — that is, those with estates worth $60,000 or more. All told, only 4 per cent of the adults in this country have estates as large as $60,000, counting *everything* they own, including cash in hand or under the mattress, and the mattress itself. But within that group, a minute number of Americans make up the real owners of America.

The Rose Bowl's 104,696 seats would still be half empty if only every adult American who owns $1 million or more in corporate stock came to cheer, and it would be even emptier if only those who have $100,000 in state and local bonds got a seat. If you counted all state, local, and Federal bonds (except U.S. Savings Bonds), and added Treasury bills, certificates, notes, and mortgages — and even foreign bonds — held by Americans in amounts of at least $200,000, you would still find well over a quarter of the Rose Bowl seats not taken. Only 55,400 adults have $1 million or more in corporate stock. A mere 40,000 have $100,000 or more in state and local bonds (all Federal tax exempt), and 73,500 adults have $200,000 or more if we count all bonds and debtholdings.

This tiny owning class at the tip of the top, barely more than one-twentieth of 1 per cent of American adults, has a fifth of *all* the corporate stock, nearly two-thirds of the worth of *all* state and local bonds, and two-fifths of *all* bonds and notes. No wonder it took five years of trying by an outstanding economist, James D. Smith, to get the IRS to allow him to study its information — and by then some of the data had been destroyed.

Contrast what this propertied class owns to what the rest of us have. Nine out of ten adults in the United States could sell everything they own, pay off their debts, and have no more than $30,000 left. Worse, more than half of all Americans would have a total "net worth" of no more than $3,000. The bottom half of all American families combined have only three cents of every dollar's worth of all the wealth in the country.

Back at the top, if we count up what the richest 1 per cent of the population own, we find that they have a seventh of all the real estate in the country, more than half the corporate stock, and almost all the trust assets. They even had a seventh of all the *cash* in every checking and savings account and pocket and purse in America.

Summed up, that is a quarter of the net worth of the entire population held by the top 1 per cent. If we take a slice as large as the richest 4 per cent — everyone whose total net assets (i.e. subtracting debts) are worth at least $60,000 — their combined wealth is more than a trillion dollars — enough to buy the entire national product of the United States and have plenty left over to pick up the combined output of a few small European countries, including Switzerland, Norway, Denmark, and Sweden.

So it's clear who owns America — but has this propertied class been slipping in its hold on the nation's wealth? Maybe, but if it slipped at all, it was not because of any egalitarian tendencies in American capitalism. It took the country's worst crash, the Great Depression, when many fortunes (and even a few of the fortune-holders) took the plunge from the pinnacle, to make a dent on what they own. Even the modest shrinkage that supposedly took place then is probably more apparent than real, because just before the crash there was a phenomenal rise in the price of stock, the biggest asset in the portfolios of the rich.

But since the end of World War II, there has been no change in their share of the nation's wealth; it has been constant in every year studied, at roughly five-year intervals, since 1945. The richest 1 per cent own a quarter, and the top half of 1 per cent a fifth, of the combined market worth of everything owned by every American. Remarkably, economic historians who have culled manuscript census reports on the past century report that on the eve of the Civil War the rich had the same cut of the total: The top 1 per cent owned 24 per cent in 1860 and 24.9 per cent in 1969 (the latest year thoroughly studied). Through all the tumultuous changes since then — the Civil War and the emancipation of the slaves, the Populist and Progressive movements, the Great Depression, the New Deal, progressive taxation, the mass organization of industrial workers, and World Wars I and II — this class has held on to everything it had. They owned America then and they own it now.

Any notion that *income* has been redistributed, even though *property* is intact, is also illusory: The higher the income bracket, the higher the percentage in it that derives its income from the ownership of property. At the top, almost all income is in dividends, rents, royalties, and interest. Among all American families and unrelated individuals combined, not more than one in eight receives any stock dividends at all. Not one in a hundred receives even a dollar from any "trust or estate." But among those with incomes of $100,000 or more, 97 per cent receive stock dividends and more than half receive inherited income directly from a trust or estate.

The 5 per cent of Americans with the highest incomes take in almost half of all the income from property in the country. They receive sixty-four cents out of every dollar in dividends earned on publicly traded stock and ninety-three cents of the dividends on stock owned in "closely held corporations" (those having just a few owners). Furthermore, they take in thirty cents of every dollar earned in interest, thirty-seven cents in rents and royalties, and sixty-four cents of every dollar in America coming from trusts and estates.

If we divide Americans into five brackets from low to high, and count all known income, the top fifth gets about forty cents of every dollar of personal income. The bottom fifth gets just one nickel. That is a ratio of eight to one, and that ratio has remained almost exactly the same in every year since World War II ended. (Here, in the capitalism celebrated by the Advertising Council and Bob Hope, the gap between the top and bottom fifths is wider than in Britain, Holland, West Germany, or even Japan. Among industrial nations, only France has a wider gap.) And the *real income* gap between the top and bottom has been growing, though the ratio has stayed the same: The average real income difference between the top and bottom fifth, measured in constant 1969 dollars, rose from $11,000 to $19,000 in the twenty years between 1949 and 1969.

All those "redistributive efforts" and wars on poverty we have heard about have not made a dent in income distribution. The overall tax burden has probably become more *regressive* since World War II — taxes are taking an increasing bite of the incomes of people in the lower rather than in the higher brackets. One reason is that state and local taxes, which are typically more regressive than Federal taxes, have grown in comparison to Federal taxes — from forty-two cents to every dollar of Federal taxes collected in 1950 to fifty-one cents in 1961 and fifty-eight cents in 1970.

But even Federal taxes have become more regressive during the same years. Corporate taxes have gone down, from twenty-seven cents of every Federal tax dollar received in 1950 to only sixteen cents in 1970, and at the same time Social Security and payroll taxes have jumped from just nine cents to twenty-six cents of each tax dollar pumped into Washington. So, when the impact of all taxes and all Government spending is taken into account — even though there has been a sizable increase in Government "benefits" to low-income Americans — the level of income inequality ("post-fiscal") has not changed since 1950.

The notion that classes are withering away in America rests not only on the mistaken assumption that the propertied have been lopped off at the top, but on the equally unfounded notion that the working class itself has been vanishing and the "white collar" strata of the so-called middle class have been multiplying. So renowned a pundit as Harvard's John Kenneth Galbraith, among many others, believes the class struggle is a "dwindling phenomenon" because "the number of white-collar workers in the United States almost fifteen years ago overtook the number in the blue-collar working force and is, of course, now greater."

Of course? The sort of counting done here misses and distorts what has really happened; it confuses occupational composition with class lines. Since the 1900s, especially during World War II, and in quickening pace in recent years, women — and increasingly married women — have been moving into the labor force. About four out of ten people in the labor force are now women, and almost half of all women now have paying jobs or are looking for them. It is this influx of women into paying jobs that accounts for the growing number of "white-collar" jobs — mainly in "clerical or sales" work — in the past few decades. Of all working women, not even one in ten was a "clerical or sales" worker in 1900. By 1940, on the eve of World War II, the figure jumped to almost three in ten, and it climbed until it reached more than four in ten in 1970.

At the same time, the proportion of women working in crafts or as operatives and laborers (except on the farm) dropped. It also dropped in so-called "service" occupations which, for women, are typically dirty and menial jobs as domestics or "food service" workers. Some "white-collar" jobs are now almost entirely filled by women — and ten occupations alone, among them waitress, typist, cashier, hairdresser and beautician, nurse and dietician, sales clerk, and teacher, account for more than two out of five employed women. Of all clerical and sales jobs, two out of three, and the same ratio in service jobs, are filled by women. In contrast, of all those working in crafts or as operatives and laborers (off the farm), only one in six is a woman.

Among men, meanwhile, the portion with clerical and sales jobs has not risen in three decades. Only seven in a hundred men at work had clerical or sales jobs in 1900, and it rose to just twelve in a hundred by 1940. In the three decades since, the ratio has not grown at all: It is still about twelve in a hundred. In the same years, though, there has been a significant rise in the proportion of men classified as "professionals and technicians" by the U.S. Census — from three, to six, to fourteen in a hundred. But many such "professionals" are vocational school products, and about four out of ten in the rapidly growing category of "technicians" are not college graduates. This, of course, is scarcely the image evoked by the terms "professional" or "technician." Many are really highly skilled workers; advanced education or certification is not required to fill their jobs, nor does their work differ much in independence and control from the work done by those classified as "craftsmen."

The plain fact is that the category of "manual workers" has not shrunk at all in this century. Fewer than forty in a hundred men worked in 1900 as a "craftsman, operative, or nonfarm laborer." In 1920, the figure rose to forty-five in a hundred, and it has barely changed since: In 1970, forty-seven out of every hundred men in the labor force were classified as manual workers. But to this figure we must add many if not most of the men who are called "service workers" — a U.S. Census category that hides a host of blue-collar jobs within its semantic recesses; janitors, porters, waiters, garage mechanics, dishwashers, and laundry workers. How many of the seven in a hundred

men in such service jobs in 1970 should be identified as "real workers" is anybody's guess — and mine is that it is most. We must also add an uncounted number of jobs that strangely get catalogued in the Census as "white collar" — among them stock clerks, baggagemen, newspaper carriers ("sales"), and even mailmen. Their work is certainly — and often heavily — "manual labor."

A safe estimate, then, is that more than five of every ten men who work in this country are manual workers, maybe as many as six in ten — and this does not count the three out of a hundred who work as agricultural laborers. Perhaps the only real difference in the working class today compared to past decades is that many working men now count on their wives' (or daughters') earnings to make the family's ends meet.

In fact, their wives are typically manual workers themselves, for among employed women, the division is sharp between those whose husbands are workers and those who are married to "professionals" or "managers." Among the latter's working wives, only one in six is in manual (or service) jobs. But among the working wives of craftsmen, two in five have such jobs; among the working wives of operatives, almost one out of two; and among the wives of laborers, about two out of three. They certainly are not smuggling any middle-class values, loyalties, or way of life into the working class based on their own experience at work. For them, on the contrary, as for most men in America, the "yoke of manual labor" is yet to be lifted.

Besides, whatever the social images "manual labor" evokes or whatever pain it involves, in real class terms the distinction between it and "nonmanual" or "white-collar" employment is, at best, misleading. How does wearing a white collar lift you into another class? Perhaps there is more prestige attached, though even this is doubtful, particularly among workers themselves. For some "white-collar" workers there may be increased security, but how many cashiers, typists, or beauticians get "salaries" rather than hourly wages, or are less subject to layoffs than highly organized manual workers?

Since most "white-collar" employes are women, and don't wear collars, white or otherwise, anyway, the name itself surely fools us about what it represents. The vast majority of the clerical and sales workers of today are, in any event, not the respectable clerks of yesteryear. Their work is not only routinized and standardized, but they often work in offices that are larger than (and even as noisy as) small manufacturing shops — tending steno machines, typewriters, accounting machines, data processors, or keypunch equipment. They work in supermarkets and department stores with hundreds of others who punch in and punch out and wait to be relieved before they take a break. They are as bereft of control over their work and the products of their work as "manual" workers — in fact, they have *less* independence and control than such workers as crane operators and longshoremen. Beneath their nice clean collars (if they wear them at all), they are propertyless workers, entirely dependent for their livelihoods on the sale of their capacity to work. And this is the essence of working-class reality.

So, neither the working class nor the propertied class has yet departed our fair land. But do the propertied really make up a *capitalist* class? Haven't they, because ownership of the large corporations has become so dispersed, lost *control* of these decisive units of production in America? Of all the pseudofacts behind the notion that classes have withered away in America, none is as persistent as the doctrine of the "managerial revolution" or "unseen revolution" implied by these questions.

The claim is that there has been a "separation of ownership and control" in large corporations — that as the corporations have grown immense, as the original founders have died off or their fortunes supposedly dwindled, as their kids have taken to mere coupon-clipping and jet-setting, and as stock ownership has spread out widely, the capitalists have lost control of the means of production. The result, we are told, is that not capital but bureaucracy, not capitalists but "anonymous administrators," now control large corporations and hold decisive power in contemporary America. The "managers" have usurped their capitalist predecessors.

With the capitalists gone and the managers no longer their mere agents, the inherent conflict that used to exist between labor and capital also supposedly becomes a relic of the past. Instead, we now have not a system of class domination but an occupational order based on merit: "rewards" get distributed according to ability ("functional importance"). What's more, with capital dissolved and new managers motivated by other urges and the pride of professionalism in control, pumping out profit is no longer what drives the corporations in the new "post-capitalist society" we are alleged to be living in. Instead, they have become the "trustees," as Prudential's chairman said — and he was just paraphrasing Harvard economist Carl Kaysen's words of twenty years ago — for all of us in the "new industrial state."

The intent of such notions is clear: We are to believe that "labor" and "management" are just parts of the same team, doing different tasks. It is a theoretical shell game that hides the fact of class domination — of the ownership *and* control of the mines, mills, and factories by a class whose lives are certainly made easier if we don't know they're there, right behind the "anonymous bureaucrats." It hides the simple but profound fact that they live on what the rest of us produce.

One reason that the illusion of managerialism persists is that it is incredibly difficult to figure out who does control a large corporation. And the illusion is nurtured, as the late Senator Lee Metcalf put it bluntly and accurately, by a "massive cover-up" of the principal owners. There are several closely related ways that capital really controls the corporations. First, the real owners do not actually have to *manage* the corporation, or hang around the executive suite with its top officers or directors, or even be formally represented on the board, in order to have their objectives realized — that is, to exert *control*. And how much stock it takes to control a corporation is neither fixed nor standard.

The few recent studies that claim to find "management control" in most large corporations simply assume that it always takes at least 10 per cent of the stock in one pair of hands in order to assure control, but it does not work that way. If you own 10 per cent of the stock in a corporation, you are supposed to report it to the Securities and Ex-

change Commission (SEC), but if the same percentage is split among several of your close associates, without any formal ties between you, or with a few of your relatives, you don't have to report it — and even if you *are* required to report, who is to know if you don't? When Senator Metcalf died, he had been trying for years to get at such information, but his staff so far has had to rely on its own investigations and volunteered data.

How much stock is needed to control a corporation depends on how big the other stockowners are — and who they are, and how they are connected — and how dispersed the rest of the stock is; it also depends on how deeply the firm is indebted to the same few large banks or other creditors. What sorts of ties the corporation has to others, and especially to big banks and other "financial institutions" allied with it, is also crucial. The ability to exert control grows with the number of other major firms in which any family, individual, or group of associates has an interest or actual control.

What a particular large holding of stock implies for any attempt at control depends to an unknown extent on who holds it. If it is held, say, by a leading capitalist family like the Mellons — who control at least four firms in the top 500 nonfinancials (Gulf, Alcoa, Koppers Co., Carborundum Co.) as well as the First Boston Corp., the General Reinsurance Corp., and Mellon National Bank and Trust (the fifteenth largest bank in the country, measured by deposits), and perhaps also, through the Mellon Bank's 7 per cent shareholding, Jones and Laughlin Steel — the meaning is just not the same as if some otherwise unconnected shareowner held it.

Even in corporations that a family like Mellon does not control, the presence of its representative among the principal shareowners, or on the board, can be critical. So the late Richard King Mellon as one of the principal shareowners in General Motors carried a rather different clout in its corporate policy than, say, Billy Rose did in AT&T, though he was reputed to be one of its biggest shareowners. Precisely because the number of shareowners is so large and their holdings typically so minute compared to the few biggest shareowners in a large corporation, it may not take more than 1 or 2 per cent of a company's stock to control it.

The critical holdings and connections that make control possible are invisible to the uninformed eye, and often even to the seasoned investigator. Senator Metcalf's staff found, for instance, that Laurance S. Rockefeller owns a controlling block of almost 5 per cent of the voting stock in Eastern Airlines, though his name did not appear on the required listing of its thirty top stockholders for the Civil Aeronautics Board. Neither the SEC nor the CAB nor Eastern itself could find all the accounts in which his shares were held and aggregate them until they asked *him* to do it for them — in response to Metcalf's prodding.

This helps explain why even the "insiders" who work as financial analysts at *Fortune, Forbes,* or *Business Week,* with their immense research resources and excellent files, have to rely heavily on gossip to estimate the holdings of even the leading families in corporations they have long controlled. These holdings are hidden in a welter of accounts held by brokers, dealers, foundations, holding companies, other corporations, associates, intermediaries, and "street names" (as the fictitious firms that just hold stock for someone are called on Wall Street) or other "nominees."

The extent of a leading capitalist family's holdings is also concealed by a finely woven though tangled web of kinship relations. Apparently unrelated persons with entirely different surnames can be part of a single cohesive set of kindred united to control a corporation. In Dow Chemical Company, for instance, there are seventy-eight dependents (plus spouses) of H.W. Dow who own a total of 12.6 per cent of Dow's stock. So, without research aimed at penetrating the web of kinship, any effort to find out who really controls a large corporation is hobbled at the outset.

In an outstanding recent study, Philip Burch Jr. mined the "inside information" presented over the years in the financial press and found that at least 60 per cent of the 500 top industrial corporations are "probably" (236) or "possibly" (64) under the control of an identifiable family or group of associates. Even these estimates are probably short of the mark because, in Ralph Nader's words, "no one really knows who owns the giant corporations that dominate our economic life." My own guess is that behind the thick veil of nominees, there are real controlling owners in most if not all of the large corporations that now appear to be under so-called management control.

Even if some large corporations were not really controlled by *particular* owning interests, this would not mean power had passed to the "new princes" from the old economic royalists. The higher executives would still have only *relative* independence in their activities and would be bound by the *general* interests of capital. The heads of the large corporations are the main formal agents or functionaries of capital. Their personal careers, interests, and commitments are closely tied to the expansion of corporate capital. Some are among the principal shareholders of the companies they run, and most own stock that not only provides much of their income but ranks them among the population's largest stockowners — and puts them in the propertied few.

Typically, the managers also move in the same intimate circles as the very rich. You'll find them together at debutante balls, select clubs, summer resorts and winter retreats, and other assorted watering places; and their kids attend the same private schools and rush the same fraternities and sororities — and then marry each other. Scratch a top executive and the chances are he will prove to be related to a principal shareowner. Intimate social ties and entangling kinship relations, common interests and overriding commitments unify the families of the heads of the largest corporations and their principal owners into the same cohesive, dominant class in America.

Finally, even if "management" alone had full control of the corporations, it would still have to try to pump the highest possible profits out of their workers and make the most of their investments. The conduct of management is shaped above all by the imperatives of capital accumulation — the competitive struggle among the giants (now global rather than national), the types of investments they make and markets they penetrate, and the relations they have with their workers. High managerial income and status depend, directly and indirectly, on high corporate profits. "Stock options" and bonuses and other forms of executive "compensation" aside from salaries are closely tied to corporate profit rates. Whatever their so-called professional motivations or power urges, their technocratic teamwork and bureaucratic mentality, managers' decisions on how to organized production and sales have to be measured against the bottom line: They dare not imperil corporate profitability.

The recent spate of articles in the financial press on "how to fire a top executive" — you have them "take early retirement" — and the new placement services now catering to them, are rather pointed indicators of what happens to supposed "management control" in times of receding profit margins. In 1974, a year of severe economic crisis around the world, about half of all the chief executives in the nation's top 500 firms were expected to be replaced — in what a weekly newsletter to corporate heads called "a wave of executive ousters" that would "cause the greatest disruption in the business community since the 1929 depression."

Any obvious lowering in profit rates is also reflected in a drop in the price of the corporation's stock; this squeezes its capital base and makes it an attractive — and vulnerable — target for takeover. And this, in turn, leads to executive ousters. In addition, with the marked centralization of huge shareholdings in the trust departments of a few of the biggest banks that administer the investment portfolios of the very rich — typically, they will not take a trust of under $200,000 — the tremors would be deep and the impact rather painful for any managers who turned out a below-average rate of return. The banks must unflinchingly act as "trustees" only for the top investors and real owners who control the large corporations.

Any political strategy that ignores or distorts these realities or is blind to the deep class divisions in our country cannot meet the common needs of the majority of Americans. So long as the illusion persists that our economic life has been "democratized" or that a "silent revolution" has already interred capital, emancipated labor, and redistributed wealth and income, we can be sure that a real effort to achieve those aims will be slated for yet another postponement.

Handouts for the able-bodied man in the gray flannel suit.

CORPORATE WELFARE OUT OF CONTROL

GREGORY FOSSEDAL

Gregory Fossedal works for the editorial page of *The Wall Street Journal.*

RONALD REAGAN has elevated the anecdote to an art form—and an effective weapon against the welfare state. Whether relating the tale of a woman receiving $65,000 in undeserved benefits, or wondering aloud whether there are really many unemployed people in "South Succotash," Reagan has effectively portrayed a social welfare budget riddled with "waste, fraud, and abuse." Now it's time he turned to perhaps the largest, fastest growing, yet least discussed public relief program of the federal government: corporate welfare or, as the Congress Watch lobbying group has dubbed it, "Aid for Dependent Corporations."

Corporate welfare has emerged as a pet theme among many free-enterprise liberals and supply-side conservatives. Both Bill Bradley and Jack Kemp, when attacked about the revenue implications of their tax reform plans, propose trimming corporate welfare as a means of cutting the budget deficit. Yet the subject has received little comprehensive research or analysis. When an aide to Kemp was asked two years ago for specific corporate welfare cuts, he could only offer, "Synthetic fuels . . . the Chrysler and big bank bailouts . . ." before his voice trailed off. Nothing beyond those two? "Well, some others. There really isn't any long list. Jack would love to see one, but right now it doesn't exist."

What research has been done suggests that corporate welfare is more costly than even Kemp or Bradley realizes. Annual studies by Ralph Nader's Congress Watch place the figure at $80 billion to $100 billion. A 1984 paper by the Congressional Budget Office estimates $90 billion. But both studies omit the defense budget, possibly the largest single source of such spending, and most "indirect subsidies"—that is, the impact of programs and regulations that help large corporations and cost the taxpayer money, but do not show up in any well-defined line-item. Add in a conservative estimate for those types of subsidies and for

defense spending, and you arrive at the annual corporate welfare check: $140 billion.

The problem with the corporate welfare freeloaders is that, like the social welfare cheaters, they are hard to find. "Instead of being listed as line-items in the budget, like the Food Stamp program," explains Congress Watch, "corporate welfare resides between the lines—in tax revenue not collected and loans not repaid. . . . While the budget process involves open debate of social programs and military spending, corporate subsidy programs easily escape scrutiny." Even CBO's vast staff expressed frustration in its modest attempt to list the most direct forms of corporate welfare. "Many industrial support program costs are hidden and not voted on explicitly by the Congress," a CBO report says. "It would be beyond the scope of this paper" to identify such items line by line. What is needed is a few Reagan-like vignettes to make all the waste, fraud, and abuse understandable to the average citizen.

The Corporate Welfare Cadillac: Reagan touches a nerve when he tells stories about poor people who, at taxpayer expense, lead lives of moral dissipation. Remember the one about the guy who bought vodka with his food stamps? Reagan might take a look at the International Monetary Fund and at Continental Bank of Illinois. The IMF was bailed out with $8 billion in federal money in 1983. The money was intended, the IMF said, to help Third World countries "restructure" their debt, and to prevent the collapse of the entire world banking system. The money, however, was not used to promote any real reforms in economic policy. Its chief effect was to save the careers of loan officers at large banks, whose ill-advised orgy of foreign lending created the threat to the "system" in the first place. In fact, in 1983 and 1984 a record number of small and medium-sized banks went belly up, more than at any time since the Depression. Not to worry, though: when Continental Bank teetered near the brink, the Reagan administration and the Federal Reserve quickly put together a $4.5 billion rescue package. The banking "safety net" may not catch everyone, but it misses few of the biggies.

Private Sector Public Assistance: Worse than the sleazy recipients who exploit overly generous benefits, however, are the miscreants who go on the dole even though they are well off. Many of the country's largest corporations fit into this category. For example, Exxon and other big energy companies not only receive research grants from the government amounting to $1.9 billion. In 1983 they also enjoyed $4.75 billion in tax "incentives" to encourage oil exploration in 1984. Just as the Reagan administration has proposed tighter rules for those on the social welfare dole, it might raise "eligibility standards" for corporate welfare recipients. In 1983 Congress did cut off one of the wealthiest welfare mothers of them all, the Clinch River Breeder Reactor, thus saving $8.5 billion. But it left intact the energy research expenditures, 84 percent of which go to the nuclear power programs of the big utilities—even though not a single nuclear plant has been ordered in the United States since 1974.

Also intact is the $7.4 billion in loans to the nuclear industry made by the Export-Import Bank from 1981 to 1984, and the $13.5 billion which the Synthetic Fuels Corporation is authorized to hand out. Lest anyone think that the Synfuel Corporation will offer support to Gilderesque entrepreneurs developing a miracle formula for turning chicken feathers into gasoline, guess again. Of 52 important synthetic fuel patents, 49 are owned by the major oil companies.

OTHER ABUSERS can be found at the Small Business Administration and the Export-Import Bank. Both pose as friends of the little guy. Yet one popular SBA loan guarantee program devotes 65 percent of its assistance to firms worth $100,000 or more, mostly to finance large shopping centers, parking lots, and the like. The Ex-Im Bank, meanwhile, in 1982 directed $4 billion of its total $4.4 billion in lending authority to large corporations able to fill huge export orders. As Doug Bandow wrote in *The New York Times* last fall, the bank "is a classic example of corporate welfare: Roughly 70 percent of its loans enrich seven large corporations." Boeing, Westinghouse, General Electric, and McDonnell Douglas alone take up $17 billion of the bank's outstanding credit.

Stretching the Dollars: Conservatives often illustrate the excesses of a social program by noting that the dollars already spent for it would stretch from here to the moon and back. On the corporate welfare rolls, subsidies to agribusiness can be used to make the same point. They have ballooned from a modest $5 billion in the early 1970s to $20 billion or more today. Approximately 70 percent of the subsidies go to the 250,000 biggest farmers in the country. Laid end to end, 20 billion dollar bills would stretch to the moon and back four times.

The Handout That Wouldn't Die: Perhaps the greatest source of corporate welfare is the tangled web of provisions governing federal procurement. Reagan himself now likes to recount the horror stories of U.S. defense contracting—the $8,000 screwdriver and the $25,000 coffee pot. But even greater institutional waste is generated every year by Congress and the White House, as they extend the life of

endangered weapons to see if a little more research and development can fix what's wrong with the latest gun that won't shoot or plane that won't fly. The typical time needed to construct a major weapons system has grown from three to six years in the early 1960s to more than ten years today. If we accept the General Accounting Office's rule of thumb for the cost of delay—a 30 percent increase for each year tacked on to the weapons procurement cycle—then delays in weapons procurement may be the single greatest source of corporate welfare in the budget.

Other agencies and departments have not been rocked by as many recent procurement scandals. Yet they buy goods and services from the private sector in even larger amounts, among them Medicare ($61 billion in 1984), Medicaid ($21 billion), food programs ($17 billion), and housing assistance ($10 billion). More competitive procurement in these agencies, according to estimates from the GAO and the Grace Commission on waste in government, could save between $5 billion and $10 billion, most of it presently going to medium and large corporations, and all of it unjustified by the rigors of free-market price competition.

Candy from Babies: The maritime industry is the corporate equivalent of the bureaucrat who, earning a $60,000 annual salary, remodels his office with millions from the federal school lunch program. Not content with several hundred million dollars in direct subsidies, U.S. shippers have established a "cargo preference" law, under which all official government travel must be conducted in American vessels—even if foreign transport is more available and cheaper. Half of all shipments bought, furnished, or financed by the U.S. government must be shipped on American vessels, regardless of costs. The cargo preference law cost the Food for Peace program $100 million a year in 1981—money that could have gone to the starving in Ethiopia.

Last but not least on the corporate welfare ledger is the kind of abuse that the social welfare recipients never benefit from: special tax breaks. The largest, such as accelerated depreciation and investment tax credit, spread their benefits across broad classes of industries. Others—permitting the passing of exploration costs for fuel along to consumers, the exclusion of interest on state and local pollution control bonds, and so on—were quite consciously designed to benefit particular sectors.

The hodgepodge of special breaks and exemptions has gradually eroded the corporate income tax. In 1975 the government collected 32 cents in corporate income taxes for every dollar in personal income tax. This year, the figure will be closer to 23 cents on the dollar. The increased complexity of the corporate code has also created wide disparities in the taxes collected from various sectors, greatly distorting the decisions of private investors. A pair of 1983 studies by the Congressional Research Service found effective corporate tax rates as low as 13 percent in the construction industry and as high as 37 percent in the finance, insurance, and real estate businesses.

IT WOULD SEEM a simple matter to cut corporate welfare abuses from the budget and the tax code. Yet this apparently attractive fiscal target has drawn little criticism from journalists or the leaders of either party. The cost of entitlements, the military, and Social Security are regularly identified as candidates for cutbacks in articles on the deficit. Corporate welfare, by contrast, is rarely mentioned. Why?

First, several of the self-proclaimed oracles on the budget and federal spending are corporate welfare recipients themselves. The names of Lee Iacocca and J. Peter Grace come to mind. They have a vested interest in not calling attention to the corporate dole. The original draft of the Grace Commission report, for example, named numerous politicians who had been especially sycophantic toward corporations and other special interest groups. Among those singled out frequently were Senators James McClure, Robert Byrd, and Ted Stevens; and Representatives Tip O'Neill, Silvio Conte, and Marvin Leath. Grace and his colleagues decided to delete the names in the final version so as not to hurt the report's chance to win acclaim. At about this time, Grace appeared on the cover of *U.S. News & World Report* under the headline "Washington: City Without Guts."

Second, if corporate welfare is hidden, its powerful proponents are not. Business political action committees in 1984 gave as much money to political candidates as labor, liberal, and conservative PACs combined. The business PACs are bipartisan, giving mainly to incumbents and committee chairmen of both parties: $24 million to Republicans, $21 million to Democrats in 1984. Not surprisingly, the old guard in both parties is committed to protecting corporate handouts.

Of the top ten Senate recipients of business PAC money in 1984, five were Democrats, including Jim Hunt, Jay Rockefeller, and Lloyd Doggett; on the House side, six out of ten, including the top three: Jim Jones, Joseph Addabbo, and Bruce Morrison. House Majority leader Jim Wright has led the fight to preserve the synthetic fuel program. Democratic presidential candidates Walter Mondale and Alan Cranston joined the Chamber of Commerce (which is otherwise willing to criticize businessmen for feeding at the public trough) in fighting to save funding for the Export-Import Bank.

Among Democrats, then, the impetus for trimming back corporate welfare will have to come from the party's younger wing: Gary Hart, Bill Bradley, and Bruce Babbit. A similar generational split emerges among Republicans. Representatives Jack Kemp, Trent Lott, Jim Courter, Robert Walker, and other young turks who drafted the party's 1984 platform are keen to tackle corporate welfare—partly to deflect blame for the deficits from their supply-side tax cutting. Yet Republican leaders in the Senate seem determined to take the old-fashioned route, namely cutting social programs in exchange for defense cuts. The package being drawn up by Republican Senate chieftains Dole, Domenici, Simpson, and others is likely to include Social Security cuts, cost of living freezes for welfare mothers, surgical cuts in Medicare, you name it. The strategy is to get leading business groups and lobbyists behind closed doors and then barter among them to cut the deficit. The unneediest are not likely to suffer in the process.

Thus, any major assault on corporate welfare will probably have to be a joint effort by the young intellectual vanguard of the two parties—a political bridge over the Republican and Democratic establishments. Both sides have much to gain: to attack corporate welfare is to support smaller government, fairness, fiscal responsibility, and free enterprise all at once. But both sides also have to buck the corporations and the conventional wisdom that says corporate welfare is sacred. Can they pull it off anyway? That's the $140 billion question.

What Ronald Reagan could learn from Charles Dickens.

ABANDONED AMERICANS

DOROTHY WICKENDEN

ON SUNDAY, November 4, a few hours after he ended his 51-day hunger strike, Mitch Snyder appeared on "60 Minutes." Mike Wallace began by calling him "the shepherd of the homeless in Washington, the nation's capital," and, toward the end of the interview, asked in his most seductive manner: "Gandhi, Mother Theresa, Martin Luther King—Mitch Snyder?" "No," Snyder replied in a rare burst of modesty, "I wouldn't go that far." He had already gone pretty far: he had starved himself nearly to death in order to bludgeon the Reagan administration into supplying up to five million dollars to repair the moldering shelter for the homeless he runs at 425 Second Street NW, just north of the Capitol. The administration, faced with the prospect of a martyred Snyder on television's highest-rated news show two days before the election, capitulated.

Four months later, the repairs are still in the planning stage. In the meantime, the building remains, as Snyder pithily puts it, "a place fit for vermin and trash." Heavy metal screens have been affixed to all of the windows to keep out vandals. The cavernous concrete basement serves as a feeding and "drop-in" center for up to 1,000 men during the day and early evening. At 8 p.m. the upper-floor dormitories open. (A separate section of the building houses about 100 women at night. They are asked to leave at 8 a.m. There is as yet nowhere for them to go during the day.) The stairways reek of urine and many of the walls have been kicked in. Five or six live-in volunteers patrol the shelter's labyrinthine corridors and dormitory rooms with walkie-talkies in case of trouble. As I arrived one night this winter, a man was being ejected from the premises for attacking another "guest." Snyder matter-of-factly pointed out a pool of congealed blood near one stairwell: "A guy was stabbed here a few nights ago. No one's cleaned it up yet."

The First District police, who file the reports on assaults, disorderly conduct, and thefts at the shelter, refer to it as "the Second Street Hilton." Health and Human Services Secretary Margaret Heckler, who granted Snyder the ini-

tial temporary lease on the federally owned building last winter and was a guest speaker at its festive opening, billed it as "a sanctuary" and "a symbol of hope. . . . There is enough love here today to heat this building for many years. So that is no problem." Heckler's optimism proved to be premature. Snyder is well known for his imperious manner. He refuses to work with other shelter administrators in the city, and as a self-proclaimed anarchist he believes that "the federal and local governments have no right to exist." "We accept only neutral things from them," he told me, "like buildings." A few months after the opening lovefest, Snyder announced that if the lease was not extended, he and his group would set up tents in Lafayette Park across from the White House. The administration agreed to his demands, as it did when he began appearing, wraithlike, on "Nightline" and "60 Minutes."

What should we do about the homeless? Preventing people from starving to death or dying of exposure in the streets is the absolute minimal obligation of society. To his credit, Snyder has forced America to recollect that obligation. Yet the sprouting of emergency shelters like the one at Second Street are hardly "symbols of hope." These new "sanctuaries," chronically underfunded and poorly staffed, are often dangerous as well as squalid. They are the end product of a long chain of abysmal social failures. They started off as temporary havens. In the absence of any coherent policy, they have evolved into an alternate form of public housing and psychiatric care. The truth is that they resemble nothing so much as the poor houses and insane asylums of the past.

There is still considerable confusion about how many homeless people there are in America, who they are, why they are on the streets, and how they should be provided for. And it's not for lack of attention. Over the past several years, countless reports have been written, congressional hearings held, task forces formed, and lawsuits filed on behalf of a group of people that was once politically powerless and socially invisible. Politicians and the public, dismayed by accounts of rapidly growing numbers of people living in alleys, cars, and cardboard boxes, are beginning to address an issue that used to concern only Salvation Army workers and religious charities.

Yet the causes of homelessness are not a mystery. There is the massive release from large state hospitals of mental patients over the last 20 years, in a movement known as "deinstitutionalization"; the ever-dwindling supply of affordable housing for the poor; continuing high unemployment; and the shaving of welfare benefits and the tightening of eligibility requirements. Solutions are harder to come by.

The administration has been called to task in two congressional hearings. The first was for a report issued last May by the Department of Housing and Urban Development that, according to critics, whitewashed the crisis. The other, in November, focused on the administration's failure to fulfill its pledge to supply empty federal buildings and surplus food for the homeless. At the time of the hearing, only three buildings had been obtained, including Mitch Snyder's shelter. The food distributed through 190 military commissaries was found to be negligible. And $7.1 million of the eight million dollars Congress had appropriated to the Department of Defense to renovate empty military facilities had been spent on routine defense maintenance instead.

HUD's *Report on the Homeless and Emergency Shelters* became a cause célèbre for concluding, among other things, that there were "only" 250,000 to 350,000 homeless people nationwide seeking shelter on an average night in December 1983 and January 1984. "For most people who become homeless," the report says cheerily, "their condition is recent and likely to be temporary." Most studies judge the correct number to be two or three million. An enraged Mitch Snyder demanded that HUD retract its figures. For a time, this was one of the conditions for ending his fast. The congressional hearing showed fairly convincingly that the methodology of the report was indeed slipshod and that the numbers were too low.

But the HUD report, for all its inaccuracies and complacency, implicitly confirmed what other studies and newspaper stories have been saying. First, the problem is getting worse, and the rapid proliferation of shelters cannot keep pace. Even using HUD's figures, there are only about half as many beds in emergency shelters as there are people in need of them. And second, the widespread impression that most of the homeless are chronically alcoholic or mentally ill is wrong. The shelter population is actually getting younger; the average age is usually judged to be 34. HUD says that at least 35 percent to 40 percent of the total is recently unemployed. And this group is getting to look more like the typical poor: there are more minority people, particularly blacks, and more single-parent families.

MUCH HAS BEEN made of the failures of deinstitutionalization. A widely cited clinical study published last December in *The American Journal of Psychiatry* claimed that at one supposedly typical shelter in Boston at least 40 percent of the residents were psychotics, 29 per-

cent were chronic alcoholics, and 21 percent had severe personality disorders of one kind or another. The implication is that 90 percent of homeless people are drunks or lunatics. That's a big exaggeration. The Task Force Report of the American Psychiatric Association, *The Homeless Mentally Ill*, the most thorough and widely respected investigation of the subject, estimates that of about two million homeless people in the United States, perhaps "as many as half suffer from alcohol, drug abuse, or mental health problems." Most other nationwide studies confirm this conclusion.

Clearly a lot of homeless people got that way as casualties of a cruelly ineffective mental health system, and emergency shelters are a poor substitute for sustained psychiatric care. Many of the deinstitutionalized who had been living relatively independent lives lost their Social Security Disability Insurance and Supplemental Security Income—and subsequently their homes—in the Reagan administration's 1981 paring down of benefits and purging of the rolls. What's more, a new generation of "space cases," as they are known among other street people, is beginning to show up in city shelters. Many of them are schizophrenics; others are strung out on drugs like PCP. Apart from occasional trips to hospital emergency rooms, most have received no professional help of any kind.

Nevertheless, the composition of the homeless population is changing. The hundreds of thousands who crowd through the doors of city shelters, welfare hotels, churches, and synagogues each night for a meal and a mattress are not only the traditional social outcasts—the bag ladies, skid-row alcoholics, and muttering schizophrenics who are a familiar part of the urban landscape. In growing numbers they are being joined there by battered women, elderly poor and disabled, and—most significantly—unemployed people with their entire families.

IN THE MIDST of the recession a few years ago, the papers were filled with stories of lines at soup kitchens, Great Depression-style. Today, in the midst of the economic recovery, the stories are about unemployed workers in the industrial Midwest whose benefits have expired and who can no longer afford their rent; or about people living in cars; or about families seeking temporary shelter at city welfare offices. It is becoming apparent that many of the poor have not shared in the economic recovery. Indeed, many of them have suffered from it.

Every major recent study cites neighborhood gentrification and the decline in low-income housing (particularly single-room occupancy hotels, or SROs) as principal causes of homelessness. *The Making of America's Homeless*, the latest report by the nonpartisan research group, the Community Services Society, estimates that 2.5 million Americans every year lose their homes, and about 500,000 low-rent apartments vanish as a result of conversion, arson, abandonment, inflation, and demolition. In Denver, which is experiencing both rapid redevelopment and an influx of unemployed from the industrial belt, the problem is particularly severe. Boarding houses in the low-rent districts are being replaced by condominiums; the number of boarding-room beds decreased from about 1,300 to about 400 over the last eight years, according to the National Coalition on the Homeless. Numerous shelter administrators emphasized that most of their charges are the new poor.

In mid-February Ruth Marcus reported in *The Washington Post* that shelters in the suburbs are now being inundated by the working poor. "Often working at service jobs for the minimum wage of $3.50 an hour . . . they may be hit by a run of bad luck, or their housing situation may simply collapse under the strain of skyrocketing suburban rents." Even when the overall unemployment rate is going down, people still lose their jobs—and their homes. A report by the U.S. Conference of Mayors, *Homelessness in America's Cities*, concluded that although unemployment had dropped in the ten cities it studied, the population in need of emergency shelter had increased. Spokesmen in San Francisco said that 63 percent of those in shelters have "marketable skills." New York City's Human Resources Administration, which runs the city shelter system, says that about 30 percent of recent arrivals were there because they had recently lost their jobs. As the Community Services Society explains in *Hardship in the Heartland*, "Something happens—a job is lost, unemployment benefits run out, creditors and banks move in to foreclose, eviction proceedings begin—and quite suddenly the respectable poor find themselves among the disreputable homeless."

One especially vulnerable group is poor young families. They have suffered at the hands of the Reagan administration over the last four years: in slashes in housing assistance ($1.8 billion), Aid to Families with Dependent Children ($4.8 billion), child nutrition ($5.2 billion) food stamps ($6.8 billion), and low-income energy assistance ($700 million). For many years shortsighted local housing policies have fostered urban renewal but have given scant attention to those removed from condemned buildings. And families that lose their homes soon discover that social service bureaucracies are already overextended.

In New York City the number of homeless families housed by the city in hotels has more than doubled since January 1983, rising from 1,400 to 3,285 last December. On January 9 this year, New York's shelters and hotels took in an unprecedented 20,000 people; 63 percent of them were families. Tens of thousands of other poor families are believed to be "doubling up" with friends and relatives. Even more disturbing, according to Robert Hayes, counsel to the National Coalition for the Homeless, there are now more children under the age of 16 than there are single adults staying in the city's emergency shelter system. A wrenching story by Jane Gross in *The New York Times* in January chronicled the seven-month ordeal of a pregnant woman and her five children who spent countless days and nights being sent from local welfare offices to overcrowded shelters to an HRA Emergency Assistance Unit—none of which had so much as a bed to spare. "Often, those in the shelters yearn for a berth in a single-room occupancy hotel. But those who have braved the

hotels, where they say they are often robbed and molested, return gratefully to the shelters they once clamored to leave. Some say they prefer the streets to the degrading and debilitating process of finding a bed, but are chased indoors by fear, cold, illness, or terror that the Bureau of Child Welfare will separate them from their children."

Here in Washington, the city currently copes with family homelessness through what is known as the "open market" system. Homeless families must go each day to the aptly named Pitts Hotel at 14th and Belmont Streets NW, where they receive their meals and a room assignment for the night. If the Pitts is full, they are given bus fare and sent to one of two other dismal hotels on the outskirts of the city, or to the Greentree Shelter in Bethesda, Maryland. The next day they return to the Pitts, and begin the process again. Many families shuttle among the hotels for months as they search frantically for an apartment they can afford.

Some of the luckier open-market families wind up just down the road from the Pitts, at the Community of Hope,

housed in a renovated apartment building on Belmont Street. The organization, which is funded by the city, is run by Tom Nees, a minister in the Church of the Nazarene. Families pay a small rental fee to live temporarily in the building. The money is put into an escrow account and given to the family when it leaves, ideally within 90 days. Nees's group includes health and social services, legal aid, job assistance, emergency housing assistance, and counseling, and so on.

"Family homelessness," Nees says, "is primarily an economic problem. Street people are traumatized, and will be dependent regardless. That's not true with families, where homelessness produces the trauma." The families at the Community of Hope rarely include a husband or father. Five of the dozen women staying there at the time of my visit worked full-time, but didn't earn enough to rent apartments of their own. Others were welfare mothers who had parceled out their children to friends and relatives or foster care. Nees tries to get such families back together. Most of the women had been living in cramped quarters with friends or relatives. Their families broke up when overcrowding in a small apartment became intolerable, or when the landlord threatened to revoke the lease, or when they realized the impossibility of finding a place cheap and big enough for all of them. Washington's public housing office is still processing applications filed ten years ago; there are no federal funds to speak of.

Nees also tries to urge the women on to greater self-sufficiency. But he can help only the employable—"We don't know how to begin with the others." And for many of the women, a minimum-wage job would hardly help. "A woman with five or six kids could be getting $1,000 a month in food stamps and AFDC. She'd have to earn $12,000 a year to compare with that. It's a terrible dilemma. There is now a disincentive to enter the job market at the minimum wage—you can't raise yourself above the poverty line."

Cities are spending considerable sums on emergency measures like the Pitts that do little or nothing to solve these families' problems: no housing and no jobs. The D.C. government shells out between $80 and $250 a day for each open-market family. Nees's costs are $40-$45 a day. New York spends a minimum of $1,200 a month to put up a family of four in a city shelter. As the Task Force Report of the American Psychiatric Association describes it, "City policy toward the homeless is best described as one that lurches from court order to court order. . . . Harvests of waste rather than economies of scale are reaped when crisis management becomes the modus operandi of housing and social service agencies." Or, as Nees puts it, "They're just putting out fires and picking up the bodies."

THESE PIECEMEAL, insufficient, and expensive efforts are an accurate reflection of ambivalent policies and beliefs. Two decades ago, during the Kennedy administration, the wards of state mental hospitals were emptied out at the urging of progressive politicians and psychiatrists who justifiably denounced the mistreatment of inmates and the wretched conditions, and who believed that the mentally ill had the right—and, with proper medication and counseling, the ability—to live productive lives in the community.

Today the betrayal of that vision is well known. Patients were precipitously released regardless of whether local facilities could provide adequate follow-up care—indeed, regardless of whether those facilities even existed. Communities fought the establishment of halfway houses and clinics in residential neighborhoods, and local governments were reluctant to fund them. The mental health centers that were established were designed more for treatment of people with occasional problems than for chronic patients. Families often found themselves unable to cope with the strains of caring for a disturbed sibling or parent or child. And the new miracle drugs proved to be less of a cure-all than the psychiatrists had hoped. Though

untold numbers successfully made the transition from years of custodial care to independent lives outside, many thousands of the most needy did not.

One of the deeply held principles of the Reagan administration is that people not only have a right to self-determination, but a duty as well. Last winter when President Reagan was asked on "Good Morning America" about the widespread impression that his policies are causing misery among the poor, he replied: "What we have found in this country—and maybe we're more aware of it now—is one problem that we've had, even in the best of times, and that is the people who are sleeping on the grates, the homeless who are homeless, you might say, by choice." That is, if people choose not to get a job, and not to care for themselves responsibly, it must be a matter of life-style. In any case, it should not be a matter of pressing concern to the federal government.

The failures of deinstitutionalization, the sluggishness of city bureaucracies, and the Reagan administration's laissez-faire precepts have led to a contrary notion among those concerned about the homeless: the "right to shelter." The 1979 case of *Callahan* v. *Carey* in New York state's Supreme Court established that the city had a legal obligation to provide shelter for the homeless. A few weeks later, in one of the most ironic repercussions yet of the community mental health movement, New York City opened the Keener Shelter on Wards Island—an empty building in one of those large, isolated state psychiatric hospitals that had been shut down. But the city balked when it came to overseeing the shelter: two subsequent lawsuits were brought—and won—against the city for failing to maintain adequate health standards, and for allowing severe overcrowding. A facility designed to hold up to 180 men was taking in 600 each night.

Many citizens are ready to recognize the right to shelter, but not to welcome the homeless into their neighborhoods. This point was neatly made in Washington recently. On election day an initiative—conceived by Mitch Snyder's group, the Community for Creative Non-Violence—requiring the District to provide shelter to everyone who requests it was passed by a resounding 72 percent, despite the opposition of virtually every politician and activist in the city. A few weeks after the vote, during a town meeting in Georgetown to discuss the possible opening of a small shelter for women in the neighborhood, a woman serving on the Advisory Neighborhood Commission stood up and objected, "What do you mean support services? I voted for Initiative 17, but I thought I was just voting for mattresses on the floor."

PARTLY for this reason, some are now advocating a return to the days of asylum. On "Nightline" recently, George Will made the case bluntly. "We constantly in this country talk about every problem in terms of a clash of individual rights," he said. "The community has some rights here. If it is illegal, and it is, and ought to be illegal, to litter the streets, frankly it ought to be illegal for people who must survive in panhandling among other things to sleep on the streets. Therefore there is a simple matter of public order and hygiene in getting these people somewhere else. Not arrest them, but move them off to someplace where they are simply out of sight and no longer a visible, in some cases intrusive, in some cases even an aggressive, public nuisance." The trouble with Will's trash removal solution is that the problem is not a "simple matter of public order"—or a simple matter of anything else. For the vast majority of the homeless, reinstitutionalization is not a sensible solution.

The first, most obvious, step is to create respectable, affordable, permanent housing. The National Low Income Housing Coalition estimates that at least 750,000 new apartments a year are needed. City and state governments are now beginning to recognize the urgency of the situation. Since 1983 New York has renovated for the homeless 4,500 vacant apartments owned by the city. Mayor Koch—under relentless pressure from advocacy groups and City Council members Ruth Messinger and Carol Bellamy, his opponent in the mayoral race—has stopped awarding tax breaks to real estate developers eager to convert SROs into luxury condominiums. New York governor Mario Cuomo and Massachusetts governor Michael Dukakis have made specialized housing programs for the poor, disabled, and elderly—closely connected to mental health and social service programs—a top priority.

The Reagan administration, on the other hand, appears to have decided to renounce once and for all any meaningful federal support. HUD's budget authority for assistance to additional households was cut from $30 billion to $11 billion in Reagan's first term. In his fiscal 1986 budget, he proposes to chop that by an additional 95 percent, to $499 million. The impact of these cuts, which are spread over a period of 20 years, has hardly been felt yet. Most housing analysts agree that although cities and states and private organizations may be better suited to administer effective housing programs, they simply don't have enough money for the initial investment, especially in cities like New York, where the need for low-income housing has become desperate.

IN THE LONG RUN, emergency shelters will cost everyone a great deal more than permanent apartments, group homes, and a mental health system that values patients' well-being as much as their freedom. Public policy is being driven by defensiveness and a failure of nerve. There are efficient and even modestly successful organizations out there that have put to good use whatever truncated services are available, without placing undue strain on the public purse.

Doubtless a small percentage of the chronically mentally ill will need continuing supervised care in a structured setting. The St. Francis Residence on Manhattan's East Side and now the St. Francis Residence II on the West Side are repeatedly cited as examples of decent, long-term, inexpensive care for the mentally ill. Both were former SRO hotels that were renovated through donations to the St.

Francis of Assisi Friends of the Poor. "Our intention," says Father John Felice, who founded the homes, "is to make the social service system work." Unlike the huge armories and flophouses run by the city, St. Francis demands that the dignity and privacy of each resident be respected. Tenants are guaranteed a room of their own, for which they pay $145-$210 per month out of their welfare payments, Social Security, SSI, or—if they have a job—their paychecks. Occasionally one of the men or women will require a period of hospitalization, in which case his or her room is held open. It costs St. Francis a modest $15-$20 a day for each of its residents. Many men are afraid to spend a single night at the city shelters. The tenants at St. Francis consider it their home. There is very little turnover.

For those whose suffering is less existential than economic, there are any number of possibilities. In Washington the Community of Hope, which assists families, is only one of them. There is McKenna House, which takes in unemployed men, assists them in finding jobs, and helps them to become fully independent again. There is the Reverend John and Erna Steinbruck's "N Street Village" at Luther Place on Thomas Circle, which includes—in addition to an emergency shelter for homeless women inside the Luther Place Church—a health clinic for the neighborhood poor and three group homes for women, where they are helped to find jobs and permanent living arrangements.

THESE UNDERTAKINGS share several fundamental principles. Insofar as it is possible, they reduce the need for shelter rather than perpetuate it. They attack both institutional and welfare dependency with strong doses of old-fashioned practical self-help. They are small and admittedly selective, recognizing that homelessness can't be effectively treated as long as people are being housed in vast warehouses, or as long as it is considered a mere matter of "mattresses on the floor."

The Steinbrucks emphasize that the most fragile of their charges—the women, most of them mentally ill, who spend each night on the floor of their chapel—would be better served at St. Elizabeth's mental hospital, where at least they would be safe. One woman was assaulted on the steps of the Luther Place Church. Another, 80 years old, was beaten while she was out on the streets. Erna Steinbruck says, "Some of them can't make a decision for their own well-being. But St. E's doesn't want them; it wants to get them out." One night recently a schizophrenic woman was sent from The District of Columbia General Hospital to St. Elizabeth's to the streets because no psychiatrist had been willing to sign an involuntary committal form and she herself couldn't cope with the paperwork. She showed up at Luther Place the next morning.

Still, the Steinbrucks have shown an adroitness at coaxing casseroles and clothing from their parishioners and neighbors; at convincing students to staff their group homes and doctors to work in their clinic; and at negotiating the complex of city welfare offices, zoning ordinances, police emergency units, and the recalcitrant mental health system. They have had less success with the biggest proponent of voluntarism: Ronald Reagan. The most the Steinbrucks have received from the administration is a few consultations with Harvey Vieth, the chairman of the Federal Task Force on the Homeless, and a visit from some of the cabinet wives, who stopped by one day at Christmastime laden with toiletries for the women.

Some of the solutions for the homeless will not be cheap or politically popular. But the Community of Hope, the St. Francis Residences, and Luther Place have demonstrated that providing for the majority of the homeless need not entail hiding them away. Neither passive acceptance of places ''fit for vermin and trash'' nor calls for a return to custodial care are the only ways out of this quandary. They are simply the least imaginative. □

HOW WELL POOR FAMILIES FARE IN THE YEARS AHEAD WILL DETERMINE THE STABILITY OF THE ECONOMY AND THE STRENGTH OF THE SOCIAL FABRIC

After steadily declining for most of the past two decades, poverty among children recently has begun to climb. Cutbacks in federal aid to low-income families have combined with inflation and limited economic opportunities to increase the number of poor children to more than one in every five. The problems created by widespread family poverty are complex, but the nation can ill afford to neglect them further since America's future depends on the well-being of today's children.

In response to this challenge, the National Council of State Human Service Administrators, a component of the American Public Welfare Association (APWA), has adopted the following policy statement. With ratification of the statement, the Council inaugurates an eighteen-month project to redirect public policies and programs in order to better support poor children and their families. Endorsed by the APWA Board of Directors, the statement questions the shortsightedness of reducing public support for programs serving the poor and outlines both short-term and long-term recommendations for reform. The project will be financed by state human service agencies and private sources.

As state human service executives, we are charged under the laws of our states with administering programs for the most disadvantaged of America's citizens. Further, we are obligated to carry out this responsibility in the most cost-effective manner possible. We are both advocates for and critics of national social policy and programs. We see the strengths and weaknesses of existing programs and understand the history of their development.

It is from this vantage point that we now call for a nationwide investment in the well-being of poor children and the strength and self-sufficiency of their families. America's ethical, moral, and religious precepts place such an effort high on the list of national priorities. The future economic strength of our society and the durability of the nation's social fabric critically depend on how well this challenge is met.

Today, more than one-fifth of the nation's children live in poverty—an astounding figure given our vast wealth. Aside from the lack of income, poverty in America often entails a host of other social problems that afflict poor children and their families disproportionately. Abuse and neglect, poor health and malnutrition, inadequate education and substandard housing, crime and delinquency—all these occur with greater frequency among the poor than among the rest of the population. Poor children are more likely to become parents out-of-wedlock while still in their teens. Our foster-care system is mainly populated by the children of low-income families. Poor youth experience the highest levels of unemployment and, owing to the lack of education and skills, face the dimmest prospects for joining society's mainstream as adults. And the likelihood of most of these social ills increases for minority poor families. All told, the problems add up to a sizable poverty gap that cannot be defined in strictly economic terms.

A reinvigorated effort to help the nation's poor children and their families is in the self-interest of all Americans. The family, in its various forms, continues to be the basic building block of our society. It is within the protection of the family that children are nurtured, learn about their roles in society, and prepare to meet the challenges of adulthood. An investment in strong, healthy, productive families is an investment in ourselves and in the society we seek to maintain and enhance.

Family poverty is a national problem that requires a national effort involving all levels of government and the public and private sectors in the search for creative, workable, and compassionate answers. In this spirit, states today are testing a variety of new programs designed, for example, to

- help welfare recipients obtain gainful employment;
- prevent teenage pregnancy and support already pregnant or parenting adolescents in their efforts to become independent;
- broaden poor families' access to adequate health care;
- reunite foster children with their families or, when necessary, place them in caring adoptive homes; and
- curb the incidence of child abuse and neglect.

But the task is much larger than the states can handle individually, for the resources and ingenuity demanded by the problem can be secured only through collaboration—among states and localities, between them and the federal government, and between the public and private arenas. The federal government's role in this task is especially important, owing to its existing investment in programs for low-income people, its unique ability to marshall needed resources, and the national scope of family poverty.

There is an urgency to our concern about the federal role. We fear families and children in poverty will not fare well in near-term decisions that are made to reduce the federal deficit. In fact, low-income families have already borne a disproportionate share of budget reductions. The deficit has been characterized as a "mortgage on our future" that is coming due with alarming speed. We fully accept both this characterization and the necessity to reduce the mortgage now and in subsequent years. However, we also believe that a deficit reduction plan is counterproductive if it further erodes basic life support programs, services to reduce dependency, and efforts to enhance the life options of millions of America's children. Such a strategy will surely undermine our only real hope for a mortgage-free future—a healthy, self-sufficient population contributing to the well-being of our society.

From *Public Welfare*, Summer 1985, pp. 5-8. Reprinted by permission of the American Public Welfare Association.

There are those who would counter our concerns with statements that

- the "truly needy" have not been hurt by budget reductions;
- programs for poor families and children have not "worked" and, therefore, need to be cut back, if not eliminated; or
- programs for poor families and children are essential sacrifices to economic necessity.

To all of these arguments we offer the following rebuttal.

The Economy and the Cuts

Poor families and children have suffered a five-way financial squeeze over the past several years.

- Their living costs have increased faster than their incomes.
- Benefit programs they look to for support have failed to keep pace with the rise in living costs.
- Federal funding of these benefits has been reduced.
- The burden of payroll and income taxes has increased for those at or below the poverty line.
- And the severe recession of the 1981-83 period drove many low-income families deeper into poverty.

The declining standard of living of low-income families and children has been a long-term trend. Inflation has been seriously eroding the value of public assistance since the early 1970s. From 1970 through 1984, for example, the purchasing power of aid to families with dependent children (AFDC) benefits declined 37 percent. Even with food stamps added in, the income of families on AFDC still fell in real terms by 25 percent during this period. Inflation also took its toll on social and health-care services for low-income families and children, as federal funding of these services failed to keep pace with the rising cost of providing them.

In the late 1970s, the first steps toward reducing federal support for public "safety net" programs, while not severe, only added to the erosion. All in all, poverty was on the rise before the start of the current decade. In this regard, the current administration's emphasis on curbing inflation, and its recent success in doing so, has helped all Americans, including those with low income. Unfortunately, this success has not appreciably narrowed the gap between the support actually available to poor children and their families and the real cost today of maintaining a minimally decent standard of living. Indeed, for many of the poor, recent cuts in federally financed benefit programs have widened the gap.

Programs for low-income families and children, while constituting less than 10 percent of federal expenditures, sustained 30 percent of all the budget cuts in the last four years. As the numbers of people living in poverty grew by 9 million, an increase of 35 percent in four years, 500,000 low-income families headed by an employed adult lost their AFDC benefits and 700,000 children were deprived of medical coverage. Emergency-food agencies in many areas across the country reported an increase of 50 percent in those seeking their services, while the food stamp program dropped 1 million recipients from its rolls and reduced real

benefits to nearly all others, half of whom were children. As natural-gas prices increased, the low-income energy assistance program was funded at a level that would cover only one-third of the eligible population. The list goes on in social services, school lunch programs, low-income housing. In short, most programs most affecting the well-being of the nation's poorest families and children experienced reductions in funding or restrictions of eligibility.

The effects of the cuts have been statistically verified by the U.S. General Accounting Office. Up to 60 percent of the families losing AFDC had no health-care coverage, more than half reported running out of food, and more than a fourth had utilities shut off in their homes. These families were pushed deeper into poverty; and their children lost health, nutrition, and day-care services. As these events occurred, one state's investment in fact-finding disclosed the disturbing fact that the death rate of children born in poverty is three times higher than that of nonpoor children.

Further cuts in the federal budget are being sought this year. Compared with the cuts made four years ago, the reductions being considered now would entail a broader sharing of the burden for lowering the deficit by curbing programs that benefit middle- and upper-income people. Nevertheless, programs for low-income people remain highly vulnerable to large reductions, evidenced by the fact that the administration's fiscal year 1986 budget request would cut those programs by $34 billion over the next three years.

The Congress should reject proposals to curtail programs that provide assistance to low-income families. These already have been cut more deeply than other domestic programs. Moreover, it would be irresponsible for the nation to further erode essential support services and benefits for poor families even more, while continuing to enlarge national defense expenditures and to accept tax policies that depress federal revenues.

Appraising Programs

There are those who allege tht most programs providing life support for poor families and children do not really work, and they use that allegation to support budget cuts as a necessary exercise in fiscal and social responsibility. Central to this point of view is the contention that public human service programs promote dependency. While we *do not* accept the idea that public programs *create* dependency, we do believe that public policy and human services must do more than accommodate it. Indeed, programs increasingly must be designed and implemented so as to reduce dependency. And both the public and private sectors must take a more active role in moving people toward self-sufficiency through a variety of methods.

To carry out programs aimed at increasing self-sufficiency, we must make honest assessments of what it will take, in terms of philosophy, resources, and management, to do this effectively. It is hard to accept or understand the view that the public resources provided to our children should be reduced when their *only chance to be self-sufficient* depends on the nutrition, education, nurturing, and protection they receive in their formative years. Furthermore, although we agree with the principle that adults should be self-sufficient, we accept the fact that many nonetheless are dependent. Their situation can be changed if we face the reality of their problems and those of the labor market and provide the interim support they need to achieve or regain self-sufficiency. We cannot pretend, however, that dependency of all kinds can be eliminated. Our national purpose should take into account all people who cannot work or maintain a home or even maintain themselves. To do otherwise is to give up the notion of a humane society.

An honest appraisal of human service programs should be carried out to deal with the factors that unintentionally encourage dependency, but this cannot be done while basic maintenance and life support to poor families and children are being eliminated or curtailed. To advocate moving people toward maximum self-sufficiency while ignoring the fact that they are hungry, homeless, unhealthy, uneducated, or unskilled is unrealistic and cruel.

Public programs provide the life supports that make self-sufficiency a real possibility rather than a distant dream for poor families and children. Examples abound.

- The original studies conducted by the Field Foundation in 1968 when only 2 million people received food stamps reported widespread hunger and malnutrition. These studies, repeated about ten years later when 18 million received food stamps, still found poverty, but much less hunger and malnutrition.
- There now are approximately 200,000 fewer children in substitute care than there were in 1977, a tribute, in part, to adoption assistance programs and efforts to reunite families.
- Although infant mortality rates still are alarmingly high, especially among poor children, the rates have been declining steadily since 1965.
- At a time when poverty has increased, 11 million people, two-thirds of them children, receive income support through AFDC and therefore are eligible for Medicaid services. Many of the adults in these families are actively engaged in job-related activities as part of the publicly supported effort to move them toward self-sufficiency.
- Child-support enforcement is increasing significantly the amount of income available to poor children from their legally liable parents, while reducing and preventing welfare dependency.

A national consensus about the plight of the nation's older citizens has produced well-focused public programs to reduce the poverty in their ranks. Dramatic evidence of how well these programs have worked is the fact that from 1970 to 1983 the proportion of persons 65 years or older in poverty declined from 24.5 percent to 14.1 percent. *By contrast*, inflation, limited economic opportunity, and cutbacks in public support for children and their families have resulted in an increase in the percentage of children in poverty—from 14.9 percent to 22.2 percent.

In short, public programs do work—not for enough of the population, and not perfectly—but they work and, we are convinced, can be made to work better for poor families and children.

Economic Necessity Versus Political Choice

Despite evidence that public human service programs

work—and even when there is agreement about the impact of budget cuts on those in poverty—there is still a persistent myth that these programs must be sacrificed to the economic necessity of deficit reduction. *Such is not the case.* No significant dent can—or should—be made in the $200 billion federal deficit by more cuts in programs for our low-income citizens. These programs constitute only one-tenth of all federal expenditures and, as noted above, have already contributed more than their fair share to reducing the deficit.

If our nation is to deal realistically with the deficit, it must take a broader look at the budget policies that have produced that deficit. In particular, closer scrutiny needs to be given to defense spending and taxes.

In 1980, defense spending stood at $136 billion and the federal deficit was $60 billion. In 1984, defense spending totaled $230 billion and the federal deficit was $172 billion. Eliminating waste in the swollen defense budget would not only ease the burden of the deficit but would also free up funds to meet our pressing domestic needs. For example, putting an end to the duplication in just one area of defense procurement (fighter and attack aircraft) would save $5.4 billion this year—more than the cost of all federal maternal, infant, and child nutrition programs combined. Our nation needs a strong defense, but not an excessive one which drains away resources that could be put to better use helping needy children and their families.

Inequities in the tax system work against humane efforts to reduce the deficit as well. In 1960, corporate income taxes contributed 25 percent of all federal tax revenues; by 1984 corporate tax contributions were less than 9 percent. Individual taxpayers have had to make up the difference, evidenced by the fact that the tax burdens of families at the poverty line in 1983 have typically doubled or tripled since 1978. Census data show that the number of families in poverty required to pay federal income tax has doubled in the past five years. Since 1981, the tax bills of the affluent have gone down while those of the working poor have gone up. In addition, the poor have had to pay these increasing taxes on a declining share of national income. In 1983, the percentage of national income received by the poorest two-fifths of all American families was 15.8, the lowest level since 1947, while the wealthiest two-fifths received 67.1, the highest level since 1947.

Poor tax enforcement also impedes deficit reduction. If the taxpaying public met its legal obligation to the federal government, the Internal Revenue Service estimates an additional $96 billion or more would be available to shore up the federal budget.

Public dollars used to help low-income families and children are not subject to decisions based on economic necessity but rather on *political choice*. The Reagan administration and Congress have not reduced government spending, but shifted it from domestic to military purposes and interest payments on the accumulating national debt. Our nation is neither so poor nor so politically paralyzed that other choices cannot be made. As we noted at the beginning of this statement, it is our intent that appropriate choices be made on behalf of poor families and their children.

Action Is Needed at All Levels

Although reordering national priorities to improve the life chances of the poor will not be easy, the honesty, humanity, and common sense of the American people do make the task possible. We offer our experience as a catalyst to the effort. We also commit ourselves and our agencies to using more effectively the substantial federal, state, and local resources that have been committed to our stewardship. That is to say, while the struggle over national priorities goes on, we pledge to seek greater results here and now in promoting self-sufficiency, protection, and increased opportunity for low-income children and their families.

State agencies administering human service programs serve a substantial majority of the nation's low-income families with children. In the AFDC program we provide assistance to over 3 million families and 7.5 million children. More than three-quarters of the nearly 8 million poor households receiving food stamps through our agencies include children. Some 9.3 million low-income children receive health care from our Medicaid programs. State human service agencies also are charged with the responsibility for child protection. Through these and related efforts, our departments have unique obligations and opportunities to assure the well-being of poor children and foster the independence of their families.

The National Council of State Human Service Administrators calls on all state human service agencies to strengthen their commitments to respond effectively to the basic needs of low-income families, to help prevent injury to children from abuse and neglect, and to help members of poor families take full advantage of the training, educational, and employment opportunities they need to achieve self-sufficiency. We accept the criticism that our agencies too often have been more concerned with the effects of deprivation and abuse than with the causes of the problems that afflict low-income families. Toward redressing this imbalance, we pledge increased emphasis on efforts to intervene early in these problems and to prevent them from occurring whenever and wherever possible. We also recognize that permanent or long-term dependency of families for whom reasonable alternatives exist is in the best interest neither of these families nor of society. Consequently, we will encourage our states to seek greater effectiveness in helping poor families with children capitalize on the alternatives available to them.

The state human service agencies cannot achieve these goals on their own, however. The federal government and the private sector must be willing and active partners. Therefore, the Council makes a twofold pledge. *First*, we will work for federal policies and programs that can help states and localities overcome the existing deficiencies in efforts to help the poor. And *second*, we will pursue the restoration and strengthening of intergovernmental and public-private partnerships committed to helping low-income families meet their basic needs, to protecting and nurturing poor children, and to assisting low-income adults toward self-support. The future standard of living of all Americans critically depends on how well we do in the years ahead in helping those people now existing on the margins of society to become productive members.

The long-term effort that we envision will include: (1) a full reexamination of existing human service programs compared with other means of assuring basic life support for the poor and providing alternatives to dependency; (2) an assessment of the effects of tax policies on the capacity of low-income families to support themselves; and (3) a structured and continuous exchange of information on successful human service programs—to better determine what works at what cost—with a strategy for sharing such information with the public. A refined and clarified call to state action will be the result of these initiatives.

In the short term, we will support

- a fiscal year 1986 budget that does not further reduce resources or restrict eligibility in terms of the basic programs that sustain human life (for example AFDC, nutrition assistance, Medicaid, health-care block grants, social services, low-income energy assistance, legal services, employment and training);
- federal efforts to provide special services to prevent adolescent pregnancy and help teen mothers and fathers and their children;
- increased emphasis on preventing family violence and child abuse and neglect, particularly among low-income people;
- reauthorization of the food stamp program as basic income security for poor families and improved integration of food stamp policies and procedures with those of cash assistance programs;
- efforts to enhance services, dollars, and evaluations of the effectiveness of programs affecting the nation's poorest families and children; and
- greater access of welfare recipients to job training and job placement programs, such as the Job Training Partnership Act.

Furthermore, we will continue

- to improve our own efforts to analyze the unintended effects of the programs we administer, such as whether they abet dependency or impair family functioning; and
- to strengthen our relationships with other sectors of society and other levels of government that do or can help poor families and children and that can serve as management resources to our agencies.

We urge all organizations, associations, governmental agencies, and interested persons who share our concerns to join us or, as appropriate, *lead* us in efforts to achieve policy and program improvements for the nation's poorest children and their families. One of those leading organizations, the U.S. Catholic bishops, has articulated the essential message of our task—"the dignity of the human person is the criterion against which all aspects of economic life must be measured." We call ourselves and our colleagues to the challenge of this measurement.

The National Council of State Human Service Administrators represents the chief human service officials of the states, U.S. territories, and the District of Columbia. The council provides a forum for state administrators to discuss and develop positions on national policy issues affecting state programs and to exchange information on state management practices and experience.

The Black Underclass

William Julius Wilson

William Julius Wilson, 48, is Lucy Flower Professor of Urban Sociology at the University of Chicago. Born in Derry Township, Pennsylvania, he received a B.A. from Wilberforce University in 1958 and a Ph.D. from Washington State University in 1966. His books include The Declining Significance of Race: Blacks and Changing American Institutions *(1978) and the forthcoming* The Hidden Agenda: Race, Social Dislocations, and Public Policy.

It is no secret that the social problems of urban life in the United States are, in great measure, associated with race.

While rising rates of crime, drug addiction, out-of-wedlock births, female-headed families, and welfare dependency have afflicted American society generally in recent years, the increases have been most dramatic among what has become a large and seemingly permanent black underclass inhabiting the cores of the nation's major cities.

And yet, liberal journalists, social scientists, policymakers, and civil-rights leaders have for almost two decades been reluctant to face this fact. Often, analysts of such issues as violent crime or teenage pregnancy deliberately make no reference to race at all, unless perhaps to emphasize the deleterious consequences of racial discrimination or the institutionalized inequality of American society.

Some scholars, in an effort to avoid the appearance of "blaming the victim," or to protect their work from charges of racism, simply ignore patterns of behavior that might be construed as stigmatizing to particular racial minorities.

Such neglect is a relatively recent phenomenon. Twenty years ago, during the mid-1960s, social scientists such as Kenneth B. Clark (*Dark Ghetto*, 1965), Daniel Patrick Moynihan (*The Negro Family*, 1965), and Lee Rainwater (*Behind Ghetto Walls*, 1970) forthrightly examined the cumulative effects on inner-city blacks of racial isolation and class subordination. They vividly described aspects of ghetto life that, as Rainwater observed, "are usually forgotten or ignored in polite discussions." All of these studies attempted to show the connection between the economic and social environment into which many blacks are born and the creation of patterns of behavior that, in Clark's words, frequently amounted to a "self-perpetuating pathology."

Why have scholars lately shied away from this line of research? One reason has to do with the vitriolic attacks by many black leaders against Moynihan upon publication of his report in 1965—denunciations that generally focused on the author's unflattering depiction of the black family in the urban ghetto rather than on his proposed remedies or his historical analysis of the black family's special plight. The harsh reception accorded to *The Negro Family* undoubtedly dissuaded many social scientists from following in Moynihan's footsteps.

The "black solidarity" movement was also emerging during the mid-1960s. A new emphasis by young black scholars and intellectuals on the positive aspects of the black experience tended to crowd out older concerns. Indeed, certain forms of ghetto behavior labeled pathological in the studies of Clark et al. were redefined by some during the early 1970s as "functional" because, it was argued, blacks were displaying the ability to survive and in some cases flourish in an economically depressed environment. Scholars such as Andrew Billingsley (*Black Families in White America*, 1968), Joyce Ladner (*Tomorrow's Tomorrow*, 1971), and Robert Hill (*The Strengths of Black Families*, 1971) described the ghetto family as resilient and capable of adapting creatively to an oppressive, racist society.

In the end, the promising efforts of the early 1960s—to distinguish the black community, and to identify the structural problems of the U.S. economy that affected minorities—were cut short by calls for "reparations" or for "black control of institutions serving the black community." In his 1977 book, *Ethnic Chauvinism*, sociologist Orlando Patterson lamented that black ethnicity had become "a form of mystification, diverting attention from the correct kinds of solutions to the terrible economic condition of the group."

Meanwhile, throughout the 1970s, ghetto life across the nation continued to deteriorate. The situation is best seen against the backdrop of the family.

 From *The Wilson Quarterly*, Spring 1984, pp. 88-89. Copyright 1984, by The Woodrow Wilson International Center for Scholars.

In 1965, when Moynihan pointed with alarm to the relative instability of the black family, one-quarter of all such families were headed by women; 15 years later, the figure was a staggering 42 percent. (By contrast, only 12 percent of white families and 22 percent of Hispanic families in 1980 were maintained by women.) Not surprisingly, the proportion of black children living with both their father and their mother declined from nearly two-thirds in 1970 to fewer than half in 1978.

In the inner city, the trend is more pronounced. For example, of the 27,178 families with children living in Chicago Housing Authority projects in 1980, only 2,982, or 11 percent, were husband-and-wife families.

TEENAGE MOTHERS

These figures are important because even if a woman is employed full-time, she almost always is paid less than a man. If she is not employed, or employed only part-time, and has children to support, the household's situation may be desperate. In 1980, the median income of families headed by black women ($7,425) was only 40 percent of that of black families with both parents present ($18,593). Today, roughly five out of 10 black children under the age of 18 live below the poverty level; the vast majority of these kids have only a mother to come home to.

The rise in the number of female-headed black families reflects, among other things, the increasing incidence of illegitimate births. Only 15 percent of all births to black women in 1959 were out of wedlock; the proportion today is well over one-half. In the cities, the figure is invariably higher: 67 percent in Chicago in 1978, for example. Black women today bear children out of wedlock at a rate nine times that for whites. In 1982, the number of black babies born out of wedlock (328,879) nearly matched the number of illegitimate white babies (337,050). White or black, the women bearing these children are not always mature adults. Almost half of all illegitimate children born to blacks today will have a teenager for a mother.

The effect on the welfare rolls is not hard to imagine. A 1976 study by Kristin Moore and Steven B. Cardwell of Washington's Urban Institute estimated that, nationwide, about 60 percent of the children who are born outside of marriage and are not adopted receive welfare; furthermore, "more than half of all AFDC [Aid to Families with Dependent Children] assistance in 1975 was paid to women who were or had been teenage mothers." A 1979 study by the Department of City Planning in New York found that 75 percent of all children born out of wedlock in that city during the previous 18 years were recipients of AFDC.

WHY NO PROGRESS?

I have concentrated on young, female-headed families and out-of-wedlock births among blacks because these indices have become inextricably connected with poverty and welfare dependency, as well as with other forms of social dislocation (including joblessness and crime).

As James Q. Wilson observed in *Thinking About Crime* (1975), these problems are also associated with a "critical mass" of young people, often poorly supervised. When that mass is reached, or is increased suddenly and substantially, "a self-sustaining chain reaction is set off that creates

What Went Wrong?

W.E.B. DuBois (*The Negro American Family,* 1908) and E. Franklin Frazier (*The Negro Family in the United States,* 1939) were among the first scholars to ask this question about poor black families. Both came up with essentially the same answer—slavery.

Slavery, they noted, often separated man from wife, parent from child. Slave "marriage" had no basis in law. Negroes thus entered Emancipation with a legacy of "sexual irregularity" (Du Bois) that fostered "delinquency, desertions, and broken homes" (Frazier). Discrimination and migration perpetuated such patterns.

The "slavery hypothesis" was challenged during the 1970s by the works of Eugene Genovese (*Roll, Jordan, Roll,* 1974) and Herbert Gutman (*The Black Family in Slavery and Freedom,* 1976). Genovese shows, for example, that blacks *did* establish strong families in slavery. And Gutman notes that as late as 1925, roughly 85 percent of black families in New York City were headed by a married couple.

If slavery did not undermine the black family, what did? Scholars as diverse as Jessie Bernard (*Marriage and Family among Negroes,* 1966), Elliot Liebow (*Tally's Corner,* 1967), William Julius Wilson (*The Declining Significance of Race,* 1978), and Stephen Steinberg (*The Ethnic Myth,* 1981) point the finger at economic hardship and urban unemployment. The rise of a "matriarchal family pattern" in the ghetto, Steinberg writes, was "an inevitable by-product of the inability of men to function as breadwinners for their families." Joblessness, in turn, eroded the black male's sense of manhood and family responsibility.

The disruptive impact of welfare on some black families is generally conceded but not easily quantified. Kristin A. Moore and Martha R. Burt (*Teenage Childbearing and Welfare,* 1981) suggest that Aid to Families with Dependent Children (AFDC) *may* influence a pregnant woman to bear and rear her child (and head up a new household) rather than marry the father, resort to adoption, or submit to abortion. Because AFDC is available only to single-parent families in half of the 50 states, the program may also encourage the break-up of married couples and deter unwed parents from marrying or remarrying.

Whatever its causes, the black family's worsening plight has belatedly been acknowledged by black leaders. So has the need for remedies. A 1983 report by Washington's Joint Center for Political Studies, *A Policy Framework for Racial Justice,* asserted flatly that "family reinforcement constitutes the single most important action the nation can take toward the elimination of black poverty and related social problems."

an explosive increase in the amount of crime, addiction, and welfare dependency." The effect is magnified in densely populated ghetto neighborhoods, and further magnified in the massive public housing projects.

Consider Robert Taylor Homes, the largest such project in Chicago. In 1980, almost 20,000 people, all black, were

THE SECOND GREAT MIGRATION, 1940–1960

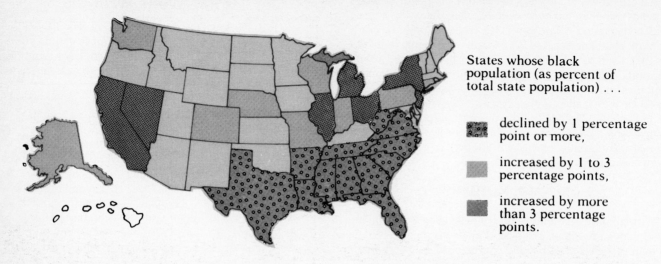

States whose black population (as percent of total state population) . . .

- declined by 1 percentage point or more,
- increased by 1 to 3 percentage points,
- increased by more than 3 percentage points.

Millions of Southern blacks migrated northward after World War II, just as the industrial base of America's older cities began to erode. The declining industries (e.g., steel, textiles, automobiles) were those in which unskilled blacks most often sought employment.

URBAN BLACK POPULATION GROWTH

Black population as percent of total city population

	1920	1950	1980
Los Angeles	2.7	8.7	17.0
Chicago	4.1	13.6	39.8
New York	2.7	9.5	25.2
Washington, D.C.	25.1	35.0	70.3
Boston	2.2	5.0	22.4
Atlanta	31.3	36.6	66.6

THE CHANGING JOB MARKET

Number of jobs gained or lost in 18 Northern U.S. cities, 1960–1970

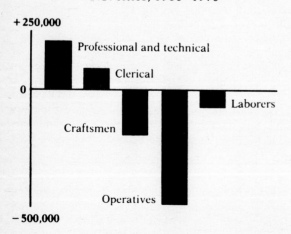

UNEMPLOYMENT RATES

for nonwhite males, by age group

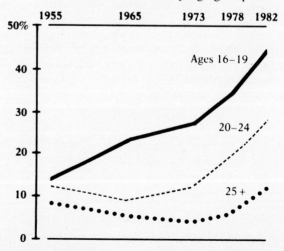

Source: U.S. Department of Labor; U.S. Department of Commerce, Bureau of the Census; John D. Kasarda, "Urbanization, Community, and the Metropolitan Problem," in *Handbook of Contemporary Urban Life*, ed. by David Street.

THE FEMINIZATION OF POVERTY
How income correlated with family status in 1982

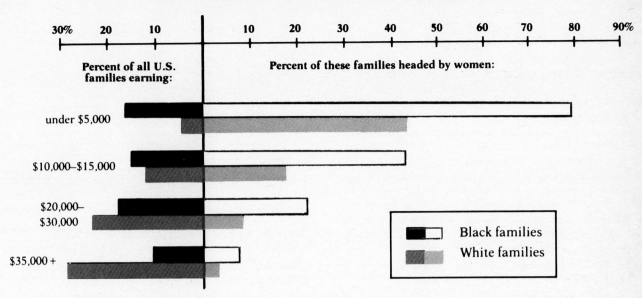

The proportion of blacks living below the poverty line ($9,862 for a family of four) grew to 35.6 percent in 1982. The number of black, female-headed households continued to rise. Some 49 percent of all black children today live with only one parent. One black child in 10 lives with neither.

ILLEGITIMATE BIRTHS

Percentage of white and black children born out of wedlock since 1950*

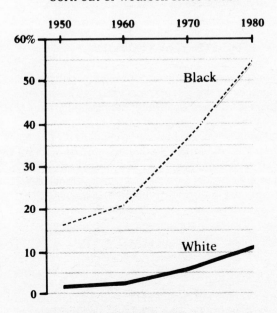

*Figures for 1950 and 1960 include small numbers of "other" nonwhites.

BLACK MEDIAN FAMILY INCOMES

As percent of white median family incomes, by family status

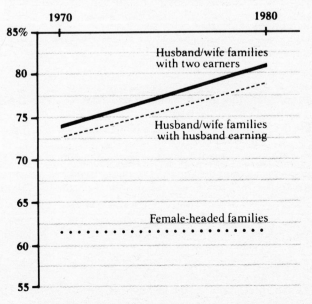

Source: U.S. Department of Commerce, Bureau of the Census.

officially registered there, but according to one report "there are an additional 5,000 to 7,000 who are not registered with the Housing Authority." Minors made up 72 percent of the population and the mother alone was present in 90 percent of the families with children. The unemployment rate was estimated at 47 percent in 1980, and some 70 percent of the project's 4,200 official households received AFDC. Although less than one-half of one percent of Chicago's population lived in Robert Taylor Homes, 11 percent of all the city's murders, nine percent of its rapes, and 10 percent of its aggravated assaults were committed in the project in 1980.

Why have the social conditions of the black underclass deteriorated so rapidly?

Racial discrimination is the most frequently invoked explanation, and it is undeniable that discrimination continues to aggravate the social and economic problems of poor blacks. But is discrimination really greater today than it was in 1948, when black unemployment was less than half of what it is now, and when the gap between black and white jobless rates was narrower?

As for the black family, it apparently began to fall apart not before but after the mid-20th century. Until publication in 1976 of Herbert Gutman's *The Black Family in Slavery and Freedom,* most scholars had believed otherwise. "Stimulated by the bitter public and academic controversy over the Moynihan report," Gutman produced data demonstrating that the black family was not significantly disrupted during slavery or even during the early years of the first migration to the urban North, beginning after the turn of the century. The problems of the modern black family, he implied, were a product of modern forces.

Those who cite racial discrimination as the root cause of poverty often fail to make a distinction between the effects of *historic* discrimination (that is, discrimination prior to the mid-20th century) and the effects of *contemporary* discrimination. That is why they find it so hard to explain why the economic position of the black underclass started to worsen soon after Congress enacted, and the White House began to enforce, the most sweeping civil-rights legislation since Reconstruction.

MAKING COMPARISONS

My own view is that historic discrimination is far more important than contemporary discrimination in understanding the plight of the urban underclass; that, in any event, there is more to the story than discrimination (of whichever kind).

Historic discrimination certainly helped to create an impoverished urban black community in the first place. In his recent *A Piece of the Pie: Black and White Immigrants since 1880* (1980), Stanley Lieberson shows how, in many areas of life, including the labor market, black newcomers from the rural South were far more severely discriminated against in Northern cities than were the new white immigrants from southern, central, and eastern Europe. Skin color was part of the problem, but it was not all of it.

The disadvantage of skin color—the fact that the dominant whites preferred whites over nonwhites—is one that blacks shared with Japanese, Chinese, and others. Yet the experience of the Asians, whose treatment by whites "was of the same violent and savage character in areas where

Manchild in the Promised Land *(1969), by Phillip Lindsay Mason.*

they were concentrated," but who went on to prosper in their adopted land, suggests that skin color per se was not an "insurmountable obstacle." Indeed, Lieberson argues that the greater success enjoyed by Asians may well be explained largely by the different context of their contact with whites. Because changes in immigration policy cut off Asian migration to America in the late 19th century, the Japanese and Chinese populations did not reach large numbers and therefore did not pose as great a threat as did blacks.

Furthermore, the discontinuation of large-scale immigration from Japan and China enabled Chinese and Japanese to solidify networks of ethnic contacts and to occupy particular occupational niches in small, relatively stable communities. For blacks, the situation was different. The 1970 census recorded 22,580,000 blacks in the United States but only 435,000 Chinese and 591,000 Japanese. "Imagine," Lieberson exclaims, "22 million Japanese Americans trying to carve out initial niches through truck farming."

THE YOUTH EXPLOSION

If different population sizes accounted for a good deal of the difference in the economic success of blacks and Asians, they also helped determine the dissimilar rates of progress of urban blacks and the new *European* arrivals. European immigration was curtailed during the 1920s, but black migration to the urban North continued through the 1960s. With each passing decade, Lieberson writes, there were many more blacks who were recent migrants to the North, whereas the immigrant component of the new Europeans dropped off over time. Eventually, other whites muffled their dislike of the Poles and Italians and Jews and saved their antagonism for blacks. As Lieberson notes, "The presence of blacks made it harder to discriminate against the new Europeans because the alternative was viewed less favorably."

The black migration to New York, Philadelphia, Chicago, and other Northern cities—the continual replenishment of black populations there by poor newcomers—predictably skewed the age profile of the urban black community and kept it relatively young. The number of central-city black youths aged 16-19 increased by almost 75 percent from 1960 to 1969. Young black adults (ages 20-24) increased in number by two-thirds during the same period, three times the increase for young white adults. In the nation's inner cities in 1977, the median age for whites was 30.3, for blacks 23.9. The importance of this jump in the number of young minorities in the ghetto, many of them lacking one or more parent, cannot be overemphasized.

Age correlates with many things. For example, the higher the median age of a group, the higher its income; the lower the median age, the higher the unemployment rate and the higher the crime rate. (More than half of those arrested in 1980 for violent and property crimes in American cities were under 21.) The younger a woman is, the more likely she is to bear a child out of wedlock, head up a new household, and depend on welfare. In short, much of what has gone awry in the ghetto is due in part to the sheer increase in the number of black youths. As James Q. Wilson has argued, an abrupt rise in the proportion of young people in *any* community will have an "exponential effect on the rate of certain social problems."

The population explosion among minority youths occurred at a time when changes in the economy were beginning to pose serious problems for unskilled workers. Urban minorities have been particularly vulnerable to the structural economic changes of the past two decades: the shift from goods-producing to service-providing industries, the increasing polarization of the labor market into low-wage and high-wage sectors, technological innovations, and the relocation of manufacturing industries out of the central cities. During the 1970s, Chicago lost more than 200,000 jobs, mostly in manufacturing, where many inner-city blacks had traditionally found employment. New York City lost 600,000 jobs during the same period, even though the number of white-collar professional, managerial, and clerical jobs increased in Manhattan. Today, as John D. Kasarda has noted, the nation's cities are being transformed into "centers of administration, information exchange, and service provision." Finding work now requires more than a willing spirit and a strong back.

BEYOND RACE

Roughly 60 percent of the unemployed blacks in the United States reside within the central cities. Their situation, already more difficult than that of any other major ethnic group in the country, continues to worsen. Not only are there more blacks without jobs every year; many, especially young males, are dropping out of the labor force entirely. The percentage of blacks who were in the labor force fell from 45.6 in 1960 to 30.8 in 1977 for those aged 16-17 and from 90.4 to 78.2 for those aged 20-24. (During the same period, the proportion of white teenagers in the labor force actually *increased*.)

More and more black youths, including many who are no longer in school, are obtaining no job experience at all. The proportion of black teenage males who have *never* held a job increased from 32.7 to 52.8 percent between 1966 and 1977; for black males under 24, the percentage grew from 9.9 to 23.3. Research shows, not surprisingly, that joblessness during youth has a harmful impact on one's future success in the job market.

There have been recent signs, though not many, that some of the inner city's ills may have begun to abate. For one, black migration to urban areas has been minimal in recent years; many cities have experienced net migration of blacks *to* the suburbs. For the first time in the 20th century, a heavy influx from the countryside no longer swells the ranks of blacks in the cities. Increases in the urban black population during the 1970s, as demographer Philip Hauser has pointed out, were mainly due to births. This means that one of the major obstacles to black advancement in the cities has been removed. Just as the Asian and European immigrants benefited from a cessation of migration, so too should the economic prospects of urban blacks improve now that the great migration from the rural South is over.

Even more significant is the slowing growth in the number of *young* blacks inhabiting the central cities. In metropolitan areas generally, there were six percent fewer blacks aged 13 or under in 1977 than there were in 1970; in the inner city, the figure was 13 percent. As the average age of the urban black community begins to rise, lawlessness, illegitimacy, and unemployment should begin to decline.

Even so, the problems of the urban black underclass will remain crippling for years to come. And I suspect that any significant reduction of joblessness, crime, welfare dependency, single-parent homes, and out-of-wedlock pregnancies would require far more comprehensive social and economic change than Americans have generally deemed appropriate or desirable. It would require a radicalism that neither the Republican nor the Democratic Party has been bold enough to espouse.

The existence of a black underclass, as I have suggested, is due far more to historic discrimination and to broad demographic and economic trends than it is to racial discrimination in the present day. For that reason, the underclass has not benefited significantly from "race specific" antidiscrimination policies, such as affirmative action, that have aided so many trained and educated blacks. If inner-city blacks are to be helped, they will be helped not by policies addressed primarily to inner-city minorities but by policies designed to benefit all of the nation's poor.

I am reminded in this connection of Baynard Rustin's plea during the early 1960s that blacks recognize the importance of *fundamental* economic reform (including a system of national economic planning along with new education, manpower, and public works programs to help achieve full employment) and the need for a broad-based coalition to achieve it. Politicians and civil-rights leaders should, of course, continue to fight for an end to racial discrimination. But they must also recognize that poor minorities are profoundly affected by problems that affect other people in America as well, and that go beyond racial considerations. Unless those problems are addressed, the underclass will remain a reality of urban life.

Blacks in School:
Trying to Catch Up

When black children finally gained access to "mainstream" public schools, they arrived during the turmoil of the late 1960s. Schools were beset by falling standards, lax discipline, and rising rates of crime and vandalism, not to mention repeated efforts to achieve greater racial balance. The big-city public schools, in particular, were in poor condition to help an influx of black underclass youths overcome the cumulative effects of family instability, poverty, and generations of inferior education. When family finances permitted, blacks, like whites, often put their offspring in private schools or moved to the suburbs.

Blacks have nevertheless made some gains through public education. At the grade school level, the gap in school attendance rates between whites and blacks has been closed. Between 1970 and 1982, the proportion of blacks graduating from high school (now 76.5 percent) grew twice as fast as that of whites. The National Assessment of Educational Progress (NAEP) reveals that blacks in grade school and junior high are improving their skills more quickly than are whites, though they still lag behind.

But high school students of neither race are doing better now than their counterparts were 10 years ago. Indeed, the NAEP reports that the proportion of 17-year-old blacks scoring in the "highest achievement group" in reading tests actually declined from 5.7 to 3.9 percent between 1971 and 1980. In the Age of Technology, blacks are still less likely than whites to take science and math courses. The modest gains by blacks during the past decade on the Scholastic Aptitude Test (SAT) still produced an average combined (math and verbal) score in 1983 of only 708 out of a possible 1600. The National Assault on Illiteracy Program estimates that 47 percent of all black Americans still read at a fourth-grade level or lower. As more blacks finish high school and college, such "functional illiteracy" will decline.

A Struggle for Freedom

Blacks seek a land that never has been yet

VINCENT HARDING

Vincent Harding is professor of religion and social transformation at the Iliff School of Theology in Denver.

O, let America be America again—
The land that never has been yet—
And yet must be—
The land where *every* man is free.
The land that's mine—
The poor man's, Indian's, Negro's, ME—
Who made America,
Whose sweat and blood, whose faith and pain,
Whose hand at the foundry, whose plow in the
   rain,
Must bring back our mighty dream again.
                              —*Langston Hughes*

At its best, the black freedom movement was meant to liberate the entire nation and all of its people from the antihuman commitments of our past. As such, it could rightly be conceived as a movement for the re-creation of the United States.

At the heart of this regenerative process were the children. When the courts declared that separate-but-equal schools were neither equal nor constitutional, black children were thrust into pioneering roles. Many keepers of the old, unjust order understood the powerful mission of these young and tender warriors from the black community, so the children's movement often met with fierce opposition.

Inside the schools, black youngsters faced diverse threats and obstacles: ink or hot soup poured over them; ostracism, curses, and assaults; teachers who treated them as second-class students. But the children persevered, and in so doing became a generation of young black men and women born into the struggle for a new America. As they faced the mobs and the more subtle threats, they were reconstituting themselves as part of "We the People"—redeemers of the land.

But students were not the only challenging force in that period. In 1957, Martin Luther King Jr. and a group of black Baptist ministers organized the Southern Christian Leadership Conference (SCLC), hoping to mobilize the transformative power sweeping the black South. Their goal, as they announced it, was "to redeem the soul of America," and they chose nonviolent action as their means.

By the end of the 1950s, the nonviolent, church-based movement was only one of many approaches. Many blacks were open to the way of armed self-defense. The Nation of Islam had expanded its influence, due in part to the status of Elijah Muhammad, who had served a jail sentence for encouraging Muslims not to join the military during World War II. Much of Muhammad's popularity derived from the power and personal charisma resident in his chief spokesman, Malcolm X.

Malcolm, an indefatigable worker and gifted leader with an intense and powerful speaking style, denounced the enemies of black freedom and spread the word of the Nation of Islam. He and the Nation recruited more followers, especially among younger urban black men in search of a mission, a purpose. One appeal to this group was the Muslims' projection of the "eye-for-an-eye" philosophy, which they

> Now, general reaction is gratefully to extol Dr. King as a loving moderate, contrasted with the angry black radicals, and to forget for how many years he demanded what his furious critics called "socialistic" responsibility for one another in our country, the "Freedom Budget" of Marshall Plan proportions to begin to mitigate American poverty, and his somber outrage and eloquence in opposing an undeclared war draining money from the aims of "The Great Society." So it is a little hard to recognize him in the mournful tributes, the exaltation of his gentleness, the chorus of *Amens* to his nonviolence, and the soothing forgetfulness of his troublesome and persisting direct action, his "creative tension" and civil disobedience, at which most of our society raged and fumed only yesterday.
>   *Margaret Long*
>   *1968*

never tired of contrasting with the nonviolent action advocated and practiced by King and his widening circle of comrades.

But history is constantly full of surprises, and it was neither King nor Malcolm who opened the way to the next explosive stage of the black freedom movement. Rather, it was the children, baptised in the rising flood of expectation—the children strengthened by the exploding bombs, the taunting mobs, the soup and ink poured down their backs.

These children, now in their teens or early twenties, first appeared at the lunch counters of the South in February 1960. On the surface they were asking for hamburgers and cokes. But at a deeper level they were insisting that they be seen and heard and encountered. In their neat suits and shirts and ties, in their carefully ironed dresses, with books in hand, gracing hundreds of lunch counters, eventually filling scores of jails, singing their songs of struggle and hope, they provided the possibility of a new beginning.

As they besieged public accommodations with their determined presence, the Southern students—aided by the rising power of television—discovered each other, and soon sensed that they were part of a movement. In the spring of 1960, they took the initial steps to form the Student Nonviolent Coordinating Committee (SNCC); their goal, they said, was the establishment of "the beloved community in America."

One year later, groups of white and black men, inspired by the Congress of Racial Equality (CORE), a Northern-based interracial organization committed to radical nonviolent action for justice, decided to test recent court rulings requiring desegregation of buses crossing state lines. This courageous band became known as the Freedom Riders, and in their daring venture to ride as brothers of the beloved community from Washington, D.C., to Jackson, Mississippi, they had their heads cracked open, their buses attacked and burned (often with the connivance of local law enforcement officials and the hidden acquiescence of the FBI).

More than any other single setting, the march on Birmingham in the spring of 1963 dramatized the Southern freedom struggle. The Reverend Fred Shuttlesworth had been waiting and working for years in Birmingham. He had been beaten in front of television cameras, had been threatened, harassed, and shot at, but had insisted on staying in that most dangerously segregated of American cities and fighting for a new order. The hard-working, hard-talking, high-strung, wiry-bodied man invited Martin Luther King Jr. and SCLC to join him in mounting a broad-based challenge to Birmingham's segregation.

Like others across the South, black people in Birmingham had found their nonviolent army. When the hoses blasted them down onto the hard pavement, they stood up and marched again. When the dogs lunged at them, they dodged and cried and laughed and kept marching. When the police and firemen formed angry human lines of defense against them, they rushed around the ends and headed downtown to sit in, to sing, to challenge the past. And when Public Safety Commissioner Eugene "Bull" Connor's forces rounded them up and stuffed

them in vans and buses to take them by the hundreds to makeshift, outdoor prisons, they sang the songs from all the struggles of the past. When Bull Connor heard them singing, he said so much more than he knew: "If this is religion, I don't want no part of it."

That freedom religion was everywhere, spreading all over the South. Shortly after the Birmingham demonstrations had reached their height, plans were drawn up for continuing massive actions of civil disobedience that would compel the society to face squarely the issues of racism and white supremacy. Washington, D.C., with its Government offices, its transportation centers, and its large black population, was proposed as the focus for the first phase of nonviolent action.

In its own way, the March on Washington, drawing some 300,000 persons to the capital, was an important symbolic event in the freedom struggle. One of its accomplishments was the affirmation of the place accorded to white allies in the movement. On that steamy August afternoon in 1963, Martin Luther King's eloquent dream allowed white Americans to follow their own longings and participate in this movement that was shaking the nation.

But the march had its critics. Many justifiably questioned the significance of such a well-mannered, non-confrontational gathering at that moment in history. Malcolm X, for instance, charged the marchers with ignoring the plight of the black underclass in America and demanded more militant, independent black action. Others were deeply troubled when John Lewis, the courageous chairman of SNCC, delivered his angry, radical criticism of the Kennedy Administration; his call for extensive civil disobedience was censored by white liberal supporters of the movement.

Following the march, SNCC and CORE continued to work at the harsh and harrowing task of registering voters in the resistant, rural interiors of the deep South. By the winter of 1964, the SNCC-led Council of Federated Organizations sent out a call for help. Co-workers were needed to register people for participation in the Mississippi Freedom Democratic Party, the alternative to the segregated regular Democrats. On an even deeper level, the black organizers felt they needed hostages from the mainstream of white America, hostages whose presence would draw press coverage and governmental attention to the Mississippi battlefront.

Hundreds came to work in Mississippi Summer from eighteen states and many backgrounds. Mostly, but with notable exceptions, they were white and Northern and young. Even before the first wave of volunteers had a chance to settle in, even as the orientations were still being carried on, word came: Three young men were missing, last seen near the Neshoba County seat of Philadelphia, Mississippi. After a day or two of desperate hope in that last week of June, everyone knew they were dead. A few of the summer volunteers returned home, but most remained to work, register voters, teach in the freedom schools, mobilize national attention, and fight the fears.

Although the fierce struggle in Mississippi was central to the freedom movement, it was not being carried on in a vacuum. In Washington, the Civil Rights bill that had taken more than a year—and too many lives—to move through Congress was fi-

Several months ago I received a telephone call from a stranger. "Just a few years ago," he said, "civil rights leaders were saying that the creative and radical thing to do was to break down Jim Crow by integrating white neighborhoods." So he and his bride met the challenge and battled their way into a lily white suburb. They overcame the vandalism and survived the physical threats and the isolation. They made it. "Now," he went on, "Negroes call us Uncle Toms and ex-colored folk for living out here with all these white people."
James Farmer
1968

nally passed in July, but everyone knew that there would be no automatic changes just because a law had been enacted. Shortly after the signing of the Civil Rights Act, New York's Harlem exploded. Several other black Northern communities soon followed suit, and in almost every instance the focus was on the bitter relationships between the black community and the occupying, mostly white, police force.

In such settings, black nationalism and the calls to black solidarity and political power seemed more appropriate than new Civil Rights bills. With Malcolm X at the center, these militant elements were, indeed, on the rise in the North. By the spring of 1964, Malcolm had broken with Elijah Muhammad and the Nation of Islam for compelling personal and political reasons. Now, like a man driven by history, he sought to mobilize and unify the power of the black Northern communities into a new force that he called the Organization for Afro-American Unity. Education, culture, politics, economics, and the right of armed self-defense were all part of his program.

At the end of 1964, King came to Lowndes County, Alabama, to join Stokely Carmichael and Courtland Cox of SNCC, who were conducting a grass-roots organizing campaign. During a demonstration, King was arrested. While King was in jail, Malcolm accepted SNCC's invitation and came to express his solidarity with the Southern movement and to assure Coretta Scott King that he was in much closer accord with her husband's vision and work than was readily apparent.

Less than two weeks later, the crushing news flashed through the movement: Malcolm was dead, assassinated in Harlem. In his death, he became a catalyst for a great revival of black world consciousness—another powerful flame in the continuously transformative black fire. In his memory "the angry children of Malcolm X" found much of the sustenance they sought, and they began disengaging themselves from their white comrades, calling on whites to turn their attention to the racism of the white community.

By 1965, a profound period of transition had begun, nurtured and deepened by a politically conscious cultural revival that was challenging the yardstick of white supremacy. Out of the cauldron of black struggle, out of the memory of Malcolm X, a new poetry, music, and material art were emerging to deepen the meaning of the struggle.

The shaking of the foundations had begun at deep levels in the black South; now it was spreading like some great fissure in the ground of America. Nowhere was this more evident than in the explosive uprising that broke loose in August 1965 in a dreary-looking, lower-middle-class black community in Los Angeles called Watts.

For five days Watts became a battleground, etching its name into the consciousness of the nation. Smaller uprisings soon followed in Chicago and Philadelphia, and the passage of the 1965 Voting Rights Act seemed ironically remote from the new scenes of battle.

At the same time, blacks were increasingly questioning participation in the Vietnam war. By the beginning of 1966, SNCC had formally and publicly linked opposition to the war with the ongoing black struggle, raising fundamental questions about the nation's real commitment to "free elections" and "democracy" in Vietnam when "the United States Government has never guaranteed the freedom of oppressed citizens and is not yet truly determined to end the rule of terror and oppression within its own borders."

The idea of rebellion was in the air in 1966. Urban revolts spread again across the black North, and they bore some strange fruit: Edward Brooke of Massachusetts was elected as the first black Senator since Reconstruction, and basketball star Bill Russell became the first black man to coach an NBA team.

By then it was clear that the ground of the movement had shifted. The Southern bastions of overt segregation had been cracked open by the sustained black thrust. But the long-festering problems of the Northern urban black communities now burst into history.

However, the streets of the urban North were not the only locus of action. By 1967, the nation was deeply engaged in the war against the Vietnamese, and black soldiers were fighting and dying in disproportionate numbers. The issue could no longer be avoided, nor was it possible to ignore the relationship of the war to the black cause and to the needs of the poor in America. King knew he had to take on the war and its meaning.

He did that in April 1967, one year to the day before his assassination. His platform was the pulpit of the highly visible Riverside Church in New York City. Unequivocally condemning this nation's role in the war, calling attention to the destruction of the hopes of poor people here and in Vietnam, identifying the United States as "the greatest purveyor of violence in the world today," King urged Americans to move with urgency toward "a revolution of values": to turn away from racism, but also to see the destructive connections among racism, militarism, materialism, and anticommunism.

The Northern ground continued to burn, and the summer of 1967—in Detroit, Newark, and elsewhere—brought the hottest explosions. President Johnson, his intelligence apparatus monitoring the situation, set up a national advisory commission on civil disorders that was supposed to tell the nation what was wrong and what needed to be made right, as if black people did not already know.

Meanwhile, King seemed to sense how little time he had. Toward the end of the fiery summer, at the annual meeting of the Southern Christian Leadership Conference, he pressed the logic of his own condemnations of militarism and imperialism. America's leadership, King said, was "preoccupied with war," so "Negroes must therefore not only formulate a program; they must fashion new tactics which do not count on government goodwill but serve, instead, to compel unwilling authorities to yield to the mandates of justice."

This was a major departure for King (and for anyone else who understood it). He was still convinced that the black-led freedom movement needed allies, but now the alliance he proposed would no longer be focused on the middle-class, white liberal force of "goodwill," nor would it be dependent on the Federal Government. "The dispossessed of this nation—the poor, both white and Negro—live in a

---

An obvious characteristic of President Kennedy's first fifteen months in office is his cautious, almost timid approach in dealing with Congress, and in no area has this approach skirted the issues more glaringly than in the field of civil rights.

Editorial
1962

cruelly unjust society," King declared. "They must organize a revolution against that injustice, not against the lives of . . . their fellow citizens, but against the structures through which the society is refusing . . . to lift the load of poverty."

He was moving toward the unknown territory of nonviolent revolution. He said he realized that the black struggle was "exposing the evils that are deeply rooted in the whole structure of our society. It reveals systemic rather than superficial flaws and suggests that radical reconstruction of society itself is the real issue to be faced."

While King was making vague plans to conduct a campaign of nonviolent direct action in Washington, D.C., he was asked to assist an overwhelmingly black union of garbage collectors striking in Memphis for just wages and humane working conditions. When police provoked some of the city's angry black young people, they turned a march led by King into a frightening, portentous experience. Stubbornly, courageously, against the advice of many persons, he returned to Memphis a few days later, trying to vindicate the potential of nonviolent struggle.

Stubbornly, courageously, he died. Even a confused, beleagured, searching Martin Luther King was too great a threat to the forces of racism, injustice, and exploitation. They were suspicious of what energies, what new life he and his unpredictable armies of hope might release in Washington, and their suspicions cost King his life.

For those of us who lived through the momentous years of the 1960s, with their inspiriting sense of collective action, transformative power, great victories, and tragic wounds, the decade of the 1970s was a long, hard winter to endure.

Since chronology has never controlled history, we can say that the 1960s actually ended when black folk, joined temporarily by hundreds of thousands of white people—especially the young—jammed themselves against the limits of this country's liberal vision of itself. The story of the 1970s can be seen in large degree as the story of what happened when black folk of many kinds and convictions began to recognize the frightening depths of our own most fundamental challenges to the nation.

The quieter, but deeply troubling and almost contemplative mood of the 1970s was not clear at first. The period of changeover was filled with much of the residual energy of the struggles of the 1960s. There were echoes of urban rebellions, and in the South, at places like Jackson State and Southern University in Baton Rouge, local police responded to student organizing with deadly force.

While black men and women were being shot down in the streets and in the jails of Soledad and Attica, while black unemployment continued to mount, while black students were taking over administration buildings, while black intellectuals were looking again at Marxist ideology as a way of dealing with American reality—while these things were happening, on another level black people were being elected to a variety of public offices on the strength of the new black voting power that emerged out of Southern voter registration struggles and the continuing black migration to the cities. Here was another possible blow to white hegemony, though it

was and is fraught with difficulty in light of the continuing financial domination of white private businesses.

Taking the electoral path appeared to be less a statement of belief in American political, economic, and social structures than an expression of weariness, the admission of unclarity and occasional despair about how change of this colossus might be brought about.

It was not surprising that one of the major developments of the decade was the proliferation of essentially apolitical groupings of black people who were in search of some significant expression of black spirituality. Some went the way of Islamic splinter movements. Some searched for other African-rooted alternatives. Many persons looked toward the modernized versions of essentially conservative Christian churches that emphasized privatistic salvation. Still other black people were scattered among the millions of seekers after the revived truths of various Eastern religions.

Few, if any, of the black participants in these numerous experiences seemed to see their faith as a basis for continued confrontation with the "basically flawed economics and politics" or "cultural degradation" of America. The historic connection between black religion and black struggle for change, which had been magnificently represented in different ways by Malcolm and Martin and their companions, was in jeopardy.

Perhaps the new time will require a new kind of connection, a new kind of community, a new basis for hope. At least three crucial developments of the 1970s worked against reliance on the old connections, communities, and hopes. First was the absence of a mass movement. Second was the corollary tendency to individualism and privatism that marked so much of the decade. Third was the victory in breaking the power of segregation at crucial levels in the public and private sectors of the society. That victory carried with it a certain draining off of the solidarity that the black community had once been forced to experience.

There is much more to the 1980s than the agonies of the Reagan Presidency or even the prospects of another one. Nothing in this young decade has spoken to the issues of our struggles more provocatively than the Presidential campaign of Jesse Jackson. Emerging out of deep engagement in the black freedom movement, bearing a sometimes ambiguous personal legacy of ambition, charisma, and perserverance, Jackson and his campaign provide some important guideposts to past and future.

His connections with King and SCLC were important elements in his development. More than fifteen years as head of PUSH (People United to Save Humanity) led to the variety of positive and negative elements that are expected when one man runs an organization for that long. For some, the major difficulty with Jackson's organization was its appearance of being too intimately tied to the health and welfare of the capitalist system, too easily satisfied with the superficial inclusion of thin layers of the black community in that system. Somehow, the phrase "economic parity" sounded far from his mentor's call for "radical redistribution of economic and political power."

The wartime record of our struggle against the multitudinous abuses heaped upon Negro soldiers reveals conclusively that the Government shows little response to moral appeals, indignant editorials, impressive delegations—or even dead bodies.
A. Phillip Randolph 1948

Jackson's bid has raised and revived a spirit in the black communities that is unlike anything we have seen since the most vibrant stages of the freedom movement. What this means about the hopes and dreams still residing in black lives and hearts— about the desire to become part of something larger— is crucial. Also critical is what these hopes and dreams will become if Jackson proves to be little more than a black version of Democratic politics.

The last time a search for a "Rainbow Coalition" took place—without the colorful title—was at the end of King's life, when he called for poor people of all backgrounds (as well as those committed to the poor) to organize themselves as a revolutionary force. Obviously, this meant much more than casting votes for a black Presidential candidate, and it certainly did not mean that the movement's members were to be bargaining chips at a Democratic convention.

Will the dependence on the mechanisms of electoral politics advance the needs of the poor within and beyond America? Will it assist those who hold anything like the vision that King held— and died for—in his last days? It would seem that no coalition is sufficient if it serves only the purposes of the political system, even a reformed or enlarged version of America's present system. History suggests, instead, that those who work within existing structures are only as strong as the movement which builds outside.

Perhaps the 1980s will be judged not by who is nominated or elected but by whether or not new forces are gathered to take our best hopes of the past and transform them into the goals of the future. Even now we can say that 1984 will not overcome us unless we give up our vision, forget our history.

A great life force has been moving through the black freedom movement, and in that flow we will be freed—if we are willing—to work on the needy places in our own lives and those of others, and to move forward, reconstituting ourselves as that new manifestation of "We the People" who are needed "to create a more perfect Union" for us all.

Social Change and the Future

- New Population Issues (Articles 35-37)
- New Technology Issues (Articles 38-40)
- New Era (Articles 41-43)

Fascination with the future is an enduring theme in literature, art, poetry, and religion. Human beings are anxious to know if tomorrow will be different from today and in what ways. Coping with change has become a top priority in the lives of many. One component of change is stress. When the future is uncertain and the individual appears to have little control over what happens, stress can be a serious problem. On the other hand, stress has positive effects on our lives in many ways if the changes can be perceived as challenges and opportunities.

Any discussion of the future must begin with basic demographic trends and then consider how new technologies will affect these and other trends. This section begins with the demographic trends in the world and in the United States. Next some of the problems produced by new technologies are discussed. Finally, three efforts to identify the crucial dangers and opportunities for the future of America are presented.

In 1984 the United Nations held the International Conference on Population in Mexico City. It was ten years after the Bucharest conference, and the concern about the population explosion in the Third World had increased substantially during the decade. The first selection is a *Time* magazine article which, at the time, reviewed the issues of the conference and assessed the world population situation. To illustrate the issues, it described in detail the problems of Mexico City that resulted from its rapid growth.

The next two articles detail demographic issues in the United States. Richard Stengel reviews dozens of demographic statistics which indicate important ways that the country is changing geographically, in family structure and life-style, in employment and income, and in age and age-related activities. The following report relates the stories of a variety of immigrants to America and considers some of the dominant opinions on current immigration issues.

Technology is a dynamic force which influences the course of history and the shape of tomorrow. The next three articles focus on new technologies and their problems. The most dangerous technology is the nuclear bomb. Carl Sagan explains how the nuclear bomb could cause a nuclear winter that would kill hundreds of millions of people. Other dangerous substances are more common to our industrial society. Robert Engler describes how

American corporations are irresponsibly endangering workers and the public by unsafe production practices. They are responsible for the sickness and death of hundreds of thousands of people over the years. Some new technologies may not cause physical illness or endanger lives but they do cause social problems. Fred Best explains how computers, robots, and other innovations will greatly affect the workplace. Workers will be displaced, but he predicts that new jobs will open up as a result. Only if America embraces these technologies, he argues, will the economy become strong, standards of living rise, and unemployment be kept relatively low.

America is entering a new era. The volume ends with three visions of the future. Richard D. Lamm sees the near future as a series of crises of American institutions: the current political system cannot adequately deal with the problems of the twenty-first century; the economy has become almost static; medical costs will soon exceed what society can pay; care for the elderly will practically bankrupt society; resource usage is extravagant; and waves of legal and illegal immigration are creating social problems. Lamm is not sure that the United States can resolve all of these crises. The second view of the future is presented by a team of journalists and is based on ten basic current trends which are extrapolated a decade or two into the future. Demographic and technical trends are included, though medical technology is emphasized. In addition the implications of the women's movement and various political forces are pondered. The final view of the future is more exhortative. Newt Gingrich sees both dangers and opportunities in America's future. The main driving force is the communications revolution which will reshape both the economy and personal life-styles. An information explosion will require people to constantly adapt to changes and update their education and it will also restructure most of the institutions of society.

Looking Ahead: Challenge Questions

What are the significant factors bringing about social change at the present time?

In what ways will social change accelerate? How can it slow down?

What are some ways to deal with social change?

People, People, People

Despite some progress, global population is still growing at an alarming rate

Diplomats and demographers, economists and family planners, the elite brigades of global social science, will converge on Mexico City next week to tackle a formidable issue: the relentless growth of world population. They will hear some good news. In the ten years since the last United Nations–sponsored International Conference on Population, which was held in Bucharest, the annual growth rate of the world's population has declined from 2% to 1.7%.

But that positive statistic stands out amid an otherwise sobering array. During the past decade, the number of people on earth increased by 770 million, to 4.75 billion. The World Bank estimates that in 2025, a date within the foreseeable lifetime of most Americans under 30, global population could nearly double, to about 8.3 billion. Of that total, about 7 billion will be residents of the undercapitalized, undernourished Third World.

The consequences of a failure to bring the world's population growth under control are frightening. They could include widespread hunger and joblessness, accompanied by environmental devastation and cancerous urban growth. Politically, the outcome could be heightened global instability, violence and authoritarianism. Says Science Fiction Writer Isaac Asimov, the author of numerous essays on demography: "Population growth at current rates will create a world without hope, gripped by starvation and desperation. It will be worse than a jungle because we have weapons immensely more destructive and vicious than teeth and claws."

The U.N.'s decision to hold its population conference in Mexico City could hardly be more appropriate. In all its splendor and squalor, the Mexican capital is the archetype of Third World megacities that are climbing to the top of the list of the world's major urban centers (*see following story*). Says Allan Rosenfield, director of Columbia University's Center for Population and Family Health: "We in the West haven't done very well managing our big cities. How Indonesia, In-dia, Mexico and other Third World countries can handle them is beyond my comprehension."

Among those who have tried to focus increased attention on the population issue is former World Bank President Robert McNamara. Writing in the latest issue of *Foreign Affairs,* he argues that the much heralded drop in the world's population growth rate during the '70s has led to overconfidence and the mistaken idea that "efforts to deal with [population] problems can therefore be relaxed." McNamara points out that the global figures for the past decade have been distorted by the experience of China, where a draconian birth control program that includes financial rewards and penalties to encourage one-child families has reduced the fertility rate by half.

There has been no such improvement in many other areas. In black Africa, some national fertility rates have actually increased in the past decade. The average number of children born to a woman in Kenya is now eight; when that is combined with a declining infant mortality rate, the country's population could balloon from 20 million today to 83 million in 2025. In Bangladesh, the fertility rate figure is 6.3, which means that 266 million people (nearly three times the present population) might be squeezed into an area the size of Wisconsin by 2025. With a fertility rate of 4.7, India will become the world's most populous country by about 2045, with 1.5 billion people. By comparison, Soviet women now have an average of 2.4 children, while American women have 1.8 children; the figure for Western Europe is even lower, 1.6.

Although in the past two decades Third World economies have had higher growth rates than those of the U.S. and Western Europe, in many countries that advance has been severely diluted by rapid population growth. Between 1955 and 1980, for example, per capita income in the U.S. grew from $7,000 to $11,500 (expressed in constant 1980 dollars), while in India it increased from $170 to $260, nearly doubling the disparity between the two countries. By the year 2000, some 630 million young adults will join the Third World's labor force, while industrialized countries will add only 20 million young workers. As a result, Third World wages will probably remain at their low levels. That may encourage the flow of manufacturing jobs from industrialized countries to developing nations, but it could also provoke protectionist threats to the international free-trade system.

Some of the baleful effects of excessive population growth are already evident. In addition to unrestrained urban growth, McNamara notes the increasing inadequacy of Third World agriculture, owing in part to rural overpopulation and economic distortions caused by efforts to palliate the rising tide of urban consumers. In such countries as Tanzania and India, where people depend on firewood for fuel, deforestation is damaging flood control, speeding erosion and adding to the hardship of merely staying alive. Citing the example of China, McNamara warns that rapid population growth may also lead to greater and more coercive state intrusions into private life, ranging from forced sterilization to restrictions on freedom of movement.

Many population experts accept McNamara's facts, while objecting to the tone of his conclusions. According to Rafael Salas, executive director of the United Nations Fund for Population Activities (UNFPA) and chief organizer of the upcoming Mexico City conference, "There is room for concern, but not panic." He points out that countries in the Third World increasingly recognize the importance of population control. In its 1984 *Development Report,* the World Bank notes that 85 nations in the Third World, containing about 95% of its population, now provide some form of public support, however inadequate, to family-planning programs. An additional 27 countries do not. Almost half of these are in Africa, where incomes are the lowest and population growth rates the highest in the world.

While the conference delegates debate whether the world's Malthusian nightmare is lifting or drawing closer to reality, they will also face a challenge from the Reagan Administration. As part of its vocal antiabortion stance in a U.S.

presidential election year, the Administration has announced sharp new restrictions on family-planning assistance for any organization or country that sanctions abortion. The impact of the policy change may be substantial: it is estimated that U.S. contributions of $240 million represent nearly one-quarter of total worldwide aid spent on family planning. The Administration will also inject its free-market philosophy into the population debate. In Mexico City, the U.S. delegation, headed by Radio Free Europe Director James Buckley, will argue that government interference with economies is a major reason why world population growth has changed "from an asset in the development of economic potential to a peril."

The Administration's policy requires that family-planning aid be allotted in ways that prevent its use in population-control programs that include abortion. The real loss may fall upon private organizations that currently receive about $100 million of the $240 million annual U.S. allotment. Groups that promote abortion would be cut off entirely. Ironi-

cally, the policy is unlikely to accomplish the one thing that its right-to-life supporters might expect. An estimated 50 million abortions are now performed each year around the globe; perhaps half of those occur in Third World countries that have antiabortion laws.

One encouraging sign for the future, according to U.N. experts, is the substantial "unmet demand" for population control among Third World residents. In a survey of 17 slowly developing countries, the U.N. found that while the average number of children per family ranged from 3.8 to 8.3, the average number of children desired was 3.7 to 4.7. The difference between desire and reality is due to the lack of available family-planning education and services.

One of the most impressive examples of a Third World country that has made progress in curbing population growth is Thailand (pop. 49 million). In the past three decades, the Thai birth rate has declined by nearly 40%, from 46.6 per 1,000 people to 28.6. The population growth rate has dropped from about 3.4% to

1.95%. One reason for the change is a determined effort to extend health care and family planning to rural areas. Thailand has more than 4,000 village health centers staffed with 220,000 paramedics in addition to village doctors and local assistant midwives. One Thai private group offers farm production and marketing assistance to contraceptive users; as a result, rates of contraceptive use have risen as high as 80% in some villages.

Such efforts, however, require not only will but money. The World Bank estimates that $7.6 billion will be necessary if the Third World is to achieve a rapid decline in fertility by the year 2000. That figure pales against the estimated $600 billion a year that the world spends on armaments. Indeed, the funds spent on population control would probably turn out to be a bargain. Says Conference Organizer Salas: "There is a lack of understanding among policymakers of the links between population and global stability."

—*By George Russell.*
Reported by Raji Samghabadi/New York and Barrett Seaman/Washington

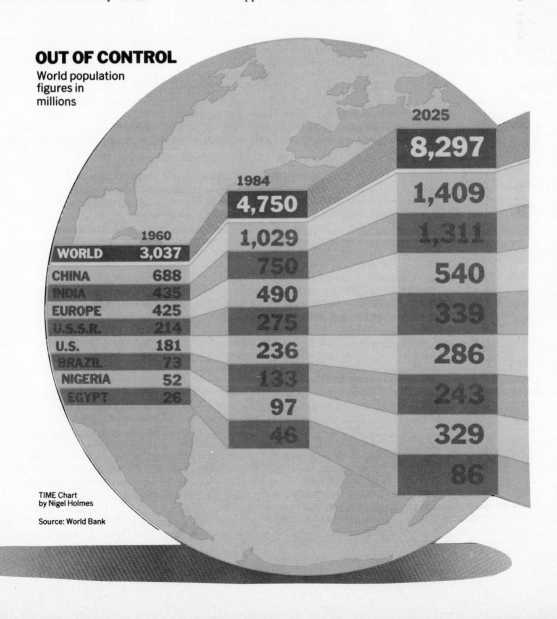

OUT OF CONTROL
World population figures in millions

	1960	1984	2025
			8,297
		4,750	1,409
WORLD	3,037	1,029	1,311
CHINA	688	750	540
INDIA	435	490	339
EUROPE	425	275	286
U.S.S.R.	214	236	243
U.S.	181	133	329
BRAZIL	73	97	86
NIGERIA	52	46	
EGYPT	26		

TIME Chart
by Nigel Holmes

Source: World Bank

Snapshot of a Changing America

The U.S. population is growing older and thinking smaller

"The United States themselves," wrote Walt Whitman, "are essentially the greatest poem." That epic is remade by every new generation, and today its rhythm, structure and content are unlike any that went before. The nation is growing middle-aged and more solitary. Men and women are delaying marriage, delaying childbirth, having few or no children at all. Real income, once expected to rise as naturally as a hot-air balloon, has leveled off. For many, home ownership, once thought of as practically a constitutional right, has become a dream denied. Demography is destiny, and Americans of today, in ways both obvious and subtle, are inventing the America of tomorrow.

Most of the changes have been triggered by the baby-boom generation. Born between 1946 and 1964, they are 75 million strong, one out of every three Americans, the largest generation in U.S. history. Next year the oldest of them will turn 40. The generation that could hum TV jingles before it could hum the national anthem, that made rock 'n' roll and protest into rites of passage, and swore never to trust anyone over 30, is becoming middle-aged.

In 1983 the median age of the population reached 30.9, the oldest ever, and is expected to exceed 36 by the year 2000. People who fox-trotted to Tommy Dorsey now outnumber those who hip-hop to Cyndi Lauper; for the first time in history, there are more Americans over 65 than there are teenagers. Notes Karl Zinsmeister, an economic demographer at the American Enterprise Institute: "By the late 1980s, one-half of our households will be headed by baby boomers. One-fourth of our population will be elderly. These two groups will define our society for a very long time."

Single people now account for 23% of all U.S. households. As many as 8% of today's adults will never marry.

Remember when unmarried men were called bachelors and unmarried women spinsters? Many of the 50 million "singles" in America are too young to recall. The Census Bureau reports that from 1970 to 1983 the proportion of never married singles ages 20 to 24 increased from 36% to 56% among women and from 55% to 73% among men. During that period, single-person households increased by 8.5 million. According to the Census Bureau, the increasing number of unmarried people in the pivotal 30-to-34 age bracket "suggests that an increasing proportion of persons may never marry."

Families with single heads grew by 69% from 1970 to 1983. One out of every five children, and more than half of all black children, lives in a one-parent household.

"Typical" is no longer an adjective that can describe the American household. Fifteen years ago, 40% of all households consisted of husband, wife and children; today that figure is 28.5%. The stereotypical nuclear family of mom, dad and two kids now accounts for only 11% of all households.

The number of female-headed households with one or more children under 18 doubled from 1970 to 1982, from 2.9 million to 5.9 million. During the 1970s the divorce rate shot up by half. Although it has dropped slightly, the U.S. rate remains the highest among all Western nations. Out-of-wedlock births jumped by 67% from 1970 to 1980.

Since 1970, the number of first births to women age 25 and older has more than doubled, while first births to women under 25 have declined. As many as one-fourth of all women of childbearing age may remain childless. The lowest total fertility rate in American history, 1.7, occurred in 1976.

Many working women of childbearing age have decided against having a child, while women with children are working in unprecedented numbers. In 1960 only 19% of women with children under six were in the work force; today half of them are. In general, women are waiting longer to have children and having fewer of them. From 1970 until 1982 the number of first births among women ages 30 to 34 tripled.

The total fertility rate declined from 3.7 births per woman in 1960 to 2.5 in 1970, and has wavered between 1.7 and 1.9 since 1976. The years from 1965 to 1976 are often called "the baby bust." While there was something of a "baby boomlet" in the late 1970s, it was due mainly to the enormous increase in women of childbearing age.

Immigration will keep the U.S. from shrinking. Without transplants, the population would crest at about 245 million in the year 2000 and then start declining. If the projected rates of immigration and fertility are realized, 100 years from now America will have a population of about 300 million, of whom 16% will be black, 16% Hispanic, 10% Asian and a diminishing majority of 58% non-Hispanic whites.

One out of four Americans is over the age of 50. By the turn of the century, more than 100,000 Americans will be 100 years or older, about three times the number today.

Demographers call them the new old. Healthy, vigorous and solvent, they confute the view that old age, as William Butler Yeats put it, is nothing but a tattered coat upon a stick. The 26% of the population over 50 controls three-quarters of the nation's financial assets and, with $130 billion in discretionary income, half of its spending power. "Today's elderly, especially the young elderly under 70, are a marketer's dream," says Alma Triner of Arthur D. Little Inc., a consulting firm based in Cambridge, Mass.

The over-65 set is doing almost as well. In 1965 one-third were classified below the poverty line; today only 14% are. But in 2025, when there will be some 64 million people over 65, the nation will have fewer than four working-age individuals for every retirement-age person. "This is the lowest ratio ever," says Gordon Green of the Census Bureau, "and has serious implications for the solvency of the Social Security system."

The "old old," or the "superelderly," as they are sometimes called, represent the fastest-growing segment of the U.S. population. The number of Americans over 85 could double by the year 2000.

In 1980, for the first time, the majority of Americans lived in the South and West. During the 1970s, California, Florida and Texas had 42% of the U.S.'s total growth.

Imagine that every American had the same weight and was placed on a flat, rigid map of the entire country. The balancing point would be just west of De Soto in Jefferson County, Mo. The center of population has been inching west by about 40 miles a decade, from outside Baltimore in 1790 and finally crossing the Mississippi in the 1970s.

"During the 1970s," says Calvin Beale, chief of population research at the U.S. Department of Agriculture, "every Sunbelt state had a rate of population growth that was higher than the U.S. as a whole." Some of the Sunbelt, however, is now in the shade; in the 1980s, population growth in Alabama, Mississippi, Arkansas, Tennessee and Kentucky has been lower than in the U.S. as a whole.

Migration drained the Frostbelt in the late 1970s. More than 1 million New Yorkers, for example, packed their suitcases and headed for the Sunbelt between 1975 and 1980, 375,000 of them bound for Florida. But in the past two years, states that were once synonyms for exhaustion have had small revivals: Ohio, Indiana, Illinois and Michigan have gained population.

For two centuries, cities were an irresistible magnet for internal American migration. In the 1970s, however, that path was reversed as nonmetropolitan areas grew by 14.4% and metropolitan areas by 10.5%. Since 1980, however, that "rural turnaround has again turned around, with metro areas. But one aspect of the 1970s trend endures. "People are moving to smaller, less crowded communities," says Peter Morrison of the Rand Corp.'s population research center, "particularly those with a population under a quarter-million."

Notes Bryant Robey, founder of *American Demographics:* "America's past has been one of steady centralization; its future is likely to be one of steady population deconcentration."

The workers most in demand since the 1970s have been secretaries. In the next ten years, the economy will need 800,000 custodians and 425,000 truck drivers.

Calvin Coolidge notwithstanding, the business of America today is service. Since World War II, the U.S. has made the transition from smokestacks and assembly lines to copiers and computers. Today, two-thirds of all people work in wholesale and retail trade, communications, government, health care and restaurants. The buzz word of the 1970s job market was high tech. In the next decade it will downshift to low tech. There will be tremendous expansion in such decidedly unglamorous occupations as cashier, registered nurse and office clerk.

Average household income in constant dollars is dropping steadily: from $21,400 in 1980 to $20,600 today. In 1981 less than a third of all households headed by a person under 35 had any discretionary income.

Baby boomers are having a hard time matching the living standards to which they were accustomed to as children. Demographers call it the promotion squeeze. There is not enough room at the top. Today the combined income of a young married couple, both of whom are working, is likely to be less than what either of their fathers earned at the same age. Baby boomers are not able to afford the houses they grew up in, and home-ownership rates have fallen for the first time since World War II.

The BMW-driving, Reebok-clad, madly acquisitive yuppies so beloved of Madison Avenue have proved to be something of a myth. They account for only about 6% of all baby boomers. The reality,

says Ralph Whitehead Jr., an associate professor at the University of Massachusetts and an adviser to the Democratic Party, is the "new-collar" voter. The new collars are the college-educated sons and daughters of blue-collar parents; they earn between $20,000 and $40,000 and outnumber yuppies at least 5 to 1.

Between 1985 and 1995, there will be a drop of 18% in college-age Americans. In 1982, there was a decrease of 3% in both violent and nonviolent crime.

Colleges, the military and fast-food merchants depend on an endless supply of 18-year-old recruits. As Americans grow grayer, says Leon Bouvier of the Population Reference Bureau, "there could be real shortages in the labor force and the military." Baby boomers turned higher education into a multibillion-dollar business that employed more people than the automobile industry. Now universities will have to scale back.

Serious crime, traditionally a youthful failing, rose by 232% between 1960 and 1975, when baby boomers were in their teens and 20s. With fewer teenagers around, it should decline sharply by the end of the decade.

The skimpier the generation, the more room at the table. Demographer Richard Easterlin has a theory that economic well-being yields earlier marriages and higher fertility. Then fertility swings back and forth like a pendulum, from boom to bust, bust to boom. Members of the baby-bust generation will not face the teeming competition their parents did. They will struggle less and earn more. Rather like their grandparents. Sound familiar? Past being prologue, they could just produce another baby boom and start the cycle over again. —*By Richard Stengel.* ***Reported by Joelle Attinger/Boston and Patricia Delaney/Washington***

The Changing Face of America

"Just look down Broadway. That guy is Indian, next to him is a Greek, next to him is a Thai . . ."

"These States are the amplest poem,
Here is not merely a nation but a teeming Nation of
nations."

—Walt Whitman

Reina came from El Salvador because of "horrible things." She says simply, "I got scared." When she finally reached Los Angeles and found a job as a housekeeper at $125 a week, her new employer pointed to the vacuum cleaner. Vacuum cleaner? Reina, 24, had never seen such a thing before. "She gave me a maid book and a dictionary," says Reina, who now writes down and looks up every new word she hears. "That's how I learn English. I don't have time to go to school, but when I don't speak English, I feel stupid, so I must learn."

Manuel Martins Simões had been a truck driver in Lisbon, but when he got to Newark in 1974, he worked on a construction gang during the week and waited on tables weekends. Eventually, he saved enough money to buy a restaurant. "The building was really broken down and dirty," Simões says, "but my wife and I rebuilt the whole thing and put in a private dining room and a barbecue in the back." After seven years, he sold the place for a $185,000 profit and returned to Lisbon to set himself up in business and live like a lord. But Simões was miserable. "All business in Portugal now is bad," he says, "and the kids are a headache, always wanting to go back to the U.S." Next week the family is emigrating all over again. "The first thing we will do," says Simões, "is become American citizens."

Lam Ton, from Viet Nam, is already a U.S. citizen, and he too did well with a restaurant, the Mekong, at the inter-

by Chuck Fishman

The moment of arrival stirs feelings of hope, anxiety, curiosity, pride. These emotions and many others show in the faces on the following pages. The photos were taken within an hour after the newcomers had landed at New York's Kennedy Airport.

section of Broadway and Argyle Street in Chicago. "When I first moved in here, I swept the sidewalk after we closed," he recalls. "People thought I was strange, but now everyone does the same." Lam Ton's newest project is to build an arch over Argyle Street in honor of the immigrants who live and work there. "I will call it Freedom Gate," he says, "and it will have ocean waves with hands holding a freedom torch on top. It will represent not just the Vietnamese but all the minorities who have come here. Just look down Broadway. That guy is Indian, next to him is a Greek, next to him is a Thai, and next to him is a Mexican."

They seem to come from everywhere, for all kinds of reasons, as indeed they always have. "What Alexis de Tocqueville saw in America," John F. Kennedy once wrote, "was a society of immigrants, each of whom had begun life anew, on an equal footing. This was the secret of America: a nation of people with the fresh memory of old traditions who dared to explore new frontiers . . ." It was in memory of Kennedy's urging that the U.S. in 1965 abandoned the quota system that for nearly half a century had preserved the overwhelmingly European character of the nation. The new law invited the largest wave of immigration since the turn of the century, only this time the newcomers have arrived not from the Old World but from the Third World, especially Asia and Latin America. Of the 544,000 legal immigrants who came in fiscal 1984, the largest numbers were from Mexico (57,000, or more than 10%), followed by the Philippines (42,000) and Viet Nam (37,000). Britain came in ninth, with only 14,000.

This enormous migration is rapidly and permanently changing the face of America. It is altering its racial make-up, its landscapes and cityscapes, its taste in food and clothes and music, its entire perception of itself and its way of life. There have long been Chinatowns in American cities, but now there is Little Havana in Miami, Koreatown in Los Angeles, Little Saigon in Orange County, Calif., Little Odessa in Brooklyn, N.Y. Monterey Park, Calif., was the first U.S. city to have a Chinese-born woman as mayor, and the five-member city council includes two Hispanics and a Filipino American; Hialeah, Fla., has a Cuban-born mayor; Delaware, a Chinese-born Lieutenant Governor.

"It's fascinating," says New York Governor Mario Cuomo, the son of Italian immigrants. "For those of us who have been in the city for 50 years, it's wonderful to see the faces on the street now. Our diversity level has gone up." The new immigrants' contribution to America, Cuomo says, is "plus, plus, plus."

In addition to the half-million immigrants who are allowed to come to the U.S. each year, a substantial number arrive illegally. Estimates of the total vary widely. The Immigration and Naturalization Service apprehended 1.3 million illegal immigrants last year (many of them more than once) and guessed that several times that many had slipped through its net. The Census Bureau, however, estimated the total of illegal immigrants in the U.S. at between 3.5 million and 6 million in 1978. A National Academy of Sciences study issued last week denounced the INS statistics as "woefully inadequate" and put the total of illegals at no more than 2 million to 4 million. These include anyone from German students who deliberately overstay their visas to Haitian boat people who scramble ashore in South Florida, but roughly 60% of the illegals are Hispanics, and about two-thirds of these are Mexicans driven by poverty and unemployment across the highly porous 2,000-mile southern frontier.

The newest wave raises many questions: How many immigrants can the country absorb and at what rate? How much unskilled labor does a high-tech society need? Do illegals drain the economy or enrich it? Do newcomers gain their foothold at the expense of the poor and the black? Is it either possible or desirable to assimilate large numbers of immigrants from different races, languages and cultures? Will the advantages of diversity be outweighed by the dangers of separatism and conflict?

When asked about such issues, Americans sound troubled; their answers are ambiguous and sometimes contradictory. In a TIME poll taken by Yankelovich, Skelly & White Inc.,* only 27% agreed with the idea that "America should keep its doors open to people who wish to immigrate to the U.S. because that is what our heritage is all about." Two-thirds agreed that "this philosophy is no longer reasonable, and we should strictly limit the number." Some 56% said the number of legal immigrants was too high, and 75% wanted illegal immigrants to be tracked down. On the other hand, 66% approved of taking in people being persecuted in their homelands.

"One of the conditions of being an American," says Arthur Mann, professor of history at the University of Chicago, "is to be aware of the fact that a whole lot of people around you are different, different in their origins, their religions, their life-styles." Yet most Americans do not know exactly what to make of those differences. Of those polled by Yankelovich, 59% believe that immigrants generally end up on welfare (the best estimate is that less than 20% do), and 54% think they add to the crime problem. Yet 58% feel that immigrants are basically good, honest people, and 67% think they are productive citizens once they become established. One out of every two knows someone who came to the U.S. in the past few years; of them, a majority says this knowledge has changed their views for the better.

"Such a mess," says Roger Conner, director of the Federation for American Immigration Reform (FAIR), which advocates stronger restrictions. "We imagine ourselves as responsible for the whole world's problems, but immigration over the next 40 years will mean 50 million more people, and once they get here, they have children." "Our kids can't get jobs because the illegals take them," says Harold Ezell, Western commissioner of the INS. "If we don't control this border, we're going to lose control of this country." Says Conner: "The politicians don't want to talk about what is happening and what will happen."

But they do. "Every house needs a door, and every country needs a border," says Colorado's Democratic Governor Richard Lamm. If the U.S. fails to stop illegal immigration, he warns, "we shall leave a legacy of strife, violence and joblessness for our children." Florida's Senator Lawton Chiles is equally alarmist. "If we do not regain control of our borders . . . I think that within ten years, we will not recognize the United States as the United States we see today."

Much of the concern comes from people who favor continued immigration, but who fear the consequences if a slowdown in the economy were to heighten the sense that immigrants, especially illegal ones, take jobs away from Americans. "We could have a terrible backlash, a terrible period of repression," warns the Rev. Theodore Hesburgh, president of Notre Dame and chairman of the Select Commission on Immigration that was established by Congress in 1978. "People tend to forget that twice in our lifetime, this country has rounded up hundreds of thousands of Mexicans and pushed them back over the border.* That was a terrible thing . . . but it could very well go on. Police sweeps from house to house, rounding up millions of people, pushing them back over a border, turning that border into a kind of armed camp."

Senator Alan Simpson, the Wyoming Republican who joined with Kentucky Democrat Romano Mazzoli to turn the Select Commission's findings into an immigration reform bill, estimates that Mexico would have to generate 700,000 new jobs every year (200,000 more than it is currently creating) just to keep its unemployment from getting worse. Simpson and Mazzoli have failed three times to get their bill passed, but Simpson, undaunted, presented yet another bill in May.

Xenophobia is not the force behind today's serious efforts to reform immigration. Simpson and other proponents recognize that most new immigrants, like the generations who came before them, work long and hard, and as much as possible on their own. Says Melvin Holli, professor of history at the University of Illinois, Chicago: "Their work ethic serves them well, and it serves us well. In a sense, they are refurbishing our work ethic." The new immigrants, says Lawrence H. Fuchs, chairman of American Studies at Brandeis, "have gumption, courage, ambition. They want to make it." This quality, which Fuchs has dubbed the "X-factor," is evident also among the children of immigrants. "They have a double X-factor: they are unencumbered by homesickness, alienation or the psychology of exile."

The American schoolroom has traditionally provided a hopeful glimpse of the nation's future, and some people still imagine it to be a Rockwellian scene of mostly pink-cheeked children spelling out the adventures of Dick and Jane. But come for a moment to the playground of the Franklin elementary school in Oakland, where black girls like to chant their jump-rope numbers in Chinese. "See you *mañana,*" one student shouts with a Vietnamese accent. *"Ciao!"* cries another, who has never been anywhere near Italy. And let it be noted that the boy who won the National Spelling Bee in Washington last month was Balu Natarajan,

---

*The findings are based on a telephone survey from April 30 to May 2 of 1,014 registered voters. The potential sampling error is plus or minus 3%.

*About 500,000 were expelled in the early 1930s and 2.2 million from 1953 to 1955. Some were actually U.S. citizens, and some were thrown out more than once.

13, who was born in India, now lives in a suburb of Chicago, and speaks Tamil at home. "Milieu" was the word with which he defeated 167 other competitors. Let it also be noted that Hung Vu and Jean Nguyen in May became the first Vietnamese-born Americans to graduate from West Point.

The number of newcomers is large in itself (an amazing two-thirds of all the immigration in the world consists of people entering the U.S.), but their effect is heightened because they have converged on the main cities of half a dozen states. Nowhere is the change more evident than in California, which has become home to 64% of the country's Asians and 35% of its Hispanics. Next comes New York, followed by Texas, Florida, Illinois and New Jersey. Miami is 64% Hispanic, San Antonio 55%. Los Angeles has more Mexicans (2 million) than any other city except metropolitan Mexico City, and nearly half as many Salvadorans (300,000) as San Salvador.

These population shifts change all the bric-a-brac of life. A car in Los Angeles carries a custom license plate that says SIE SIE LI, meaning, in Chinese, "thank you." Graffiti sprayed in a nearby park send their obscure signals in Farsi. A suburban supermarket specializes in such Vietnamese delicacies as pork snouts and pickled banana buds. The Spanish-language soap opera *Tu o Nadie* gets the top ratings among independent stations every night at 8.

Such changes require adaptation not only in the schools and the marketplace but throughout society. The Los Angeles County court system now provides interpreters for 80 different languages from Albanian and Amharic to Turkish and Tongan. One judge estimates that nearly half his cases require an interpreter. Sometimes the results are freakish. A police officer testified that he had read a Chinese suspect his Miranda rights in Chinese, in the Tai-shan dialect. The suspect only understood Cantonese. The judge thereupon ruled out his confession.

These changes do not represent social decline or breakdown. The newcomers bring valuable skills and personal qualities: hope, energy, fresh perspectives. But the success stories should not blot out the fact that many aliens face considerable hardships with little immediate chance of advancement. Avan Wong, 20, came from Hong Kong in 1983 and hoped to go to college. She lives in the Bronx with her aged father, commutes two hours by bus to a job of up to twelve hours a day in a suburban restaurant. "I don't even read the newspapers," she says. "You don't have time. Once you go home, you go to sleep. Once you get up, you have to go to work. The only thing I'm happy about is that I can earn money and send it back to my mother. Nothing else. You feel so lonely here." College is not in sight.

José Luis Villa, who slipped across the Mexican border last fall, has even worse prospects. He makes his home on a ragged mattress, one of about 30 lying in a row underneath the roaring traffic of Los Angeles' San Diego Freeway. Next to Villa's mattress stands a cardboard Perrier carton that contains most of his worldly possessions: a toothbrush, a tube of Colgate toothpaste, a cracked and yellowing bar of soap, a flashlight and a beginner's manual of English. Villa looks 13, but he claims to be 16. Every morning he hikes over to the "slave market" on Sawtelle Boulevard and hangs around with other youths until someone drives up and offers him $30 for a day's work shoveling gravel or moving furniture. "It's better than picking crops in Mexico," he says. "I'd rather go home than stay here forever, but I don't know when I can do that. I don't think about it, really."

Many immigrants are still the tired, the poor, the huddled masses whom the Statue of Liberty traditionally welcomed to New York Harbor. But the newcomers disembarking at Kennedy Airport or Miami or Los Angeles also include the successful. Baron Guy de Rothschild, for example, recently took refuge in New York City from the vagaries of French Socialism. Australia's publishing tycoon Rupert Murdoch, who has made a deal to buy seven television stations in the U.S., announced in May that he would become a U.S. citizen. The roster of Soviet immigrants includes not only the black-garbed babushkas huddled over their knitting in Brooklyn's Little Odessa but such artists as Alexander Solzhenitsyn and Mikhail Baryshnikov.

In greeting them with a mixture of sympathy and anxiety (lightly flavored with hypocrisy), Americans express one of their oldest national traditions. Thomas Jefferson, who proclaimed it self-evident that all men are created equal, felt considerable doubts about whether they were all equally well suited to be U.S. citizens. He complained of "the unbounded licentiousness" some of the newcomers displayed, and he warned that they would turn the nation into "a heterogeneous, incoherent, distracted mass." This at a time when the U.S. population was only 2 million, and still 80% from the British Isles.

Early in the 19th century came the great flood of Irish (2 million between 1815 and 1860) and Germans (1.5 million), some driven westward by political persecution, more by hunger and hardship. Philip Hone, mayor of New York in the 1820s, regarded both the Irish and the Germans as "filthy, intemperate, unused to the comforts of life and regardless of its proprieties." "Nativists" in Philadelphia raided Irish Catholic churches and burned Irish homes.

The next wave was more than twice as large—10 million from 1860 to 1890—but these were still mostly Northern Europeans: English, Dutch, Swedes, Norwegians. The third wave was even bigger: 16 million from 1890 to 1914, including a still unmatched record of 1.3 million in 1907 (when the total U.S. population was only 87 million). And to the dismay of the now established Irish and Germans, more than 80% of the newcomers were Eastern and Southern Europeans: Sicilians, Bulgarians, Greeks, Russian Jews fleeing the Czar's pogroms. This was the era in which Emma Lazarus wrote the Statue of Liberty's welcome to the huddled masses yearning to breathe free, but it was also the era in which the eminent Thomas Bailey Aldrich, editor of the *Atlantic Monthly,* composed a poem entitled "Unguarded Gates":

> Wide open and unguarded stand our gates,
> And through them presses a wild motley throng—
> Men from the Volga and the Tartar steppes,
> Featureless figures of the Hoang-Ho
> Malayan, Scythian, Teuton, Kelt, and Slav . . .
> These bringing with them unknown gods and rites,
> Those, tiger passions, here to stretch their claws . . .
> Accents of menace alien to our air,
> Voices that once the Tower of Babel knew!

Even with the best intentions on all sides, the question of how to fit all these varieties of strangers into a relatively coherent American society remains difficult. Linda Wong, a Chinese-American official of the Mexican-American Legal Defense and Education Fund, sees trouble in the racial differences. "There is concern among whites that the new immigrants may be unassimilable," says Wong. "Hispanics and Asians cannot melt in as easily, and the U.S. has always had an ambivalent attitude toward newcomers. Ambivalent at best, racist at worst."

Many historians disagree. Hispanics, says Sheldon Maram, a professor of history at California State University at Fullerton, "are moving at about the same level of acculturation as the Poles and Italians earlier in the century. Once they've made it, they tend to move out of the ghetto and melt into the rest of society." Asians often have it easier because they come from urban middle-class backgrounds. "They are the most highly skilled of any immigrant group our country has ever had," says Kevin McCarthy, a demographer at the Rand Corp. in Santa Monica, Calif.

Immigrants struggling to make good in the U.S. often express dismay at what they see around them. "Many American values and customs which are very much part of the American way of life are seen [by Indians] as 'evil,' " writes Parmatma Saran, associate professor of sociology at Baruch College in Manhattan. "The American attitude toward sex . . . is viewed as immoral." Gaspar Ortega, a onetime Mexican prizefighter who is now a social worker in New Haven, Conn., is concerned about American treatment of the family. "I get disgusted when I see families separated. I blame the pressure of the dollar when both mother and father have to work and leave the kids in day care. In Mexico, babies are breast-fed with the milk of life. We were poor, but we were a family."

Still, the process of assimilation is inexorable. "As these students become Americanized, they want to eat hot dogs and hamburgers and pizza," says Mark Palermo, a teacher at Chicago's Senn High School. "They want designer jeans and bicycles and calculators and digital watches. We're taught maybe it's an error to be materialistic, but material things are what they want."

The genes change too. Statistically, according to one study, about 80% of European immigrants marry outside their own ethnic groups by the time they reach the third generation. Among Japanese Americans, at least in the Chicago area, the comparable figure is 15% in the second generation, 50% in the third.

How long, how complete and how painful the process of Americanization will be remains unclear. It is true that ethnic elitists have bewailed each succeeding wave of Irish or Germans or Greeks, but it is also true that the disparities among Korean merchants, Soviet Jews, Hmong tribesmen, French socialites and Haitian boat people are greater than any the U.S. or any other country has ever confronted. On the other hand, Americans are probably more tolerant of diversity than they once were. "America is much more of a pluralistic society now," says Peter Rose, professor of sociology at Smith College. "You don't hear so much talk about the melting pot today. The old ideology, the concerted effort to make people the same, has been overtaken by reality."

The question is not really whether the new Americans can be assimilated—they must be—but rather how the U.S. will be changed by that process. Economically, there will inevitably be strains, but most evidence indicates that the immigrants create more wealth than they consume. Socially and culturally, the diversity can hardly help benefiting the U.S. by acting as an antidote to everything that is bland and homogenized. The sad fact, indeed, is that uniformity is exactly what the immigrants' children will probably strive for, and their grandchildren achieve.

Politically, the prospects are uncertain. A large majority of immigrants—some illegal, some ineligible, some anxious, some apathetic—do not vote at all. Hispanic registration drives are trying to change that, but even in Los Angeles only 12% of the voters (vs. nearly 33% of the population) are Hispanic. Asians appear even more wary of political activism, though some are beginning to seek clout through financial contributions. By one estimate, they provided 25% of Los Angeles Mayor Tom Bradley's last campaign fund.

Historically, immigrants have tended to vote Democratic, but this is no longer so predictable. Many Cubans, Koreans, Taiwanese and Vietnamese came with strong anti-Communist fervor, and President Reagan's appeal has broken open many traditionally Democratic groups. In Miami there was a bizarre confrontation over the Memorial Day weekend as exiled Cubans and Nicaraguans waved U.S. flags to welcome Reagan, while native-born Americans brandished placards denouncing his Latin American policies. "Go back to Russia," one Nicaraguan shouted at an Anglo demonstrator. "Y'all go back to Cuba," came the answer.

The new wave of immigrants, says former California Governor Jerry Brown, is gradually changing the country's angle of vision. "The Pacific Rim is becoming the focal point for economic and political concerns," he says. "This immigration will eventually move Europe to a lower priority in the way we look at the world." It is a mistake, though, to think of immigrants as an undifferentiated clump, politically or otherwise. Not only do they differ by national origin and social class and ideology but also according to whether they plan to stay permanently or eventually return home. "What binds Americans to one another, regardless of ethnicity or religion, is an American civic culture," says Brandeis Professor Fuchs. "It is the basis for the *unum* in *E pluribus unum*. It is a complex of ideals, behaviors, institutions, symbols and heroes connected by American history and its great documents, the Declaration of Independence, the Bill of Rights, the Gettysburg Address. It is backed by a civil religion giving transcendent significance to those ideals. And it is the basis for accepting ethnic diversity while protecting individual rights. An American can be as ethnic as he or she wishes in private actions, but in public actions, the rules of the civic culture are binding."

Lam Ton, the Vietnamese restaurateur who wants to build a freedom arch in Chicago, says these things differently because he is not a professor at Brandeis, but he feels very strongly about the civic culture. "This is the last stand," he says. "There is nowhere else to run. We have to stick to this country and help it do better."

—By Otto Friedrich. Reported by Douglas Brew/Los Angeles and Sidney Urquhart/New York

We Can Prevent NUCLEAR WINTER

New studies suggest that we must overhaul our thinking about nuclear weapons

Carl Sagan

As the readers of *Parade* know, recent evidence suggests unexpectedly that a nuclear war might raise an enormous pall of smoke and dust that would cover, darken and cool much of the Earth. The main effect would come from the sooty smoke produced in the burning of cities, so that even a "small" nuclear war could trigger a "Nuclear Winter"—if cities are targeted, as is certainly the case today.

The clouds of fine particles would rise up over the targets, spreading out rapidly in longitude around the Earth and a little more slowly in latitude. Quite apart from the radioactivity, the toxic smogs, the later enhancement of ultraviolet light from the sun and other effects, it is clear that if the lights are turned out and the temperatures plunge—for months, if not for years—our global civilization and the human species will be profoundly imperiled.

The massive fires produced by bombing in World War II were not extensive or simultaneous enough to have produced significant climatic consequences. The above-ground nuclear testing by the United States and the Soviet Union between 1945 and 1963 (ended by the Limited Test Ban Treaty) also did not produce significant climatic effects, in part because they caused very little burning.

The original Nuclear Winter study has now been corroborated in part by many other quantitative studies, performed, for example, at the National Center for Atmospheric Research, the Lawrence Livermore National Laboratory and the Computing Center of the USSR Academy of Sciences. Scientists all over the world are subjecting these findings to constructive criticism, with total budgets in the tens of millions of dollars now projected for the research. A number of new points have come up that will be pursued in future research. Several of these may ameliorate the consequences somewhat; others make the consequences of nuclear war still more severe. Even if the chance of a worldwide climatic catastrophe following nuclear war were one percent or less, it would have to be taken very seriously: The stakes are unprecedentedly high.

In the 1950s, the American nuclear strategist Herman Kahn imagined what he called a "Doomsday Machine." If even a small nuclear war occurred, Kahn proposed, the Doomsday Machine would automatically be activated and all life on Earth would be destroyed. The idea of this "thought experiment" was to illuminate the nature of strategic deterrence.

But it may be that the Doomsday Machine is not just an intellectual exercise. Since the early 1950s, the United States has had the capability, as far as we can tell, to trigger a Nuclear Winter. The Soviet Union did not reach this level of technological advancement until the middle 1960s. From those years to today, the leaders of the United States, the Soviet Union and other nuclear powers have made decisions of unprecedented importance—possibly involving the extinction of the human species—in total ignorance of the world climatic catastrophe that might follow nuclear war.

Stanley Kubrick's motion picture masterpiece *Dr. Strangelove* clearly brought out one important aspect of Doomsday Machines: Their existence must be known by all the contending parties. A secret Doomsday Machine will do nothing to discourage the other side.

Is the existence of Nuclear Winter understood by the Russians? And, not incidentally, what about the Americans? Fortunately, both American and Soviet scientists have worked on the problem and have discussed the issues with each other. Nuclear Winter has been given some, but by no means overwhelming, attention in both nations. It has been discussed in major stories in *The Washington Post* and in *Pravda,* on ABC's *Nightline* and on the all-USSR television news program *Vnanie.* The U.S. intelligence and uniformed military communities have been open to serious discussions of these issues. At a meeting on Nuclear Winter in January of this year at the Vatican, the leader of the Soviet delegation, Y.P. Velikhov—who is also vice president of the Soviet Academy of Sciences—told me that he had provided extensive briefings on Nuclear Winter to Soviet Foreign Minister Andrei Gromyko and Soviet Defense Minister Dimitri Ustinov. I wish I had been able to assure Dr. Velikhov that U.S. Secretary of State Shultz and Secretary of Defense Weinberger had received comparable briefings. But a real start has been made in these two adversary nations on understanding the nature and implications of Nuclear Winter, and there are strong signs that many other nations are becoming involved.

The unanticipated prospect of Nuclear Winter challenges some of the conventional thinking about nuclear deterrence and nuclear war. Here are a few of the possible implications:

• *First strike.* A considerable part of the mutual fear and hostility between the United States and the Soviet Union is due to concerns by each side that the other will launch a disabling first strike. The development of highly accurate MIRV'd missiles (a single booster rocket with many nuclear warheads) has in recent years increased the incentives for a first strike: Destroying an enemy missile might prevent, say, 10 of your cities from being destroyed while expending only one of your nuclear warheads. So, many of the weapons-system developments of both nations are now designed with the idea very much in mind of such first strikes against land-based fixed-site missiles.

But Nuclear Winter raises the prospect that a major first strike is self-deterring. Even in the very unlikely case that not a single city were burned in a nuclear war, the destruction of more than 1000 missile silos, airfields, submarine facilities and other urgent strategic targets would—through dust and soot—probably lower the temperature and cause an unprecedented agricultural catastrophe. One nation could launch a disabling first strike against the other and be utterly destroyed without the opponent lifting a finger to retaliate. It would take about 10 days for the pall of fine particles to drift back from the target nation to the aggressor nation, soon thereafter devastating both. But if such first strikes are suicidal for the aggressor, and if both nations recognize this to be true, the mere knowledge of Nuclear Winter might produce some additional restraint, a new stabilizing influence.

• *Civilian shelters and crisis relocation.* Even before Nuclear Winter was discovered, severe and fundamental criticism had been leveled at the idea of civil defense in a nuclear war. In the sorts of nuclear war that are discussed in both countries, something like 10,000 warheads would fall. The idea of the population of one city fleeing to another, or to a benign and receptive countryside, is reminiscent of the victims of Hiroshima who made their way to Nagasaki for medical care. Nuclear Winter makes the idea of crisis relocation much less sensible still. And as for civilian shelters, we must now imagine deep underground shelters, adequate to supply all needs for a year—perhaps many years—with a dark, frigid, radioactive wasteland waiting up above: a dismal and largely untenable prospect for the citizens of either nation for technical, fiscal and psychological reasons.

• *Other nations.* Just as there appears to be no sanctuary for the populations of the United States and the Soviet Union, it is now beginning to look as though there may be no sanctuaries anywhere on the planet. As a result, nations that thought they could sit out a nuclear war between the United States and the Soviet Union must now recognize that they can be fundamentally destroyed without a single nuclear weapon falling on their territories. The stake that other nations have in the relations between the United States and the Soviet Union now appears to be very high.

• *Star Wars.* It is natural to wish for some impenetrable shield placed over the United States (and the Soviet Union) that would render incoming missiles, in the words of Ronald Reagan, "impotent and obsolete." Perhaps it would include laser, particle-beam and small homing weapons. However, a wide range of studies by independent scientists, by those in the Department of Defense and by the Office of Technology Assessment of the Congress indicate that—because of the laws of physics and such noncontroversial matters as the fact that the Earth is round—nothing like an impenetrable defense can be established in the foreseeable future. And a ballistic-missile defense system that is porous, that lets in a significant fraction of incoming warheads, may be much more dangerous than no shield at all. Only a small fraction of incoming warheads need hit their targets for a Nuclear Winter to be triggered. Also, its imminent deployment might be understood as an indication of a forthcoming first strike and therefore lead, in a time of crisis, to nuclear war. After all, the deployment of an effective shield by the United States would be tantamount to the involuntary strategic disarmament of the Soviet Union, and vice versa. Neither nation is likely to acquiesce to such a development.

• *Massive reductions in the nuclear arsenals.* It is monumental foolishness to accept a world in which Nuclear Winter could be triggered. Even if we were entirely confident of the sanity, sobriety and prudent judgment of the present leaders of the United States and the Soviet Union and of the perfect reliability of their computers and other technological systems, that confidence cannot extend to all leaders of all nuclear nations and all machines for all times to come. Even neglecting the more than 30,000 tactical nuclear weapons in the world, there are some 18,000 strategic and theater weapons. Fewer than one percent of them could probably trigger a Nuclear Winter.

But fewer than one percent of these weapons would also be adequate to maintain the doctrine of strategic deterrence—an invulnerable retaliatory capability. A single U.S. strategic submarine can destroy some 160 Soviet cities. There are roughly 30 such submarines on active duty, to say nothing of the cruise missiles, intermediate range missiles, ICBMs and aircraft of the U.S. Strategic Air Command. The Soviets have a comparable capability. If a Soviet or an American leader would not be restrained by the knowledge that the sure and certain destruction of a few hundred of his largest cities was in the hands of his adversary, what *would* restrain him? Massive cuts in the world nuclear arsenals can be carried out—bilaterally, verifiably, safely. A feasible goal is to move the world nuclear arsenals out of the realm where Nuclear Winter is likely, while still preserving deterrence.

. . . I ask whether a further increase in these bloated and grotesque nuclear arsenals is in the best interest of our nation, our planet and our species.

■ MANY BHOPALS:

Technology Out of Control

ROBERT ENGLER

Robert Engler is the author of The Politics of Oil *and* The Brotherhood of Oil *(both from* The University of Chicago Press*). A former assistant to the president of the National Farmers Union, he is a professor of political science at Brooklyn College and the Graduate School of the City University of New York.*

We, civilized men and women, know everything, we have settled opinions upon everything, we take an interest in everything. We only know nothing about whence the bread comes from which we eat—even though we pretend to know something about that subject as well—we do not know how it is grown, what pains it costs to those who grow it, what is being done to reduce their pains, what sort of men those feeders of our grand selves are . . . we are more ignorant than savages in this respect.

—*Pëtr Kropotkin, 1898*

Last December, a toxic cloud escaping from a Union Carbide pesticide plant brought death to at least 2,500 residents of the shantytowns crowding its edges. The alchemy that overnight transformed the Indian city of Bhopal into a gas chamber injured perhaps 200,000 and brought terror and suffering to hundreds of thousands more. From a count of burial shrouds sold and other indicators, some observers estimate the total killed at between 4,000 and 10,000. Exactly how many died we may never know.

Only weeks earlier in Mexico City an explosion of liquefied-gas tanks belonging to Pemex, the government oil corporation, killed at least 450 dwellers in nearby slums. The two disasters evoked memories of Séveso, Italy, where in 1976 the dioxin from an exploding chemical reactor hospitalized hundreds and contaminated many acres. In the United States, the 1979 radiation leak from a nuclear power plant at Three Mile Island forced the evacuation of some 60,000 people in the surrounding areas. And the percolation into the soil of twenty-year-old lethal wastes stored in a corporate chemical dump site brought ailments and anxiety to 1,200 residents of Niagara Falls, New York, rendering their modest homes in the Love Canal neighborhood uninhabitable.

Each time, the headlines suggest that the calamity is isolated, unique. The search for causes begins with human error and bureaucratic ineptitude and moves on to mechanical failure and inadequate design. The limited education and rote-learned skills of the workers at Bhopal, as well as the simplicity of the surrounding populace, experts assert, hinder the developing world's introduction to better living through chemistry.

Western pundits joined in the widespread lament over the deaths in India; some offered the consolation that the disaster might have been much worse. And, as one pointed out, "Progress has always involved a certain amount of trial and error." A historian of technology calculated that half of those killed at Bhopal "would not have been alive today if it were not for that plant and the modern health standards made possible by wide use of pesticides." Thus the dead at Bhopal could be regarded as a necessary human sacrifice to the gods of modernization. *The Economist* concluded, "Thousands will not have died in vain if multinationals now build safer plants, even when local government regulations discourage them from doing so."

The question asked in the United States was, Could it happen here? Unaccustomed to the spotlight, Union Carbide took the precaution of closing a much larger plant in Institute, West Virginia, which also stockpiled the chemical that escaped at Bhopal. Named methyl isocyanate (MIC), it is used in making the pesticides Temik (banned by a number of American communities) and Sevin. A Congressional investigation of the plant, which is the only one of its kind in the country, found that twenty-eight accidental leaks (the figure was later raised to sixty-two) had occurred during the previous five years. All of them were minor, Union Carbide spokesmen assured the public, and "represented no threat to the local community." The plant was "absolutely safe." After another review of its records, the company announced that there had been 107 in-plant leaks of phosgene, which is poisonous and volatile, and twenty-two leaks of a mixture of phosgene and MIC, but not in illegal or harmful quantities. It also disclosed that only three months before the Bhopal tragedy there had been an internal safety warning about the storage of the unstable methyl isocyanate at Institute. The plant had no equipment for automatically detecting MIC leaks. Instead, its managers relied on "odor and/or eye irritation [of personnel]," although such sensitivity might not be apparent until safety levels had been exceeded. The plant was found unprepared to cope with a potential "runaway reaction" in time to prevent a major catastrophe.

The recommendations from corporate headquarters resulted in additional safety measures at Institute. But no comparable message had been sent to the Indian sister plant. Meanwhile, Du Pont, heretofore a customer for Union Carbide's MIC, announced it would produce the chemical itself in a closed loop system, that is, "whip it through a pipe" for instant use in its own pesticide product so as to minimize the transportation and storage of the lethal chemical. Its plant is located outside Houston. In mid-February Union Carbide declared it would resume production in West Virginia following some procedural changes and the installation of a computer system to trace chemical leaks.

Could It Happen Here?

When one studies disasters like that at Bhopal not as freak happenings against all expectations but as integral to industrial development, and when one views American occupational and environmental casualties in aggregate terms, then the answer to the question, Could it happen here? becomes clear: it already has and will continue to.

Although a precise body count is difficult to arrive at, the illnesses and deaths each year in this country caused by the production and use of arsenic, asbestos, benzene, coal and cotton dust, silica, toxic dyes, uranium, vinyl chloride and hazardous waste chemicals number in the hundreds of thousands. A complete history of American mining, foundries, mills and farming, along with a host of other industries, would yield a staggering casualty list. Yet this continuing chemical warfare against the American people has remained largely unanalyzed; it is considered an incidental cost of growth or played down as hysteria. Periodically, in the wake of a dramatic shock to the public conscience, the issue is "discovered" and a burst of reform fervor triggers demands for greater corporate responsibility and more stringent public regulation.

Despite the repeated wonder at these recent occurrences, they are nothing new. In 1908 Dr. Alice Hamilton began investigating lead and other industrial poisons and fighting against them. In 1924, oil refinery workers went into convulsions and died from "loony gas," tetraethyl lead. The dust raised by the blasting of a West Virginia water tunnel by a Union Carbide subsidiary in the early 1930s killed almost 500 workers and disabled another 1,500, most of them unskilled and black. Sixty years ago asbestos companies were refused insurance, yet only recently has asbestos received public recognition as a major cause of cancer—a

costly consequence of making employee health information a privilege of private ownership.

The cumulative record for the developing world is even more shocking, though figures are imprecise. In India, where the permissible limits on workplace exposure to lead are much higher than in the United States, one-fourth of the employees who were examined at battery plants had lead poisoning. Almost one-third of the workers at an Indian plant making DDT, which increasingly has been restricted in the United States, were found to be sick. An Oxfam report cites 15,000 cases of pesticide poisoning in Sri Lanka in 1978, 1,000 of which resulted in death. There is a global double standard that places a greater value on Western lives. Corporations generally operate under laxer safety regulations in the Third World, as a recent issue of *Multinational Monitor* stated:

> U.S. chemical corporations . . . export from the U.S. at least 150 million pounds of pesticides each year that are totally prohibited, severely restricted, or never registered for use in this country. Oxfam estimates that 375,000 pesticide poisonings, 6,700 of which are fatal, occur each year in the Third World.
>
> Little noticed was the battery plant on the outskirts of Jakarta, Indonesia that was operated by Union Carbide. . . . At one point, more than half the work force of 750 were diagnosed as having a kidney disease linked to mercury exposure. Little noticed, too, was the mass poisoning in Al Basrah, Iraq in 1971. Cargoes of American barley and Mexican wheat arrived in Al Basrah treated with methylmercury, a fungicide prohibited for use in the U.S. and other countries. The grain, intended as seed only, had been chemically treated to prevent rot and had been sprayed with a bright pink dye to indicate the presence of the mercury solution. The shipments were not, however, marked in Arabic, the language of Iraq. The grain was sold to hundreds of thousands of Iraqis. One observer estimated that as many as 6,000 persons died and 100,000 were injured.

Americans have no guarantee of immunity from such tainted imports, for we consume fruit and coffee that enter the country after having been treated with dubious or banned chemicals. But it was the widespread spraying of Agent Orange over Vietnamese fields and jungles to destroy crops and deny cover to the enemy that brought Americans fully into the "circle of poison." Many Vietnam veterans have complained about skin diseases and birth defects in their children, which they suspect resulted from exposure to the defoliant. "I died in Vietnam and didn't even know it," said one terminal cancer victim. A class action suit filed in 1979 charged Dow, Monsanto and several smaller chemical manufacturers with withholding information about the toxic properties of dioxin, a byproduct of one of the principal herbicides (2,4,5-T) in Agent Orange. The defendants responded that they had been conscripted to fill military orders for one of the safest and most carefully studied agricultural products. Scientists recognize that the use of herbicides causes unbalanced growth in plants, which can destroy weeds and clear brush. But no one knows exactly how they work. The companies also insisted that the government knew at least as much as they did about the dangers inherent in these efforts to alter the chemistry of life. More than 200,000 individual claims have been filed since the recent settlement.

Dumping People Off the Land

America's abundant resources in relation to population size and its unfolding industrial prospects have helped sustain an excessive readiness to liberate people from agricultural work through chemistry (or, more accurately, to liberate work from people). In bringing about the shift from an agrarian economy to one devoted to the production of industrial goods and services, the major reliance was placed on the incentives of the marketplace. But many farmers, both whites and blacks, found themselves excluded from the rewards of individual opportunity. Today they continue to be more driven than lured from the old agrarian order. Corporate research and development as well as national farm policies and practices are oriented to agriculture as big business rather than to family farmers who respect the soil and want to live close to it. A lingering frontier ethic makes it difficult for Americans to perceive that the forced migration has been a major source of the urban crisis and its related racial tensions. It is less disturbing to accept these dislocations as technologically ordained than to analyze social forces and explore alternative possibilities. "Land reform" has an un-American ring. It remains esoteric terminology, reserved for less developed countries.

India, in contrast, has been burdened throughout its history by low productivity and poverty in what Mohandas Gandhi once described as "700,000 dung heaps which today pass muster as villages." At the time of its independence it also possessed a slender industrial base. Following their victory over the British, the leaders of the new nation turned to rebuild the rural economy in tandem with new machine-tool and heavy industries. Planned development was seen as the swiftest and surest path to economic reconstruction with social justice.

The adoption of Western agricultural methods to create the food surpluses needed to feed the cities resulted in the dumping of many farmers onto the fringes of urban areas. Although he wrote the following for an Indian publication in 1961, E.F. Schumacher might have been at Bhopal last December:

> It is a familiar sight in so-called underdeveloped countries to find somewhere, in the midst of great poverty and a primitive way of life, a gleaming, steamlined new factory, created by foreign private enterprise and producing consumer goods of just the kind that poor people need. Such a factory, as a factory, may be in no way inferior to anything that could be found in Western Europe or the United States, superbly equipped and well-managed and attaining, with native labour, as high a level of productivity as might be attained in the country of its origin. When inspecting the factory you might think you were in America. But you would not think so the moment you stepped outside. Not only that there might be a huge barbed wire fence, heavily guarded, around the whole property, but immediately outside the gates you might find a shanty town of the most miserable kind teeming with thousands of people most of whom are unemployed and do not seem to have a chance of ever finding regular employment of any kind. The contrast is so striking, even overwhelming, that you begin to wonder, not merely what this factory represents by itself—on this point the management have provided you with excellent and convincing literature—but what it means to the society into which it has been planted.

The displaced Indians have remained marginal producers and consumers. Meanwhile, three-fourths of the population of 720 million (expected to reach 1 billion by the year 2000) still dwell on the land. Nearly half those people live at a bare subsistence level.

The New Scientific Farming

As Americans recognize from the experiences of their own country, the Bhopal plant is part of an industrial process that integrates agriculture into the international business system. At its best, farming was a local nurturing activity by which those who loved the land worked with nature rather than, in E.B. White's phrase, attempting to beat it into submission. Now farming has become largely an extractive industry, responsive to global market fluctuations and controls.

Pesticides have been central to the transformation. They are used to protect crops from insects and rodents in the field and in storage. Similarly, herbicides ward off diseases and parasitic plants. The bumper yields resulting from this "scientific" agriculture are, at least in the short run, impressive. According to Union Carbide, pesticides save about 10 percent of India's annual food crop, enough to feed more than 70 million people. But the price is heavy. Indiscriminate or poorly planned use of chemical pesticides has reduced the soil's nutrients, the plants' natural resistance to disease and the land's ability to retain moisture. The standard response to these warnings from nature has been to step up the application of fertilizer and to intensify irrigation, increasing the runoff of chemical-laden soil, which contaminates waterways and aquatic life.

More than twenty years ago Rachel Carson sounded the alarm about the dangers to animals and humans of pesticides like DDT. Yet the destruction of species continues, including those that prey on many pests. As Carson noted, the pests have developed increased resistance to many of the magical chemicals, and hardier breeds have consequently emerged.

The new agricultural order is also dependent on high-yield, genetically identical crops or those having only a few strains. Such crops are grown from hybrid seeds which the farmer purchases each year from seed companies, many of them now controlled by oil and petrochemical corporations, including Union Carbide. Artificial fertilizer and pesticides are needed to increase the productivity of the seeds; also, it is more cost effective to sow and spray a broad, one-crop field by machine. All those techniques heighten the crop's vulnerability to insects or disease, raising the possibility of catastrophic losses for the farmer. In contrast, as the Council on Environmental Quality, poet-farmer Wendell Berry and others have pointed out, a more diversified agriculture with crop rotation and care by experienced farmers can deal with such dangers naturally.

Scientific farming, together with expensive, high-powered machines, requires a substantial capital outlay. The farmer borrows the money, adding interest to his fixed costs. Productivity becomes his overriding concern. The concentration of agricultural holdings accelerates as small farmers are forced out and those who survive grow dependent on the banks, the government and overseas markets. Rural people are removed from the land as effectively as they were by the British enclosure acts of the eighteenth century and the forced collectivization in the Soviet Union.

The output of the factories in the field is generally celebrated as a triumph of technology wed to scientific management—the Green Revolution. American textbooks glowingly record how one mechanized (and now computerized) farmer feeds x times as many consumers as he did in Thomas Jefferson's day. We still pay homage to the sage of Monticello for his democratic ideals, but we have forgotten his dictum that broadly diffused land ownership is essential for an independent citizenry. Similarly, the people of India often forget Gandhi's precept that independence must begin at the bottom, with every village self-sufficient. Even less is said about what the return in healthy crops might be from a balanced husbandry with educated farmers, aided by the best tools and by renewable resources, intensively working manageable holdings, individually and cooperatively.

The emerging agribusiness is hooked on chemicals produced from nonrenewable fossil fuels. The farmer, encouraged by the interlocking research network of scientists, academics and industry-backed development centers with professional stakes in such dependence, becomes tightly linked to the international petrochemical and energy industry. Union Carbide has been an integral part of this structure. The third-largest chemical company in the United States (after Du Pont and Dow), its $9.5 billion in sales placed it thirty-fifth among the 1985 Fortune 500, and its assets of $10.5 billion make it the twenty-third largest in that category. While consumers are familiar with its Eveready batteries, Prestone antifreeze and Glad wrap, its primary dealings in chemicals, gases, plastics, metals, technological processes, uranium research and, until recently, enrichment, have been with other corporations and governments. It has plants, mills, mines and laboratories in thirty-eight countries, and it is a major supplier for the $7 billion pesticide market.

Union Carbide owns a 50.9 percent share of the Bhopal plant, well over the 40 percent limit on foreign ownership set by India. This compromise by the Indian government, which preferred a state-owned industrial sector, was attributed to the country's need for high technology and the multinational's superior bargaining position. (Also, co-ownership can temper popular pressures for nationalization, often without surrendering basic technological knowledge.) The remainder of the shares are held by Indian interests. After

the disaster, Union Carbide was quick to emphasize that Union Carbide India Ltd. (U.C.I.L.), of which the pesticide facilities are a part, is managed by Indians and operates as a totally separate company. Yet the American corporation has an executive vice president on U.C.I.L.'s board. U.C.I.L., with headquarters in Bombay, reports directly to Union Carbide Eastern, in Hong Kong. Four executives of Union Carbide Eastern, including its chair, sit on the Indian company's board. Budgets, major capital expenditures, policy decisions and company reports must be cleared with the Danbury, Connecticut, headquarters. While precise details about the working relationships are beginning to emerge from the litigation, the central issue when appraising the accident is more than one of formal ownership. After all, Pemex, successor to international corporate oil operations that were nationalized by Mexico in 1938, an event still marked as a national holiday in that country, is owned by the government.

Secret Lethal Substances

Union Carbide was producing the highly toxic chemical methyl isocyanate as a component of its pesticide Sevin. Pesticides are designed to kill, and although the intent may be selective, the consequences often are not. All kinds of life may be threatened by such chemicals. In humans they cause liver damage, nervous-system dysfunction, respiratory failure, cancer and genetic defects, among other ailments. Rachel Carson concluded that a more appropriate name for them would be biocides.

Field, factory and warehouse workers throughout the world are exposed daily to lethal chemicals about which they may understand little, other than that their eyes tear, they cough harshly and they suffer recurring rashes and headaches. In the United States, the hard-won laws of the 1970s—the Environmental Protection Act, the Occupational Safety and Health Act and the Federal Insecticide, Fungicide and Rodenticide Act—along with other laws, provide some safety standards for regulating toxic chemicals and wastes in the workplace and in the community. Pesticides must be reviewed and registered before being put on the market.

Manufacturers have resisted such procedures, claiming they interfere with progress and profits. They insist that the ingredients of their products are proprietary information and that disclosure of such trade secrets upsets competition. They have warned local communities, as Union Carbide did in Marietta, Ohio, in 1971, that clean-air laws would result in layoffs or shutdowns. They have also said such regulation of pesticides jeopardizes the world food supply.

The Reagan Administration has used budget cuts and cost-benefit analysis to curtail enforcement of environmental laws. Scientists and administrators sympathetic to the laws have been purged, and the industry, rather than the public, has become the constituency of the regulatory agencies. Corporate officials have been invited to participate in the regulatory process, reviewing projects, budgets and reports in their early stages. A conscious effort has been made to reduce public information and involvement.

7. SOCIAL CHANGE AND THE FUTURE: New Technology Issues

A policy of industry self-policing has resulted in fraudulent and inadequate testing and has kept questionable pesticides on the market. Henry Waxman, chair of the House Subcommittee on Health and the Environment, which held hearings on the safety of Union Carbide's West Virginia plant, concluded that although the Environmental Protection Agency has no idea what is going on inside such facilities, "it blithely reassures the public that they are safe." The E.P.A. has made no attempt to regulate underground storage of chemicals like methyl isocyanate and has not set waste-emission standards, thus making it easier to claim with a straight face that no violations have taken place. Even after Bhopal the agency continues to give the review of MIC a low priority, explaining, "It is never expected to be emitted into the air under normal circumstances." As a top E.P.A. administrator reasoned, "You can't predict against a random incident like what happened over in Bhopal."

According to Jonathan Lash's *A Season of Spoils*, published last year, "Of 600 registered generic pesticides in common use today, 79 to 84 percent have not been adequately tested for their potential to cause cancer, 60 to 70 percent have not been tested for their potential to cause birth defects, and 90 percent have not been tested for genetic mutations." The substantial cancer-producing effects of ethylene dibromide (EDB) as a grain, fruit and soil fumigant have been played down. One E.P.A. official proposed giving pesticides a better image. Labeling them "hazardous" and "toxic," he explained, conveys "a lack of trust in the producer of the chemicals, the government which regulates the industry and the applicators who apply these chemicals." His suggestion: refer to them as "crop protection chemicals." Joan Claybrook and the staff of Public Citizen note in their recent *Retreat From Safety* that chemicals and pesticides "are presumed safe until proven dangerous." And judging by the frequency of authorizations for emergency use of banned or unregistered pesticides, "an observer might conclude that the election of Ronald Reagan has sparked a nationwide insect outbreak."

The Bhopal disaster has prompted groups in a number of states to press for the introduction or strengthening of "right to know" laws which require that the public be informed about chemical and other potentially dangerous plant operations. Labor unions continue to fight for accurate labeling of the chemicals workers handle, training in their use, and power to close down unsafe operations.

In contrast, the petrochemical industry laments the emotional fallout from the Indian disaster. "The public's fear of toxic chemicals is grossly exaggerated but nevertheless it is very real," Edwin Holmer, chair of the Chemical Manufacturers Association and president of Exxon Chemical, warned a National Academy of Engineering symposium at Stanford University last month. "This fear can be translated into laws and regulations so punitive and so excessively expensive that they would make our operations prohibitive, make new products difficult to develop and commercialize, and make our industry noncompetitive in the international trade arena." On March 27, *The New York Times* reported that

officers of major chemical companies, "reversing their longtime position, joined members of Congress . . . in calling for stricter Government controls over toxic air pollutants." Warren Anderson, chair of Union Carbide, urged Congress "to improve regulatory control over hazardous air pollutants" through "uniform, nationwide and coordinated standards" which would assure communities the right to know about hazardous chemicals in their vicinity. Other corporate voices have suggested nationwide health and safety regulations. Given the political climate under the Reagan Administration, such rules and their enforcement would be relatively tame, and they would take precedence over tougher regulations pushed through by local community groups. Thus does corporate America move in the wake of Bhopal to define the parameters of national debate and policy, while asserting that we are all in it together when it comes to concern about unruly chemicals.

In New Jersey, a pioneering Worker and Community Right to Know Act, effective last August, was challenged in Federal court by the state Chamber of Commerce and major chemical and oil corporations. They argued that OSHA regulations, which require description of the hazards but not specific identification of chemicals (presumably to protect trade secrets), pre-empt the new state legislation, which requires precise chemical labeling and registration. In a partial victory for business, the court held that the law cannot be applied to the petrochemical industry or other manufacturers. The labor/environmental coalition that fought for the act is mobilizing for new state legislation. Meanwhile, representatives of the companies involved in the suit, all of which have been charged by state or Federal agencies with releasing hazardous substances into the environment, sit on the state's Right to Know Advisory Council, which was created to oversee implementation of the law. Heading the eleven-member council is the manager of safety and environmental affairs for the Specialty Chemicals Division of Union Carbide.

Third World nations ardently pursuing industrial and agricultural development are even less rigorous in evaluating potential risks from chemical plants and imported chemicals. (Pollution is a disease of the affluent, it is sometimes said. And the preoccupation with the environment is their privileged indulgence.) Developing nations often lack the resources for independent appraisal and control of pesticides, and some have become pollution havens for multinational corporations. About 29 percent of the 522 million pounds of pesticides shipped from the United States in 1976 was not registered for domestic use, according to a 1979 General Accounting Office report. About 20 percent of those unregistered pesticides had been suspended or canceled by the E.P.A. because of health or environmental risks. And some 25 percent of the products exported either had never been studied or had been deemed too hazardous for use in the United States. A 1984 environmental study of development in Malaysia reveals that test data for fifty-six pesticides imported from the United States had been deliberately falsified.

Attempts to publicize adverse findings and curb such exports have been opposed by corporations as unwarranted intrusions on the free market. The Administration contends that this country must not become a "global nanny" and combats U.N. efforts to restrict the dumping of unsafe pesticides. Even while the Bhopal story was on the front pages, the United States was the only nation in the General Assembly (the vote was 148 to 1) to oppose the continued publication of a reference directory of restricted or banned pesticides. It argued that the $89,000 expenditure was wasteful and discriminated against the companies listed.

In the headlong rush to industrialize, it is sometimes forgotten that the purpose of the emerging global food system is to meet basic human needs, not to advance technical prowess or promote corporate expansion. The urban consumer has been integrated into that food system, trained to accept as food a growing number of synthetic or chemically treated products, whether artificially ripened, tasteless tomatoes, beguilingly labeled "vine grown," or squeezable bread made with fumigated grain, from which much of the nutrition and most of the taste have been removed. "It is one of the miracles of science and hygiene," Wendell Berry has observed, "that the germs that used to be in our food have been replaced by poisons."

Every day we read that farmers in this country find it increasingly difficult to survive. Yet as food becomes more expensive to produce, process, package and transport, the likelihood diminishes that the hungry of the world, including the rural poor, will be the ones to eat better or more. The grim irony of this organizational achievement is that in many regions of the world, single crops are produced for export in order to earn the foreign exchange to pay for technical sophistication. Where that happens, the bulk of the farm population may remain as underemployed industrial field hands, vulnerable to the profit expectations of a remote international order which snuffs out their livelihood as well as their life.

Who Was to Blame in Bhopal?

Warren Anderson's disclaimer—"It never entered my mind that an accident such as Bhopal could happen"—begs the question of culpability. Although Anderson insisted that the $20 million "state of the art" MIC facility left "nothing . . . to be desired" technologically, considerable evidence of corporate neglect, stupidity, arrogance and greed has surfaced. An affidavit from Edward A. Munoz, a former high-level official of Union Carbide who was active in the development of the Bhopal plant and had been managing director of U.C.I.L., describes how the engineering department of the American company was responsible for the conceptualization and the design work of the plant. It monitored the engineering and construction and pushed to store the highly volatile chemical in large bulk tanks. It "imposed" that procedure over the objections of U.C.I.L., which he represented. While experts and lawyers are determining how water entered the MIC storage tank, producing the buildup of temperature and pressure beyond safe levels,

others are wondering about the extent of fundamental flaws in the plant's design and instrumentation.

For a few days prior to the accident, workers had been unable to pressurize with nitrogen a storage tank in order to move the MIC to the nearby pesticide production facility. The amount of MIC in the tank exceeded specifications. It was unclear by which route the nitrogen left the tank. Meanwhile, safety systems failed to work or were bypassed by the escaping MIC. A cooling unit had been shut down; a vent scrubber to neutralize escaping gas with a caustic soda solution was also inoperative (it has been charged that its capacity would have been inadequate anyway); and a flare tower to burn off escaping gas was not working.

At the time of the accident, Anderson said that safety precautions for working with MIC were the same at Institute and Bhopal. Union Carbide spokesmen have since explained that safety equipment and procedures in Bhopal were less sophisticated, in part to provide more jobs. Although the MIC unit was closed for maintenance the day of the fatal leak, it is obvious that the Indian management had routinely cut corners on upkeep and safety. Workers reported that critical valves did not always respond and defective fail-safe mechanisms were not promptly replaced. They had learned to accept the gauges as unreliable. Operating crews had been cut back. A maintenance engineer had been dropped from each shift. Warnings from workers, their local unions and the press were ignored. Two years previous the union representing most of the plant's 632 workers had put up thousands of posters predicting the release of toxic vapor over Bhopal. "Nobody listened," one maintenance supervisor said, and there were inadequate responses to earlier inspection reports from the American parent. It has also been disclosed that for some time the international company had been searching quietly for a buyer for its holding because of disappointing financial returns. Production was down and the plant lost more than $4 million last year.

Inspection by the Indian government was casual and possibly corrupt. The State of Madhya Pradesh did little to insure that the plant had adequate warning and evacuation plans for the work force and the community. C. Arjun Singh, the state's Chief Minister, who was responsible for the speedy arrest of Anderson and of the two top officers of U.C.I.L., cited their "criminal liability" for this "cruel and wanton negligence." Yet in 1982, after leaks had caused several accidents and one death, he rejected calls to shut down the facility, reminding petitioners of its importance to the economy. "We cannot suddenly shift or close down factories. The Bhopal plant is safe and will always be safe."

The billions of dollars in liability suits Union Carbide faces far exceed its insurance coverage, and initially there were doubts about the company's ability to avoid bankruptcy. But Anderson expressed confidence to a Congressional committee that "the victims can be fairly and equitably compensated without a material adverse effect on the financial condition of Union Carbide Corporation." The company had no intention of seeking the protection of Federal bankruptcy laws, as the Manville Corporation had done after it was inundated by lawsuits from victims of asbestos poisoning. At a meeting with investment analysts shortly after the news came from India, and in a subsequent letter to stockholders, officials announced that the quarterly dividend was safe.

Net income for fiscal 1984 was $323 million, up from $79 million the previous year, when Union Carbide was covering the costs of closing some of its petrochemical facilities. Earnings per share were $4.59, up from $1.13. The beleaguered company has maneuvered to reach settlements or to have the suits tried in Indian courts, where lifetime earnings and hence compensation would be estimated much lower than they would be in the United States. Obviously no sum will compensate for the lost lives, and neither India nor the United States has laws for holding corporations and governments accountable for shattered families, despoiled resources and ravaged communities.

During the early 1970s, Union Carbide's lack of concern about the environment earned it a reputation for being indifferent to public opinion. Since the accident, *Business Week* has awarded Anderson high marks as a business diplomat for his courage in promptly flying to the scene to gather facts, arrange relief and head off lawsuits. There, in a sequence worthy of Brecht, after his arrest and speedy release on bail, he pledged financial aid and offered to convert the company's modern guest house, in which he had been detained, into an orphanage.

Capitalism rewards corporations not for taking risks but for shifting them. The social costs of pesticide production have been transferred beyond corporate fences, beyond national boundaries, beyond the lifetime of executives and stockholders. What economists call externalities are now other people's pain.

To dwell on Bhopal as a regrettable accident is to learn little from the experience. American chemical corporations are capital intensive and employ relatively few workers; overall, their safety records are considered good compared with many other industries. Union Carbide has introduced new safety mechanisms and organizational procedures in Institute and undoubtedly will in Bhopal, should that plant ever reopen. The company has considerable experience and a cash stake in an efficient operation. And where governmental agencies have responsibility for reviewing these precautions, there will be new vigilance, sharpened by an awareness that they may be under the scrutiny of a morally aroused public.

'Normal' Accidents

Large questions about the limits of technology remain. Intervening in the natural order with only partial understanding of relationships and consequences is always a chancy business. Too often we trust untested processes which reveal their flaws only when the casualties come in. The Bhopal plant's operating manual contains a brief and not very helpful discussion of how to deal with major leaks which concludes, "We will learn more and more as we gain actual experience." Public health experts admit they have done little research on many of the chemicals involved in making pesticides, including methyl isocyanate.

The extremely adverse effects of much of the normal usage and handling of chemicals seldom command front pages, at least not until their cumulative impact becomes impossible to ignore. The spectacular breakup of a supertanker is featured news; prior understanding of the profit considerations shaping its construction and performance would remove the element of surprise. Floating oil slicks, the increasing industrial pollution of the ocean and the daily practices of tankers along major shipping lanes are not considered news. Giant irrigation projects, including the Aswan Dam on the Nile and those in California's Central Valley, are cited as triumphs of energetic civilizations because of the magnificent increases in arable land and yields. There is less discussion of how they waterlog the soil or how the heavy salts deposited on the surface ultimately will threaten productivity, unless complex and costly draining is introduced.

Some areas of technology, like nuclear power and recombinant DNA experiments, are attracting public attention because of their high potential for disaster. This despite assurances from many reputable scientists that those frontier research areas, although certainly not accident proof, are expertly controlled. As Charles Perrow points out in his 1984 book *Normal Accidents*, the public's gut fear of catastrophe should be heeded. His study offers an illuminating framework for understanding what happened at Bhopal. When potentially toxic or explosive raw materials are chemically transformed (what Lewis Mumford calls the resynthesis of nature), the risks are great. In production systems involving a relatively loose coupling of stages, each of which has the space for its own process to unfold and to incorporate shocks, engineers are able to isolate the breakdown of the component parts. The elements of an assembly line may be loosely or tightly linked, but since only linear reactions take place, it is relatively easy to pinpoint difficulty and close down the line or temporarily bypass the trouble spot. These systems, Perrow writes, tend to have preventable or manageable accidents. In contrast, complex technological systems, with their tightly coupled units and feedback loops, have baffling and not immediately comprehensible interactions occurring in a not necessarily predictable sequence. Multiples of sometime small failures, making unexpected connections and moving along unplanned or hidden paths, may set off a large and catastrophic accident, leaving the managers uncertain about how or where to intervene. (In chemical plants, such reactions are almost instantaneous.) Warnings can get swamped by a medley of signals "that fit our expectations, and thus can be discounted as 'noise' in the system," Perrow writes. And, he asks, what does one do when, as happens quite frequently, "warning systems do not warn us that they can no longer warn us?"

The conventional explanations presented after Bhopal and other disasters, blaming design or operator failure, may be inadequate and deceptive, as is the rationalization that no system is perfect. The trouble certainly lies not in Indian genes but in Western industrial systems. Hence, accidents may be ''normal,'' and we may not always learn enough from them to avoid future ones—indeed, nuclear power accidents can be expected to increase. Many mishaps have been concealed from the public by governments and corporations. Three Mile Island came close to being a holocaust. As Perrow writes, nuclear power ''is quite new and has not been given a chance to reveal its full potential for danger.'' He concludes that because the risks outweigh the benefits, we should shut down all nuclear power plants.

Does that analysis apply to pesticide plants? Surely they can be made safer. There are less hazardous (if, perhaps, less profitable) chemical substitutes for MIC, and there are also alternatives to storing large amounts of unstable chemicals, as was done at the Bhopal plant. Given the tightly coupled nature of the petrochemical production process, however, Perrow's argument that systems accidents are inevitable is compelling.

The search for alternative technological and organizational systems and safeguards in pesticide manufacture will continue, but the wisdom of producing and using such chemicals has yet to be addressed. A pest-free agricultural abundance is an attractive prospect but not if it entails making the world ecologically less stable and depleting fossil fuels to produce the pesticides.

The continued use of complex systems and the related search to make them fail-safe, as well as the acceptance of accidents as fate, will increase the centralization of bureaucratic controls and the dependence on distant offices. Computers encourage the assumption that the radius of effective control can be extended bit by bit until technological and organizational breakdowns are eliminated.

Yet complex organizations may generate more error rather than less. And, as Perrow suggests, individuals on the scene in decentralized operations are more likely to anticipate errors and correct them if they occur. Certainly the Bhopal story has something to add here, given the workers' uneasiness about conditions in the plant and the union's warnings to management and the state government about the possibility of disaster. On March 20, several weeks before the Indian government brought suit against Union Carbide in a United States Federal court on behalf of the victims, the company released a study by a team of scientists and engineers which found that ''this incident was the result of a unique combination of unusual events.'' The ''events and circumstances'' of what went wrong at Bhopal, explained Anderson, ''were not in compliance with standard operating procedures.'' But safety was the responsibility of the Indian personnel. It was ''a local issue.'' Anderson added that while it disturbed him tremendously ''that any Union Carbide plant could have operated with such total disregard for procedures . . . you can't run a . . . $10 billion corporation all out of Danbury. You can't be there day in and day out, week in and week out.'' Nevertheless, ''the appropriate people'' at Union Carbide ''should have known.'' In contrast, the company said, the Institute plant was well run and very safe. Indeed it has been made safer: ''a Bhopal-type situation is inconceivable.''

Responsibility is so often blurred in big organizations that its precise locus is concealed from the rulers as well as the ruled. Nevertheless, those in corporate, political and military authority in the United States are driven to transcend all known limits to attain the ultimate pesticide, the ultimate industrial process for production and profits, the ultimate weapons and the ultimate defense systems against an adversary who only seeks the same. The objective is effective control; the consequence is authoritarian madness.

In reviewing what went wrong at Bhopal, industrial experts have placed human errors caused by carelessness, ignorance, confusion and fright high on the list. Although the larger issue of democratic accountability appears uncomfortably ideological to the business world, the need for disciplined, predictable human behavior does not. ''You can design the best system,'' the technical director of the Chemical Manufacturers Association contended, ''but when you deal with people you can create a problem.'' To others, speculating whether human beings are becoming obsolete in industrial development is academic—particularly in populous countries like India. The heart of the matter is not careful training or automation. It is assumed that workers from traditional agricultural societies can be taught to perform specific tasks, but because of their lack of sufficient experience with industrialization, they are considered incapable of coping with breakdowns. As an official of the United Nations Environment Program explained, in an unfortunate choice of words, ''They have not internalized the technological culture.''

At the same time that experts were crafting explanations in the United States, survivors in Bhopal were still burying the dead and trying to put their broken lives back together. When the alarm had sounded on the day of the accident, some of them had raced from their homes to help put out what they thought was a fire. That was the innocence of their former lives. They now know that Union Carbide India Ltd. was not producing medicine for the soil or for humans.

The Faustian Dream of Science

The issue Bhopal presents is not technology versus no technology. But technology is never neutral; its use always has consequences. The engineering mentality assumes that technological problems will be solved by more technology and its improved administration, that we can bank on what conservative philosopher Herman Kahn viewed as ''the curative possibilities inherent in technological and economic progress.''

This Faustian faith in the ultimate technological fix invokes the ideals of scientific inquiry, imaginative and free-spirited, beholden only to the disciplined search for truth. ''What science has to teach us,'' Jacob Bronowski wrote some thirty years ago, defending its contribution even amid the ruins of Nagasaki, ''is not its techniques but its spirit: the irresistible need to explore.'' Dispassionate inquiry, what Veblen called idle curiosity, is an indispensable element of creative work, and it can enhance the lives of all. As scientists expand our knowledge of the behavior of microorganisms in the soil, we may discover that there are peaceful alternatives to the pesticidal violence against nature that erupted at Bhopal to become violence against humans.

But science is also deeply embedded in society. Public and private funding tends to go to proposals that accord with prevailing systems of belief and power. The commercial potential of herbicides and pesticides made them more attractive than natural alternatives like microorganisms that prey on unwanted weeds and insects. Chemicals have the added attraction of military utility. That preference may shift with the heightened interest in biological warfare and the prospects for big profits from bioengineering. The celebration of applied research downplays how heavily, and often secretly, science draws on our national resources in support of often morally indefensible goals of the state and of corporate empires. A science pledged to technology is indifferent to the environment within which it functions, whether in Bhopal or Institute. Promising "more" for all of us, it forestalls moves toward a modicum of economic justice for each of us.

Fundamental science should be cherished; its open deliberations, like those of a free society, are humankind's first defense against the tyranny of established ignorance. But people must have the right to know what hazards science has created. They didn't at Séveso, at Three Mile Island, at Love Canal. The immediate consequence of not knowing was that local health and fire departments could not prepare for the "unlikely" or know what to do when the "impossible" happened, as at Bhopal. Technological decisions that will affect communities should first be debated by the people who live there. If we are to be participating citizens rather than enthralled consumers with whom experts play Russian roulette, we cannot permit petrochemical companies to conceal information behind the claim of "proprietary rights," akin to the government's claim of "national security."

Gandhi's Truth

The tragedy of Bhopal challenges us to ask basic questions: Technology for what ends, with what limits, susceptible to what constraints and to whose controls? The temptation to do things because they can be done and are profitable must be countered by a humbler commitment to understand the needs of mankind and then ask what might be helpful. An appreciation of the richness and pride of the world's many cultures, and the right of all people to worthwhile employment and to wholesome food, the end of gross inequalities of opportunity and power, a firm foundation for peaceful relations with nature and one's fellow human beings, the right of coming generations to find a plentiful and unravaged earth on which they can live in freedom— these are among the more broadly accepted goals for a responsible technology.

Gandhi posed moral and political concerns when appraising the likely impact of industrialization on daily life. One need not accept his complete philosophy, including the sometimes blanket condemnation of machinery, to comprehend his fears that his country would embrace technology indiscriminately. He imagined Indian society as an association of independent villages, each a democratic polis of about 1,000 citizens, whose economic and cultural resources would be utilized along peaceful, cooperative principles. He believed that a healthy rural India could better withstand a foreign invasion than an urban one with huge factories, enslaved mill hands, a top-heavy central government and a highly equipped professional army.

He feared dependence on foreign economic forces whose control of the industrial process would give them control of all social processes. He related artificial chemical fertilizers to a desire for quick returns, heedless of eventual soil exhaustion, and he saw that pesticide use served absentee owners interested in the profits from shipping crops long distances. His answer again was regional self-sufficiency. Heavy machinery was acceptable where human effort was inadequate for the task, but such machinery had to be controlled by government for the public good, lest it enrich the few and displace the many. If Gandhi's plan appears to condemn millions to drudgery, one must remember that his focus was on the enforced idleness of the bulk of the population, who lived on the border of starvation.

Following independence, India's leaders knew that their socialist model required planned economic development and rapid mechanization. They wanted this planning to be democratic and to respect community values derived from tradition and Gandhi's political vision. With a series of five-year plans, India made sizable strides in its industrial revolution. The task was so overwhelming, however, that the planners became frustrated and felt they were not making sufficient impact on the squalor in which the masses, rural and now also urban, lived. Nor had they succeeded in radically altering the structure of the economy. They increasingly wanted capital and technology from overseas, and they wanted to cut down on the exchange drain of imports. But the arrangements were often unfavorable to India, especially when corporations preferred to guard their technical know-how.

The pesticide plant in Bhopal thus did not spring up as a weed from the soil. Nor was it washed up on the shores of India by chance. Although the terms have yet to be disclosed fully, it was a product of an agreement between a government hungry for "advanced" technology and a corporation looking overseas for markets and profits.

Lessons of Bhopal for the U.S.

In the United States the most valuable first step would be to reappraise the overextended and irresponsible aspects of the domestic political economy. Questions about technology are very much in order, despite the remarkable achievements seen in this abundant land. Americans must challenge the assumption that the marketplace is the sole arbiter of what technologies should be introduced at home and the assertion that their transfer abroad is a private affair, except perhaps when the government raises the flag of national security. Decisions on what basic technologies are needed and how and where they are to be introduced must involve people in the affected communities and workplaces. Conversely, if it is decided that the plant at Institute and its products are too dangerous and should be phased out (a concern among residents), alternative employment or income protection must be provided so that the costs of environmental moral outrage are not shifted to those dependent on the pesticide industry for their livelihood. A search for benign alternative technologies is essential. But unless we insist on technologies that do not further the concentration of industrial control, we may be introducing simply another technological fix, even if it is more desirable than those that prevail under the present business system.

Much of this effort will require public planning. To many Americans the term "planning" raises the specter of unaccountable bureaucrats drafting blueprints that only they can understand and apply. Yet the private sector and the military employ extensive planning. Union Carbide did in penetrating the Third World. Such private planning exercises considerable control over our lives. If technological decisions are to be dealt with democratically they must be brought into the political process, and on levels where citizens can be involved. Establishing the Bhopal plant was a political decision; only the citizens were excluded.

The tragedy gives credibility to the fear that the human race may perish by its own violent cleverness. The continued tribal thumpings of national leaders, armed with unprecedented means to engineer weapons and public assent, who demand that other nations knuckle under, does nothing to lessen such concern. Bhopal was murder, if not genocide. To mumble "Sorry" and offer cash is an intolerable response in light of the organized effort that profited from the conditions that produced the disaster. To accept the proposition that people of less technologically advanced regions, abroad and at home, are unfortunate but necessary industrial fodder so that the rest of us may progress to unlimited splendor is unconscionable. It suggests how much we have yet to learn about our common humanity, how genuine freedom may have to be shared before it can be thoroughly lived and enjoyed.

A deeper fear is that we will continue to accept such authority and its pervasive myths. The consolidation of power over nature in the name of science and service to mankind surrenders social power to technicians and their institutional masters, who have no special sensitivity to human needs and certainly no sanction to serve as guardians of humanity's future. If we concede that vast, complex and un-limited expansion is technologically inevitable and ultimately desirable, we cut ourselves off from nature, other human beings and ultimately ourselves. Accepting the image of ourselves as incompetent and powerless, we abdicate our obligation to shape history.

An alternative vision for a peaceful and productive world requires the emergence of the political will to insist that a future of unlimited technological growth, self-anointed managers and "normal" accidents is unworthy of the best in human potential and may well be unendurable. There is already vigorous resistance everywhere from people determined to live as though it mattered. One finds them in India: for example, the women of a village who linked hands to protect a stand of trees that was to be chopped down. In saving the forest from further destruction by outside timber merchants the women gave economic hope to their community. And they sparked a rural grass-roots movement called Chipko (meaning "embraced"). Green, environmental and antinuclear organizations in Europe and the United States, along with worker health, safety and economic democracy groups, are all asking that technology be brought to account. How to move from resistance to reconstruction remains the challenge.

E.F. Schumacher, who devoted much of his life to the search for technologies appropriate to satisfying work and responsible institutions, had a suggestion for beginning. Like Gandhi, he feared the potential for disaster in highly concentrated technological systems. He rejected a Keynesian model of unlimited expansionism powered by human self-ishness as a suitable path to an abundance that only then would allow the luxury of ethical considerations. The global emergence of a privileged technocracy and a permanent underclass troubled him. National planning seemed too monstrous to control, and Gandhi's village idyll was too limited to produce the diversity necessary for a good life. In terms reminiscent of Pëtr Kropotkin, Albert Einstein and Paul Goodman, he wrote: "Any third-rate engineer or researcher can increase complexity; but it takes a certain flair of real insight to make things simple again."

Whether for the production of food for all, the generation of energy from renewable sources or the peaceful and democratic governance of our communities, the struggle to retain our humanity may require nothing less than a technology bound by human-size institutions committed to the goals of a just world.

Technology and the Changing World of Work

Fred Best

Fred Best, president of Pacific Management and Research Associates (1208 Seventh Avenue, Sacramento, California 95818), has written extensively on management and human resources, economic development, and the impacts of new technologies. His books include *The Future of Work, Flexible Life Scheduling,* and *Work Sharing.* This article is excerpted from his report *The Future of Work: A View from the United States,* prepared for the Swedish Secretariat for Future Studies.

The United States and other industrial nations are now experiencing wave after wave of innovations that bring profound changes in our personal and occupational lives. At the core of these changes is the computer. More than 3 million Americans purchased home and personal computers during 1982, with that figure doubling to 6 million in 1983. If the cost of purchased or rented computer time continues to decline at its historical rate of 50% every two and one-half years, and if the complexity of utilization is reduced by "user-friendly" software, computers and allied technologies will soon be assimilated into every aspect of our lives.

The impacts of such technological change on the economy, the world of work, and our personal lives will be phenomenal. These innovations are likely to alter the nature of work activities within all economic sectors, dramatically affect the growth and location of employment opportunities, and shift the relationships between our jobs and personal lives.

Changing Skill Requirements

Up to 45% of existing U.S. jobs will be significantly altered by technological changes over the next

Computers and other technological innovations are changing the nature of work and the balance between our jobs and our personal lives. Here, an expert on the impacts of new technologies offers some long-term speculations on the future of work.

20 years, many through an upgrading of skills.

The historical trend toward mechanization is becoming increasingly sophisticated as robots and computer-coordinated operations take over routine and dangerous tasks now performed by workers. For example, the installation of robots in the United States has been growing by 30% per year, increasing from 200 in 1970 to 3,500 in 1980. Moderate estimates indicate that there will be 35,000 installed robots in America by 1990 and that applications will skyrocket during the last decade of the twentieth century.

Small computers, sophisticated sensors and servo-mechanisms, and design and control instruments that are easier to understand and use are moving us rapidly toward the "cybernetic promise" of highly integrated and flexible production systems. For example, the growing application of CAD/CAM systems (computer-assisted design/computer-assisted manufacturing) now allows industrial planners to design products on computer screens and then reformat machinery on the shop floor to produce products by centralized programming. The implications for increased productivity and product diversity are spellbinding.

Many workers will have to be reassigned to new tasks. While some of these new tasks might not require greater skill, many necessitate an understanding of new and more complex technologies. For example, General Motors Corporation predicts that 50% of its work force in the year 2000 will be categorized as skilled tradespersons (technicians, inspectors, monitors, etc.), compared with 16% in 1980. Thus, there will be a need for more highly trained personnel such as engineers, technicians, computer specialists, and managers with basic technical skills.

Technological innovations will also profoundly affect the nature of work in both office and service occupations. Just as we have moved from manual typewriters and carbon copies to memory typewriters and photocopy machines over the last few decades, newer technologies will vastly increase the efficiency and output of information processing.

Dramatic reductions in the cost of computers, the development of user-friendly software, and the availability of high-speed printers and telecommunication systems will create a fundamental shift from paper to electronics as the main medium of operation. Typewriters, file cabinets, and mail systems will increasingly be replaced by word processors, computerized data retrieval systems, and video transmissions between computer terminals.

As in the case of manufacturing

From *The Futurist*, April 1984, pp. 61-66, published by the World Future Society, 4916 St. Elmo Avenue, Bethesda, MD 20814. Reprinted by permission.

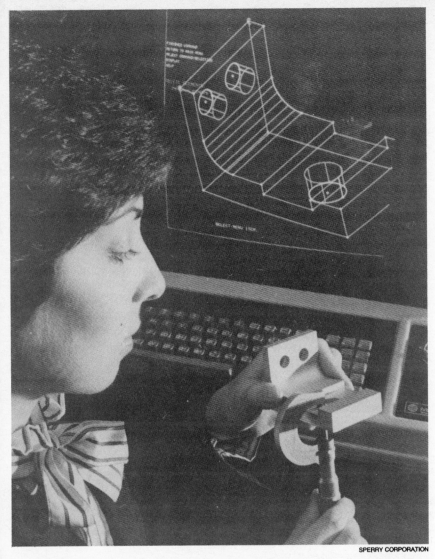

SPERRY CORPORATION

Applications analyst compares computer-generated drawing with finished bracket produced by computer-assisted design and manufacturing system. Innovations such as this CAD/CAM system are increasing demand in manufacturing sectors for computer specialists, engineers, technicians, and managers with basic technical skills.

isolated cases of worker dislocation, most experts believe that technological advances have generally fostered economic and job growth by increasing the quality and quantity of products while lowering the costs.

Because costs are lower, producers can afford to sell at lower prices, which in turn commonly causes consumers to buy more. As a result of increased demand, producers generally employ as many or more workers than before technological innovation began to increase output. When this process occurs throughout the economy, the result is economic growth, with higher real wages and an increase of employment.

Two historic examples illustrate this process. First, during the early stages of the Industrial Revolution, the introduction of the Hargreaves jenny in 1770 ultimately allowed one worker to produce as much as 200 spinners could without the jenny. Yet employment in Britain's textile industry increased from less than 100,000 in 1770 to about 350,000 in 1800 because productivity allowed major reductions in price, leading to even more dramatic increases in market demand for textiles.

A second example is the introduction of the assembly line by Henry Ford. As a result of this combination of machinery and industrial organization, it took 56% fewer hours to produce the average car in 1920 than it did in 1910, leading to a 62% reduction in the real dollar price of an automobile. Consumers who previously could not afford a car began to make purchases, sales increased tenfold, and Ford employment rose from 37,000 to 206,000 in just 10 years. Workers may have been shifted to new assignments, but there was no overall loss of jobs.

From the standpoint of preserving and creating jobs, there appear to be few alternatives to technological innovation. While these changes are likely to cause considerable displacement and reassignment of workers, failure to modernize will cause affected industries to lose pace with national and international competition and

and material processing, many jobs will become unnecessary. Demand will gradually disappear for mail deliverers, file clerks, stenographers, and other workers. Familiarity and skill with computers will become essential to all office workers, from manager to secretary.

Displacement and Realignment

National Cash Register reduced its U.S. work force from 37,000 to 18,000 between 1970 and 1975 because of productivity gains from using microelectronic rather than mechanical parts. The General Motors plant in Lordstown, Ohio, reduced its work force by 10%

after increasing productivity 20% through the introduction of welding robots. In Providence, Rhode Island, the *Journal Bulletin* cut its printing staff from 242 workers in 1970 to 98 in 1978 as a result of new typesetting technology. These examples underscore the fact that workers have indeed been displaced by technology; however, the question remains as to how extensive such displacement will be in coming years.

Concern over job loss due to the higher productivity of machines has historical roots, beginning with Luddite resistance to industrial mechanization in early-nineteenth-century England. However, despite

Work in a High-Tech Future

The proportion of American workers involved in agriculture and manufacturing declined from 83% to 30% between 1860 and 1980, while services expanded proportionately. Recent trends indicate that this historical transformation will continue, if not accelerate. In the medium-range future, this will not mean an *absolute* decline of jobs in agriculture and manufacturing sectors, but a *relative* decline as the size of the work force increases. However, as advanced technology is applied to heavy industry during the last decades of the twentieth century, some analysts speculate that the proportion of the work force employed in manufacturing will gradually decline to about 3% over the next 50 years.

The relative decline of employment in manufacturing and agriculture does not indicate that they will become less important to our economy; rather, these sectors will produce more with fewer workers. Just as the number of persons fed by the average American farmer increased from 9 to 25 between 1940 and 1962, advances in technology and management will allow workers in manufacturing and other sectors to produce far more per hour of labor.

California, a recognized center of technological innovation, exhibited shifts in the distribution of its work force that parallel national trends. Many forecasters speculate that the large and growing proportion of businesses involved in the development and production of high-technology products within California will foster a rate of change that is faster than that seen nationally. To provide an overview, the number of jobs within the United States is projected to increase 15.9%, from 103 million to 119 million, between 1981 and 1990; the number of jobs in California will increase some 24.9%, from 11 million to 14 million.

Projections to 1985 from the California Employment Development Department indicate considerable variation of job growth among different occupations. These forecasts, which roughly parallel those for the nation, indicate a greater than average growth rate for most technical occupations, as well as skilled craft and operative positions. However, many observers feel that these forecasts are conservative due to the growth of California's high-tech industries and the demand for highly skilled labor.

As in the past, shifts in the skills required for employment will be due primarily to technological change. The high-technology sectors will increasingly account for new jobs created in the coming decades and will change the skills required throughout the entire economy.

These high-technology industries include computers, communication equipment, instruments, electronic components, and computer services. The aerospace industry is occasionally included in the high-tech category, as are a variety of fledgling enterprises such as energy innovations, biotechnology, robotics, chemicals, new materials, selected medical products, and home entertainment equipment.

Although high technology now employs a relatively small proportion of the total work force, job growth within these sectors has been phenomenal. Between 1970 and 1980, job growth for the five core high-tech industries within California was 80.3%, compared with 38.8% for the state work force as a whole. During the 1980s, job growth for these same industries is projected to be 47.6%, compared with 24.9% for the entire state economy. Moderate projections indicate that the number of California jobs in these core high-tech industries will increase from 591,795 to 726,700 between 1980 and 1990.

The aerospace industry is expected to add at least 24,400 new jobs (possibly more due to defense contracts) to the California economy during the 1980s, and fledgling high-tech enterprises are likely to add another 10,000 jobs during the same period. Consolidation of all high-tech related industrial growth suggests that these sectors will account for approximately 268,900 new jobs during the next decade. To put these figures into historical perspective, these high-tech industries and enterprises directly created 6.9% of overall California job growth during the 1970s and are expected to account for 9.7% during the 1980s. Some studies have forecast even greater growth.

These high-tech sectors will require workers with more extensive and diverse training than the work force in general. Engineers, scientists, technicians, and computer specialists, representing 5.7% of the total California work force, will make up about 28.7% of the employees in the state's five core high-tech industries by 1990.

The growth of California's high-technology industries will foster an increasing demand for technical, scientific, and skilled workers. Demand for computer specialists will increase 106% among the five core high-tech industries between 1980 and 1990. The demand for technicians will increase by about 46% and for qualified assemblers and operatives by about 30% over the same period.

As a result, high-technology industries will probably need 19,000 additional technicians, 21,000 additional skilled craft persons, and 44,000 more qualified assemblers and operatives by 1990. Correspondingly, there will be increased demand for managers, clerical workers, and other support personnel who are familiar with basic technical issues.

—Fred Best

The Evolution of Work

The social, institutional, and human roles associated with work have changed dramatically as human civilization has evolved. The work of antiquity was essentially direct physical toil, required for immediate survival. For primitive peoples, "work" and "leisure" were almost completely integrated. As civilization developed, work and nonwork activities continued to be integrated within families and tribes.

With the emergence of agriculture, economic surpluses, and culturally transferable knowledge, work became easier and more distinct as a social activity. Specialization and individual roles and responsibilities began to emerge as key elements of human existence.

As economic surplus, development of productive tools, and specialization continued to grow, the goals and conditions of work continued to change. Work became increasingly oriented toward the improvement of the human condition rather than bare survival. The resulting surpluses gave rise to increasingly productive tools, and ultimately machinery, which correspondingly allowed and required further refinement of skills and increased specialization.

While work dominated life, the concept of "leisure" as distinct from "work" began to crystallize. Industrial society was a natural outgrowth of these trends. As machinery became increasingly important and sophisticated, work became progressively specialized and oriented toward the use of tools and capital within the context of complex human organizations.

Organizational interdependence and division of labor gave rise to the ultimate predominance of employment. While productive human activity continued to be performed outside the context of employment, work became commonly viewed as an activity performed by "holding a job."

These dramatic shifts have caused a near inversion of the concepts of "work" and "leisure." As defined by classical philosophers, leisure was restricted to reflection and the fine arts; it was commonly viewed as nonmanual activities within preindustrial societies. Commerce, science, politics, writing, and all arts came to be viewed as the freely chosen "leisurely" pursuits of the elites.

Today, as progressively larger proportions of the work forces in advanced industrial societies become employed in "white-collar" jobs doing "knowledge work," the work activities of today are increasingly like the "leisure" activities of the past. While contemporary work conditions are commonly far from utopian, today's jobs tend to require more autonomy, creativity, freedom of expression, and skill than that required during the pre-industrial and early industrial eras.

While the work of the foreseeable future is likely to resemble much of what we do today, historical perspective suggests the importance of keeping an open mind to the possibility of radical changes in the medium- and long-range future. Just as the all-encompassing struggle for physical survival that commonly epitomized primitive humanity has little resemblance to "jobholding" within the offices of today, the nature of work in the future may take on new dimensions that we can scarcely perceive.

—Fred Best

ultimately cause even greater loss of employment and economic growth.

Technology and Non-Job Work

There are increasing signs that technological change may also alter the balance between job activities and our personal lives. If we define work as "productive human activity," it is clear that work has never been confined to "holding a job." There have always been people who are self-employed, who build their own houses, raise children, provide voluntary social services, and perform countless other productive actions outside the context of employment. The balance of productive activity inside and outside the workplace has undergone many changes in recent years and will probably change considerably in the future.

Just as the development of heavy machinery drew work out of the home and into factories and offices during the Industrial Revolution, new technologies may cause households and neighborhood groups to become more self-sustaining and to abandon institutional settings for many productive activities. Harbingers of such realignments are suggested by the emerging uses of many new technologies:

• **Home and personal computers.** The potential of home and personal computers, which didn't exist 10 years ago but now are an increasingly common new "home appliance," has scarcely been explored. This technology, which is greatly expanding in power and diminishing in price, is already being used for home entertainment centers, long-distance communication and mail systems, cookbooks, medical advisors, high-speed typewriters, portable offices, family business and tax filing systems, art and graphics devices, educational tutors, library reference services, financial planning, and control of other household appliances. Countless new uses, many of which are integrated with other new technologies, are being developed daily.

• **Video recorders.** Like home

and personal computers, video recorders and disc players have emerged from nowhere in the course of only a few years. As archives of television and motion picture entertainment are rapidly transferred to video tapes and discs, a progressively larger portion of entertainment is likely to be pulled back into the home. The use of video recorders as substitutes for home movie cameras also affects the entire film development and processing industry.

• **Decentralized energy production and conservation.** A variety of new, improved, and rediscovered technologies are being developed as alternatives to centralized energy sources. Photovoltaics, solar heating, windmill generation, a variety of conservation measures, and other energy-related technologies are replacing or reducing dependence on central energy sources. These devices are likely to become more attractive as prices decline and the costs of central energy increase.

• **Decentralized medical care.** A number of affordable devices and services are being developed that provide patient-utilized and home-based medical care. For example, new technologies make it both desirable and less expensive to undertake sophisticated "do-it-yourself" medical treatments such as kidney dialysis, cancer chemotherapy, and intravenous feeding.

• **Decentralized and interactive communication systems.** Home-linked and controlled communication technologies are being developed that greatly expand the choice of information and provide options for interaction and local control. Cable and satellite television greatly enhance viewer choice, provide the potential for two-way communication, and open the option of local and neighborhood stations. Teleconferencing expands the concept of conference calls on the telephone to include visual communication. Satellite and microwave transmission greatly reduce the cost and difficulty of long-distance communication. When these communication systems are used with other technologies such as personal computers, work tasks that formerly had to be located and coordinated

COURTESY OF DIGITAL EQUIPMENT CORPORATION

Computer terminal and telephone allow office work to be done at home. Individuals can move work activities out of formal organizations and create new balances between their jobs and personal lives.

at a central location can be decentralized.

While the ultimate impact of these and other technologies is uncertain, their utilization will dramatically change the activities and skill required for work. They might significantly alter the timing, location, and organizational context of work in the future. These same technologies will increase self-sufficiency, open new options for individual business ventures, and generally reduce the need for "holding a job."

An Exploratory Scenario: Toward a Home-Based Economy?

Many novel developments are emerging that might make it desirable, efficient, and necessary to reduce traditional jobholding as the focus of "purposeful and pro-

ductive human activity." High unemployment and growing job instability suggest the need for individuals to find backup modes of activity that are economically and psychologically rewarding.

The emergence of relatively inexpensive and user-friendly technologies may make it economically efficient and personally rewarding to move both job and non-job work activities out of formal work organizations. Greater flexibility in work arrangements could allow many individuals and groups to meet personal and economic needs through a better balance of job-linked work and other productive efforts.

There are already countless jobholders with computer-based home businesses and flexible worktime and workplace arrangements that allow them to perform job responsibilities without having to be "at work" in the usual sense of the term.

If such conditions become more prevalent, the average worker of tomorrow might work "full time" for six or seven years within a traditional work environment. Then, in order to better handle family responsibilities, the worker might arrange to perform most job responsibilities at home using information technologies. He or she might then reduce worktime given to employment and develop an auxiliary business enterprise, perhaps to increase home-based self-sufficiency. Ultimately, the worker might return to work on a part-time or part-year basis while retraining for new skills.

Without doubt, such arrangements would pose some costs and dangers to individuals, employers, and the economy. For example, the worker might worry about being able to return to suitable employment after an extended period away from an organization. Organizations might have trouble de-emphasizing and re-emphasizing the roles of individual workers. There might also be concern with the loss of social-professional networks, problems of maintaining income during de-emphasis of employment, and discontinuance or reduction of fringe benefits.

Certainly such a system would entail individual responsibility, initiative, and accountability. However, more people might be willing to confront the costs and dangers if recurrent unemployment and job insecurity make it necessary, if individual preferences for more autonomy within work settings increase, and if institutional and social policies provide the necessary options and resources.

While new balances between household- and employment-

Couple tries out program on home computer. About 6 million Americans bought home and personal computers in 1983—twice as many as the year before. The impact of computers and other new technologies will be felt in every aspect of our personal and working lives, says author Best.

based economies may emerge primarily via individual initiative, they could be encouraged by a number of institutional and social policies. Policies that might support such developments include:

• Tax incentives to defer use of earnings for utilization during periods of de-emphasized employment.

• Guaranteed credit and loans.

• Individually vested retraining vouchers.

• Guidelines for job-return rights.

• Subsidies and tax incentives for the purchase and use of home-based technologies.

• Options for flexible worktime arrangements.

• Financial incentives to encourage use of homes as offices and to reduce job-related travel.

• Standardization of selected information technologies.

• Options for selecting and continuing fringe benefits during de-emphasized employment.

• Options for using income maintenance payments to start

small business enterprises.

The costs of such policies are not likely to be undertaken unless private and public expenditures for other policies such as income maintenance, retraining, public transportation, public service employment, and general social services are reduced. Clearly, the political consensus for such a tradeoff is not likely to emerge until a significant number of individuals have developed nontraditional home-job work patterns on their own.

Although jobholding will probably continue as the prevalent pattern of work for the immediate future, ongoing transitional instability, shifting human preferences toward work, and new technologies may foster continued growth of hybrid balances between job and household activities. We can only speculate on whether such patterns will develop into a major trend or prevalent pattern; however, private and public policy makers must begin now to think about the implications, costs, and benefits.

Copernican Politics

It's Time to Ask Heretical Questions

We can't find solutions to today's problems because we're not asking the right questions, says the governor of Colorado.

Richard D. Lamm

Richard D. Lamm is in his third term as governor of Colorado. He co-authored *The Angry West* (Houghton Mifflin, 1982, $13.95), which is available from the World Future Society Book Service (pre-payment required; please include $1.50 for postage and handling). Lamm's earlier article on "Why the U.S. Closed Its Borders" appeared in the December 1982 issue of THE FUTURIST. His address is Executive Chambers, 136 State Capitol, Denver, Colorado 80203.

Copernicus made his lasting contribution to history by asking the right question: "Instead of the sun going around the world, could the world go around the sun?"

It was a heretical question but an indispensable one.

Clearly, if one is to discover the correct answer, one must start with the right question. But solutions are often obscured by existing doctrines. As *New York Times* columnist James Reston observes, "The history of mankind is strewn with habits, creeds and dogmas that were essential to one age and disastrous in another."

In the United States today, our problems are clearly outrunning our solutions: We have chronic unemployment, political stalemate, economic stagnation, and social unrest. Contributing to this turmoil is the lack of agreement on the correct questions—let alone the solutions. How we describe the situation often dictates the answer.

Is the public policy glass half empty or half full? Is the energy crisis a matter of inadequate supply or is it a matter of excessive demand? Are immigrants an asset as they always have been or have they become a liability? Do we best reduce our international vulnerability through foreign policy or through domestic policy? Should we continue our massive spending for "illness care" or should we invest in health promotion?

How many of our once essential dogmas are still valid and how many are now disastrous? We need to ask some hard Copernican questions, remembering T.H. Huxley's admonition that every important truth begins as heresy.

Is our political system equal to the problems of the twenty-first century?

We now have our fifth paralyzed presidency. The voters, ever hopeful, elected Presidents Johnson, Nixon, Carter, and Reagan with the expectation that they could give us leadership, prosperity, and peace. Each of these men devoutly believed he could solve America's problems and each clearly failed.

There has not been a happy presidency since Dwight Eisenhower. Each successive administration has ended in defeat or disaster. Given the national and international pressures, one must ask, "Can anyone run the country?"

We ask fragile people to do an impossible job without adequate tools or institutions and then complain when they don't solve our country's problems. Political parties are in a similar position.

Has the question become not *which* political party has the answers to today's problems, but does *either* of them?

Can politicians of either persuasion resist the special interests who come bearing campaign contributions? Can the new wave of Democrats withstand an attack from the old wave when they talk, as they must, about "productivity" and "capital formation"? Can enlightened labor leaders support politicians who talk, as they must, about corporate earnings going into plant modernization instead of wages and benefits? Can the Republican politicians talk freely, as they must, about corporate management's excesses and weaknesses? Can any president or either political party meet the expectations they themselves have built up in the public?

 ## Are we entering the world of the static economic pie?

Almost imperceptibly, the U.S. economy has faltered and begun sliding backward. Family income was actually less in 1980 than it was in 1973. All wage increases and benefits since 1975 have been wiped out by inflation, and in 1980 the average American saw a 5.5% drop in real income. In 1982, the national economy registered a 1.7% negative growth rate. The economic pie, sad but true, is shrinking.

To divide a static pie we have to take from one sector to give to another, instead of distributing the "growth dividend" that has been the historical solution to our problems. Without a growth dividend, we politicians can't fulfill our hopes and promises of a better life for all.

"But," you will say, "what's to prevent the good old days from returning and the pie from growing again?" Nothing could be better—and as a politician I long for a return of those days. But it is unlikely to happen.

The good old days of 5% economic growth could never last. No economy in world history has ever sustained anything like that increase in growth and never could. Five percent economic growth, in real terms, for 100 years, would give us an economy producing 131 times the volume of goods and services produced in 1982.

America's economy has undergone a dramatic structural change. In contrast, the growth of the Gross National Product (GNP) per employed worker has only been 0.1% per year since 1973. At that rate, the output per worker would take 700 years to double and produce a traditional growth dividend.

We begin to see why Giscard d'Estaing said, shortly before leaving office as president of France, that "all modern day curves lead to disaster." A new world of international competition has shaken our economy. It is going to take more than an upturn in the economic cycle to cure our problems:

- In 1965, General Motors earned twice as much as the 30 largest German and the 30 largest Japanese industrial companies combined. In 1980, General Motors reported a loss while virtually all of the Japanese and German companies prospered.
- In 1965, American industrial companies, with sales of over $1 billion, represented 70% of all such companies in the world. By 1980, our share had fallen to 40%.
- In 1970, the American GNP represented 30% of the total world GNP. By 1980, our share had fallen to approximately 20%.

While it is my fervent hope that America's economy will grow again, it is my prediction that at least in the 1980s it will not grow substantially. We must get over the idea that God is an American who especially watches out for us and recognize that our economy is in deep trouble.

The static pie will require a series of hard decisions. For virtually the first time, we will be unable to initiate new programs funded by our growth dividend. We will, instead, be forced to allocate scarcity as we rob the mass transit programs in St. Petersburg to pay the heating bills of the elderly in St. Paul.

If we are condemned to live, at least temporarily, in a no-growth or slow-growth economy, how will that affect our political, social, and economic institutions? The public, the special interests, and the political parties have formed platforms, goals, and agendas based on an economic system that ranked first in the world among industrial market economies in per capita GNP. It now ranks ninth.

Our political grasp formed in the optimism of the 1960s while our reach is confined by the realities of the 1980s. Yesterday's luxuries have become today's necessities and yesterday's hopes the expectations of tomorrow. But the political system cannot deliver all the promises and expectations that have been made and built up over the years.

Our chief political question of the 1980s will have to be "How do we allocate resources more efficiently and fairly?" I believe that if we, like Copernicus, ask the heretical questions, we can devise a better system.

 ## Can society afford what medical technology can invent?

Medical costs already account for 9.4% of the GNP and are growing astronomically—at about twice the rate of inflation.

On top of the already skyrocketing medical costs, the "Barney Clark syndrome" is developing. Thirty-four thousand people per year will need the artificial heart when it is perfected, at a cost of at least $3 billion to a health-care system already out of control. The Medicaid-funded Kidney Dialysis Program cost $150 million the first year (1976). It is already up to $2 billion. The costs of hip-replacement surgery will soon be an estimated $1 billion annually—borne mostly by federal taxpayers in the form of Medicare. Clearly, medical science can invent more technology than society can pay for.

What happens if the coronary bypass graft operations are shown to be effective for all patients with coronary artery disease? Or if an artificial pancreas now being investigated is developed and made available to the four million Americans with diabetes? How much of our resources would that take?

Does increased spending on health care bring increased health?

The cost of the health-care system has increased dramatically—threatening federal, state, local, and individual budgets. Yet we seldom ask: Is it really worth it?

We have been led to believe that spending money on the health-care system leads inextricably to better national health, when, in fact, our massive spending really supports an "illness care" system that plays a small role in our national health.

The U.S. Surgeon General states clearly that one's life-style and environment are the main determinants of health: "Perhaps as much as half of all U.S. mortality in 1976 was due to unhealthy behavior or lifestyle; 20% to environmental factors; 10% to human biological factors; and only 20% to inadequate health care."

If the best medical care in the United States were available to everyone, it would only increase the life expectancy by about three years. But if everyone were to eat sensibly, stop smoking, and exercise moderately, life expectancy would increase by 11 years.

We must challenge the illusion that better health is for sale and that if we spend enough on doctors and hospitals it will be available. In a world of limited resources, it would seem more reasonable to invest a higher proportion of our dollars in health promotion, education, and motivation.

Can we continue to be so generous to the elderly?

The facts are simple and well known. In 1900, 4% of the population was over 65; today 11% is over 65; by the

U.S. DEPARTMENT OF ENERGY

Cars line up in a typical bumper-to-bumper freeway scene. The United States uses 30,000 gallons of petroleum every second, with one-ninth of that going to fuel automobiles. America's dependence on oil puts the country in a vulnerable position. Conservation efforts that lessen reliance on unstable, volatile oil producers offer more security than military might, says author Lamm.

year 2000, about 17% will be over 65. The "old-old" category (75 and over) is rising at almost twice the rate of the "young-old" (65-74). Some 1,500 Americans turn 65 every day. We have become a four-generation society.

In fiscal 1981, the elderly got one dollar in four in the federal government's budget—up 30% from 1979 and growing.

The pension system in America is a chain letter to the future, with ominous implications. Social Security has an unfunded liability of anywhere from one to four trillion dollars—far more than the national debt.

Military pensions last forever and are accelerating. Last year, we still had 158 widows and needy children of Civil War veterans on the pension roles. We may be paying veterans of the Vietnam War and their dependents until the year 2097. Veterans over 65 receive five times as much health care as those under 65, and by the mid-1990s the number of elderly veterans drawing public services will have *tripled.*

Pensions and medical costs of the elderly are a fiscal time bomb ticking away in the heart of our federal budget. As the number of the elderly increases, the question must change from "Have we done enough?" to "Have we done too much for the elderly?"

Are energy shortages a matter of inadequate supply—or excessive demand?

America has always solved shortages by increasing the supplies. Pushed by our belief in the infinite and boundless frontier, we move to solve the energy problem as we have solved so many others: We roll up our sleeves, use our Yankee ingenuity, call upon our national heritage, push aside the doubters, and drill, mine, produce, and refine. Former Energy Secretary James Edwards argues that the way to solve the nation's energy problems is to "produce, produce, produce." What is the first joint letter Democrats in Congress sent to President Reagan? Save the synfuels program!

Clearly, the American character defines shortages as a matter of inadequate supply. Yet increasingly and virtually unanimously, thoughtful studies point out that the energy crisis is largely a matter of excessive demand.

It is heretical but important to ask, "Are we not still doing exactly the opposite of what our nation really needs?" As energy expert Amory Lovins observed, "Like someone who cannot fill a bathtub because the hot water keeps running out, we need not a bigger water heater but a plug."

Supply-side approaches have not produced solutions. Despite massive drilling, oil production is static; natural gas and coal production is up, but not dramatically. America's energy dependence has eased not because we have produced more but because we are consuming less.

Conservation is a clear energy source. Growth in the use of electricity has dropped from approximately 8% per year to 2%. Energy conservation has a proven record: In 1980, the United States reduced its consumption of energy below the 1979 figure by an amount equal to the entire output of the nation's 74 nuclear plants.

America, some say, wastes more energy every year than is used by two-thirds of the world's population. One must ask if more energy self-sufficiency is found in the frugal use of present supplies or in oil shale. It is a trillion-dollar question.

 ## Can we protect our resource supplies or must we reduce our demands?

The energy and resource crisis is not only a matter of supply but a matter of availability in a world where the geopolitical situation is changing rapidly. Two-fifths of America's oil imports are highly susceptible to a cutoff by revolution, terrorism, or embargo.

Studies show that a stoppage of Middle East oil would cause a 10-20% drop in the GNP—the magnitude of the Great Depression. In Japan and parts of Europe it would be twice as bad.

Energy economist Walter Levy points out the foolishness of risking the free world's economies in the most politically unstable region in the world, where over half of the present Arab heads of state reached power by forcibly removing their predecessors. In the past 15 years, Arabs have fought Arabs in 12 fierce wars. We have all focused on the Strait of Hormuz, but few know that 60% of the Persian Gulf exports pass through *three* ports with *eight* critical pump sites controlling the flow of oil. A terrorist act at the Saudi Arabian Ras Tannurah oilfield complex alone could interrupt the flow of 6 million barrels of oil a day and cripple a large part of the free world's economy.

But our vulnerability goes far beyond energy supplies. The American Geological Institute and others warn that America is already involved in a "resource war," with our economy dependent upon a number of imported minerals vitally necessary for the production of strategic equipment such as oil refineries, power stations, and computers. For example, the United States imports from southern Africa 93% of its platinum, 42% of its manganese, 76% of its cobalt, and 48% of its chromium.

Tragically, the United States has tied its energy and mineral destiny to the two most anachronistic regimes in the world—Saudi Arabia and South Africa. That dependency portends serious harm for the free world.

Conventional wisdom suggests protecting our supply through military strength. But as heretical as it may seem, the solution to dependency on the Middle East may lie with middle-American self-sufficiency. The vulnerability of the United States can be reduced in Detroit—and in our attics—by innovation, recycling, and reuse.

The world today uses approximately 30,000 gallons of petroleum every second and the United States uses one-third of that, with one-ninth going to fuel the American automobile. Considering the geopolitical forces of a volatile world, it seems doubtful that we can

continue to exact the lion's share of the world's resources.

Availability is not, however, the only concern. In 1980, the United States spent $10 million an hour— more than the total earnings of the Fortune 500 corporations—buying imported petroleum, creating a staggering drain on our national wealth.

Either the finiteness of the resources, or their geopolitical vulnerability, or their prices will force us to dramatically restructure our society to use less.

 ## Can the "nation of immigrants" continue its traditional immigration policies?

Historian Arnold Toynbee said that the same elements that build up an institution eventually lead to its downfall, an observation that applies to the question of immigration. When the United States was a vast frontier, it needed immigrants to people an empty continent. Those days are gone, never to return, yet the myth lingers on.

The America of the empty frontier has been replaced by an America of 9.5% unemployment—with dramatically higher unemployment in many industries and appallingly high unemployment among youth. We are overdue in re-examining our immigration policies and goals.

At present, the United States doesn't have much of an immigration policy. What policy we do have is reactive, set by the ingenuity and imagination of individuals seeking to come here, or by Fidel Castro, or by an increasing number of smugglers who, for a price, will slip anyone into this country.

Someone once defined maturity as a recognition of one's own limitations. Sooner or later America will come to the conclusion that it is demographic insanity to continue to accept twice as many immigrants as the rest of the world combined. The United States must recognize that we can't be the home of last resort to all the displaced people in the world.

Legal and illegal immigration accounts for half of the population growth rate in the United States and a rising percentage of its crime and welfare statistics. Whatever the pressures are now, they will soon grow dramatically worse.

For example, the population of Mexico has tripled since 1945 and is expected to double within the next 20 years. Mexico has a labor force of 19 million people, of whom 50% are unemployed or seriously underemployed. By the year 2000, it will be 45 million. Lowering the birthrate will not change the situation; most people who will make up the labor force in the year 2000 have already been born. Per capita annual income in 1977 was $1,020 in Mexico, compared with $8,520 for the United States, creating an incredible pull.

More than a billion people today have an annual per capita income of $150—what an American earns in a week. This dangerous discrepancy must be corrected, but the numbers are so large as to render large-scale immigration an impossible solution. Demographers tell us that we will add 1 billion people to the world's population in the next 11 years.

Demographer Kingsley Davis estimates that, for Europe as a whole, the 1970 population without emigration would have been 1.08 billion rather than the actual count of 650 million. Italy alone had 25 million emigrants over the last 100 years—a large exodus compared with its present population of 57 million. But there are no more continents left; the Third World, unlike Europe, will never have a chance to solve overpopulation through emigration.

The United States is no longer a frontier; our humanity can no longer be boundless. The United States cannot possibly absorb the hundreds of millions of poor people throughout the world who, quite understandably, would love to settle in this country. Our increasingly scarce resources and our own multiple economic problems are already substantial enough without encouraging the entrance of many millions of new immigrants who would compound these problems and diminish our standard of living significantly.

Can democracy survive lowered expectations?

No author ever hoped more fervently that he was wrong. A world of scarcity is a world of bitter struggle, and no rational person wishes this kind of world on his children. Yet the harbingers of a distressful new world are too obvious to ignore. One must speak the unspeakable, which leads us to the ultimate Copernican question: Can democracy survive the static pie?

Democracy has always prospered on growth. The pie usually grew and fostered social and political expectations of progress. The legitimacy of governments has not been based so much on justice or religious freedom as on material advancement. Everyone could and did

have a better tomorrow. If these conditions disappear, perhaps the legitimacy of our governmental structure will also disappear.

Politics is the management of expectations. Progress and growth are inextricably interrelated with our political system. If, despite our best efforts, the geopolitical forces turn against the United States, we must ask how Americans will react. We are not a disciplined people. Nor are we a patient people. We are accustomed to instant gratification. The glue that holds us together as Americans is in danger of coming unstuck.

When will we face up to our hard choices?

We are not getting the correct solutions because we are not asking the right questions. We have been assuming that the future will be an extension of the recent past. It will not be. New economic and geopolitical forces will dramatically change past patterns.

We must stop chasing short-term solutions that often turn out to be counterproductive. The emerging guideline for public policy in this difficult time is a test of long-term sustainability: We should adopt only those life-styles, industries, processes, and institutions that, when pursued over the long term, do not lead to disasters, but rather to a future that can be sustained by the resources of this planet.

This path will be difficult and may be impossible. Mankind has a history of denying the inevitable—especially in a society such as the United States that has no tradition of doing with less, no tradition of the English "stiff upper lip." We drift along, vainly hoping we will not have to make hard choices, hoping that some Keynesian on the left or supply sider on the right will rescue us. But it's not happening.

We forget the Hegel aphorism: "Freedom is the recognition of necessity." We forget to ask the hard, heretical Copernican questions of our time.

10 Forces Reshaping America

Family life, the economy, health and education, national power—all have been transformed in little more than a generation. Ahead: Even faster change.

ALVIN P. SANOFF

From Eisenhower to Reagan—it is a span of only 20 years, yet a period of change so dramatic that it has left many Americans both dazzled and bewildered.

In virtually no aspect of life does the U.S. of the early 1980s resemble what it was in the relatively simple days of the late 1950s. What's more, the pace of change will quicken as the turn of the century approaches.

Already, family life has been turned inside out by the rush of women into the work force. The youth cult of the '60s is fast giving way to an older and more settled lifestyle. Once powerless minorities, aided by strides in education and a flurry of door-opening laws, are demanding a bigger role in business, politics and community life.

People from every age and racial group are staggered and challenged by rapid technological advancements, especially the computer. Cancer, heart disease and other killers are less of a threat as medical breakthroughs extend life spans.

On the national scene, the traditional pacesetters in commerce and politics—the Northeast and Midwest—are losing ground to the booming sun belt. Increasingly, too, big government is viewed with suspicion, prompting more people to look for local solutions to problems.

Old friends, new attitudes. In dealings with other nations, the U.S. no longer gets its way as it did when it engineered the rebuilding of war-torn Europe and Japan. In fact, brisk competition from many of those same nations is spurring sweeping changes in factories and offices.

Together, these forces not only have made life more exciting but also have created stresses and aftershocks that show up in higher divorce rates, the loss of whole categories of jobs and, some would say, a leadership crisis. For support and comfort, many have turned to religion—sparking a spiritual revival in the United States—or to small self-help groups.

Indeed, what surprises many observers is that Americans are coping so well. "There's a tremendous resilience in our society," says social historian Leon Botstein, the president of Bard College. "Despite all the change, there has been more continuity than one would expect."

Yet the indelible marks of change are everywhere, and the seeds for future twists and turns are sprouting.

Given projections that 75 percent of women will be on the job by the year 2000, there will be a rising need for products and services ranging from day-care centers and household help to convenience foods and restaurants.

The postwar baby-boom generation that strained the resources of schools and colleges for so many years now is moving into the prime buying years, a prospect that pleases home builders, furniture producers and auto makers.

An aging population poses problems, too. On a practical plane, the country faces enormous health bills for senior citizens. An older society also could mean less tolerance for new ideas. Says Botstein: "It is no accident that there is more interest in nostalgia than in fads emanating from the young."

Like it or not, change will be even swifter in the future, predicts Marvin Cetron, president of Forecasting International in Arlington, Va. People will be pressed as never before to update their education. An expansion of leisure will prompt renewed interest in recreation, voluntary activities, self-improvement.

Meanwhile, on the international front, the gap between rich and poor will widen, adding to world tensions. Other challenges, says Theodore Gordon, president of the Futures Group, include terrorism and the nuclear buildup.

Even so, Gordon's view of the future contains more positive than negative developments: Improved communications, medical breakthroughs, an agricultural boom from genetic research. A proven ability to adapt, he believes, will keep Americans from being paralyzed by the even greater technical revolution that lies ahead. "People talk about future shock, but it hasn't happened," he says.

Following, in more detail, are some of the major forces that are shaping the way Americans live—forces so strong and so widespread that they will dominate U.S. society well into the next century.

FORCE ONE — A Maturing Society

"Don't trust anyone over 30" was a slogan of the youth culture in the decades now past.

But that phrase is being turned on its head as America undergoes a transformation from a youth-oriented society

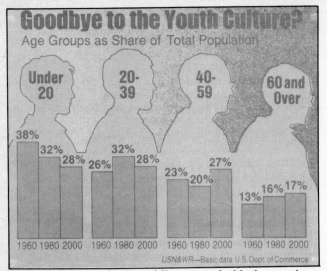

Goodbye to the Youth Culture?
Age Groups as Share of Total Population

Under 20: 38% (1960), 32% (1980), 28% (2000)
20-39: 26% (1960), 32% (1980), 28% (2000)
40-59: 23% (1960), 20% (1980), 27% (2000)
60 and Over: 13% (1960), 16% (1980), 17% (2000)

USN&WR—Basic data: U.S. Dept. of Commerce

into a nation in which middle-age and elderly people set the pace by sheer force of numbers.

For the first time in U.S. history, there are more people 65 and over in the population than teenagers, and by 1990 the number of older citizens is expected to surpass 31 million, while the teenage population shrinks to 23 million. "We are older than we have ever been as a society and we will get even older," says Gregory Spencer, a demographer at the Census Bureau.

Relatively stagnant birth rates along with big jumps in life expectancy are the causes of America's aging. Another factor: The vast baby-boom generation, born between 1946 and 1964, is now moving into middle age. By 1990, the number of people between the ages of 30 and 44 is expected to surge by 20 percent and total 60 million.

These shifts are reshaping the social, economic and political landscape. Already, what some call the narcissism of the '70s is on the wane as maturing members of the baby boom look for close relationships and commitments. Once content to live for the moment, they are increasingly concerned about planning for the future.

For business, the surge of 30 and 40-year-olds means an expanding market for housing, furniture, computers and other high-tech goods.

Rand Corporation demographer Peter Morrison says the increase in middle-age Americans, along with the rise in dual-career families, portends "an explosion of buying power" as large numbers of people have more to spend.

Over 50. Further along on the age spectrum, businesses are discovering a growing market for luxury items and travel services among "active affluents" over 50. Products aimed at this segment range from magazines to shampoo.

These changes are bringing a new look to advertising. "There is more realism and less fixation on youth," says Adam Hanft, a New York advertising executive. Couples with children as well as older people are now commonly shown in ads for everything from cars to frozen foods.

In cosmetic commercials, the models, while still glamorous, often are more mature. Actress Catherine Deneuve, now 40, is featured in ads for skin lotion.

Films are changing, too, as more movies deal with themes of interest to adults. Two recent box-office hits that appeal to an older audience: "The Big Chill," which looks at how time has changed a group of friends who were once campus activists, and "Terms of Endearment," exploring the relationship between a mother and her grown daughter.

The aging of the population is also producing a drop in the crime rate. Studies show that young people are more likely to be lawbreakers. As their numbers dwindle, so does crime.

Spending priorities, too, are being affected. Researchers say that the growth of the elderly population helps explain why so many communities are putting more emphasis on keeping property taxes down, even if that means spending less on schools. "We may see schools become less important and long-term health care more important as America becomes a society with fewer small children and more old people," says Robert Binstock, director of the Policy Center on Aging at Brandeis University.

Some analysts worry about the potential for conflict between generations, as the elderly and young battle over spending priorities. Social Security costs are already a source of debate, and now there is intensifying controversy over the health costs of the elderly.

Though older people are healthier than at any time in U.S. history, one of the fastest growing segments of the population—85 and over—contains many who suffer from chronic illnesses. The ranks of those 85 and up are expected to reach 3.5 million by 1990—a jump of almost 1 million over the present level, and that is expected to drive up medicare costs.

"We're living longer into the pathway of chronic conditions that reduce the quality of life and are very expensive," says Binstock.

States with concentrations of elderly such as Florida, California and Arizona and central cities that include large numbers of less-well-to-do elderly may face especially difficult financial problems.

"Queuing up for promotions." The graying of the society will pose thorny dilemmas in the workplace, too, as large numbers of middle-age workers jockey for advancement.

A nearly 60 percent increase in the number of 35-to-44-year-olds in the labor force is expected over this decade. "There will be a lot of people queuing up for promotions, but there will be fewer slots opening up than there will be people eager to fill them," says demographer Morrison.

This could lead to frustration and an increase in midlife career changes, although some experts predict that, instead of fretting, people will pour more of their energies into hobbies or into family and community pursuits.

For society, though, the maturation of the work force clearly has a positive side: More employes will be in the midst of their most productive years.

Young people coming into the work force after 1990 also can look forward to expanding opportunities. These members of the "baby bust" generation will face less competition for jobs than their older brothers and sisters did. Employers, unable to fill jobs from this shrinking pool of new entrants, may turn more to older, part-time employes.

With the number of young workers dropping, the military may find recruits in short supply, producing more pressure to renew the draft or to hike pay and benefits to entice volunteers.

In the political realm, there is likely to be greater voter participation, since men and women over 30 are more likely to cast ballots than the young. Some political scientists expect higher turnouts to begin with this year's presidential election.

Analysts warn that in assessing America's future, the aging of the population cannot be considered in isolation. Such factors as the state of the economy, immigration and technological change could modify the impact of a more mature society.

Nonetheless, notes psychologist David Campbell of the Center for Creative Leadership in Greensboro, N.C., as America gets older there will be more seasoned hands around to solve whatever problems crop up. Says he: "We are going to be blessed with a pool of talent and experience that we have not had before."

Window of Opportunity

Newt Gingrich

Newt Gingrich, a U.S. congressman from Georgia, was first elected to the House of Representatives in 1978. His previous article for THE FUTURIST, "Post-Industrial Politics: The Leader As Learner" (co-written by his wife, Marianne Gingrich), appeared in December 1981. His address is U.S. House of Representatives, Washington, D.C. 20515.

There exists today a window of opportunity through which we can look and—with luck and hard work—reach to create a bright and optimistic future for our children and grandchildren.

At the moment, this window of opportunity is open and the optimistic future is reachable, but reaching it will require changes in our current behavior and institutions. This optimistic future will necessitate accepting the possibilities inherent in our emerging technologies and accelerating the transition to a high-technology, information-based society.

There is hope for a continuing revolution in biology that will allow us to feed the entire planet; hope for jobs, opportunities, and adventures in space; hope that computers and information science will allow us to work at home, to help everyone live fuller lives, to save energy and resources by expanding our potential while exchanging transportation for communication.

The Communications Revolution

Distance will evaporate as a limiting social factor when communication replaces transportation as the primary mode of human interaction. We already see geographic neighbors being replaced by electronic neighbors: Your best friend is probably not the person next door but a person you talk to on the phone.

Our grandchildren, as we view them through our window of opportunity, will be using a complex information-set telephone as easily as we dial the directory-assistance operator or call our best friends. They will utilize the library by telephone, shop by telephone, send information to and from their workplaces by telephone. As satellites and computers keep bringing down long-distance rates, people will make calls to any spot on the globe—and perhaps to friends on

> Advances in space, communications, and biotechnology are creating a window of opportunity and hope for the future. A U.S. congressman identifies the major opportunities for the United States— and the challenges that first must be met.

space habitats or on the moon—as routinely as we now call friends across town.

Many of our grandchildren will do much of their work from their homes by connecting keyboards to their telephones to write letters, books, and purchase orders. Hotels will routinely have full information-set connections in every room. Wherever you are in the world, you will be able to work, shop, and learn.

This decentralized work system will almost certainly mean a decline in 9-to-5 jobs and the re-emergence of piecework. People who love freedom will rapidly adapt to working on their own schedules and being paid for the product on delivery, creating an extremely fluid marketplace of skills and services.

Home occupations have always existed, to some extent, in America, but the new possibilities inherent in advanced technology will soon allow millions of people to work at home. People will contract to produce 10,000 words of material per day or to do a particular project over a week, month, or year, and the employer will not be concerned with how or when the work is done—while the baby is asleep or late at night—because the employer is buying the product, not the process.

Working people will find no single change more valuable in increasing their leisure time and real income than the development of workstations in the home. Consider, first, the hidden costs. Today, most working people pay for transportation to and from work, parking while they work, and a commercially prepared lunch. Deduct these hidden costs and take-home pay decreases drastically. If we further deduct the cost of dressing for work, there is an additional decline in real income.

Today, big companies deduct the costs of providing a work environment; tomorrow, when people work at home, they will be able to benefit personally from deduction for work rooms and work-related expenses that increase their after-tax income.

Our work force will, however, gain benefits in lifestyle that outshine those in income when workstations are common in American homes. Today, millions of people spend hours in their cars or on mass transit commuting to and from work. Because work is currently a process rather than a product, and because most people work the same hours, we endure seemingly inevitable traffic jams and surges of peak traffic unrelieved by our attempts to create freeways and augment mass transit to meet our growing needs.

People who work at home gain an average of an hour of travel time, each way, which amounts to the equivalent of 12 weeks per year. These extra hours of new free time gained by working from home can be devoted to earning more money or used for leisure.

Neighborhoods will be revitalized when more people are in their homes during the day; there will be fewer burglaries, less crime, and a significant increase in neighborhood businesses as well as a return to utilizing the neighborhood as a community center.

More importantly, the family unit will be strengthened by the shift to working at home: Once you control your own time, you are free to schedule that birthday party or Cub Scout meeting, which used to be so troublesome. Home workstations will allow both male and female partners to share in parenting and family chores and permit a far more flexible lifestyle in which self-directed work choices rather than the coercion of an inflexible employer-dictated routine dominate our lives.

The coming era of expanded machine-accounting may allow us to build a more free and open society in terms of work, pensions, and government. We might build personal pension accounts that will keep track of us all our lives: Credits toward retirement could be transferred when we move to a new job as easily as computers now convert currencies when we buy goods in one country and pay for them in another.

"Home workstations will allow both male and female partners to share in parenting and family chores."

COURTESY OF KATHERINE ACKERMAN AND ASSOCIATES

Information broker Katherine Ackerman of East Lansing, Michigan, and her son, Bradley. Ackerman, a former librarian at the Chicago *Tribune*, began her home-based computer-research and information service in 1983, shortly after the boy's birth. The communications revolution will allow more people to work in their homes, resulting in strengthened family ties, says author Newt Gingrich.

Opportunities in Space

Many of the opportunities we glimpse through our window have little to do with developments here on earth. One of the great revolutions in our lifetime has been man's leap beyond the planet. As astronomer Carl Sagan is fond of noting, for all the rest of human history there will have been only one magic moment when we first left the planet, braved the near-vacuum of space, and reached our nearest neighbor, the moon.

Since 1969 and the landing on the moon, we have been waiting for someone to give us a new vision of our purpose and role in space. We are *still* waiting for such a visionary, someone able and willing to translate technological capability into human opportunity.

If visionary thinking succeeds, by our grandchildren's time we will have factories in space producing medical goods, special alloys, vacuum-formed surfaces, and a host of other materials. In medicine alone, for example, we may find that the effect of weightlessness on

certain manufacturing processes carried on in the relatively sterile and pure environment of space will result in a multi-billion-dollar industry.

If we will make an intensive effort to develop space, we will create millions of jobs on earth and thousands more in space, while ensuring a solid balance of payments in foreign trade by producing goods and services others want but cannot produce for themselves. The late futurist Herman Kahn once suggested that the biggest growth industry of the twenty-first century will be space tourism. As people grow wealthier and the cost of space transportation comes down, spending a week's vacation on a space station or a honeymoon on the moon may become commonplace. People aboard space shuttles—the DC-3s of the future—will fly out to the Hiltons and Marriotts of the solar system, and mankind will have permanently broken free of the planet.

Breakthroughs in Biology

While space is an important area

of growth for the next generation, it may not be the most dramatic. The greatest changes ahead may come in the area of biology.

Biology is entering a period of intellectual flowering like that which transformed physics after the turn of the century. The discovery of the structure of DNA by Watson and Crick is symbolic of a new era in biology that may reveal the very secrets of life.

This biological revolution may enable us to feed a world with a population vastly greater than that of any current projection. The next two generations may see such significant breakthroughs in our understanding of the biological world that we will develop sustainable farming that will improve and enhance nature while producing nutrition for humans.

The biological revolution will transform far more than food production. Already there have been enormous advances in health care, and the lessons we are learning in microbiology may soon remove cancer from the list of life-threatening diseases.

The exercise boom is the first major step toward the form that preventive medicine may take in years to come. Our grandchildren may invest time and money in avoiding illness by staying in shape; they will recognize that the greatest enemies to our health are no longer

the viruses of the past but our own behavior and habits.

There is a growing market of future senior citizens who believe that their own habits can determine whether they spend their last years in a nursing home or in productive pursuits. As we discover that understanding and manipulating the biology of aging will allow us to

FLORIDA DEPARTMENT OF COMMERCE/DIVISION OF TOURISM

Space shuttles may become the "DC-3s of the future" as people begin traveling in space regularly, says author Gingrich.

remain young far longer, people will begin to develop a different outlook on the prospects for life in their 80s and 90s.

As life-spans of longer than 75 years become commonplace, our children must inevitably change their image of retirement. Most people have no wish to spend 25 years or longer in enforced inactivity. The desire to remain active will increase as jobs become more knowledge-oriented and less physical.

Youth in the Information Age

I first came to realize how much the information age will change our vision of youth when I was teaching a federal executive seminar in Washington. One of the seminar's members owned a small software company in partnership with her husband. The couple got summer-job applications from 12- and 13-year-olds—young people with home computers who were adept enough in their use to be employable at a much higher wage than the average teenager could expect to earn from a menial summer job.

Recently I heard a story about an eighth-grader in Florida who built a successful business as a weather consultant serving large corporations by processing free information—information that the government had on its computers but that normally could not be processed for two or three months. This young man, who was doing the processing and sending out weekly reports via electronic mail to more than 40 national corporations each week, was making money by providing his clients with a valuable service for less than they could obtain it elsewhere.

It is conceivable that, by our grandchildren's time, adolescence will have become a thing of the past: Future historians may conclude that adolescence was an invention of nineteenth-century parents to protect their children from exploitation in textile and steel mills.

If young people enter the labor force earlier, there might be a revival of the concept of apprenticeship. Youngsters could be paid a modest wage to work and study under a

NATIONAL INSTITUTES OF HEALTH

Improvements in biomedicine will help people lead longer, healthier lives.

master of their chosen trade. Anyone familiar with Benjamin Franklin's autobiography or the pre-industrial lifestyle will recognize that there is much to be said for learning while working.

Education for Change

Our children and grandchildren, having seen the costs of subsidizing those who will not change, may take the position that society owes its members only the *opportunity* to change, *not* the right to avoid change.

The retraining and reinvestment programs of the next century will be gigantic by today's standards. An information society requires as much investment in adult retraining and re-education as the industrial society required in public schooling. The greatest single problem we face in trying to manage the coming transition is that of making it relatively easy for people to adapt.

No society as wealthy as America's should allow people to suffer simply because they took the wrong job—or because the right job one year became the wrong job a decade later. Once a system for continuing self-education is developed, the able-bodied should be required to throw themselves into the game of life, instead of sitting on the sidelines with subsidies in their hands.

Reforming the Great Bureaucracies

America today is in thrall to a number of monolithic bureaucratic structures, all of them expensive and personally burdensome to the public. These entrenched structures require real and innovative reform:

- The legal system.
- Health care.
- Education.
- Welfare.
- The Defense Department.
- Public bureaucracy.

These bureaucracies share certain characteristics. Each structure's insiders regard themselves as a professional elite serving society in a way that people outside their spe-

TIMBERTECH COMPUTER CAMP

Youngsters find computers fun and easy to use. The youth of the information age, adept at computer-based knowledge work, may start their work lives much sooner than preceding generations.

cialty can't really understand. In each area, the structure has now grown so large that most of the professionals spend their time talking only to other professionals. And any proposals for substantive reform by "outsiders" are derided as the views of amateurs who fail to grasp the sophisticated problems of these professionals.

In an age of change, such antiquated systems are expensive and inefficient, yet the inherent capacity of each structure to resist reform has prevented the growth of approaches that might benefit the public.

A More Just Justice System

The United States is today the most lawyered and litigious society in the world. There are more lawyers in Georgia (population 5.7 million) than there are in Japan (population 119 million). Despite our wealth of attorneys, most Americans would agree that we have a dearth of justice: Criminal justice is too slow, too lenient, and too random; civil actions are too expensive and too protracted.

We must de-emphasize courtroom activity and expand the use of mediators and arbitrators who need not be lawyers. In most cases, law should be simple; only the more complex matters should require more legal sophistication.

A legal system that met the needs of ordinary citizens would differ markedly from the current model. For example, the criminal-justice system should make life easier for victims and witnesses. After reasonable notice, the burden of being prepared and being in court should be on the accused and the defense attorney.

We should also reduce the legal fees now built into the American business system that raise costs and make the United States less competitive overseas because of the overhead earmarked for possible litigation.

Finally, we must simplify the intricate processes of the legal profession that have resulted in additional paperwork, complicated formulas and procedures, and increasingly complicated systems for adjudicating claims.

Better Health Care for All

Health care today is the most expensive single factor in American life, and its cost is increasing faster than any other element in the economy. The central problem with our approach to providing adequate health care at reasonable cost has been its focus on tactical, or operational, changes within the existing vision and strategies of health care. What is needed for the opportunity society, however, is a new vision.

"People who know that another year without hospitalization might bring them a $1,000 bonus may watch their diet and exercise a little more carefully."

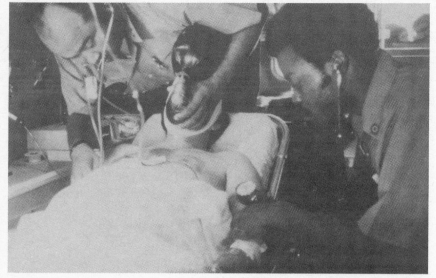

THE WASHINGTON HOSPITAL CENTER

Paramedics revive victim. Well-trained paramedics can provide many health-care services, relieving the burden on doctors and hospitals.

CHARLES BETHEL

Volunteer mediators help individuals settle disputes without costly lawyers and time-consuming court appearances. Expanding the use of arbitrators and mediators is one key to reforming the legal bureaucracy, says author Gingrich.

An example of a visionary change is the elimination of polio as a major threat. Inventing a better iron lung would have been a significant tactical breakthrough, but it would not have altered the world. The discovery of a polio vaccine, on the other hand, represented a paradigm shift—a response to a vision so great that it did indeed alter the world.

One new vision of health care in the opportunity society is to focus on preventive medicine and good health. We must convince people to watch their diets and habits. We may try rewarding people who do not need health care: In Mendocino, California, for example, the teachers' association gave people money at the end of the year for not using their health-care plan.

Changing our third-party payment system so that the individual is once again directly involved in the market costs might mean that insurance companies could find it worthwhile to offer bonuses to people who had not used their insurance for a period of time. People who know that another year without hospitalization might bring them a $1,000 bonus may watch their diet and exercise a little more carefully.

We should also increase research at the vision and strategy level to transform specific areas. There are a number of definable problems that are extremely expensive and that deserve major investments to solve.

Decision-making in health care should be decentralized so that we can move more rapidly to new technologies and procedures. We need to make it relatively easy for local doctors, hospitals, and communities to experiment, and new medical knowledge must be spread more widely and systematically so that people can adopt new methods without professional involvement. We must get new technology into the hands of the general public as rapidly as possible. Many of the procedures currently available could be used by laymen. New software for home computers will allow an individual to become proficient with relatively little training.

As in the legal profession, much health care can be done by "semi-professionals." It is in everyone's interest that individuals do for themselves as much as possible; when they cannot, a large, well-trained corps of paramedics should be available. For example, the return of midwifery is a good start toward decentralizing and de-bureaucratizing health care. There are many other procedures that, if encouraged, would lead to better-informed, more self-reliant citizens and to a more appropriate structure of health care.

The home health-care industry has been developing a number of systems and processes that allow people to take care of themselves or to be taken care of by their friends and relatives. It would be worthwhile to develop a system wherein your family could earn a tax credit, or even a direct payment from the government, for every day that the doctor certifies you would have been hospitalized, had not your family taken care of you instead.

Rethinking Education

Ours is the first generation in American history to educate its children less well than itself. Of the major Western nations, the United States scores close to the bottom in math and science. What we are doing is not working.

The most important step in improving education today is not merit pay, tuition tax credits, or increased funds at any level, but rethinking the educational process and system. You would expect educators to be in favor of intellectually re-examining education; in reality, educators tend to be a special interest like any other.

We must shift the focus of education from teaching to learning. There are many strategies for successful learning—a reward system for learning, for instance, could change the speed with which individuals focus on achieving their next objective. One experiment worth trying would be to offer a $500 bonus for any child who enters the first grade reading at a fourth-grade level.

This shift would also recognize the need for lifetime learning. As our culture and society change with new technology, new medicine, and new government rules, people will have to keep learning until they die. The challenge to keep learning will be even larger in the future. Our grandchildren will have to plan multiple careers in a working lifetime.

The priorities for schools should be mastery of learning fundamentals and the development of academic discipline. We don't need to go back to the fundamentals of 1900. Instead, we need to move forward to the "triliteracy" that futurist Alvin Toffler prescribes for our schools—the traditional basics of reading, writing, and arithmetic alongside the new basics of computer literacy and information management. The truly autonomous citizen of the twenty-first century must be able to handle all five layers of competence to continue learning at the pace and in the systems that will dominate the information society.

"No one must fall beneath a certain level of poverty, even if we must give away food and money."

WILLIAM SCHELL, JR./*NATIONAL GUARD* MAGAZINE

Army National Guardsmen receive briefing before live-fire exercises at Fort Carson, Colorado. Reforming the military bureaucracy may mean expanding the role of guardsmen and military reservists, who are paid only during training or when called into service.

There are a host of learning opportunities available in our society that the educational bureaucracy simply ignores: public libraries, newspapers, and educational television, to name just a few. An opportunity society would also develop apprenticeship programs as an alternative to high school, offering tax advantages and subsidies to both the apprenticer and the community. Many skills and trades are learned better through apprenticeship than in academia. There are young people who simply do not fit well into school but would love to learn a trade.

We have grossly neglected the potential educational resources of new technologies. The potential linkage between the home computer, the telephone, cable television, and the local newspaper is enormous. For a modest sum, we could build a software package that would make a large library available to home computers by telephone hookup.

From Welfare to Workfare

We must compassionately reconsider poverty, unemployment, and the culture of being poor. Our present, inadequate solutions are no longer useful and must be reformed.

Let me suggest just a few guidelines around which we might build an opportunity-society welfare system:

● Individuals, families, and poor communities should receive cash and credit-card vouchers directly in order to increase their choices and give them power over their own lives.

● Services going to the very neediest should be seen as state charity and should be generous rather than stingy. Our current system crimps those at the bottom of the welfare ladder. No one must fall beneath a certain level of poverty, even if we must give away food and money.

● Those who are able-bodied and under the age of retirement should work or study if they wish to receive aid—including unemployment compensation. Among other things, this principle could encourage the establishment of day-care centers where some welfare mothers care for the neighborhood children while others go out to work.

● The tax and welfare laws should be changed so that those trying to work their way out of the welfare system gain more than they lose at each step. Taxes, child care, and the cost of going to work should be set against gross pay in calculating welfare eligibility.

Our goal must be to help the helpless and the elderly so that they can lead full lives and to empower the poor to control their lives and rise from poverty. If we design the right programs now, then no members of the next generation will be able to say they live in poverty for lack of choice.

Military Reform

While the Department of Health and Human Services may disburse more money in the form of transfer payments, there is no other system in the federal government remotely comparable to the Defense Department in size and complexity.

Everything that conservatives have said about bureaucracies in general applies in particular to the Pentagon: It is well protected by its allies on Capitol Hill and in the

TIMBERTECH COMPUTER CAMP

Tree-climbing boy reads his computer textbook. Computer literacy and the ability to use information media are the new "basics" of education, according to author Gingrich.

military-industrial complex; it is hidebound by traditions, some of them going back nearly 200 years; and it is a hive of internal political squabbles.

There are some weaknesses in the current military system that need to be dealt with directly. The most serious is the underuse of the national guard and the reserves. A regular-duty soldier is nine times as expensive as a reservist or a guardsman. Regular soldiers are paid every day, while the reserves and guard are paid only when they train. Further, the regulars retire after 20 years on half-pay pensions. Our military today is too small to meet all its potential commitments—and too expensive besides.

The time is ripe for a thorough overhaul of our military management system. There is no excuse for focusing on the smaller bureaucracies while ignoring this one.

Deregulating the Federal Bureaucracy

Most federal civil servants want to do a good job and are as totally frustrated by irrational, obsolete bureaucratic systems as the people ill-served by them.

A free people may indicate public policy through their elected offi-

cials, but they can only implement those policies through a professional staff. In the information age, even a lean federal government is going to be an enormous structure to manage.

We have the capacity to revamp the federal government into an exciting, dynamic place to work. If we combine technology with a system of merit pay, idea bonuses, individual retirement accounts for those who desire them, and other steps toward a more flexible and desirable style of work, then I think that, in the twenty-first century, we can once again be proud of the quality of our civil service.

In each area of government there are great opportunities for an age of improvement. The time to start making those improvements is now.

Peering into the future through our window of opportunity, I am confident that our children and grandchildren *can* live in a positive, optimistic America—*if* we regain our morale and elan as a society. I am equally convinced that an America confident enough to take risks in space, computers, and biology can regain its capacity to lead the world economically, militarily, and politically.

Glossary

This glossary of 459 sociology terms is included to provide you with a convenient and ready reference as you encounter general terms in your study of sociology which are unfamiliar or require a review. It is not intended to be comprehensive but taken together with the many definitions included in the articles themselves it should prove to be quite useful.

Absolute Poverty A condition in which one lacks the essentials of life such as food, clothing, or shelter. *See* Relative Poverty.

Achieved Status The position of an individual within a system of social stratification based on changeable factors such as occupations, high income, or marriage into hgiher social strata. *See* Ascriptive Status.

Agents of Socialization The people, groups, and organizations who socialize the individual. *See* Socialization.

Alienation A sense of separation from society. In the context of the bureaucracy, one's feeling of not having control over or responsibility for one's own behavior at work. *See* Bureaucracy.

Altruism Behavior motivated by a desire to benefit another individual, or sacrifice by individuals for the benefit of the group as a whole.

Androgyny A combination of male and female characteristics. The term may be used in a strictly physical sense or it may apply to a wider, social ideal.

Anomie The loosening of social control over individual behavior that occurs when norms become ineffective.

Ascriptive Status The position of an individual within a system of social stratification based on factors such as sex, age, race, over which the individual has no control. *See* Achieved Status, Social Stratification, Status.

Assimilation The absorption of a subordinate group into the dominant culture.

Authority Power that people recognize as just, legitimate, and necessary; the basis for compliance with a government's laws.

Authority Systems Systems by which authority is legitimated. According to Max Weber, in a traditional system, positions of authority are obtained by heredity. In a charismatic system, leaders are followed because of some extraordinarily appealing personal quality. In a legal-rational system, the office is the source of authority, rather than the officeholder.

Autocratic Leader The type of group leader who is authoritarian and impersonal and who does not participate in group projects. *See* Democratic Leader, Laissez-Faire Leader.

Awareness Context The "total combination of what each interactant in a situation knows about the identity of the other and [about his or her] own identity in the eyes of the other."

Belief System Groups of basic assumptions about general concepts such as the existence and nature of God, the meaning of life, or the relationship of the individual and the state held by a culture.

Bilineal Kinship Kinship system in which descent is traced through both parents and all grandparents. *See* Kinship, Lineal Kinship.

Biological Determinism The view of behavior as a product of genetic makeup.

Biological-Instinctual Theories Theories of behavior that stress the importance of instinct. *See* Environmental Theories.

Biosocial Interaction The ways in which interrelationships with society influence and are influenced by biological factors. *See* Biosociologists.

Biosocial Systems Systems of social organization such as those among insects, which survive because behavior patterns are biologically controlled.

Biosociologists Sociologists who are concerned with the implications of biology in the study of society. They study the genotype-environment interactions in the production of behavior. *See* Genotype/Phenotype, Sociobiology.

Birth Rate (Crude) The number of people born in a single year per 1,000 persons in the population.

Bourgeoisie The class that owns the means of production. *See* Proletariat.

Bureaucracy An authority structure arranged hierarchically for the purpose of efficient operation.

Case Study A research method which involves intensive examination of a particular social group over time. *See* Sample Survey, Participant Observation, Research.

Caste A rigid form of social stratification, rooted in religious standards, in which individuals spend their lives in the stratum into which they were born. *See* Class, Estate, Social Stratification.

Census A periodic count and collection of demographic information about an entire population. *See* Demography.

Central City The core unit of a metropolitan area. The term is also used to mean "inner city" or "ghetto," with its urban problems of poverty, crime, racial discrimination, poor schools and housing, and so on.

Centrality of the Leader A concept of group interaction formulated by Sigmund Freud which considers the group leader's power and authority to be centrally important to the group.

Charisma Exceptional personal leadership qualities which command authority as contrasted to legal or formal authority. A driving, creative force that attaches both to individuals and to social movements.

Clan A lineal kinship group. *See* Kinship, Lineal Kinship.

Class A form of social stratification in which groups are divided primarily by economic positions. According to Weber, people with the same amount of property belong to the same class. *See* Caste, Estate, Social Stratification.

Class Conflict According to Marxist theory, the dynamics for change created by the conflict between ruling classes and subordinate classes in society.

Class Consciousness According to Marxist theory, the awareness of what it means to be a member of a certain class.

Classless Society According to Marxist theory, the goal of socialism and the state in which all social stratification on the basis of class is eliminated. *See* Class, Social Stratification.

Cliques Tight clusters of friends and acquaintances who share relatively intense feelings of belonging. Cliques are primary groups. *See* Primary Groups.

Closed Community A type of community in which families within tight kinship groups cooperate closely and are closed to non-relatives. *See* Open Community.

Closed System A social stratification system which offers an individual no way to rise to a higher position; based on ascriptive status. *See* Ascriptive Status, Open System.

Coercion The power to compel people to act against their will, by using force or the threat of force. The constraint of some people by others. According to conflict theorists, it is that glue that binds society together. *See* Conflict Model, Power.

Coercive Organization According to Amitai Etzioni, an organization in which force is the major means of control. Examples include prisons and custodial mental hospitals. *See* Normative and Utilitarian Organizations, Compliance Patterns.

Cognitive Category Category of knowledge and experience into which people organize their perceptions of the world.

Cognitive Development A theory of psychology which states that cognitive processes such as thinking, knowing, perceiving, develop in stages although they function and influence even newborns' behavior. *See* Behaviorist.

Collective Behavior The behavior of a loosely associated group which is responding to the same stimulus. The concept embraces a wide range of group phenomena, including riots, social movements, revolutions, fads, crazes, panics, public opinion, and rumors. All are responses to as well as causes of social change. Elementary forms of collective behavior (panics, rumors) are relatively spontaneous and unstructured, but longer-lasting activities (social movements) require more planning and coordination. *See* Social Aggregate.

Communalism The need for scientific discoveries to be made available to the whole community. *See* Universalism.

Communism A political-economic system in which wealth and power are shared harmoniously by the whole community. The concept today refers mainly to the revolutionary socialism of Karl Marx and to the political systems that adhere to his principles. *See* Socialism.

Community The spatial, or territorial, unit in social organization; also the psychological feeling of belonging associated with such units. *See* Metropolis.

Competitive Social System A social system in which the dominant group views the subordinate group as aggressive and dangerous and thereby in need of suppression. *See* Paternalistic Social System.

Compliance Patterns According to Amitai Etzioni, the (three) ways in which formal organizations exercise control over members. *See* Coercive, Normative, Utilitarian Organizations.

Comte, Auguste (1798-1857) French philosopher who coined the term "sociology" and is considered the founder of the modern discipline.

Concentric Zone Theory A proposal by the Chicago School founders, Park and Burgess, saying that cities grew from a central business district outward in a series of concentric circles. Each zone was inhabited by different social classes and different types of homes and businesses. *See* Multiple-Nuclei Theory, Sector Theory.

Conflict Model The view of society that sees social units a sources of competing values and norms. See Equilibrium Model.

Conforming Behavior Behavior that follows the accepted standards of conduct of a group or society. See Deviance.

Conjugal Family A family type in which major emphasis is placed on the husband-wife relationship. See Consanguine Family.

Consanguine Family The family type in which the major emphasis is on the blood relationships of parents and children or brothers and sisters.

Contagion Theory A theory of collective behavior, originated by Gustave LeBon, which states that the rapid spread of a common mood among a large number of people is what forms a crowd.

Conventional Morality According to Lawrence Kohlberg, the second level of moral development, at which most adults remain. This level involves conformity to cultural or family norms, maintenance of, and loyalty to, the social order. See Preconventional, Postconventional Morality.

Convergence Theory A theory of collective behavior which states that people with certain tendencies are most likely to come together in a crowd. This theory assumes that crowd behavior is uniform.

Core of the Aggregate People in a particularly visible location within a social aggregate who may induce action by the aggregate. See Social Aggregate.

Crimes Without Victims Violations of criminal law, such as homosexuality, drug addiction, prostitution, or abortion, which raise questions about the enforcement of morality by legal controls. See Crime, Sin.

Criminality Deviant behavior that is punishable through formal sanctions, or penalties, applied by political authorities. See Crime, Deviance.

Criminalization The labeling of individuals as criminals, especially by the criminal justice system. See Criminal Justice System, Stigmatization.

Criminal Justice System Authorities and institutions in a society concerned with labeling and punishing criminals according to formal social sanctions.

Criminology The social science that analyzes crime as a social occurrence; the study of crime, criminality, and the operation of the criminal justice system. See Crime.

Crowd A type of social aggregate in which all participants are in the same place at the same time, and they interact in a limited way. See Social Aggregate.

Cults Small groups whose teachings stress ritual, magic, or beliefs widely regarded as false by the dominant culture. See Religion.

Cultural Adaptation The flexibility of a culture that allows it to change as the environment changes.

Cultural Diffusion The adaptation of a culture as it encounters another and undergoes social change.

Cultural Lag The condition that exists when values or social institutions do not change as rapidly as social practices.

Cultural Relativism The principle of judging a culture on its own terms. See Ethnocentrism.

Culture The knowledge people need to function as members of the particular groups they belong to; our shared beliefs, customs, values, norms, language, and artifacts.

Culture of Poverty As defined by Oscar Lewis, ''an effort to cope with the feelings of hopelessness and despair that arise [when the poor realize] the improbability of their achieving success in terms of the prevailing values and goals.''

Death Traditionally defined as the end of all vital functions. Some states define the cessation of breathing and absence of heartbeat as death. Others say death occurs when brain activity stops.

Death Rate (Crude) The number of deaths in a single year per 1,000 persons in the population. See Demography.

Democratic Leader A type of group leader who encourages group decision-making rather than giving orders. See Autocratic and Laissez-Faire Leader.

Democratization The process of making something democratic. According to Max Weber, political democratization is related to the growth of the bureaucratic state.

Demographic Transition The pattern in which death rates fall with industrialization, causing a rise in population and ensuing drop in birth rate which returns the rate of population growth to nearly the same level as before industrialization.

Demography The study of human population, focusing on birth rate, death rate, and migration patterns.

Dependent Variable The factor that varies with changes in the independent variable. See Independent Variable.

Desegregation Elimination of racial segregation in a society. See Discrimination.

Determinism The view of social change proposing that an inevitable pattern of change occurs in societies because of a universal principle, or dynamic, of the historic process. See Deterministic.

Deterministic Any theory that sees natural, social, or psychological factors as determined by preceding causes.

Deterrence Theory A theory held by some criminologists that punishment will prevent as well as control crime.

Deviance The label for all forms of behavior that are considered unacceptable, threatening, harmful, or offensive in terms of the standards or expectations of a particular society or social group. See Conforming Behavior, Norm, Secondary Deviance.

Dewey, John (1859-1952) American philosopher and educator, a functionalist, whose ideas about education had a strong effect on schooling. He pressed for a science of education and believed in learning by doing. Individualized instruction and experimental learning can be traced to his theories.

Dialectical Materialism The philosophical method of Karl Marx, who considered knowledge and ideas as reflections of material conditions. Thus the flow of history, for example, can be understood as being moved forward by the conflict of opposing social classes. See Communism.

Discrimination Unfavorable treatment, based on prejudice, of groups to which one does not belong. See Prejudice.

Disinterestedness The quality of not allowing personal motives or commitments to distort scientific findings or evaluations of scientific work. See Communalism, Organized Skepticism.

Division of Labor The separation of tasks or work into distinct parts that are to be done by particular individuals or groups. Division of labor may be based on many factors, including sex, level of technology, and so on. See Task Segregation.

Double Standard A moral judgment by which sexual activity of men is considered appropriate or excused while that of women is considered immoral. See Sex Role.

Doubling Time The time it takes a population to double its size.

Dramaturgical Perspective The point of view, favored by Erving Goffman, that social interaction can be compared to a dramatic presentation.

Durkheim, Emile (1858-1917) French sociologist and one of the founders of modern sociology. Deeply influenced by the positivism of Auguste Comte, Durkheim's major concern was with social order, which he believed to be the product of a cohesion stemming from a common system of values and norms.

Dying Trajectory A graph that plots the time span from the terminally ill patient's hosptial admission until the moment of death, and the course of the patient's physical deterioration. See Thanatology.

Ecological Determinism The point of view stressing how environment affects behavior. See Urbanism.

Economic Determinism The doctrine, supported by Karl Marx, that economic factors are the only basis for social patterns.

Economic Modernization Shift from an agricultural-based economy to an industrial one.

Education The social institution by which a culture is transmitted from one generation to the next. See Institutions, Sociology of Education.

Egalitarianism Emphasis within a society on the concept of equality among members of social systems.

Egocentricity The characteristic quality of very young children, their awareness of only their own point of view.

Elaborated Code According to Basil Bernstein, the formal type of language available to the middle class only. See Restricted Code.

Elements of Culture Factors such as customs, language, symbols, and values shared by members of a cultural group.

Elite Those at the top of a hierarchy based on status and on economic, social, or political power. See Hierarchy.

Elite Groups Members of the top ranks of society in terms of power, prestige, and economic or intellectual resources. See Power Elite.

Emergent Norm Theory A theory of collective behavior stating that social aggregates form in response to specific problems that cannot be solved through institutionalized action. See Crowd, Social Aggregate.

Encounter Groups Groups of individuals who meet to change their personal lives by confronting each other, discussing personal problems, and talking more honestly and openly than in everyday life. See Group Therapy.

Endogamy Marriage within one's social group. See Exogamy.

Environmental Theories Theories of behavior that stress the influence of learning and environment. See Biological-Instinctual Theories.

Equilibrium Model A view of society as a system of interdependent parts which function together to maintain the equilibrium of the whole system. *See* Conflict Model, Functionalism.

Erikson, Erik (1902-) Danish-born psychoanalytic theorist who lives in the United States. He supplemented Freud's theory of psychosexual development with a separate theory of psychosocial development. He theorized that individuals move through a series of psychosocial stages throughout life, with the integrity of the personality depending largely on the individual's success in making appropriate adaptations at previous stages.

Estate A form of social stratification based on laws, usually about one's relationship to land. *See* Social Stratification.

Ethnic Group A social group distinguished by various traits, including language, national or geographic origin, customs, religion, and race.

Ethnicity The act or process of becoming or being a religious, racial, national, cultural, or subcultural ethnic group. *See* Ethnic Group.

Ethnocentrism The tendency to judge other groups by the standards of one's own culture and to believe that one's own group values and norms are better than others'. *See* Cultural Relativism.

Ethology The comparative study of animal behavior patterns as they occur in nature.

Eugenics The science of controlling heredity.

Evolution A process of change by which living organisms develop, and each succeeding generation is connected with its preceding generation.

Evolutionary Change A gradual process of social change. *See* Revolutionary Change.

Exchange Theory The viewpoint that stresses that individuals judge the worth of particular interactions on the basis of costs and profits to themselves.

Exogamy Marriage outside one's social group. *See* Endogamy.

Experiment A research method in which only one factor is varied at a time and efforts are made to keep other variables constant in order to isolate the causal or independent variable. *See* Research, Independent Variable.

Extended Family A family type consisting of two or more nuclear families. Also characterized as three or more generations who usually live together. *See* Modified Extended Family System.

Facilitating Conditions In a model of suburban growth, those factors that make movement from city to suburb possible. Such factors include commuter transportation systems and communications technology. *See* Motivating Conditions.

Family A set of people related to each other by blood, marriage, or adoption. Family membership is determined by a combination of biological and cultural factors that vary among societies.

Family Life Cycle The process of characteristic changes that a family's task (such as child-rearing) undergo over time.

Family Planning The theory of population control that assumes that parents should be able to determine and produce the number of children they want, spaced at the intervals they think best. *See* Population Control.

Fashioning Effect The tendency for role categories to determine people's behavior and thus to help shape their self-concepts. *See* Role Selection.

Feral Children Children who are not socialized because they have been, according to unconfirmed reports, brought up by wild animals. *See* Social Isolates.

Fertility Rate The number of births in relation to the number of women of childbearing age in a population.

Folk Taxonomy Classification system used by a culture to organize its cognitive categories.

Formal Organization A large social unit purposely set up to meet specific, impersonal goals. *See* Informal Organization.

Freud, Sigmund (1856-1939) Viennese founder of modern psychology and originator of psychoanalysis. Basic to Freud's theories are the beliefs that much of human behavior is unconsciously motivated and that neuroses often have their origins in early childhood wishes or memories that have been repressed. He developed an account of psychosexual development in which he said that sexuality was present even in infants, although the nature of this sexuality changed as the individual progressed through a sequence of stages to mature adult sexuality.

Freud also proposed a division of the self into the *id* (instinctual desires), the *ego* (the conscious self), and the *superego* (conscience). The ego mediates between the pressures of the other two parts in an effort to adapt the individual to the demands of society, and personality formation is largely the result of this process. *See* Psychoanalytic Theory.

Functionalism A dominant school in modern sociology which assumes that each part of the social structure functions to maintain the society and which views social change according to the equilibrium model; also called structural-functionalism. *See* Equilibrium Model.

Game Theory The study of situations in which the outcome of interaction depends on the joint action of the partners.

Gemeinschaft/Gesellschaft Simple, close-knit communal form of social organization/impersonal bureaucratic form. Typology of social organization devised by Tönnies and used to understand variety and changes in societies' social structure. *See* Tönnies.

Gender Identity A child's awareness of being either male or female. *See* Sex Role.

Gene Pool The total of genes present in the population.

Generalized Others According to George Herbert Mead, the developmental stage in which children adopt the viewpoint of many other people or, in short, of society in general. *See* Significant Others.

Genetic Engineering Altering the reproductive process in order to alter the genetic structure of the new organism.

Genetic Load The presence of genes in a population that are capable of reducing fitness. *See* Adaptive.

Genocide Deliberate destruction of a racial or ethnic group.

Genotype/Phenotype Genotype is the entire structure of genes that are inherited by an organism from its parents. Phenotype is the observable result of interaction between the genotype and the environment.

Gerontology The study of the problems of aging and old age.

Group Two or more people who know each other, interact regularly or systematically, share ideas or goals, and think of themselves as a unit.

Group Marriage Marriage among two or more women and two or more men at the same time.

Group Processes The dynamics of group functioning and decision-making and of the interactions of group members.

Group Space A concept of Robert Bales, from his research on social groups. Bales correlated many factors and then constructed dimensions, such as dominance, likeability, task orientation, along which group members could be placed. When these dimensions are combined in three dimensions, they form the group space.

Group Therapy A form of psychotherapy in which interaction among group members is the main therapeutic mode. Group therapy takes many forms but essentially requires a sense of community, support, increased personal responsibility, and a professionally trained leader.

Hierarchy The relative positions of individuals or groups within a body or society and their relationship to power and control. *See* Social Sciences.

Hobbesian Question The term referring to the question of the 17th-century philosopher Thomas Hobbes, who asked how society could establish and maintain social order. Today, sociologists apply this question to the problem of conformity within the social order.

Hobbes, Thomas (1588-1679) British philosopher and writer who theorized about social order and social confict. He was the first social conflict theorist.

Human Ecology Term used by geographers to define the impact of changes in human populations in the broader environment; refers to the relationship between humans and their environment.

Hypothesis An "educated guess," a statement of a probable relationship between variables in a research design. *See* Research, Scientific Method, Theory.

Ideal Type A conceptual model or tool used to help analyze social occurrences. It is an abstraction based on reality, although it seldom, if ever, occurs in exactly that form.

Identity According to Erik Erikson, a person's sense of who and what he or she is.

I/Me According to George Herbert Mead, the I is the spontaneous, natural, self-interested aspect of the self. The me is the socialized part that has adopted the norms of the community.

Imperialism According to Lenin, a nation's policy of building empires by extending its power and domination.

Independent Variable The causal variable, or factor that changes. *See* Dependent Variable.

Individuation The development and recognition of the individual as a distinct being in the group.

Industrialization The systematic organization of production through the use of machinery and a specialized labor force.

Industrial Society Society characterized by mechanized means of production for its goods and services, a high degree of economic development, and a specialized labor force. *See* Postindustrial Society, Traditional Society.

Infant Mortality Rate The number of children per 1,000 dying in the first year of life.

Influence A subtle form of power involving the ability to sway people to do what they might not otherwise do. *See* Power.

Informal Norms The rules governing behavior generally set by an informal group instead of the formal requirements of an organization. *See* Informal Organization.

Informal Organization In contrast to and within a formal organization, those groups of people or roles they play that cut across the official bureaucratic pattern. *See* Formal Organization.

Instinct An unlearned fixed action pattern that occurs in response to specific stimuli as a result of complex hormonal and neurological processes.

Institutions Complex and well-accepted ways of behaving aimed at meeting broad social goals. The major social institutions are government, family, religion, education, and the economy. *See* Organization.

Intelligence A capacity for knowledge. There is not agreement on a precise definition, although intelligence has come to refer to higher-level abstract processes.

Intelligence Quotient (IQ) A measurement of intelligence, defined as a relation between chronological and mental ages. Measured IQ is a good indicator of school performance. Relative contributions of genetic inheritance and environment are not known.

Interest Groups Political factions made up of citizens who associate voluntarily and who aim to influence communal action. *See* Pluralism.

Intergenerational Learning Learning by one generation from another. It is found generally among nonhuman primates as well as among humans.

Intergenerational Status Transmission The passing of the parents' socioeconomic status onto their children.

Internalization In the process of socialization, the taking into oneself of attitudes, values, and norms so that they are part of one's personality. *See* Socialization.

Interpersonal Space The physical distance between people. Cultures vary in the amount of space people leave between themselves when they interact in various ways.

Iron Law of Oligarchy According to Robert Michels, the tendency of formal organizations to give their officers a near monopoly of power. *See* Formal Organization.

Kin Selection A process in which individuals cooperate, sacrifice themselves, or do not reproduce so that their kin can survive and reproduce.

Kinship A system of organizing and naming relationships that arise through marriage (affinal kinship) and through birth (consanguine kinship). *See* Lineal Kinship, Bilineal Kinship.

Kinship Networks Family systems.

Labeling Theory The school of thought that sees deviance or criminality as a status imposed by societal reaction. *See* Criminality, Opportunity Theory, Secondary Deviance, Status.

Laissez-faire Leader A type of group leader who makes few suggestions and allows the group great freedom to do what it wants. *See* Autocratic Leader, Democratic Leader.

Language A means of communication using vocal sounds that make up units of meaning (words) and arranged according to rules of usage and order (grammar and syntax).

Leisure Class The social stratum which exists on inherited wealth. *See* Social Stratification.

Level of Interaction The way in which people relate to one another. Interactions may be subtle and nearly undetectable, or they may be clear and obvious. People may relate on a number of different levels with each statement or gesture. *See* Group Processes.

Lineal Kinship Kinship traced through one parent only. *See* Clan, Kinship, Bilineal Kinship.

Linguistic Relativity The concept that different languages analyze and portray the universe in different ways.

Locke, John (1632-1700) British philosopher and political theorist who put forward a social contract theory of government, which saw people as rational and dignified and entitled to overthrow any government that grew tyrannical. *See* Social Contract.

Macrosociology The sociological study of relations between groups. Some sociologists consider it the study of the entire society or social system. *See* Microsociology.

Malthusian Theory Pessimistic pronouncements by Thomas Malthus (1766-1834) about population growth outstripping increases in food production, thus resulting in starvation. *See* Demography, Thomas Malthus.

Malthus, Thomas (1766-1834) British economic and demographic theorist who predicted that population increases would outrun increases in food production, with starvation as a result.

Marriage The social institution that sanctions, or gives approval to, the union of husband and wife and assumes some permanence and conformity to social custom. Marriage patterns differ among societies.

Marx, Karl (1818-1883) The German-born economic, political, and social thinker whose ideas provided the inspiration for modern communism. Marx's social theory is based on a determinist view of history: according to the "materialist method" that Marx elaborated, the mode of production in any particular society determines the character of the economy of the society and hence the society's cultural characteristics. The economic base constitutes the substructure of society, and all other social and cultural phenomena, such as law, religion, or art, form a superstructure that is ultimately conditioned by the economic base. Social change comes about through a dialectical process of conflict between opposing classes; all history is but the history of class conflict. In capitalist society, class conflict reaches its most antagonistic form; the struggle between the bourgeoisie and proletariat will result ultimatley in the creation of a classless society. In such a society people will finally realize their own potential, no longer feeling themselves alien in the social world they have created.

Mass A type of social aggregate in which separate individuals respond to a common stimulus, but with little or no communication or interaction. For example, all of the people who watch the same television program constitute a mass. *See* Mass Society, Social Aggregate.

Mass Communications Those forms of communication, including especially the mass media, which involve the transmission of ideas and attitudes from a communications center to a diverse mass of people. *See* Mass, Mass Media.

Mass Media The press (newspapers and magazines) and broadcasting (radio and television). The mass media are important agents of socialization. *See* Agent of Socialization.

Mass Society The complex, industrialized society that displays a basic uniformity of material goods, ideas, roles, and lifestyles. Also used in the sense of those at the bottom of the social scale who produce a nation's goods and perform its services. *See* Mass, Mass Media.

Matrilineal Kinship The tracing of one's descent through the mother and her side of the family. *See* Patrilineal Kinship.

Matrilocal A pattern of residence in which a married couple lives with or near the wife's family. *See* Patrilocal.

Mead, George Herbert (1863-1931) American social psychologist and philosopher whose theories of mind, self, and society had a major influence on sociological approaches such as role theory and symbolic interactionism. *See* I/Me, Significant Others.

Measures of Central Tendency Descriptive statistical techniques used to measure the central tendency of distribution of group scores or results.

Mechanisms of Perpetuation In a model of suburban growth, factors that assure that successive generations of target populations will exist and will be drawn to the suburbs. Such factors include movement of industry from city to suburbs and cheaper land, taxes, and facilities in the suburbs. *See* Target Population.

Median Age The age that divides the population in half. Half of the population is older and half younger than the median age.

Megalopolis Urban areas made up of more than one metropolis, "supercities." The area between New Hampshire and nortnern Virginia is one megalopolis. *See* Metropolis.

Methodology The logic of applying the scientific perspective and the set of rules for conducting research. *See* Scientific Method.

Metropolis Urban area made up of separate cities, towns, and unincorporated areas which are interrelated. *See* Standard Metropolitan Statistical Area.

Microsociology The sociological study of interaction between individuals. *See* Macrosociology.

Migration The movement of people, a variable affecting the size and composition of population. Migration may be internal, within a country, or international, between countries. *See* Demography.

Milling The physical moving about of people in a crowd who spread emotions as their contact increases. Milling is an important factor in the escalation of excitement in collective behavior. *See* Collective Behavior.

Mills, C. Wright (1916-1962) The leader of mid-20th-century American sociological thought, who attempted to develop a radical sociological critique of capitalist society. His social-interactionist position, derived from Max Weber and Herbert Spencer, also influenced his thinking.

Miscegenation Mingling of races, particularly marriage or cohabitation between whites and other races. *See Race.*

Modernization The process of gradual change in a society from traditional social, economic, and political institutions to those characteristic of modern urban, industrial societies. *See Industrialization, Social Modernization.*

Modified Extended Family System A middle-class urban family pattern of related nuclear families participating in a kinship structure based on ties of affection rather than ties demanded by tradition. *See Extended Family.*

Monasticism An organized system of withdrawal from everyday life and devotion to religous principles.

Monogamy Marriage of one woman and one man. *See Polygamy.*

Moral Absolutism The idea that one's own moral values are the only true ones and that they are the proper basis for judging all others. *See Cultural Relativism.*

Moral Development The growth of a child into an adult who is willing to make the sacrifices necessary for social living. Study of moral development has focused on how people come to adopt their culture's standards of right and wrong and how they resist the temptation to defy the rules of acceptable conduct.

Mores Folkways or customs to which group members attach social importance or necessity; standards of behavior that carry the force of right and wrong. *See Socialization.*

Motivating Conditions In a model of suburban growth, factors that stimulate the shift of population from city to suburb. Such factors include deteriorating conditions in the cities and rising economic productivity. *See Facilitating Conditions.*

Multiple-Nuclei Theory Theory of urban development stating that a city grows from a number of centers rather than from a single point. *See Concentric Zone Theory, Sector Theory.*

Natural Increase Births minus deaths per 1,000 population.

Natural Selection The evolutionary process by which those individuals of a species with the best-adapted genetic endowment tend to survive to become parents of the next generation. *See Evolution.*

Negative Rites According to Emile Durkheim, rites which maintain taboos or prohibitions. *See Piacular Rites.*

Neoidealism A philosophy that rejects the positivist approach to social phenomena as inadequate. Neoidealists believe that a full explanation must take into account the experience and subjective values of the social actors. *See Positivism, Verstehen.*

Non-participant Observations A research method used in case studies by social scientists who come into contact with others but do not interact and behave primarily as a trained observer. *See Participant Observation.*

Nonperiodic Assemblies Gatherings that occur sporadically and whose membership is rarely the same over a period of time. Parades, protest demonstrations, and rallies are examples. *See Periodic Assemblies.*

Norm A shared standard for judging the behavior of an individual. Norms are elements of culture.

Normative Organization According to Amitai Etzioni, a formal organization to which people belong because of personal interest or commitment to the organization's goals. Examples include religious, political, and professional organizations. *See Coercive and Utilitarian Organizations.*

Nuclear Family The smallest family type, consisting of parents and their children. In Western society, custom has broadened the basic definition to include childless couples and single parents.

Open Community A type of community in which families interact with relatives and friends and have selective attachments to a variety of associations and secondary social groups which offer relatively impersonal relationships. *See Closed Community.*

Open System A social stratification system which allows an individual to rise to a higher position; based on achieved status. *See Achieved Status, Closed System.*

Opportunity Theory The school of criminology that sees criminality as conduct. It is based on the writings of Robert Merton, who reasoned that deviance results from pressures within the social structure. *See Criminology, Labeling Theory.*

Organization A deliberately formed group of people who achieves the aims of a social institution. For example, the aims of the educational institution are carried out by organizations such as schools and colleges. *See Institution.*

Organization Development A field of endeavor that seeks to help organizations adapt to a difficult and changing environment by techniques such as sensitivity training, and which aims to humanize and democratize bureaucracies. *See Formal Organization, Sensitivity Training.*

Organized Skepticism The suspension of judgment until all relevant facts are at hand and the analysis of all such facts according to established scientific standards. *See Communalism, Disinterestedness.*

Parsons, Talcott (1902-1979) An American sociologist and one of the most controversial and influential of social theorists. Although clearly identified with the functionalist approach to social analysis, Parsons avoided becoming personally involved in the debates surrounding that concept. His career has passed through a number of phases, ranging from a substantive approach to social data involving a moderate level of abstraction to an analytic approach of almost metaphysical abstraction. *See Functionalism.*

Participant Observation A research method used in case studies by social scientists who interact with other people and record relatively informal observations. *See case study, Non-Participant Observations.*

Party According to Max Weber, made up of people who share political interests. Parties are goal-oriented, and they aim to acquire social power.

Paternalistic Social System A social system in which people or groups are treated in the manner in which a father controls his children. *See Competitive Social System.*

Passive Euthanasia The practice of letting a very ill person die naturally when there is no hope of recovery.

Pathological Behavior Conduct that results from some form of physical or mental illness or psychological problem. *See Deviance.*

Patrilineal Kinship The tracing of one's descent through the father and his side of the family. *See Matrilineal Kinship.*

Patrilocal A pattern of residence by which married couples reside with or near the husband's family. *See Matrilocal.*

Pecking Order A hierarchical relationship of dominance and submission within a flock, herd, or community.

Peer Group Group of people with whom one has equal standing.

Periodic Assemblies Gatherings that are scheduled in advance, have a preset time and place, and draw repeated attendance if they are part of a series. *See Nonperiodic Assemblies.*

Personality The individual's pattern of thoughts, motives, and self-concepts.

Phenomenology A scientific method that attempts to study an individual's awareness of experience without making assumptions, theories, or value judgments that would prejudice the study. *See Relativism.*

Piacular Rites According to Emile Durkheim, religious rites which comfort or console individuals, help the community in times of disaster, and ensure the piety of the individual. *See Negative Rites.*

Piaget, Jean (1896-1980) Swiss biologist and psychologist who has demonstrated the developmental nature of children's reasoning processes. He believes that humans pass through a universal, invariant development sequence of cognitive stages. Intelligence is at first a purely sensorimotor phenomenon. But it develops through a hierarchical process until it can finally be applied to formal, hypothetical thinking.

Pluralism A state of society in which a variety of groups and institutions retain political power and distinctive cultural characteristics.

Pluralistic Society A society in which power is distributed among a number of interest groups which are presumed to counterbalance each other.

Political Modernization The shift in loyalty or administrative structure from traditional authorities, such as tribal and religious leaders, to large-scale government organizations or from regional to national government. *See Social Modernization.*

Political Socialization The social process by which political values are acquired, particularly by young children. *See Socialization.*

Political Sociology The sociological study of politics, which, in turn, involves the regulation and control of citizens; closely related to political science. Traditionally, politcal scientists have been concerned with the abstract qualities of the political order and the formal behavior of citizens, especially in voting and political party participation. Sociologists generally claim that they are more inclined to focus on the actual power relations cloaked by the formal political structure. *See Political Science.*

Polyandry The marriage of one woman to several men. *See* Polygamy, Polygyny.

Polygamy The marriage of one woman to several men. *See* Monagamy.

Polygyny The marriage of one man to several women. *See* Polygamy, Polyandry.

Population Control Lowering the rate of natural increase of population. *See* Natural Increase.

Population Explosion A sudden, dramatic growth in the rate of natural increase of population. *See* Natural Increase.

Positivism A philosophy that rejects abstract ideas in favor of a factual, scientific orientation to reality. *See* Neoidealism.

Postconventional Morality According to Lawrence Kohlberg, the final level of moral development, which few people ever attain. This level is concerned with the moral values and individual rights apart from the group or society. *See* Conventional, Preconventional Morality.

Postindustrial Society A "service" economy of relatively recent development, in which the principal economic activity has advanced from industrial production to services that depend on significant inputs of knowledge. *See* Industrial Society.

Power The ability of people to realize their will, even against others' opposition. *See* Coercion, Influence.

Power Elite According to C. Wright Mills, the leaders in an organization or society who have a near monopoloy on policy making. *See* Elite Groups.

Preconventional Morality According to Lawrence Kohlberg, the first level of moral development. At this level, children know cultural labels of good and bad, although they judge behavior only in terms of consequences. *See* Conventional, Post Convention Morality.

Prejudice A biased prejudgment; an attitude in which one holds a negative belief about members of a group to which one does not belong. Prejudice is often directed at minority ethnic or racial groups. *See* Stereotype.

Primary Groups Groups such as the family, work group, gang, or neighborhood, which are characterized by face-to-face contact of members and which are thought to significantly affect members' personality development. *See* Secondary Group.

Products of Culture Religion, art, law, architecture, and all the many material objects used and produced by a given cultural group.

Projection According to Sigmund Freud, the tendency for people to attribute to others beliefs or motives that they have but cannot bring themselves to recognize or admit consciously. *See* Prejudice.

Proletariat According to Karl Marx, the working class. *See* Bourgeoisie.

Protestant Ethic According to Max Weber, the belief that hard work and frugal living would ensure future salvation.

Psychoanalytic Theory A theory of personality development, based on the work of Sigmund Freud, which maintains that the personality develops through a series of psychosexual stages as it experiences tension between demands of society and individual insticts for self-indulgence and independence. *See* Personality.

Public A loose, heterogenous social aggregate held together for a specific period by a shared interest in a public event or issue. Participants are not usually in the same physical location. *See* Social Aggregate.

Public Opinion Open verbal or nonverbal expressions by members of a social aggregate who are giving attention to a particular controversial point at a particular time. *See* Collective Behavior, Public, Social Aggregate.

Race Biologically, the classificiation of people by observed physical characteristics; culturally, the meaning we give to physical characteristics and behavior traits when identifying in- and outgroups.

Race Relations Social interactions among members of different groups that are based on, or affected by, an awareness of real or imagined racial or ethnic differences. *See* Race.

Racial Group As defined sociologically, any collection of people that other groups treat as a distinct race. *See* Race.

Racism A belief in racial superiority that leads to discrimination and prejudice toward those races considered inferior. *See* Discrimination, Prejudice, Race.

Rationalization According to Max Weber, the systematic application of impersonal and specific rules and procedures to obtain efficient coordination within modern organizations. *See* Formal Organization.

Recidivism The return to criminal behavior after punishment has been administered. *See* Deterrence Theory.

Relative Poverty Poverty of the lower strata of society as compared to the abundance enjoyed by members of higher strata. *See* Absolute Poverty.

Relativsm The idea that different people will have different experiences and interpretations of the same event. *See* Phenomenology.

Reliability A criterion for evaluating research results that refers to how well the study was done. A reliable study can be duplicated and its results found by other researchers. *See* Validity.

Religion A communally held system of beliefs and practices that are associated with some transcendent supernatural reality. *See* Sect.

Replacement Level The rate of population increase at which individuals merely replace themselves. *See* Zero Population Growth.

Research In the application of scientific method, the process by which an investigator seeks information to verify a theory. *See* Scientific Method, Theory.

Resocialization Major changes of attitudes or behavior, enforced by agents of socialization, that are likely to occur in institutions in which people are cut off from the outside world, spend all day with the same people, shed all possessions and identity, break with the past, and lose their freedom of action. *See* Socialization.

Restricted Code According to Basil Bernstein, the kind of ungrammatical, colloquial speech available to both middle-class and working-class people. *See* Elaborated Code.

Revolutionary Change Violent social change, most likely to occur when the gap between rising expectations and actual attainments becomes too frustrating for people to bear. *See* Evolutionary Change, Rising Expectations.

Rising Expectations The tendency of people to expect and demand improved social, economic, and political conditions as social change progresses within a society.

Rite of Passage A ceremony that dramatizes a change in an individual's status. Weddings and funerals are examples.

Role The behavior of an indivdiual in relations with others. Also, the behavior considered acceptable for an individual in a particular situation or in the performance of a necessary social function. *See* Role Allocation, Role Label, Role Performance.

Role Allocation Assignment of people to separate jobs, such as cook, table setter, and dishwasher. *See* Division of Labor.

Role Convergence A growing similarity in roles that were formerly segregated and distinct. As men and women come to share domestic tasks, for example, their roles converge. *See* Sex Role.

Role Label The name assigned to an individual who acts in a particular way. Role labels may be broad ("laborer") or specific ("people who get colds easily").

Role Performance The actual behavior of individuals in a particular role.

Role Portrayal The adapting of roles to fit one's style of interaction. *See* Fashioning Effect, Role Selection.

Role Selection The process of choosing a role that allows one to fulfill one's self-concept. *See* Fashioning Effect, Role Portrayal.

Rumor Unconfirmed stories and interpretations. They are the major form of communication during the milling process in collective behavior. *See* Collective Behavior, Milling.

Rural Areas Settlements of fewer than 2,500 residents or areas of low population density, such as farmlands. *See* Urban Areas.

Salience The degree of importance of a group to its members; its impact on members. Generally, the smaller the group, the more salient it can become. *See* Small Groups.

Sample Survey A research method in which a representative group of people is chosen from a particular population. Sample surveys may be conducted by interview or questionnaire. *See* Case Study, Experiment.

Scapegoat A person or community that is made the undeserving object of aggression by others. The aggression derives from the need to allocate blame for any misfortune experienced by the aggressors. *See* Prejudice.

Scientific Method The process used by scientists to analyze phenomena in a systematic and complete way. It is based on an agreement that criteria must be established for each set of observations referred to as fact and involves theory, research, and application. *See* Research, Theory.

Secondary Group A social group characterized by limited face-to-face interaction, relatively impersonal relationships, goal-oriented or task-oriented behavior, and possibly formal organization. *See* Primary Group.

Sect A relatively small religious movement that has broken away from a larger church. A sect generally is in opposition to the larger society's values and norms.

Sectarianism Having characteristics of sects, such as opposition to and withdrawal from, the larger society. *See* Sect.

Sector Theory Theory of urban development which states that urban growth tends to occur along major transportation routes and that new residential areas are created at the edges of older areas of the same class. These developments produce more or less homogeneous pie-shaped sectors. *See* Concentric Zone Theory, Multiple-Nuclei Theory.

Secularization The displacement of religious beliefs and influences by worldly beliefs and influences.

Segmental Roles Specialized duties by people in a bureaucratic society and over which they have little control. *See* Role, Specialization.

Segregation Involuntary separation of groups, on the basis of race, religion, sex, age, class, nationality, or culture.

Sex Role The culturally determined set of behavior and attitudes considered appropriate for males and females. *See* Gender Identity.

Shaman The individual in a tribal or nonliterate society who is priest, sorcerer, and healer all in one. The shaman treats diseases, exorcizes evil spirits, and is considered to have supernatural powers.

Significant Others According to George Herbert Mead, parents and other relatives or friends whose viewpoints children learn to adopt. *See* Generalized Others.

Simmel, Georg (1858-1918) German sociologist and conflict theorist who proposed that a small number of stable forms of interaction underlie the superficial diversity of manifest social occurrences. *See* Conflict Model.

Small Group An interaction system in which members have face-to-face contact and which tend to have important effects on members' behavior. *See* Primary Group.

Social Aggregate A relatively large number of people who do not know one another or who interact impersonally. Aggregates have loose structures and brief lives. There are basically three types of aggregates: the crowd, the mass, and the public. *See* Collective Behavior, Crowd, Mass, Public.

Social Bonding The quality of forming relatively permanent associations, found in both human and some animal and insect societies.

Social Change An alteration of stable patterns of social organization and interaction, preceded or followed by changes in related values and norms.

Social Conflict Disagreement over social values and competing interests. *See* Conflict Model.

Social Constraints Factors that produce conformity to the behavioral expectations of society, such as ridicule, expulsion from a group, or punishments. Knowledge of social constraints is taught during socialization. *See* Socialization.

Social Contract An agreement binding all parties that sets up rights, responsibilities, powers, and privileges and forms a basis for government.

Social Control Techniques and strategies for regulating human behavior.

Social Darwinism The view which sees society as an organism that grows more perfect through the natural selection of favored individuals. In this view, the wealthier and better-educated classes are more "fit" because they have competed their way to success. Social Darwinism applies Darwin's theory of biological evolution to social groups. *See* Evolution, Natural Selection.

Social Disorganization The breakdown of institutions and communities, which results in dislocation and breakdown of ordinary social controls over behavior.

Social Distance The relative positions of members or groups in a stratified social system; the degree of social acceptance that exists between certain social groups in a society.

Social Dynamics All the forces and processes involved in social change.

Social Engineering Systematic planning to solve social problems.

Social Epidemiology The study of illness rate in a population within a specific geographic area. *See* Sociology of Medicine.

Social Group A collection of interrelating human beings. A group may consist of two or more people. The interaction may involve performing a complex task—a surgical team—or simple proximity—all the drivers on a road during rush hour. Groups may be classified as primary or secondary. *See* Primary Group, Secondary Group, Small Groups.

Social Interaction The effect that two or more people have on each other's behavior, thoughts, and emotions through symbolic and nonsymbolic modes of expression.

Socialism An economic system in which means of production (land, equipment, materials) are collectively owned and controlled by the state rather than by private individuals. *See* Capitalism, Communism.

Social Isolates Children who have had minimal human contact because of abandonment or parental neglect. Also refers to people cut off from social contact voluntarily or involuntarily. *See* Feral Children.

Socialization The complex process by which individuals learn and adopt the behavior patterns and norms that enable them to function appropriately in their social environments. *See* Agents of Socialization, Personality.

Social Mobility The movement of people up or down a social hierarchy based on wealth, power, and education.

Social Modernization A process of change in social institutions, usually viewed as a movement from traditional or less-developed institutions to those characteristic of developed societies. *See* Economic Modernization.

Social Movement A long-term collective effort to resist or to promote social change. See collective behavior.

Social Organization A general term used in different ways in different contexts, but usually referring to organizational aspects of societies, communities, institutions, and groups. Perhaps the most basic aspect of social organization is a common understanding among members of the organization about the interpretation of social reality.

Social Relations Perspectives A view which emphasizes factors other than intelligence, such as family, in determining an individual's economic positions. *See* Technocratic Perspective.

Social Sciences Branches of learning concerned with the institutions of human societies and with human behavior and interrelationships. Social sciences draw their subject matter from the natural sciences.

Social Stratification A system of social inequality in which groups are ranked according to their attainment of socially valued rewards.

Social System The arrangement or pattern of organization of any social group. A system is a whole made up of interacting parts.

Society A social group that is relatively large, self-sufficient, and continues from generation to generation. Its members are generally recruited through the process of socialization. *See* Conflict Model, Functionalism, Socialization, Sociology.

Sociobiology A realtively new field which is a branch of behavioral biology that studies the biological bases of the social behavior and social organization of all animal species. *See* Biosociology.

Sociocultural Social organization in which patterns of behavior are largely governed by a network of learned values, norms, and beliefs. *See* Culture, Norm.

Sociogram A diagram showing the interaction among group members. A sociogram of a group might show, for example, who is most liked and who is least liked. *See* Group Processes.

Sociological Perspective The point of view of the sociologist. It aims at precision and objectivity through the scientific method. *See* Scientific Method.

Sociology The social science concerned with the systematic study of human society and human social interaction. *See* Society.

Sociology of Death The inquiry into the impact of dying on a patient's relationship to self, to others, and to the social structure as a whole. *See* Thanatology.

Sociology of Education The scientific analysis of both formal and informal learning in a society. *See* Education.

Sociology of Medicine The study of the definition, causes, and cure of disease in different societies and social groups. The sociology of medicine also studies the social organization of modern medical care and the social roles of staff and patients at various medical facilities.

Sociology of Work A study of the relations of production and consumption and the influence of work on social organization and social change. *See* Social Change.

Specialization A concentration of work in a specific area. According to Max Weber, specialization is a characteristic of an ideal type of bureaucratic organization. *See* Bureaucracy, Ideal Type.

Spencer, Hebert (1820-1913) British philosopher whose descriptive sociology was very influential and formed the basis for Social Darwinism. *See* Social Darwinism.

Standard Metropolitan Statistical Area (SMSA) A Census Bureau concept for counting population in core cities, their suburbs, satellite communities, and other closely related areas. SMSAs ignore usual political divisions, such as state boundaries. *See* Metropolis.

State The political-legal system that represents a whole country, its territory, and people. A state is a more formal legal and technical entity than the broader concept, "society." *See* Society.

Statistics A method for analyzing data gathered from samples of observations in order to: describe the amount of variation in each of the variables; describe hypothetical relationships among variables; to make inferences from the results to the larger population from which the sample was drawn.

Status The position of the individual (actor) in a system of social relationships. *See* Achieved Status, Ascribed Status.

Status Group According to Max Weber, people with similar lifestyles and social standing.

Stereotype An exaggerated belief associated with some particular category, particularly of a national, ethnic, or racial group. *See* Racial Group, Sex Role.

Stigmatization The labeling of individuals in such a way that they are disqualified from full social acceptance and participation. Criminalization is part of this process. *See* Criminalization, Deviance.

Structural Differentiation The specialization of institutions, social roles, and functions that accompanies social change.

Structural-functionalism *See* Functionalism.

Structuralism An intellectual approach which emphasizes studying the underlying structures of human behavior rather than obvious, surface events.

Subcultures Various groups within the society who share some elements of the basic culture but who also possess some distinctive folkways and mores. *See* Culture.

Surrogate Religion A belief system that substitutes for a traditional religion. Communism is an example.

Symbol Anything that stands for something else. For example, words may be symbols of objects, ideas, or emotions.

Symbolic Interactionism A theory in academic sociology founded by George Herbert Mead that says humans communicate through symbols—words and gestures—and develop self-images through others' responses.

Symbolic Interactions Interactions conducted through the use of symbols.

Target Population In a model of suburban growth, a group of people who are affected both by facilitating and motivating conditions. This population consisted of young to middle-age white married couples. *See* Facilitating and Motivating Conditions.

Task Segregation A division of labor based on a feature such as the sex or age of the participants. Task segregation is common in most societies. *See* Division of Labor.

Taxonomy A classification system of cognitive categories. *See* Folk Taxonomy.

Technocracy The domination of an industrial society by a technical elite. *See* Elite Groups, Technocratic Perspective.

Technocratic Perspective The view which sees the hierarchical division of labor as a result of the need to motivate the ablest individuals to undertake the most extensive training, which will allow them to perform the most difficult and important occupations in a society. *See* Technocracy.

Thanatology The study of theories, causes, and conditions of death.

Theory A set of generalized, often related, statements about some phenomenon. A theory is useful in generating hypotheses. Middle-range theories interrelate two or more empirical generalizations. Grand theory organizes all concepts, generalizations, and middle-range theories into an overall explanation. *See* Hypothesis, Research.

Tönnies, Ferdinand (1855-1936) Classical German sociologist who was the first to recognize the impact of the organic point of view on positivism. He identified the social organization concepts of *Gemeinschaft* and *Gesellschaft*. *See Gemeinschaft/Gesellschaft*.

Totemism Religious belief in which a totem—a representation of some natural object in the environment—figures prominently. Totems serve as symbols of clans and sacred representations. *See* Clan.

Traditional Society Rural, agricultural, homogeneous societies characterized by relatively simple means of production. *See* Industrial Society.

Tylor, Sir Edward Burnett (1832-1917) British pioneer anthropologist upon whose central ideas about culture all modern definitions are based.

Typology A classification system of characteristics. An example is *Gemeinschaft/Gesellschaft,* two types of social organization.

Universalism A rule for scientific innovation, according to Robert Merton. It refers to an objectivity which does not allow factors such as race, religion, or national origin to interfere with scientific inquiry. *See* Communalism, Disinterestedness, Organized Skepticism.

Urban Area According to Census Bureau definitions, a settlement of 2,500 or more persons. *See* Rural Area.

Urbanism The ways in which the city affects how people feel, think, and interact.

Urbanization The movement of people from country to city as well as the spread of urban influence and cultural patterns to rural areas. Also refers to the greater proportion of the population in urban areas than in rural areas. *See* Urban Society.

Urban Society A form of social organization in which: (1) economic exchange and markets are very important; (2) social roles are highly specialized; (3) centralized administrative and legal agencies provide political direction; and (4) interaction tends to be impersonal and functional. *See* Urbanization.

Utilitarian Organization According to Amitai Etzioni, a formal organization that people join for practical reasons, mainly jobs and salaries. Examples include blue-collar and white-collar industries. *See* Coercive and Normative Organizations.

Validity A criterion for evaluating research results that refers to how well the data actually reflect the real world. *See* Reliability, Research.

Value-added Theory Neil Smelser's theory which postulates five stages in the development of collective behavior. *Social conduciveness* describes situations that permit collective behaviors to occur. *Structural strain* refers to problems in the social environment. The growth of a *generalized belief* involves the interpretation of structural conduciveness and strain in a way that favors collective behavior. *Precipitating factors* are events that trigger collective behavior. *Mobilization for action* is the ''organizational'' component and usually involves explicit instruction and/or suggestions. *See* Collective Behavior.

Values Individual or collective conceptions of what is desirable. This conception usually has both emotional and symbolic components. *See* Norm.

Variables Factors that can change. Reserachers must state the specific variables they intend to measure. An independent variable is causal. A dependent variable changes according to the independent variable's behavior. *See* Research, Scientific Method.

Verstehen Subjective understanding which, according to Max Weber, must be employed in sociological investigation. *See* Neoidealism, Positivism.

Weber, Max (1864-1920) German sociologist whose work profoundly influenced Western sociological thought and method. The key to Weber's analysis of the modern world is his concept of *rationalization*—the substitution of explicit formal rules and procedures for earlier spontaneous, rule-of-thumb methods and attitudes. The result of this process was a profound ''disenchantment of the world,'' which had been carried to its ultimate form in capitalist society, where older values were being subordinated to technical methods. The prime example of the rationalized insitution was bureaucracy.

Weber's writings on methodology have been singularly influential. He argued that the social sciences were inherently different from the natural sciences, for a full understanding of social action must involve *Verstehen* (empathetic understanding). He firmly believed that, although true objectivity was impossible, the sociologist should attempt to remain value-free. *See* Rationalization, *Verstehen*.

Woman Suffrage The right of women to vote. *See* Women's Movement.

Women's Movement A social movement by women to gain equal social, economic, and legal status with men. *See* Feminists, Social Movement.

Zero Population Growth The point at which population stops increasing. *See* Population Control, Replacement Level.

Source for the Glossary:

This glossary of 459 terms is reprinted from *The Study of Society, Second Edition.* ©The Dushkin Publishing Group, Inc. Guilford, CT 06437.

Index

Credits/ Acknowledgments

Cover design by Charles Vitelli

1. The Discipline
Facing overview—New York Convention & Visitors Bureau.
2. Culture
Facing overview—UN Photo/Paula Fridman. 18-21—Courtesy of
Colin M. Turnbull.
3. Socialization
Facing overview—UN Photo/Jeffrey Foxx. 66—WHO photo by K.
Kalisher. 76—Clemens Kalischer. 78-81—Courtesy of E. Richard
Sorenson.
4. Groups and Roles in Transition
Facing overview—Dover *Pictorial Archive* Series. Dover
Publication. 123-127—*Aging* magazine.

5. Social Institutions
Facing overview—UAW Solidarity Photo by Robert Gumpert.
6. Stratification and Social Inequalities
Facing overview—UAW Solidarity Photo by Robert Gumpert.
172—Guy Billout.
7. Social Change and the Future
Facing overview—IBM Corporation.

We Want Your Advice

ANNUAL EDITIONS: SOCIOLOGY 86/87
Article Rating Form

Here is an opportunity for you to have direct input into the next revision of this volume. We would like you to rate each of the 43 articles listed below, using the following scale:

1. **Excellent: should definitely be retained**
2. **Above average: should probably be retained**
3. **Below average: should probably be deleted**
4. **Poor: should definitely be deleted**

Your ratings will play a vital part in the next revision. So please mail this prepaid form to us just as soon as you complete it.
Thanks for your help!

Annual Editions revisions depend on two major opinion sources: one is our Advisory Board, listed in the front of this volume, which works with us in scanning the thousands of articles published in the public press each year; the other is you—the person actually using the book. Please help us and the users of the next edition by completing the prepaid article rating form on this page and returning it to us. Thank you.

Rating	Article	Rating	Article
	1. The Sociological Imagination		24. Washington: The Three Fiscal Crises
	2. Invitation to Sociology: A Humanistic Perspective		25. America's Management Crisis
	3. Why I Love America		26. The American Family in the Year 2000
	4. The Mountain People		27. Why Johnny Can't Think
	5. Penny Capitalism on an Urban Street Corner		28. Between Pro-Life and Pro-Choice
	6. The New Lost Generation		29. Who Owns America? The Same Old Gang
	7. Brave New Wave of the '80s		30. Corporate Welfare out of Control
	8. Radical Departures		31. Abandoned Americans
	9. Childhood Through the Ages		32. How Well Poor Families Fare in the Years Ahead Will Determine the Stability of the Economy and the Strength of the Social Fabric
	10. The Loss of Childhood		
	11. Erik Erikson's Eight Ages of Man		
	12. Growing Up as a Fore		33. The Black Underclass
	13. Sexism in the Schoolroom of the '80s		34. A Struggle for Freedom
	14. What Is TV Doing to America?		35. People, People, People
	15. Alex Haley: The Secret of Strong Families		36. Snapshot of a Changing America
	16. Restoring the Traditional Black Family		37. The Changing Face of America
	17. Jonestown as a Perverse Utopia		38. We Can Prevent Nuclear Winter
	18. Cities Won't Drive You Crazy		39. Technology out of Control
	19. Work: The Right to Right Livelihood		40. Technology and the Changing World of Work
	20. The Politics of Motherhood		41. Copernican Politics
	21. Another Stereotype: Old Age as a Second Childhood		42. 10 Forces Reshaping America
	22. Where Have All the Heroes Gone?		43. Window of Opportunity
	23. Tocqueville's Mistake		Glossary

(cont. on next page)

ABOUT YOU

Name _____ Date _____

Are you a teacher? ☐   Or student? ☐

Your School Name _____

Department _____

Address _____

City _____ State _____ Zip _____

School Telephone # _____

YOUR COMMENTS ARE IMPORTANT TO US!

Please fill in the following information:

For which course did you use this book? _____

Did you use a text with this Annual Edition?   ☐ yes ☐ no

The title of the text: _____

What are your general reactions to the Annual Editions concept?

Have you read any particular articles recently that you think should be included in the next edition?

Are there any articles you feel should be replaced in the next edition? Why?

Are there other areas that you feel would utilize an Annual Edition?

May we contact you for editorial input?

May we quote you from above?

SOCIOLOGY 86/87